United Kingdom Law Society Library

Catalogue of the Library of the Law Society of the United Kingdom

United Kingdom Law Society Library

Catalogue of the Library of the Law Society of the United Kingdom

ISBN/EAN: 9783337132606

Printed in Europe, USA, Canada, Australia, Japan

Cover: Foto ©ninafisch / pixelio.de

More available books at **www.hansebooks.com**

THE
𝕷𝖆𝖜 𝕾𝖔𝖈𝖎𝖊𝖙𝖞'𝖘
LIBRARY CATALOGUE

LONDON: PRINTED BY
SPOTTISWOODE AND CO., NEW-STREET SQUARE
AND PARLIAMENT STREET

CATALOGUE

OF

THE LIBRARY

OF

𝔗𝔥𝔢 𝔏𝔞𝔴 𝔖𝔬𝔠𝔦𝔢𝔱𝔶

OF THE

UNITED KINGDOM

Incorporated by Charters 2 Wm. IV. and 9 Vict.

London
PRINTED FOR THE SOCIETY
1869

CATALOGUE.

DEFINITIONS.

C. S. Pa.	Camden Society's Papers.
Par. S. Pa.	Parker Society's Papers.
Col. Jur.	Collectanea Juridica.
L. T.	Law Tracts. 1688-89.
L. T. & A.	Law Tracts and Arguments. 1641.
Har. L. T.	Hargrave's Law Tracts.
Jac. Col.	Collection of Law Tracts by Mr. Jacob.
His. L. T.	Historical Law Tracts. 1761.
Fr. Law	French Law.
U. S. Law	United States Law.
Ita. Law	Italian Law.
Pam.	Pamphlets.
M. R. Pub.	Refers to Chronicles and Memorials of Great Britain and Ireland during the Middle Ages, published under the direction of the Master of the Rolls.

Abbott (B. V. & A.) National Digest of Reports of U.S. Courts & Acts of Congress. 3 vols. 8vo. 1867-68 (and *See* America—United States Digest)

—— (C.) Jurisdiction & Practice of Great Sessions of Wales upon the Chester Circuit . . 8vo. 1795

—— (F. G.) Forms of Writs in the Petty Bag Office 12mo. 1849

—— (G.) The Question of Rating Tithes (Joddrell's Case). Vol. 1, Pam. 1839

—— (Charles, Lord Tenterden) on Merchant Ships & Shipping 8vo. 1802

———————————————————— 4th ed. 8vo. 1812

———————————— (J. H. Abbott). 5th ed. 8vo. 1827

———————————————— (W. Shee). 6th ed. 8vo. 1840

———————————————————— 8th ed. 8vo. 1847

———————————————————— 10th ed. 8vo. 1856

———————————————————— 11th ed. 8vo. 1867

Abdicated, Debate between Lords & Commons on this word in the Commons Vote . . . 12mo. 1695

A'Beckett (T. T.) Railway Litigation, How to Check it. Vol. 21, Pam. 1846

—— on Law Reform. Vol. 6, Pam. 1849

B

Aberconway Abbey, Register, &c. of. C. S. Pa.
No. 39 C. M. Vol. 1 (ed. Sir H. Ellis) . . . 1846
Abingdon, Chronicon Monasterii de (ed. Rev. J.
Stevenson) No. 2 M. R. Pub. 1858
Abjuration, Thoughts on the Oath of, in Letter to
Earl Aberdeen, by a Member of late Parliament.
Vol. 9, Pam. 1853
Abrahall (B. H.) Second Letter to Sir Richard
Bethell on Bankruptcy & Insolvency Reform.
Vol. 13, Pam. 1861
Abrahams (S.) The Palace Court, its Constitution
& Practice 12mo. 1848
Absence, Process in (*see* Historical Law Tracts) . 1761
Acland, on Associate in Arts. Oxford Examination . . . . 2nd ed. 8vo. 1858
Acton (T. H.) Reports of Cases before the Commissions of Appeals in Prize Causes
2 vols. in 1, 8vo. 1811
Acts, Black Letter, 1543–1848 . . . 192 folio
Acts, Drafts of, 1653 . . . . 4to. 1653
Acts of Council in Civil Causes (Scotland) . folio 1839
Acts of Lords—Auditors of Causes in Scotland
(Record Commission) 1468–95 . . . . folio 1839
Acts of Parliament of Scotland (*see* Scotland)
Acts & Ordinances of Parliament, Collection (*see*
Parliament)
————— temp. Cromwell, 1656–57 (*see* Cromwell)
Adams (J.) Index Villaris, or an Alphabetical Table
of Cities, &c. in England & Wales . . folio 1680
——— (*Rev. J.*) on Self-Murther . . . 12mo. 1700
——— (Jno.) on the Action of Ejectment. 3rd ed. 8vo. 1830
——————————————— 4th ed. 8vo. 1846
——— on Police & Criminals. Vol. 5, Pam. . . 1838
——— Jun.) Doctrine of Equity 8vo. 1849
——— (T.) History of Antient Town of Shaftesbury. Partly selected from Hutchins . . 8vo. 1808
Adamson (T.) Acts & Ordinances in force in Victoria, 1825–56 . . . . . 2 vols. 8vo. 1855–56
———Acts of Parliament of Victoria . . . 8vo. 1857

Addams (*Dr.* J.) Reports, Ecclesiastical Courts,
    1822–26 . . . . 3 vols. 8vo. 1823–26
Adderley (C. B.) Letter to B. D'Israeli, Esq. on
    Present Relations of England with the Colonies.
    Vol. 18, Pam. 1861
Addington (W.) Abridgment of Penal Statutes. 8vo. 1775
    ——————————————— 2nd ed. 4to. 1782
Addison (C. G.) History of the Knights Templars,
    the Temple, & its Church 4to. 1842
—— on Contracts, & Rights & Liabilities of Con-
    tractor 8vo. 1845
    ————————————— 3rd ed. 2 vols 8vo. 1853
    ————————————— 5th ed. 8vo. 1862
    ————————— (L. W. Cave) 6th ed. 8vo. 1869
—— on Wrongs & their Remedies, being a Treatise
    on the Law of Torts 8vo. 1860
    ————————————————— 2nd ed. 8vo. 1864
Admiralty Courts, Parliamentary Report on. folio 1833
—— Statutes to 8 Geo. III. 4to. 1768
Adolphe (C.) (*see* Carre)
—— & Helie (F.) Théorie du Code pénal & Ap-
    pendice (*Fr. Law*). 4th ed. 7 vols. 8vo. 1861 1863
Adolphus (J. L.) & Ellis (T. F.) Reports, K. B.
    1834–41 . . . . 12 vols. 8vo. 1835, &c.
—— Q. B. new series, 1841–52. 18 vols. 8vo. 1842, &c.
—— (*see* Barnewall, R. V.)
Advocate's Library (Doctors' Commons) Catalogue
    MSS. 8vo. 1818
Ærodius (*see* Ayrault)
Æsopi Fabulæ 4to. 1675
Agarde (A.) Tractatus Pacis (*see* Ayloffe's Calendar)
Aikin (*Dr.* J.) History of Manchester . . 4to. 1794
Ainsworth (R.) Latin & English Dictionary, by
    Dr. T. Morell & *Dr.* J. Carey. 2nd ed. 2 vols. 4to. 1823
Airlie Peerage, Cases of W. & D. Ogilvy. Vol. 1,
    3rd series. Evidence, Vol. 8 1813
Airth Peerage, Evidence. Vols. 14 & 17, H. L.
    Sess. Papers, 1839 1839

Aiton (W.) Inquiry into the Pedigree, &c. of the
 Hamilton Family 4to. 1827
Akerman (J. Y.) (see C. S. Pa. No. 52)
Alauzet (J.) Commentaire du Code de Commerce
 (Fr. Law) . . . . 4 vols. 8vo. 1856–57
Albericus de Rosate. In primam Codicis partem
 Commentarii . . . . 4 vols. folio 1586
Albin (J.) History of the Isle of Wight . . 8vo. 1795
Albion Newspaper . . . . 2 vols. folio 1835
Alcock (J. B.) on Personal Property in India. 8vo. 1850
—— (J. C.) (see Cooke, J. R.)
—— & Napier (J.) Reports, Irish K. B. & Exch.
 Chamber, 1831–33 . . . . 8vo. 1834
Alderson (E. H.) (see Barnewall)
Aldobrandini (Silv.) (see Justiniani)
Alexander (W.) Abridgment of Acts of Sederunt
 from 1532 . . . . 8vo. 1838
—— Acts of Scotch Parliament, with Notes, 1424–
 1707 . . . . 8vo. 1841
—— Digest of Bankrupt Act of Scotland, 1839
 2nd ed. 8vo. 1842
Aleyn (J.) Reports, K. B. 1646–1649 . . folio 1681
Alison, Practice of Criminal Law of Scotland. 8vo. 1833
——(Sir A.) Military Life of Duke of Marlboro'. 8vo. 1848
—— History of Europe, from the commencement
 of the French Revolution to the Restoration of
 the Bourbons, 1789–1815. 20 vols. 12mo. 1847, &c.
—— from Fall of Napoleon, 1815, to Accession of
 Louis Napoleon, 1852, and Index. 9 v. 8vo. 1853, &c.
Allen (J.) on the Royal Prerogative in England
 (B. Thorpe) 8vo. 1849
—— (T.) History of Lambeth 4to. 1827
———— History of Surrey . . 2 vols. 8vo. 1831
———— History of Yorkshire. 3 vols. 4to. 1836, 1839
Allibone (S. A.) Critical Dictionary of English
 Literature & British & American Authors. 8vo. 1859
Allnutt (G. S.) Practice of Wills . 4th ed. 8vo. 1860
—— (H.) Auctioneers', &c. Directory 4th ed. 12mo. 1866
Almack (R.) C. M. Vol. 3, No. 61

Almanac, British, & Companion. 40 vols. 12mo. 1828–68
—— British, Index to Companion to, 1828–43. 12mo. 1844
—— Collections, 1774 and 1799 . 2 vols. 12mo.
—— Companion to. 12mo. 1752
—— Dublin Registry & Directory, 1742–1849
49 vols. 12mo.
—— Edinburgh (New). 12mo. 1822
—— London 8vo. 1841
—— Stationers' Company Book, 1792–1867 (except 1816) . . . . 74 vols. 12mo.
Almon (J.) Extinct Peerage 12mo. 1769
—— Baronetage . . . . 3 vols. 12mo. 1769
—— Trial of, for Selling Junius' Letters (see Morris, R.) (Letter) Libel L. T. Vol. 3 . . . 1770
—— Peerage . . . . 2 vols. 8vo. 1789
Ambler (C.) Chancery Reports, 1760–86 . folio 1790
——————— 1737–86 (Blunt) . 2nd ed. 2 vols. 8vo. 1828
America—United States Digest of Decisions of Courts of Common Law & Admiralty, by T. Metcalf, J. C. Perkins, & G. T. Curtis. 3 v. 8vo. 1860–63
————————— Supplement to, by J. P. Putnam
2 vols. 8vo. 1860–61
—— Table of Cases, by G. P. Sanger (contained in above 5 vols.) 8vo. 1864
—— Digest of Equity Decisions reported up to 1847, by J. P. Putnam . . . . 2 vols. 8vo. 1864
—— Annual Digest of Decisions of Courts of Common Law, Equity, & Admiralty in the United States & England, 1847 to 1865, by Putnam, Hale, Hale & Smith, Smith, Frost. 19* vols. 8vo.
—— The Public Statutes at large of the United States of America, from 1789 to 1845, in chronological order, with Notes of the Decisions of Courts, &c. . . . . 8 vols. 8vo. 1861–62
—— The Statutes at large and Treaties and Proclamations from 1845 to March 1867, arranged in chronological order, Edited by Minot, Minot & Sanger, Sanger . . 6 vols. 8vo. 1862–68

* The first four Volumes relate to United States only.

America—Synoptical Index to the Laws & Treaties
 of United States of America, 1789 to 1851, 8vo. 1856
—— U. States Consular Regulations. 3rd ed. 8vo. 1868
—— History of (*see Dr.* W. Robertson's Works)
—— Bankruptcy Rules, &c. bound up with Henry
 (J.) French Law as to Foreigners, &c. . . . 1842
—— Papers on Foreign Affairs, being the United
 States Version of the Differences with Great
 Britain . . . . 2 vols. 8vo. 1865
—— New York Book of Forms 8vo. 1865
—— New York Political Code. 8vo. 1860
—— New York Civil Code 8vo. 1865
—— New York Penal Code 8vo. 1865
American Correspondence on the Present Relations
 between Great Britain & United States, in Let-
 ters from Mr. Loring to Mr. Field. Vol. 22 Pam.
American Law Review. . . . . 3 vols. 8vo. 1866–69
—— Literature Catalogue 8vo. 1856
—— Mining Companies, Inquiry concerning. Vol.
 2, Jac. Col. 1825
—— Securities, Hints & Warnings to British In-
 vestors, by an Anglo-American. Vol. 13, Pam. 1860
—— Slavery, Pamphlets on, and Report of American
 Anti-Slavery Society for 1860. Pam. Vol. 22
Americans, History of, in Greek . 4 vols. 12mo.
Ames (S.) (*see* Angell, J. E.)
Amicable Society's Charter, &c. 8vo. 1823
Amos (A.) on Laws of Parochial Settlement by
 Equitable Estate. Jac. Col. Vol. 1 1823
—— Lecture on Study of English Law. Jac.
 Col. Vol. 7. 1829
—— on the Constitution (temp. Car. II.) . 8vo. 1857
—— & Ferard (J.) on the Law of Fixtures. 8vo. 1827
Amsinck (P.) History of Tonbridge Wells . 4to. 1810
Ancient Universal History . . . 9 vols. folio 1736–41
Ancren Riwle, Duties of Monastic Life. C. S. Pa.
 No. 57 (J. Morton) 1852
Anderson (A.) Origin of Commerce . 2 vols. folio 1764

Anderson (C. H.) Digest of Examination Questions . . . . 2 vols. 8vo. 1867
—— (*Sir* Edm.) Reports, C. P. (temp. Eliz.) in 2 parts . . . . folio 1664–65
—— (G. C.) Laws of the Bahamas, 1729–1868
        2 vols. 8vo. 1862–68
—— (J. C.) History of Shropshire . . . 8vo. 1864
André (St.) Rabbit Woman of Godalming . 8vo. 1727
Andrews (G.) Reports K. B., 1737–38 . . folio 1754
———————————————— 2nd ed. 8vo. 1791
Angelus. Commentaria in quatuor Institutionum libros . . . . folio 1513
Angell (J. K.) Property in Tidal Waters, by J. W. May (Boston) . . . . 2nd ed. 8vo. 1847
—— on Insurance, Fire & Life (Boston, U. S.) 8vo. 1855
—— Limitation of Actions &c., by J. W. May (Boston). . . . . 4th ed. 8vo. 1861
—— & Ames (S.) on Corporations, by Lathrop
      7th ed. 8vo. (Boston) 1861
—— & Durfee (T.) on Highways, by Lathrop
       8vo. (Boston) 1857
——————— . . (G. F. Chaote). 2nd ed. 8vo. 1868
Anglesea Peerage. Case of Viscount Valentia & another. Vol. 1, 3rd series, pp. 33–51
—— Evidence. Vol. 3, p. 1, & Vol. 14 . . . 1760
Anglesey (*Lord*) on Privileges of Parliament, 12mo. 1702
—— (*Earl*) (*see* Annesley)
Angliæ et Hiberniæ Cat., MSS. . . . . folio 1697
Anglicas ad res et Hibernicas Rotuli Selecti spectantes. (J. Hunter) (*see* Record Commission) 8vo. 1834
Angliæ et Walliæ Taxatio Ecclesiastica (Astle, Aycough & Caley) (*see* Record Commission) folio 1802
Anglois des Livre à Geneve 8vo. 1831
Anglo-Saxon Chronicle (B. Thorpe). No. 23 M. R. Pub. . . . . 2 vols. 8vo. 1861
Anjou, Margaret of. C. S. Pa. No. 86 (C. Monro) 1863
Annandale Peerage Case, 1825–44, of Sir F. G. Johnstone & others. Vol. 1, 2nd series, p. 1

Annandale Peerage, Case of J. J. H. Johnstone & of J. H. G. Johnstone. Vol. 1, 3rd series, p. 54
―――― Evidence. Vol. 3, p. 67; Vol. 8, p. 26(*b*); Vol. 14; & Vol. 16, House of Lords Sessions Paper . 1844
Annesley Craig dem. *v.* Earl Anglesey, Trial. folio 1744
Annual Biography & Obituary (Vols. 3, 6, 8 wanting)
. 6 vols. 8vo. 1818–26
Annuities, Instructions for Establishing Parochial Societies for (*bound up with Fairman on Stocks*)
8vo. 1837
Anstey (Henry, M.A.) Munimenta Academica (*see* M. R. Pub. No. 50)
Anstey (J.) Pleader's Guide . . 5th ed. 12mo. 1808
―――― (T. C.) Law as to Roman Catholics . 8vo. 1842
―――――――― on the Reform Act 8vo. 1867
Anstis (J.) Essay on the Knights of the Bath 8vo. 1725
Anstruther (A.) Biography of (*see* Eminent Lawyers) 1790
―――― Reports, Exchequer, 1791–96 3 vols. 8vo. 1792–98
Antigua Acts, 1690–1760. . 2 vols. in 1, folio 1734–64
―――― Acts, 1857–67 . . . . 2 vols. folio 1857–68
―――― Laws of, and Acts of Leeward Islands in force there, 1668–1864 (Snagg, W.) . . . . folio 1865
Antiquarian Itinerary of Architecture, &c.
4 vols. 8vo. 1815–16
―――― Society, MSS. at the Society of, Catalogue
4to. 1816
―――― Map of London, as it appeared in 1578 . . 1738
Antrobus (R.) & Impey (T.) Collection of Writs. 12mo. 1663
Apothecaries' Society, Address of, to Practitioners of Medical Profession on Medical Bill. Vol. 11, Pam. 1844
―――― Society, Statement of, on Medical Reform; & Practitioners' Address to, on Bill. Vol. 5, Pam. 1845–46
Archbishop's Claim to dispose of Sees. Vol. 2, Col. Jur.
Archbold (J. F.) Practice, K. B. . 2 vols. 12mo. 1819
―――― Forms, K. B. & C. P. 12mo. 1825
―――― Practice, C. P. . . . . . 3 vols. 12mo. 1829
―――― Practice, K. B. (Chitty) 4th ed. 2 vols. 12mo. 1835
――――――――――――――― 5th ed. 2 vols. 12mo. 1836

Archbold(J. F.) Practice, K. B. 6th ed. 2 vols. 12mo. 1838
—— Practice, Q. B. . . 7th ed. 2 vols. 12mo. 1840
—— Practice, Q. B. (Thomas Chitty)
                        8th ed. 2 vols. 12mo. 1845–47
———————— (S. Prentice) 9th ed. 2 vols. 12mo. 1855–56
————————————————— 11th ed. 2 vols. 12mo. 1856
—— Practice, Q. B. Supplement to . . . 12mo. 1856
—— Practice, Q.B.(S. Prentice)11th ed. 2 vols. 8vo. 1862
————————————————— 12th ed. 2 vols. 8vo. 1866
—— New Practice, Q. B. . . . 2 vols. 12mo. 1844
—— on Bankruptcy 8vo. 1825
———————————————— 2nd ed. 8vo. 1827
————————————— (Flather) 4th ed. 8vo. 1831
————————————————— 5th ed. 8vo. 1834
————————————————————— . 8vo. 1844
————————————————— 9th ed. 8vo. 1842
————————————————— 10th ed. 12mo. 1849
————————————————— 11th ed. 8vo. 1859
—— on Bankruptcy & Insolvency . . . 8vo. 1861
—— Criminal Pleading & Evidence (Jervis)
                        6th ed. 8vo. 1835
————————————————— 8th ed. 8vo. 1841
————————————————— 9th ed. 8vo. 1843
—————————(W. N. Welsby) 13th ed. 8vo. 1855
————————————————— 14th ed. 8vo. 1859
————————————————— 15th ed. 8vo. 1862
————————————(W. Bruce) 16th ed. 8vo. 1867
—— Country Attorneys' Practice 8vo. 1838
—— Criminal Statutes Consolidated . . . 8vo. 1851
—— Lunacy (Pauper) 8vo. 1854
—— Landlord & Tenant . . . 2nd ed. 12mo. 1855
————————————————— 3rd ed. 8vo. 1864
—— Justice of the Peace, 6th ed. 4 vols. 12mo. 1855–60
—— Quarter Sessions Practice . . 2nd ed. 8vo. 1857
———————————— (C. W. Lovesy) 3rd ed. 8vo. 1869
—— Poor Law . . . . . . 10th ed. 12mo. 1860
————————————————— 11th ed. 12mo. 1863
—— on Awards & Arbitration 12mo. 1861
—— Magistrate's Pocket-Book (*see* Robinson, W.)

Archbold & Shaw's Parish Officer & Parish Law
(J. Paterson) . . . . 4th ed. 12mo. 1864
Archer (F. J.) Digest Common Law (Irish) 8vo. 1842
—— (T. E.) Index to Unrepealed Statutes. 8vo. 1851
Arcot, Nabob of, Letter of (*see* East India Company)
Arden (*Sir* R.) Biography of (*see* Eminent Lawyers) 1790
Argou (M.) Institution au Droit françois, par M.
A. C. B. d'Argis . . 11th ed. 2 vols. 12mo. 1787
Armstrong (R.), Macartney (J.) & Ogles' (J. C.)
Reports (*Civil & Criminal*) Irish N.P. 1840–43
8vo. 1843
Army & Marine List (& *see* East India Company)
42 vols. 8vo. 1801–62
—— & Navy Gazette . . . . folio. 1860
—— Service Act 1847, & Mutiny Act 1854
12mo. 1847, 1854
Arnold (T. J.) (*see* Barron, A.)
—— New Term Reports (Common Pleas) 1838–39
8vo. 1840
—— Municipal Law 8vo. 1851
—— Justice of the Peace 8vo. 1860
Arnot (H.) Scotch Criminal Trials (*see* Trials) 4to. 1785
Arnould (J.) on Marine Insurance . 2 vols. 8vo. 1849
———————— 2nd ed. 2 vols. 8vo. 1857
———————— (Maclachlan) 3rd ed. 2 v. 8vo. 1866
Arrest & Imprisonment, for Debt, on the Law of,
by an Attorney 12mo. 1742
—— & Imprisonment for Debt, Thoughts on Present State of Law. L. T. Vol. 3 1821
—— & Imprisonment, Observations on the Law
of, by an Attorney. L. T. Vol. 5 1827
—— & Imprisonment, Remarks on, by a Barrister.
Vol. 1, do. 1830
Arrowsmith (A.) Map of Mexico & Provinces adjacent, in case 4to. 1810
—— (R. G.) on Occupation, or a Glance at the
Property Tax & Income Tax, dedicated to Taxpayers. Vol. 21, Pam. 1851

Arrowsmith's (J.) Universal Geography 1818
—— London Atlas . . . . folio 1838
—— Map of Asia 1801
—— Map of West Indies, & Spanish Provinces of
North America 1803
—— Map of Africa 1804
—— Map of Europe, South of, & Alpine Country 1804
—— Map of Italy, South, & Coasts adjacent . . 1807
—— Map of Europe 1810
—— Map of Germany 1816
—— Map of France, Belgium, & part of Switzerland 1817
—— Map of Delhi & Constantinople District
between . . . . n. d.
—— Map of India . . . . n. d.
—— Map of North & South America . . . . n. d.
——————————————— . . . . n. d.
Art & Nature, British Curiosities in, 2nd ed. 8vo. 1728
Articled Clerk's Manual 12mo. 1836
Arts, Transactions of Society of, in 1851–52, 5
parts 1836–39
Arundel, Antiquities of, by Master of Grammar
School 8vo. 1766
—— MSS. in the College of Arms, Catalogue, 8vo. 1829
—— MSS. in British Museum, Catalogue, N.S.
Vol. 1, p. 1 . . . . folio 1834
—— & Burney Catalogue, Index to, in British
Museum. P. 3 . . . . folio 1840
Arundell (W.) on Mines & Mining Cos. . . 8vo. 1862
Ashbourne, History &c. of (Derby) . . . 8vo. 1839
Ashburton (*Lord*) Biography of (*see* Roscoe's Lives
of British Lawyers) 1790
Ashby *v.* White, Debate on, in House of Commons,
Elector denied his Vote for M.P., 1704
2nd ed. 8vo. 1721
—— White, on Free Parliaments (*see* Pam. Vol. 11)
Ashe (T.) Table of Coke's Reports . . 12mo. 1606
Ashmole (E.) History of the Order of the Garter, &
the several Orders of Knighthood extant in
Europe 8vo. 1715

Ashurst (*Sir* W. H.) Biography of (*see* Roscoe's
Lives of British Lawyers). 1790
Aspin (J.) Chronology, or Universal History
Abridged 8vo. 1813
Assessed Taxes Acts, 1803-17 . . . . . 8vo.
—— Taxes, Judges' Decisions on, 1823-65
7 vols. folio
Assize, Expenses of Judges of, on Western & Oxford Circuits, 1596-1601, 73 C. S. Pa. . 4to. 1858
Asso (Ig. & J.) & Manuel's (M.) Civil Law of
Spain, translated by L. F. C. Johnston . 8vo. 1825
Astle (T.) on Origin of Writing . 2nd ed. 4to. 1803
—— & others, Antiquarian Repertory. 4 v. 4to. 1707-8
Aston (J.) Description, &c. of Warwickshire. 8vo. 1817
—— (J. J.) Letter to Lord Chancellor Westbury
for Further Assimilation of Courts of Law &
Equity, or Fusion Practicable. Vol. 17, Pam. 1863
—— (R.) Book of Entries & Precedents
3rd edit. 4to. 1673
Astry's (*Sir* J.) Charge to Grand Juries . 12mo. 1703
Athenæum (The) 1856-68 . . . 22 vols. 4to.
—— Library, Liverpool, Catalogue . . . 8vo. 1820
Athenry Peerage Case of E. Birmingham. Vol. 1,
2nd series, p. 153-174
—— Evidence. Vol. 3, p. 119, 1826-36
Atherley (E. G.) on Settlements 8vo. 1813
Athol (Duke of) Claims on the Isle of Man (*see* Isle
of Man)
Atkinson (G.) Sheriff Law 8vo. 1839
———————————— . . . . . 2nd ed. 1842
———————————— . . . . . 3rd ed. 1854
———————————— . . . . . 4th ed. 1861
———————————— . . . . . 5th ed. 1869
—— (R. W.) Observations on the Scheme of the
Solicitor-General to simplify Title & Transfer of
Land. Vol. 19, Pam. 1859
——'s Precedent Book, MS. . . . . . folio n. d.
Atkyns (J. T.) Reports, temp. Hardwick, 1736-64
3 vols. folio 1765

Atkyns (J. T.) Reports, temp. Hardwick, 1736–64
    3 vols. 8vo. 1781
———— (by F. W. Sandars) 3rd ed. 3 vols. 8vo. 1794
—— (L. C. B.) Speech to Sir William Ashurst. Atk. L. T.
—— (*Sir* R.) Parliamentary & Political Tracts Containing   8vo. 1678
<blockquote>
Power, Jurisdiction, & Privilege of Parliament
Argument in the Great Case concerning the Election of M.P.'s (Case of Barnardistone *v.* Soame)
Enquiry into Power of Dispensing with Penal Statutes, with Animadversions upon a Book writ by Sir Edwd. Herbert, & a Short Account of the Authorities in Sir Edwd. Hale's Case
Discourse on Ecclesiastical Jurisdiction in the Realm of England
Defence of late Lord Russell's Innocence
Further Defence of late Lord Russell's Innocence
Speech to Sir Wm. Ashurst at time of his being sworn in Lord Mayor
</blockquote>

—— The Ancient & Present State of Gloucestershire . . . . 2nd ed. 1768
Atlas Newspaper (The) 1826-7-8 .   3 vols. folio
Atterbury, Pope's Letters to him. Ed. J. G. Nichols. No. 73, C. S. P. C. M. Vol. 4 . . 1859
Atthill (*Rev.* W.) (*see* C. S. Pa. No. 38) 1847
Attorney, by an, Proposals for Remedying the great Charge & Delay of Suits at Law & Equity. 7th ed. L. T. Vol. 1 . . . . n. d.
Attorney's Academy & Almanac 4to. 1623
—— Guide 8vo. 1773
—— Law Hints, or Recreations 8vo. 1759
—— Pocket Book . . . . 5th ed. 2 vols. 8vo. 1764
—— Practice . . . . . . 4th ed. 2 vols. 8vo. 1737
—— & Solicitor's Companion 12mo. 1725
——————————————— . . 2nd ed. 12mo. 1725
——————————————— Compleat. 3rd ed. 8vo. 1732
——————————————— . . 3rd ed. 8vo. 1739
—— Employment, &c. of, & Charges (extracted from Monthly Law Magazine, February 1830). Vol. 3, Pam.
—— Law of 8vo. 1764

Attorneys & Solicitors, List of, presented to the House
of Commons by Order of Jan. 26, 1729. folio 1729–31
―― Additional ditto, by Order of Feb. 22, 1730 folio 1731
Attorneys' New Scrutiny, a Poem (Dublin). 12mo. 1807
―― of Ireland, Remonstrance on behalf of, by one
of their Body. Vol. 16, Pam. 1859
―― of Ireland, Report of Sub-Committee of
Dublin on the State of the Registry of Deeds.
Vol. 16, Pam. 1862
―― of Ireland, Detail of the Report of ditto.
Vol. 16, Pam. 1862
Attwood *v.* Eyre, on quashing a Significant. Col.
Jur. Vol. 1
Aubrey's (J.) Natural History of Wilts . . . 4to. 1847
Auckland (*Lord*) (*see* Eden, W.)
Auction Laws . . . . . . Excise ed. 8vo. 1828
Aungier (G. J.) Chroniques de London. C. S. Pa.
No. 28 1844
―― Syon & Isleworth 8vo. 1800
Austen (J.) on Jurisprudence 8vo. 1832
―― Sequel to . . . 2nd ed. 3 vols. 8vo. 1862–63
――'s Bankrupt Register, 1831–48. 8 vols. 4to.
Austin (A.) (*see* Barron, A.)
―― (R. C.) on Metropolitan Poor Act (bound up
with Glen) 12mo. 1867
―― on Union & Parish Officers' Superannuation
Acts, 1864–66 . . . . 12mo. 1867
Australia—*see* New South Wales
―― Zealand
Queensland
South Australia
Tasmania
Victoria
Western Australia
Australian Agricultural Company Act & Charter,
1824. . . . . folio
Autograph Letters, &c., Catalogue of, exhibited
in the Library of the Incorporated Law Society
by John Young, Esq. in 1862 . . . . 4to.

Avebury, The Old Serpentine Temple of the Druids at (1793), bound up with Dodsworth (W.) on *Salisbury Cathedral*
Ayckbourn's (H.) Chancery Practice. 2nd ed. 8vo. 1846
———————————————————— 3rd ed. 8vo. 1849
———————————————————— 4th ed. 8vo. 1854
———————————————————— 6th ed. 8vo. 1858
———————————————————— 7th ed. 8vo. 1861
——————————— (J. N. Higgins). 8th ed. 8vo. 1866
—— Chancery Forms . . . . . 4th ed. 8vo. 1854
————————————— and Orders 8vo. 1866
Aylmer Peerage Case. ' 4to. 1859
Ayliffe (John, LL.D.) A new Pandect of Roman Civil Law . . . . folio 1734
—— Parergon Juris Canonici Anglicani; or, a Commentary by way of Supplement to the Canons & Constitutions of the Church of England . . . . 2nd ed. folio 1734
Ayloffe (*Sir* J.) Calendar of Ancient Charters, & of the Welsh & Scottish Rolls in Tower of London: Account of Public Records from the Conquest to the present time; also Calendars of Treaties of Peace between England & Scotland
4to. 1772
————————————————— (another copy) . 4to. 1774
Ayrault (P.) or *Ærodius*. Pandectæ rerum ab omni tempore judicatarum . . . . . . folio 1589
————————————————————————— folio 1615
Ayres (W. T.) Comparative View between English & Irish Law . . . . 2 vols. 8vo. 1780
Ayrton (S.) Bankruptcy Bond Practice . 12mo. 1840
—— Bankruptcy Law (*see* Montagu, B.) . . . 1834
—— Bankruptcy Reports (*see* Montagu, B.) . 1837-39
—— on Act for Land Transfer 8vo. 1863
—— Proposal for Act for Composition Deeds. Vol. 3, L. T.
—— Suggestions for an Act to give an Indefeasible Title to Land, addressed to the Legislature. Vol. 11, Pam.

Ayscough, Works of Lord Lyttelton
3rd ed. 2 vols. 8vo. 1776
———— (Saml.) Cat. of Additional MSS. in British Museum . . . . 2 vols. 4to. 1782

B

Babington (C.) (*see* Pecock) 19 M. R. Pub.. . . . 1860
———— (R.) on Auctions 8vo. 1826
Back (Capt.) Expedition to Arctic Regions. 8vo. 1838
Bacon (Francis, *Viscount*, St. Alban's) Essays, 1598.
    Apophthegmes, 1625 . . . . . . 12mo.
———— Annals of Henry VII. . . . . . folio 1629
———— Common Law Maxims 4to. 1636
———— Elements of the Common Law . . . 4to. 1636
———— Discourses on the Law . . . 4th ed. folio 1739
———— on Advancement of Learning (G. Wats) 4to. 1640
———— Law Tracts . . . . . . 2nd ed. 8vo. 1741
    Proposal for Amendment of Laws
    Offer of a Law Digest
    Elements of the Common Laws of England, &c.
    The Use of the Law for the Preservation of our Persons, Goods, &c.
    Cases of Treason, Felony, Premunire, Prerogative of the King's Office of Constable
    Arguments in Law in Difficult Cases
    Ordinances in Chancery for the better Administration of Justice
    Reading on Statute of Uses
———— Works by Montagu . . . 17 vols. 8vo. 1825
———— Argument on Writ de Rege Inconsulto. Vol. 1, Coll. Jur.
———— & others, Opinions of in answer to Letter from Lord Ellesmere as to Precedents in Chancery for Relief against Judgments at Common Law, temp. James & Charles. MS. folio
———— Opinion as to Relief in Chancery against Judgments in Common Law. MS. temp. James & Charles
———— (F. Roger) The Opus Tertium & Opus Minus (ed. T. S. Brewer) 15 M. R. Pub. . . 1859

Bacon (J.) Liber Regis 4to. 1786
—— (M.) Abridgment of the Law. 5 v. folio 1736–66
———————————————————— 4th ed. 3 v. folio 1778
———————————————————— (*Sir* Henry
Gwillim & C. E. Dodd). 7th ed. 8 vols. 8vo. 1832–37
Bagehot (W.) Essay reprinted from " National Review " of the History of the Unreformed Parliament. Vol. 15, Pam.
—— On Parliamentary Reform. Vol. 21, Pam. . . 1859
Bagley (W.) Practice at Judges' Chambers . 8vo. 1834
—— General Practice 8vo. 1840
Bagshaw (S.) Kent Gazetteer, &c. . 2 vols. 8vo. 1847
—— & Spencer, Chancery Case, 22 Geo. II.
Vol. 1, Coll. Jur.
Bailey (H.) Bankrupt List, 1772–93 . . . 8vo. 1794
————————————————— 1771-99 . 2nd ed. 8vo. 1799
Baillie (Jac.) (*see* Craig's Jus feudale)
Baily (F.) on Annuities 8vo. 1810
Bainbridge (W.) on Mines & Minerals. 2nd ed. 8vo. 1856
———————————————————— 3rd ed. 8vo. 1867
Baines (E.) Lancashire Directory, &c. 2 vols. 8vo. 1824
—— Strictures on the new Government measure
for Education. Vol. 9, Pamphlets 1853
Baker (G.) History of Northamptonshire
2 vols. folio 1822–41
—— (J.) on Salmon Fisheries 12mo. 1866
———————————————— . 2nd ed. 12mo. 1868
—— (*Sir* R.) Chronicles of English Kings
8th ed. folio 1684
—— (T.) on Burials . . . . 2nd ed. 12mo. 1859
—— Public Health 8vo. 1865
—— (W.) on Coroners 12mo. 1851
Baldwin (*Abp.*) Itinerary thro' Wales in 1188 by
G. de Barri (translated by Sir R. C. Hoare),
with Life of Barri . . . . . . 2 vols. 4to. 1806
—— (R.) New London Guide . 12th ed. 12mo. 1770
—— (S.) on the Customs 4to. 1770
Bale (John *Bp.*) King John (a play). No. 2 C. S.
Pa. (ed. J. P. Collier) 4to. 1838

Bale (*Bp.*) Works.. Par. Soc. Pub. 1849
Balfour of Burleigh Peerage.—Cases of F. M.
   Balfour & R. Bruce. Vol. 1, 3rd series, page 129 1861
Ball (T.) & Beatty (F.) Reports (Irish Chy.)
   1807–14 . . . . 2 vols. 8vo. 1824
—— (W.) Index to Statutes, Great Britain & Ireland, 1800 . . . . folio 1804
—— Appendix to Abridgement of Irish Statutes,
   33–4–5–6–7 Geo. III. 5 (1793–7) . . 4to. 1794–97
Ballantine (W.) (*see* Boote, R.)
Banbury Peerage: Case of William Earl of Banbury. Vol. 1, 2nd series, p. 179, & Vol. 2, 3rd
   Series, p. 194 1809
—— Evidence. Vol. 8, p. 107, & Vol. 2, p. 247 . 1809
—— Pedigree of Knollys Family 1809
Banda and Kirwee Booty: Case & Papers, &
   Judgment of Dr. Lushington in Court of
   Admiralty. . . . . 10 vols. folio 1866
Bandinel (*Rev.* B.) (*see* Caley)
Bank of England Charter, 6 W. & M. . . 12mo. 1679
———————————— Report . . . . folio 1832
———————— On the Crisis of 1847, with an
   Examination of certain Fallacies in Mr. Disraeli's
   Life of Lord G. Bentinck. Vol. 9, Pam. . . 1854
Bankers' & Notaries' Law Manual (New York)
   (Dr. W. R. Wedgwood & J. S. Homan) . 8vo. 1867
Bankruptcy Act, 6 Geo. IV. with Notes . 8vo. 1826
—— Act, 1826–39 . . . . 8vo. 1843
—— Act to establish Uniform System in America.
   Pam. 8vo. 1842
—— Act, Alphabetical List of Applicants under.
   Pam. 8vo. 1843
—— Considerations on 8vo. 1818
—— Consolidation, Letter to Lord Lyndhurst,
   from a Barrister. Vol. 6, Pam. 1849
—— Digest, an Article for Lord Brougham, by a
   Practical Man. Vol. 6, Pam. 1849
—— Gazette, 1861–62 . . . . 3 vols. folio. 1861–63
—— & Insolvency Reports, 1853–4 . . . 8vo. 1855

Bankruptcy, Letter to Sir R. Bethell on Law of,
by a Registrar of the Court. Vol. 10, Pam. . . 1859
Bankruptcy, Orders in 8vo. 1842–68
—— Pamphlets on the Court of, bound up with
Humphreys on Real Property . . . 8vo. 1829–34
—— Practice Epitomised . . . . . 6th ed. 8vo. 1808
—— Reports of Parl. Commissioners . folio, 1849–54
—— Rules & Regulations in Circuit & District
Courts of. Pam. 8vo. 1842
—— Statutes relating to 8vo. 1765
Bankrupts, Weekly List of . . . . folio, 1811–12
—————————————— 1817–19 . . . 8vo. 1819
Banks (T. C.) Extinct Peerage. 4 vols. 4to. 1807–37
—— Dormant Peerage . . . . . 2nd ed. 8vo. 1812
—— Family History of Marmyon 4to. 1817
—— Stirling Peerage Case 4to. 1826
Bannister (J.) on New Colonies 8vo. 1830
—— (S.) (*see* Sir O. Bridgman)
—— Grammar Schools. Vol. 2, Jac. L. T. . . 1820
—— North American Indians. Do. 1823
Bar (The) Sketches of Eminent Judges, &c. a
Poem. 12mo. 1825
Barba (A. A.) Collection of Treatises upon Metals,
Mines, &c. 8vo. 1738
Barbadoes Orders in Chancery, 1653–1811. folio
—— Laws, 1666–1863 . . . 2 vols. 8vo. 1855–64
—————————— 1864–67 . . . . . . 1 vol. 8vo.
Barcelona. Codico de las Costumbras, Maritimas,
&c. 4to. 1791
Baretti (J.) Dictionary, Spanish & English (& *see*
Neuman & Baretti) . . . . . 2nd ed. folio 1778
—— Dictionary, Italian & English, by J. Daven-
port & G. Comelate . . . . . . 2 vols. 8vo. 1860
Barker (C.) Joint Stock Company's Directory. 8vo. 1864
Barlow (F.) Peerage . . . 2nd ed. 2 vols. 8vo. 1765
————————————— . . . . 2 vols. 8vo. 1772
Barnardistone (R.) K.B. Reports, 1724–34
2 vols. folio 1744
—— (T.) Chancery Reports, 1740–41 . . . folio 1742

Barnardistone and Soames, as to Election of M.P.
(*see* Atkyns, Sir R. *Tracts*)
Barnes (H.) Notes of Cases . . . 2 vols. 8vo. 1754
——————————————— . . . 2nd ed. 4to. 1772
Barnes (H.) Notes of Cases. 1736-1756, 3rd ed. 8vo. 1790
—— (Joshua) History of Edward III. . . folio 1688
—— (R.) Report of Exeter Deanery Case. Vol. 2, Pam. 1841
—— Equity Practice, Enquiry into, &c. Vol. 6. Jac. L. T. 1827
—— (W. E.) (*see* Sir J. Bayley)
Barnett (J. D.) & Buckler (H.) Central Criminal Court Trials, 1847–67 . . . . 41 vols. 8vo.
(and *see* Buckler, H.)
Barnewall Peerage Case, 1st series, Part 1, Evidence, Vol. 11, p. 275 1813
—— (R. V.) & Adolphus (J. L.) K. B. Reports, 1830 1834 . . . . 5 vols. 8vo. 1831–35
—— & Alderson (E. H.) ditto, 1818–22
5 vols. 8vo. 1818–22
—— & Cresswell (C.) ditto, 1823–30
10 vols. 8vo. 1823–32
Barnham (T. C.) Questions for Law Students (Jones) . . . . 4th ed. 12mo. 1840
Baron & Feme 12mo. 1700
Baronages & Peerages, British Compendium
11 vols. 12mo. 1719–46
—— Extinct 12mo. 1769
——————— 8vo. 1807
Barrett (B.) Code Napoléon (translated) (*see* Code Napoléon, translated by a Barrister; also Richards)
2 vols. 8vo. 1811
Barri (G.) (*see* Baldwin, *Abp.*)
Barrington (*Sir J.*) Memoirs of Ireland. 2 v. folio 1833
Barrister, Thoughts of a Junior, on his Position & his Prospects. Vol. 17, Pam. 1852
Barron (A.) & Arnold (T. J.) Election Cases, 1843–46 . . . . 8vo. 1846
—— (A.) & Austin (A.) Election Cases, 1842. 8vo. 1844

Barrow (G.) Rights of Britons . . . . . 4to. n. d.
—— (J. H.) Mirror of Parliament, 1828–37
       38 vols. folio 1828–37
     ————1838–41. 24 vols. 8vo. 1838–42
Barry (M.) on Calculation of Time (*see* Lectures,
 Ireland) 1842
—— (W. W.) Statutory Jurisdiction of Court of
 Chancery 8vo. 1861
—— Conveyancing Practice 8vo. 1865
—— Law & Practice of Benefit Building & Free-
 hold Land Societies 12mo. 1866
Barstow (D.) Secular Diary . . . . . 12mo. n. d.
Barter(W. G. T.) on Homer & English Metre. 12mo. 1862
—— Essays on Law Life & Literature . 12mo. 1863
Bartolus de Saxoferrato. Lectura . . . . folio 1471
Barton (C.) Suit in Equity 8vo. 1796
—— Elements of Conveyancing . 5 vols. 8vo. 1802–5
—— Precedents in ditto 8vo. 1802
Barwick (W.) Report of Trial, Tatham *v.* Wright,
 before Mr. Baron Gurney. 12mo. 1834
Bassett, Law Catalogue 12mo. 1682
Bate (J.) on Emigration to British Colonies, show-
 ing Extent, &c. of, Vol. 18, Pam 1862
—— Letter to Lord Lyttelton on the National Im-
 portance of Emigration, Vol. 18, Pam. . . . 1863
Bateman (I.) on Turnpikes, & Supplement
         2 vols. 12mo. 1823
————————————— . . . 3rd ed. 12mo. 1836
—— on Highways (Welsby) . . 2nd ed. 12mo. 1863
—— (J.) on Auctions (Rouse) . . . 4th ed. 8vo. 1863
—— on Excise Laws 8vo. 1843
—— (T.) on Tithes 8vo. 1770
Bather *v.* Brayne: Trial 8vo. 1848
Bathurst (*Earl*) Biography of (*see* Eminent
 Lawyers) 1790
Batteley (J.) History of Bury St. Edmunds. 4to. 1745
—— Antiquities of Richborough 8vo. 1711
       ———— 2nd ed. 4to. 1745
Batten (E. C.) & (H.) Ludlow, Equity Jurisdic-
 tion of County Courts 8vo. 1866

Battista (Giov.) Consolato del Mare . . . 4to. 1612
Battle of the Blocks, bound up with Hogan's Appeal to the Public 1809
Baugh's Map of Shropshire . . . . . . folio 1808
Bawdwen (*Rev.* W.) Domesday Book for Derbyshire 4to. 1809
—— Domesday Book (translation) for Middlesex, Hertford, Bucks, Oxford, & Gloucester . 4to. 1812
—— & Hutchins (*Rev.* J.), Domesday for Dorset; & Dissertations . . . . folio 1815
—— Domesday Book (translation) for Yorkshire; Amounderness, Lonsdale, & Furness, in Lancashire; parts of Westmoreland & Cumberland, Derby, Nottingham, Rutland, & Lincoln . 4to. 1809
Baxter (J.) Agricultural, &c. Library
3rd ed. 8vo. 1834
Bayle (F.) General Dictionary . 10 vols. folio. 1731–41
Bayley (*Sir* J.) on Bills of Exchange (W. E. Barnes)
3rd ed. 12mo. 1813
———————————————— 4th ed. 8vo. 1822
———————————————— 5th ed. 8vo. 1830
—— on Common Prayer 8vo. 1816
—— (J.) History of the Tower of London
2nd ed. 8vo. 1830
—— (W. D.) Account of the House of D'Oyley (*see* Grimaldi's Tracts, Vol. 3) 1845
Bayly (J. B.) Commentaries 8vo. 1840
Beames (J.) Chancery Orders 8vo. 1815
—— on Equity Costs 8vo. 1822
———————————— . . . . 2nd ed. 8vo. 1840
———————————— on Writ of Ne Exeat Regno, bound up with Beames on Costs . . . 2nd ed. 1824
—— (*see* Vesey, F.)
Bearblock (J.) on Tithes 8vo. 1813
———————————————— . . . . 5th ed. 8vo. 1818
Bearcroft (*Dr.* P.) Biography of Sutton . . 8vo. 1737
Beasley (T. J.) Precedents in Masters' Office, Irish Chancery 8vo. 1837
———————————————— 2nd ed. 8vo. 1840

Beasley (T. J.) Precedents in Masters' Office, Irish
    Chancery . . . . 3rd ed. 8vo. 1843
—— Duties of Attorneys & Solicitors (*see* Irish
    Pamphlets)
—— Lectures on the Profession of Attorney &
    Solicitor, at the Law Institute, Dublin (*see* Irish
    Pamphlets)
—— on Irish Records (*see* Irish Pamphlets) . . 1842
Beatson's (Jos.) Political Index or Register of
    Hereditary Honours . . . . . 3 vols. 8vo. 1806
—— Parliamentary Register . . . 3 vols. 8vo. 1807
—— Biographical Index of present House of Lords
                                         12mo. 1808
Beatty (F.) (*see* Ball)
—— Reports (Irish Chancery), temp. Manners &
    Hart, 1827–29 . . . . 8vo. 1829
Beaufort (*Dr.* D. A.) Memoir Illustrating Topo-
    graphy of Ireland 4to. 1792
Beaufoy (H. B. H.) Catalogue of the London
    Traders' Tokens current in the 17th Century. 8vo. 1853
—— (J. H. Burn) . . . . . . 2nd ed. 8vo. 1855
—— (Col. M.) Hydraulics Experiments . 4to. 1834
Beaumont (G.) on Insurance, Fire & Life . 8vo. 1833
—— (G. B. D.) on the Code for Real Property.
    Vol. 5, Jac. L. T. 1827
—— (J.) on Bills of Sale 12mo. 1855
—— (Josh.) Letters on Marriage with a Deceased
    Wife's Sister; to Earl of Ellesmere. Vol. 2, Pam. 1851
—— Peerage: Case of M. T. Stapleton. Vol. 1,
    2nd series, p. 204
—— Peerage Evidence. Vol. 21, 1840. House
    of Lords' Sessions Paper 1840
Beaurain *v.* Sir William Scott: Trial for Excom-
    munication 8vo. 1814
Beavan (C.) Chancery Orders 8vo. 1842
—— Reports (Rolls), temp. Langdale & Romilly,
    1838–65 . . . . 35 vols. 8vo. 1841–65
—— (E.) *Railway & Canal Cases* (*see* Oliver, L.)
—— *Statutes* (*see* Chitty, J.)

Beavan & Parkins (W. T.) Addenda to Chitty's
  Statutes, 1854–63 . . . . . . 2 vols. 8vo. 1858–63
Beawes (W.) Commercial Law. 5th ed. (T. Mortimer)
  folio 1792
Beccaria (C.) dei Delitti e delle Pene . .12mo. 1801
  ——————————————————— . . 8vo. 1828
—— on Criminal Law of Tuscany . . . 8vo. 1828
—— (G.) on Artificial Electricity (translated) 4to. 1776
Becke (G.) Letter to Lord Campbell, proposing a
  Cheap & Simple Substitute for the County Court
  Extension Bill in the Superior Courts. Vol. 20,
  Pam. 1850
Beckwith (W.) on Chancery Delays . . . 8vo. 1810
Becon (T.) Works (Parker Society's Papers) . 1842–44
Bedarride (J.) des Commerçants 8vo. 1854
—— des Sociétés . . . . . 5 vols. 8vo. 1857–59
—— du Commerce maritime . . . 5 vols. 8vo. 1859
—— de la Lettre de Change . . . 2 vols. 8vo. 1861
—— des Achats et Ventes 8vo. 1862
—— des Bourses de Commerce 8vo. 1862
—— Traité des Faillites & Banqueroutes
  4th ed. 3 vols. 8vo. 1862
—— des Commissionnaires 8vo. 1863
—— de la Jurisdiction commerciale . . . 8vo. 1864
Bedford (*Duke* of) Anecdotes of 8vo. 1796
—— Level Acts (C. N. Cole) . . . 5 vols. 4to. n. d.
Bedfordshire, Topographical & Historical Descrip-
  tion of 8vo. 1801
Beer & Malt Reducing Duties, Enquiry as to,
  Vol. 5, Pam. 1830
Beesley (A.) History of Banbury 8vo. 1841
Belfast, Historical Collection as to . . . 8vo. 1817
Belhaven Peerage: Case of W. Hamilton. Vol. 1,
  3rd series, 262, &c. 1799
Bell (*Major* E.) on the Mysore Reversion
  2nd ed. 8vo. 1866
—— (G. J.) Scotch Law Principles . 3rd ed. 8vo. 1833
—— Commentaries on Scotch Law (Shaw)
  6th ed. 2 vols. 8vo. 1858

Bell (H. N.) on Huntingdon Peerage. . . . 4to. 1820
—— (J. S.) Scotch Appeals to House of Lords,
1848–52 . . . . 7 vols. 8vo.
—— (R.) Dictionary of Scotch Decisions (W. Bell)
3rd ed. 2 vols. 8vo. 1826
—— (Robt.) Scotch Election Law . . . 8vo. 1812
—— (T.) Crown Cases, 1858–60 . . . . 8vo. 1861
—— (Thos.) (*see* Dearsley, H. R.)
—— (W.) Digest of Scotch Law, by G. Ross 8vo. 1861
——'s Weekly Messenger, 1805–42 . 11 vols. folio
Bellarmin (R.) Disputationes . 4 vols. in 3, folio 1608
Belt (R.) (*see* Vesey's (Senr.) *Chancery Reports*)
—— *Chancery Reports* (*see* Brown, W.)
Beltz (G. F.) on Chandos Peerage . . . 8vo. 1834
Benefices, List of, in Lord Chancellor's patronage
(*see* Vol. 3 House of Lords Sess. pap.). . . . 1863
Bengal Gazette 1868–69
Bengal Presidency, Regulations & Acts of (*see*
East India Company)
Benjamin (T. P.) on Sale of Personal Property. 8vo. 1868
Benloe (W.) & (W.) Dalison's Reports, temp. Hen.
VIII. to Elizabeth (*French*). . . . . folio 1689
Bennet (W. H.) Practice in Masters' Office . 8vo. 1834
—— on Receiver in Chancery 8vo. 1849
Bennett (J.) History of Tewkesbury (Gloucester)
8vo. 1830
Benson (T.) Vocabularium Anglo-Saxonicum. 8vo. 1701
Bentham (J.) History & Antiquities of the
Cathedral Church of Ely, &c. 4to. 1771
———————— Supplement to, &c. & Memoirs of
Rev. J. Bentham, by W. Stevenson, F.S.A. 4to. 1817
—— Usury . . . . 12mo. 1790 ✓
—— Judicial Evidence (Dumont) . . . . 8vo. 1825 ✓
—— Vindication respecting Lord Eldon, Vol. 1,
Jac. L. T. . . . . 1825 ✓
—— on General Registry. Vol. 10, Jac.L. T. . . 1831
—— Packing Special Juries . . . . . 8vo. 1831 ✓
—— Traité de Législation (Dumont). . . 8vo. 1858 ✓
Bentley (R.) Miscellany. Vols. 44 to 64
18 vols. 8vo. 1858–68

Benwell (J. B.) New Formulæ in the Valuation of Annuities on Lives, &c. (bound up with Fairman, Wm.) 1830

Bergenroth (G. A.) Calendar of Letters, Despatches, and State Papers, relating to the Negotiations between England & Spain, preserved in the Archives of Simancas and elsewhere. Vol. 1: Hen. VII. 1485–1509. Vol. 2: 1509–25. Supplement to Vols. 1, 2 (*see* Calendar of State Papers) . . . . imp. 8vo. 1862–68

Berkeley Peerage: Case, 1799, of W. F. Berkeley & others. Vol. 1, 2nd Series, 228

—— Evidence. Vols. 1, 2, 3 1799–1811

—— New Case, & Evidence. 3 vols. folio 1858, &c.

Berkshire, Historical Description of . . . 8vo. 1802

—— Pedigrees, MS. . . . . folio 1623

—— Poll Book 8vo. 1818

Bermuda Acts, 1691–1860 (J. H. Darell) . . . 1862

—— Acts, 1857–1867 . . . . . . 3 vols. folio

Bernardy (C. W. de) Register of Unclaimed Property, 1754–1856 . . . . 8vo. 1858

Berner's Peerage: Case of R. Wilson. Vol. 1, 2nd series, p. 295 . . . .

—— Vol. 1, 3rd series, p. 274 . . . .

—— Evidence. Vol. 3, p. 476, and Vol. 9, p. 1 . 1822

Berry (W.) County Genealogies. Pedigrees of the Families in the County of Kent, collected from the Heraldic Visitations and other authentic Manuscripts in the British Museum, and in the possession of private individuals, and from the information of the present resident families. folio 1830

—— Pedigrees of the Families in the County of Sussex . . . . folio 1830

—— Pedigrees of the Families in the County of Hants . . . . folio 1833

—— Pedigrees of Hertfordshire Families, collected by Wm. Berry, transferred from his own hand-writing, & printed in lithography by F. Alvey . . . . folio

Berry (W.) Pedigrees of Essex Families, bound up with the above
—— History of Guernsey, from the remotest period of antiquity to the year 1814; with particulars of the neighbouring Islands of Alderney, Serk, & Jersey 4to. 1815
Berton (G. F. S.) Acts of New Brunswick, 1776–1836 . . . . 4to. 1838
Best (W. M.) Witnesses' Examination. Vol. 4, L. Tr. 1836
—— Right to Begin & to Reply 8vo. 1837
—— Law of Presumptions 8vo. 1844
—— on Evidence . . . . . . 3rd ed. 8vo. 1860
———————— . . . . . . 4th ed. 8vo. 1866
—— & Smith (P.). Reports, Q. B. 1861–65
4 vols. 8vo. 1862–65
Betham (Rev. W.) Genealogical Tables . . folio 1795
—— on Baronetage . . . . . 4 vols. 4to. 1801–4
—— (Sir Wm.) Irish Antiquarian Researches
2 vols. 8vo. 1826–27
—— on Feudal Dignities 8vo. 1830
Bever (Dr. T.) Legal Policy of the Roman Law. 4to. 1781
Bibliotheca Britannica Catalogue . 8 vols. 8vo. 1813–19
—— Hibernica . . . . 5 vols. 8vo. 1834
Bickersteth (Rev. R.) & Others: Opinions on the Lawfulness of Marriage with a Deceased Wife's Sister. Vol. 24, Pam. 1851
Biggs (J.) Railway Regulation Acts, 1838–47
12mo. 1849
—— Clauses Consolidation Acts, 1845–66 . 12mo. 1866
—— Standing Orders in Parliament, 1839–67
6 vols. 12mo.
Bigland (J.) Yorkshire, Historical Description of
8vo. 1819
—— (R.) Observations on Marriages, Baptisms, &c. as presented in Parochial Registers . . 4to. 1764
Bills of Exchange 8vo. 1760
Bilton (S. F.) Law & Practice in Divorce . 12mo. 1860
Bingham (P.) (see Broderip, W. J.)

Bingham (P.) Reports, C.P., 1822–34
        10 vols. 8vo. 1824–34
—— New Cases, 1834–40 . . . 6 vols. 8vo. 1835–41
Binnell (R.) Thames Conservancy, &c. History of
            8vo. 1758
Binney (T.) Argument on the Levitical Marriage Law, as to Marriage with a Deceased Wife's Sister. Vol. 24, Pam. 1851
Binns (J.) Map of Lancaster 1821
Biographical Dictionary . . . . 11 vols. 8vo. 1761
Birch (A. N.) & William Robinson, Colonial Office List . . . . . . 7th ed. 8vo. 1868, & continued
Bird (C.) Letter to Attorney-General on the Malpractices in the Crown Courts at Exeter. Vol. 18, Pam. 1842
—— (G.) Practising Scrivener & Modern Conveyancer . . . . folio 1729
—— (J. B.) Pocket Conveyancer
       3rd ed. 2 vols. 12mo. 1816
Birléy (W. R.) Election Rules 12mo. 1869
Births, Deaths, & Marriages in England. 8th & 9th Reports of Registrar-General . . 2 vols. folio 1848
————————————————— Monthly Record. 8vo. 1861
Bishop (J. P.) Criminal Law (U.S.)
       2nd ed. 2 vols. 8vo. 1858–59
————————————————— 3rd ed. 2 vols. 8vo. 1865
—— Marriage & Divorce (U.S.) 4th ed. 2 vols. 8vo. 1864
—— First Book of the Law (U.S.) . . . 8vo. 1868
Bishops' Right to Vote in Parliament . . 12mo. 1680
Bishops (Seven) Trial of the 8vo. 1739
Bisset (A.) *Precedents in Conveyancing* (*see* Bythewood, W. M.)
—— on Estates for Life 8vo. 1842
Bittleston (A.) & Wise (E.) New Practice Cases, 1844–48 . . . . 3 vols. 8vo. 1846–48
Blackburn (*Sir* Colin) (*see* Ellis, T. F.)
—— Q. B. Reports (*see* Ellis, T. F.)
—— The Effect of Contract of Sale on the Legal Right of Property and Possession in Goods, &c. 8vo. 1845

Blackie (W. G.) Imperial Gazetteer . 2 vols. 4to. 1856
Blackstone (H.) Reports, C. P. 1788–1796. 2 vols.
folio 1793
———————————————————2nd ed. 2 vols. 8vo. 1801
—— (*Sir* W.) on Law of Descents in Fee Simple.
Vol. 1, L. T. 1759
—— Arguments in Exch. Chamber on giving
Judgment in Perrin *v.* Blake. Har. L. T. on a
Devise
—— Tracts, chiefly relating to the Antiquities &
Laws of England . . . . 3rd ed. 4to. 1771
CONTENTS:—
   I. Analysis of the Laws of England
  II. Essay on Collateral Consanguinity (1750)
 III. Considerations on Copyholders
 IV. Observations on the Oxford Press
  V. Introduction to the Great Charter, &c.
      Magna Carta. Carta de Foresta, &c.

—— Analysis of the Laws of England. 6th ed. 8vo. 1762
—— Commentaries, MSS. . . . . . 4 vols. 8vo.
—— Commentaries, Dr. Bever's MSS. 2 vols. folio
—— Commentaries . . 1st ed. 4 vols. 4to. 1765–69
————————————————— 3rd ed. 4 vols. 4to. 1768
————————————————— 7th ed. 2 vols. 8vo. 1775
————————————————— 8th ed. 4 vols. 8vo. 1778
———————————————(Dr. Burn) 10th ed. 3 vols. 8vo. 1787
——————————————(Christian) 12th ed. 4 vols. 8vo. 1793
————————————————— 14th ed. 4 vols. 8vo. 1803
———————(Sir J. T. Coleridge) 16th ed. 4 vols. 8vo. 1825
————————— New edition (J.Chitty) . 4 vols. 8vo. 1826
—— Select Extracts from (S. Warren) . 12mo. 1837
————————————————— (J. M. Kerr) . 4 vols. 8vo. 1857
————————————————— 3rd ed. 4 vols. 8vo. 1862
—————————— Commentaires sur les Loix anglaises
6 vols. 8vo. 1774
—— Biography of; containing also a Catalogue of
his Works, published & in manuscript, and The
Nomenclature of Westminster Hall . . 8vo. 1782
—— & *see* Roscoe's Lives of Lawyers 1790
—— Reports, K. B. 1746–79 . . 2 vols. folio 1784

Blackstone (*Sir* W.) Reports (C. H. Elsley)
2nd ed. 2 vols. 8vo. 1828
—— Judgment in Perrin *v.* Blake. Vol. 1, Hargrave's L. T. 1787
Blackwood's Magazine, with Index. 104 vols. 8vo. 1817–68
Blaine (D. R.) Suggestions on Copyright Works of Art Bill. Vol. 13, Pam. 12mo. 1861
Blair (*Dr.* J. B.) Chronology (J. W. Rosse) 12mo. 1856
Blake (M.) Account of Blandford Fire in 1731. 12mo. 1736
—— (W.) Observations on Rev. R. Jones's Pam. on Rating Tithes to the Poor. Vol. 1, Pam. . 1839
Blankley (T. R.) Naval Expositor . . . 4to. 1750
Blatchford (Saml.) Reports of Cases in Prize (U.S.) 1861–65 . . . . 8vo. 1866
Blesinton Rental (Dublin) 4to. 1836
Blewert (W.) Stock Table . . . 4th ed. 12mo. n. d.
Blewitt (R. G.) Satirical Poem on Court of Chancery 8vo. 1827
Bligh (R. J.) Reports, House of Lords, 1819–21
4 vols. 8vo. 1823–27
———————— N. S. 1827–37. 11 vols. 8vo. 1827–37
—— (R.) Bankruptcy Reports (*see* Montagu, B.)
Blome (R.) Britannia, with plates of Arms . folio 1673
Blomefield (*Rev.* F.) History of Norfolk, continued by *Rev.* C. Parkin . . . 11 vols. 8vo. 1805–10
—— History of Norwich . . . . 2 vols. 8vo. 1806
—— History of Thetford 4to. 1739
—— (*Rev.* R.) Collectanea Cantabrigiensia, or Collections relating to Cambridge University, Town, & County 4to. 1750
Blonde of Oxford, No. 72 C. S. P. [P. de Reimes] (ed. M. de Roux de Lincy) 4to. 1858
Blore (T.) History of South Winfield (Derby)
2nd ed. 4to. 1816
Blount (T.) Law Dictionary 4to. 1670
—— Fragmenta Antiquitatis, or Ancient Tenures of Land, & Jocular Customs of Manors, by H. M. Beckwith 4to. 1815
Bloxam (R.) Chamber Regulations in Chancery. 8vo. 1857

Blundell (B.) Parliamentary Privilege, Considerations on the Judgment in Stockdale v. Hansard 1839
—— Memorial of Abingdon Free Grammar School. Vol. 16, Pam. 1863
—— (Benson) on Separate Use Clauses in Tullet v. Armstrong. Vol. 4, L. T. 1839
Blunt (J. E.) History of the Jews in England. Vol. 7, Jac. L. T. 1839
Boat Building Company by Machinery. Vol. 13, Pam. 1861
Bode (*Baron* de) Address to House of Commons. Vol. 5, Pam. 1833
—— Statement for Counsel's Opinion, & Opinions of several Foreign Counsel. Vol. 16, Pam. . . 1845
Bodman (J.) Concise History of Trowbridge, 1814, bound up with Dodsworth (W.) on Salisbury Cathedral
Bocce (H.) History of (*see* No. 6 M. R. Pub.). . 1858
Boetius (H.) Scotorum Historia . . . . folio 1526
Bohn (H. G.) on Foreign Copyright . . . 8vo. 1851
Bohun (W.) Institutio Legalis, or K.B. & C.P. Practice . . . . 3rd ed. 8vo. 1724
———————————————— K.B. . 5th ed. 8vo. 1764
—— Laws & Customs of London . . 3rd ed. 8vo. 1723
—— Tithes . . . . 2nd ed. 8vo. 1731
—— Chancery Practice 8vo. 1715
—— Attorneys' Practice . . . . 2nd ed. 8vo. 1726
———————————————— 8vo. 1764
Bolton (G.) Criminal Practice 12mo. 1825
—— (S.) Extinct Peerage 8vo. 1769
Bombay Gazette 1868–69
Bombay Almanac & Directory . 2 vols. 8vo. 1867–68
—— Presidency, Regulations & Acts of (*see* East India Company)
Bond (T.) East & West Looe, Historical Sketches of 8vo. 1823
Bonds, Bills, & Notes—Substitute for Sir John Campbell's Summary Law for obtaining Judgment. By an Attorney. Law Tracts, Vol. 8 . 1835

Bonney (*Rev.* H. K.) Historical Notices of Fotheringhay 8vo. 1821
Bonnycastle's Arithmetic (Maynard) 19th ed. 12mo. 1862
Boote (R.) Action at Law 8vo. 1766
——————————————— . . . 2nd ed. 8vo. 1781
——————————— (W. Ballantine) 5th ed. 8vo. 1814
——————————————————— . 6th ed. 8vo. 1823
Booth (G. R.) Observations on Defective Plan of London Sewerage Question. Vol. 2, Pam.
—— (J.) on Statute of Uses (1791). Vol. 1, Col. Jur. 1791
Boothby (R.) on Indictable Offences . . . 8vo. 1842
———————————— 2nd ed. (S. Temple) 8vo. 1854
—— Suggestions of a Plan for adapting the Superior Courts of Common Law, Circuit Courts of Assizes, & Sessions of the Peace, to the increased demands of the Country Local Courts; being the Remedy for the Law's Defects. Vol. 20, Pam. . 1844
Boothroyd (B.) History of Pontefract . . 8vo. 1807
Borcholten (J.) Commentarii in quatuor Institutionum Juris Civilis libros . . (Geneva) 4to. 1640
Borlace (E.) Account of Latham Spa . 12mo. 1670
Borlase (D. W.) Natural History of Cornwall
folio 1758
—— Historical & Monumental Account of ditto
2nd ed. folio 1769
Borsari (L.) Il Civile Codice Italiano. 2 vols. 8vo. 1865–67
Borthwick (W.) on Feudal Dignities . . . 8vo. 1775
—— Peerage Cases, 1st series, p. 9 (of J. & W. Borthwick). Vol. 1, 3rd series, 293
—— Evidence, Vol. 2, p. 359 1809
———————— Vol. 9, p. 76 1814
Bosanquet (*Sir* J. B.) & (Puller C.) Reports, C. P., Ex. Chamb. & House of Lords, 1796–1800
3 vols. folio 1800
———————————— 1796–1804. 3rd ed. 3 vols. 8vo. 1826
———————— New ditto, 1804–7. 2nd ed. 2 vols. 8vo. 1827
—— (S. B.) Regula Generalis 8vo. 1835
—— Tithe Commutation Act 12mo. 1837

Bosanquet (W. H.) on Producing Documents before
the Hearing. Vol. 2 Chy. Pam. & Vol. 12 Jac.
Col. 1836
Boston (America) Directory . . 2 vols. 8vo. 1856–1858
Boswell (E.) The Civil Division of the County of
Dorset 8vo. 1795
Botetourt Peerage; Case of N. Berkeley. Vol. 1,
3rd series, p. 305 1764
Bott (E.) Poor Law (F. Const) 3rd ed. 2 vols. 8vo. 1793
———————————— (J. T. Pratt) 6th ed. 2 vols. 8vo. 1827
Bottin (D.) Annuaire Almanach du Commerce
(Paris) 8vo. 1867
Boucher (Jonathan) Glossary . . . 2 vols. 8vo. 1832
Bouillet (Nicholas) Dictionnaire Universel d'His-
toire et de Geographie 8vo. 1864
Boundaries of England & Wales, Reports. 4 vols. fo. 1832
—— England, Small Boroughs, Report . . folio 1832
———————————— & Wales (large paper). 2 vols. folio 1837
—— Ireland, Small Boroughs ditto . . . . folio 1832
—— Scotland, Small Boroughs, ditto . . . folio 1832
Bourchette (J.) British Dominion in North America,
or Canada . . . . 2 vols. in 1, 4to. 1832
Bourget (Dom. Jno.) History of the Royal Abbey
of Bec, near Rouen (bound up with J. N.'s Alien
Priories) 1779
Bourke (R.) Parliamentary Precedents, 2nd ed. 8vo. 1857
Boutell (C.) Heraldry, Historical and Popular
3rd ed. 8vo. 1864
Bouvier (J.) Institutes of American Law
4 vols. 8vo. 1854
—— Law Dictionary of America. 11th ed. 2 vols. 8vo. 1862
Bowdler (C.) Queen's College, Cambridge, Case:
Report, Vol. 2, Jac. L. T. 1821
Bowen's English Atlas . . . . folio 1777
Bowes' Peerage: Case of Jno. Bowes, 1st series,
Vol. 1; 2nd series, Vol. 1 1821
Bowles (J.) on Rights of Judge & Jury on Trials
for Libel (*see* Libel L. T. Vol. 4)

D

Bowles (J.) Two Letters to Mr. Fox on his intended Libel Bill, & Appendix to Second Letter (*see* Libel L. T. Vol. 4.)
—— (*Rev.* W. L.) History of Lacock Abbey. 4to. 1835
Bowman (E.) English Pleader 8vo. 1734
———— (T.) History of Richmond (York) 12mo. 1814
Bowyer (*Sir* G.) Statutes of Italian Cities . 8vo. 1838
—— Commentaries on Civil Law 8vo. 1848
Boyd (*Dr.* R.) Justice of the Peace . 2 vols. 4to. 1787
Boyer (E.) Belgian Traveller . . 4th ed. 12mo. 1810
Boyer (M. A.) Dictionary, English & French. (L. du Mitand) . . . . 2 vols. 4to. 1816
—— Political State of Great Britain, 1711–32
                                                 38 vols. 8vo.
Boyle (W. R. A.) on Charities 8vo. 1837
——'s Court Guide, 1794–1867 . . 69 v. 12mo.
—— (R.) Philosophical Works . . . 3 vols. 4to. 1725
Brabant (John of) & Henry & Thomas of Lancaster, Account of the Expenses of, in 1292-3 (J. Burtt), No. 55 C. M. Vol. 2 . . . 4to. 1852
Bracton, De Legibus . . . . folio 1569
——————————— 4to. 1640
—— & his relation to the Roman Law, by C. Guterboch, translated by B. Coxe, Philadelphia
                                                 8vo. 1866
Bradby (J.) on Distress 8vo. 1808
Bradford (J.) Works (A. Townsend) Par. S. Pa. . 1848
Bradshaw's Railway Guide, 1846–68 . 50 v. 12mo.
—— Railway Maps
—— Continental Guide, 5 vols. . . . 12mo. 1864–68
—— Continental Guide, with Plans of Towns
                                                12mo. 1864–68
—— Shareholder's Manual 8vo. 1866
Brady (Robt.) Introduction to the Old English History, with a Glossary of Words in Ancient Records, Laws, & Historians . . . . . folio 1684
—— (F.) on Cities, &c. 8vo. 1777
—— (J.) Clavis Calendaria, 3rd edit. 2 vols. 8vo. 1815
—— Lectures (*see* Irish Pamphlets)

Braithwaite (J. W.) Oaths in Chancery 1854
———————————————— 2nd ed. 12mo. 1864
—— Record & Writ Practice 8vo. 1858
—— Times of Procedure in Chancery . . . 8vo. 1864
Brakelonda (J. de) Chronica, 1173-1202, C. S.
Pa. No. 13 (J. G. Rokewode) 4to. 1840
Bramley's (H.) Catalogue of Engraved British
Portraits 4to. 1793
Bramston (*Sir* J.) Autobiography of (temp. Ch. I.
& Ja. II.) C. S. Pa. No. 32 (T. W. Bramston) 1845
Bramwell (G.) Table of Private Acts, 1727-1834
2 vols. 8vo. 1835
—— House of Commons Practice 8vo. 1837
—— Parliamentary Bills 4to. 1837
Brand (J.) History of Newcastle (Nor.) 2 vols. 4to. 1789
Brandon Peerage : Case of Duke of Hamilton. 1st
series, Pa. 33 1782
—— (W.) on the Customary Laws of London on
the Distribution of Freeman's Personal Estate.
Vol. 20, Pam. 1843
—— on Foreign Attachment in Lord Mayor's
Court 8vo. 1861
—— Mayor's Court Practice 8vo. 1864
Brant (S.) Concilium Basiliense. 4to. 1499
Brantone (P. de) Mémoires . . . 9 vols. 12mo. 1666
Brasseur (J.) French Grammar . 17th ed. 12mo. 1863
Brathwait (R.) Barnabæ Itinerarium, or Barnabee's
Journal . . . . 7th ed. 12mo. 1818
Bratiorio (D.) Correspondence with Lord Dudley
C. Stuart on the Danubian Principalities of
Wallachia & Moldavia. Vol. 9, Pam. 1853
Bray Peerage : Cases of Sir P. H. Dyke & Another.
2nd series. Vol. 1, p. 297
—— Evidence. Vol. 1, p. 1 1836
—— Vol. 2, p. 301 1836
—— Vol. 19. H. L. Sess. Pa. 1837-38
—— Vol. 17 . . do. 1839
—— (W.) (*see* Manning, *Rev.* O.)

D 2

Bray (R.) Sketch of a Bill to promote the Extinction of Manorial Tenures 8vo. 1835
—— (W.) Tour in Derbyshire, Leicestershire, Northamptonshire, Nottinghamshire, Warwickshire, Yorkshire . . . . . . 2nd ed. 8vo. 1783
Brayley (E. W.) Topographical & Historical Description of Kent . . . . . . 2 vols. 8vo. 1808
—— Topographical & Historical Description of London & Middlesex . . . . . . 5 vols. 8vo. 1810–16
—— History of Isle of Thanet & Cinque Ports
2 vols. 8vo. 1817
—— History of Surrey . . . . . 5 vols. 4to. 1850
—— & Britton (J.) History of Westminster. 8vo. 1836
Bretherton (E.) on Registration of Voters . 8vo. 1863
Brewer (J. N.) History of Oxfordshire . . 8vo. 1818
—— (J. S.) Calendar of Letters & Papers, Foreign and Domestic, of the Reign of Henry VIII. preserved in Her Majesty's Public Record Office, the British Museum, &c. . Vol. 1, 1509–14. Vol. 2 (in two parts), 1515–18. Vol. 3 (in two parts), 1519–23 . . . . . . Imp. 8vo. 1862–67
—— Monumenta Franciscana (see No. 4 M. R. Pub.) 1858
—— "Opus Tertium," & "Opus Minus" of Roger Bacon, 15 M. R. Pub. 1859
—— Works of G. Cambrensis. Vols. 1, 2, 3. 21 M. R. Pub. 1861–63
—— (J. S.) & Bullen (Wm.) Calendar of the Carew Papers, preserved in Lambeth Library.
  Vol. 1. 1515–1574. Vol. 3. 1589–1600.
  Vol. 2. 1575–1588.
3 vols. 8vo. 1867–69
—— (T.) Life of John Carpenter, Founder of City School 8vo. 1856
Brewster (Rev. J.) Antiquities of Stockton-on-Tees, Durham 4to. 1796
Brice (A.) Mobiad (Exeter Election) . . . 8vo. 1770
Brickdale (M. L. F.) on Settled Estates, Leases, & Sales Act 12mo. 1856
—————————————— another ed. 12mo. 1861

Bridges (J.) History of Northamptonshire (Whalley). . . . . 2 vols. folio 1791
Bridgman (*Sir* J.) Reports K. B. 1615-20 . folio 1659
—— (*Sir* O.) Conveyancing (T. P. Johnson) folio 1682
———————————————— . . 3rd ed. folio 1699
———————————————— 5th ed. 2 vols. in 1, folio 1725
Bridgman (*Sir* O.) Reports C. P. (S. Bannister), 1660-67 . . . . 8vo. 1823
—— (R. W.) (*see* Buller, Sir F.)
—— Thesaurus Juridicus; Decisions of Equity Courts, High Court of Parliament, and of the Courts of Equity and Parliament in Ireland, from the Revolution to E. T. 1798. Vols. 1,2. 8vo. 1799-1800
—— (R. W.) Reflections on Law Study. 12mo. 1804
—— View of Legal Bibliography 8vo. 1807
—— Equity Digest, Companion, & Supplement
3rd ed. 5 vols. 8vo. 1822-32
Bridgwater Treatises (various authors)
12 vols. 8vo. 1836
Brieves, History of (*see* Hist. L. T.)
Bright (J. E.) on Husband & Wife . 2 vols. 8vo. 1849
Brightley (F. C.) Digest of Decisions of the Federal Courts, from the Organisation of the Government (U.S.) to the present time. . . . 8vo. 1868
Brighton (New), Cheshire, Plan of
Bristol Poll Books 8vo. 1722-38
—— Charities (by a Barrister) 8vo. 1823
Bristow (S. B.) Private Bill Practice . . 12mo. 1859
Britain, Present State of Court of . . . 12mo. 1742
Britannia Newspaper . . . . folio 1841
British Colonies in America, Charters of . . 8vo.
—— Compendium of Peerage. 11 vols. 12mo. 1719-46
—— Critic . . . . . . 42 vols. 8vo. 1795-1813
—— Guiana Ordinances, 1856-65 (1863 wanting)
2 vols. folio
—— Imperial Kalendar . . 1812-50. 36 vols. 8vo.
—— Museum Acts & Votes, 1752-1808 . . 8vo. 1808
—— Museum, Addition to MSS. in 1836-45
2 vols. 8vo. 1843-52

British Museum, Catalogue of Printed Books in
Mus.: A to Assurimus . . . . . . folio 1841
—— Museum, Catalogue of Printed Books of
Reference in Reading Room 8vo. 1859
—— Museum, Observations on Reading Room. folio 1850
—— Museum, Statutes & Rules . . . 12mo. 1754
—— Provinces of North America, Review of
Law of 8vo. 1790
Britton (J.) (*see* Brayley)
—— History of Lancashire 8vo. 1815
—— Survey of Borough of Marylebone . . 4to. 1834
—— Architectural & Archæological Dictionary. 8vo. 1838
—— Biography of Aubrey 4to. 1845
—— Catalogue of Books as to Wilts . . 12mo. 1857
—— Law. Edited & translated from the French
by F. M. Nichols . . . . . . 2 vols. 8vo. 1865
—— Essay on Topography . . . . . . 4to.
—— & Hosking on Rebuilding Church of St.
Mary Redcliffe 4to. 1842
Broderip (W. J.) (*see* Callis)
—— & Bingham (P.) C. P. Reports, 1818–22
3 vols. 8vo. 1821–23
Brook (Robt.) upon Statute of Magna Charta. L.
T. & A. 1641
—— (N.) England's Glory 12mo. 1660
Brooke (Ralph) Catalogue of Succession of Kings
& Nobility . . . . folio 1619
——————————————— 2nd ed. folio 1622
—— (Ralph) on Camden's Errors & Camden's
Answers 4to. 1723
—— (Richard) Notary Office & Practice . 8vo. 1839
———————————————(L. Levi) 2nd ed. 1867
—— (*Sir* Robt.) Grand Abridgment . . . 4to. 1576
——————————————— . . . folio 1586
—— Reading on Statute of Treason. Magna
Carta Cap. 16, L. T. 1641
—— New Cases (March), temp. Hen. VIII. &c. 12mo. 1651
Broom (H.) Legal Maxims . . 2nd ed. 8vo. 1848
——————————————— . . 3rd ed. 8vo. 1858

Broom (H.) Legal Maxims . . 4th ed. 8vo. 1864
—— Commentaries on the Common Law. 2nd ed. 8vo. 1861
———————————————————— 3rd ed. 8vo. 1864
—— Constitutional Law 8vo. 1866
Brougham (Henry, *Lord*) on Colonial Policy
         2 vols. 8vo. 1803
—— Speech of, in House of Commons 1828, on
Present State of the Laws 8vo. 1828
—— An Estimate of his Local Court Bill, by an
Observer. 7 Jac. Col. L. T. 1830
—— Opinion on Negro Slavery. Vol. 13, Jac. Col.
L. T. 1830
—— Speech of, in the House of Lords, on Legislation & the Law. 8vo. 1848
—— Letter to Sir Jas. Graham on the Making &
Digesting of the Law. Vol. 6, Pam. . . . 1849
—— on British Constitution 12mo. 1861
—— Acts & Bills 8vo. 1867
Broun (R.) Peerage 8vo. 1841
Browell (W. F.) Objections to Lord Cottenham's Judgment in Whitworth *v.* Gargani—Judgment Creditor after Execution as Equitable Mortgagee.
Vol. 21, Pam. 1844
—— Real Property Statutes. 12mo. 1846
Brown (A.) Civil Law . . 2nd ed. 2 vols. 8vo. 1802
—— (E. C.) Letters to J. Bright on the Supply of
Cotton from India. Vol. 18, Pam. 1865
—— (Josiah) Reports, H. L., 1701–79
       7 vols. folio 1779–83
———————————— 1779 . . 7 vols. 8vo. 1784–89
———————————— by Tomlins, 1702–1800
       2nd ed. 8 vols. 8vo. 1803
—— (Jos.) Trial by Jury, the Dark Side of.
Vol. 12, Pam. 1859
—— (Rawdon) Calendar of State Papers & Manuscripts, relating to English Affairs, preserved in the Archives of Venice, &c. Vol. 1, 1202–1509.
Vol. 2, 1509–19 (*see* Calendar of State Papers)
       Imp. 8vo. 1864–67

Brown (S.) Account of Plan of International Association on Decimal System of Measures, Weights, & Coins.   Vol. 12, Pam. 1858
—— (T.) State Treaties. 8vo. 1702
—— (W.) Entries . . . . folio 1675
—— (W.) Fines & Recoveries, or Modus Transferendi Status per Recorda 8vo. 1698
———————————————————— 8vo. 1700
———————————————— 6th ed. 8vo. 1725
—— Entering Clerk's Introduction to Pleading
3rd ed. 8vo. 1702
—— (W.) Reports in Chancery, 1778-94
8vo. 4 vols. 1785-94
—— (W.) Reports in Chancery, 1778-1794
2nd ed. 4 vols. fol. 1794
———— 1778-1794 (R. Belt) 5th ed. 4 vols. 8vo. 1820
—— on Agency and Trusts 12mo. 1868
Browne (G.) Entering Clerk's Vade Mecum
2nd ed. 8vo. 1695
—— (G.) on Divorce 12mo. 1864
—————— . . . . . . 2nd edit. 12mo. 1869
—— (G. L.) on the Companies Act, 1862 . 8vo. 1867
—— Manual of the Companies Act, 1867 . 8vo. 1867
—— (J.) Law List . . . . 17 vols. 8vo. 1775-98
—— (J.) Chancery, Clerk's Tutor in. 2nd ed. 8vo. 1694
—— Chancery Practice . . . . 2 vols. 8vo. 1830
Browning (W. E.) on Divorce 8vo. 1862
Brownlow (R.) Entries . . . . folio 1693
—— & Goldesborough (J.) Reports of divers ⎫
Choice Cases in Law in the Common Pleas ⎪
(temp. Eliz. & Jas.) . . . . ⎬ 4to.
Part 1. 3rd ed. . . . . ⎪ 1675
Part 2. 2nd ed. . . . . ⎭
Bruce (Alexander) Abridgment of Acts of Parliament, 1707-26 (bound up with Sir Jas. Stewart's Abridgment) 12mo. 1726
—— (J.) Calendar of State Papers, Domestic Series, of the Reign of Charles I. preserved in Her Majesty's Public Record Office

Vol. 1.—1625-26.   Vol. 7.—1634-35.
Vol. 2.—1627-28.   Vol. 8.—1635.
Vol. 3.—1628-29.   Vol. 9.—1635-36.
Vol. 4.—1629-31.   Vol. 10.—1636-37.
Vol. 5.—1631-33.   Vol. 11.—1637.
Vol. 6.—1633-34.

        Imp. 8vo. 1856-68
Bruce (J.) History of the Arrival of Edward IV.
 1471, No. 1, C. S. Pa. 4to. 1838
—— Sir Kenelm Digby's Voyage, 1628, No. 96,
 C. S. Pa. 1868
—— (W.) (*see* Archbold, Criminal Pleading)
—— (W. D.) Land Transfer Act 8vo. 1862
Brunswick-Lunenberg, History of the House of. 8vo. 1715
Brut y Tywysogion, or the Chronicle of the Princes
 of Wales. Ed. Rev. J. Williams. No. 17 M. R.
 Pub. 1860
Brydall (J.) Jus Sigilli; or, the Law of England
 touching the Seals 12mo. 1673
Brydall (J.) Camera Regis, or a Short View of
 London 12mo. 1676
—— Decus et Tutamen; or, Prospect of the Laws
 of England 12mo. 1679
—— Jus Imaginis apud Anglos, or the Law of
 Nobility & Gentry 12mo. 1675
—— on the Law of Lunacy 8vo. 1700
Buchan Peerage (Petition of Sir C. Mackenzie)
 2nd series, Vol. 1 1841
Buchanan (D.) History of Reformation in Church
    of Scotland . . . . fol. 1644
—— (W.) Family History, &c. of Extinct Scottish
 Surnames, by W. Buchanan 4to. 1723
Buck (J. W.) Reports, Bankruptcy (temp. Eldon)
 1816-20 . . . . 8vo. 1820
Buckingham (George Villiers, Duke of). The Fate
 of Families exemplified in the Fall of (Grimaldi
 Tracts, Vol. 2)
Buckinghamshire, Historical Description of . 8vo. 1801
—— Character of John Sheffield, Duke of (Grimaldi
 Tracts, Vol. 3)

Buckler (H.) Old Bailey Sessions Papers, 1824–34
8 vols. 4to.
—— Reports of Trials at Central Criminal Court
(and *see* Barnett, J. D.) . . 26 vols. 8vo. 1835–47
—— (R.) Stemmata Chicheliana, & Supplement.
Genealogical Account of some Families so named
4to. 1765
Buckworth *v.* Thirkill: Replevin Case in K. B.
1785. Vol. 1, Col. Jur.
Bull (Jno.) Letter from Thos. Bull, reprint of.
Vol. 9, Pam. 1807
Bullar (J.) Guide to Isle of Wight (*see* Hampshire
Tracts)
Bullen (E.) on Distress 12mo. 1842
—— & Leake (S. M.) Precedents in Pleading 8vo. 1860
———————————————— 2nd ed. 8vo. 1863
———————————————— 3rd ed. 8vo. 1868
Buller (*Sir* F.) Biography (*see* Eminent Lawyers)
8vo. 1790
—— Nisi Prius (A. Onslow) . . . . . 4th ed. 4to. 1785
———————————————— . . new ed. 8vo. 1789
———————————————— . . . 5th ed. 8vo. 1790
———————————————— . . . 6th ed. 8vo. 1793
———————————————— (R. W. Bridgman) 7th ed. 8vo. 1817
Bullingbroke(E.) Irish Ecclesiastical Law 2 v. 4to. 1770
Bullinger's (H.) Works, P. S. Pa. 4 vols. 8vo. 1849–52
Bullion (Gold) Report of H. C. Committee . 8vo. 1810
Bullock (*Col.*) on Municipal Corporation & Public
Health Acts: their practical working exemplified
in the case of Le Feuvre *v.* Lankester. Vol. 9,
Pam. 1854
—— (H. A.) History of Isle of Man, &c. . 8vo. 1816
Bulstrode (E.) Reports, 2nd ed. 1603–49 . folio 1688
Bunbury (W.) Reports . . . . folio 1755
———————————————— 1714–60 . . . . . 8vo. 1791
Bunny, History of Newbury 8vo. 1839
Bunyon (C. J.) on Fire Assurance . . . 8vo. 1866
—— Life Assurance 8vo. 1854
———————————————— . . . . . 2nd ed. 8vo. 1868

Burchell (Jos.) Digest, K. B. & C. P. 1756–94 8vo. 1796
Burge (W.) Colonial & Foreign Law. 4 vols. 8vo. 1838
—— Observations on the Supreme Appellate
Jurisdiction of Great Britain 1841
Burge (W.) The Temple Church, an Account of, &
of its restoration & repairs 8vo. 1843
Burges (J. B.) on Insolvency 8vo. 1783
Burgo (J. de) Pupilla Oculi. 4to. 1514
Burke (*Sir* B.) Vicissitudes of Families
2nd ed. 2 vols. 8vo. 1860
—— Dictionary of the Peerage & Baronetage of
the British Empire . . . . . 29th ed. 8vo. 1867
———————————————————— 30th ed. 1868
———————————————————— 31st ed. 1869
—— (Edmund) Speeches . . . . 4th ed. 8vo. 1738
—— Letter as to his Pension . . 14th ed. 8vo. 1796
—— on Attacks on Himself & Pension in 1796.
Vol. 12, Jac. Coll. . . . . New ed. 1831
—— Speech on Reform in 1792. Vol.12, Jac. L. T. 1831
Burke (J.) Extinct Peerage Dictionary . . 8vo. 1831
—— History of the Commoners. . . 4 vols. 8vo. 1836
—— Peerage & Baronetage, 1832–64 . 9 vols. 8vo. n. d.
—— (J. B.) Dictionary of the Landed Gentry of
Great Britain & Ireland . . . 2 vols. 8vo. 1850
———————————————————— 4th ed. 8vo. 1863
———————————————————— 4th ed. revised 1869
—— (J. & J. B.) Extinct & Dormant Baronetcies
of England 8vo. 1838
Burlamaqui (J. J.) Natural Law 8vo. 1748
———————————— (Nugent) 2nd ed. 2 vols. 8vo. 1763
Burman (J.) Statute Laws of the Isle of Man
since 1848 (continued by J. C. Lamothe) 8vo. 1853
Burn (*Dr.*) on Crime & Insanity: their Causes,
Connexion, & Consequences. Vol. 9, Pam. . . 1852
—— (J. B.) Marine Insurance 12mo. 1801
—— (J. H.) (*see* Beaufoy)
—— (J. S.) The Fleet Registers, comprising the
History of Fleet Marriages, &c. & Notices of
the May Fair, Mint, & Savoy Chapels . 8vo. 1833

Burn (J. S.) Notices of the Court of the High Commission & its Proceedings 8vo. 1865
—— (R.) Justice of the Peace, 7th ed. 3 vols. 8vo. 1762
Burn (R.) Justice of the Peace. 13th ed. 4 vols. 8vo. 1776
———————————————— 15th ed. 4 vols. 8vo. 1785
———————————————— 16th ed. 4 vols. 8vo. 1788
———————————— (J. B.) 18th ed. 4 vols. 8vo. 1797
———————————————— 19th ed. 4 vols. 8vo. 1800
———————— (W. Woodfall) 20th ed. 4 vols. 8vo. 1805
———————— (C. D. Durnford & John King)
        21st ed. 6 vols. 8vo. 1810
———————————— (J. King) 22nd ed. 5 v. 8vo. 1814
———————————— (G. Chetwynd) & Sup.
      23rd ed. 6 v. 8vo. 1820–23
———————— (J. & T. Chitty) 26th ed. 6 v. 8vo. 1831
———————————————— 28th ed. 6 v. 8vo. 1837
———————— (T. Chitty & M. Bere) 29th ed. 6 v. 8vo. 1845
———————— Supplement (by E. Wise) 8vo. 1852
—— Poor Law 8vo. 1764
—— Ecclesiastical Law . . 2nd ed. 4 vols. 8vo. 1767
Burn (R.) Ecclesiastical Law . 4th ed. 4 vols. 8vo. 1781
———————————————— 5th ed. 4 vols. 8vo. 1788
———————— (S. Fraser) 7th ed. 4 vols. 8vo. 1800–1
———————— (R. P. Tyrwhitt) 8th ed. 4 v. 8vo. 1824
———————— (R. Phillimore) 9th ed. 4 v. 8vo. 1843
Burnett (*Bp.*) History of his Own Time, 4 vols. 8vo. 1810
—— History of the Reformation. . . 6 v. 4to. 1816
Burney (*Dr.* C.) Catalogue of MSS. in British Museum, Parts 2, 3 . . . . . . 2 vols. folio 1840
———— (M. C.) Index to Journals of H. C., Vols. 56–75, 1801–20 . . . . folio 1825
Burning Shame (The) (*see* Hants County Tracts) 1812
Burrough (Samuel) History of the Chancery, relating to its Judicial Power, & Rights of the Masters 12mo. 1726
—— The Legal Judicature in Chancery stated
            8vo. 1727
Burrow (*Dr.*) Letter on Davis's Case. Vol. 7, Jac. L. T. 1830

Burrow (Jas.) Report on Literary Property, Millar
v. Taylor, in 1769 . . . . 4to. 1773
—— (*Sir* J.) Reports, 1756–72, 3rd ed.
        3 vols. folio 1777–80
      —————————— 4th ed. 5 v. 8vo. 1790
      —————————— 5th ed. 5 v. 8vo. 1812
—— Settlement Cases, 1732–76 . . . 2nd ed. 4to. 1786
Burton (*Dr.* J.) Ecclesiastical History of Yorkshire . . . . folio 1758
—— (J. B.) Scotch Law Manual 8vo. 1839
—— (P.) (*see* Cases and Opinions)
—— Exchequer Practice 8vo. 1770
——————————— . . . . . 2 vols. 8vo. 1791
—— (W. H.) Compendium of Real Property. 8vo. 1828
——————————————— 4th ed. 8vo. 1837
——————————— (by E. P. Cooper) 6th ed. 8vo. 1845
——————————————— 8th ed. 8vo. 1856
Burtt (J.) C. M. No. 55
Bury, Wills & Inventories, No. 49 C. S. Pa.
1370–1652 (S. Tymms) 4to. 1850
Bushby (H. J.) Election Manual. 3rd ed. 12mo. 1868
Buswell (J.) Historical Account of the Knights of
the Garter 8vo. 1757
Butler (C.) Horæ Juridicæ Subsecivæ. 2nd ed. 8vo. 1807
—— (G. C.) on Property Law 8vo. 1866
—— (H.) Tale—The Mayor of Wigan. Lancashire County Tr. 1759
—— (T.) White and Black Lists . . . 12mo. 1762
—— (W.) on the Globes, Exercises in
        2nd ed. 12mo. 1800
——'s Practical Observations in Conveyancing
(MSS.) . . . . 4to.
Butterworth (H.) Memoir from Gentleman's Magazine, February 1861
Buttevant's Peerage (Evidence only), Vol. 9, p. 39 1825
Byles (*Sir* J. B.) on Bills . . . 2nd ed. 12mo. 1834
——————————— . . . 4th ed. 12mo. 1843
——————————— . . . . 5th ed. 8vo. 1847
——————————— . . . . 6th ed. 8vo. 1851

Byles (Sir J. B.) on Bills . . . . 7th ed. 8vo. 1857
——————————————— . . . . 8th ed. 8vo. 1862
——————————————— . . . . 9th ed. 8vo. 1866
—— on Usury 12mo. 1845
Bynkershoek (C.) Opuscula Juridica (D. F. C. Conrad) . . . . 2 vols. 4to. 1729
—— Opuscula : & Observationum Juris Romani Libri quatuor (J. G. Heineccius) 2 v. 4to. 1719–23
Byrne (J. P.) on Patents . . . 2nd ed. 12mo. 1860
Bythewood (W. M.) & Jarman (T.) Selection of Precedents, forming a System of Conveyancing; with Index by G. Sweet . . 11 vols. 8vo. 1829–36
—— & Jarman (T.) Selection of Precedents, forming a System of Conveyancing; with Dissertations, Practical Notes, & a Copious Index, by J. Stewart & W. Parker; with an Appendix by J. Stewart . . . . . . 2nd ed. 9 vols. 8vo. 1834
—— Selection of Precedents, &c., by G. Sweet & A. Bisset (Part 1, Vol. 8, by W. Stokes)
11 vols. 1841–49
The remainder of the 8th vol. & Vol. 10 are in the press)
—— & Jarman (T.) Selection of Precedents, forming a system of Conveyancing; with additional Precedents & Notes by T. Jarman; with Appendix by Parker & Stewart, showing the Alterations effected by the recent Acts, by J. Stewart . . . . . . 2nd ed. 9 vols. 8vo.
(General Index *wanting*)
*B. (T.) Law Dictionary, or Termes de la Ley. 8vo. 1667
——————————————————— —— 8vo. 1685
——————————————————— 8vo. 1721

* Lord Coke ascribes this work to Wm. Rustal (*see* 10th Report).

LAW SOCIETY LIBRARY. 47

C

Cabinet Lawyer (The) . . . . 22nd ed. 8vo. 1866
Cadière (M. C.), et Girard (J. B.). Recueil général
des pièces concernant le Procez entre 4 vols. 8vo. 1731
Cadière (M. C.) et Girade (J. B.) Accusation &
Defence 8vo. 1731
Caernarvon—The Record of; Registrum vulgariter
Nuncupatum, 26 Edw. III. c. Codice MSS.
Harl. 696 descriptum [Sir H. Ellis] . . folio 1838
   (This Vol. contains Leges et Consuetudines Walliæ & Extentæ
   Com. Meryonneth). *See* Record Commission.
Cæsarean Operation, inquest on case of, Report
from Lancet. Pam. Vol. 3 1833
Cæsaris (J.) Commentarii. 8vo. 1544
———————— ———————— 12mo. 1759
———————— ———————— 12mo. 1804
Calais, Chronicle of, 1435-1540 (J. G. Nichols)
No. 35 C. S. Pa. 1845
Caldecott (T.) Settlement Cases, 1776-85 . 4to. 1786
Caldwell (J. H.) on Arbitration 8vo. 1817
Calendar of Letters, Despatches, & State Papers
relating to the Negociations between England
& Spain, Hen. VII. 1485 & Hen. VIII. 1525
(G. A. Bergenroth) . . . . . 2 vols. 8vo. 1862
—— Supplement to Vols. 1, 2 . . . . . 8vo. 1868
—— of Letters & Papers, Foreign & Domestic,
temp. Hen.VIII. 1509-23 (J. S. Brewer)
           3 vols. in 5, 8vo. 1862-67
Calendar of State Papers, Domestic Series, 1547-
90, temp. Edw. VI., Mary & Elizabeth (Robt.
Lemon) . . . . 2 vols. 8vo. 1856-65
————————————— Domestic Series, of the
Reign of Elizabeth (continued), preserved in Her
Majesty's Public Record Office (M. A. E. Green)
1591-97 . . . . 2 vols. 8vo. 1867-69
————————————— Foreign Series, temp.
Edw. VI. 1547-53 (W. B. Turnbull) . . 8vo. 1861

Calendar of State Papers, Foreign Series, temp.
Mary, 1553–58 (W. B. Turnbull) . . . 8vo. 1861
———————— temp. Eliz. 1558–62 (Rev.
Jos. Stevenson) . . . . . 5 vols. 8vo. 1862–65
———————— temp. Jas. I. 1603–25 (M.
A. E. Green). . . . . . 4 vols. 8vo. 1857–59
———————— temp. Car. I. 1625–37 (J.
Bruce) . . . . 11 vols. 8vo. 1858–68
———————— temp. Car. II. 1660–67 (M.
A. E. Green). . . . . . . 7 vols. 8vo. 1860–66
—— of Letters relating to Scotland (M. J.
Thorpe) . . . . 2 vols. 8vo. 1858
Vol. 1. temp. Hen. VIII. to Eliz. 1509–89.
Vol. 2, temp. Eliz. & Mary Queen of Scots, 1589–92.

———————————— relating to Ireland (H. C.
Hamilton). . . . . 2 vols. 8vo. 1860–67
Vol. 1, temp. Hen. VIII. to Eliz. 1509–73.
Vol. 2, temp. Eliz. 1574–85.

———————————— Colonial Series (W. N. Sainsbury) . . . . 2 vols. 8vo. 1860–62
Vol. 1, America & West Indies, 1574–1660.
Vol. 2, East Indies, China, & Japan, 1513–1616.

———————————— & MSS. relating to English
affairs, 1202–1519 (R. Brown) . . 8vo. 1864–67
—— of the Carew Papers, preserved in Lambeth
Library, 1515–1600 (J. S. Brewer & W. Bullen)
3 vols. 8vo. 1867–69
—— of Treasury Papers, 1557–1696 (J. Redington) 8vo. 1868
Calendarium Catholicum 12mo. 1662
–—— Ducatus Lancastriæ temp. Edw. I. to
Car. I., & Calendar to the Pleadings, Hen.
VII. to 14th Eliz. (ed. R. J. Harper, J. Caley,
W. Minchin) (*see* Record Commission)
3 vols. folio 1823–34
—— Genealogicum for reigns of Hen. III. & Edw.
I. (C. Roberts) . . . . . 2 vols. 8vo. 1865
—— Inquisitionum post mortem sive Escaetarum.
Hen. III.—Ric. III.; cum Appendice de quam-

plurimis aliis Inquisitionibus Hen. III.—Jac. I.
(ed. J. Caley) (*see* Record Commission)
         4 vols. folio 1806-28
Calendarium Rotulorum Patentium in Turri Londinensi. 3 John—23 Edw. IV. (S. Ayscough)
(*see* Record Commission) . . . . . . folio 1802
—— Chartarum & Inquisitionum ad quod damnum Joh. & Hen. VI. (ed. J. Caley) (*see* Record Commission) . . . . folio 1803
Caley (J.) (*see* Calendarium)
—— Ellis (H.) & Bandinel (*Rev.* B.) Anglicanum Monasticon . . . . 8 vols. folio 1818-30
Calfhill (*Bp.* J.) Answer to Martiall's (J.) Treatise of the Cross. Par. S. Pa. 1846
Callis (R.) Reading on Statute of Sewers, 28 Hen. VIII. 4to. 1647
————————————————— 2nd ed. 4to. 1685
————————————————— 2nd ed. 4to. 1686
——————————— (W. J. Brodcrip) 4th ed. 8vo. 1824
Calthrop (*Sir* H.) Reports of Special Cases relating to the Customs of London . . '. 12mo. 1670
Calvert (F.) Parties to Suits 8vo. 1837
—— (M.) History of Knaresborough (York) 8vo. 1844
Calvinus (J.) Lexicon Juridicum . . . . folio 1670
Cambrensis (Giraldus) Works of (J. S. Brewer). 21 M. R. Pub. . . . . . . 3 vols. 8vo. 1861-63
Cambriæ Annales (*see* Rev. J. Williams) 20 M. R. Pub. 1860
Cambrian Directory 8vo. 1800
Cambridge Calendar, 1801-67 . . 50 vols. 8vo.
—— Graduati Cantabrigiensis; sive Catalogus exhibens nomina eorum quos ab anno 1659 usque ad decimum diem Octobris 1823, &c. . . . 8vo. 1823
———————————— 1750—Octobris 1856
(cura J. Romilly) 8vo. 1856
—— University Election Poll Books . 8vo. 1754-80
———————————— (*see* Hertford) 1784-1826
———— Commissioners' Report, &c. 3 vols. folio 1852

E

Cambridge, County of, Topographical and Historical description of (and *see* Carter). . . 8vo. 1801
Camden(*Earl*) Biography of (*see* Eminent Lawyers)
             8vo. 1790
—— (Wm.) Britannia (in Latin) . . . 12mo. 1586
———————————— (in English) . . . folio 1637
———————————— (Rd. Gough). 3 v. fol. 1789
—— Annals of England & Ireland, temp. Eliz. 8vo. 1725
Camden Society's Papers:—
 1. Edward IV. Historie of Arrivall in England,
   1471 (ed. J. Bruce) 4to. 1838
 2. Kynge Johan. A play [Bp. J. Bale] (ed. J.
   P. Collier) 1838
 3. Alliterative Poem on Deposition of Richd. II.
   (R. Maydiston; ed. T. Wright) . . . 1838
 4. Plumpton Correspondence. Series of Letters
   written temp. Edw. IV. Richd. III. Hen.
   VII. VIII. & Edw. VI. 1460–1551 (ed.
   T. Stapleton) 1839
 5. Anecdotes & Traditions of Early English
   History, 1838 (W. J. Thoms) 1838
 6. Political Songs of England, from John to
   Edw. II. 1199–1327 (T. Wright) . . . 1839
 7. Annals of the First Four Years of Queen
   Elizabeth, 1558–1562 [Sir J. Hayward];
   (ed. J. Bruce) 1840
 8. Ecclesiastical Documents (Rev. J. Hunter) 1840
 9. Norden's (J.) Speculi Britanniæ pars: Description of Essex, 1594 (Sir H. Ellis) 1840
 10. Edward IV., Chronicle of First Thirteen
   Years of, 1461–74 (Dr. J. Warkworth;
   ed. J. O. Halliwell) 1839
 11. W. Kemp's Nine Daies Wonder, 1600
   (Rev. A. Dyce) 1840
 12. The Egerton Papers, 1558–1625 (ed. J. P.
   Collier) 1840
 13. Chronica Jocelini de Brakelonda, 1173–1202
   (J. G. Rokewode) 1840

LAW SOCIETY LIBRARY. 51

Camden Society's Papers—*continued*
14. Irish Narratives, 1641-90 (ed. T. C. Croker) 1841
15. Rishanger's Chronicle (ed. J. O. Halliwell) 1840
16. Poems of Walter Mapes (ed. T. Wright) . 1841
17. Travels of Nicander Nucius, Book II. (Rev. J. A. Cramer) 1841
18. Three Metrical Romances (ed. J. Robson) . 1842
19. Diary of Dr. Jno. Dee, 1554-1601 (ed. J. O. Halliwell) 1842
20. Apology for the Lollard Doctrines (Wycliffe; ed. J. H. Todd) 1842
21. Rutland Papers, 1485-1522 (ed. W. Jerdan) 1842
22. Diary of Bishop Cartwright, 1686-67 (ed. Rev. J. Hunter) 1843
23. Letters of Eminent Literary Men, 1549-1799 (Sir H. Ellis) 1843
24. Proceedings against Alice Kyteler, 1324 (ed. T. Wright) 1843
25. Promptorium Parvulorum, sive Clericorum, circa A.D. 1440 (ed. A. Way) Vol. 1, A—L 1843
26. Suppression of the Monasteries, 1528-55 (ed. T. Wright). 1843
27. Leycester Correspondence, 1585-86 (ed. J. Bruce) 1844
28. French Chronicle of London, 1260-1343 (ed. G. J. Aungier) 1844
29. Polydore Vergil, 1422-85 (ed. Sir H. Ellis) 1844
30. The Thornton Romances (ed. J. O. Halliwell) 1844
31. Verney's Notes of Long Parliament, temp. Car. I. (Sir R. Verney; ed. J. Bruce) . 1845
32. Autobiography of Sir J. Bramston, temp. Car. I. & Jas. II. (ed. T. W. Bramston) 1845
33. Correspondence of Earl of Perth, 1688-96 (ed. W. Jerdan) 1845
34. Liber de Antiquis Legibus, 1178-1274 (ed. T. Stapleton) 1846

Camden Society's Papers—*continued*

35. The Chronicle of Calais, 1485–1540 (ed. J. G. Nichols) 1846
36. Polydore Vergil's History, Vol. 1, prior to Conquest, 1066 (ed. Sir H. Ellis) . . 1846
37. Italian Relation of England, 1500 (C. A. Sneyd) 1847
38. Middleham Church, Yorkshire (Rev. W. Atthill) 1847
39. The Camden Miscellany, Vol. 1, which *see* . 1847
40. Life of Lord Grey of Wilton, 1530–47 (Sir P. G. Egerton) 1847
41. Diary of Walter Yonge, Esq. 1604–28 (ed. G. Roberts) 1848
42. Diary of Henry Machyn, 1550–63 (ed. J. G. Nichols) 1848
43. Visitation of Huntingdonshire, 1613 (ed. Sir H. Ellis) 1849
44. Obituary of Richard Smyth, 1627–74 (ed. Sir H. Ellis) 1849
45. Sir R. Twysden on Government of England (ed. J. M. Kemble) 1849
46. Letters of Elizabeth & James VI. 1582–90 (ed. J. Bruce) 1849
47. Chronicon Petroburgense, 1122–1295 (T. Stapleton) [With Introduction by J. Bruce] 1849
48. Chronicle of Queen Jane & Queen Mary, 1553–54 (ed. J. G. Nichols) 1850
49. Bury Wills & Inventories, 1370–1650 (ed. S. Tymms) 1850
50. Mapes de Nugis Curialium, 1160–82 (ed. T. Wright) 1850
51. Pilgrimage of Sir R. Guylforde, 1506 (ed. Sir H. Ellis) 1851
52. Secret Services of Car. II. & Jas. II. 1679–88 (ed. J. Y. Akerman) 1851

Camden Society's Papers—*continued*

53. Chronicle of Grey Friars of London, 1189-1556 (ed. J. G. Nichols) 1852
54. Promptorium Parvulorum, sive Clericorum, circa A.D.1440 (ed. A.Way), Vol.2,M—R 1853
55. The Camden Miscellany, Vol. 2 1853
56. Verney Papers down to 1639, Edw. I. to Car. I. (ed. J. Bruce) 1853
57. The Ancren Riwle (duties, &c. of Monastic Life) (ed. J. Morton) 1853
58. Letters of Lady B. Harley in 1625-43 (ed. T. T. Lewis) 1853
59. Roll of Bishop Swinfield, Vol. 1, 1289-90 (Rev. J. Webb) 1854
60. Grants temp. Edward V. 1483 (J. G. Nichols) 1854
61. The Camden Miscellany, Vol. 3 1855
62. Roll of Bishop Swinfield, Vol. 2 (Rev. J. Webb) 1855
63. Letters of Car. I., 1646, to Queen Henrietta Maria (ed. J. Bruce) 1856
64. English Chronicle of Reigns of Richard II., Henry IV., V. & VI., 1377-1461 (ed. Rev. J. S. Davies) 1856
65. The Knights Hospitallers in England, 1338 (ed. Rev. L. B. Larking & J. M. Kemble) 1857
66. Diary of John Rous, 1625-42 (ed. M. A. E. Green) 1856
67. The Trevelyan Papers, prior to 1558, Part 1 (ed. J. P. Collier) 1857
68. Journal of Dr. Davies, 1689-90 (ed. R. Caulfield) 1857
69. The Domesday of St. Paul's, 1222, by Archdeacon Hale 1858
70. Liber Famelicus of Sir Jas. Whitelock, 1609-31 (ed. J. Bruce) 1858
71. Saville Correspondence (ed. W. D. Cooper) 1858

Camden Society's Papers—*continued*

72. Blonde of Oxford (P. de Reimes; ed. M. Le Roux de Lincy) 1858
73. Camden Miscellany, Vol. 4 1859
74. Diary of Rd. Symonds, 1644–45 (ed. C. E. Long) 1859
75. Papers relating to Milton (ed. W. D. Hamilton) 1859
76. Letters of George, Lord Carew, 1615–17 (ed. J. Maclean) 1860
77. Narratives of the Reformation [John Foxe] (ed. J. G. Nichols) 1859
78. Correspondence of James VI. with Sir Robert Cecil (ed. J. Bruce). 1861
79. Jno. Chamberlaine's Letters, temp. Elizabeth 1597–1602 (ed. S. Williams) 1861
80. Proceedings in Kent in 1640 (ed. Rev. L. B. Larking & J. Bruce) 1862
81. Parliamentary Debates, 1610 (S. R. Gardiner) 1862
82. Foreigners resident in England, 1618–88 (ed. W. D. Cooper) 1862
83. Wills from Doctors' Commons, 1495–1695 (ed. J. G. Nichols & J. Bruce) . . . 1863
84. Trevelyan Papers, Part 2, 1446–1643 (ed. J. P. Collier) 1863
85. Life of Marmaduke Rawdon, of York (ed. R. Davies) 1863
86. Letters of Margaret of Anjou, &c. (ed. C. Monro) 1863
87. Camden Miscellany, Vol. 5 1864
88. Letters of Sir Robert Cecil to Sir George Carew, 1600–2 (ed. J. Maclean) . . . 1864
89. Promptorium Parvulorum, sive Clericorum, circa A.D. 1440 (ed. A. Way), Vol. 3, R—Z (*see* Nos. 25, 54) 1865
90. Relations between England & Germany, 1618–19 (ed. S. R. Gardiner) 1865

Camden Society's Papers—*continued*
91. Registrum Prioratus Wigorniensis, 1240
 (W. H. Hale) 1865
92. Alexander VII. and his Cardinals [By John
 Hargrave, 1662-80] (J. C. Robinson) . 1867
93. Mary, Queen of Scots (A. J. Crosby & J.
 Bruce) 4to. 1866
94. Dingley (Thomas) History from Marble,
 Compiled temp. Charles II., Part 1 (J.
 G. Nichols) 4to. 1867
95. Manipulus Vocabulorum [By Peter Levins,
 A.D. 1570] (H. B. Wheatley) . . 4to. 1867
96. Sir Kenelm Digby's Voyage, 1628 (J. Bruce)
 4to. 1868
97. Dingley (Thomas) History from Marble,
 Compiled temp. Charles II., Part 2 (J.
 G. Nichols) 1868
98. Relations between England & Germany
 (Gardiner) 4to. 1868
99. Diary of John Massingham 4to. 1868
Catalogue of Camden Society's Papers . 4to. 1862
Camden Miscellany, C. S. Pa. . . . 5 vols. 4to.
 Vol. I. No. 39 :—
 Register & Chronicle of the Abbey of Abercon-
 way, from the Harleian MSS. (ed. Sir H. Ellis) 1846
 Chronicles of the Rebellion in Lincolnshire in
 1470 (ed. J. G. Nichols) 1847
 Bull of Pope Innocent VIII. on the Marriage
 of Henry VII. with Elizabeth of York
 (J. P. Collier) 1847
 Journal of the Siege of Rouen in 1591 [Sir T.
 Coningsby] (ed. J. G. Nichols) 1847
 Letter of George Fleetwood, describing the
 Battle of Lützen & Death of Gustavus
 Adolphus (ed. Sir P. de M. Grey Egerton) 1847
 Diary of Dr. Edward Lake, Chaplain & Tutor
 to the Princesses Mary & Anne, 1677-78
 (ed. G. P. Elliott) 1846

Camden Miscellany, C. S. Pa.—*continued*
  Vol. II. No. 55:—
    Account of the Expenses of John of Brabant & Thomas & Henry of Lancaster, 1292–93 (ed. J. Burtt) 1853
    Household Account of the Princess Elizabeth, 1551–52 (ed. Visct. Strangford) 1853
    The Request & Suite of a Truehearted Englishman, written by Wm. Cholmeley, 1553 (ed. W. J. Thoms) 1853
    Discovery of the Jesuits' College at Clerkenwell, in March 1627–28 (ed. J. G. Nichols) 1852
    Trelawny Papers, temp. Car. I. (ed. W. D. Cooper) 1853
    Autobiography of Wm. Taswell, D.D., 1651–82 (ed. G. P. Elliott) 1852
  Vol. III. No. 61:—
    Papers relating to Proceedings in the County of Kent, 1642–46 (ed. R. Almack) . . . 1854
    Ancient Biographical Poems of the Sixteenth Century, from the Norfolk MSS. in the Bodleian Library (ed. J. P. Collier) . . 1855
    A Relation of Abuses committed against the Commonwealth, 1629 (ed. Sir F. Madden) 1854
    Inventory of the Wardrobe, Plate, &c. of Henry Fitzroy Duke of Richmond & of the Wardrobe, &c. of Catharine of Arragon at Baynard's Castle (ed. J. G. Nichols) . . 1855
  Vol. IV. No. 73:—
    London Chronicle during the Reigns of Henry VII. & VIII. (ed. C. Hopper) 1859
    Expenses of Judges of Assize riding Western & Oxford Circuits, 1596–1601 (ed. W. D. Cooper) 1858
    The Incredulity of St. Thomas (the Skryvener's Play at York) (ed. J. P. Collier) 1859
    The Child of Bristow, a Poem, by Jno. Lydgate (ed. C. Hopper) 1859

Camden Miscellany, C. S. Pa.—*continued*
  Sir Edward Lake's Interviews with Charles I.
    (ed. T. P. Langmead) 1858
  Letters of Pope to Atterbury when in the
    Tower of London (ed. J. G. Nichols) . . 1859
  Supplementary Note to the Discovery of the
    Jesuits' College at Clerkenwell, in March
    1627-28 (ed. J. G. Nichols) 1859
Vol. V. No. 87 :—
  Five Letters of King Charles II., communi-
    cated by the Marquis of Bristol 1864
  I. Letter of the Council to Sir Thomas Lake
    relating to Sir Edward Coke's proceedings
    at Oatlands
  II. Documents relative to Sir Walter Raleigh's
    Last Voyage (S. R. Gardiner). . . . 1864
  III. Catalogue of Early English Miscellanies, for-
    merly in the Harleian Library (ed. W. C.
    Hazlitt) 1862
  IV. Letters collected from the Collection of
    Autographs in the possession of Wm. Tite,
    Esq., M.P. 1864
  V. Sir Francis Drake's Memorable Service done
    against the Spaniards in 1587. Written by
    Robert Leng, Gentleman, one of his co-ad-
    venturers & fellow-soldiers (ed. C. Hopper) 1863
  VI. Inquiry into the Genuineness of a Letter
    dated February 3, 1613, & signed ' Mary
    Magdalene Davers ' (J.B.) 1864
Cameron (J. H.) Q.B. Reports for Upper Canada,
  1843-62, & continued by Robinson 18 vols. 8vo.
Campbell (*Dr.* J.) Political Survey of Great Bri-
  tain . . . . 2 vols. 4to. 1774
—— (*Lord* J.) N.P. Reports . . 4 vols. 8vo. 1809-16
—— Lives of the Chancellors. 3rd ed. 7 vols. 8vo. 1848-50
—— Lives of the Chief Justices. 2 vols. 8vo. 1849-57
Campbell (late *Lord*) Lives of Lord Lyndhurst &
  Lord Brougham 8vo. 1869

Campbell (S.) & others. Revised Statutes of Nova
 Scotia. 3rd Series 8vo. 1864
Campin (T. W.) Law of Patents as to the Protection of Designs & Trade Marks . . . 12mo. 1869
Canada, Act granting Charter to Company . . . 1825
—— Minutes for arrangement of a Charter, 19th
 Aug., 7 Geo. IV. 1826 . . . . } Fo.
—— Act to alter Act for granting Charter,
 1828. . . . .
—— Code of Laws for Quebec . . . . . folio 1774
—— Directory for 1857 . . . . 8vo. 1857
—— Lower, Index to Statutes, 1776–1856 (G. W.
 Wichsteed) 8vo. 1857
—— Chronological Table of ditto, 1777–1857
 (G. W. Wichsteed) 8vo. 1857
—— Lower, Civil Code for . . . . . . 8vo.
———————————— (T. McCord) 12mo. 1867
———————————— Reports on. 3 vols. folio 1855
—— Statutes, 1857 to 1st Parliament of the Union,
 1867–68 inclusive (1861 wanting) 13 vols. 8vo.
—— Statutes, Consolidated 8vo. 1859
———————————— (Upper) . . 8vo. 1859
—————— of 31 V. 1st Parliament . 8vo. 1867
Canning (G.) Speech to his Liverpool Constituents, in 1820, at the Celebration of his Fourth
 Election. Vol. 27, Pam. 1820
—— Claim to Public Confidence; The Grand
 Vizier Unmasked. Remarks on. Jac. Col. Vol.
 7, L. T. 1827
—— (T.) On Assignment of Wife's Interest.
 Vol. 1, Jac. Col. L. T. 1820
Canons (English) of 1603 (*see* E. Gibson's Codex)
Cantalupe (N.) & Parker (Rev. R.) History &
 Antiquities of Cambridge University; Description of the Colleges, with an account of their
 Founders, &c. 8vo. 1721
Canterbury, Account of, & Proposal of Abp. &
 other Bishops to H. M. L. T. 1688–89

Cantrell (J. T.) Letter to Lord Chancellor on the
  Separate Use Clause. Vol. 6, L. T. 1839
Cantuariensis, Historia Monasterii S. Augustini,
  by Thomas of Elmham (*see* C. Hardwick)
  8, M. R. Pub. 8vo. 1858
Cape of Good Hope (*see* Martin's British Colonies)
—— Report on the Railways of, at Meeting at
  Gresham House, London. Vol. 12, Pam. . . . 1858
—— Acts, 1854, 1865 . . . . 3 vols. folio
Capgrave (J.) Chronicles of England. No. 1, M. R.
  Pub. (Hingeston) 8vo. 1858
——Liber de illustribus Henricis (Hingeston)
  No. 7, M. R. Pub. 1858
Capital Punishment, the effects of, as applied to
  Forgery & Theft. Bound up with Tracts by
  B. Montagu
Cardigan (*Earl* of) Trial of, in House of Lords. 8vo. 1841
Care (Hen.) on English Liberties . 4th ed. 8vo. 1719
—— on British Liberties . . . . 2nd ed. 8vo. 1767
Carew *v.* Burrell Trial (bound up with R. Barnes'
  Exeter Deanery Case)
Carew (Geo. *Lord*) Letters of, to Sir Thomas Roe,
  1615-17. C. S. Pa. No. 76 (ed. J. Maclean) . 1860
—— (*Sir* G.) Letters to him by Sir R. Cecil.
  C. S. Pa. No. 88 (ed. J. Maclean). 1864
Carew Papers, Calendar of the Carew Papers (*see*
  Brewer & Bullen)
—— (G.) Precedents of Bills of Costs in the Court
  of Probate 4to. 1869
—— (R.) Cornwall, Survey & History . . 4to. 1769
—— Index to Solicitors' & Stamp Fees under
  Chancery New Orders 8vo. 1857
Carey (Hy.) *Irish Reports* (*see* Jones, Thos.)
—— (J.) Plans of Canals in Great Britain . folio 1795
—— (*Dr.* J.) (*see* Ainsworth)
—— (P. S.) Borough Court Rules . . . 8vo. 1841
Carkesse (C.) Book of Rates & Collection of Cus-
  toms Statutes. . . . . folio 1726

Carlisle (*Bp.*) Border Laws 8vo. 1705
———————————— 8vo. 1747
Carlisle (Dean & Chapter of) Substance of Letter to an M.P. on a Scheme concluded by, with the Ecclesiastical Commissioners. Vol. 9, Pam. . . 1853
—— (N) Dictionary of England . . 2 vols. 4to. 1808
———————————— Ireland 4to. 1810
———————————— Wales 4to. 1811
—— Endowed Grammar Schools . 2 vols. 8vo. 1818
Carneiro (M. B.) Diréito Civil de Portugal (Lisbon)
  3 vols. in 1, 4to. 1826-28
Carpmael (W.) on Patents . . . 2nd ed. 8vo. 1836
———————————— . . . 6th ed. 8vo. 1860
Carr v. Hood, Trial for Libel 4to. 1808
Carré (G. L. J.) Lois de la Procédure, par C. Adolphe . . . . . 4th ed. 9 vols. 8vo. 1862-63
Carrighan (T.) on Doctrine & Practice of Court of Chancery, 5 Jac. Col. Jur. 1826
Carrington (F. A.) Criminal Law . 2nd ed. 8vo. 1827
—— & Kirwan's (A. V.) Reports, Nisi Prius, 1843-52 . . . . 3 vols. 8vo. 1845-52
—— & Marshman (J. R.) ditto, 1842 . . 8vo. 1843
—— & Payne (J.) ditto, 1823-41. 9 vols. 8vo. 1825-41
Carrow (J. M.) & Oliver (L.) Railway & Canal Cases, 1842-46 1846
Carrow (J. M.) & Oliver (L.) Railway & Canal Cases. Beavan (E.) & Lefroy (T. E. P.) 1842-46
  8vo. 1848
—— (*see* Nicholl, H. J.)
Carte & Carew Papers (*see* Hardy, T. D., & Brewer, J. S.)
Carte (T.) Catalogue des Rolles Gascons, Normans et François . . . . 2 in 1, folio 1743
Carter (S.) Reports in C. P. 1664-7 . . . folio 1688
———————— on Copyholds (Lex Custumaria). 8vo. 1696
—— (Edmd.) History of Cambridgeshire & Isle of Ely 8vo. 1819
—— History of Colchester . . 2 vols. in 1, 8vo. 1803

Carteret (*Lord*) Address to him on his Appointment as Lord Lieutenant of Ireland. MS. folio n. d.
Carthew on Uses. Reading on 3rd Wm. & M. Vol. I. Col. Jur.
—— (T.) Reports K.B. . . . . folio 1728
———————————— 1688–99 . 2nd ed. folio 1741
Carts, City Orders as to Standing (*see* London Tracts)
Cartwright's (Edmd.) Rape of Bramber, Parochial Topography (*see* Dallaway's Sussex, pt. 1) 4to. 1830
—— (*Bp.*) Diary, 1686–87, C. S. Pa. No. 22 . . 1842
Carwardine (H. H.) on Parochial Assessment, Vol. 4, Pam. 1841
Cary (*Sir* G.) Reports in Chancery, 1601 (Reprint)
12mo. 1820
—— (H.) on Juries 12mo. 1826
Cases in Chancery, 1660–78
3rd ed. 3 vols. in 1, folio 1735
—— temp. Sir John Holt, K.B. 1688–1710. folio 1738
—— temp. Talbot (J G. Williams) 2nd ed. folio 1753
——————————————— . 3rd ed. 8vo. 1792
—— Special, in Chancery, 1669–93 . . . 8vo. 1694
—— temp. Car. I. to Anne, 1625–1714
3 vols. in 1, folio 1736
—— & Opinions of eminent Counsel in matters of Law, Equity, and Conveyancing, arranged by P. Burton . . . . 2 vols. 8vo. 1791
Casley (D.) Catalogue of Royal MSS. in British Museum 4to. 1734
Cassell & Co., Map of London, in case 1867
Cassilis Peerage: Case of Earl Ruglen. 1st Series, page 37
—— Case of Sir Thomas Kennedy. 1st Series, page 42
Castellane Dictionary . . . . folio 1780
——————————— . . . . . 3rd ed. folio 1791
Castle (H. J.) Remarks on Union Assessment Act
8vo. 1863

LIST OF THE BOOKS IN THE

Castle & E. J. Castle, Remarks on Rating & Assessment of Railways, &c. 8vo. 1869

CATALOGUES :—

Bassett	12mo. 1682
Walthoe	12mo. 1716
Walthoe, 1720 & 1726	. 2 vols. 12mo.
Worrall, 1732 & 1736	. 2 vols. 12mo.
Worrall & Brooks . . . . ,	2 vols. 12mo. 1788–1800
Law List—Brown	. 8vo. 1775–98
Law List—Stamp Office . . . ,	8vo. 1798–1869
Clarke (J.)	. 12mo. 1819
Stevens & Sons	. 12mo. 1833
Clarke, J. & W. T.	. 12mo. 1833
Stevens, V. & R. & C. S. Norton . .	. 12mo. 1840
Little & Brown (American) . . .	. 12mo. 1843
Butterworth	12mo. 1845 & 1850
Stevens & Norton . . , , .	. 12mo. 1848
Maxwell, W.	. 12mo. 1850
Maxwell & Sons	. 12mo. 1867
H. G. Stevens & R. W. Haynes . . .	. 12mo. 1868
Catalogue of MSS. at Corpus Christi College, Cambridge	4to. 1722
Royal MSS. in British Museum—Casling . .	. 4to. 1734
Earl Powis Estate at Hendon . . .	4to. 1756
MSS., Abp. Parker in Corpus Christi College, Cambridge— Nasmith	4to. 1777
Additional MSS. in the British Museum—Ayscough 2 vols.	4to. 1782
Catalogue, or Repertory of Endowments of Vicarages in the Dioceses of Canterbury & Rochester—Ducarel	. 8vo. 1782
Catalogue of the Works of Sir Wm. Blackstone. See his Biography	1782
Des Livres de la Bibliothèque du Duc de la Vallière, par G. de Bure . . . . . . , .	3 vols. 8vo. 1783
MSS. of Lord Chancellor Hardwick . . .	4to. 1794
Cottonian MSS. in British Museum . . .	Fol. 1802
Harleian MSS. in British Museum . .	4 vols. fol. 1808-12
Archiepiscopal MSS., Registers & Records at Lambeth Palace	Fol. 1812
Bibliotheca Britannica	8 vols. 8vo. 1813–19
Printed Books at the Society of Antiquaries . .	4to. 1816
Advocates' Library at Doctors' Commons . . .	8vo. 1818
Advocates' Library at Doctors' Commons, on Sale of .	8vo. 1861
Hargrave MSS. in the British Museum . .	4to. 1818
Lansdowne MSS. in the British Museum . .	Fol. 1819
Athenæum Library at Liverpool—Burrell . . .	8vo. 1820
Library of the Corporation of London , , ,	8vo. 1828
Library of the Corporation of London . , .	8vo. 1840
Library of the Corporation of London . . .	8vo. 1859
Library of the Corporation of London, Supplements .	1860–67

LAW SOCIETY LIBRARY. 63

Catalogues—*continued*
Library of the Corporation of London, of Sculpture, &c., part 1 1867
Library of the Corporation of London, of Sculpture, &c., part 2 1868
Arundel MSS. in the College of Arms . . . 8vo. 1829
Maps, &c., in the Library of George III. in the British Museum . . . . Fol. 1829
Maps, &c., in the Library of George III. in the British Museum . . . . 2 vols. 8vo. 1829
Maps, &c., in the British Museum . . . 2 vols. 8vo. 1844
Library of the House of Commons . . . . Fol. 1830
Library of the Inner Temple 8vo. 1833
Red Book of the Exchequer—Dodsworth MSS. in the Bodleian MSS. in Lincoln's Inn Library . . . 8vo. 1833
Bibliotheca Hiberniana . . . . . 5 vols. 8vo. 1834
Fellows, &c., of College of Physicians . . . 8vo. 1835
Library of the London Institution, Charter, &c. . 8vo. 1832
Library of the London Institution, Charter, &c. 3 vols. 8vo. 1835-43
Library of Lincoln's Inn 8vo. 1835
Library of Lincoln's Inn of MSS. 8vo. 1838
Library of Lincoln's Inn, 2 Supplements . . . 8vo. 1862, 67
Library of Lincoln's Inn, of Books on Ancient Law of France
        8vo. 1849
Catalogue of Printed Books & MSS. of Fras. Douce, Esq., bequeathed to the Bodleian Library, Oxford . . Fol. 1840
Library of the Harvard University, Cambridge, Massachusetts, N. A. 8vo. 1841
Printed Books in the British Museum, Ato—Azzurimus Fol. 1841
Catalogue or List of Members of House of Lords, whose Ancestors have occupied the Judicial Seat of England, showing the Grandeur of the Law—Phillips, 12mo. 1685; Foss, 4to. 1842
Catalogue of the Contents of Strawberry Hill—Earl Waldegrave 4to. 1842
Catalogue or Chronological List of Books & Papers as to Rate of Mortality, Annuities, & Life Assurance—Pocock (2nd edit.) 8vo. 1842
Arundel MSS. in British Museum, N.S., vol. 1 . . Fol. 1834
Codicum Manuscriptorum Orientalium, qui in Mus. Brit. asservantur, Catalogus . . . . . 4 parts, fol. 1838-52
Burney MSS.—N.S., vol. 1 . . . . Fol. 1840
Arundel & Burney MSS., Index to Catalogue—Part 3 Fol. 1840
MSS. Music in British Museum 8vo. 1842
MS. in Library of—Phillips, Esq. . . . . Fol.
MSS. Music in British Museum 8vo. 1842
MSS. in British Museum, List of Additions, 1836-1840 8vo. 1843
MSS. in British Museum, List of Additions, 1841-1845 8vo. 1852
Middle Temple Library, 1845 & 1863
Catalogue of Home Office Library . . . 8vo. 1852
MSS. in Caius College Library—Smith . , , 8vo. 1849
Manchester Law Society Library . . . 8vo. 1854

Catalogues—*continued*
Descriptive of Historical MSS., in Arabic & Persian Languages in Asiatic Library—Morley . . . 12mo. 1854
American Literature 8vo. 1856
Patent Office Commissioners' Library . . 2 vols. 4to. 1858
Catalogue of Books of Reference in the Reading Room of the British Museum 8vo. 1859
Catalogue of Camden Society's Works—Nichols . 4to. 1862
Catalogue of Materials relating to the History of Great Britain & Ireland (T. D. Hardy) 26 M.R. Pub. 1862–65
Catholique Ballad, or Invitation to Popery. MS. temp. James & Charles
Cato (M. Portius) De Re Rustica . . . 12mo. 1543
Catton (C.) English Peerage . . 3 vols. folio. 1780–90
Catulli, Tibulli, et Propertii Opera . . . 4to. 1772
Caulfield (R.) (*see* C. S. Pa. No. 68)
Cause Lists, 1833–63 . . . . 95 vols. folio
Causes Célèbres . . . . . . 12 vols. 12mo.
—————— by M. Richer . 22 vols. 12mo. 1772–88
Causton (G. K. S.) The Howard Papers . 8vo. 1862
Cave (L. W.) (*see* Leigh, E. C.)
—— List of Lords & Commons 1734–1735
Cay (J.) Abridgment of Statutes, & Supplement, Hen. III. to 1 G. III. . . . 3 vols. folio 1739–66
Cecil (*Sir* Robt.) Letters to Sir Geo. Carew. No. 88, C. S. Pa. (J. Maclean) 1864
Cervantes' (M. de) Don Quixote (Por D. M. F. de Navarrete) 8vo. 1855
Ceylon Acts, 1796–1851 . . . . . 2 vols. 4to. 1854
—— Institutes of Laws of (H. B. Thomson)
2 vols. 4to. 1866
—— Ordinances, 1857–65 . . . . . 3 vols. folio
Chadwick (S.) Probate Court Manual . . 8vo. 1861
Chaffers (W.) on Hall Marks on Gold, &c. Plate. 8vo. 1863
—— Marks & Monograms in Pottery & Porcelain; with Notices of each Manufactory, & an Essay on the Vasa Victitia of England 8vo. 1863
Chalmers (A.) General Biographical Dictionary
32 vols. 8vo. 1812–17

Chalmers (G.) Opinions of Eminent Lawyers 8vo. 1858
Chamberlain (A.) on the Commercial System of the
  Stamp Laws, Vol. 21, Pam. 1841
—— (E. & J.) Present State of Britain
                        36 vols. 8vo. 1669-1755
—— (H.) History of London . . . . . folio 1769
Chamberlaine (J.) Letters temp. Eliz. C. S. Pa.
  No. 79 1861
Chambers (C. H.) on Leases 8vo. 1819
—— (Sir H.) on Estates 8vo. 1824
—— (J.) History of Malvern 8vo. 1816
—— (J. D.) on Errors in Reform Act. Vol. 11,
  Jac. Col. & Vol. 4, Pam. 1832
—— Dictionary of Elections 8vo. 1837
—— on Infants 8vo. 1842
Chambers (J. D.) Gorham Case, Review of, and Ex-
  amination of Judgment, in Letter to Bishop of
  Salisbury. Vol. 7, Pam. 1850
Chambers (Thos.) & Peterson (A. T. T.) on the Law
  of Railway Companies, with Forms. . . 8vo. 1848
Chamney (W. G.) Report of Warren's Trial (Dublin)
                                    8vo. 1867
Chance (H.) on Powers . . . . . 2 vols. 8vo. 1831
Chancellors & Lord Keepers of the Seal, temp.
  John (*see* Foss's Grandeur of the Law)
Chancery, Authority of the Master of the Rolls in
                                    8vo. 1827
—— Bar, Observations on. Vol. 5, Jac. Col. . . 1816
Chancery Calendars of Proceedings in, temp. Eliz.
  (J. Bailey) (*see* Rec. Com.) . . . 3 vols. folio 1832
—— Choice Cases in, & Practice . . . 12mo. 1672
—— Clerk of Court in, or Practising Solicitor. 8vo. 1,726
—— Commissioners' Reports to Parliament
                        3 vols. folio 1826-56
—— Compensation Statement. Vol. 3, Pam. . . 1845
—— Compensation Statement. Parts 1 & 2, in
  Support of Mr. Watson's Renewed Motion, ditto 1846

F

Chancery, Considerations on, by Lord Redesdale.
Vol. 3, Jac. Col. 1826
—— Considerations on Reform in, by an Equity
Draftsman, Vol. 2, Ch. Pam. 1842
—— Court, Bill for Reform of. Vol. 8, Jac.
Col. 1831
—— Court of, its Inherent Defects, by a Solicitor.
Vol. 17, Pam. 1849
—— Court Jurisdiction Vindicated, & King James's
Judgment on Controversy between Lord Chancellor Ellesmere & Lord Coke, 16 Jas. I. Vol. 1,
Col. Jur.
—— Delays, Enquiry into. Vol. 1, Jac. Col. . . 1824
—— Discourse on the Judicial Authority belonging to the Office of the Master of the Rolls,
in the High Court of 12mo. 1727
—— General Orders in 12mo. 1669
———————————— 8vo. 1739
———————————— . . . . . 4th ed. 8vo. 1839
———————————— temp. Hardwicke . 12mo. 1744
———————————— Strictures on. Vol. 8, Jac.
Col. 1829
—— Irish Fees in, Schedule of 8vo. 1836
—— Irish Orders . . . . 12mo.
—— Judges of Court of: Letter by a Barrister.
Vol. 9, Jac. Col. 1829
—— Masters in (author unknown). Vol. 1, Har.
L. T.
—— Modern Index 8vo. 1807
—— Office, Facts & Suggestions respecting. Vol.
2, Ch. Pam. 1841
—— Master's Office, by a Master's Clerk. Vol. 11,
Jac. Col. 1831
—— Orders in. Vol. 12, Jac. Col. . . . 8vo. 1828
—— Orders in, & Rules, Equity Jurisdiction,
County Courts 8vo. 1865
—— Practice, by a Chancery Barrister . . 12mo. 1834
—— Practice in Libels, Vol. 1, Jac. Col. . . . 1823

Chancery Practice, Questions & Answers on Practice 12mo. 1842
—— Proceedings (*see* Proceedings)
—— Reform, Propositions as to. Vol. 17, Pam. 1830
—— Rolls, Master of, Authority in . . . 8vo. 1727
—— Select Cases in, temp. King, 1724–33 . folio 1740
———————————— (S. Macnaghten) 8vo. 1850
—— Special Cases in, temp. Car. to 2 Anne
        3 vols. in 1, folio 1736
—— Suits in (from Cotton MSS.). Har. L. T. Vol. 1
—— Vindication of Solicitors, Essay. Vol. 5, Jac. Col. 1836
Chandler (R.) Biography of Waynflette (Bishop of Winchester) 8vo. 1811
Chandos Peerage: Case of Rev. T. Brydges, Clk. Vol. 1, 2nd Series, 468, & Vol. 1, 3rd Series, p. 311. Evidence, Vol. 2, p. 522 1802–3
Chaplain (F.) Remarks on Certain Acts of the late Session of Parliament on Life Assurance, Vol. 9, Pam. part 2 1853
Chapman (F.) Practice, K. B., with 1st, 2nd, & 3rd Addenda 12mo. 1831
———————————————. . 2nd ed. 12mo. 1833
———————————————. . 3rd ed. 8vo. 1834
Characteristicks, an Enquiry concerning Virtue & Merit . . . . Vol. 2, 8vo. 1723
Charitable Donations, 1787–1788. 2 vols. large folio
—— Trust Bill, Address to Parliament, showing cause why it should not pass into a Law. Vol. 18, Pam. 1846
Charity Commissioners' Parliamentary Reports, 1819–42, & Indexes . . . . 42 vols. folio
———————— (New Commission) 1–12. folio 1851, 1864
Charles I. An exact Collection of all Remonstrances, Declarations, Votes, Ordinances, Proclamations, Petitions, &c. between the King & Parliament. Dec. 1641 to March 1643 . 4to. 1643

Charles I., Calendar of State Papers, Domestic
Series, 1625–37. Ed. by J. Bruce 11v. imp. 8vo. 1858–68
—— *Sir* E. Lake's interviews with (ed. T. P.
Langmead). No. 73, C. S. Pa., C. M. Vol. 4 . 1858
—— Letters of, 1646, to Queen Henrietta Maria.
No. 63, C. S. Pa. (ed. J. Bruce) 1855
—— II. Calendar of State Papers, Domestic Series,
1660–67. Edited by M. A. E. Green
                            7 vols. imp. 8vo. 1860–66
—— Letters of, communicated by the Marquis
of Bristol. No. 87, C. S. Pa., C. M. Vol. 5 . . 1864
———————— & James II., Secret Services of, 1678–
88. No. 52, C. S. Pa. (ed. J. Y. Akerman) . 1851
Charles V. History of the Emperor (*see* Dr. Wm.
Robertson's Works)
Charlton (L.) Whitby, History of, & its Abbey. 4to. 1779
Charnock (R.) on General Issue (bound with
Mansel on Limitation) 1837
Chartarum Antiquarum in Turr. Lond. Catalogus
(*see* Ayloffe's Calendar)   1772
Charterhouse Prize Essays, 1814–32 . . 12mo. 1833
Charter Rolls Calendars, 1199–1483, & Inquisitiones
ad Quod Damnum (*see* Record Commission) folio 1803
—— Rotuli Chartarum, 1199–1216 (*see* Record
Commission) . . . . folio 1837
Charters, Collection of (*see* East India Company) . 1817
Chatham, *Earl of* (Biography) . . . 3 vols. 8vo. 1794
Chauncy (H.) History of Hertfordshire. 2 vols. folio 1700
———————————————— reprint, 2 vols. 8vo. 1826
Cheetham Hospital, Manchester, Founder's Will,
1651, & Charter . . . . 4to.
Chelmsford Poll Book 8vo. 1763
Chelsea Charities, Report of Vestry Committee, folio 1863
Cheshire, History of . . . . 2 vols. 8vo. 1778
—— Description of (*see* Leigh's Natural History
of Lancashire)
Chester Miscellany 4to. 1750
Chesterfield's, *Earl of*, Will 4to. 1713

Chevalier ( ) & others. The Patent Question
    under Free Trade . . . . . . 2nd ed. 8vo.
Chichester (*Abp.*) Life of . . . . folio 1765
Child (*Sir J.*) Discourse on Trade . 4th ed. 12mo. 1698
Childrey (J.) Rarities of England & Wales. 12mo. 1661
Chipping Wycombe, Charters & Grants relating
    to. 4to. 1817
Chitty (Ed.) Equity Index . . . . 4 vols. 8vo. 1837
—————————— (Macaulay). 3rd ed. 4 vols. 8vo. 1853
—— (Edw.) & Forster's (F.) Index to Reports in
    Common Law Conveyancing & Bankruptcy. 8vo. 1841
—— (Hen.) Descent 8vo. 1825
—— (J.) on Bills 8vo. 1799
————————— . . . . . 2nd ed. 8vo. 1807
————————— . . . . . . 6th ed. 8vo. 1822
————————— . . . . . . 8th ed. 8vo. 1833
————————— (J. A. Russell & D. Maclachlan)
    10th ed. 8vo. 1859
—— (Jos.) Contracts 8vo. 1826
————————— . . . . 2nd ed. 8vo. 1834
————————— (T. Chitty) . 3rd ed. 8vo. 1841
————————— (Russell) . . 4th ed. 8vo. 1850
————————— (Do.) . . . 7th ed. 8vo. 1863
————————— (Do.) . . . 8th ed. 8vo. 1868
—— Law of Nations 8vo. 1812
—— Game & Fish Laws. . . . 3 vols. 8vo. 1812–16
—— Criminal Law . . . . . . 4 vols. 8vo. 1816
————————— & Pleading. 2nd ed. 4 vols. 8vo. 1826
—— Commerce & Manufactures . 4 vols. 8vo. 1820–42
—— Reports, 1819-20 . . . . 2 vols. 8vo. 1820–23
—— Stamp Laws 8vo. 1829
————————————— (Hulme). 2nd ed. 8vo. 1841
————— Statutes . . . . . . 4 vols. 8vo. 1829–37
Chitty (J.) Statutes. (W. N. Welsby & Ed. Pearson)
    2nd ed. 7 vols. 8vo. 1853–63
————————————— 3rd ed. 4 vols. 8vo. 1865
—— Summary of Practice 8vo. 1832
—— General Practice . . . 3 vols. 8vo. 1833–1835

Chitty (J.) Medical Law 8vo. 1834
—— Forms . . . . 2nd ed. 12mo. 1835
—————— . . . . 3rd ed. 12mo. 1836
—————— . . . . 4th ed. 12mo. 1838
—————— . . . . 5th ed. 8vo. 1840
—————— . . . . 6th ed. 8vo. 1847
—————— . . . . 7th ed. 8vo. 1856
—————— . . . . 9th ed. 8vo. 1862
—————— . . . . 10th ed. 8vo. 1866
—— (Jun.) Precedents in Pleading. Pt. 1. 3rd ed.
8vo. 1836
——————— by T. Chitty & others . 3rd ed. 8vo. 1837
——————— (T. Chitty, L. Temple, R. G. Williams, & C. Jefferys) 3rd ed. 2 vols. 8vo. 1867-68
—— (& T.) Pleading 8vo. 1809
————————————— . . 2nd ed. 2 vols. 8vo. 1811
————————————— . . 5th ed. 3 vols. 8vo. 1831
—— Concise View 8vo. 1835
——————— . . . . 6th ed. 3 vols. 8vo. 1836-37
—— (J. J.) (*see* Deacon, E. E.)
—— (T.) (*see* Archbold)
—— & Temple (L.) on Inland Carriers . . . 8vo. 1856
Chiuso (G. de C.) Description of King's Bench Prison, &c. . . . . . 4th ed. 2 vols. 8vo. 1821
Cholmeley (W.) Request & Suite of a Truehearted Englishman. No. 55, C. S. Pa. C. M. Vol. 2. Ed. W. J. Thoms 1852
Christian (E.) Bankruptcy Practice
2nd ed. 2 vols. 8vo. 1818
—— Ethics : Extracts from Theological Review of 1864, & the Westminster Review
Vol. 27, Pam. 1866
—— Instructor . . . . . 2nd ed. 2 vols. 8vo. 1820
——————— . . . . . 3rd ed. 3 vols. 8vo. 1822
——————— Prayers & Meditations. Par. S. Pa. 8vo. 1842
Christie (J. T.) (*see* Crabbe, Geo.)
—— (R.) & Newmarch (W.) Hints to Agents & Friends of Assurance Offices. Vol. 9, Pam. . 1852

Chronicles & Memorials of Great Britain & Ireland,
published under direction of Master of the Rolls:—
1. Chronicles of England, Jno. Capgrave. Ed.
    Rev. F. C. Hingeston 8vo. 1858
2. Chronicon Monasterii de Abingdon, 675–
    1189. Ed. Rev. J. Stevenson 2 vols. 8vo. 1858
3. Lives of Edward the Confessor. Ed. H. R.
    Luard 8vo. 1858
4. Monumenta Franciscana, 1226–1351. Ed.
    J. S. Brewer 8vo. 1858
5. Fasciculi Zizaniorum Magistri Johannis
    Wyclif, cum Tritico. Ascribed to Thomas
    Netter of Walden. Ed. Rev. W. W.
    Shirley 8vo. 1858
6. The Buik of the Croniclis of Scotland, a
    metrical version of the History of Hector
    Boece, by W. Stewart. Ed. W. B. Turn-
    bull . . . . 3 vols. 8vo. 1858
7. Johannis Capgrave Liber de Illustribus
    Henricis. Ed. F. C. Hingeston . 8vo. 1858
8. Historia Monasterii S. Augustini Cantu-
    ariensis, by Thomas of Elmham. Ed. C.
    Hardwick 8vo. 1858
9. Eulogium (Historiarum, sive Temporis):
    Chronicon ab Orbe condito usque ad
    annum Domini 1366, a Monacho quodam
    Malmesburiensi exaratum. Ed. F. C.
    Haydon . . . . . . 3 vols. 8vo. 1858–63
10. Memorials of Henry the Seventh. Ed. Jas.
    Gairdner 8vo. 1858
11. Memorials of Henry V. Ed. C. A. Cole. 8vo. 1858
12. Munimenta Gildhallæ Londoniensis. Ed.
    H. T. Riley . . . . 4 vols. 8vo. 1859–62
13. Chronica Johannis de Oxenedes, 449–1292.
    Ed. Sir H. Ellis 8vo. 1859
14. A Collection of Political Poems & Songs
    relating to English History, from Acces-
    sion of Edward III. to that of Richard
    III. Ed. T. Wright . 2 vols. 8vo. 1859–61

Chronicles—*continued*

15. The Opus Tertium—' Opus Minus,' &c., of F. Roger Bacon. Ed. J. S. Brewer. 8vo. 1859
16. Bartholomæi de Cotton Monachi Norwicensis Historia Anglicana, 449–1298. Ed. H. R. Luard 8vo. 1859
17. Brut y Tywysogion, or the Chronicle of the Princes of Wales. Ed. Rev. J. Williams ab Ithel 8vo. 1860
18. Royal & Historical Letters during the Reign of Henry IV., 1399–1404. Ed. Rev. F. C. Hingeston. Vol. 1 . . . 8vo. 1860
19. The Repressor of Over-much Blaming of the Clergy, by Reginald Pecock, Bishop of Chichester. Ed. C. Babington. 2 vols. 8vo. 1860
20. Annales Cambriæ. Ed. Rev. J. Williams ab Ithel 8vo. 1860
21. The Works of Giraldus Cambrensis. Ed. J. S. Brewer & J. F. Dimock
  5 vols. 8vo. 1861–67
22. Letters & Papers illustrative of the Wars of the English in France during the Reign of Henry VI. Vol. 1 and Vol. 2 (in 2 parts). Ed. Rev. J. Stevenson
  3 vols. 8vo. 1861–64
23. The Anglo-Saxon Chronicle, according to the several original authorities. Edited with a Translation by B. Thorpe
  2 vols. 8vo. 1861
24. Letters & Papers illustrative of the Reigns of Richard III. & Henry VII. Ed. J. Gairdner . . . . 2 vols. 8vo. 1861–63
25. Roberti Grosseteste Episcopi quondam Lincolniensis epistolæ. Ed. H. R. Luard
  8vo. 1861
26. Descriptive Catalogue of Materials relating to the History of Great Britain & Ireland, to the end of the Reign of Henry VII. Vol. 1 (in 2 parts), Anterior to the

Chronicles—*continued*

Norman Invasion. Vol. 2, From A.D. 1066–
1200. Ed. T. D. Hardy . 2 vols. 8vo. 1862-65
27. Royal & other Historical Letters, illustrative of the Reign of Henry III. From the originals in the Public Record Office, 1216–25. Ed. Rev. W. W. Shirley
2 vols. 8vo. 1862–66
28. Chronica Monasterii S. Albani. Ed. H. T. Riley:—
   (1) Thomæ Walsingham Historia Anglicana. Vol. 1, 1272, 1381. Vol. 2, 1381, 1422
1863–64
   (2) Will Rishanger, Chronica et Annales, 1259–1307
   (3) J. de Trokelowe et Henrici de Blaneforde, Chronica et Annales, 1259–1406 . . . 1866
   (4) Gesta Abbatum Monasterii S. Albani, a Thoma Walsingham, regnante Ricardo Secundo, ejusdem Ecclesiæ præcentore, compilata. Vol. 1, 793–1290. Vol. 2, 1290–1349 1863–67
29. Chronicon Abbatiæ Eveshamensis, auctoribus Dominico priore Eveshamiæ et Thoma de Marlberge abbate, a Fundatione ad annum 1213 una cum continuatione ad annum 1418. Ed. W. D. Macray . . . 8vo. 1863
30. Ricardi de Cirencestria speculum Historiale de Gestis Regum Angliæ. Vol. 1, 447–871. Ed. J. E. B. Mayor . . . 8vo. 1863
31. Year Books of the Reign of Edward I. Years 20 & 21, 1292–93; 30 & 31, 32 & 33, 1302–5. Ed. & translator, A. J. Horwood
3 vols. 8vo. 1863, 1864, 1866
32. Narratives of the expulsion of the English from Normandy, 1449–1550.—Robertus Blundelli, de Reductione Normanniæ. Le Recouvrement de Normendie, par Berry, Herault du Roy

Chronicles—*continued*

Conferences between the Ambassador of France & England. Ed. from MSS. in the Imperial Library at Paris, Rev. L. J. Stevenson 8vo. 1863

33. Historia et Cartularium Monasterii S. Petri Gloucestriæ. Ed. W. H. Hart. 3 v. 8vo. 1863-67
34. Alexandri Neckam de Naturis rerum libri duo; with Neckam's Poem. de Laudibus Divinæ Sapientiæ. Ed. J. Wright . 8vo. 1863
35. Leechdoms, Wortcunning, & Starcraft of Early England, being a collection of Documents illustrating the History of Science in this Country before the Norman Conquest. Collected & ed. by R. O. Cockayne
3 vols. 8vo. 1864, 1865, 1866
36. Annales Monastici. Vol. 1, Annales de Margan, 1066-1232. Annales de Theokesberia, 1066-1263. Annales de Burton, 1004-1263. Vol. 2, Annales Monasterii de Wintonia, 519-1277. Annales Monasterii de Waverleia, 1-1291. Ed. H. R. Luard . . . . 2 vols. 8vo. 1864-65
37. Magna Vita S. Hugonis Episcopi Lincolniensis; from MSS. in the Bodleian Library, Oxford, & the Imperial Library, Paris. Ed. Rev. J. F. Dimock 8vo. 1864
38. Chronicles & Memorials of the Reign of Richard I.:—

    Vol. 1, Itinerarium peregrinorum et gesta regis Ricardi

    Vol. 2, Epistolæ Cantuarienses: the Letters of the Prior & Convent of Christchurch, Canterbury, from 1187-99. Ed. W. Stubbs . . . . . . 2 vols. 8vo. 1864-65
39. Recueil des Chroniques et Anchiennes Istories de la Grant Bretaigne, a present nommé Engleterre, par T. de Waurin, Alb. 688. Ed. W. Hardy . . . 8vo. 1864

Chronicles—*continued*

40. A Collection of the Chronicles & Ancient Histories of Great Britain, now called England, by J. de Waurin, from Albina to 688 (translation of the preceding). Ed. & translated by W. Hardy . 8vo. 1864
41. Polychronicon Ranulphi Higden; with Trevisa's translation. Ed. C. Babington. Vol. 1 . . . . 8vo. 1865
42. Le Livere de Reis de Brittanie et Livere de Reis de Engleterre. Ed. J. Glover . 8vo. 1865
43. Chronica Monasterii de Melsa, A.D. 1150, usque ad annum 1400, auctore Thoma de Burton Abbate. Ed. E. A. Bond. Vols. 1, 2, 3 . . . . 8vo. 1866–68
44. Matthæi Parisiensis Historia Anglorum, sive, ut vulgo dicitur, Historia Minor. Vols. 1 & 2, 1067–1245. Ed. Sir F. Madden. 8vo. 1866
45. Liber Monasterii de Hyda—Chronicle & Chartulary of Hyde Abbey, Winchester, 455–1023. Ed. Ed. Edwards . . 8vo. 1866
46. Chronicum Scotorum—A Chronicle of Irish Affairs, from earliest times to 1150. Ed. & translated by W. M. Hennessey . 8vo. 1866
47. The Chronicle of Pierre de Langtoft from the earliest period to Death of Edward I. Ed. T. Wright 8vo. 1866
48. War of the Gaedhill with the Gaill, or Invasions of Ireland. Ed. J. H. Todd 8vo. 1867
49. Gesta Regis Henrici Secundi Benedicti Abbatis. The Chronicle of the Reigns of Henry II. & Richard I., 1169–92; known under the name of Benedict of Peterborough. Vols. 1 & 2. Edited by William Stubbs, M.A. 1867
50. Munimenta Academica, or Documents illustrative of Academical Life & Studies at Oxford (in two Parts). Edited by the Rev. Henry Anstey, M.A. 1868

Chronicles—*continued*
   51. Chronica Magistri Rogeri de Houedene.
      Vol. 1. Edited by William Stubbs, M.A. 1868
Chronicon Petroburgense, 1122–95. No. 47, C.
   S. Pa. (J. Bruce) 1849
Church of England, Apology for, as to the persecuting spirit of which she is accused. Tract 1688–89
Church of England, Vindication of, & Penal Laws
   of. Tract 1688–89
—— Question (The) in England. The Piccadilly
   Papers, No. 2. Vol. 15, Pam. 1860
Churcher's College, Petersfield, Hants, History of
                                                     8vo. 1823
Churton (E.) County Kalendar 8vo. 1847
Cicero, a Drama (Moile) 4to. 1847
Cicero's Letters, Paris. Vol. 4 . . . . 12mo. 1725
Cinque Ports, Charter of 12mo. 1682
Circuits of the Judges, 1838–67 . . . . folio
City Press Newspaper
Civil & Canon Law. Latin Tracts on, 1720–30. 8vo.
Civil Engineers, Charter to 1867
Clarendon (*Lord*) Trial 8vo 1700
—— Life, & his Collection of State Papers
                                       3 vols. folio 1759
—— History of the Rebellion . . . 8 vols. 8vo. 1826
Clark (C.) House of Lords Cases, 1850–66
                                    9 vols. 8vo. 1853–66
—————————— Index to, 1814–66. . 8vo. 1868
—— (Law Reports) . . . . 3 vols. 8vo. 1866–68
—— (C.) (*see* Dow, P.)
—— Commentarius Juris Anglicani . . . folio 1734
—— Summary of the Colonial Law . . . 8vo. 1834
—— & Finelly (W.) Reports, H.L., 1831–46
                                   12 vols. 8vo. 1833–46
Clarke (C.) & Finelly (W.) Reports, H. L., N. S.,
   1847-50 . . . . 2 vols. 8vo. 1849–51
—— (E.) On Extradition 12mo. 1867
—— (F.) Ecclesiastical Praxis (T. Bladen)
                                    2nd ed. 4to. 1684

Clarke or Clerke (F.) Praxis Curiæ Admiralitatis Angliæ in Latin and English, the Practice of the Court of Admiralty of England, written originally in Latin 12mo. 1722
―――――――――――――― (Rowghton) . 12mo. 1743
―― (G.) Penal Statutes Abridged (Wilson)
2nd ed. 12mo. 1777
―― (G.R.) History of Ipswich & Villages near. 8vo. 1830
―― Unanimity of Trial by Jury Defended; addressed to Earl Derby. Vol. 12, Pam. . . 1859
―― (G. R.) Letter to Lord Chelmsford as to Relief of Trustees. Vol. 12, Pam. 1859
―― Yorkshire Gazetteer (York) 8vo. 1828
―― (G. S.) Hebrew Criticism & Poetry . 8vo. 1810
―― (J.) Bibliotheca Legum 12mo. 1819
―― (Jas.) Survey of Lakes of Cumberland & Westmoreland . . . . folio 1789
―― (R.) East India Regulations for Madras, 1802-34 . . . . 4to. 1840
――――――――― for Bombay, 1799-1834 . 4to. 1851
――――――――― & Acts for Bengal, 1793-1834
2 vols. 4to. 1854
―― (S. R.) Lancashire Gazetteer. 8vo. 1830
―― (T.) Ecclesiastical Jurisdiction . . . 8vo. 1840
―― (W.) History of Knighthood . . . 8vo. 1784
―― (W. R.) Parochial Topography of the Hundred of Wanting, with other Miscellaneous Records of the County of Berks 4to. 1824
Classiques français, Tome 2 (Gonzalve de Cordoue)
12mo.
Clayton v. Duchy of Cornwall: Trial. . . 8vo. 1834
―― (W. C.) on Conveyancing 8vo. 1855
――'s Reports & Pleas of Assizes at York. 12mo. 1651
Cleaveland (Jno.) Banking System of New York
(G. S. Hutchinson) . . . . . 2nd ed. 8vo. 1864
Clergy List (*see* Cox)
Clerical Guide & Ecclesiastical Directory . 8vo. 1836
Clerk (J.) on Election Committees. . . . 8vo. 1852
―――――――――――――――――― . . . 8vo. 1857

Clerk's Manual 12mo. 1672
—— Guide . . . . 3rd ed. 12mo. 1653
Clifford Peerage: Case of Richard, Earl of Burlington, 1st Series, p. 49 1735–39
—— (H.) on Southwark Election 8vo. 1797
—— (*Sir* Thos.) History of Tixall, Staffordshire
            4to. 1817
Clift (H.) Entries . . . . . . 2nd ed. folio 1719
Clinton Peerage: Case of R. W. G. Trefusis. Vol. 1, 3rd Series, 353 1794
Clive (*Lord*) Jaghire, Opinions on, of Eminent Counsel. Vol. 1, Col. Jur.
Clode (C. M.) on the Military Forces of the Crown, their Administration & Government. Vol. 1, 8vo. 1869
Clubb (*Rev.* W.) History of Wheatfield, &c., Suffolk, bound up with Morant's Colchester . . . 1758
Clun, Documents relating to Borough of . . 4to. 1858
Clutterbuck (R.) History of Hertford, 3 vols. folio 1815
Coates (*Rev.* C.) History, &c. of Reading . 8vo. 1802
Coburg (*Duke of*) Pamphlet on Russia. Vol. 12, Pam. 1859
Cochrane (G.) on the Economy of the Law, especially in Chancery. Vol. 11, Pam. . . 3rd ed. 1857
——————————— Vol. 17, Pam. . . . 5th ed. 1863
——'s (*Lord*) Trial 8vo. 1814
Cockburn (A. E.) & Rowe's (W. E.) Election Cases 8vo. 1835
—— (*Rev.* D. W.) Ecclesiastical Practice
           4th ed. 8vo. 1792
—— (F.) Lord Chief Justice Cockburn's Charge at Old Bailey, in Regina *v.* Nelson . . . 8vo. 1867
Cocking (W.) Essay on Reading 8vo. 1775
Code, Frederician, of Prussia, translated from the French . . . . 2 vols. 8vo. 1761
—— Napoléon (*see* Barrett)
——————— (*see* Richards)
——————— translated by a Barrister . 8vo. 1823
—— Pénal, of France. Paris . . 4th ed. 12mo. 1777

Code for Russia, Instructions to frame, translated
 by Tatischeff 4to. 1768
Codes, les Six 8vo. 1828
Codigo de Commercio. Madrid 4to. 1829
Cohen (B.) on Finance. 8vo. 1822
Coke (*Sir* E.) Biography of (*see* Roscoe's Lives
 of Eminent British Lawyers) 12mo. 1830
—— (*Sir* Edw.) Reports (in French) 4 vols. 4to. 1601–8
 ———————————————————— 2nd ed. folio 1680
 ———————————————————— . . . folio 1697
—— Reports (G. Wilson) . . . . 7 vols. 8vo. 1793
 —————— Table to (Ashe) 12mo. 1606
—— 5th Report, Answer to (Parsons) . . 4to. 1606
 —————— New edition, with Notes, &c., by J.
 H. Thomas & J. F. Fraser. Index by R. P. Tyrwhitt . . . . 6 vols. 8vo. 1826
—— Book of Entries . . . . folio 1614
 ———————————————— . . . . 2nd ed. folio 1671
—— Compleat Copyholder 12mo. 1644
—— Institutes of the Laws of England, or a
 Commentary upon Littleton. 1st Institute
 2nd ed. folio 1629
 ———————————— 2nd Institute . . 3rd ed. folio 1669
 ———————————————— . . 6th ed. folio 1681
 ———————————— 3rd & 4th Institute . . . . folio 1644
 ———————————————————— 6th ed. folio 1680–81
—— upon Littleton; also Three Tracts by same
 Author; by F. Hargrave, with Additional Notes
 by C. Butler, 1795 . . . . . . 13th ed. folio 1775
 ———————————————— F. Hargrave & C.
 Butler, including the Notes of Chief Justice Hale
 & Lord Chancellor Nottingham, &c. 14th ed. folio 1789
 ———————————————— 15th ed. 2 vols. 8vo. 1795
 ———————————————— 16th ed. 3 vols. 8vo. 1809
 ———————————— (C. Butler) 19th ed. 2 vols. 8vo. 1832
 ———————————————— A systematic arrange-
 ment on the plan of Sir M. Hale's Analysis, &c.
 (J. H. Thomas) . . . . 3 vols. 8vo. 1818

Coke (*Sir* E.) Three Law Tracts, by Wm. Hawkins
8vo. 1764
1. The Compleate Copyholder
2. Reading on 27 Edw. I. de Finibus Levatis
3. Bail & Mainprize. To which are added the Old Tenures, & some Notes & Additions to Lord Coke's Commentary (W. Hawkins)

Coker (J.) Antiquities of Dorsetshire . . folio 1732
Colburn's New Monthly Magazine, 1831, & continued
8vo.
—— United Service Magazine, 1838, & continued
8vo.
Cole (C. A.) Memorials of Henry V., No. 2, M. R. Pub. 1858
—— (C. N.) Bedford Level, Law & History of the Drainage 8vo. 1761
———————————————— 2nd ed. 8vo. 1803
———————————— Regulations as to. 8vo. 1821
———————————— Map . . . folio
———————————— Statutes. 5 vols. 4to. n. d.
—— (H.) Record Commission Letters . 8vo. 1835–36
—— English History & Documents illustrative of the 13th & 14th Centuries. Selected from Records of Queen's Remembrancer of Exchequer. folio 1844
—— (Hy. Thos.) (*see* Saunders, T. W.)
—— (W. R.) on Criminal Information and Quo Warranto (bound up with Flather's Bankruptcy)
8vo. 1842
—— Domicil of Englishmen in France . 12mo. 1857
—— on Ejectment 8vo. 1857
Coleman (E.) on Chancery Costs . 2nd ed. 8vo. 1857
Coleridge (H. N.) Six Months in the West Indies
2nd ed. 8vo. 1826
Colinii Gasparis Vita 12mo. 1575
Collectanea Juridica: Tracts on English Law (collected by F. Hargrave) . . . . 2 vols. 8vo. 1791
Vol. 1.
No. 1. Case of the Commendams before the Privy Council, in 16 Jac. I.
No. 2. Vindication of the Jurisdiction of the Court of Chancery, with King James's Judgment on Controversy between Lord Chancellor Ellesmere & Lord Coke, 16 Jac. I.

Collectanea Juridica—*continued*

3. Lord C. J. Reeves' Instruction to his Nephew on the Study of the Law
4. Sir James Marriott's Argument in giving Judgment in Admiralty Court as to Ship Columbus
5. The Duke of Newcastle's Letter to Monsieur Michell, in Answer to the Prussian Memorial respecting Capture of Vessels & Property of Neutrals in time of War
6. Lord Bacon's Argument, when Attorney-General, on the Writ de Rege Inconsulto, in the case of the Grant of the Office of Supersedeas in the C. P., 13 Jas. I.
7. Case on the Validity of Equitable Recoveries, & Opinions of several eminent Counsel thereon
8. Opinions of several eminent Counsel on the Case of Lord Clive's Jaghire
9. Lord Hale's Preface to Rolle's Abridgment
10. Case of Perrin & Blake in K.B., with Judges' Arguments therein
11. Case of the Duchess of Kingston's Will made in France, with Opinion of Monsieur Target thereon
12. Case of Buckworth *v.* Thirkill, in K.B., in replevin, reserved at Cambridge Assizes, 25 Geo. III.
13. Case of Willoughby & Willoughby, in Chancery, on Priority of Mortgage Debt
14. Serjt. Carthew's Reading on the Law of Uses, 3 W. & M.
15. Case of Bagshaw & Spencer, in Chancery, 22 Geo. II.
16. Case on the operation of the Statute of Uses, with opinions of Mr. Booth and other Counsel thereon
17. Select Cases determined in Chancery by Lord Hardwicke, on Statute of Mortmain
18. Decree of Lord Chancellor Northington in remarkable case of Norton *v.* Reilly
19. Case of West *v.* Erissey, in Exchequer. T. 1726
20. Case of Attwood *v.* Eyre, in Chancery, in quashing a Significavit
21. Case of Devise of Real & Personal Estate, and Mr. Peere Williams's Opinion
22. Observations on the Great Expense of Prosecuting Suits at Law, with a Plan proposing a Remedy
23. Case of Elizabeth Dunn, on a Trial for Forgery

Vol. 2.

No. 1. Treatise on the Court of Star Chamber, by W. Hudson
2. Opinions of three Eminent Modern Counsel on the doctrine of Tacking prior & subsequent Securities, & on Statute 4 & 5 W. & M. c. 16, respecting Frauds by Clandestine Mortgages
3. Opinions on a Devise of Real and Personal Estate
4. Opinions on a Surrender of Copyholds
5. Opinions on a Revocation of a Will
6. Opinions on Terms in Gross, & attendant on the Inheritance

G

Collectanea Juridica—continued

7. Opinions on an Estate in Fee-simple defeasible on leaving no issue
8. Opinions on the Grant of a Perpetual Post Obit Annuity
9. The Option: Inquiry into Grounds of Claim made by the Archbishop on all consecrated & translated Bishops of the disposal of any preferment belonging to their respective Sees that he shall make choice of
10. Of the Public Councils of this Kingdom, & of affairs of War and Peace therein debated
11. Lord Loughborough's Argument in C.P. on Fines payable on Admission to Copyhold Estates
12. On Construction of Marriage Articles & Cross Remainders, in case of Duke of Richmond; with Mr. Booth's Opinion, Mr. Wedderburn's Argument, & Decree of Lord Chancellor Apsley
13. The Rules of Customs pertaining unto West Sheen, Petersham, & Ham
14. Arguments of the Lord Chancellor & Lord Chief Justice of the K.B. on the Douglas cause in the House of Lords, Feb. 27, 1769
15. Speech of Lord Chancellor Jefferies on occasion of creating Sir Edward Herbert L.C.J. of the K.B., 23rd Oct. 1685
16. On the Interest of the Husband in the Real & Personal Estates & Chattels of the Wife
17. Analysis of the Theory & Practice of Conveyancing

Colles (R.) Reports H. L. (Supplement to Brown), 1697–1709 . . . . 8vo. 1789
Collier Dock Act . . . . folio 1826
—— (J. P.) (see C. S. Pa. Nos. 2, 12, 39)
—— (see C. M. Vol. 4, No. 73)
—— (J. R.) (see Millar, F. C. J.)
—— (R. P.) Railway Precedents 12mo. 1845
—— on Mines 12mo. 1849
Collieries of South Wales: Evidence Vol. 13, Jac. Col. 1810
Collins (A.) The Peerage of England; or an Historical and Genealogical Account of the Present Nobility, &c. . . . . 1 vol. 8vo. in 2 1709
——————————— 2nd ed. 2 vols. 8vo. in 3 1710–11
—— another copy of Vol. 2, in 2 vols. 1711
——————— 2nd ed. (with a Supplement) 2 vols. 8vo. 1714
——————— 3rd ed. ——————— 2 vols. 8vo. 1714

LAW SOCIETY LIBRARY. 83

Collins (A.) The Peerage, Supplement to
       2nd ed. 1 vol. 8vo. 1716
—————————————————4th ed. 2 vols. 8vo. 1717
——— containing a Genealogical & Historical Account
of all the Peers of England, &c. 3 vols. in 4, 8vo. 1735
——— very much enlarged . . 2nd ed. 4 vols. 8vo. 1741
——— Supplement to . . . 2nd ed. 2 vols. 8vo. 1750
————————————— . . . 3rd ed. 5 vols. 8vo. 1756
————————————— . . . 4th ed. 7 vols. 8vo. 1768
————————————— . . . 5th ed. 8 vols. 8vo. 1779
——— Supplement (by Longmate) . . 1 vol. 8vo. 1784
——— another edition (by *Sir* E. Brydges). 9 v. 8vo. 1812
——— another copy
——— The Baronetage of England . . 2 vols. 8vo. 1720
——— The English Baronage. . . . 1 vol. 4to. 1727
——— Proceedings, Precedents, & Arguments on
Claims & Controversies concerning Baronies by
Writ . . . . 1 vol. folio 1734
Collinsen (G. D.) on Lunacy . . . 2 vols. 8vo. 1812
——— (*Rev.* J.) History of Somersetshire (Bristol)
          3 vols. 4to. 1791
Collyer (J.) (*see* Younge, E.)
——— on Partnership 8vo. 1832
————————————————— . . . . . . 2nd ed. 8vo. 1840
——— Reports in Chancery, V. C. Bruce, 1844–46
          2 vols. 8vo. 1845–47
Colonial Gazette . . . . . . 9 vols. folio 1839–46
——— Office List . . . . 1868 & continued
——— Series. Calendar of State Papers, 1574–
1660. Edited by W. Noel Sainsbury
  Vol. 1. America & West Indies, 1574–85
  Vol. 2. East Indies, China, & Japan, 1513–1616
       2 vols. imp. 8vo. 1860–62
Colquhoun (P.) on Police of Metropolis. 5th ed. 8vo. 1796
————————————————————— 6th ed. 8vo. 1800
Columbine (D. E.) on County Courts . . 12mo. 1850
Comberbach (R.) K.B. Reports, 1685–95 . folio 1724
Commendams, Case of, before the Privy Council
(*see* Col. Jur. Vol. 1)

Commentaire sur l'Ordinance de la Marine, 1669
& 1673 . . . . 12mo. 1761
Commentaries in the Order of Sir Wm. Blackstone
8vo. 1819
Commercial & Notarial Precedents 4to. 1802
Common Assurance . . . . folio 1651
—— Law Commissioners' Proposed Regulations &
Forms of Process, &c. Vol. 9, Jac. Col. . . . 1829
—— Law Commissioners' Reports. 3 vols. folio 1829–32
———————————————————— folio 1851–53
—— Law, History & Analysis 8vo. 1713
—— Law Reports, 1853–55 . . 5 vols. 8vo. 1854–55
—— Pleas, Court of, MSS. History of . . folio
—— Prayer, with Act of Uniformity . . . folio 1724
Commons & Commoners, Law of . 2nd ed. 8vo. 1720
—— House of, Catalogue of Library . . . folio 1830
———————— Fees' Reports . . . . . folio 1833
———————— Reports, 1715–1803, & Index
16 vols. folio 1803
Commonwealth: A Relation of Abuses committed
against, in 1629. No. 61, C. S. Pa. C. M. Vol. 3.
Ed. Sir F. Madden 1854
Company (*Mr.* John): Familiar Epistles to Mr.
John Bull, reprinted from Blackwood's Magazine. Vol. 19, Pam. 1858
Compleat Attorney & Solicitor 12mo. 1676
—— Solicitor 12mo. 1668
——————— . . . . 4th ed. 12mo. 1672
——————— Entering Clerk, & Attorney 12mo. 1683
Complete Justice 12mo. 1642
Comyns' (*Sir* J.) K. B. Reports . . . . folio 1744
——————— (Rose) 2nd ed. . 2 vols. 8vo. 1792
—— Digest . . . . 5 vols. folio 1785
——————— (Hammond) . . 5th ed. 8 vols. 8vo. 1822
Concanen (M.) Observations on the Use & Abuse
of the Practice of the Law. 3rd ed. Vol. 2, L. T. n. d.
—— (M., Jun.) & Morgan (D.) History of St.
Saviour's, Southwark 8vo. 1795
Conelly (*Dr.* J.) on Insanity 8vo. 1830

Conkling (A.) Admiralty Jurisdiction, Law &
Practice in U.S. . . . 2nd ed. 2 vols. 8vo. 1857
—— On the Origin, Jurisdiction, & Practice of the
U.S. Courts . . . . 4th ed. 8vo. 1864
Connor (H.) & Lawson (J. A.) Irish Chancery
Reports, 1841–43, temp. Sugden 2 vols. 8vo. 1842–44
Conrad (*see* Bynkershoek)
Conset (H.) Ecclesiastical Practice . . . 8vo. 1685
——————————————————— . 2nd ed. 8vo. 1702
Const (F.) (*see* Bott)
Constable (H. S.) on the Cattle Plague; with Remarks on the Drainage of Farm Buildings &
Stables. Vol. 27, Pam. 1866
Conti, Prince of, the Works of, with a Short
Account of his Life 8vo. 1713
Contius (A.) Codex Justiniani (*see* Justinian)
Convention, Letter to Member of, & Answer,
L. T. 1688–89
Conveyancing, Analysis on Theory & Practice of,
Col. Jur. Vol. 2
—— Commissioners. 3rd Report. . . . folio 1838
—— Observations on (Butler) MSS . . . 4to.
—— Scotch System of . . 3rd ed. 2 vols. 8vo. 1826
Coode (G.) on Legislative Expression, or the Language of the Written Law. Vol. 21, Pam. . . 1845
Cooke, Cases & Rules in C.P., 1706–40 . . folio 1742
—— & Alcock, Irish Common Law Reports,
1833–34 . . . . 8vo. 1834
—— (E.) on Trusts 8vo. 1843
—— (E. R.) Local Management Act . . 12mo. 1855
—— Construction of Metropolitan Buildings. 12mo. 1856
—— (G. A.) Description of Lancashire . . 8vo. 1797
—— (G. W.) on Defamation 8vo. 1844
—— on Inclosures . . . . . . 2nd ed. 8vo. 1853
——————————— . . . . . . 3rd ed. 8vo. 1856
——————————— . . . . . . 4th ed. 8vo. 1864
—— (H.) & Harwood (R. G) on the Charitable
Trusts Acts . . . . 2nd ed. 8vo. 1867
—— (J. A.) General Orders in Chancery. 12mo. 1835

Cooke (J. H.) Report of Carew & Burrell, Sussex
Assizes. Vol. 2, Pam. 1840
—— Report of Judgment in H.R.H. Prince Albert
v. Strange, of Property in Works of Art. Vol.
23, Pam. 1849
—— (John) Map of Hendon 4to. 1796
—— Insolvency Practice 12mo. 1827
—— (Wm.) on Bankruptcy 8vo. 1785
———————————————————— . . . 3rd ed. 8vo. 1793
———————————————————— . . . 4th ed. 8vo. 1797
———————————————————— . 5th ed. 2 vols. 8vo. 1804
———————————————————— (Gregg) 6th ed. 8vo. 1812
———————————————————— (Roots) 7th ed. 2 vols. 8vo. 1817
—— (W. F.) on the Electric Telegraph; was it
invented by Professor Wheatstone or W. F.
Cooke? . . . . 2 vols. 8vo. 1857
Cooper (*Bp.*) Answer to the Apology for Private
Mass. Par. S. Pa. 1850
Cooper (C. P.) Chancery, Defects in, &c. . 8vo. 1828
—— Jurisprudence 8vo. 1828
—— Cour de la Chancellerie d'Angleterre . 8vo. 1830
—— Registration of Deeds 8vo. 1831
—— Proposal for General Record Office . . 8vo. 1832
—— Reports (temp. Brougham) 1832-4 . . 8vo. 1835
—— Account of Public Records . . 2 vols. 8vo. 1837
—— (temp. Cottenham) 1845-47 . 2 vols. 8vo. 1847-48
—— Chancery, Delays in Offices of the Masters,
& Remedy. 1st & 2nd ed. Vol. 17, Pam. . . 1849
—— Lunatics, as to Custody of. Vol. 6, Pam.
3rd ed. 1849
—— on Appellate Jurisdiction. Vol. 7, Pam. . . 1850
—— on V.-C. Shadwell ceasing to Adjourn his
Court for leading Counsel. Vol. 7, Pam. . . . 1850
—— on Points of Practice, 1837-38 . . . 8vo. 1851
—— on Ultra-Romanists, & Extract Letters of Roman Catholic Peers. Vol. 8, Pam.
4th ed. 1851
—— Notes of some Conclusions as to the Pope's
Brief. Vol. 8, Pam. 1854

Cooper (C. P.) Nine Letters to him relative to his proposal for Analysing our Reports. Vol. 15, Pam. 1858
—— Memorandum respecting our Statute Book. Vol. 15, Pam. 1860
—— Memorandum of a proposal to Analyse our Reports. Vol. 15, Pam.
—— Speech on Lady Hewley's Charity, L. T. Vol. 3
—— (E. P.) (*see* Burton, W. H.)
—— (G.) Reports in Chancery 8vo. 1815
—— (J.) Trial of Thornton, on Appeal, for Murder
            8vo. 1818
—— (W. D.) (*see* C. S. Pa. Nos. 71, 82. C. M. Vol. 2, No. 55. Vol. 4, No. 73)
—— Age of Sussex Families, Edwd. II. IV. 8vo. 1860
—— The Oxen Bridge of Brede Place, Sussex
            8vo. 1860
Coote (H. C.) Admiralty Practice 8vo. 1860
————————————————— 2nd ed. 8vo. 1868
————————————————— & Supplement 1869
—— Ecclesiastical Practice 8vo. 1847
—— (H. E.) Probate Court Practice. 2nd ed. 8vo. 1859
—— & Tristram (T. H.) Probate Court Practice
          3rd ed. 8vo. 1860
————————————————— 4th ed. 8vo. 1863
————————————————— 5th ed. 8vo. 1866
—— (R. H.) on Mortgage 8vo. 1821
————————————— . . . . 2nd ed. 8vo. 1837
————————————— (R. Coote) 3rd ed. 8vo. 1850
—— & Harrington (C. M.) on General Registry
          8vo. 1829–31
—— & Harrington (C. M.) on proposed General Registry. Vol. 10, Jac. L. T. 1829
Copyhold Enfranchisement, Form of Award. Vol. 1, L. T.
—— Opinions on Surrender of. Col. Jur. Vol. 2
Copyholders by Copy, whether they are entitled to Vote? Vol. 1, L. T.

Copyright, Proposed Alterations in the Law of,
 1826-41. Vol. 7, L. T.
Corbett (U.) & Daniell's (E. R.) Election Cases,
 1819 . . . . 8vo. 1821
Cordovas (J. de) Lectures as to the Cultivation of
 Cotton in Texas. Vol. 12, Pam. 1858
Corfe Castle, Description of (*see* Sydenham's Poole)
Corneille (Pierre) Commentaires sur le Théâtre
            12mo. 1764
—— Le Théâtre 12mo. 1723
—— Le Cid, Tragédie 12mo. 1860
Cornellus (F.) (*see* Justinian)
Corner (R. J. & A. B.) Crown Practice . 8vo. 1844
Cornish (W. F.) on Purchase Deeds (G. Horsey)
            8vo. 1855
Cornwall, Description of 8vo. 1802
—— Duchy of, Petition as to Manor of Kennington.
 Vol. 10, Pam. 1854
—— Laws, &c. of Stannaries of 12mo. 1752
Cornwall, Laws, &c. of Stannaries of. 2nd ed. 8vo. 1824
—— Tables of Costs & Fees 8vo. 1837
Coroners, Election of, Orders as to . . . 8vo. 1831
Corpus Christi College, Catalogue of MSS. at . 4to. 1722
—— Juris Civilis (Amsterdam) 8vo. 1700
Corrie (Wm.) Letter to Sir J. Jervis, A.G., on the
 Uses, &c. of Special Pleading, Suggestions.
 Vol. 21, Pam. 1850
Corry (J.) History of Bristol (Bristol), 2 vols. 8vo. 1816
—— Tim Bobbin's Work (Lancashire Dialect). 8vo. 1819
—— History of Lancashire . . . 2 vols. 4to. 1825
Cort (C. F.) Tribute to Learning, Fame, Science,
 & Genius 4to. 1834
—— (R.) Observations on the Real Value of Iron
 for Free Trade. Vol. 14, Pam. 1856
Corvinus Enchiridium, seu Institutiones, per Ero-
 temata digestæ 12mo. 1649
Cory (J. P.) on Accounts 8vo. 1839
Coryton (J.) on Letters Patent . . . 8vo. 1855

Cosens (Jas.) Non-Jurors' Names (List). . 8vo. 1745
Costs in Chancery 8vo. 1807
Costs, Bills of 12mo. 1832
——————— in Bankruptcy. 12mo. 1832
————————————————. . . . 3rd ed. 8vo. 1839
Cottage Life, Economy of: Letters & Essays on the Improvement of Arigricultural Labourers. By the Wife of an Essex Gentleman. Vol. 13, Pam. 1847
Cotton (B. de) Monachi Norwicensis Historia Anglicana (Luard). No. 16 M. R. Pub. 8vo. 1859
—— (*Sir* R.) Abridgment of Parliamentary Records in Tower of London, from Edw. II. to Ric. III., by W. Prynne . . . . . . folio 1657
————————————————————————— folio 1679
—— Posthuma, by Howell (*see* Howell J.) . 12mo. 1679
Cottonian Library, & other Public Records, Report of House of Commons Committee (bound up with Attorneys & Solicitors, List of)
Cottonian Library MSS. Catalogue of, in British Museum . . . . folio 1802
Cottu (M.) on Criminal Justice 8vo. 1832
Counties, Proposed Division of, Report E. & I. folio 1832
Country Solicitors, Suggestions to 8vo. 1837
County Court Forms (settled by Judges) . 8vo. 1847
——————— Judges 8vo. 1865
——————— Rules, &c. . . . . . . folio 1851
—— Common Law & Equity Jurisdiction, Rules, Orders, & Forms 8vo. 1868
Courier Newspaper . . . . . 16 vols. folio, 1834–41
Court Kalendar, 1739–42 & 1744 3 vols. . 12mo.
—— of Requests' Returns . . . . . . folio 1833
Courtenay (Wm.) on Projected Improvements in Chancery. Jac. Col. Vol. 11 1828
Courts, History of, His. L. T. 1761
—— of Justice at Westminster, Fees of Officers of
                                    3rd edit. 12mo. 1697
————————————————————— Officers of. folio 1731

Courts of Justice at Westminster, Removal of: Facts for Consideration of Parliament. Vol. 4, Pam. . 1841
———— at Westminster, Review of Evidence taken before Committee of the House of Commons. . 1842
———— of Law & New Houses of Parliament: Extracts from Evidence taken before the Committee of the House of Commons in 1841 and 1842, proving the necessity for removal. Vol. 17, Pam. 1843
Courvoisier's Trial . . . . folio 1840
Coventry (T.) Conveyancing Evidence . . 8vo. 1832
———— Stamp Laws 8vo. 1833
———— & Hughes (S.) Analytical Digest to the Common Law Reports, from Hen. III. to Geo. III. . . . . 2 vols. 8vo. 1827
Coverdale's (*Bp.*) Works, Par. S. Pa. . . . 1844–46
Covert (N.) Scrivener's Guide (Bohun)
        3rd ed. 2 vols. 8vo. 1716
—————————————————— 5th ed. 8vo. 1740
Cowardisze, Doome of (*see* Prynne, W.)
Cowell (*Dr.*) Law Interpreter (Manley). . folio 1672
——————————————————2nd ed. folio 1684
———— (J. W.) Letter on Southern Secession, addressed to Capt. Maury, Confederate Navy, on his Letter to Admiral Fitzroy. Vol. 16, Pam. 1862
Cowie (*Rev.* M.) Letter to Duke of Buccleuch on Education at Putney College. Vol. 6, Pam.
Cowper (H.) K. B. Reports. 8vo. 1794
——————————————— 1774 & 1778
         2nd ed. 2 vols. 8vo. 1800
Cox on the Cattle Plague Law 12mo. 1866
———— Consolidation Acts, (*see* Tayler)
———— (C.) Clergy List, 1845, & continued . 8vo.
———— (E.) Probate Act and Rules 8vo. 1858
———— Orders 8vo. 1861
———— (Edw.) Chancery Forms at Chambers . 8vo. 1847
————————————————— 2nd ed. 8vo. 1858
————————————— (Biddle) 3rd ed. 8vo. 1863

Cox (E. W.) The Advocate, his Duties, &c.   8vo. 1852
—— & Grady (S. G.) on Registration & Elections
　　　　　　　　　　　　　　　10th ed. 12mo. 1868
—— Joint Stock Companies . . . 4th ed. 12mo. 1857
————————————————————— 6th ed. 8vo. 1862
—— Criminal Cases, 1843-67, & continued . 8vo.
—— Joint Stock Companies' Cases, 1864-67. 8vo. 1869
—— & Lloyd (M.) on County Courts. 4th ed. 12mo. 1851
—— (H.) Institutions of English Government. 8vo. 1863
—— History of Reform Bills, 1866 & 1867. 8vo. 1868
—— Antient Parliamentary Elections . . 8vo. 1868
—— (S. C.) Chancery Reports, 1788-96
　　　　　　　　　　　　　5th ed. 2 vols. 8vo. 1816
Coxe (E.) History of Monmouthshire. 2 vols. 4to. 1801
Crabb (G.) English Synonyms 4to. 1826
—— Precedents in Conveyancing . . 2 vols. 8vo. 1835
————————————————————— by J. T. Christie;
　　　　　　　5th ed. by L. Shelford, 2 vols. 8vo. 1859
—— Digest of Statutes . . . . 4 vols. 8vo. 1841-47
Craig (*Sir* T.) Jus Feudale (L. Menckenii). 4to. 1716
————————————————————— (Jac. Baillie)
　　　　　　　　　　　　　　　3rd ed. folio 1732
—— Scotland's Sovereignty Asserted . . 8vo. 1695
—— (R. D.) (*see* Mylne, J. W.)
—— on Trees & Woods 12mo. 1866
—— (R. D. C.) & Phillips' T. G. Chancery Reports, 1840-41 . . . . 8vo. 1842
Craigie (J.), Stewart (J. S.) & Paton (T.) Reports on Scotch Appeals to House of Lords
　　　　　　　　　　　　　　6 vols. 8vo. 1821-22
Cramer (*Rev.* J. A.) (*see* C. S. Pa. No. 17)
Cranch's Reports, U. S. (*see* Curtis)
Cranmer's Writings & Remains. Par. S. Pa.
　　　　　　　　　　　　　2 vols. 8vo. 1843-46
Crawford, Scotch Peerage Case . . . . folio 1716
—— & Lindsay, Peerage Cases of J. L. Crawford & another . . . . Vol 2, 2nd series
————————————————————— Vol. 1, 3rd series

Crawford & Lindsay Peerage, Evidence, Vol. 17, 1845; Vol. 21, 1846; House of Lords Session Paper, Vol. 16
—— (G. M.) on Copyright 8vo. 1839
Crawfurd, Genealogy of the Stewarts, 1034–1710
            folio 1710
Creasy (E. S.) Text Book of the Constitution. 8vo. 1848
—— (Jas.) History of Sleaford 8vo. 1825
Creech, Trial of Brodie & Smith (Scotch)
          2nd ed. 8vo. 1788
Cresswell (C.) (*see* Barnwall, R. V.)
Crew's Proceedings in Parliament, 1628 . 12mo. 1707
Criminal Law (*see* His. L. T.) 1761
—— Considerations on 8vo. 1772
—— Trials, abridged, 1678–90 . . . . . 8vo. 1690
———— Tuscany Edict (Warrington) . 8vo. 1789
———— published by Society for Diffusion of Useful Knowledge, & reported in State Trials
            12mo. 1832
———— Gunpowder Plot . 2 vols. 8vo. 1802–35
Cripps (H.W.) Reports, Clergy Law . . 8vo. 1846–50
—— Church & Clergy Law 8vo. 1852
———————————————— . . 3rd ed. 8vo. 1857
———————————————— . . 4th ed. 8vo. 1863
Cripps (H. W.) Church & Clergy Law. 5th ed. 8vo. 1869
Crisp (Jno.) Conveyancer's Guide (bound up with Anstey's Pleader's Guide) 8vo. 1832
Croke (A.) Report of Horner *v.* Lidiard . . 8vo. 1800
—— (*Sir* G.) K.B., &c. Reports, 1581–1641
          3 vols. 4to. 1661
———————————————— 2nd ed. 3 vols. folio 1669
Croker (T. C.) (*see* C. S. Pa. No. 14)
Crompton (*Sir* C.) & Jervis (*Sir* J.) Exchequer Reports, 1830–32 . . . . . 2 vols. 8vo. 1832–33
—— & Meeson (R.) Do. 1832–34 . 2 vols. 8vo. 1834–35
—— & Roscoe (H.) Do. 1834–36. 2 vols. 8vo. 1834–36
—— (G.) Practice . . . . . 2 vols. 8vo. 1780
———————————— . . . . 3rd ed. 2 vols. 8vo. 1786
—— (R.) on Jurisdiction of Courts . . . 4to. 1637

Crompton (R.) New Star Chamber Cases. Law Tr. & Arg.
Cromwell, Acts of Protector, 1656-57 . . folio 1657
—— (T.) History of Colchester (Colchester)
         2 vols. in 1 8vo. 1825
—— History of Clerkenwell 8vo. 1828
Crosby (A. J.) & Bruce (J.) (see C. S. P. No. 93)
Cross (Jno.) on Lien & Stoppage in Transitu. 8vo. 1840
—— (T.) Hints on House Property. 4th ed. 12mo. 1854
Crossley (J. T.) & Martin (W.) Intellectual Calculator . . . . 68th ed. 12mo.
Crown Lands, Account of . . . . . . folio 1789
Crowther (P. W.) History of Law of Arrest. Jac. Col. Vol. 12. 1828
Cruise (W.) Fines & Recoveries . 2nd ed. 8vo. 1786
——————————————— 3rd ed. 2 vols. 8vo. 1794
—— on Uses 8vo. 1795
—— on Dignities 8vo. 1823
—— Digest of Real Property Law
         3rd ed. 6 vols. 8vo. 1824
———————————— (White). 4th ed. 7 v. 8vo. 1835-36
Cudden (J.) on Copyhold Acts 8vo. 1865
Cullen (A.) on the Bankruptcy Laws . . 8vo. 1800
—— (C. S.) on Bankruptcy Court Reform. Jac. Col. Vol. 8 1830
Cullum (Sir J.) History of Hawksted & Hardwick, & Notes by T. G. Cullum . . . 2nd ed. 1813
Cumberland, Description of, & Isle of Man . 8vo. 1803
Cumin (P.) Civil Law . . . . . 2nd ed. 8vo. 1865
Cunningham, Index to House of Commons Journals. 1st 7 vols. 1547-1659 . . . . folio
—— (T.) Tithes . . . . . . 3rd ed. 8vo. 1748
—— on Bills of Exchange 8vo. 1760
—— History of Taxes from William the Conqueror to 1764 . . . . 8vo. 1764
—— Law Dictionary . . . . . . 2 vols. folio 1764
—— Reports, 1733-36 . . . . . 2nd ed. fo. 1770
—— on Elections 8vo. 1783
—— Simony 8vo. 1784

Curiæ Regis Rotuli, 1191–99 . . . 2 vols. 8vo. 1835
Curialium Nugæ Mapes, 1160–82, No. 50,
  C. S. Pa. 1850
Curson (P.) Laws of Great Britain. 2nd ed. 12mo. 1716
Curteis (*Dr.* W. C.) Reports (Ecclesiastical) 1834–
  44 . . . . 3 vols. 8vo. 1834–44
Curtis (G. T.) on Copyright in England &
  America (Boston) 8vo. 1847
—— on Patents (U. S.) 8vo. 1849
————————————— . . . 3rd ed. 8vo. 1867
—— (*Rev.* J.) History of Leicestershire . 8vo. 1831
—— (R. B.) Reports of Supreme Court & Digest
  (U. S.) 1790–1854 . . . . 22 vols. 8vo. 1855–56

Vol. 1 contains Vols.		2, 3, 4	—Dallas
————————	,,	1, 2, 3	—Cranch
,, 2	,,	4, 5, 6, 7	⎫
,, 3	,,	8, 9	⎬ ,,
	,,	1	—Wheaton
,, 4	,,	2, 3, 4, 5	⎫
,, 5	,,	6, 7, 8	⎪
,, 6	,,	9, 10, 11	⎬ ,,
,, 7	,,	12	⎭
————————	,,	1	—Peters
Vol. 8 contains Vols.		2, 3	⎫
,, 9	,,	,, 4, 5	⎪
,, 10	,,	,, 6, 7	⎪
,, 11	,,	,, 8, 9	⎬ Peters
,, 12	,,	,, 10, 11, 12	⎪
,, 13	,,	,, 13, 14	⎪
,, 14	,,	,, 15, 16	⎭
	,,	1	—Howard
,, 15	,,	,, 2, 3	⎫
,, 16	,,	,, 4, 5, 6	⎪
,, 17	,,	,, 7, 8	⎪
,, 18	,,	,, 9, 10, 11	⎬ ,,
,, 19	,,	,, 12, 13	⎪
,, 20	,,	,, 14, 15	⎪
,, 21	,,	,, 16, 17	⎭
,, 22	,,	Digest	

Curwen (J. C.) Bill as to Tithes, & Baron Wood's
Observations on . . . . folio 1817
Cust (R. J.) on the West Indian Incumbered
Estates Acts . . . . 2nd ed. 12mo. 1865
Customs' Frauds, Report of Committee of House
of Commons (Attorneys, List of) 1733
Cutler (J.) The International Law of Navigable
Rivers. Vol. 21, Pam. 1863
—— (J. C.) Forms of Writs . . 2nd ed. folio 1687
—— City of London Charters 12mo. 1745
Czymski (J.) Diebreignesse, or Revolution in
Warsaw, 1831. Vol. 13 Jac. Col. 1832

D

Daily News (The) 1846–68, & continued
—— Telegraph, 1862–68, & continued
Dale (J. M.) Clergyman's Handbook. 2nd ed. 12mo. 1859
—— (R.) Catalogue of the Nobility . . 12mo. 1697
—— (Sam.) History of Harwich & Dover Court
4to. 1730
Dalison (W.) (*see* Benloe)
Dallas' Reports U. S. (*see* Curtis)
Dallaway (*Rev.* J.) History of Sussex
2 vols. 4to. 1815–19
Dalrymple (*Sir* J.) on Feudal Property. 4th ed. 8vo. 1759
—— Memoirs of Great Britain & Ireland
2nd ed. 2 vols. 4to. 1771
D'Alton (Jno.) History of County of Dublin. 8vo. 1838
—— Memoirs of Archbishops of Dublin . 8vo. 1838
Dalton (M.) Country Justice . . . 3rd ed. 4to. 1626
———————————— (Nelson) . . . folio 1727
—— Sheriff . . . . folio 1670
———————— . . . . folio 1682

Daly (B.) Handy Book on the Practice of the
Mayor's Court 12mo. 1861
Dance (H.) Letter to Mr. Jones on the Insolvent
Debtors' Act. Vol. 5, Jac. Col. 1827
—— Remarks on Law Expenses. Vol. 8, Jac.
Col. 1830
Daniel (W. T. S.) Letter to Sir R. Palmer on the
Present System of Law Reporting: its Evils, &
Remedy Suggested. Vol. 20, Pam. 1863
Daniell (E. R.) Reports (Equity Exchequer) 1817–
20 . . . . 8vo. 1824
—— On the Practice of the High Court of Chancery, with some Practical Observations on the Pleadings in that Court . . . 3 vols. 8vo. 1837–41
———————————————————— with
Additions by T. M. Headlam . . 2 vols. 8vo. 1845
———————————————————— adapted
to the present Practice of the Courts. (T. E.
Headlam) . . . . 2 vols. 8vo. 1857
———————————————————— with
Alterations & Additions, incorporating the
Statutes, Orders, & Cases to the present time,
& Braithwaite's Record & Writ Practice. (L.
Field, E. C. Dunn, J. Biddle) 2 in 3 vols. 8vo. 1865–67
—— On the Practice of the High Court of Chancery; Forms & Precedents of Pleadings &
Proceedings (L. Field, E. C. Dunn, J. Biddle)
8vo. 1865–67
Danish Laws used in America by English Inhabitants 8vo. 1756
Dansey (Wm.) on Rural Deans, Origin, &c.
2nd ed. 2 vols. 4to. 1844
Danson (F. N.) & Lloyd (J. H.) Mercantile Cases
in the Courts of Common Law, 1828–29 . 8vo. 1830
Darby (J. G. N.) & Bosanquet (F. A.) on the
Statutes of Limitations, England & Ireland. 8vo. 1867
Darell (J. H.) (*see* Bermuda Acts)
—— (Wm.) History of Dover Castle, temp. Eliz.
4to. 1797

Dart (*Rev.* J.) History of Canterbury . . folio 1726
——— (J.) History of Westminster Abbey
      2 vols. folio 1774–80
——— (J. H.) On Vendors & Purchasers of Real
 Estate . . . . 2nd ed. 8vo. 1852
 ———————————————— . 3rd ed. 8vo. 1856
Davenant, Discourse on Public Revenues & Trade
 of England. 8vo. 1698
Davenport (*Sir* H.) Synopsis, or an exact Abridgment of Lord Coke's Commentaries upon Littleton 12mo. 1652
——— (J. M.) Oxfordshire Annals 8vo. 1869
——— Lords Lieutenant & Sheriffs of do. . 8vo. 1868
——— (R. A.) Dictionary of Biography . . 8vo. 1831
Davers (Mary Magdalene) Inquiry into the Genuineness of a Letter dated Feb. 3rd, 1613, & signed as 'Mary Magdalene Davers.' C. M. No. 87, Vol. 5 1864
Davidson (C.) Precedents and Forms in Conveyancing, by C. Davidson, T. C. Wright, J. Waley, & J. Whitehead . . . 2nd ed. 5 vols. 8vo. 1855–65
——————————————— by Davidson (C.), Wright (T. C.), & Waley (J.) . 3rd ed. 2 vols. 8vo. 1860–64
——— & Stapylton (M. B.) Concise Precedents in Conveyancing . . . . 6th ed. 12mo. 1865
Davidson (C.) & Stapylton (M. B.) adapted to the Act to Amend the Law of Real Property. 7th ed. 1867
Davies (*Rev.* D. P.) History of Derbyshire . 8vo. 1811
——— (*Dr.*) Journal, No. 68, C. S. Pa. 1689–90 (ed. R. Caulfield) 4to. 1857
——— (Jno.) History of Caribby Islands, or West Indies . . . . folio 1666
——— (*Rev.* J. S.) (*see* C. S. Pa. No. 64)
——— (R.) (*see* C. S. Pa. No. 85)
——— (R. R.) Handy-Book on Land, Assessed, & Income Taxes 8vo. 1864
——— (T.) On Bankruptcy . . . . . folio 1744
——— (*Sir* J.) Reports, Ireland, 1603–10 . . 8vo. 1762

H

Davies (*Sir* J.) Argument upon Impositions, Tonnage, Poundage, &c. 1656
—— (John) Important Cases respecting Patents of Inventions and Rights of Patentees . . 8vo. 1816
Davis (J. E.) County Court Practice. 2nd ed. 8vo. 1857
—— County Court Act, 1867 . . . . . 8vo. 1868
—— on Master & Servant Act 12mo. 1868
—— on Registration & Elections 8vo. 1868
—— Criminal Law Consolidation Acts . . 8vo. 1861
—— (J.) Patent Cases, 1785–1816 . . . 8vo. 1816
—— Metropolis Map of County Courts . . 8vo. 1848
—— County Court Equity Jurisdiction . 12mo. 1865
—— (*Dr.* Jno.) Origines Divisianæ; or, the Antiquities of the Devizes, 1754, bound with Dodsworth (W.) on *Salisbury Cathedral*
Davison (H.) & Merivale (H.) Reports, in Queen's Bench & Exchequer Chamber, 1843–44 (*see* Perry (T. C.) & Gale (C. J.) 8vo. 1844
Davys, or Davies (*Sir* John) Argument upon the Question of Impositions. MS. temp. James, Charles
Daw (M. E.) Map of the World 1867
Dawes (M.) on Dean of St. Asaph's Case. Two Letters, Libel Law T. Vol. 3 1785
Dax (E. T.) Letter to Lord Lyndhurst on Appellate Jurisdiction (bound up with Burge, W.) . . . 1842
—— on Costs in Superior Courts of Common Law 8vo. 1847
—— (T.) The Practice on the Plea Side of the Court of Exchequer 8vo. 1831
—— the Practice of the Offices of the Masters on the Plea Side of the Common Law Courts. 8vo. 1844
Day (J. C. F. S.) (*see* Finlason, Markham, Stephen)
—— Common Law Procedure Acts, 1852–60. 12mo. 1861
———————————————— 2nd ed. 8vo. 1863
———————————————— 3rd ed. 8vo. 1868
Deacon (E. E.) Game Laws 8vo. 1831
—— & Chitty's (E.) Bankruptcy Reports, 1832–34 . . . . 4 vols. 8vo. 1834–37

Deacon (E. E.) Bankruptcy Reports, 1835–40
　　　　　　　　　　　　4 vols. 8vo. 1837–40
—— on Bankruptcy (Langley) 3rd ed. 2 vols. 12mo. 1864
Dean (J.) on the Beneficial Employment of the
　Surplus of Labouring Classes in Agriculture &
　Garden Allotments System. Vol. 19, Pam. . . 1845
Deane (J. P.) on Blockade 8vo. 1855
—— Ecclesiastical Reports, 1855–57 . . . 8vo. 1858
—— on Wills Act 8vo. 1858
Dearsley (H. R.) Crown Cases, 1852–56 . 8vo. 1858
—— & Bell (T.) Crown Cases, 1856–58 . 8vo. 1858
De Balrath Peerage: Case of A. Lord Aylmer.
　Vol. 1, 3rd Series, p. 376
Debates, Parliamentary, 1610. C. S. Pa. No. 81
Debating Society's Minutes & Rules. 2 vols. 4to. 1786–89
Debrett (J.) Baronetage . . . . 2 vols. 12mo. 1804
——————————— . . . 2 vols. 12mo. 1808
——————————— 3rd, 4th, 5th, 6th, & 7th ed.
　　　　　　　　　　8 vols. 12mo. & 8vo. 1815–35
—— Peerage . . . . . . 45 vols. 12mo. 1802–40
——————— & Baronetage . . . 2 vols. 12mo. 1866
Debtor & Creditor, Suggestions on Law of. Vol. 3,
　Pam. 1844
Debtors' Laws, with a Word to their Victims 8vo. 1838
De Bure, (G. F.) Traité de la Connoissance des
　Livres rares et singuliers . . 9 vols. 8vo. 1763–69
De Burgh (W.), Maritime International Law. 8vo. 1868
Deccan Booty Papers in P. C. 2 v. fo. & 1 v. 4to. 1833
Dee River, Acts, Laws, & Rules. 2 vols. 12mo. 1820–40
—— (Dr. J.) Diary, 1554–1601, No. 19, C. S. Pa. 1841
Deering (C.) History of Nottingham . . . 4to. 1751
De Fer (Sir S.) Map of Paris & Environs . . . 1766
De Fougasses, History of Venice, translated by
　Wm. Shute . . . . folio 1612
De Gex (J. P.) (see Montagu, B.)
—— Reports in Bankruptcy, decided in Court
　of Review by V.-C. Sir J. L. Knight Bruce,
　& Lord Chancellors Lyndhurst & Cottenham
　1844–48 . . . . 8vo. 1852

H 2

De Gex & Smale(J.) Reports in Chancery, V.-C.C., Sir J. L. Knight Bruce & Sir James Parker, 1846–52 . . . . 5 vols. 8vo. 1849–53
—— Macnaghten (S.) & Gordon (A.) Reports of cases determined by Lord Chancellor & Court of Appeal in Chancery, 1851–57. 8 vols. 8vo. 1853–58
—— & Jones (H. C.) Reports, ditto, 1857–59
           4 vols. 8vo. 1858–61
—— Fisher (F.) & Jones (H. C.) Reports, ditto, 1859–61 . . . . 3 vols. 8vo. 1861–67
—— Jones (H. C.) & Smith, Reports, ditto, 1863–65 . . . . 2 vols. 8vo. 1866
—— & Smith (R. H.) Arrangements between Debtor and Creditor 8vo. 1867
———————— 2 Supplements . . . 8vo. 1868–69
Degge (*Sir* S.) The Parsons' Counsellor. 3rd ed. 8vo. 1681
———————————————— 4th ed. 8vo. 1685
———————————————— 7th ed. 8vo. 1820
Deheque, (F. D.) Dictionary (Greek & French). 8vo. 1826
De la Croix on Constitution of European States
          2 vols. 8vo. 1783
Delamer (Henry *Lord*) Works (Henze) . . 8vo. 1694
Delane (W. F. A.) Decisions of Revising Courts
            8vo. 1836
Delaune (Thomas) Angliæ Metropolis; or present State of London 12mo. 1690
De Lincy (M. Le Roux) C. S. Pa. No. 2
De Lisle Peerage: Sir J. S. Sidney's Case. No. 13, Vol. 2, 2nd Series; & 3rd Series, Vol. 1. Evidence, Vol. 5 1824
De Lolme (J. L.) on the Constitution of England (Hughes) 8vo. 1834
Del Mar (E.) Modélos de la Literatura Española
           12mo. 1854
Del Rio & Rodriguez, Civil Law of Spain
Delphin Classics, cum Variorum Notis (Valpy)
         141 vols. 8vo. 1840
Demerara Ordinances (*see* British Guiana)

Demolombe (C.) de l'Absence . . . 2nd ed. 8vo. 1860
—— de la Publication, &c. 2nd ed. 8vo. . . . 1860
—— Traité des Mariages. 2nd ed. 2 vols. 8vo. 1860-61
—— de l'Adoption . . . . . . 2nd ed. 8vo. 1861
—— de la Distinction des Biens. 2nd ed. 2 v. 8vo. 1861
—— de la Minorité . . . . 2nd ed. 2 vols. 8vo. 1861
—— des Successions . . . 2nd ed. 5 vols. 8vo. 1862
—— de Servitude . . . . . . 3rd ed. 8vo. 1863
—— des Donations entre Vifs et des Testaments
      2nd ed. 3 vols. 8vo. 1863-6
—— de la Paternité et de la Filiation
      2nd ed. 8vo. 1862
Dempsey (J. J.) on the Coroner's Court, its Uses
  & Abuses. Vol. 10, Pam. 1858
De Nevill Testa, sive Liber Feodorum in Curia
  Scaccarii, temp. Hen. III. et Edw. I., 1216–
  1306 (*see* Record Commission) . . . . folio 1807
Denham (*Sir* J.) Poems & Translations, with the
  Sophy 12mo. 1666
Denholme (J.) History of Glasgow & Greenock.
  With Weir's Greenock . . . . 3rd ed. 8vo. 1804
Denisart (J. B.) Décisions nouvelles
      9th ed. 4 vols. 4to. 1777
Denison (E. B.) Substance of his Article in Fraser's
  Magazine, January 1850, Marriage with a De-
  ceased Wife's Sister. 3rd ed. Vol. 24, Pam. . . 1851
—— Letter to Bishop of Exeter on his Speech on
  Bill for legalising Marriage with a Deceased
  Wife's Sister. Vol. 24, Pam.
Denison (J. C.) Crown Cases, 1844-52
      2 vols. 8vo. 1850-52
Denmark & Germany & the Scandinavian Question
Dennes (G. E.) on County & Borough Franchise.
  Vol. 7, Pam. 1850
Denton (H. B.) Lord Brougham's Local Courts
  Bill Examined. Vol. 5, L. T.
Deptford, Charters to Trinity House . . . 8vo. 1730
—————————————————— . . . 8vo. 1835

Dequignes (M.) des Huns, Turcs, Moguls, &c.
Histoire Générale, 4 vols. in 5 . . . . 4to. 1756
Derbyshire, Description of 8vo. 1803
De Reimes (P.) C. S. Pa. No. 72
Derwentwater (*Earl of*) Speeches on Judgment against, in 1715 (*see* Impeachment of Lords)
folio 1701
—— Report of House of Commons Committee as to the Sale of his Estates (bound up with List of Attorneys) . . . . folio 1731
Descent & Distribution, by a Solicitor . . 8vo. 1834
Desno, Map of Paris & Environs . . in portfolio 1766
De Trévoux ( ) Dictionnaire françois et latin universel . . . . 8 vols. folio 1771
Devencenzi (G.) Report of Minister of Agriculture, &c., on the Cultivation of Cotton in Italy. Vol. 18, Pam. 1862
Devise of Real & Personal Estate, Opinions on. Vol. 2, Col. Jur.
Devon Peerage: Case of William Viscount Courtney. Vol. 2, 2nd Series. Evidence, Vol. 9 1831
—— (F.) Pell Records, Issue Rolls, 44 Ed. III., 1370 . . . . 8vo. 1835
——————————————temp. Jas. I. 8vo. 1836
—— Issues of the Exchequer, Henry III., 1216, to Henry VI., 1461 . . . . 8vo. 1837
Devotional Poetry, temp. Elizabeth. Par. S. Pa.
2 vols. 12mo. 1842-47
Dew (E. L.) (*see* Power, D.)
De Wit's General Atlas . . . . . folio impft.
Dibden (*Rev.* J. F.) Library Companion
2nd ed. 2 vols. 4to. 1825
—— Reminiscences of a Literary Life . 2 vols. 8vo. 1836
Dicey (T.) Historical Account of Guernsey from its first Settlement before the Norman Conquest to the present time 12mo. 1751
Dickens (Jno.) Reports in Chancery, 1559-1792 (J. Wyatt) . . . . 2 vols. 8vo. 1803

Dickenson (W.) Quarter Sessions Practice (T. N.
    Talfourd). . . . . 5th ed. 8vo. 1841
Dickson (*Lieut.-Col.*) Address to British Army on
    his Displacement, & Addenda. Vol. 13, Pam.;
    Vol. 18, Pam. . . . . 6th ed. 1861
—— (N. W.) Lancashire Agriculture (Stevenson)
                                              8vo. 1815
Dictionnaire des Faillites, 1848-63. . . . 4to. 1864
Dictionary, Historical, Genealogical, & Poetical
                                          12mo. 1703
Digby (K. E.) on Shares in Companies . . 12mo. 1868
Digby (*Sir* Kenelm) Voyage, 1828 (J. Bruce).
    No. 96, C. S. P. 4to. 1868
Dilapidations, Royal Institute of British Artists on
                                                8vo. 1824
Dilworth (T.) on the Use of the Globes. 2nd ed. 8vo. 1794
Dingley (Thos.) History from Marble [compiled
    temp. Charles II.] Parts 1, 2, Nos. 94, 97,
    C. S. Pa. (J. G. Nichols). 4to. 1867–68
Diprose (J.), Account of the Parish of St. Clement
    Danes past & present 8vo. 1869
Discourse against Jurisdiction of the K.B. over
    Wales by Latitat. Har. L. T.
—— on Ecclesiastical Jurisdiction. Atkyn's Tracts
Disney's (J.) Collection of Acts as to Elections. 8vo. 1811
—— Collection of Irish & Scotch Election Acts. 8vo. 1812
Dissenters' Chapel Bill, Report on Debate of. 8vo. 1844
Distress & Replevin . . . . . . 3rd ed. 8vo. 1746
——————————— . . . . . 4th ed. 8vo. 1761
Divorce Acts & Rules 12mo. 1858
Dixon (H. H.) The Law of the Farm . . 8vo. 1858
———————————————— 3rd ed. 8vo. 1863
—— (J.) Partnership 8vo. 1866
—— (R.) on Proposed Real Property Code.
    Vol. 3, L. T. 1827
————————————— Vol. 4, Jac. Col. . . . 1827
—— Title Deeds 8vo. 1858
Doctor & Student . . . . . . 3 vols. 12mo. 1590

Doctor & Student, Abridgment 12mo. 1630
Doctors' Commons, Wills from, No. 83, C. S. Pa. . 1863
Doctrina Placitanti [Sampson Euer] . . . 4to. 1677
Documents, &c., in the Exchequer relating to History of Scotland 8vo. 1837
Dod (C. R.) Parliamentary Companion
       17 vols. 12mo. 1837–65
—— Electoral Facts, 1832–52 . . . . 12mo. 1852
Dodd (C. E.) (*see* Bacon, M.)
—— on Election Law. Vol. 6, Jac. Col. . . . 1826
—— (P. W.) & Brooks (G. H.) Probate Court Practice 8vo. 1865
—— (S.) History of Woburn, Beds . . . 8vo. 1818
Doddridge (J.) Compleat Parson, L. T. & A. . . 1641
Dodridge (*Sir* J.) History of the Ancient & Modern Estate of the Principality of Wales, Dutchy of Cornwall, & Earldom of Chester . . . 8vo. 1630
———————————————— 2nd ed. 12mo. 1714
Dodsley (J.) Annual Register, 1758–1866
       108 vols. 8vo.
—— Index, 1758–1819 . . . . 8vo.
———— N. S. 1867
Dodson (*Sir* John) Admiralty Reports, 1811–22
      4th ed. 2 vols. 8vo. 1815–28
Dodsworth (R.) *see* Dugdale's Anglicanum Monasticon . . . . 2nd ed. 3 vols. folio 1655–73
—— The Manuscripts in the Bodleian Library (*see* Hunter)
Dodsworth (W.) a Guide to the Cathedral Church of Salisbury 12mo. 1792
Dogherty (T.) Crown Assistant 8vo. 1788
—— Circuit Companion . . . . 7th ed. 8vo. 1799
Doleman on Succession to Crown 8vo. 1681
Domat (J.) Civil Law in its Natural Order together with the Public Law, Translated by Dr. Wm. Strahan: with some Additional Remarks on some Material Differences between the Civil Law and the Law of England . . . . 2 vols. folio 1722
———————————————2nd ed. 2 vols. folio 1737

Domesday Book, sive, Liber Censualis Wil. primi (or Survey of the Kingdom in 1086) (*see* Record Commission)
  Vol. 1. Kent, Sussex, Surrey, Hants, Berks, Wilts, Dorset, Somerset, Devon, Cornwall, Middlesex, Hertford, Buckingham, Oxford, Gloucester, Worcester, Hereford, Cambridge, Huntingdon, Bedford, Northampton, Leicester, Warwick, Stafford, Salop, Chester, Lancashire,* Derby, Nottingham, Rutland, York, Lincoln, Lindsey . . folio 1783
  Vol. 2. Essex, Norfolk, & Suffolk . . folio 1783
  Vol. 3. General Introduction & Indices. folio 1816
  Vol. 4. Exon Domesday, Inquisitio Eliensis, Liber Winton, Boldon Book . . . folio 1816
  The General Introduction (contained in Vol. 3) by Sir Henry Ellis, with further Indices
    2 vols. 8vo. 1833
Domesday Book for Derbyshire (W. Bawdwen) 4to. 1809
—— for Middlesex, Hertford, Bucks, Oxford, and Gloucester (Translation) (W. Bawdwen) 4to. 1812
—— for Dorsetshire (W. Bawdwen & J. Hutchins) folio 1815
—— for Yorkshire : Amounderness, Lonsdale, & Furness in Lancashire; parts of Westmoreland and Cumberland, Derby, Nottingham, Rutland, and Lincoln (Translation W. Bawdwen) . 4to. 1809
Domevesu (E. A.) Road Book of Germany 12mo. 1830
Dominica & Virgin Islands, Act establishing Courts in. 8vo. 1802
—— Acts, 1763-1859 . . . . 2 vols. 4to. 1858-60
—— Acts, 1860-66
Donaldson & ano^r v. Beckett & others : Case in House of Lords as to Literary Property (reversing Lord Chancellor Apsley's decree) . . . 4to. 1774
—— (T. L.) Pompeii . . . . folio 1827
—— Heraldic Architecture 8vo. 1837

* Lancashire is placed, in part, in other counties.

Donelly (R.) Minutes of Cases in Chancery . 8vo. 1837
Donovan (*Dr.*) Analysis of his Edition of Annals of
   Four Masters, of Celtic Records in Ireland. 8vo. 1852
Doria (A.) & Macrae (D. C.) on Bankruptcy
                              2 vols. 12mo. 1861–63
Dorset—Letter from Lords of the Treasury as to
   quota of Timber from Dorset for the Royal Navy
   —MS., temp. James & Charles.
Dorsetshire Election Poll Book 8vo. 1805–16
Douce (F.) Cat. of Books & MSS. bequeathed
   to Bodleian Library, Oxford . . . . . folio 1840
Douglas Cause: H. L. Arguments, Col. Jur. Vol. 2 1769
—— Court-martial, Proceedings on . . . 8vo. 1849
—— Lady, Letters of 8vo. 1767
Douglas (*Sir* R.) Peerage of Scotland . . folio 1764
—— Baronage of Scotland · . . . . folio 1798
—— Peerage of Scotland (J. P. Wood)
                         2nd ed. 2 vols. folio 1813
—— (S.) Reports of Cases determined in the
   K. B., 19, 20, & 21, Geo. III. . . . . folio 1783
———————————————————2nd ed. folio 1786
————————————— (1778–81) 3rd ed. 1790
—— ———————————— 4th ed. with additions by Serjt. Frere, 2 vols. 8vo, 1813, with Reports of Cases determined in the Courts of King's Bench in the 22nd, 23rd, 24th, & 25th Geo. III., from Manuscripts of S. Douglas (Baron Glenbervie), Mr. Justice Laurence, Mr. Justice Le Blanc, and Mr. Geo. Wilson. By Mr. Serjt. Frere & H. Roscoe. 2 vols. 8vo. 1831 (Vols. 3 & 4) . . . . 4 vols. 8vo. 1813–31
—— Election Cases, 1775–76. 2nd ed. 4 vols. 8vo. 1802
Dover, Corporation of, Report . . . . . folio 1835
Dow (P.) Reports H. L. 1812–18 . 6 vols. 8vo. 1814–19
—— & Clark (C.) Reports, 1827–32
                                2 vols. 8vo. 1827–32
Dowling (A. S.) Colonial Statutes. 2 vols. 12mo. 1830–31
—— Reports of Cases in K. B. Practice Courts, with the Points of Pleading & Practice

decided in the Courts of C. P. & Exchequer
1830–41 . . . . 9 vols. 8vo. 1833–42
Dowling (A. S.) Reports of Cases in Practice
Courts, K. B. & C. P. 12mo. 1834
—— New Series Practice Reports, 1841–43. By
A. S. & V. Dowling . . . 2 vols. 8vo. 1843–44
—— & Lowndes (J. J.) ditto Reports, 1844–49
7 vols. 8vo. 1845–51
—— (J. A.) Report on Inquest on Jno. Lees, who
died of Sabre Wounds 8vo. 1820
—— (Jas.) & Ryland (A.) Reports, 1822–28
9 vols. 8vo. 1822–31
—— (Josh.) Report on Beckwith v. Wood: London
Riots, London Tracts 1818
—— (V.) (*see* Dowling, A. S.) Reports
D'Oyly, Account of House of (*see* Grimaldi's
Tracts, Vol. 3)
—— (*Rev.* G.) & Mant's (*Rev.* R.) Bible (Oxford)
3 vols. 4to. 1817
—— (*Serjt.* T.) on Rating, &c. Tithes, Pam. Vol. 1. 1839
Draining (*see* Dugdale on Embanking, &c.)
Drake (F.) History, &c. of York . . . . folio 1736
—— (*Sir* F.) Memorable Service done against the
Spaniards in 1587; written by Robt. Leng,
Gentleman, one of his fellow-soldiers. No. 87
C. M., C. S. Pa. (C. Hopper) 1864
Drapers' Company Reports, Irish Estates, 1817–39
8vo. 184.
Dream (The): Law Tracts, 1688–89
Drewry (C. S.) on Patent Law, Vol. 4, L. T. . . 1839
—— on Injunctions 8vo. 1849
—— Reports (V.-C. Kindersley), 1852–59
4 vols. 8vo. 1853–60
—— on Equity Pleading 12mo. 1858
—— & J. J. Smale (V.-C. Kindersley), 1859–65
2 vols. 8vo. 1862–67
Dring (T.) List of Lords who Compounded for
Estates 12mo. 1655
Druid's Temple at Avebury, bound up with Dodsworth (W.)

Drury (W. B.) Reports, Irish Chancery (temp.
Sugden) 8vo. 1843
—— Select Cases, Irish Chancery (temp. Napier)
8vo. 1860
—— & Walsh (F. W.) Reports, &c., Irish
Chancery, 1837–40 . . . . 2 vols. 8vo. 1839–42
—— & Warren (R.) Reports, &c., Irish Chancery,
1841–43 . . . . 4 vols. 8vo. 1843–46
Dublin Almanac & Directory, 1742–1849
50 vols. 12mo. &c.
—— Gazette, 1862–68 & continued . . . folio
—— Law Institute Rules. Vol. 16, Pam. . . . 1843
———————— Papers on the Law as it relates
to the Economic Condition of a People, Vol. 16,
Pam. 1843
—— Law School, Proceedings of. Vol. 16, Pam. 1843
—— University Commissioners' Report, &c. folio 1853
Dubourdieu (*Rev.* John) Statistical Survey of
County Antrim . . . . 2 vols. 8vo. 1812
Du Calcul des Probabilités. Vol. 13, Jac. Col. 1806
Du Cange (C. D.) Glossarium ad Scriptores Mediæ
Latinitatis . . . . 10 vols. folio 1733–66
Ducarel (A. C.) Account of Doctors' Commons
Society, MSS. . . . . folio 1753
—— Repertoire of Endowments in Dioceses of
Canterbury & Rochester 8vo. 1782
Ducarel, Croydon, Account of Church & Palace
4to. 1783
Ducatus Lancastriæ, Pars Prima, Calendarium In-
quisitionum post mortem, Edward I.—Chas. I.
Pars Secunda, Calendar to the Pleadings, Hen.
VII.—P. & M. . . . . folio 1823
Vol. 2, Pars Tertia do. do. Hen. VII.—13
Eliz. . . . . folio 1827
Vol. 3, Pars Quarta, 14 to 45 Eliz. (*see*
Record Commission) . . . . . . folio 1834
Duck (S.) Poems on several subjects, by S. Duck,
lately a poor Thresher . . . . . . 7th ed. 1730

Duer (J.) on Marine Insurance. New York. 2 v. 8vo. 1845
Dufour (G.) Traité général de Droit administratif
      2nd ed. 7 vols. 8vo. 1854–57
Dugdale (J. S.) Table of Punishments at Quarter
 Sessions 8vo. 1866
—— (*Sir* Wm.) Antiquities of Warwickshire. folio 1656
 ——————————————— (W. Thomas,
 D.D.) . . . . 2nd ed. 2 vols. folio 1730
—— Monasticon Anglicanum, sive Pandectæ
 Cœnobiorum Benedictinorum Cluniacensium,
 Cisterciensium, Carthusianorum, a primordiis ad
 eorum usque dissolutionem, per R. Dodsworth
 et G. Dugdale. Vol. 1, 2nd ed. (1682). Vol. 2
 (1661). Vol. 3 (1673) . . . 3 vols. folio 1661–82
—— Monasticon Anglicanum, or the History of
 Ancient Abbies, Monasteries, Hospitals, Cathe-
 drals, & Collegiate Churches, &c., with exact
 Catalogues of the Bishops of the several Dioceses
 to 1717; with two additional volumes by John
 Stevens . . . . 3 folio 1718–23
 ———————————————— New Edition,
 enriched with large accession of materials, &c.,
 by John Caley, H. Ellis, & Rev. B. Bandinel
       6 vols. folio 1817–30
 ———————————————— & Index Monasticus (*see* Taylor, R.)
—— Origines Juridicales, or Historical Memorials
 of the English Laws, &c.; also a Chronologie of
 the Lord Chancellors, &c. . . 2nd ed. folio 1671
—— The Baronage of England: or, An Historical
 Account of the Lives & most Memorable Actions
 of our English Nobility . 3 vols. in 2, folio 1675–76
—— (*see* Grimaldi's Tracts, Vol. 3)
—— History of St. Paul's Cathedral, by Edw. Maynard, D.D. 1716
—— Ditto, with Continuations and Additions, including the Re-publication of Sir W. Dugdale's
 Life, from his own Manuscript, by H. Ellis. folio 1818

Dugdale (Sir W.) History of Embanking & Draining Fens & Marshes, &c., by C. N. Cole. 2nd ed. folio 1772
—— Ancient Usage of Arms, with Additions, containing An Introduction to the Science of Heraldry and Art of Emblazonry; to which is added a Brief Discourse touching the Office of Lord High Chancellor, by John Selden; with Catalogues of Lord Chancellors, &c. by Sir W. Dugdale; whereto is superadded Honores Anglicani, or Titles of Honor, by T. C. Banks . . folio 1812
Duhigg's (J. B.) History of the King's Inns, or An Account of the Legal Body of Ireland (Dublin) 4th ed. 2 vols. in 1, 8vo. 1806
Duke (G.) The Law of Charitable Uses, with the Reading of Sir F. Moor; to which is added the Law of Mortmain . . . . folio 1676
——— with continuations (R. W. Bridgman) 8vo. 1805
Dunboyne Peerage: Case of D. F. Butler. Vol. 1, 3rd Series, p. 409 . . . . 4to. 1858
Duncker (C.) Map of London . . . . . folio 1647
Duncombe (A. J.), Laws of Turks & Caicos Islands, 1799–1860 . . . . 8vo. 1862
Duncum (J. M.) Parochial Ecclesiastical Law of Scotland 8vo. 1864
Duncumb (J.) Collection towards the History of Herefordshire (Hereford) . . . . 2 vols. 4to. 1804
Duncumbe (G.) Nisi Prius, or Trials per pais
           5th ed. 8vo. 1718
——————————————— 6th ed. 8vo. 1725
——————————————— 7th ed. 8vo. 1739
Dundonald Peerage: Case of F. B. Earl of. Vol. 1. 3rd Series
Dunkin, History of Bicester and Alchester . 8vo. 1816
—— (J.) & Kempe (A. J.) History of Bromley & Holwood Hill, Kent 8vo. 1815
Dunn (Elizabeth) Case of, on a Trial for Forgery. Vol. 1, Col. Jur.
—— (S.) Index to House of Commons Journals. Vols. 35, 55, 1774–1800 . . . . folio 1796–1827

Dunsford (M.) History of Tiverton . . . 4to. 1790
Durand (M.) Histoire du Droit canon (Lyons)
              12mo. 1770
Durfee (T.) (*see* Angell, J. E.)
Durham, Estates in, of Greenwich Hospital. folio 1805
—— Poll Book 8vo. 1790
—— Yard, Remarks on Encroachments on Thames,
 near 8vo. 1771
Durnford (C.) & East (E. H.) Reports of Cases
 in K. B. 1785–1800 . . . 8 vols. folio 1787–1800
—— Term Reports in the Court of K. B.
       4th ed. 8 vols. 8vo. 1794–1802
—— (*see* Willes)
—— (*see* Term Reports)
Du Roy (Tapisseries) . . . . folio 1687
Duvergier (J. B.) Le Droit civil des Français
           6 vols. 8vo. 1835–43
Dwarris (*Sir* F.) Letter to Lord Chancellor on
 proposed Scheme to Consolidate the Statute
 Law. Vol. 23, Pam. 1833
—— on the Statutes (Amyott) . 2nd ed. 8vo. 1848
Dyce (*Rev.* A.) (*see* C. S. Pa. No. 11)
Dyer (Geo.) University of Cambridge Privileges
           2 vols. 8vo. 1824
Dyer (*Sir* J.) Les Reports, 4 Hen. VIII.—24 Eliz.
             folio 1672
——————————————— 1513–82, translated, with
 Additional References, by J. Vaillant. 3 vols. 8vo. 1794
 (To this edition a Life of the Author is prefixed.)

E

Eadon's Map of United Provinces (portfolio) . . 1789
Eagle (*Dr.* F. K.) & Younge (E.) Reports on Tithe
 Cases, 1204–1820 . . . . 4 vols. 8vo. 1826

Eagle (W.) on Tithes. Vol. 10, Jac. Col. . . . 1834
—— on the Law of Tithes . . . . 2 vols. 8vo. 1830
Earnshaw (Wm.) Colonial Law Digest . . 8vo. 1819
East, Routes to the: Letter to Lord Palmerston, by
    an old Indian, as to opening the Suez Canal.
    Vol. 10, Pam. 1857
—— (E. H.) of the Pleas of the Crown. 2 vols. 8vo. 1803
—— Reports of Cases in the, K.B., 1800–14
                  16 vols. 8vo. 1801–14
East India Company :—
    Collection of Treaties & Grants, 1736–72 . 4to. 1774
    Papers relating to Restoration of King of
        Tanjore . . . . 2 vols. 4to. 1774
    ——————————— do. considered 4to. 1777
    Letter of Nabob of Arcot, as to Tanjore . 4to. 1777
    Appendix to do. . . . . . . 3 vols. 4to. 1777
    Defence of Lord Pigot . . . . 2nd ed. 4to. 1778
    Proceedings on Coroner's Inquest on do. . 4to. 1778
    Stuart's Letter to Directors 4to. 1778
    Collection of Charters 4to. 1817
    ——————————— 1601–26 . . . . 4to. 1827
    ——————————— establishing Courts in the
        three Presidencies 8vo. 1849
    Law of. 1st, 2nd, 3rd, & 4th edits.
                  4 vols. 4to. 1840–43
    Acts of Governor, &c. of, 1834–67
                  12 vols. 4to.
    Bengal Regulations and Acts, 1793–1834
    Acts of Bengal Presidency, 1867
    Bombay Regulations and Acts, 1799–1834
    Acts of Bombay Presidency, 1862–64
                  2 vols. 8vo.
    ———————————————————— 4to. 1865–7
    Madras Regulations and Acts, 1802–34
    Acts of Madras Presidency, 1864
    Army List, 1861–67 . . . . 12 vols. 12mo.
    Register, 1800–60 . . . . . 46 vols. 12mo.
    Maritime Officers of, Compensation to. Debate.
        Vol. 5, Pam. 1834

East London Waterworks Acts 8vo. 1808
Eastern Counties, Sections of intended Railway
from London to Norwich and Yarmouth. . 4to. 1835
Eastmead (*Rev.* W.) History of Kirby Moorside,
Yorkshire 8vo. 1824
Ebsworth (J.) on Infants 12mo. 1861
Ecclesiastical Benefices, Valuation of . . 12mo. 1680
—— Commissioners, Proceedings before, against
the Bishop of London. L. T. 1688
Ecclesiastical Commissioners' Acts & Orders in
Council . . . . 20 vols. 8vo. 1844–63
—— Courts, H. C. Reports . . 3 vols. folio 1832–33
—— Documents No. 8 C. S. Pa. (J. Hunter). . 1839
—— Gazette 4to. 1857–61
—— Legal Guide 8vo. 1839
—— Revenues, E. & W. Reports . . . . folio 1835
—— Revenues, Ireland, do. . 3 vols. folio 1833–1837
Economic Life Assurance Society: Report of Quin-
quennial Meeting. Vol. 10, Pam. 1859
Economist (The). Vol. 26 & continued . . folio. 1868
Ecton (J.) Liber Valorum et Decimarum . 8vo. 1711
—— Thesaurus Rerum Ecclesiasticarum . 8vo. 1742
Eden (R.) Jurisprudentia Philologica. . . 4to. 1744
—— (R. H.) on Injunctions 8vo. 1821
Eden (R. H.) Analysis of Bill for Consolidating the
Bankrupt Laws. Vol. 1, Jac. Col. 1823
—— Observations on Bankrupt Laws. Vol. 1,
Jac. Col. 1824
—— on Bankruptcy 8vo. 1825
———————————— . . . . . 3rd ed. 8vo. 1832
—— Reports of Cases in Chancery from MS. of
Lord Northington, 1757–66 . 2nd ed. 2 vols. 8vo. 1827
—— (Wm. *Lord* Auckland) Principles of Penal
Law 8vo. 1771
—— (Wm.) Letters to Earl Carlisle. 3rd ed. 12mo. 1780
Edgar (A.) Transactions of Social Science, 1868
8vo. 1869
Edinburgh (New) Almanac 12mo. 1822

Edinburgh (New) Directory 8vo. 1867
—— Gazetteer . . . . 6 vols. 8vo. 1822
—— Gazette, 1862–66, & continued . . . folio
—— Review & Three Indices, 1802–68
     2nd ed. 132 vols. 8vo.
Edmondson (J.) Heraldry . 5 vols. in 3, folio 1764–84
—— Peerage, & Supplement . 5 vols. folio 1764–84
—— Family History of Greville 8vo. 1766
—— Peerage, Companion to 8vo. 1776
————————————— 8vo. 1785
Edmunds' Exchequer Practice 8vo. 1794
Education Journal 4to. 1835–36
—— Lecture on, at Witham Institution. Vol. 5,
Pam. 1845
Education, Observations on System of. 10th ed.
Vol. 5, Pam. 1845
Educational Times 1867–8
Edward the Confessor, Lives of. Ed. H. R. Luard
(*see* No. 3, M. R. Pub.) 1858
—— III. to Richard III. Political Poems and
Songs relating to English History. Ed. T.
Wright (*see* No. 14, M. R. Pub.) 1859–61
—— IV., Historie of Arrivall of, No. 1, C. S. Pa. 1838
—— Chronicle of (first 13 years), No. 10 C. S. Pa.
(J. O. Halliwell) 1839
Edward IV. (temp.) Report (5th Anno 1465). folio 1638
—— V., Grants, &c. from the Crown during his
Reign, No. 60, C. S. Pa. (J. G. Nichols) . . 1854
Edward VI., Mary, & Elizabeth. Calendar of
State Papers, Domestic Series. Ed. by Robert
Lemon, F.S.A.
 Vol. 1, 1547–1580   Vol. 2, 1581–1590.
       imp. 8vo. 1856–1865
Edward VI. Calendar of State Papers, Foreign
Series, 1547–1553. Ed. by W. B. Turnbull
       imp. 8vo. 1861
Edwards (Edwd.) Letter to Mr. Hawes as to the
British Museum. Vol. 4, L. T. 1836
—— (Edwin) on Ecclesiastical Jurisdiction. 8vo. 1853

Edwards (*Dr.*T.) Reports, Admiralty, 1803–10. 8vo. 1812
—— on Admiralty Jurisdiction 8vo. 1847
—— (T.) Notanda Digest (in progress) . . 4to. 1863
—— (W. F.) Suggestions for Improving the state of the Court of Chancery, in a Letter to Lord Lyndhurst. Vol. 17, Pam. 1859
Egan (C.) on Extradition 8vo. 1846
Egerton Papers, No. 12, C. S. Pa., 1558–1625 . . 1840
—— (*Sir* P. G.) (*see* C. S. Pa. Nos. 39, C. M. Vol. 1, & 40) 1847
Ejectment, Law & Practice of 8vo. 1734
Eldon (*Lord*) Examination of an Article on, in 'Edinburgh Review.' Vol. 1, Jac. Col. . . . 1823
—— Judgment in Wellesley *v.* Duke of Beaufort. Vol. 6, Jac. Col. 1827
Election Cases, Determinations of House of Commons on . . . . 6th ed. 8vo. 1780
—— Irish, 1795–1814 . . . . 8vo. 1814
—— Reports 8vo. 1741
——————— 8vo. 1774
—— Statutes relating to 12mo. 1747
Elector denied his Vote for M.P., Debate on, in 1704 . . . . 8vo. 1721
Electoral Abuses considered by a defeated Candidate. Vol. 10, Pam. 1859
Elizabeth (*Queen*), Reign of, Calendar of State Papers, Domestic Series (in continuation of R. Lemon). Ed. by M. A. E. Green.
Vol. 3, 1591–94.   Vol. 4, 1595–97.
2 vols. imp. 8vo. 1867–69
——————————————— Foreign Series.
Ed. by the Rev. Joseph Stevenson
Vol. 1, 1558–59.   Vol. 3, 1560–61.
Vol. 2, 1559–60.   Vol. 4, 1561–62.
Vol. 5, 1562.
5 vols. imp. 8vo. 1863–67
Elizabeth (*Queen*) Annals of first four years of, 1558–62, No. 7, C. S. Pa. [Sir J. Hayward] (ed. J. Bruce) 1840

Elizabeth (*Queen*) Injunctions given concerning the Clergy both & Laity. L. T. & A. Vol. 1 . 1641
—— Letters, temp. [*see* Chamberlaine] C. S. Pa. No. 79 1861
—— Letters of, & of James VI. 1582–92, No. 46, C. S. Pa. (ed. J. Bruce) 1849
—— (*Princess*) Household Account of, 1551–52, C. S. P. No. 55, Cam. Mis. Vol. 2 (ed. Viscount Strangford) 1852
Ellesmere (Thomas, *Lord*) on the Privileges and Prerogatives of the Court of Chancery. MS. temp. Jas. I.
Elliott (G. P.) C. S. Pa. Nos. 39, C. M. Vol. 1, 55, C. M. Vol. 2.
Ellis (C.) on Insurance, Fire, Life, & Annuities. 8vo. 1832
———————————————— 2nd ed. 8vo. 1846
—— (C. T.) Parliamentary Precedents . . 8vo. 1802
———————————————— 2nd ed. 8vo. 1810
—— (H.) (*see* Caley, J.)
—— (*Sir* H.) Introduction to Domesday (*see* Record Commission)
—— Chronica Johannis de Oxenedes (*see* No. 13 M. R. Pub.) 1859
—— (*see* C. S. Pa. Nos. 9, 23, 29, 36, 39, 43, 44, 51)
—— (T. F.) (*see* Adolphus)
—— & Blackburn (C.) K. B. Reports, 1852–58 8 vols. 8vo. 1852–58
—— & Ellis (F.) do. 1858–61 . . 3 vols. 8vo. 1863–67
Elmer (J.) on Lunacy 8vo. 1844
———————————— 8vo. 1857
—— on Lunacy Regulations 8vo. 1862
———————————————— . 4th ed. 8vo. 1864
Elmes (J.) on Dilapidations . . . 3rd ed. 8vo. 1829
—— Dictionary of London 8vo. 1831
Elstob (Eliz.) English Saxon Grammar . . 8vo. 1715
Elsynge (Hen.) Declaration of Parliament on Commission of Array under 5 Hen. IV. (*see* Tracts, Parliament, Privileges of) 1642

Elsynge (Hen.) Manner of Holding Parliaments,
MSS. . . . . folio 1680
———————————————— 3rd ed. 8vo. 1675
———————————————— 4th ed. 8vo. 1679
—— Manner of Holding Parliaments, MSS. 8vo. 1768
Elton (C. J.) Tenures of Kent 8vo. 1867
—— on Commons and Waste Lands . . 12mo. 1868
Elwick (G.) Bankrupt Directory, 1829–43 . 8vo. 1843
Ely, Isle of (*see* Carter, E., History of Colchester)
—— Peerage: Minutes on Marquis of Ely's Claim
to Vote. Vol. 2, 3rd Series
Emerignon, Traité des Assurances et des Contrats
à la grosse (Marseilles) 2 vols. 4to. 1783
—— on Insurances; translated from the French
by S. Meredith 8vo. 1850
Emerson (T.) on City of London Courts . 8vo. 1794
Emigration, National Colonial Society, Report of
Meeting. Vol. 18, Pam. 1863
Encyclopædia Britannica . . 8th ed. 22 vols. 4to. 1860
Enderbie (Percy) Cambria Triumphans . . folio 1661
Enfield (Wm.) History of Liverpool . . . folio 1774
England, Ancient Laws, &c. of: Ethelbert to
Hen. I., &c. (*see* Record Commission) . . folio 1840
—— Chronicles of [Capgrave] Hingeston, Nos.
1, 7, M. R. Pub. 1858
—— Foreigners resident in, 1618–33, No. 82 C.
S. Pa. (W. D. Cooper) 1862
—— & Germany, Relations between, No. 95 C. S.
Pa. (S. R. Gardiner) 1865
—— Italian Relation, or Account of, 1500, No. 37
C. S. Pa. (C. A. Sneyd) 1846
—— Enlistment Question in, Remarks on
—— History of the Royal Family of (abridgment
of Sandford's Genealogy of the Kings) . . 8vo. 1741
—— National MSS. . . . . . . 3 vols. 4to. 1868
—— & Wales: Maps showing the Railways,
Canals, &c., in cases . . . . folio 1852
English Compendium of Peerages, 1753–66
9 vols. 12mo.

Elizabeth (*Queen*) Injunctions given concerning
the Clergy both & Laity. L. T. & A. Vol. 1 . 1641
—— Letters, temp. [*see* Chamberlaine] C. S. Pa.
No. 79 1861
—— Letters of, & of James VI. 1582–92,
No. 46, C. S. Pa. (ed. J. Bruce) 1849
—— (*Princess*) Household Account of, 1551–52,
C. S. P. No. 55, Cam. Mis. Vol. 2 (ed. Viscount
Strangford) 1852
Ellesmere (Thomas, *Lord*) on the Privileges and
Prerogatives of the Court of Chancery. MS.
temp. Jas. I.
Elliott (G. P.) C. S. Pa. Nos. 39, C. M. Vol. 1,
55, C. M. Vol. 2.
Ellis (C.) on Insurance, Fire, Life, & Annuities. 8vo. 1832
———————————————————— 2nd ed. 8vo. 1846
—— (C. T.) Parliamentary Precedents . . 8vo. 1802
———————————————————— 2nd ed. 8vo. 1810
—— (H.) (*see* Caley, J.)
—— (*Sir* H.) Introduction to Domesday (*see* Record
Commission)
—— Chronica Johannis de Oxenedes (*see* No. 13
M. R. Pub.) 1859
—— (*see* C. S. Pa. Nos. 9, 23, 29, 36, 39, 43, 44, 51)
—— (T. F.) (*see* Adolphus)
—— & Blackburn (C.) K. B. Reports, 1852–58
8 vols. 8vo. 1852–58
—— & Ellis (F.) do. 1858–61 . . 3 vols. 8vo. 1863–67
Elmer (J.) on Lunacy 8vo. 1844
——————————— 8vo. 1857
—— on Lunacy Regulations 8vo. 1862
———————————— . 4th ed. 8vo. 1864
Elmes (J.) on Dilapidations . . . 3rd ed. 8vo. 1829
—— Dictionary of London 8vo. 1831
Elstob (Eliz.) English Saxon Grammar . . 8vo. 1715
Elsynge (Hen.) Declaration of Parliament on Com-
mission of Array under 5 Hen. IV. (*see* Tracts,
Parliament, Privileges of) 1642

Elsynge (Hen.) Manner of Holding Parliaments,
MSS. . . . . folio 1680
―――――――――――――――――― 3rd ed. 8vo. 1675
―――――――――――――――――― 4th ed. 8vo. 1679
―― Manner of Holding Parliaments, MSS. 8vo. 1768
Elton (C. J.) Tenures of Kent 8vo. 1867
―― on Commons and Waste Lands . . 12mo. 1868
Elwick (G.) Bankrupt Directory, 1829–43 . 8vo. 1843
Ely, Isle of (*see* Carter, E., History of Colchester)
―― Peerage: Minutes on Marquis of Ely's Claim
to Vote. Vol. 2, 3rd Series
Emerignon, Traité des Assurances et des Contrats
à la grosse (Marseilles) 2 vols. 4to. 1783
―― on Insurances; translated from the French
by S. Meredith 8vo. 1850
Emerson (T.) on City of London Courts . 8vo. 1794
Emigration, National Colonial Society, Report of
Meeting. Vol. 18, Pam. 1863
Encyclopædia Britannica . . 8th ed. 22 vols. 4to. 1860
Enderbie (Percy) Cambria Triumphans . . folio 1661
Enfield (Wm.) History of Liverpool . . . folio 1774
England, Ancient Laws, &c. of: Ethelbert to
Hen. I., &c. (*see* Record Commission) . . folio 1840
―― Chronicles of [Capgrave] Hingeston, Nos.
1, 7, M. R. Pub. 1858
―― Foreigners resident in, 1618–33, No. 82 C.
S. Pa. (W. D. Cooper) 1862
―― & Germany, Relations between, No. 95 C. S.
Pa. (S. R. Gardiner) 1865
―― Italian Relation, or Account of, 1500, No. 37
C. S. Pa. (C. A. Sneyd) 1846
―― Enlistment Question in, Remarks on
―― History of the Royal Family of (abridgment
of Sandford's Genealogy of the Kings) . . 8vo. 1741
―― National MSS. . . . . . . 3 vols. 4to. 1868
―― & Wales: Maps showing the Railways,
Canals, &c., in cases . . . . folio 1852
English Compendium of Peerages, 1753–66
9 vols. 12mo.

English Endowments, Report of Attorney-General
 v. Pearson, before Lord Cottenham. Vol. 2,
 L. T.
—— Hexameter, Translations 8vo. 1847
—— History, Documents illustrative of 13th & 14th
 Centuries (ed. by Cole) (*see* Record Commission)
           folio 1844
—— History: Political Poems & Songs relating to,
 Edw. III. to Rich. III. *Ed.* H. Wright (*see*
 No. 14, M. R. Pub.) 1859–61
—— Law, Discourse on 12mo. 1673
———— Grounds of, or Institutions . 12mo. 1556
———— Introduction to 8vo. 1763
—— Lawyer: or, Every One his Own Lawyer.
 By a Student of the Inner Temple . . 8vo. n. d.
—— Miscellanies (early), Cat. of, formerly in
 Harleian Library. No. 87 C. M. Vol. 5 (W. C.
 Hazlitt) 1864
—— Peerage . . . . 2 vols. 8vo. 1779
—— Reformation, Letters relative to. Par. S. Pa.
           8vo. 1846
—— (H. S.) Laws of Pews in Churches, 3rd ed.8vo. 1826
Enjuiciamiento sobre los Negocios, y Causas de
 Comercio . . . . (Madrid) 4to. 1830
Enquire within for Everything 8vo. 1866
Equitable Life Assurance Society, Deed of Settlement
           8vo. 1778
Equity Cases, abridged . . 4th ed. 2 vols. folio 1756
————————————— Vol. 1, 5th ed.; Vol. 2, 2nd
 ed. . . . . 2 vols. folio 1769–93
—— Exchequer (Ireland) Orders 8vo. 1844
—— Pleading 8vo. 1780
·—— Reports, 1853–55 . 3 vols. in 4, 8vo. 1854–55
—— Treatise on 8vo. 1737
Erasmus, Colloquia Familiaria 32mo. 1524
Erck (J. C.) Repertory of Patent Rolls in Chancery
 of Ireland, commencing James I. . . . 8vo. 1846
Erdeswick (J.) Survey of Staffordshire . . 8vo. 1820

Erle (*Sir* Wm.) on Trade Unions Law . 12mo. 1869
Errors, Law of 8vo. 1703
Erskine (Jno.) Scotch Law . . . 7th ed. 8vo. 1791
—— Scotch Law, Principles . . 12th ed. 8vo. 1827
—————————————————— (J. G. Smith). 8vo. 1860
Erskine (Thomas, *Lord*) Biography of (*see* Roscoe's Lives of Lawyers)
—— Speeches (Jas. Ridgway). . 5 vols. 8vo. 1810
—— Speech in case of Dean of St. Asaph's Trial for Libel before Mr. Justice Buller. Libel L. T. Vol. 3 1784
Espinasse (J.) on Defects of the Law. Vol. 5, Jac. Col. 1827
—— Law of Actions & Trials at Nisi Prius
2nd ed. 2 vols. 8vo. 1793
————————— . . . . . 4th ed. 2 vols. 8vo. 1812
————————— Reports, 1793–1807
6 vols. 8vo. 1798–1811
Essex Poll Book 8vo. 1722–39
————————— 8vo. 1751–80
—— (*Earl of*) Account of his Death. L. T. 1688-9
—— did not Murder himself. L. T. 1688-9
Established Church, Five Reports (H. C.) on State of . . . . folio 1835–37
Estate in Fee Simple Defeasible on Leaving no Issue: Opinions . . . . . Vol. 2, Col. Jur.
Estates Gazette, 1858–68 & continued . . 4to.
Eton (*see* Hakewell's Windsor)
Euclid's Elements of Geometry . (Paris) 8vo. 1830
Euer (Sampson) System of Pleading . . 4to. 1771
Eulogium (Historiarum sive Temporis): Chronicon ab Orbe condito usque ad annum Domini 1366; a Monacho quodam Malmesburiensi exaratum. Edited by F. S. Haydon. No. 9, M. R. Pub. Vols. 1, 2, 3 1858–63
Europe, Annals of, 1739–43 . . 6 vols. 8vo. 1739–43
—— History of, 1643–1700 . . . 3 vols. 8vo.

Falconer (W.) New Universal Dictionary of the Marine, with a Vocabulary of French Sea Phrases, &c., by Dr. Wm. Burney . . . 4to. 1815
Falle (P.) Cæsarea, or, An Account of Jersey; to which are added, in a Letter to the Author, Remarks on the 19th Chap. of the 2nd Book of Mr. Selden's Mare Clausum, by P. Morant. 8vo. 1734
————— 4to. 1797
Fane (C.) on Jurisdiction of Bankruptcy Court to Commit for Contempt. Vol. 2, Pam. 1837
—— on Bankruptcy Reform — Letter to Mr. Hawes. Vol. 6, Pam. 1848
————————————— Ditto to Sir R. Peel. Vol. 6, L. T.
Fanshaw (*Sir* T.) The Practice of the Exchequer Court (bound up with Vernon) 1658
Farley (E.) on Imprisonment for Debt . . 8vo. 1788
Farmer (J.) History of Waltham Abbey . 8vo. 1735
Farnborough Road, Kent. Mr. Nolan's Speech on Bill for Repealing Act of 1810 for Repairing. Vol. 13, Jac. Col.
Farnham Quay, Litigation as to, between Barfoot & Burgess—Review of Facts 8vo. 1778
Farren (E. I.) Life Contingencies 8vo. 1844
—— (G.) on Life Insurance. 8vo. 1823
—— on Law of Mortality 8vo. 1826
—— on Key to the Statutes 12mo. 1837
Farrer (W. D.) on Contributories . . . 12mo. 1850
Farrington (*Serjt.* E.) Charter of St. Albans 8vo. 1813
Faulkner (T.) History of Chelsea 8vo. 1810
————————————— Fulham 4to. 1813
————————————— Kensington . . . 4to. 1820
————————————— Hammersmith . . 8vo. 1839
Faux (W.) Tour in America (an English farmer). 8vo. 1823
Fawcett (J. H.) & Littler (R. D. M.) Practice in Referees Court in Parliament. 8vo. 1866
Fea (*Dr.* J. W.) Eldoniana Dialogue between a Reformer & a Chancery Barrister. Vol. 3, Jac. Col. 1826

Fearne (C.) on Remainders 8vo. 1772
——————————————— . . . 2nd ed. 8vo. 1773
——————————————— . . . 3rd ed. 8vo. 1776
——————————————— . . . 4th ed. 8vo. 1795
——————————————— . . . 5th ed. 8vo. 1795
——————————————— . . . 6th ed. 8vo. 1809
——————————————— (C. Butler) 9th ed. 8vo. 1831
——————————————— (W. Smith)
                       10th ed. 2 vols. 8vo. 1844
—— Works (including Remainders) & Posthumous
(T. M. Shadwell) . . . . 3 vols. 8vo. 1795-97
Fees of House of Commons Report . . . folio 1833
———————————— on Private Bills & Evidence. folio 1834
—— of Officers of Courts, List . . . 12mo. 1697
—— Table of Fees of all the Courts at Westminster, as delivered to Parliament by order, 19th Nov. 1693 . . . . 12mo. 1697
—— Claimed by Officers & their Deputies of ditto, presented to House of Commons by order, 4th March 1730 (bound up with Attorneys, List of)
—— Report of Committee of House of Commons on (bound up with Attorneys, List of)
—— in Law & Equity, Parliamentary Committee's Report . . . . folio 1847-50
Fell (W. W.) on Mercantile Guarantees. 2nd ed. 8vo. 1820
Fellowship Porters, Reply to the Statement of, contained in Reports of Committee of Control over Coal & Corn Meters 1818
Feltham (J.) a Tour through the Isle of Man in 1797-8, comprising Sketches of its Ancient & Modern History 8vo. 1798
Fenn—Compendium of English & Foreign Funds, Banks, Railways, &c. (R. L. Nash). 9th ed. 8vo. 1867
Fenning (D.) & Collyer (J.) Geography
                     4th ed. 2 vols. folio 1772
Fens, History of the, extending over parts of the Counties of Cambridge, Isle of Ely, Huntingdon, Lincoln, Norfolk, Northampton, & Suffolk (*see* Coles' Bedford Level) 1761

Fenton (R.) History of Pembrokeshire . . 4to. 1811
Ferard (J.) on Fixtures 8vo. 1847
—— (*see* Amos, A.)
Ferguson (J. F.) on Limitation of Actions (Irish)
    Bill (*see* Irish Pamphlets) 8vo. 1843
Ferrall (S. A.) Pamphlet on Parliamentary Privi-
    lege raised in Stockdale *v.* Hansard . . 8vo. 1837
Ferrar (J.) History of Limerick 8vo. 1737
Field (B.) Analysis of Blackstone's Commentaries
                                             8vo. 1811
—— (C. D.) on Evidence in India . . . 8vo. 1867
—— (E. W.) on Defects in Equity Courts' Prac-
    tice & System of Costs. Vol. 2, Chancery Pam. 1840
—— on Recent & Future Law Reforms, Judicial
    Procedure, &c. Vol. 20, Pam. 1843
—— on the Right of the Public to form Limited
    Liability Partnerships. Vol. 9, Pam. . . . 1854
—— Letter to (*see* Loring, C. G.)
—— (W.) History of Warwick & Leamington. 4to. 1815
Fielding (H.) on Increase of Robbers. 2nd ed. 12mo. 1751
—— Plan for Preventing Increase of Robbers. 8vo. 1755
—— Plan for Universal Register Office for Sale of
    Property (bound up with above) 1753
—— (Jno.) Account of Origin of a Police (do.) . 1758
—— Peerage . . . . 3 vols. 12mo. 1786–91
—— (*Sir* M.) Penal Laws as to Metropolis. 8vo. . 1762
Fienne's Trial (Prynne & Walker) bound up with
    Prynne (W.) 1644
Filmer (*Sir* R.) on Government . . . 12mo. 1696
—— on Power of Kings 12mo. 1680
Finance, H. C. Report on . . . . 4 vols. 8vo. 1799
Finch (*Sir* H.) Discourse on the Law . . 12mo. 1627
—————————————————— . . . 8vo. 1678
—— Chancery Reports, 1673–80 . . . . folio 1725
—— (T.) Chancery Reports, 2nd ed. 1689–1722
                                             8vo. 1786
Fine Rolls—Fines, sive pedes finium: sive finales
    Concordiæ. Vol. 1, 1185–1214 (*See* Record
    Commission) 8vo. 1835

Fine Rolls—Fines, sive pedes finium: sive finales
Concordiæ. Vol. 2, 1195-1214 (J. Hunter) (*see*
Record Commission) 8vo. 1844
—— Excerpta e Rotulis Finium, 1216-72 (C.
Roberts) (*see* Record Commission) 2 vols. 8vo. 1835-36
—— Rotuli de Oblatis et Finibus, temp. Regis
Johannis (T. D. Hardy) (*see* Record Commis-
sion). 8vo. 1835
Fines 8vo. 1751
——— 8vo. 1753
Finlaison (A. G.) Succession Duty Tables   12mo. 1856
—— (John) on the Law relating to the Public
Rights over Wastes & Commons Lands . 8vo. 1867
Finlason (W.) Leading Cases on Pleading . 8vo. 1847
—— Law & County Courts & Actions. Vol. 7,
Pam. 1850
—— (W. F.) on Charitable Trust Act . 12mo. 1855
——————————————————— 12mo. 1860
—— Common Law Procedure Act, 1852-54 (*see*
Day, Markham, & Stephens). . . . 12mo. 1855
—— Lawyer's Companion and Diary . . . 8vo. 1859
—— Martial Law 8vo. 1866
Firth (J. F.) Royal Hospitals of London . 8vo. 1836
Fisher (R. A.) Digest of Reports, 1865-66 . 8vo. 1866
—— (R. B.) on Copyhold . . . 2nd ed. 8vo. 1803
—— (W. R.) on Mortgage 8vo. 1856
——————————— 2nd ed. 2 vols. 8vo. 1868
Fishermen, Thames, &c. Rules 1785
Fisk (Geo.) Analysis of Coke upon Lyttleton
2 vols. 8vo. 1824
Fitch (G.) Letter to Lord Campbell on the Bill to
Lessen Expense attending the Transfer of Lands
of Small Value. Vol. 19, Pam. 1843
Fitzgibbon (J.) K. B. Reports, 1728-32. . folio 1732
Fitzherbert (Anthy.) Abridgement of Statutes folio 1577
—— Natura Brevium (W. Rastall) . . . 8vo. 1652
——————————————— 8vo. 1687
——————————————— . . 7th ed. 4to. 1730
——————————— (Hale) . 8th ed. 4to. 1755

Fitzherbert (A.) Natura Brevium. 9th ed. 2 v. 8vo. 1794
Fitzwalter Peerage: Case of Sir B. W. Bridges.
Vol. 2, 2nd Series
────── Evidence. Vol. 16, 1842 & 1844; Vol. 19,
1843; & House of Lords Session Papers, Vol. 16,
1842-43
Flanagan (S. W.) & Kelly (C.) Irish Chancery
Reports (Rolls) 1840-42 . . . . . . 8vo. 1843
Flather (J.) (*see* Archbold)
Flaxman (*Dr.*) Index to House of Commons Journals. Vols. 8, 11, 1660-97 . . . . . folio
Fleetwood (Geo.) Letter describing the Battle of
Lützen & Death of Gustavus Adolphus. No. 39,
C. M. Vol. 1. (Sir P. de M. Grey Egerton) . 1847
──────'s (*Bishop of Ely*) Works . . . . . folio 1737
────── Life of St. Winefrede . . 2nd ed. 12mo. 1713
Fleta sive Commentarius . . . 2nd ed. 4to. 1685
Floyer (P.) Proctors' Practice 8vo. 1794
Flügel, English & German Dictionary. 2 vols. 8vo 1861
Flux (W.) Law of Sale of Poisons . . . 12mo. 1869
Fœlix, Traité du Droit international, par Demangent . . . . 2 vols. 8vo. 1856
Foley (R.) Poor Laws . . . . . 3rd ed. 8vo. 1751
────────────────── . . . . . 4th ed. 8vo. 1758
Follett (T. L.) on Good Government. Vol. 13,
Jac. Col. 1838
Fonblanque (J.) on Equity . 5th ed. 2 vols. 8vo. 1820
────── (J. S. M.) on Bankrupt Consolidation Bill.
Jac. L. T. Vol. 4 1824
────── on Bankruptcy 8vo. 1825
────── (J. W. M.) Reports of Bankruptcy Commissioners, 1849-52 . . . . 8vo. 1852
Fougasses (Thos. de) History of Venice, translated
by Shute . . . . folio 1612
Foote (Wm.) on Improvement of Criminal Law
2nd ed. 12mo. 1843
Forbes (*Dr.* J.) Critical Examination of Bill for
Representation, &c. of the Medical Profession.
Vol. 21, Pam. 1845

Forbidden Book; or American Medical Inquirer. 8vo. 1850
Forcellinus (Ægidius). Totius Latinitatis Lexicon, consilio et cura Jacobi Facciolati, opera et studio Ægidii Forcellini lucubratum; edidit, Anglicam interpretationem in locum Italicæ substituit, appendicem Patavinam Lexico passim intertexuit, auctorium denique et Horatii Tursellini de Particulis Latinæ orationis libellum, Gerrardi Siglarum Romanum et Gesneri Indicem Etymologicum adjecit J. Bailey . . . 2 vols. 4to. 1828
Ford (W.) Chancery Practice 8vo. 1847
—— Observations on Publication of Notices of Warrants of Attorney, &c. Vol. 2, Pam. . . 2nd ed. 1858
—— Remarks on 514th Sect. of Bankruptcy & Insolvency Bill. Vol. 13, Pam. 1860
Fordun (J. de) Scotichronicon cum Boweri Supplementis. Ed. W. Goodall . . . 2 vols. folio 1759
Forfeiture, Tract on . . . . 3rd ed. 1748
—— Scotch Law of 12mo. 1778
Foreign Office List
Foreigners resident in England, C. S. Pa. No. 82 (W. D. Cooper) 1862
Formy ( ) French Exercises . . 6th ed. 12mo. 1789
Forrest (R.) Exchequer Reports, 1800-1 . . 8vo. 1802
Forrester (*see* cases temp. Talbot) . 3rd ed. 8vo. 1792
Forster (F.) (*see* E. Chitty, Index to C. L., &c. Reports)
—— (Nat.) Index to H. C. Journals. Vols. 12–17, 1697–1713 . . . . folio
Foster (G. J.) Doctors' Commons, its Courts & Registries, being a Treatise on Probate Business
8vo. 1868
Forsyth (R.) Beauties of Scotland. 5 vols. 8vo. 1806-8
—— (W.) on Composition Deeds. . 3rd ed. 12mo. 1854
Fortescue de Laudibus Legum Angliæ (Selden)
12mo. 1672
———————————————————— folio 1737
———————————— (Selden). 2nd ed. folio 1741
————————————————(Amos) 8vo. 1823

Fortescue (John, *Lord*) K.B. Reports, 1711-31. folio 1748
—— (*Sir* John) The Difference between an Absolute and Limited Monarchy, &c. (Sir J. F. Aland) 8vo. 1714
—————————————————— 3rd ed. 8vo. 1734
Fortune on Life Annuities bound up with Fairman (W.) on Stocks 1808
—— (E. F. T.) Epitome of the Public Funds (Evans) . . . . 17th ed. 12mo. 1856
Fosbrooke (T. D.) Berkeley MSS., History of Castle, &c. & Smythe's Lives of the Berkeleys . . 4to. 1821
—— (*Rev.* T. D.) History of Gloucester . . 8vo. 1819
Foss (Edwd.) Grandeur of the Law 4to. 1842
—— on Lord Chancellors of Reign of King John. 1847
—— on Cursitor Baron 4to. 1855
—— Lineage of Sir Thomas More . . . . 4to. n. d.
—— Biography of English Judges 1066-1864 9 vols. 8vo. 1848-64
—— Tabulæ Curiales 8vo. 1865
Foster (*Sir* M.) Crown Cases 8vo. 1767
—— Crown Cases (Dodson) . . . 2nd ed. 8vo. 1776
—— (T. C.) on Scire Facias 8vo. 1851
—— & Finlason (W. F.) Nisi Prius Reports, 1856-67 . . . . 4 vols. 8vo. 1860-67
Fowler (C.) on Site for Houses of Parliament. Vol. 5, Pamphlet 1836
—— (D. B.) Exchequer Practice . . 2 vols. 8vo. 1795
—————————————— 2nd ed. 2 vols. 8vo. 1817
—— (T. C.) on Collieries & Colliers . . 12mo. 1861
Fox (R.) History of Godmanchester, Hunts. 4to. 1831
Foxe (J.) Days of the Reformation, C. S. Pa. No. 77 (J. G. Nichols) 1859
France, Carte Orléanois 1761
—— Code Pénal . . . . . . 4th ed. 12mo. 1777
Francillon (J.) Lectures on English Law . 8vo. 1860
Francis (J.) History of the Bank of England, its Times & Traditions . . 3rd ed. 2 vols. 8vo. n. d.
—— (R.) Equity Maxims . . . . . . folio 1728
——————————————————— . . 2nd ed. folio 1739

Franciscana Monumenta (*see* No. 4, M. R. Pub.)
Fraser (A.) Report of Trial, Rex *v.* Kinnear (Conspiracy) 8vo. 1819
—— Report of Trial of Doe dem. Gibson *v.* Hargreaves, 1837 . . . . 8vo. 1838
—— (J.) Election Cases, 1790-91 . . . 8vo. 1791
—— (Jas.) on Patents & Copyright . . 12mo. 1860
——'s (Jas.) Magazine, Vol. 7 to Vol. 77, 1833-1868 . . . . 71 vols. 8vo.
Freeman (R.) Reports, by Dixon . . ⎫ 2vols.
    Common Law, 1679-1783   ⎬ in 1, folio 1742
    Chancery, 1676-1706 . . . .   ⎭
—— Chancery Reports, Hovenden, 1660-1706
                                2nd ed. 8vo. 1823
Freeman (W.) Index to 'The Times,' 1862 . 8vo. 1863
—————————————————————— 1863 . 8vo. 1864
Free Trade, Sophisms of (by a Barrister) . 12mo. 1849
French Claims, Baron de Bodé's Address to H. C. 1833. Vol. 5, Pam.
—— Law, Catalogue of Law Books in Lincoln's Inn Library 8vo. 1849
—— Midwife's Murder of her Husband in January 1687. L. T.
—— Ministers who fled to Germany on account of persecution. Law Tract, 1688-9
Frend (H. T.) & Ware (T. H.) Railway Precedents relating to Transfer of Land (D. Sturges & T. M. Browne). . . . . 2nd ed. 8vo. 1866
Frere (C.) on House of Commons Committees 8vo. 1847
Freshfield (J. W.) Speech on Equity Courts. Vol. 2, Chancery Pam. 1839
—— Speech on Breach of Parliamentary Privilege. Pam. 1839
—— Papers on Factors & Brokers. . . . folio
Friend (*Sir* J.) Trial (*see* Impeachment of Lords)
Frost (C.) History of Hull & its Harbour . . 4to. 1827
—— (H. W.) (*see* United States Digest)
Froude (J. A.) History of England, 1527-73
                        2nd ed. 10 vols. 8vo. 1858-66

K

Fry (D. P.) Vaccination Acts . . 2nd ed. 12mo. 1865
—— (Edward) on Specific Performance of Contracts 8vo. 1858
Fulbecke, (W.) A Parallele, or Conference of the Civil Law, the Canon Law, and the Common Law of this Realme of England . . Small 4to. 1618
Fulke (*Dr.* Wm.) Works. P. S. P. 2 vols. 8vo. 1843–48
Fuller (John) History of Berwick-upon-Tweed, Northumberland 8vo. 1799
—— (Nich.) Argument against Ecclesiastical Commission. L. T. 1641
—— (Thos.) Worthies of England (J. Nichols)
2 vols. 4to. 1811
Furetière (A.) Dictionnaire Universel. 2nd ed. 8vo. 1701
Furneaux (*Dr.* P.) on Toleration Act. 2nd ed. 8vo. 1771
Fynn (R.) British Consuls Abroad. Hand-book
3rd ed. 12mo. 1851
F. (H.) Jamaica Laws 8vo. 1683
F. (J. S.) Citizen's Pocket Chronicle . . 8vo. 1827

G

Gabbett (J.) Digest of or Comparative View of the Statute Law of England & Ireland
2 vols. in 3, 8vo. 1812
Gage (J.) History of Hengrave, Suffolk (bound up with Cullum's Hawsted) 1822
—— History of Thingoe Hundred, Suffolk. folio 1838
Gaill (A.) Practicarum Observationum Libri II. 4to. 1621
Gairdner (J.) Memorials of Hen. VII. (*see* M. R. Pub. No. 10) 8vo. 1858
—— Letters and Papers illustrative of the Reigns of Rich. III. & Hen. VII. (*see* M. R. Pub. No. 24)
2 vols. 8vo. 1861–63

Gaius. Commentaries of the Roman Law, with
Translation, &c. By T. Tomkins & M. G.
Lemon 8vo. 1869
Gale (C. J.) Exchequer Reports, 1835–36
          2 vols. 8vo. 1836–38
—— on Easements . . . . 2nd ed. 8vo. 1849
————————————— (Willes) . . . 3rd ed. 8vo. 1862
Gale (C. J.) & Whatley (C.W.) on Easements. 8vo. 1839
—— & Davidson (H.) K. B. Reports, 1841–43
          3 vols. 8vo. 1841–45
—— (Roger) Registrum Honoris de Richmond. folio 1722
Galignani (A. & W.) Paris Guide. 10th ed. 12mo. 1822
Gallison (Jno.) Reports Circuit Court, U.S. 1812–
15 . . . . 2 vols. 8vo. 1845
Gambia (River) Laws, 1843–67 1868
Gambier (*Sir* E. J.) on Parochial Settlements. 8vo. 1828
Gamesters, Laws as to 12mo. 1711
Gank (the Brothers) Madras Almanac & Directory
          8vo. 1868
Gaol Delivery in Kent, 1788, MSS. . . . folio 1799
Gardiner (R.) Instructor Clericalis, K.B. & C.P.
Practice . . . . 7th ed. 8vo. 1727
—— on Newcastle Coal Trade 8vo. 1796
—— (S. R.) C. S. Pa. Nos. 81, 90; C. M. Vol. 5,
No. 87
—— (Thos.) History of Dunwich, Blithburgh, &
Southwold (Suffolk) 4to. 1754
Gardner's Peerage (no case) Evidence, Vol. 5 . . 1825
Garfield (S.) & Snyder (F. A.) Laws of California,
U. S., 1850–53 . . . . 8vo. 1853
Garrett (W. A.) on Chancery Reform. Vol. 2,
Chancery Pam. 1837
Garrow (*Rev.* D. W.) History of Croydon . 8vo. 1818
Gas Company, Memorial to Sewer Commissioners,
London Tracts
Gateshead, History of (*see* McKenzie's Newcastle)
Gazette des Tribunaux, 1839–67 . 46 vols. folio
Gell (J.) Statute Laws of the Isle of Man since
1836 (continued by J. Burman) . . . 8vo. 1848

K 2

Gem (H.) Considerations on Government Bill for Ecclesiastical Reform. Vol. 18, Pam. & Vol. 8 L. Tracts 1844
General Registry, Tracts on & Reasons for
           4to. 1678, &c.
—— Record Office, Papers relating to . . 8vo. 1835
Geneste (G.) Statute Laws of the Isle of Man since 1821 (continued by J. M. Jeffcott) . 8vo.
Gentleman's Magazine, 1731–1868, with 5 Indices
        226 vols. 8vo. 1731–1868
—— Register 12mo. 1749
Geoffrey of Monmouth. The British History, translated from the Latin by A. Thompson (J. A. Giles) . . . . New ed. 8vo. 1842
George (J.) on Joint Stock Companies. Vol. 7, L. Tr. 1825
—— III., Catalogue of Maps in his Library in British Museum . . . . folio 1829
———————————————— 2 vols. 8vo. 1829
Germany & Italy. Vol. 10, Pam. . . . 2nd ed. 1859
—— Denmark, & the Scandinavian Question
         Vol. 14, Pam. 1861
Gesvres, Marquis & Marchioness of, Trial
         2 vols. 12mo. 1714
Gibbon's (D.) Limitations & Prescriptions . 8vo. 1835
—— on Dilapidations & Nuisances . . . 8vo. 1838
—— (E.) Rise & Fall of the Roman Empire
           8vo. 1841
—— (H. F. & W. C.) Harvey on Equity of the County Court 12mo. 1865
Gibbs (F. W.) Recognition, a Chapter from the History of the North American & South American States. Vol. 16, Pam. 1863
—— on the Foreign Enlistment Act. Vol. 18, Pam. . . . . 2nd ed. 1863
Gibson (Edmd.) Codex Juris Ecclesiastici Anglicani . . . . 2nd ed. 2 vols. folio 1761
—— (Jno.) History of Glasgow 8vo. 1777
—— (W. S.) Memoir of Lord Lyndhurst . 8vo. 1866

Giffard (J.) English Lawyer . . . 5th ed. 8vo. 1821
―― (J. W. de L.) Reports, V.-C. Stuart, 1858–
65 . . . . 4 vols. 8vo. 1859–69
Gilbert (*Ld. Ch.* B.) Reports (Chancery) . folio 1734
―― Reports (Chancery) 1706–25 . 2nd ed. folio 1742
―――――― (Chancery & K. B.) 1713–14 . 8vo. 1760
―― on Uses 8vo. 1734
―――――― (Sugden) 8vo. 1811
―― History & Practice of Court of Common Pleas
8vo. 1739
――――――――――――― . . . 7th ed. 8vo. 1761
―― Devises & Revocations 8vo. 1739
―――――――――――― 8vo. 1756
―― Replevin 8vo. 1755
―― History & Practice of the High Court of
Chancery 8vo. 1756
―― the Law &Practice of Distresses & Replevin
8vo. 1757
――――――― (by a Barrister) . . 2nd ed. 8vo. 1780
――――――― (W. J. Impey) . . 4th ed. 8vo. 1823
―― Tenures . . . . 3rd ed. 8vo. 1757
――――――― (Watkins) . . . . 4th ed. 8vo. 1796
―― Treatise on the Court of Exchequer . 8vo. 1758
―― the Law of Executions 8vo. 1763
―― the Law of Evidence . . . 4th ed. 8vo. 1777
――――――― (Sedgwick) . . . 6th ed. 8vo. 1861
―― Biography of 8vo. 1793
―― (C. S.) Survey of Cornwall . 2 vols. 4to. 1817–20
―― (P.) Les Codes annotés de Sirey. Vol. 1,
Code Napoléon 8vo. 1862
―― Code Procédure civile et Code de Commerce. Vol. 2 . . . . 8vo. 1863
―― Codes d'Instruction criminelle, pénal et
forestier. Vol. 3 . . . . 3 vols. 8vo. 1863
Gill (J.) on Insolvency 8vo. 1836
―― (H.) Comments on his connection with the
Birmingham Manufactures. Vol. 16, Pam. . . 1844
Gillingwater (E.) Lowestoft 4to. 1790
―― History of Bury St. Edmunds . . 12mo. 1804

Gilmour (J.) Record of Sequestrations, 1842–45
                                                              folio 1845
—— Alphabet of ditto . . . . . 2 vols. 4to. 1850–51
—— On County Court Act, 1867 . . . 12mo. 1868
Girard's Trial (French) 8vo. 1781
Girod et Clariond, Journal de Jurisprudence commerciale maritime . . . . . . 2 vols. 8vo. 1820
Glanville (J.) Election Reports, 21 & 22 Jas. I. 8vo. 1775
—— (Ranulph de) Beames' Translation of . 8vo. 1812
———————————— de Legibus, MSS. . . . 4to.
Glastonbury, Charter & Depositions of Witnesses of Cures by Waters of, MSS . . . . . folio 1751
Glen (W. C.) Poor Law Statutes, 43rd Elizabeth to 1866 . . . . 2 vols. 8vo. 1857–66
—— on Burial Boards 12mo. 1858
—— Nuisances 12mo. 1858
—— (W. C.) Poor Law Board Orders. 4th ed. 8vo. 1859
—— on Highways 12mo. 1860
——————————— . . . . . 2nd ed. 12mo. 1865
—— Jervis's Acts . . . . . . 3rd ed. 12mo. 1868
—— Registration of Births, &c. 8vo. 1860
—— Prison Act 12mo. 1865
—— Public Health, Local Government, & Nuisance Removal Laws . . . . . . 3rd ed. 12mo. 1865
———————————————— 4th ed. 12mo. 1866
———————————————— 5th ed. 12mo. 1869
—— Rating Small Tenements . . . 4th ed. 8vo. 1866
—— Reform Act 12mo. 1867
—— Metropolitan Poor Law Act, 1867 . 12mo. 1867
Glencairne Peerage Case of Sir A. Fergusson, Vol. 2, 3rd series
Glisson (W.) & (A.) Gulston, Common Law Epitomised (Styles) . . . . . 2nd ed. 12mo. 1679
Globe Newspaper, 1834–66 . . . 56 vols. folio
Globes, one pair
Gloucester Cathedral, some account of . . 4to.
Gloucestershire Election Poll Book . . . 8vo. 1816
Glover, on Lord Brougham's Law Reform. Vol. 11, Jac. L. Tr. . . . . , 1834

Glover (S.) History & Gazetteer of Derbyshire
           2 vols. 4to. 1831
Glyn (T. C.) & Jameson's (R. S.) Bankruptcy Reports, 1821-23 . . . . . . 2 vols. 8vo. 1824-25
Godbolt (Justice J.) K. B. Reports, 1574-1633
              4to. 1653
Godefroi (H.) & Shortt (J.) on Railways . 8vo. 1869
Godolphin (*Dr.* J.) Repertorium Canonicum, or Abridgment of Ecclesiastical Law . . 4to. 1678
——————————————— 2nd ed. 4to. 1680
—— Orphan Legacy . . . . . 3rd ed. 4to. 1685
————————————— . . . . . 4th ed. 4to. 1701
Godson (R.) on Patents 8vo. 1823
——————————— . . . . . 2nd ed. 8vo. 1844
Godwin (F.) Annales of England, 1509-58 . folio 1630
Goldsmith (W.) on Equity 8vo. 1838
———————————— . . . 2nd ed. 8vo. 1842
———————————— . . . 4th ed. 8vo. 1849
———————————— . . . 5th ed. 8vo. 1862
Goodall (*Dr.* C.) Catalogue of Physicians of College of London 4to. 1684
Goode (J.) Measuring Made Easy (Atkinson) 12mo. 1760
Goodeve (J.) Letter to Lord Chancellor : Shall we Transfer Lands by a Register. Vol. 9, Pam. Pt. 2 1854
Goodinge (T.) on Bankruptcy . . 2nd ed. 8vo. 1701
Gosling's List of Lords Temporal & Spiritual, 1719 & 1728 (*see* Grimaldi's Tracts)
—— (R.) Laws of Honour 12mo. 1726
Gough (H.) Land Register Manual . . . 8vo. 1862
—— (R.) (*see* Camden, W.)
—— British Topography . . . . . 2 vols. 4to. 1780
—— History of Pleshy, Essex 4to. 1803
Gould (*Sir* W.) Biography of (*see* Lawyers)
Gouldsborough (J.) Reports, K.B., 1585-1603, 4to. 1653
Gourlay (R.) Upper Canada, Statistical Account of
           2 vols. 8vo. 1822
—— General Introduction to Statistical Account of Upper Canada . . . . . . 2nd ed. 8vo. 1822

Government, or Civil Policy, Nature of . . 8vo. 1703
Gow (N.) Reports, Nisi Prius, 1818-20. 2nd ed. 8vo. 1828
—— on Partnership . . . . . . 3rd ed. 8vo. 1830
Grady (S. G.) on Diminution of Poor Rate. 12mo. 1862
—— on Fixtures & Dilapidations . 2nd ed. 8vo. 1866
—— on the Hindoo Law of Inheritance . . 8vo. 1868
—— & Scotland (C. H.) Crown Practice . 8vo. 1844
Grafton (R.) Chronicle; or History of England,
   1189-1558 . . . . 2 vols. folio 1809
Graglia (G. A.) Italian & English Dictionary
                            15th ed. 12mo. 1829
Grain (W.) Ley Hipotecaria of Spain . . 8vo. 1867
Granada Acts, 1857-66 . . . . 8vo.
Grand Junction Canal Acts . . . . . . folio 1794
Grand Juries, or Security for Men's Lives. 12mo. 1681
—— Jurymen's Oath, &c., explained. Vol. 1,
   Libel Tr. 1680
—— Vizier Unmasked, Remarks on Mr. Canning's
   Claim to Public Confidence. Vol. 7, Jac. Col. . 1827
Grandison Peerage: Cases of Sir H. C. Bedingfield.
   Vol. 2, 3rd series; Evidence, Vol. 17 . . 1829-58
Grant (A.) Canada Chancery Reports, 1849-61
                        2nd ed. 8 vols. 8vo. 1861
—— Chancery Practice (Hurd) . 2 vols. 12mo. 1826
—————————————— 2nd ed. 2 vols. 12mo. 1829
—————————————— . 3rd ed. 2 vols. 8vo. 1833
—————————————— . 4th ed. 2 vols. 8vo. 1837
—— Chancery Questions & Answers . . 12mo. 1839
—— (C.) Memoires de la Maison de Grant . 8vo. 1796
—— (James) on Corporations 8vo. 1850
—— on Bankers and Banking 8vo. 1856
—————————————— (Fisher) 2nd ed. 8vo. 18·5
Grave (J.) History of Cleveland 4to. 1808
Gray (J.) Country Attorneys' Practice . . 8vo. 1836
—————————————— (Paterson) 8th ed. 8vo. 1861
—————————————— 9th ed. 8vo. 1869
—— Solicitors' Practice . . . . . , . . 8vo. 1837
—— on Common Law Costs 8vo. 1853
Great Britain, Present State of Court of . 12mo. 1742

Great Britain & Ireland, Catalogue of Materials
relating to History of, to end of Reign of Henry
VII. (T. D. Hardy) 26 M. R. Pub. 1862
——— & U. S. of America, Diplomatic Correspondence . . . . 2nd ed. 2 vols. 8vo. 1862
Great Charter, Introduction to. Blackstone's L. Tr. 1771
——— Session of Wales Practice 8vo. 1795
——— Chamberlain of England, Lord, Cases of
Hugh Baron Percy & others, claiming title.
1st series 1780–83
——————————————————— Memoir of the
Claim of the Dillon Family . Vol. 2, 3rd series 1780
Great Exhibition, Catalogue, British Division
2 vols. 4to. 1862
——————————————— Italian Kingdom. 1 vol. 8vo. 1862
Greaves (C. P.) Letter to Lord John Russell, on
Quarter Sessions Amendment. Vol. 4, Pam. . . 1839
——— (C. S.) on Publication of Banns of Matrimony
12mo. 1867
——— (S.) on Criminal Law Consolidation & Amendment Acts 8vo. 1861
————————————————————— 2nd ed. 8vo. 1862
Greek Grammar . . . . 12mo.
Green (Edwd.) Bankrupt Laws . 3rd ed. 8vo. 1776
————————————————— . 4th ed. 8vo. 1780
Greene (J.) Admiralty Digest 8vo. 1818
——— (John) City Privileges 8vo. 1708
—————————————————. . . . 3rd ed. 8vo. 1722
Greene (M. A. E.) Calendar of State Papers,
Domestic Series, of the Reign of Elizabeth (continued) preserved in Her Majesty's Public Record
Office (see Lemon). Vol. 3, 1581–94. Imp. 8vo. 1867
——— Calendar of State Papers, Domestic Series,
of the Reign of James I. preserved in Her
Majesty's Public Record Office :—

    Vol. 1.—1603-10   Vol. 3.—1619-23
    Vol. 2.—1611-18   Vol. 4.—1623-25

with Addenda. Imp. 8vo. 1857–59

Greene (M. A. E.) Calendar of State Papers, Domestic Series, of the Reign of Charles II., preserved in Her Majesty's Public Record Office:—
Vol. 1.—1660-61   Vol. 5.—1665-66
Vol. 2.—1661-62   Vol. 6.—1666-67
Vol. 3.—1663-64   Vol. 7.—1667
Vol. 4.—1664-65
Imp. 8vo. 1860-66

—— (N.) Survey of City of Worcester . . 8vo. 1764
—— History of City & Suburbs of Worcester
2 vols. in 1, 4to. 1796
—— (T. W.) Letter to Lord Chancellor, suggesting a Site for Superior Courts in the Temple. Vol. 20, Pam. 1862
Greenhow (W. T.) Shipping Law Manual . 8vo. 1863
Greening (H.) Forms, Statutes, & Rules . 8vo. 1852
Greenleaf (*Dr.* S.) on Evidence, U. S.
11th ed. 3 vols. 8vo. 1863
Greenwich Hospital, Account of 8vo. 1789
—— Bye Laws, &c. 8vo. 1776
—— Cumberland Estates . . . . . folio 1805
—— Durham Estates . . . . . . folio 1805
—— Report as to ditto . . . . . . folio 1823
Greenwood (C. & J.) Map of London 1827
—— (G. W.) Court Keeper . . . 9th ed. 8vo. 1730
—— Manual of Conveyancing 8vo. 1858
——————————— . . . 3rd ed. 8vo. 1865
—— (Wm.) on County Courts & Offices of Sheriff & Coroner . . . . 5th ed. 8vo. 1675
———————————————Office of Coroner
(Wilkinson) . . . . 7th ed. 8vo. 1763
Gregg (F.) Costs in Bankruptcy. Vol. 8, Jac. Col. 1826
—— Suggestions for Altering Bankrupt Law. Vol. 8, Jac. Col. 1831
—— on Bankruptcy 8vo. 1838
Gregorius XIII. Corpus Juris Canonici . . 4to. 1650
Gregorie (A.) Moot Book, or Survey of Common Law (Hughes) 4to. 1663
Gregory (*Dr.* D.) on Geometry . 10th ed. 8vo. 1787

Gregory (J.) Manual of Geography. 2nd ed. 12mo. 1740
Gregson (J.) on Geography . . . 2nd ed. 12mo. 1740
—— (M.) History of Lancashire & Duchy
    2nd ed. 4to. 1817
Gresham (*Sir* T.) Copy of Will . . . . 4to.
Gresley (R. N.) on Evidence in Equity . . 8vo. 1836
Greville, Family History of 8vo. 1766
Grey Friars of London, Chronicles of, 1189–1556.
  No. 53, C. S. Pa. (J. G. Nichols) 1851
Grey of Wilton, Life of, 1530–47. No. 40,
  C. S. Pa. (*Sir* P. G. Egerton) 1841
—— (R.) Ecclesiastical Law . . 3rd ed. 8vo. 1735
Griffith (E.) Cases on supposed Exemption from
  Poor Rate 8vo. 1831
—— (F. A.) Military Law 8vo. 1841
—— (W.) Institutes of Jurisdiction, Jurisprudence
  & Pleading in Chancery 8vo. 1868
—— (W. D.) on Bankruptcy 12mo. 1862
—— (W. D.) on Arrangements with Creditors
  under Bankruptcy Act 12mo. 1865
Grimaldi (S.) on Public Records as Sources of
  Genealogies 4to. 1828
—— Rotuli de Dominabus et Pueris et Puellis de
  donatione Regis in XII. Comitatibus . . 4to. 1830
—— Lectures on, from which Pedigrees may be
  traced from the Norman Conquest (delivered in
  the Hall of I. L. S.), Vol. 7 Law Tracts . . . 1835
—— Collection of Tracts . . . . 3 vols. 8vo.
  Vol. 1, containing :—
  1. The Fall of Villiers, Duke of Buckingham . . 1734
  2. Titles and Honours conferred by Geo. I. & Geo. II.
    (Phillips) 1728
  3. Lists of the Lords Spiritual & Temporal & Knights &
    Burgesses of Parliament (Gosling) 1719, & *see* Vol. 2 1728
  4. The Old Constitution in Church & State . . . 1718
  5. A Letter touching the late Rebellion, &c.. . . 1717
  Vol. 2, containing :—
  The case of War in Italy stated, &c. 1718
  A Full Answer to Shepheard the Assassin's Speech; & Account of Treasonable Sermon of Edward Bisse . . 1718

Grimaldi (S.) Collection of Tracts

Vol. 2—*continued*
The Resigners Vindicated, &c. 1718
Dialogue between Whig & Tory
Letter to Sir Wm. Benson, &c. 1719
Peerage Bill, Letter from Member of House of Commons 1719
———— The Plebians 1719
———— The Old Whig. 1720

Vol. 3, containing :—
Anecdotes of Olave the Black, King of Man, and the Hebridian Princes of the Somerled Family, to which are added XVIII. Eulogies on Haco, King of Norway, by Snorro Sturlson & by the Rev. J. Johnstone 1780
A Character of John Sheffield, late Duke of Buckinghamshire, with an account of the pedigrees of the Sheffield Family, to which is annexed His Grace's last Will & Testament, written with his own hand. 1729
A Biographical, Historical, &c. Account of the House of D'Oyly; by W. D'Oyly Bayley, 1845, with MSS. Errata
A small specimen of the many Mistakes in Sir W. Dugdale's Baronage; by Dr. Richard Rawlinson. Reprint . 1801

Grindall, Remains of Edmund Archbishop. Par. S.P. 1842
—— *v.* Grindall. Report of Trial . . . 8vo. 1832
Grocers' Company's Reports, Londonderry Estates, 1817–29 . . . . 8vo. 1827–29
Grose (F.) & others, Antiquarian Repertory
          4 vols. 4to. 1807–9
—— (*Sir* N.) Biography of (*see* Lawyers) . 8vo. 1790
Grosseteste (Bp. of Lincoln) Letters illustrative of Social Condition of his Time (Ed. H. R. Luard) (*see* M. R. Pub. No. 25) 8vo. 1861
Grote (G.) History of Greece . 12 vols. 8vo. 1854–57
Grotius (Hugo) de Jure Belli ac Pacis . . 8vo. 1712
———————— (Barbeyrac) . 2 vols. 8vo. 1735
—— on Peace & War (Rev. A. C. Campbell)
          3 vols. 8vo. 1814
—— Introduction to Dutch Jurisprudence, translated by C. Herbert 8vo. 1845
Grounds & Rudiments of Law & Equity digested
          folio 1749
————————————————————— folio 1751

LAW SOCIETY LIBRARY. 141

Guardian, The . . . . . 6th ed. 2 vols. 12mo. 1704
Guardian Newspaper . . . . folio 1833
Guernsey, Documens relatifs à l'Ile de Guernsey
    (in English), temp. 1607 . . . . 8vo. 1814
—— History of St. Peter's Harbour & Port. 4to. 1765
Gude (R.) Crown Practice . . . 2 vols. 8vo. 1828
Guidott (T.) Antiquities of Bath . . . 8vo. 1675
Guilford (*Lord*) Biography of (*see* Roscoe's
    Lives of Eminent British Lawyers)
Guildford, Description of Hospital, & Life of Arch-
    bishop Abbot, a Reprint, by A. Onslow . 8vo. 1777
Guizot (M.) History of Charles I. & the Revo-
    lution . . . . 2 vols. 8vo. 1854
—— History of Oliver Cromwell & the English
    Commonwealth . . . . 2 vols. 8vo. 1854
—— History of R. Cromwell & the Restoration of
    Charles II., translated by R. B. Scoble
                                2 vols. 8vo. 1856
Gunning (F.) Law of Tolls 8vo. 1833
—— (H.) Report of Poll for Cambridge Uni-
    versity Election, Vol. 7, Jac. Col. 1827
Gurdon (T.) on Courts Leet & Baron, with Rights
    of Lords and Privileges of Tenants 1731
—— on Parliament . . . . 2 vols. 8vo. 1731
Gurney (Josh.) Report of Trial of J. H. Tooke for
    High Treason . . . . . 2 vols. in 1, 8vo. 1795
—— Report of Sir John Nicholl's Judgment in
    Kemp *v*. Wicks, Refusal to bury a child baptized
    by a dissenting minister. Vol. 2, Jac. Col. . 1810
—— of Trial Rex *v*. Montague, as to Yantlett
    Creek. London Tracts 1824
—— of Proceedings in the House of Lords as to
    Lady Hewley's Charity. 8vo. 1839
Gutch (J.) Collectanea Curiosa, or Miscellaneous
    Tracts relating to the History of England &
    Ireland . . . . 2 vols. 8vo. 1781
Guterboch (C.) (*see* Bracton)
Guthrie (Wm.) Peerage 4to. 1763

Guy (W. A.) on Medical Jurisprudence
              2nd ed. 12mo. 1861
Guylforde (*Sir* R.) Pilgrimage, 1506. C. S. Pa.
  No. 51 (ed. Sir H. Ellis) 1850
Gwillim (*Sir* H.) Reports of Tithe Cases, 1285–
  1824. . . . . 2nd ed. 4 vols. 8vo. 1825
—— (J.) Display of Heraldry . . 3rd ed. folio 1638
———————————————————— . . 6th ed. folio 1724
Gwynn (J.) London & Westminster Improved. 8vo. 1766
Gwynne (T.) on Legacy Duties . . 2nd ed. 8vo. 1836
G. (J.) Highgate, Account of its Grammar School
  & Founder 8vo. 1822
G. (R.) Art of Conveyancing explained
              2nd ed. 2 vols. 8vo. 1668
—— Retorna Brevium 8vo. 1707
———————————————————— . . New, 3rd ed. 8vo. 1738
—— Instructor Clericalis, K. B. & C. P. Practice
              6th ed. 8vo. 1721
———————————————————— 7th ed. 8vo. 1727

H

Hackney, St. John, Act for Maintaining Poor, &c.
  1764 . . . . 8vo. 1793
—— St. John, Rebuilding Church
Hackney Carriage Fares, by Metropolitan Police
              12mo. 1863
Haddan (Jno.) Outlines of Chancery Procedure
              12mo. 1862
Haddon (T. H.) on Legal Education, in a Letter
  to Vice-Chancellor of Oxford 1848

Haggard (J.) Consistory Reports, 1789–1802
　　　　　　　　　　　　　　　2 vols. 8vo. 1822
—— Admiralty Reports, 1822–38. 3 vols. 8vo. 1825–40
—— Ecclesiastical Reports, 1827–33
　　　　　　　　　　　　　　　4 vols. 8vo. 1829–33
Hakewell (Jas.) History of Windsor & its Neigh-
　bourhood 4to. 1813
Hakewil (W.) on Passing Bills in Parliament. 8vo. 1641
—— the Liberty of the Subject 4to. 1641
—— Old Manner of Holding Parliaments. 12mo. 1671
Halcomb (J.) Report of Rowe *v.* Grenfell. Vol. 10,
　Jac. L. T. 1826
—— House of Commons' Practice, & Supplement
　　　　　　　　　　　　　　　2 vols. 8vo. 1836–38
Hale (*Archdeacon*) (*see* C. S. Pa. Nos. 69, 91)
Hale (*Sir* Edwd.) Case: Ld. Ch. J. Herbert's Law
　examined. L. T. 1688
—— (G. H.) United States Digest
—— & Smith (H. F.) United States Digest
—— (*Lord*) Preface to Rolle's Abridgement. Col.
　Jur. 1791
—— Sheriffs' Accounts, bound up with 3rd ed.
　Pleas of the Crown 1683
—— (*Sir* M.) Biography of (*see* Roscoe's Lives of
　Eminent British Lawyers).
—— on Mankind . . . . folio 1677
—— Original Institution, &c. of Parliament. 12mo. 1707
—— History of the Common Law 8vo. 1713
————————————————— . 2nd ed. 8vo. 1716
—————————————————(C. Runnington)
　　　　　　　　　　　　　5th ed. 2 vols. 8vo. 1794
—— Tracts . . . . 5th ed. 8vo. 1716
　　Containing:—
　　　1. Pleas of the Crown　　3. Trial of Witches
　　　2. Sheriffs' Accounts　　4. Discourse on the Poor
—— Discourse, Pleas of the Crown . 2 vols. folio 1736
————————————————— (Wilson)
　　　　　　　　　　　　　　　2 vols. 8vo. 1778

Hale (*Sir* M) Jurisdiction of the House of Lords
  4to. 1790
—— on Courts of K. B. & C. P. & Process therefrom. Hargrave's L. T.
—— Case, Inquiry into Power of Dispensing with Penal Statutes, & Animadversions thereon, 1688. Atkins' L. T. 1741
—— (W. H.) (*see* C. S. Pa.)
Haliburton (T. C.) History of Nova Scotia
  2 vols. 8vo. 1829
Halifax (Yorkshire) History of, & of the Gibbet Law there 12mo. 1712
—— (*Dr.* S.) Analysis of the Civil Law (Dr. J. W. Geldart) 8vo. 1836
Hall (F. J.) & Twell's (P.) Reports, temp. Cottenham, 1848-50. . . . . 2 vols. 8vo. 1850-51
—— (R. G.) on the General Metropolitan Registry. Vol. 11, Jac. Col. 1834
—— (S.) Family History of Echyngham . 8vo. 1850
—— (W. C.) Legal Forms 12mo. 1865
Hallam (H.) Middle Ages . 5th ed. 3 vols. 12mo. 1829
—— Introduction to Literature of Europe
  3 vols. 8vo. 1854
—— Constitutional History of England, 1485-1760 . . . . 9th ed. 3 vols. 12mo. 1857
Halliday, History of the House of Guelph, or Royal Family of Great Britain 4to. 1821
—— (*Sir* A.) Letter to Lord R. Seymour on Number of Lunatics, &c. in England & Wales. Vol. 7, Jac. Col. 1829
—— (R.) Articled Clerks' Manual . . . 8vo. 1859
—— Digest of the Examination Questions & Answers . . . . 4th ed. 1864
Halliwell (J. O.) (*see* C. S. Pa. Nos. 13, 19, 30)
—— History of New Place, Stratford (Shakespeare's Residence) . . . . folio 1864
—— Dictionary of Words, Archaisms, & Provincialisms . . . . 5th ed. 2 vols. 8vo. 1865

Halma (F.) Dictionnaire Flamend et François. 4to. 1710
Halpin, Trial for Treason at Dublin . . . 8vo. 1868
Hamel (F. H.) on International Law . . . 8vo. 1863
Hamilton (E.T.) Second Letter to 'Sydney Morning Herald,' on Augmentation of Licence Fees Paid by Occupiers of Crown Lands in New South Wales. Vol. 18, Pam. 1844
—— (H. B.) Villa Volpicelli, or the Shut School. Vol. 23, Pam. 1853
—— (H. C.) Calendar of State Papers relating to Ireland preserved in Her Majesty's Public Record Office:—
  Vol. 1—1509-73. Vol. 2—1574-85.
Imp. 8vo. 1860-67
Hamilton (*Rev.* W.) History of Northern Coast of County of Antrim 8vo. 1790
—— (W. D.) C. S. P. No. 75
Hammond (A.) Digest of Term Reports, temp. Geo. III. & IV. . . . . 2 vols. 8vo. 1820
—— (N.) Algebra . . . . . . 3rd ed. 8vo. 1764
Hamper (W.) Life, Diary, & Correspondence of Sir W. Dugdale 4to. 1827
Hampshire Repository . . . . . 2 vols. 8vo. 1799
—— Poll Books, 1779-90 . . . . . 8vo. 1780-90
—— County Tracts . . . . 8vo.
 Containing :—
1. Holdsworth (E.) Muscipula, sive Kambronmyomachia, The Welsh Mouse Trap 1709
Holdsworth (F.) Hoglandia, Latin description of Hoglandia, with its Dedication, translated into English . . 1711
2. Bullar (J.) Historical Guide to Isle of Wight . . 1806
3. The Burning Shame, a Punishment for Bad Lawyers, custom peculiar to Newport (Isle of Wight) . . . 1812
4. Account of Winchester Cathedral, extracted from Milner's Winchester . . . . . 2nd edit. 1807
5. Sketch of History of Holy Ghost Chapel, at Basingstoke
2nd edit. 1808

Hampson (*Sir* G.) on Trustees' Liabilities
2nd ed. 8vo. 1830

L

Hamst (Olphar.) Handbook of Fictitious Names. 8vo. 1868
Hanbury (*Rev.* W.) History of Church Langton,
    Leicestershire 8vo. 1767
Hancock (J. W.) on Canada Conveyancing. 8vo. 1861
Hands (Wm.) on Fines 8vo. 1782
———————————————— . . . 2nd ed. 8vo. 1807
———————————————— . . . 3rd ed. 8vo. 1817
—— on Crown Suits Practice 8vo. 1805
—— Solicitors' Assistant in Chancery . . 8vo. 1809
—— on Election Petitions 8vo. 1812
Hansard (G.) on Aliens, & Supplement
                                           8vo. 1844 & 1866
—— (J.) Book of Entries . . . . . . folio 1633
—— Parliamentary History (Cobbett), 1063–1803
                                26 vols. 8vo. 1806–20
Hansard (G.) Parliamentary History & Debates
             1st series, 1803–20 . 41 vols. 8vo. 1804–20
        ——————— 2nd series, 1820–30 . 25 vols. 8vo. 1820–30
        ——————— General Index (Philippart) 1803–30
                                    2 vols. 8vo. 1822–34
        ——————— 3rd series, 1830–68 . 193 vols. 8vo. 1831–68
Hanshall (J. H.) History of Cheshire . . 4to. 1817
Hanson (A.) Trial 8vo. 1809
—— on Succession Duty Act 12mo. 1865
Hardiman (J.) History of Galway . . . 8vo. 1820
Harding (G. R.) Ecclesiastical Law
                                  2nd ed. 12mo. 1862
Hardres (*Sir* T.) Exchequer Reports, 1655–70
                                        folio 1693
Hardwick (*Lord Chancellor*) Catalogue of MSS. of
                                        4to. 1794
—— General Orders, temp. 12mo. 1744
—— (C.) (*see* Cantuariensis Historia) 8 M. R. Pub. 1858
—— (F.) Select Chancery Cases in Mortmain.
    Vol. 1, Col. Jur.
Hardy (T. D.) Close Rolls — Rotuli Litterarum
    Clausarum, 1201–27 (*see* Record Commission)
                                    2 vols. folio 1833–34

Hardy (T. D.) Patent Rolls. Vol. 1, Part 1,
1201–16 (*see* Record Commission). . . folio 1835
—— Introduction to Patent Rolls (*see* Record
Commission) 8vo. 1835
—— Catalogue of Lord Chancellors, &c. . 8vo. 1843
—— Rotuli de Liberate ac de Misis et Præstitis,
regnante Johanne (*see* Record Commission) 8vo. 1844
—— Modus tenendi Parliamentum (*see* Record
Commission) 8vo. 1846
—— Catalogue of Materials relating to the History
of Great Britain & Ireland. 26 M. R. Pub. . . 1862
—— (Wm.) Duchy of Lancaster Charters . 8vo. 1845
—— (Dep. Kep. of Pub. Rec.) & Brewer (J. S.)
Report to M. R. upon Carte and Carew Papers
in the Bodleian and Lambeth Libraries . 8vo. 1864
Hare (J. C. L.) & H. B. Wallace, Leading Cases
on Mercantile Law, U.S. .. 4th ed. 2 vols. 8vo. 1851
—— (T.) on Discovery of Evidence . . . 8vo. 1836
—— Chancery Reports, 1841–53. 11 vols. 8vo. 1842–58
—— (T.) on the Development of Wealth in India.
Vol. 14, Pam. 1861
Hargrave (F.) Opinion of, on the case of the Duke
of Athol in respect of the Isle of Man (1788). 4to.
—— Juridical Arguments . . . 2 vols. 4to. 1797–99
Vol. 1
No.1. As to Commitment of Butler & Bond
  2. Scott *v*. Vernon, Conditional Legacy
  ————————————— 2nd Arguments
  3. Duke of Chandos' Title to Estate
  4. Same. Further Argument in Exchequer Chamber
  5. Myddelton *v*. Lord Kenyon
  ————————————— Further Argument
  6. Athol, Duke of, Case as to Isle of Man
  7. Parliamentary Aids
  8. Writs of Error in Criminal Cases
  9. Inchiquin, Earl, Appeal to Irish H.L.
 10. Mackreth's Petition for Rehearing
 11. Liverpool Corporation *v*. Corporation of London
 ————————————————— 2nd Argument
 12. Caithness Earldom, Admissibility of Vote on Election of
    Scotch Peers
 13. Fox *v*. Mackreth, Reasons of Appeal to the House of Lords

Hargrave (Juridical Arguments)—*continued.*
Vol. 1. Appendix :—
1. Case in Butler *v.* Bond
2. Do. in Duke of Chandos
3. Myddelton *v.* Kenyon, Extracts from Papers
4. Inchiquin, Earl, Case
5. London *v.* King's Lynn, Case of the latter

Vol. 2
No. 1. Thellusson's Will, Three Arguments in
2. Perry's Case of Privilege on House of Lords' Committal
3. Pardon for Perjury, Effect of
4. Mutual Wills, Walpole's Case
5. Dacre *v.* Dacre Case
6. Nabob of the Carnatic Petition
   Appendix :—
   1. Extract from Case, &c. in Thellusson's Will
   2. Morgan's Calculations of Accumulations

Hargrave (F.) & Butler (C.) (*see* Coke upon Littleton)
—— Law Tracts . . . . 8vo. & 4to. 1797
1. Lord C. J. Hale's de Jure Maris
   —— de Portibus Maris
   —— on Customs of Goods Imported & Exported
2. Considerations as to Amendment or Alteration of Laws
3. On Masters in Chancery (Author unknown)
4. On Suits in Chancery by Subpœna, from Cotton MSS.
5. Lord C. J. Hale, Discourse on Courts of K. B. & C. P.
6. Discourse against Jurisdiction of K. B. over Wales, by Latitat (Author unknown).
7. Mr. G. Norhouse on Abuses & Remedies in Chancery
8. Hargrave on Effect of Sentences of Ecclesiastical Courts in Cases of Marriage when pleaded in Temporal Courts
9. Mr. Justice Blackstone's Arguments in Exchequer Chambers on giving Judgment in Perren *v.* Blake
10. Hargrave's Argument in Appeal from Chancellor to House of Lords, Wicker *v.* Mitford
11. Hargrave's Observations on Rule in Shelley's Case

—— MSS. Catalogue of, in British Museum. 4to. 1818
Harle (W.L.) A Career in the House of Commons
                                                    8vo. 1850
—— on Distinction between Barrister & Attorney.
Vol. 8, Pam. 1852
Harleian Miscellany (W. Oldys & T. Park)
                                            10 vols. 4to. 1808–13
—— MSS. Catalogue of, in British Museum
                                            4 vols. folio 1808–12

Harley (*Lady* B.) Letters, 1625–43. No. 58,
C. S. Pa. (ed. T. T. Lewis) 1853
Harris (*Dr.* John) History of Kent . . . folio 1719
—— (W.) History of Dublin, with Map. . 8vo. 1766
—— Elementary Principles of Law, Part 1. 8vo. 1865
Harrison (J.) Chancery Practice 8vo. 1741
———————————————————— . . 5th ed. 8vo. 1767
———————————————————— . . 6th ed. 8vo. 1779
———————————————— (Parke)
8th ed. 8vo. 1796
———————————————————— (Newland)
new ed. 2 vols. in 1, 8vo. 1808
—— (J.) K. B. Practice 8vo. 1761
———— C. P. do. 8vo. 1761
—— (O. B. C.) Practice in City Sheriff's Court
8vo. 1860
—— (R. A.) New Municipal Manual of Upper
Canada 8vo. 1859
Harrison (R. A.) & Wollaston (F. L.) K. B.
Reports, 1835–37 . . . . . 2 vols. 8vo. 1836–37
—— & Robinson's (J. L.) K. B. Canada Digest,
1823–51 . . . . 8vo. 1852
—— (S. B.) Common Law Digest of Term Reports,
1756–1827 . . . . 2 vols. 8vo. 1828
———————————————————— 4 vols. 8vo. 1835–37
—— Common Law Digest of Term Reports, 1756–
1827 . . . . 2 vols. 8vo. 1838–42
———————————————————————— (R. T.
Harrison) 1756–1843 . . 3rd ed. 4 vols. 8vo. 1844
———————————————————————— (R. A.
Fisher) 1843–1855 . . . . 2 vols. 8vo. 1856
Hart (*Col.* H. G.) Annual Army List, 1840–66
& continued . . . . 8vo.
—— Monthly do. 1818–67 . . 101 vols. 12mo.
—— Quarterly do. 1842–68 . . . 36 vols. 8vo.
Harvard University Library Catalogue, Cambridge,
Massachusetts, U.S. 8vo. 1841
Harvey (D. W.) Appeal to Inner Temple (Inn of
Court) 8vo. 1832

Harvey (D. W.) Letter to Burgesses of Colchester.
Vol. 2, L. Tr. 1822
Harwood (T.) Alumni Etonenses 4to. 1797
Haslam on Insanity 8vo. 1817–18
Hasted (E.) History of Kent . . . 4 vols. folio 1778
Hastings Peerage: Case of Sir J. Astley. Vol 2,
2nd series. Vol. 2, 3rd series, Le Strange's Case
—— Evidence, Vol. 18
—— Evidence, Vol. 21 1840
—— Evidence, Vol. 20 1841
—— (G.W.) Social Science Transactions (*see* Social
Science) . . . . 7 vols. 8vo. 1862–68
—— (Warren) Impeachment (*see* The Oracle) 8vo. 1790
Hatsell (Jno.) Cases & Records in Parliament, to
1628 . . . . 4to. 1776
Hatsell (Jno.) Precedents in House of Commons
2nd ed. 3 vols. 4to. 1785
Hatton (Edwd.) New View of London (maps) temp.
Elizabeth . . . . 2 vols. 8vo. 1708
Hawke (M.) Grounds of the Law 8vo. 1656
Hawkins, Index to Records 12mo. 1739
—— (F. V.) Construction of Wills . . . 8vo. 1863
——(*Serjt.* Wm.) Pleas of the Crown. 2nd ed. folio 1724
————————————————4th ed. 2 vols. folio 1762
——————————————————— (Leach)
6th ed. 2 vols. 8vo. 1777
——————————————————— (Curwood)
8th ed. 2 vols. 8vo. 1824
Hawles (*Sir* John) on Duty of Petty Juries, or the
Englishman's Right (*see* Libel L. T. Vol. 1)
Hay (Alex.) History of Chichester & County of
Sussex 8vo. 1804
—— (*Sir* J. D.) on Reward of Loyalty. Vol. 20,
Pam.
—— (Wm.) on Accidents & Negligence . 8vo. 1860
Haydn (J.) *Beatson's* Political Index modernised.
The Book of Dignities, &c. 8vo. 1851
—— Dictionary of Dates. . . . 6th ed. 8vo. 1853
———————————————— (B. Vincent) 13th ed. 8vo. 1868

Haydon (F. S.) Eulogium (Historiarum sive Temporis): Chronicon ab orbe condito usque ad A.D. 1366, a Monacho quodam Malmesburiensi exaratum. No. 9, M. R. Pub. 3 vols. 8vo. 1858–63
Hayes (Edmd.) Irish Exchequer Reports, 1830–32
            8vo. 1837
—— & Jones (T.) Irish Exchequer Reports, 1834–38 . . . . 8vo. 1838–47
—— (W.) Real Property Law. Vol. 1, Jac. Col. 1825
—— Letter to Mr. Amos, as to his Lecture on the Study of English Law. Vol. 7, Jac. Col. . . . 1830
—— on Conveyancing 8vo. 1834
———————————— . . . . 3rd ed. 8vo. 1837
———————————— . . 5th ed. 2 vols. 8vo. 1840
—— Concise Precedents (W. B. Coltman)
          2nd ed. 8vo. 1864
Hayes (W.) on Doctrine of Equity as to Separate Estate. Vol. 11, Jac. L. T.
—— & Jarman (T.) Concise Forms of Wills
          3rd ed. 8vo. 1840
————————————(T. S. Badger) 5th ed. 1860
———————————— (T. S. B. Eastwood) 6th ed. 8vo. 1863
Haynes (F. O.) Outlines of Equity . . 12mo. 1858
———————————————— 2nd ed. 8vo. 1865
Hayward (A.) Appeal to Inner Temple, Inn of Court 8vo. 1848
—— (Sir J.) Annals, First Four Years of Queen Elizabeth. C. S. Pa. No. 7 (ed. J. Bruce) 4to. 1840
Hazlitt (W.) & Roche (H. P.) on Bankruptcy. 12mo. 1861
—— (W. C.) (see C. M. Vol. 5, No. 87)
—— Handbook of the Popular Poetical & Dramatic Literature of Great Britain to the Restoration. 8vo. 1867
Headlam (T. E.) New Chancery Acts . . 8vo. 1853
Healey (P.) on Laws of Debtor & Creditor. Vol. 6, Pam. 1849
Healthy Homes, Report of Meeting of Metropolitan Association for Improving Dwellings of Industrious Classes. Vol. 9, Pam.

Hearn (W. C.) The Government of England, its
 Structure & Development 8vo. 1867
Hearne(T.) Liber Niger Scaccarii. Accedunt Chartæ
 Antiquæ. Contains No. of Hides of Land held
 by King's Tenants . . . . 2 vols. 8vo. 1771
—— English Antiquities . . . . . 2 vols. 8vo. 1771
Heath (C.) History of Monmouth 4to. 1804
—— Excursions down the Wye 4to. 1799
—— (Sir J.) Biography (see Lawyers) 1790
—— (J. B.) Account of Grocers' Company 8vo. 1829
—— (R.) History of Cornwall & Scilly . . 8vo. 1750
Hedericus (B.) Græcum Lexicon Manuale (T.
 Morell) 4to. 1825
Heineccius (J. G.). Opera Omnia . . 8 vols. 4to. 1744
Heir-Apparent, Privilege to continue Ancestor's
 Possession, Hist. L. T. 1761
Heirs, Limited & Universal Representation of.
 Hist. L. T.
Helie (F.) Traité de l'Instruction criminelle
  9 vols. 8vo. 1845-60
Helps to English History, with Catalogue of
 Bishops, &c.
  3rd, 5th, & 6th eds. 5 vols. 12mo. 1670-1709
———————————————————— (Wright)
  8vo. 1773
Heming (G. W.) Outline of Practical Law . 8vo. 1858
Hemingway (J.) History of the City of Chester
  2 vols. 8vo. 1831
Hemming (G. W.) & Miller (A. E.) Chancery
 Reports . . . . 2 vols. 8vo. 1864-65
Henley (Lord) on Church Reform. Vol. 12, Jac.
 Col. 1832
Henricis, Liber de illustribus (see Capgrave) No. 7,
 M. R. Pub. 1858
Henry & Thomas of Lancaster. No. 55,C.M. Vol. 2 1853
—— II. Life of [Benedict of Peterborough] (Rev.
 W. Stubbs.) See M. R. Pub., No. 49
—— III. Life of, Law T. 1641

Henry III. Royal & Historical Letters illustrative of his Reign (Rev. W. W. Shirley) No. 27, M. R. Pub. . . . . 2 vols. 8vo. 1862–66
—— IV. V. VI. & Richard II. Chronicle of Reigns of, No. 64, C. S. Pa. 1377–1461. (J. S. Davies) 1856
—— IV. Royal & Historical Letters (F. C. Hingeston). No. 18, M. R. Pub. 1860
—— V. Memorials of (C. A. Cole). No. 11, M. R. Pub. 1858
—— VI. Letters, &c. illustrative of English Wars in France during this Reign (Rev. J. Stevenson). No. 22, M. R. Pub. 1862–64
—— VII. Bull of Pope Innocent VIII. on Marriage with Elizabeth of York. No. 39, C. S. Pa. Cam. Mis. Vol. 1 (J. P. Collier) 1847
—— VII. & Richard III. Letters & Papers illustrative of the Reigns of (J. Gairdner). Vols 1, 2. No. 24, M. R. Pub. 1861–63
—— VII. & VIII. a London Chronicle during. No. 73, C. S. Pa., Cam. Mis. Vol. 4 (C. Hopper) 1859
—— VIII. Calendars of Letters & Papers, Foreign & Domestic. Edited by J. S. Brewer

Vol. 1, 1509–14.   Vol. 2 (in two parts), 1515–18.
Vol. 3 (in two parts), 1519–23.

3 vols. 8vo. 1862–67
—— (J.) French Law as to Foreigners, with Appendix to Judgment of Demerara Court in Odwin *v.* Forbes (bound together) 8vo. 1823
Henshall (Saml.) & Wilkinson (J.) Doomsday Book for Kent, Surrey, Sussex 4to. 1799
Herand (J.) Legend of St. Loy, &c. . . . 8vo. 1820
—— Stamp Duties 12mo. 1824
Herapath's Railway & Commercial Journal, 1844–68 & continued . . . . 4to.
Herbert, Speech of Lord Chancellor Jeffries on his creating Lord Herbert Chief Justice. Vol. 2, Col. Jur. 1635

Herbert (*Lord* C. J.) Law in Sir Edward Hale's
 Case examined. L. T. 1688
—— (W.) Antiquities of Inns of Court . . 8vo. 1804
—— & Brayley (E.) History of Lambeth Palace
 4to. 1806
Herefordshire Election Poll Book, bound up with
 York 8vo. 1802
Herne (J.) on Conveyancing 8vo. 1656
——'s Pleader 4to. 1657
——'s Pleader & Clerk's Directory. . 2nd ed. 4to. 1658
Herodotus, translated by Rawlinson . 4 vols. 8vo. 1858
Herries' Peerage. Cases of the Maxwells. Vol. 2,
 3rd series (*see* Evidence, 1849–58, House of
 Lords Sessions Papers) 1848–52
Herrmannus (A.) Corpus Juris Civilis (Kriegellus)
 3 vols. 4to. 1844
Hersee (Wm.) Excise Board Orders, 1700–1827
 8vo. 1829
Hertfordshire (*see* Chauncey, H.)
—— Poll Books . . . . . 3 vols. 8vo. 1784–1826
Hertslet's Commercial Treaties . 11 vols. 8vo. 1840–64
—— (E.) Foreign Office List . 8vo. 1867 & continued
Hessey (J. A.) Account of Merchant Taylors'
 School 8vo. 1850
Hetley (*Sir* Thomas) C. P. Reports, 1628–31. folio 1657
Hewley (*Lady*) Charity Proceedings in Dissenters'
 Chapels Bill 8vo. 1844
—— Speech of C. P. Cooper. Vol. 3, L. T.
Heylyn (P., D.D.) Biography (Vernon) . 12mo. 1682
—— Help to English History . . 5 vols. 12mo.
Heywood (B. A.) Tour to the Antipodes through
 Victoria, Tasmania, New South Wales, Queens-
 land, & New Zealand in 1861–62 . . . 8vo. 1863
—— (S.) on Borough Elections 8vo. 1797
—— on County do . . . . . . 3rd ed. 8vo. 1812
—— (Thos.) Song of Lady Bessy. Lancashire
 County Tracts 1829
—— (L.) Glimpses at Origin, &c. of Man. 12mo. 1851

Hibernia. Inquisitionum in Officio Rotulorum Cancellariæ Hiberniæ asservatarum Repertorium (C. Hardiman) (*see* Record Commission)
2 vols. folio 1826-29
—— Rotulorum Patentium et Clausorum Cancellariæ Hiberniæ Calendarium, Hen. II.—Hen. VII. Vol. 1, Part 1 (*see* Record Commission). folio 1828
—— Reports on Public Records, 1810-28
3 vols. folio 1813-29, &c.
(*See* 18 and 19 Reports, 1828-29, bound up with 7th Report, Woods and Forests)
Hickesius (G.) Thesaurus Grammatico-Criticus et Archæologicus . . . . 2 vols. folio 1705
Higden (R.) Polychronicon of England (translated by Trevisa) 4to. 1577
Higges (J.) Justices' Guide 8vo. 1734
Higgins (J. H.) (*see* Ayckbourn)
—— (J. W.) on the Gold Companies & Costbook System, Vol. 9, Pam. 1853
Highgate & Hampstead Road Act . . . 12mo. 1734
——————————————— . . 12mo. 1821
Highmore (A.) on Bail 8vo. 1783
—— Charitable Uses 8vo. 1787
—— on Lunacy. 8vo. 1807
—— on Mortmain . . . . 2nd ed. 8vo. 1809
Highmore (A.) City Charities (Public) . . 8vo. 1814
Hill (A. S.) on Probate Court Practice . . 8vo. 1859
—— (F.) on Stannary Courts of Cornwall. Jac. L. T. Vol. 12 1835
—— (J.) on Trustees 8vo. 1845
—— (M. D.) Charge to the Jury as Recorder of Birmingham. Vol. 6, Pam. 1848
—— Do. do. on Connection between Disease & Crime. Vol. 9, Pam. 1854
Hilliard (F.) on Real Property, U.S.
3rd ed. 2 vols. 8vo. 1855
—— on Mortgage of Real & Personal Estate, U.S.
2nd ed. 2 vols. 8vo. 1856

Hilliard (F.) on Mortgage of Real & Personal
Estate, U.S. . . . . new ed. 8vo. 1867
—— on Torts . . . . 2 vols. 8vo. 1859
—— Sales of Personal Property. 2nd ed. . 8vo. 1860
Hinde (R.) Chancery Practice 8vo. 1785
Hinderwell (T.) History of Scarborough . 8vo. 1832
Hindmarsh (W. M.) on Patents 8vo. 1846
Hine (J.) Observations on Endowed Public Chari-
ties. Vol. 10, Pam. 1842
Hingeston (*Rev.* F. C.) (*see* Capgrave, No. 1, M. R.
Pub.) 1858
—— De illustribus Henricis (Capgrave). No. 7,
M. R. Pub. 1858
—— Royal, &c. Letters, temp. Hen. IV., No. 10,
M. R. Pub. 1860
Hinton (J. H,) History & Topography of North
America . . . . 2 vols. 4to. 1830
Historical, Genealogical, & Poetical Dictionary
12mo. 1703
—— Law Tracts . . . . 2 vols. 8vo. 1753
————————— . . . . 2nd ed. 8vo. 1761

  Containing:—
 1. Criminal Law
 2. Of Promises and Covenants
 3. Of Property
 4. Securities upon Land for Payment of Debt
 5. Of Privilege which an Heir-Apparent has to continue the
   Possession of his Ancestors
 6. Regalities and Privileges of Repledging
 7. Courts
 8. Brieves
 9. Process in Absence
 10. Execution against Moveables & Land for Payment of Debt
 11. Personal Execution for Payment of Debt
 12. Execution to obtain Payment after death of Debtor
 13. Limited & Universal Representative of Heirs
 14. Old and New Extent

—— Questions exhibited in 'Morning Chronicle,'
in January 1818. Vol. 1, Jac. Col.
—— Register (Sun Fire Office) 1714–35
22 vols. 8vo.

Hitch (C.) Universal Pocket Companion, containing List of Merchants . . . . 3rd ed. 8vo. 1760
—— London Guide . . . . . . 8th ed. 12mo. 1760
Hoare (*Sir* R. C.) (*see* Baldwin, *Abp.*)
—— (*see* Nichols, J. B.)
—— History of Modern Wilts. 4 vols . . folio 1822–26
Hobart (*Sir* H.) C. P. Reports . . . . folio 1641
———————————————— . . . 3rd ed. folio 1671
———————————————— 1613–44 4th ed. folio 1678
Hobbes (T.) Leviathan . . . . folio 1651
—— Tripos, Three Discourses. . . 3rd ed. 8vo. 1684
Hobler (F., Jun.) Exercises between an Attorney & Articled Clerk 12mo. 1831
———————————————————— 2nd ed. 12mo. 1838
—— Merchant's Manual 12mo. 1839
Hodges (*Sir* W.) C.P. Reports, 1835–37
3 vols. 8vo. 1836–39
—— on Railways 8vo. 1847
———————————— . . . . . . 2nd ed. 8vo. 1855
—— on Railways (C. M. Smith) . 3rd ed. 8vo. 1863
———————————————— . 4th ed. 8vo. 1865
Hodgkin (J.) on General Registry. Jac. L. T. Vol. 10 1829
Hodgson, (Christ.) Instructions to the Clergy
4th ed. 8vo. 1829
Hodgson (Christ.) Instructions to the Clergy
5th ed. 8vo. 1838
———————————————————— 8th ed. 8vo. 1860
—— (C.) Account of Queen Anne's Bounty, or Small Livings 8vo. 1826
———————————————— with Supplement, 2nd ed.
8vo. 1845–64
—— (H. J.) on Rating Railways . . . 12mo. 1851
—— (John) History of Northumberland (not complete, 6 parts). 4to. 1820–40
Hoffman (D.) Legal Studies . 2nd ed. 2 vols. 8vo. 1836
Hofmannus (J.) Lexicon Universale . 4 vols. folio 1698
Hogan (*Major*) Appeal to the Public . . 10th ed. 1809

Hogan (Wm.) Irish Rolls Report, temp. McMahon,
  1816–33 . . . . 2 vols. 8vo. 1828–33
Hoker (Jno.) Description of Exeter (*see* Vowell,
  Jno.) 4to. 1765
Holbourne (R.) on Statute of Treason . 12mo. 1781
—— (*Sir* R. O.) (*see* Tothill's Reports)
Holden (W.) London & Provincial Triennial
  Directory, 1805–8 . . . . . . 4 vols. 8vo.
Hole (C.) Brief Biographical Dictionary
                              2nd ed. 12mo. 1866
Holinshed (R.) Chronicles of England, Scotlande,
  & Irelande . . . . . . 3 vols. in 2, folio 1857
Holland (H. T.) & Chandless (T.) on Common
  Law Procedure Acts, 1852–54 . . . . 12mo. 1854
—— (T. E.) on Composition Deeds . . 12mo. 1864
Holliday (J.) Biography of Lord Mansfield . 4to. 1797
Holmes (J. H. H.) on Durham Coal Mines . 8vo. 1816
Holroyd (E.) on Patents 8vo. 1830
Holstein & Schleswig Question, Translation of
  Herr Raasloff's Reply. Vol. 14, Pam. . . . 1861
Holt (F. L.) N.P. Reports, 1815–17 . . 8vo. 1818
—— on Shipping . . . . 2 vols. 8vo. 1820
—— (John) Survey of Lancashire, Cheshire, Derby-
  shire, West Riding of Yorkshire, & part of Stafford
                                      8vo. 1797
—— (*Sir* John) K.B. Reports, 1688–1710 . folio 1738
—— (Wm.) on the Rule of the Road at Sea 8vo. 1867
Holthouse (H. J.) Law Dictionary . 2nd ed. 8vo. 1846
Home Office Library Catalogue 8vo. 1852
—— (H.) Principles of Equity . . 2 vols. 8vo. 1778
—— on British Antiquities . . . 3rd ed. 12mo. 1763
Homer's Iliad . . . . . . 2 vols. in 1, 8vo. 1839
—— Odyssey. Vol. 1, by S. Clarke . . 12mo. 1806
Homersham (S. C.) on Supply of Water. Vol. 7,
  Pam. 1850
Honduras Acts, 1765–1857 . . . . . folio
—— Acts, 1858–63 . . . . folio
Hone (W.) Three Trials 8vo. 1818

Honest Lawyer, Character of (*see* Lawyers) . . 1790
Hong Kong Laws, 1841–54 . . . . . . folio 1856
—— Acts, 1857–64 . . . . folio
—— Ordinances in Force, June 30, 1865 . 8vo. 1866
Honor, Laws of 8vo. 1726
Hook (*Dr.*) Sermon preached before the Queen, for which he was dismissed his Chaplaincy. Vol. 5, Pam.
—— (*Dr.* W. F.) Church Dictionary . 10th ed. 1867
Hooker (Rd.) Life & Works . . . . . folio 1666
—— (*Sir* W. J.) Description of Kew Gardens. 12mo. 1851
Hooper (*Bp.*) Works. Par. S. Pub. . 2 vols. 8vo. 1843
Hope (*Sir* T.) Scotch Law Praticks . . 12mo. 1726
Hopkins (M.) Handbook of Averages . 3rd ed. 1868
Hopper (C.) C. M. Vol. 4. No. 73; Vol. 5, No. 87
Hopwood (C. H.) & Philbrick (F. A.) C. B. Registration Cases, 1863–67 . . . . . . 8vo. 1868
Horatii, a Tragedy 1846
Horn, Admiralty Compendium 8vo. 1808
—— (H.) & Hurlstone (E. T.) Exchequer Reports, 1838–39 . . . . 8vo. 1840
Horne (Andw.) Mirror of Justice (French) . 8vo. 1642
——————————————————— 8vo. 1646
——————— Translation by W. H[ughes] 12mo. 1768
—— (T. H.) Admiralty Statute Law, to 8 George III. 12mo. 1768
——————————————————— 12mo. 1803
Horry (S. C.) on Licensed Victuallers . . 12mo. 1837
Horseman (G.) Conveyancing . . . 3 vols. folio 1744
——————————— 3rd ed. 2 vols. folio 1768
——————————— . . 3 vols. 8vo. 1785
Horses, Laws of 8vo. 1825
Horsfield (*Rev.* T. W.) & Mantel (G.) History of Lewes & its District 4to. 1824
—— History of Sussex . . . . . 2 vols. 8vo. 1835
Horwood (R.) Map of London, mounted, in three cases, marked West, Central, & East 1799
(A Second Copy, not mounted)

Hoskin's Observations on Reading Room at British
  Museum 8vo. 1858
Hosking (W.) Rebuilding Church of St. Mary
  Redcliffe (*see* Britton) 1842
Hotham (*Sir* B.) Biography of (*see* Lawyers) . . 1790
Houard (D.) Dictionnaire de la Coutume de Nor-
  mandie . . . . 4 vols. 4to. 1780
Houghton (T.) Complete Miner (Derby)
  2nd ed. 12mo. 1729
—— Complete Miner (*see* Barba)
—— Mineral Laws 12mo. 1734
House of Commons Cases & Bills
—— Fees of, Report of Committee on . . folio 1833
—— Journals, 1547–1864 . . . 121 vols. folio
—— Indexes . . . .
—— Manual of Practice 12mo. 1827
—— Reports & Index, 1715–1803 . 16 vols. folio 1803
—— Report of Committee on Private Bills & Evi-
  dence . . . . folio 1834
—— Sessions Papers, including Bills, Accounts, &
  Reports, 1745–1867 (*see* Parliament) . . folio
House of Lords Appeal Cases, 1700–1867. 254 vols.
  folio & 4to.
—— Calendars & Indexes, 1509–1863. 9 vols. folio
—— Journals, 1509–1867 . . . 98 vols. folio
—— Protests of the, 1641–1741 . . . . 8vo. 1745
—— Sessions Papers, including Bills, Accounts, &
  Reports, 1804–67 (*see* Parliament)
Housman (F.) Conveyancing 8vo. 1861
Houston (J.) on Stoppage in transitu . . 8vo. 1866
Hoveden (Magistri Rogeri de) Chronica. Edited by
  W. Stubbs, M.A. Vol. 1 (*see* M. R. Pub. No. 51)
Hovenden (J. E.) on Fraud 8vo. 1825
——————————— Supplement to Vesey (*see* Vesey)
Howard *v.* Gossett, Parliamentary Report of Com-
  mittee of House of Commons on Printed Papers
  folio 1844
—— (C.) Anecdotes of the Howard Family. 12mo. 1769

Howard (J. H.) Law of British Colonies in America
2 vols. 8vo. 1827
—— (P.) on the Earth & Mankind . . . 4to. 1797
—— Reports of Supreme Court, U.S. (*see* Curtis)
Howard de Walden: Peerage Case of C. A. Ellis,
   & others. 1st series
—— *Sir* J. G. Griffin. Evidence, Vol. 12, p. 1
Howell (J.) Cottoni Posthuma 12mo. 1679
    Containing :—

1. As to Proceedings against Ambassadors . . . 1679
2. Kings of England have consulted Parliament as to Marriage of their Children, &c. 1679
3. Sovereign's person required in State Councils . 1679
4. On the Legality of Combats, Duels, or Camp Fights . 1679
5. On the Question of Precedency between England & Spain 1679
6. On the Alliances between Austria & England . . 1679
7. As to Popish Recusants, Jesuits, & Seminaries . . 1679
8. How Kings of England have supported their Estate . 1679
9. Answer to Arguments of Members of House of Commons to prove that Ecclesiastical Laws ought to be enacted by Temporal Men 1679
10. Arguments by House of Commons in Conference with the Lords, on the Privilege of every Free-born Subject 1679
11. A Speech delivered in House of Commons, at Oxford, in First Year of King Charles I. 1679
12. Sir R. Cotton's Speech delivered before the Council Table on the Alteration of Coin 1679
—. The Danger wherein the Kingdom then stood, & the Remedy 1679
—. Valor Anatomised in a Fancy, by Sir Philip Sidney . 1581
14. On the Power of Parliament in point of Judicature
15. Sir Fras. Walsingham Anatomising of Honesty, Ambition, and Fortitude 1590

Howell (T. B.) State Trials, continued by, & Thos.
Jones Howell, 1163–1820, 9th Hen. II. to 1st
Geo. IV. . . . . 34 vols. 8vo. 1816–28
—— Index to do. (*see* Jardine)
Howgrave (F.) History of Stamford (Lincoln) 4to. 1726
Howlett (*Rev.* J.) Tracts, 1786–1801 . . 8vo.
    Containing :—

1. On Population of Ireland 1786
2. Influence Inclosures have on Population . . . 1786
3. Inclosures a Cause of Improved Agriculture . . 1786

M

Howlett (*Rev.* J.) Tracts—*continued*
 4. Insufficiency of the Causes to which Increase of Poor & Poor
   Rates have been attributed 1788
 5. Examination of Mr. Pitt's Speech in H. C. 12th Feb. relative
   to the Condition of the Poor 1786
 6. Dispersion of Gloomy Apprehensions on the Decline of the
   Corn Trade 1797
 7. Influence of Tithes upon Agriculture . . . 1801

Hubback (J.) on Succession to Real & Personal
 Property & Peerages 8vo. 1844
Hudson (Wm.) on the Star Chamber. Vol. 2,
 Coll. Jur. 1792
—— (W. E.) & Brooke (J.) Irish Common Law
 Reports, 1837–38 . . . . 8vo. 1839
Huet on the Dutch Trade (translated from the
 French) . . . . 2nd ed. 12mo. 1722
Hughes (Wm.) Report, Rex *v.* Bebb (Extent)
          8vo. 1811
—— on the Practice of Sales of Real Property
     2nd ed. 2 vols. 12mo. 1849
—— on the Stamp Act 12mo. 1850
—— on Conveyancing . . 2nd ed. 3 vols. 8vo. 1856
—— on the Practice of Conveyancing. 2 vols. 12mo. 1856
Hughson (*Dr.* D.) London & Neighbourhood to 30
 miles . . . . 6 vols. 8vo. 1806
—— Epitome of City Privileges. . . . 12mo. 1826
Hull Election Poll-Book 1774
Hullock (J.) on the Law of Costs 8vo. 1796
———————————————2nd ed. 2 vols. 8vo. 1819
Hulton (W. A.) on Convictions 8vo. 1835
Hume *v.* Pearson, Tithe Case 8vo. 1732
—— (D.) Essays . . . . 2 vols. 8vo. 1788
Hume (D.) History of England . . 6 vols. 8vo. 1820
—— (R. M.) on Chancery Delays & their Remedy.
 Vol. 8, Jac. L. T. 1830
Humphrey (J.) Real Property Code 1826
Humphry (W. W.) on General Registry. Vol. 10,
 Jac. Col. 1831

Hundredorum Rotuli, temp. Hen. III. & Edw. I.
(W. Illingworth) *see* Record Commission
        2 vols. folio 1812–18
Hunt (Wm.) Annuity Act 8vo. 1794
—————————————— . . . 2nd ed. 8vo. 1796
—— Collection of Cases & Practice of Registering Memorials
Hunter (*Rev.* J.) (*see* C. S. Pa. No. 22)
—— Hallamshire, History, & Topography of, Sheffield, Ecclesfield, Hansworth, Freeton, Whiston, & Chapelry of Bradfield. . . . . folio 1819
—— History & Topography of the Deanery of Doncaster . . . . 2 vols. folio 1828–31
—— Catalogue of the Red Book of the Exchequer, the Dodsworth MSS. in the Bodleian Library, & the MSS. in the Library of Lincoln's Inn. 8vo. 1838
—— Ecclesiastical Documents. C. S. Pa. No. 8 . 1840
—— Historical Defence of Lady Hewley's Charity Trustees. Vol. 1, L. T.
—— (S. J.) Suit in Equity 12mo. 1858
————————————— (Laurence)
        2nd ed. 12mo. 1862
————————————— . . . 3rd ed. 12mo. 1865
—— Property Law Amendment Act for the Relief of Trustees 12mo. 1859–60
Huntingdonshire Visitation (ed. Sir H. Ellis) 1613. C. S. P. No. 43 1840
Huntly Peerage, Case of George, Marquis of Huntly. Vol. 2, 2nd series
—— Evidence, Vol. 19, H. L. Sessions Papers, 1837–38, & Vol. 18, 1838
Hurd (P.) Report of Trial, Adams *v.* Malkin, whether an Attorney is liable to Bankruptcy Laws as a Scrivener 8vo. 1814
Hurlstone (E. T.) & Gordon (J.) Exchequer Reports, 1854–56 . . . . . . 2 vols. 8vo. 1854–56
—— & Norman (J. P.) Exchequer Reports, 1856–62 . . . . 7 vols. 8vo. 1857–62

Hurlstone (E. T.) & Coltman (F. J.) Exchequer
  Reports, 1862–65 . . . . . . 3 vols. 8vo. 1863–66
Husband & Wife, Law of 8vo. 1700
—— 's Interest in Wife's Estate, Real and Personal.
  Vol. 2, Col. Jur.
Hutchins (J.) (*see* Bawdwen) Domesday for Dorset
  folio 1815
—— History of Dorsetshire . . . 2 vols. folio 1774
—— & Antiquities. . . . 2nd ed. 4 vols. folio 1796
Hutchinson (*Bp.*) Works. Par. S. Pa. . . 8vo. 1841
—— (Wm.) View of Northumberland, with an
  Excursion to the Abbey of Mailross, Scotland
  4to. 1776
—— History of Durham . . . 3 vols. 4to. 1785–87
—— History of Cumberland . . . 2 vols. 4to. 1794
Hutton (*Dr.* C.) Compendious Measurer. . 12mo. 1700
—— (*Sir* Rd.) C. P. Reports, 1616–28 . . folio 1632
—— (Wm.) History of Birmingham . . . 8vo. 1781
—— History of Derby from the Remote Ages to
  1791 . . . . 2nd ed. 8vo. 1817
—— Description of Blackpool, 1826–41 (bound
  up with Thornber) . . . . . 3rd ed. 8vo. 1817
—— on the Court of Requests, with a Memoir.
  L. T. Vol. 7 1840
Huxley (Geo.) Second Book of Judgments (Towns-
  end) 4to. 1674
Hyde (E.) Indian Succession Act 8vo. 1865
H. (F.) Laws of Jamaica 8vo. 1683
H. (J.) Conveyancer's Light . . . 3rd ed. 4to. 1671
H. (*Sir* R.) The Young Clerk's Guide. 6th ed. 12mo. 1663

I

Ibbotson (R. W.) Legal Prompter . . . 12mo. 1860
Illingworth (C.) History of Scampton, Lincolnshire
               4to. 1810
—— (W.) on Forestalling 8vo. 1800
—— the Public Records of the Four Courts at
 Westminster 8vo. 1831
Illustrated London News . . . . . folio 1859–68
—— London Times, 185
Illustrious Dead, who died in 1711–12, Lives &
 Characters . . . . 2 vols. 8vo. 1713
Impeachment of Lords . . . . folio 1701
   Viz. :—
 1. Impeachment of Lords Wm. Earl of Portland, John Lord Somers, Edwd. Earl of Oxford, Charles Lord Halifax
 2. Speeches against Repealing Triennial Act
 3. Do. of Lord Cowper on Judgment against Earl Derwentwater, & others
 4. Commons' Proceedings as to Impeached Lords Portland, & others
 5. Trial of Sir John Friend, 1695–96
 6. Lords' Protests, 1722–23

Imperial British Calendar, 1814–50, 35 vols. 8vo.
Impey (Jno.) New Instructor Clericalis, or K.B.
 Practice & Office of Sheriff 8vo. 1782
——————————————————— 2nd ed. 2 vols. 8vo. 1788
————————————————————————— 6th ed. 8vo. 1796
————————————————————————— 7th ed. 8vo. 1807
————————————————————————— 8th ed. 8vo. 1813
————————————————————————— 9th ed. 8vo. 1818
————————————————————————— 10th ed. 8vo. 1823
————————————————————————————— 8vo. 1828
——————————————————— or C.P. Practice
              3rd ed. 8vo. 1790
————————————————————————— 4th ed. 8vo. 1794
————————————————————————— 5th ed. 8vo. 1812

Impey (Jno.) New Instructor Clericalis, or C.P.
Practice . . . . 6th ed. 8vo. 1817
———————————————————— 7th ed. 8vo. 1826
—— Modern Pleader 8vo. 1794
————————————————— . . . 2nd ed. 8vo. 1814
—— Practice of the Office of Sheriff & Coroner
3rd ed. 8vo. 1812
—— Stamp Laws 8vo. 1823
—— (T.) (*see* Antrobus)
—— (W. J.) K. B. & C. P. Practice, Questions
8vo. 1825
—— on Mandamus 8vo. 1826
Ince (H. B.) Trustee Acts 12mo. 1858
Inchiquin Peerage Case. Vol. 2, 3rd series . 4to. 1861
Income-Tax Act, Observations on
Incorporated Law Society, Reports of, 1825–65
3 vols. 8vo.
—— Observations on Proposed Concentration of
Courts of Justice. Vol. 10, Pam. 1859
Inderwick on Divorce Rules & Orders . 12mo. 1862
—— (F. A.) on the Law of Wills 8vo. 1866
India, a President in Council the best Government
for. Vol. 19, Pam. 1858
—— Army & Civil Service List 1866 & continued
12mo.
—— History (*see* Robertson's Works)
—— Memorandum of Improvements in Administration of, during the last Thirty Years. Vol. 10,
Pam. 1858
—— Reform, No. 4, The Native States of India.
Vol. 9, Pam.
—— Register 12mo. 1801
—— Report of General Meeting of Scinde Railway Company, held April. Vol. 19, Pam. . . 1862
Indian Mutiny, Report of the Committee of the
Fund for Relief of the Sufferers by 1858
—— Penal Code, prepared by Indian Law Commissioners 8vo. 1851

Inglewood Forest, Lease of (*see* Portland *Duke of*)
Ingram (T. D.) on Compensation 8vo. 1864
———————————————— . 2nd ed. 8vo. 1869
Ings (E.) on Abolition of Arrest . . . 12mo. 1840
Inland Navigation in Lancashire 8vo. 1766
Innes (J.) Summary of Scotch Law . . . 8vo. 1733
Innocent VIII. Bull of Pope, on Marriage of Henry
  VII. with Elizabeth of York, No. 39, C. M. Vol. 1,
  (J. P. Collier) 1847
Inns of Court, Reports of Commissioners, & Evidence . . . . folio 1834
—— Historical Memoranda 8vo. 1859
Inquisitiones Nonarum temp. Edwd. III. . folio 1807
Inquisitionum post mortem, sive Escaetarum Calendarium; temp. Reg. Hen. III. ad Ric. III.;
  cum Appendice a regno Hen. III.—Jac. I.
  (J. Caley). (*see* Record Commission)
                              4 vols. folio 1806-28
—— ad quod damnum Cal. Joh. &c. Hen. VI.
  (ed. J. Caley) (bound up with Charter Rolls,
  1307-1409) . . . . folio 1803
Institutiones, or Grounds of Law . . . 12mo. 1556
International Council, Observations on the Feasibility of Forming, to Adjust Disputes, & Prevent
  War (by a Solicitor). Vol. 14, Pam. . . . 1855
Investors' Manual. Vol. 7 1868
Inwood (Wm.) Estate Tables . . 7th ed. 12mo. 1837
Ipswich, Charities to 8vo. 1747
—— Poll Book, 1754-80. . . . . 8vo.
Ireland. Calendar of State Papers, 1509-1585.
  Ed. by H. C. Hamilton . 2 vols. imp. 8vo. 1860-67
—— Celtic Records of, Analysis of Dr. Donovan's
  Edition of the Annals of the Four Masters. 8vo. 1852
—— Corporation, Boundaries of . . . . folio 1836
—— Correspondence relating to, temp. Hen. VIII.
  (*see* State Papers, Vols. 2, 3)
—— Lord Stewardship of, Case of Earl of Shrewsbury & Waterford claiming Office of. Vol. 2,
  3rd series

Ireland (S.) Inns of Court of London & Westminster
8vo. 1800
—— (*Sir* Thos.) Abridgement of Coke's Reports
12mo. 1666
—— (W. H.) History of Kent . 4 vols. 8vo. 1828–30
Irish Chancery, Fees in Schedule
—————————— Orders in
—— Circuit Cases, 1841–43 . . . . . . 8vo. 1843
—— Common Law Digest (Archer) . . . 8vo. 1842
—— Common Law Report . . 2 vols. 8vo. 1867–68
—— Common Law Reports, N. S. 1850–66
16 vols. 8vo.
—— Compendium of Peerage, 1st, 2nd, 3rd, 5th ed.
5 vols. 12mo. 1725–56
—— Equity Reports . . . . 2 vols. 8vo. 1867–68
—— Fenians :——
Trial of Sullivan & Pigott
———— Halpin
———— Luby
———— Warren
(And *see* Ball)
—— Law Reports, Q. B. C. P. & Exchqr. 1838–50
13 vols. 8vo.
—— Narrative. No. 14, C. S. Pa. 1641–90 (T. C. Croker) 4to. 1841
Irish Pamphlets :——
Barry (M.) on the Legal Calculating & Division of Time 1842
Beasley (T. J.) Lectures relative to the Profession of
Attorney & Solicitor 1841
—— on Irish Records 1842
Brady (T.) on Medical Jurisprudence . . . 8vo. 1834
Ferguson (J. F.) Remarks on the Limitations of Actions
Irish Bill 8vo. 1843
Lascelles (R.) Ultimate Remedy for Ireland . . . 1831
Molyneux (E.) Introductory Lecture on Equity . . 1831
Napier (J.) Lecture on the Study of the Common Law . 1839
—— Parliamentary Register, 1781–97
17 vols. 8vo.
—— Poor, Letter to Lord Howick, Senior
—— Railway Atlas . . . . folio 1838
—— Railway Plans . . . . folio 1837

Irish Railway Sections . . . . folio 1837
—— Records, Index to, prepared by Messrs. King
folio 1832
———————————————————— Beasley
—— Reports in Equity, 1838–50 . 12 vols. 8vo.
—— Reports in Chancery, 1850–66, 16 vols. 8vo.
—— Salmon Question, socially, economically, &
commercially considered by a Naturalist & an
Epicure. Vol. 19, Pam. 1863
—— Society in Ulster, Report of Deputation &
Report of Committee respecting their Charter
8vo. 1815
—— Society in Ulster, Concise view of the Origin,
&c. of . . . . . . 2 vols. 8vo. 1822–32
—— Society in Ulster, Reports of Deputations
from Grocers' Company's Estates in Londonderry
8vo. 1827–29
—— Statutes, 1310–1761 . . . . . 8 vols. folio 1765
——————— 1310–1800 . 12 vols. 8vo. 1794–1801
——————— . . . . . 20 vols. folio. 1781–1801
——————— Index to . . . . . 2 vols. 8vo. 1818
Irving (*Dr.* D.) Introduction to Study of Civil Law
4th ed. 8vo. 1837.
Isambert (François André) Recueil général des
anciennes Loix françaises, depuis l'an 420
jusqu'à la Révolution de 1789; avec notes de con-
cordance et table, par MM. Jourdan, De Crusy,
Armet et Taillandier . . . 29 vols. 8vo. 1822–33
Isleworth, Zion's Peace 4to. 1800
Islington Cattle Market, Proposed 1850
—— Institution, Mr. Sudlow's Inaugural Address.
Vol. 5, Pam. 1837
Italian Law :—
Civil Code of Italy 8vo. 1865
Florence, Decisioni, Annali di Giurisprudenza,
Toscana e Lucca, 1860–65 . . 6 vols. 8vo.
Raccolta di Manifesti, 1814–60 . . 57 vols. 8vo.
—— Ufficiale delle Legge e Decreti, 1861–67
20 vols. 8vo.

Italian Law—*continued.*
Raccolta Ufficiale delle Legge e Decreti, Supplement, 1867 . . . . . . 7 vols. 8vo.
Sentenze della Corte di Cassazione, 1860-64
           5 vols. 4to.
Sicilia, Atti del Governo della Luogotenenza Generale, 1860–62 . . . . . . 8vo. 1862
Zappala, Leggi, Trattati 8vo. 1862–63
Italian Relation or Account of England, 1500, No. 37, C. S. Pa. (C. A. Sneyd) 1846
Italy, Kingdom of, Official Catalogue of, at Great Exhibition 8vo. 1862
Ivory (Wm.) Catalogue of Law Books in Signet Library, Edinburgh 8vo. 1856
Izacke (R.) History of Exeter (S. Izacke)
          3rd ed. 8vo. 1734
———————————— & Devon Charities
(Saml. Izacke) 8vo. 1736

J

Jackson (G. T.) Remarks on Reports of Commissioners on Registration of Title, 1857. Vol. 23, Pam.
Jacob (*Rev.* A.) Peerage (English) 2 vols. folio 1766–67
—— (E.) History of Town & Port of Faversham
          8vo. 1774
—— Reports (Chancery) 1821, 1822 . . . 8vo. 1823
—— & Walker (J.) Chancery Reports, 1819–21
         2 vols. 8vo. 1821–23
—— (G.) Court Keeper . . . . 4th ed. 8vo. 1663
————————————— . . . . 3rd ed. 8vo. 1724
————————————— . . . . 6th ed. 8vo. 1764
————————————— . . . . 7th ed. 8vo. 1781
————————————— by a Barrister. 8th ed. 8vo. 1819
—— Law Dictionary . . . . . 4th ed. folio 1739

Jacob (G.) Law Dictionary (Ruffhead & Morgan)
10th ed. folio 1782
—— Lex Mercatoria 8vo. 1718
—— City of London Liberties 8vo. 1732
—— Common Law common-placed. 2nd ed. folio 1733
—— Parish Officer . . . . . 13th ed. 12mo. 1734
—— Table of Public Acts, Magna Car. to Geo. II.
5th ed. 8vo. 1748
—— Every Man His Own Lawyer. 10th ed. 8vo. 1788
Jagoe (J.) Equity Digest . . . . 2 vols. 8vo. 1851
Jamaica, Acts & History 12mo. 1683
—— Acts of Assembly . . . . . 2 vols. folio 1698
———————————— . . . . folio 1756
———————————— . . 1681–1788. 2 vols. folio 1787
———————————— . . . . . . 2 vols. 4to. 1789
—— Courts of Criminal Justice (by a Solicitor) 8vo. 1855
—— Laws, 1857–1866–67 . . . 13 parts 4to.
—— Slave Laws 8vo. 1828
James I. Calendar of State Papers, Domestic
Series. Ed. by M. A. E. Green.
    Vol. 1, 1603–1610.   Vol. 3, 1619–1623.
    Vol. 2, 1611–1618.   Vol. 4, 1623–1625.
4 vols. imp. 8vo. 1857–59
—— a Book of Proclamations published since the
beginning of his reign until 1609 . . . folio
—— II. (*see* Life in Macpherson's Original Papers
as to Great Britain) 1776
—— as to his Succession. Discourse on the Monarchy (*see* Monarchy)
—— & Charles II. Secret Services of. No. 52,
C. S. Pa. 1679–88 (ed. J. Y. Akerman) . . . 1851
—— VI. & Elizabeth, Letters. No. 46, C. S. Pa.
1582–90 (ed. J. Bruce) 1849
—— Correspondence with Sir Robert Cecil. No. 78,
C. S. Pa. (ed. J. Bruce) 1861
James (*Col. Sir* Henry) Facsimile of Domesday
Book for Cornwall . . . . folio 1861
—— (J.) What should be the Price of Bread?
Vol. 10, Pam. 1855

James (J. H.) on Redeeming Property Mortgaged
 to Building & Land Societies 12mo. 1854
—— (T. H.) Handy Book on Merchant Shipping
           12mo. 1866
—— on Salvage 8vo. 1867
—— (W. A.) Registration Guide . . . 12mo. 1855
—— County Voters' Manual 12mo. 1855
Jamieson (*Dr.* John) Etymological Scotch Dictionary 8vo. 1867
Jane (*Queen*) & Queen Mary, Chronicles of, 1553–
 54. No. 48, C. S. Pa. (ed. J. G. Nichols) . . 1849
Jani Anglorum Facies Nova (by Attwood) . 12mo. 1680
Jansson (J.) General Atlas . . . . 6 vols. folio 1656
Jardine (D.) General Index to Howell's State Trials
            8vo. 1828
—— Reading on Use of Torture 8vo. 1837
Jarman (H.) New Chancery Practice . . 12mo. 1853
———————————————— 3rd ed. 12mo. 1864
—— (T.) Conveyancing (*see* Bythewood)
—— (Thos.) on Wills . . . . . 2 vols. 8vo. 1844
———————————— (Wolstenholme & Vincent)
      2nd ed. 2 vols. 8vo. 1855
———————————— 3rd ed. 2 vols. 8vo. 1861
Jay (Wm.) Recollections of 8vo. 1859
Jeake (S.) Charter to Cinque Ports . . . folio 1728
Jebb (R.) Irish Crown Cases Reserved, 1822–40
            8vo. 1841
—— Report of Dr. Hampden, Case in K. B. &c.
            8vo. 1849
—— & Symes (A. R.) Irish Common Law Reports,
 1838–41 . . . . 2 vols. 8vo. 1840–42
—— & Bourke (R.) Irish Common Law Reports,
 1841–42 . . . . 8vo. 1843
Jeffcott (J. M.) Statute Laws of the Isle of
 Man, since the year 1832 (continued by J. Gell)
            8vo. 1837
Jefferies (*Lord Chancellor*) Biography of (*see* Roscoe's Lives of Eminent British Lawyers)

Jefferies (*Lord Chancellor*) Speech on creating Sir
E. Herbert Lord C. J. of K. B., Oct. 23, 1685.
Vol. 2, Col. Jur.
Jefferson (S.) History of Carlisle 4to. 1838
Jefferys (C.) (*see* T. Chitty on Pleading)
Jemmett (W. T.) Equity Acts 12mo. 1830
———————————————— . . 2nd ed. 12mo. 1836
Jenkins (A.) History of Exeter 8vo. 1806
——— (*Judge*) Remonstrance to Parliament by. 4to. 1647
——— on English Law and Liberty of the Subject
12mo. 1648
——— Exchequer Reports (eight centuries) 1220–
1623 . . . . folio 1734
Jenner (*Sir* H.) Judgment in Panton *v*. Williams
(supposed Forged Will Case). Vol. 1, Pam. . 1840
Jennings & Heckford, Costs 8vo. 1836
Jerdan (W.) (*see* C. S. Pa. Nos. 21, 33)
Jerden (Wm.) on Plan for Encouraging Authors.
Vol. 3 Pam. 1839
Jeremy (G.) on Equity Jurisprudence . . 8vo. 1828
——— (H.) Digest . . . . . . 6 vols. 8vo. 1838–54
Jerningham (F.) on Steam Communication to
Colonies. Vol. 6, Pam. 1848
Jersey. An Authentic Narrative of the Oppression
of the Islanders, & History of Military Actions,
Constitutions & Laws, &c. of the Island. 2 v. 8vo. 1771
Jervis (*Sir* John) (*see* Archbold)
——— on Coroners 8vo. 1829
——————————— (W. N. Welsby). 2nd ed. 12mo. 1854
——————————— (C. W. Lovesy). 3rd ed. 12mo. 1866
——— Regulæ Generales . . . . 4th ed. 8vo. 1839
——— Criminal Acts (Glen) . . . 2nd ed. 12mo. 1861
Jesuits, Three Letters from, L. T. 1688–89
——— College at Clerkenwell, Discovery of. No. 55,
C. M. Vol. 2 (ed J. G. Nichols) 1852
——— College, Supplemental Note to the Discovery
of it in 1627–28. No. 73, C. M. S. P. (ed. J. G.
Nichols) 1859

Jevons (W. S.) Pure Logic 12mo. 1864
Jewel's (*Bp.*) Letters, 1st & 2nd series (Zurich)
  Par. S. Pa. . . . . 2 vols. 8vo. 1842–45
—— Writings of . . . 4 vols. 8vo. 1845, 7, 8, 1850
Jewish Emancipation, Progress of, since 1829.
  Vol. 6, Pam. 1848
—— History (*see* Blunt)
Jewitt (A.) History of Buxton, & Visitor's Guide
  to the Peak, &c. 4to. 1811
John Bull Newspaper, 1821 to 1841. 17 vols. folio
Johnes (A. J.) on Chancery Reform . . . 8vo. 1834
—— Remarks on the Report of the Committee
  on the Bankruptcy Bill in a Letter to Lord
  Brougham. Vol. 27, Pam. 1866
Johnson (H.) New York Chancery Reports, 1816–
  24 . . . . 7 vols. 8vo.
—— (H. R. V.) Reports (V.-C. Wood) 1858–60
                                      8vo. 1860
—— & Hemmings (G. W.) Reports, 1859–62
                             2 vols. 8vo. 1861–64
—— (J.) View of the Jurisprudence of the Isle of
  Man, with the History of its Ancient Constitution
  &c. 8vo. 1811
—— (*Dr.* Samuel) Dictionary (*Rev.* H. J. Todd)
                             3 vols. 4to. 1827
—— Works . . . . 2nd ed. folio 1713
—————— Oxford edition . . . . 11 vols. 8vo. 1825
Johnston (A.) London Directory 8vo. 1818
—— (A. K.) General Gazetteer . 2nd ed. 8vo. 1855
—— (*Col.*) Trial 8vo. 1811
—— (L. F. C.) (*see* Asso & Manuel)
Johnstone (*Rev.* J.) Anecdotes of Olave, the
  Black, King of Man (*see* Grimaldi Tracts)
—— Canon Law of English Church, 610–1519
  (Burn). . . . . 2 vols. 8vo. 1850
Joint Stock Banking, Report of Committee, House
  of Commons, & Evidence, 1836 (*see* Admiralty
  Courts Report)

Joint Stock Banking, A Few Words on. Vol. 5,
Pam. 1836
—— Stock Companies' Directory 8vo. 1866
Jollie (F.) Cumberland Guide & Directory . 8vo. 1811
Jones' Attorneys' Pocket Book. 2nd ed. 2 vols. 8vo. 1798
———————————————— (Coventry)
6th ed. 2 vols. 8vo. 1826
—— (C. J.) on the Collection & Recovery of
Tithe Rent-Charge. 8vo. 1849
—— (E. C.) C. P. Canada Reports, 1848-61
11 vols. 8vo. 1861
—— (Edwd.) Index to Records called the Originalia & Memoranda . . . . . 2 vols. folio 1793-95
—— (F. R.) Two Letters, containing Proposals
to Settle the Question whether Tenant Right
Owners can be disturbed in Possession. Vol. 23,
Pam. 1861
—— (Inigo) History of Stonehenge, Dr. Charleton's
Reflections, & Mr. Webb's Vindication in Answer to Dr. C. . . . . folio 1725
—— (*Dr.* J.) Law of Libel 8vo. 1812
—— History of Wales 8vo. 1824
—— (J. W.) Translation of Greek, Latin, Italian,
& French Quotations occurring in Blackstone's
Commentaries. 8vo. 1823
—— (*Serjt.*) Letter to Lord Chelmsford on Exchequer Judgment, Furber *v.* Sturmey. Vol. 10,
Pam. 1859
—— (T.) on Government (*see* Libel Tracts, Vol. 2) 1785
—— History of Brecknockshire . . 2 vols. 4to. 1795
—— & Latouche (E. D.) Irish Chancery Reports,
temp. Sugden, 1844-46 . . . 3 vols. 8vo. 1846-49
—— (Thos.) Irish Exchequer Reports, 1834-38
2 vols. 8vo. 1838-47
—— & Carey (H.) Irish Exchequer Reports,
1838-39 . . . . 8vo. n. d.
—— (*Sir* T.) K. B. Reports, 1670-85
2nd ed. folio 1729

Jones (T. E.) Account of a Public Testimonial Dinner to John Britton. Vol. 16, Pam. 1846
—— (W.) Speeches of Isæus as to Succession to Property at Athens 4to. 1779
Jones (W.) on Insolvent Debtors Act. Vol. 5, Jac. L. T. 1827
—— (*Sir* Wm.) Biography of (*see* Roscoe's Lives of Eminent British Lawyers)
—— K. B. Reports, 1620–41 . . . . . folio 1678
—— on Bailments 8vo. 1781
———————— (Nicholls) . . 3rd ed. 8vo. 1823
———————— (Theobald) . . 4th ed. 8vo. 1833
—— Hindoo Laws 8vo. 1796
—— (W. H.) on Uses 12mo. 1862
Joyce (S.) Remarks on the County Courts Act, 9 & 10 Vict. c. 95, & Suggesting Amendments. Vol. 20, Pam. 1850
——————————————— & Suggestions for Amendment. Vol. 27, Pam. 1860
Judges' Assize Expenses on Western & Oxford Circuits, 1596-1601 (ed. W. D. Cooper). No. 73 C. S. P., C. M. Vol. 2 . . . . . . 4to. 1858
—— Expenses on Circuit in 1707, from 'Legal Observer,' Dec. 20, 1838. L.T. Vol. 7
—— Chambers. Debate on presenting a Petition to House of Commons, August 1832. Vol. 3, Pam.
—— and Officers at Westminster (*see* Attorneys, List of)
Judicature in Parliament, Treatise MSS. . folio n. d.
Junior United Service Club Rules, 1835 . 12mo.
Junius (F.) Etymologicum Anglicanum (E. Lye) folio 1743
Juries, Debate on Mr. Fox's Bill as to Functions of, in Libel Cases (*see* Law Libel Tracts, Vol. 4)
—— Duty of, & Doctrine of Libels (*see* Law of Libel Tracts, Vol. 4) 1752
—— Grand, or Securities for Men's Lives, 12mo. 1681

Juries, Guide to 12mo. 1682
—— Power of 8vo. 1729
    Containing :—
1. Enquiry into Power of, on Trials for Libel (*see* Libel Law T. Vol. 2) 1792
2. Considerations on Matter of Libel, suggested by Mr. Fox's Notice to Parliament, by J. Leach, Esq. (*see* Libel Law Tr. Vol. 2, 2nd ed.)
3. Dr. Tower's Observations on Rights, &c. of Juries, & Remarks on Law of Libel (*see* Libel Law Tr. Vol. 2) . 1784
4. Discussions on the Law of Libel (*see* Libel Law Tr. Vol. 2) 1785

—— on Libel, Enquiry into Extent of (*see* Libel Law Tr. Vol. 2)
—— Proceedings in Parliament occasioned by Lord Mansfield's Direction to Juries in Libel Cases. (*see* Libel Law Tr. Vol. 3)
Jurisprudence, Elements of Lectures . . . 4to. 1783
Jurist, The . . . . 1839-54 ⎫
—— New Series . . 1855-66 ⎬ 60 vols. 4to. 1839–66
Juris Utriusque Tractatus Varii 4to. 1512
Justice of the Peace, The complete . . 12mo. 1642
———————————— Country (E.W.) 12mo. 1661
———————————————————— 12mo. 1668
———————————— Case Law . . . 8vo. 1731
———————————— 31 vols. 4to. 1837–67
Justinian, Corpus Juris Civilis . . . 2 vols. 8vo. 1681
————————————————— 8vo. 1700
Justiniani Quinquaginta Decisiones, bound up with Mohedan's Linglois . . . . folio 1661
—— Institutiones (R. Eden) 4to. 1744
———————— (G. Harris) . . . 3rd ed. 4to. 1811
———————— (D. A. & D. M. Kriegelii) 8vo. 1 vol. in 3 1833–44
———————— with English introduction, translation, & notes by T. C. Sandars . . 3rd ed. 8vo. 1865
—— Institutiones, Roman Law . . 2 vols. folio 1782
—— Institutiones 12mo. 1670
—— Institutiones Juris Civilis cum Annotationibus S. Aldobrandini (F. Cornellus) . . . 4to. 1580

Justinien, Explication Historique des Instituts par
M. Ortolan . . . . . 7th ed. 3 vols. 8vo. 1863
Juvenalis et Persius, in usum Delphini . . 4to. 1684
J. C. Collection of Writs. . . . 2nd ed. folio 1687

K

Kain (J.) on Solicitors' Book Keeping. 7th ed. 12mo. 1864
——————————————————— 8th ed. 12mo. 1864
—— on Single & Double Entry 12mo. 1864
Katchenovsky, Prize Law, by Dr. C. F. Pratt. 8vo. 1867
Kay (E. C.) Reports (V.-C. Wood) 1853–54 . 8vo. 1854
—— & Johnson (H. R.) Reports (V.-C. Wood)
1854–58 . . . . 4 vols. 8vo. 1855–59
Keane (D.) Nuisances Removal . . 5th ed. 8vo. 1866
—— (D. D.) & Grant (J.) Registration Cases in
C. P. 8vo. 1854
Kearsley (G.) Peerage . . 7 vols. 12mo. 1778–1809
—— Tax Tables 12mo. 1808–22
Keble (J.) K. B. Reports, 1661–71 . 2 vols. folio 1685
—— (*Rev.* Jno.) Sermons 8vo. 1847
—— (Josh.) Statutes at Large, from Mag. Car.
to 32 Car. II., 1224–1681 . . . . folio 1681
Keen (B.) Chancery Reports (Rolls), temp. Langdale, 1836–39 . . . . . . 2 vols. 8vo. 1837–39
Keessel (D. G. Van Der) on the Laws of Holland &
Zetland; being a Commentary on Hugo Grotius'
Introduction to Dutch Jurisprudence, translated
from the Latin by C. A. Lorenz, with Biographical Notices of the Author, by J. de Wai
2nd ed. 8vo. 1868
Keilway (R.) K. B. Reports, 1496–1574. . folio 1688

Kelham (R.) Domesday Illustrated . . . 8vo. 1788
———— Norman, or old French, Dictionary
8vo. 1779
Kellie Peerage, no case. Evidence. Vol. 3, 1834;
Vol. 9, 1832–35
Kelly (*Dr.* B.) Biography of Dolland. 3rd ed. 4to. 1808
—— Universal Cambist, or Commercial Instructor
2nd edit. 2 vols. in 1, 4to. 1821
—— (J. B.) on Annuities 8vo. 1835
—— on Usury 8vo. 1835
——'s P. O. Directories:—
Bath, *see* Gloucestershire, 1856
Bedfordshire, *see* Berks, 1854
—— *see* Northamptonshire, 1854
Berkshire, Bedfordshire, Oxfordshire . . 8vo. 1854
—— *see* Northamptonshire, 1864
Birmingham, Warwickshire 8vo. 1860
———, Staffordshire, Warwickshire . . . 8vo. 1864
———. 8vo. 1865
—— and its Suburbs 8vo. 1867
—— Staffordshire, Warwickshire, Worcestershire 1868
Bristol, *see* Gloucestershire, 1856–63
—— *see* Somersetshire, 1861–66
Buckinghamshire, *see* Berkshire, 1864
—— *see* Northamptonshire, 1864
Cambridgeshire, Suffolk 8vo. 1858
———, Leicestershire, Derbyshire, Rutlandshire,
Suffolk 8vo. 1864
——— 8vo. 1865
Cheshire 8vo. 1857
——— 8vo. 1864
Cornwall, *see* Devonshire, 1856
Cumberland, *see* Westmoreland, 1858
Derbyshire 8vo. 1856
———————— Leicestershire, Nottinghamshire,
Rutlandshire
—— *see* Cambridgeshire, 1864
Devonshire and Cornwall 8vo. 1856

Kelly's P. O. Directories—*continued.*
Dorsetshire, *see* Hampshire, 1859
——— 8vo. 1867
Durham, *see* Westmoreland, 1858
Essex, *see* Home Counties
Gloucestershire, Bath, Bristol, Shropshire. 8vo. 1856
——————————————————— 8vo. 1863
Hampshire 1854
——— Dorsetshire, Wiltshire 8vo. 1859
Hardware District, *see* Birmingham, 1865
Herefordshire, *see* Gloucestershire, 1856
——— 8vo. 1863
Hertfordshire, *see* Home Counties
Home Counties (Essex, Herts, Kent, Surrey, Sussex) 8vo. 1845
——————————— 8vo. 1855
——————————— 8vo. 1859
——————————— 8vo. 1862
——————————— 8vo. 1866
Hull 8vo. 1857
——— *see* Lincolnshire, 1861
Huntingdonshire, *see* Berks, 1854
——— *see* Northamptonshire, 1864
Isle of Wight, *see* Dorset, 1867
Kent, *see* Home Counties
Lancashire 8vo. 1858
——— Liverpool 8vo. 1864
Leicestershire, *see* Derbyshire, 1855
——— *see* Cambridgeshire, 1864
Lincolnshire, Hull 8vo. 1861
Liverpool, *see* Lancashire, 1864
London, *see* Post Office
Norfolk, *see* Cambridgeshire, 1858-65
Northamptonshire, *see* Berks, 1854
——— Bedfordshire, Berkshire, Buckinghamshire, Huntingdonshire, Oxfordshire . . . 8vo. 1864
Northumberland, *see* Westmoreland, 1858
Nottinghamshire, *see* Derbyshire, 1855

Kelly's P. O. Directories—*continued*.
  Nottinghamshire, *see* Cambridgeshire, 1864
  Oxfordshire, *see* Berks, 1854
  —— *see* Northamptonshire, 1864
  Rutlandshire, *see* Derbyshire, 1855
  —— *see* Cambridgeshire, 1864
  Salford Hundred, *see* Lancashire, 1864
  Sheffield, *see* Birmingham, 1864
  Shropshire, *see* Gloucestershire, 1856
  —— 1863
  Somersetshire 8vo. 1861
  —— 8vo. 1866
  Staffordshire, *see* Birmingham, 1864
  Suburban 1860–63–65–68
  Suffolk, *see* Cambridgeshire, 1858–65
  Surrey, *see* Home Counties
  Sussex, *see* Home Counties
  Warwickshire *see* Birmingham, 1860–64
  West Derby Hundred, *see* Lancashire, 1864
  Westmoreland, Cumberland, Durham, Northumberland 8vo. 1858
  Wiltshire, *see* Hampshire, 1859
  Worcestershire, *see* Birmingham, 1860
  Yorkshire, W., N. & E. Ridings . . . 8vo. 1857
  —— W. Riding & York City 8vo. 1861
  ——————————————— 8vo. 1867
  —— Directory Guide 8vo. 1862
  ——————————— Maps . . . . . . 1845 & 1867
  —— European Directory 1866
Kelynge (*Sir* J.) Crown Cases, temp. Car. II.
                                        folio 1708
—— (*Lord* Wm.) Chancery Reports, 1730–35
                                        folio 1764
Kemble (J. M.) (*see* C. S. Pa. Nos. 45, 65)
—— Historical Society, Codex Diplomaticus. 8vo. 1829
Kemp (W.) Nine Days' Wonder. No. 11 C.
  S. Pa. 1600 (*Rev.* A. Dyce) 1839
Kempher (G.) Rei Venaticæ Scriptores . . 4to. 1728

Kendall (J.) on Bankruptcy & Insolvency 12mo. 1849
——————————————————— 2nd ed. 1850
Kennedy (C. K.) Address to the Mutual Law
  Association. Vol. 21, Pam. 1852
—— (C. R.) on Parliamentary Privilege of H. C.
  Pam. on Par. Priv. 1840
—— Letter to the Lord Chancellor on Revising
  Barristers. Vol. 4, Pam. . . . . n. d.
—— (L.) & Granger (T. B.), Agricultural Customs
  of Counties 8vo. 1828
—— (T.) Orders & Statutes in Chancery
  2 vols. 8vo. 1843–45
—— Practice in Chancery. . . 2 vols. 12mo. 1845–53
—— Orders & Statutes in Chancery. 2 vols. 8vo. 1850-52
—— (Wm.) Annals of Aberdeen . . 2 vols. 4to. 1818
Kennett (*Bp.*) Antiquities of Ambrosden & Bur-
  cester, Oxon & Bucks 4to. 1695
———————————— (B. Bandinel) 2 vols. 4to. 1818
—— Family History of the Dukes of Cavendish. 8vo. 1708
—— (Basil) Antiquities of Rome . 13th ed. 8vo. 1763
Kent Gaol Delivery, 1788, MSS. . . . . folio 1790
—— Papers relating to Proceedings in, 1642–46.
  No. 61, C. M. Vol. 3 (ed. R. Almack) . . . 1854
——————————————————— 1640, No.
  80, C. S. P. (ed. Rev. L. B. Larking & J. Bruce) 1862
—— Poll Books, 1734–1826 . . . 8 vols. 8vo.
—— (Chancellor) Commentaries on American Law,
  U.S. . . . . 3rd ed. 4 vols. 8vo. 1836
——————————————————— 10th ed. 4 vols. 8vo. 1859
——————————————————— 11th ed. 4 vols. 8vo. 1866
—— International Law (Abdy) 8vo. 1866
—— (Hen.) Directory (London) 1766–1826
  7 vols. 8vo.
Kenyon (*Lord*) Notes (Hanmer, J. W.) 1753–59
  2 vols. 8vo. 1819–25
—— Biography of (*see* Lawyers) 1790
Kerr (R. M.) Action at Law . 2nd edit. 12mo. 1857
——————————————— (P. Smith) 3rd edit. 12mo. 1861

Kerr (W. W.) on Injunctions 8vo. 1867
—— on Fraud & Mistake 8vo. 1868
Keyzer (Hen.) on the Law, &c. of the Stock
    Exchange 12mo. 1850
Killeen Peerage—no case. Return of Act relating
    to, of 27 Hen. 6. Vol. 12, Evidence
Kilmorey Peerage. Claim of Viscount Kilmorey
    to vote. Vol. 2, 3rd series; Evidence, Vol. 18. 1812–13
Kimbell (Jno.) Account of Gifts to Greenwich
    Parish 4to. 1816
Kimber (E.) Peerage. 1st & 2nd ed. 2 vols. 8vo. 1766–69
—— Scotch Peerage 12mo. 1767
—— Irish Peerage 12mo. 1768
—— & Johnson (R.) Baronetage . . 3 vols. 8vo. 1771
Kime (W. T.) Practical Hints on Common Law
    Proceedings 12mo. 1848
King, The, Enquiry, Do we owe him Allegiance,
    are bound to treat with & call him back? L.
    T. 1688–89
—— (*Abp.*) On the Origin of Evil
              1st vol. 2nd ed. 8vo. 1732
—— (*Sir* J.) Biography 12mo. 1855
King's Bench Prison (*see* Chiuso)
—— College Hospital Report, Vol. 7, Pam. . . 1849
—————————————— Vol. 14, Pam. . . 1861
Kingston (*Duchess*) Opinion of Monsieur Target
    on Case on her Will. Vol. 1, Col. Jur.
Kinnear (J. B.) Scotch Bankruptcy Laws
                   2nd edit. 8vo. 1862
—— Digest of House of Lords' Scotch Cases,
    1700–1864 . . . . 8vo. 1865
Kippis (*Dr.* A.) Biographia Britannica, 1778–93
              2nd ed. 5 vols. folio
Kirby (Jno.) Suffolk: Traveller from a Survey in
    1732–34 . . . . 2nd ed. 8vo. 1764
Kirwan (A. J.) (*see* Carrington, F. A.)
Kitchen (Jno.) on Courts Leet, &c. . . 12mo. 1585
——————————————————— . . 12mo. 1607

Kitchen (Jno.) on Courts Leet, &c. 4th ed. 12mo. 1663
———————————————— (Antrobus & Impey)
5th ed. 12mo. 1675
Knapp (J. W.) P. C. Reports, 1829–36
3 vols. 8vo. 1831–36
—— (J. W. & E.) Omler Election Cases, 1834–35
8vo. 1837
Knights Hospitallers in England, 1338. No. 65,
C. S. Pa. (ed. Rev. L. B. Larking). 1857
Knipe (J. A.) Map of British Isles & part of France 1844
Knox (James) County Maps of Scotland . folio 1822
—— (Jno.) Biography of (in Buchanan's History
of Church of Scotland) 4to. 1644
Koe (J. H.) & Miller (S.) on Bankruptcy
2nd ed. 3 vols. 8vo. 1844–45
Kyd (S.) on Corporations . . . 2 vols. 8vo. 1793
—— on Awards . . . . 2nd ed. 8vo. 1799
Kyteler (*Dame Alice*) Proceedings against, 1324.
No. 24, C. S. Pa. (ed. T. Wright). 1843

L

Labatt (H. J.) California Practice Act . . 8vo. 1858
Labouring Population, General Report of Great
Britain on Sanitary Condition 8vo. 1842
—— Local Report, E. & W. 8vo. 1842
—— Scotland 8vo. 1842
La Croix on European Constitutions . 2 vols. 8vo. 1792
Laidman (J.) on Bankruptcy, &c. Letter to Lord
Chancellor. Vol. 6, Pam. 1847
Laird's Rutlandshire, History & Antiquities of. 8vo. 1818

Lake (*Dr.* Edwd.) Chaplain & Tutor to the Princesses Mary & Anne, 1677–78, Diary of.
No. 39, C. M. Vol. 1 (ed. G. P. Elliott) . . 1846
—— (*Sir* E.) interviews with Car. I. No. 73, C. M.
4 (ed. T. P. Langmead) 1858
—— (*Sir* Thos. W.) Letters of the Council to, as to Sir Edward Coke's proceedings at Oatlands.
No. 87, C. M. Vol. 5 (S. R. Gardiner) . . . 1864
Lamb (J.) (*see* Master, *Rev.* R.)
—— (Jno.) Translation of Aratus, with notes . 8vo. 1849
Lambard (W.) Perambulation of Kent . . 4to. 1596
—— Justice of the Peace 4to. 1619
Lambert (B.) History & Survey of London & its Environs . . . . 4 vols. 8vo. 1806
Lambeth Palace, Cat. of MSS. Registers, &c. at folio 1812
—— St. Mary, Act for Watching, &c. . 12mo. 1820
Lamothe (J. C.) Statute Laws of the Isle of Man, 1853–61 . . . . 8vo. 1862
Lampadius de Republicâ Romano-Germanicâ 4to. 1671
Lancashire, Agricultural Survey of, & of Cheshire, extracted from History of Manchester . . 8vo. 1797
—— County Tracts . . . . 8vo.
  Containing :—

  1. Siege of Lathom House 1823
  2. Hutton's Description of Blackpool . . 3rd ed. 1817
  3. Johnson's Cobler of Preston . . . 2nd ed. 1716
  4. Happiness of Retirement & Encomium of the Town of Preston 1733
  5. Butler's Tale, the Mayor of Wigan 1759
  6: Law's Poem, scene the Vale of Todmorden . . 1772
  7. Heywood's Song of Lady Bessey 1829

Lancaster, Account of 8vo. 1867
—— Charters of the Duchy of 8vo. 1845
—— Rules of C. P. at . . . 2 vols. 12mo. 1831–32
—— & Cheshire. History of Inland Navigation of 8vo. 1766
—— Plot 8vo. 1696

Lancaster, Statement of Facts in support of Petition of Inhabitants of Liverpool to adjourn Assizes to Liverpool & Manchester. Vol. 20, Pam. . . 1833
Lancastriæ Ducatus. Vol. 1, Part 1, Calendarium Inquisitionum post mortem, Edwd. I. to Chas. I. Part 2, Calendar to the Pleadings, Hen. VII. to P. & M. . . . . folio 1823
———————— Vol. 2, Part 3, Calendar to Pleadings, Hen. VII. to 13 Eliz. . . . folio 1827
———————— Vol. 3, Part 4, 14 Eliz. to 45 Eliz. (*see* Record Commission) . . . folio 1834
Lancellott (J. P.) Institutiones Juris Canonici. 4to. 1606
Lancet's Report of Inquest on case of Cæsarean Operation. Vol. 3, Pam. 1833
Land Bills, address to Landed Gentry of England. Vol. 11, Pam. 1859
—— Equalisation, statement by Committee of Rolls Liberty. Vol. 9, Pam. 1853
—— Purchasers' Companion 12mo. 1733
—— Tax Assessment, its Inequality, &c. Vol. 8, Pam. 1852
Landowners, a few words to, on Bill for registering of, by a Barrister. Vol. 11, Pam. . . 2nd ed. 1857
Lane (R.) Exchequer Reports, 1605–12 . . folio 1657
—— (T.) Students' Guide through Lincoln's Inn 12mo. 1805
Langdale (*Lord*) Speech of, on second reading of Bill for Better Administration of Justice in Chancery. Vol. 1, Chancery Pam.; Vol. 11, Jac. Col. 1836
—— (Thos.) Dictionary of Yorkshire . . 8vo. 1809
Langley (A. G.) on the Trustees' Relief Act. 12mo. 1860
—— (Thos.) History of Desborough Hundred, Bucks, & of Wycombe Deanery, Marlow, & 16 Parishes 4to. 1797
Langmead (T. P.) Vol. 4, C. M. No. 73
Lankester (*Dr.*) (*see* Social Science)
—— Journal of Social Science Association & Sessions Papers . . . . . . 2 vols. 8vo. 1865–66

Lansdowne MSS. Catalogue in the British Museum
folio 1819
Larking (*Rev.* L. B.) & Kemble (J. M.) (*see* C. S.
Pa. Nos. 65, 80)
Lascelles (R.) (*see* Irish Pamphlets)
Lassere (L.) L'Art de procéder en Justice civile
que Criminelle 4to. 1677
Latch (J.) K. B. Reports, 1625–28 . . . folio 1661
Latham (F. L.) on Window Lights . . 12mo. 1867
Lathom House, Siege of (*see* Lancashire Co.
Tracts and Thornber's Description of Blackpool)
Lathrop (T.) (*see* Angell & Ames)
——————————— & Durfee)
Latimer's Works, Sermons, & Remains. Par. Soc.
Pa. 1844–45
Lauderdale Peerage, Case of James Earl of Lauder-
dale . . . . 1st series
Laurie (James) Interest Tables 8vo. 1836
Lavoisne's General Atlas . . . . 3rd edit. folio 1822
Law Advertiser & Index, 1823–30 . 8 vols. 4to. 1823–30
—— Amendment Society, Further Report of Com-
mittee on Equity & Masters' Offices. Vol. 17,
Pam. 1849
—— Amendment Society, 2nd Report on the Bar,
the Attorney, & the Client. Vol. 20, Pam. . .
—— Amendment Society, 5th Annual Report of
the Council. Vol. 20, Pam. 1848
—— Amendment Society. Address from Council
read at General Meeting, Nov. 12. Vol. 20, Pam. 1860
—— Amendment Society, Paper of Mr. Serjeant
Woolrych, on Opening Biddings in Chancery,
read at General Meeting, Jan. 14. Vol. 20, Pam. 1861
—— Amendment Society, Paper of Mr. Edgar on
proposed Amendments in Law as to Procedure,
&c. on Criminal Trials, Jan. 28. Vol. 20, Pam. 1861
—— Amendment Society, Paper of J. P. Taylor
on Expediency of passing an Act permitting
Defendants in Criminal Courts, their Wives, &c.,
to testify on Oath. Vol. 20, Pam. 1861

Law Amendment Society, Paper of Mr. A. Edgar and Mr. W. Hawes as Observations on Bankruptcy & Insolvency Bill. Vol. 20, Pam. . . 1861
—— Amendment Society, Report, 18th Annual, for Session 1860–61
—— Amendment Society, European Convention respecting Domicile, Paper of Mr. Serjeant Woolrych. Vol. 20, Pam. 1863
—— Amendment Society, Report of Special Committee on Convict Discipline. Vol. 20, Pam. 1863
—— Amendment Society, Mr. Serjeant Burke's Paper on Literature & Fine Arts. Vol. 20, Pam. 1863
—— Amendment Society, Dr. A. Waddilove's Paper on Sale of Benefices in connection with Augmentation of Benefices Bill. Vol. 20, Pam. 1863
Law Chronicle, 1813–24 . . . . 12 vols. folio
—— Clerks' Society's Rules 12mo. 1832
—— Courts & New Houses of Parliament, Extracts of Evidence as to removal of former. Vol. 9, Pam. 1853
—— Directory (The London) 12mo. 1848
—— A Discourse on the (Enchiridion Legum) 12mo. 1673
—— of East India Company (*see* East India Company)
—— Essay on the 12mo. 1750
—— Expense of Suits, & Plan for a Remedy. Vol. 1, Col. Jur.
Law Journal Digest, 1825, no Ed. . . . 4to.
—— 1828–31, Ed. W. Chambers 4to. 1835
—— 1831–35, Ed. J. Greenwood 4to. 1838
—— 1835–40, Ed. F. T. Streeten & E. W. Cameron 4to. 1843
—— 1840–45, Ed. F. T. Streeten & T. D. Archibald 4to. 1847
—— 1845–50, Ed. F. T. Streeten & J. H. Hodgson 4to. 1852

Law Journal Digest, 1850–55, Ed. F. T. Streeten
  & G. S. Allnut 4to. 1857
—— 1856–60, Ditto ditto 4to. 1863
—— 1860–65, Ed. F. T. Streeten & E. A. Hadley
  4to. 1868
—— Journal, with Digests, 1823–68. 95 vols. 4to.
———— Acts of Parliament, 1866–68. 3 vols. 4to.
———— Legal News, 1866–68 . folio & 4to. 1866–68
———— List of Bankrupts, 1836–40 . . 4to.
———— Notes of Cases, 1866–68. 3 vols. 4to. 1866–68
———— & Bankrupt List.
———— Tracts, published 1825–26. . . 4to.
  Containing:—

1. On Claim of Executors to Residue
2. On Title to Lands derived through Inclosure Acts
3. On Soundness of Certain Points as to Executory Limitations
4. On Mortgage of Tolls under Turnpike Acts
5. As to whether Executors can make Conveyance without concurrence of Heir-at-Law
6. On Executors' Remedies for recovering Rent, particularly under 32 Hen. VIII. c. 37
7. Analysis of Preston's Essay on Estates
8. Cases collected where Trustees take the Legal Estate

(And *see* Tracts.)

—— List of Attorneys & Fees of Officers. folio 1729–30
———————————————— Additional. folio 1731
—— List, Scotch, 1848–67 . . . 10 vols. 8vo.
—— List, Stamp Office, 1798–1869. 72 vols. 8vo.
—— Magazine, 1828–56 . . . . 55 vols. 8vo.
—— & Review, 1856–68 & continued 25 vols. 8vo.
—— Monthly, 1831–41 . . . . 10 vols. 8vo.
—— Pratick, or Compleat Attorney & Solicitor
  12mo. 1676
———————————————— 3rd edit. 8vo. 1702
—— Quibbles . . . . 2d ed. 8vo. 1726
———————— . . . . .4th ed. 8vo. 1736
—— Reflections or Hints on the (*see* also
  Simpson) 8vo. 1759

Law Reports (whole Series of Council of):—
Scotch Appeals, H. L. . . . . . . 2 vols. 8vo.
House of Lords, E. & I. 1866–68 . 3 vols. 8vo.
Privy Council . . . 1865–67 . 2 vols. 8vo.
Chancery Appeals . 1866–67 . 3 vols. 8vo.
Equity Law Reports 1866–68 . 6 vols. 8vo.
Queen's Bench . . 1866–68 . 3 vols. 8vo.
Common Pleas . . 1866–68 . 3 vols. 8vo.
Exchequer . . . . 1866–68 . 3 vols. 8vo.
 Probate & Divorce Court 1865–68
            1 vol. 8vo.
 Admiralty & Ecclesiastical 1865–68
            2 vols. 8vo.
 Weekly Notes of Cases, 1866–68 3 vols. 4to.
Law Review, 1844–56 . . . . 22 vols. 8vo.
Law Times, 1846–68. (1st 6 vols. wanting)
            39 vols. folio
Law Times Reports, New Series, 1859–68
            19 vols. 8vo.
—————— Index to 1st 10 vols. 1859–64 8vo. 1865
—— Writers, Report of Meeting of, on Lord Cranworth's New Order abolishing Old Charge by folio. Vol. 20, Pam. 1854
—— (J. T.) Ecclesiastical Statutes at Large
           5 vols. 8vo. 1847
—— (Saml.), Poem. Lancashire County. Tr.
Law (S. D.) Copyright & Patent Laws U. S., 1790–1868 . . . . 8vo. 1868
—— (T. P.) Report of Trial Reg. v. Sullivan & Pigott, Irish Fenians 8vo. 1868
—— (W. J., Mr. Commr.) on Insolvent Debtors' Law & Practice 8vo. 1843
Law's Proposal for constituting a Council of Trade for Scotland 12mo. 1751
Lawes (*Mr. Serjt.* E.) Suggestions for Alterations of the Law on Practice, Pleading, &c. No. 9 Jac. Col. 1827
—— (E.) on Charter Parties 8vo. 1813

Lawes (E.) The Declaration on Bills of Exchange,
Promissory Notes, &c. explained . . 12mo. 1842
Lawrence (E.) Letter to Lord Chancellor on Bankruptcy Law Reform. Vol. 10, Pam. 1859
—— (F.) on Common Law Procedure Act. 8vo. 1852
Lawson (*Dr.* Jno.) Lectures on Oratory . 8vo. 1759
Lawton (G.) Bona Notabilia of York Diocese. 12mo. 1825
Lawyer, Life of, written by himself . . . 8vo. 1830
Lawyers, Eminent, Biography of 8vo. 1790

   Containing :—

Lord Thurlow	Sir J. Heath
Earl Mansfield	Sir J. Wilson
Earl Camden	Sir J. Eyre
Earl Bathurst	Sir B. Hotham
Sir R. P. Arden	Sir R. Perryn
Lord Kenyon	Sir A. Thompson
Sir F. Buller	Sir A. Macdonald
Sir N. Grose	Sir John Scott
Sir W. H. Ashurst	Mr. Anstruther
Lord Loughborough	An Honest Lawyer
Sir H. Gould	

Lawyers' & Magistrates' Magazine. 6 vols. 8vo. 1790–94
Laxton (W.) Builders' Price Book, with Cases
under Metropolitan Building Act . . 12mo. 1869
Leach (Thos.) on Libel (*see* Libel L. T. Vol. 2)
—— Crown Cases, 1730–88 . . . . . 8vo. 1789
———————— 1730–1800 . . . 2 vols. 8vo. 1800
Leahy, Report of Judgment in O'Connell *v.* Regina
8vo. 1844
Leake (S. M.) (*see* Bullen, E.)
—— on Contracts 8vo. 1867
Le Beau, Code des Prises . . 3 vols. 4to. 1798–1800
Le Bland, Military Engineer 8vo. 1759
Le Cras (A. J.) The Laws, Customs, & Privileges, & their Administration in the Island of
Jersey, with Notices of Guernsey, &c. . 8vo. 1839
Lectures, &c. (Ireland) (*see* Ireland)
Ledwich (Edw.) Antiquities of Ireland . . 4to. 1790
—— Account of Aghaboe, Queen's County. 8vo. 1796

Lee (*Sir* G.) Ecclesiastical Reports, 1752–58
          2 vols. 8vo. 1833
—— (J. Y.) on Abstracts of Title . . . 8vo. 1843
—— (R.) on Captures in War . . 2nd ed. 8vo. 1803
—— (S.) Southwark Court of Requests, Commissioners' Address to. London Tr. 1819
—— (T.) Dictionary of Practice . 2 vols. 8vo. 1811–12
———————————————— 2nd ed. 2 vols. 8vo. 1825
—— Cases (temp. Hardwicke) K. B. & Chy. 1733–1836 . . . . 8vo. 1815
Leech (*Dr.*) Suggestions on the Law of Lunacy & Lunatic Asylums. Vol. 9, Pam. Pt. 2. 2nd ed. 1852
Leeds to Liverpool, Plan of proposed Canal. 4to. 1770
Leeds. Official Catalogue of Works of Art exhibited at 12mo. 1868
Leeming (H.) & Cross (R. A.) Quarter Sessions Practice 8vo. 1858
Lees (J.) on Shipping. . . . . . 9th ed. 8vo. 1865
Lefroy (J. E. P.) (*see* Carrow, J. M.)
Legal Antiquities, Writ of Protection to a Common Attorney in K. B. 1 Ric. L. T. Vol. 7
—— Bill of Costs in 1608. L. T. Vol. 7
—— Discontent, Thoughts on State & Prospects of. Vol. 15, Pam. 1860
—— Education, Report of Parliamentary Committees . . . . folio 1846
—— Practitioners, Thoughts on Condition of. Vol. 3, L. T. 1834
—— Recreations, by a Barrister . . . . 8vo.
Legibus, Liber de Antiquis, 1178–1274 (London Chronicles) No. 34, C. S. Pa. (T. Stapleton)
            4to. 1845
Legislation, Essays on the Spirit of . . . 8vo. 1772
Legulean Magazine, 1850–51 . . . . 2 vols. 8vo.
———————————— Questions & Answers, 1850–62
           2 vols. 8vo.
Leicester, Charter of Corporation of (MSS. Edw. I. & Jas. II.) & Records . . . . folio

Leicester Earldom, Case of P. A. Sidney. Vol. 2, 3rd series
—— Poll Book, 1768–1826 . . . 3 vols. 8vo.
—— Square Soup Kitchen, 1st Report: Plea for the Poor 8vo. 1850
Leigh Peerage: Case of G. Leigh. Vol. 2, 2nd series
—— Evidence. Vol. 4
—— . . . . 2 vols. 8vo. 1832
—— (Chas.) Natural History of Lancashire, Cheshire, & the Peak in Derbyshire . . . folio 1700
—— (E. C.) & Cave (L. W.) Crown Cases Reserved 1861–65 . . . . 8vo. 1865
—— (P. B.) on the Game Laws . . . 12mo. 1831
—— on Poor Laws. 8vo. 1838
Leland (J.) de Rebus Britannicis Collectanea (Hearne) . . . . 4 vols. 8vo. 1715
———————————— Appendix 2 vols. 8vo. 1715
—— Itinerary . . . . . 8 vols. in 5, 8vo. 1745
Le Marchant (Thos.) Remarques et Animadversions sur l'Approbation des Lois et Coustumier de Normandie (Reprint), History of Guernsey, 2 vols. in 1 . . . . 8vo. 1826
Lemon (Robert) Calendar of State Papers, Domestic Series, of the Reigns of Edward VI., Mary, and Elizabeth, preserved in Her Majesty's Public Record Office. Vol. 1, 1547–80; Vol. 2, 1581–90 . . . . . . Impl. 8vo. 1856–65
(Continued by Greene (M. A. E.)
Lemprière (Dr. J.) Classical Dictionary. 20th ed. 8vo. 1844
Leng (Robert) Memorable Service of Sir F. Drake against the Spaniards, A.D. 1587, (C. Hopper) No. 87, C. S. Pa. C. M. Vol. 5 1863
Lennox Dukedom, Case of J. Earl of Darnley. Vol. 2, 3rd series
Leonard (Wm.) K. B. Reports, 1582–1615, 1675 folio 1658
———————————— (W. Hughes) 2nd ed. 4 vols. in 2, folio 1687

Le Riche (E. W.) on Taxation of Costs . 12mo. 1859
—— on Bills of Costs 12mo. 1860
Le Sage, Gil Blas de Santillane (Histoire)
        3 vols. 12mo. 1787
—— Genealogical, &c. Atlas of Royal Families of
Europe. . . . . folio 1801
Leunclavius (J.) Juris Græco-Romani tam Canonici quam Civilis, Tomi duo. Curâ Marquardi
Freheri . . . . folio. 1596
Levi (Leone) International Commercial Law
       2nd ed. 2 vols. 8vo. 1863
Levinz (*Sir* C.) Entries . . . . folio 1702
—— Reports . . . . 2 vols. folio 1702
————— 1660–96. 2nd ed. 3 vols in 2, folio 1722
Lewin (F. A.) The Law of Apportionment. 12mo. 1869
Lewin (*Sir* G) Crown Cases, 1822–38
       2 vols. 12mo. 1834–39
—— (Thos.) on Trusts 8vo. 1837
————————————— . . . . . 2nd ed. 8vo. 1842
————————————— . . . . . 3rd ed. 8vo. 1857
————————————— . . . . . 4th ed. 8vo. 1864
————————————— . . . . . 5th ed. 8vo. 1867
Lewis (C. E.) Election Manual 12mo. 1865
—— (F. A.) Letter to Lord Brougham on Pseudo
Lawyers. Vol. 20, Pam. 1851
—— (H.) on Conveyancing. 8vo. 1863
—— Equity Drafting. 8vo. 1865
—— (J.) Faversham, History of Abbey & Church.
           4to. 1827
—— (John) Thanet, Isle of, History & Antiquities of . . . . 2nd ed. folio 1736
—— Statement on the delays in the Registrar's
Office of the Court of Chancery. Vol. 17,
Pam. 1860
—— (P.) Historical Enquiries into the state of the
New Forest, with Map 4to. 1811
—— (Saml.) Topographical Dictionary of England, with Atlas . . . . 5 vols. 4to. 1831

Lewis (T.) Sheriffs' Court of London Practice. 8vo. 1833
—— (T. T.) (see C. S. Pa. No. 58)
—— (W. D.) Can Remainders be too Remote?
Vol. 23, Pam. 1841
—— on Perpetuities, & Supplement . . 8vo. 1842–49
—— on the Profession of the Law. Vol. 3, Pam. 1845
Lex Custumaria (see Carter, S.) 8vo. 1696
—— Parliamentaria (G. Petyt). . 2nd ed. 8vo. 1690
Ley (Sir J.) K. B. Reports, 1619–29. . . folio 1659
Leycester (Sir P.) History of Cheshire . . folio 1673
—— Correspondence, 1585–86, during his Government of the Low Countries. No. 27, C. S. Pa. (J. Bruce) 1844
Libel, Tracts on the Law of (see Tracts)
—— Debate on Mr. Fox's Bill for removing doubts as to functions of Juries in Libel Cases. Vol. 3, (see Libel Law Tracts, Vol. 4)
—— Doctrine of, or State Law on Defamation (see Libel L. T. Vol. 4)
—— Doctrine of, & Duty of Juries, 1752. Libel L. T. Vol. 1
—— Grand Jurymen's Oaths & Office explained. Libel L. T. Vol. 1
—— Law, Summary of, 1771. Vol. 1, Libel L. T. Vol. 1
—— Letter concerning General Warrants, seizure, &c. of papers. Libel L. T. Vol. 1 . 17th ed.
—— Parliamentary Proceedings occasioned by Lord Mansfield's Judgment in Rex v. Woodfall, in 1770. Libel L. T. Vol. 3
—— Protest of the Lords in Wilkes' Case. Libel L. T. Vol. 1
—— Speech of Mr. Erskine for a new Trial in Dean of St. Asaph's Libel Case. Libel L. T. Vol. 3
Libellous & Immoral Publications, Chancery Practice as to. Libel L. T. Vol. 1
Liberty of the Press, on Personal Slander. Libel L. T. Vol. 1

Liddell (H. G.) & Scott (Robt.) Greek & English
   Lexicon . . . . 5th ed. 4to. 1861
Lilly (J.) Practical Register, Chancery & Com-
   mon Law . . . . 2 vols. folio 1719
—— Entries . . . . folio 1723
———————————— . . . . 2nd ed. folio 1741
———————————— . . . . . . 5th ed. 2 vols. 8vo. 1791
—— Conveyancer . . . . . . 3rd ed. folio 1742
Lincoln (*Bishop of*) on Gunpowder Treason, man-
   ner of Discovering 8vo. 1679
Lincoln's Inn Library Catalogue . . . 8vo. 1835
———————————————— of Ancient French
   Law Books 8vo. 1849
————————————— MSS. in (*see* Hunter)
————————————— MSS. there . . . 8vo. 1838
————————————— Return from, to Record Com-
   mission 8vo. 1801
————————————— Spanish Law, presented by
   C. P. Cooper, Esq., to Lincoln's Inn . . 8vo. 1847
Lincolnshire Rebellion, Chronicle of, in 1470. No.
   39, C. M. (ed. J. G. Nichols) 1846
Lincy (M. Le Roux de) Blonde of Oxford & Jehan
   of Dammartin: a Romance by P. de Reimes.
   No. 72, C. S. Pa. 1858
Lindenbrogius (F.) Codex Legum Antiquarum. folio 1614
Lindley (N.) on Partnership, & Addenda. 3 vols. 8vo. 1860

                        2nd ed. 2 vols. 8vo. 1867
Lindsay (R.) Etymology of Southwark. 3rd ed. 8vo. 1839
—— (*Lord*) Report on Claim of Lord Crawford
   to Montrose Dukedom . . . . . . folio 1855
Lingard (J.) History of England . 13 vols. 12mo. 1837
Linglois (P. F.) Quinquaginta Decisiones Justi-
   nianæ (bound up with Mohedan) . . . folio 1661
Lipscombe (G.) History & Antiquities of Buck-
   inghamshire 4to. 1831
Literary Fund, Summary of Facts. Vol. 11,
   Pam. 1858

Literary Men, Letters of Eminent. No. 23, C. S.
Pa. 1549–1799
—— Property Case in H. L. 4to. 1774
Littledale (W. E.) on the Origin & Progress of
the Society of King's Inn, Dublin. Vol. 14,
Pam.
Littleton (*Sir* Edw.) Tenures 12mo. 1577
——————————————— . . . 12mo. 1600
—— Tenures in French & English . . 12mo. 1671
—— C. P. Reports, 1626–32 . . . . . folio 1683
—— (H. A.) & Blatchley (J. S.) Digest of Fire
Insurance Decisions in G. B. & N. A. 2nd ed.
by S. G. Clarke 8vo. 1868
Liturgies, Catechism, &c. temp. King Edwd. VI.
Par. S. Pa. 1844
—— Catechism, Queen Eliz. do. 1847
Liturgy, New Protestant, 1688–89, L. T. . . . 1689
Liverpool, Catalogue of Athenæum Library. 8vo. 1820
—— Law Society, Remarks of, as to Registering
Titles of Landed Estates. Vol. 11, Pam. . . 1859
Livingstone (J.) Law Register, U.S. . . 8vo. 1860
Livornier (C. P.) Traité des Fiefs . 5th ed. 4to. 1771
Llorenté (J.) Leyes del Fuero Juzgo, 6 Recopila-
cion de las Leyes de los Wisigodos españoles. 4to. 1792
Lloyd (B. C.) & Goold (F.) Irish Chancery Re-
ports, temp. Plunket 1834–36 . . . . 8vo. 1839
———————————————————— temp.
Sugden, 1845 . . . . 8vo. 1845
—— (D.) State Worthies . . . . . . folio 1668
Lloyd (E.) on Trade Marks 12mo. 1862
—— on Compensation 8vo. 1867
—— (J. H.) & Welsby (W. N.) Commercial
Cases, 1829–30 . . . . 8vo. 1830
—— (R.) Costs, Bills in K.B. & C.P. . . 8vo. 1818
———————————— in Parliament, Chancery &
Exchequer 8vo. 1820
Loan Societies, Instructions to establish (bound up
with Stocks) 8vo. 1837

Local & Personal Acts, 1798–1867. 238 vols. folio
—— Courts Bill, Lord Brougham's, Estimate of,
  by an Observer. Vol. 7, Jac. Col. 1830
—— Taxation Report Poor Law Commissioners
  8vo. 1844
Locke (Edwd.) Customs of the Manor of Taunton
  Deane 12mo. 1826
—— (John) on the Understanding. 4th ed. folio 1700
—— Works . . . . 10 vols. 8vo. 1823
—— on City and Foreign Attachment . 12mo. 1853
—— on the Game Laws. . . . . 4th ed. 12mo. 1856
———————————— (G. Evans) 5th ed. 12mo. 1866
Loder (Robt.) Statutes & Ordinances of Seck-
  ford's Almshouses at Woodbridge, Suffolk 4to. 1792
——————————————————— 2nd ed. 1811
—— & Hawes (R.) History of Framlingham,
  Suffolk 4to. 1798
Lodge (E.) Peerage & Baronetage, 1843–61, &
  1863–65–68 . . . . 5 vols. 8vo.
—— (*Rev.* J.) History of Herefordshire . 8vo. 1793
—— (John) Irish Peerage . . . 4 vols. 8vo. 1754
——————————— (M. Archdall) 7 vols. 8vo. 1789
Loft (C.) K. B. Reports, 1771–74 . . . . folio 1776
London (*see* Stillingfleet's Ecclesiastical Law for
  Antiquities of) 1696
—— Almanac 8vo. 1841
—— Bishop of, Letter to, preparatory to Visitation
  in 1846, on Cases of Rees, Sealey, & Harvey.
  Vol. 5, Pam. 1846
—— Bishop of, Proceedings against, before
  Ecclesiastical Commissioners in 1686. L. T.
  1688–89
—— Bridge, Chronicles of, by an Antiquary. 8vo. 1827
—— Conduct of the Corporation of . . . 8vo. 1823
—— Proceedings as to, 1799–1819 . . . folio
—— Charities of (Endowed) 8vo. 1829
—— Charters of 12mo. 1679
—— Chronicle No. 28, C. S. P. (G. P. Aungier) . 1844

LAW SOCIETY LIBRARY. 199

London, City & Sheriffs' Court Practice. . 8vo. 1657
—— City Companies (*see* Maitland's London)
—— Corporation, Catalogue of Library . . 8vo. 1828
————————————————————— . 8vo. 1859
————————————————— Supplements. 8vo. 1860–67
————————————————————— Prints there. 8vo. 1868
————————————————— Works of Art there. 8vo. 1867
————————————————————————— 1868
—— Customs, Laws, &c. 12mo. 1658
————————————————— 12mo. 1680
————————————————— 12mo. 1702
————————————————— 8vo. 1765
—— Directories (*see* Hitch's Universal Pocket Companions, Johnson, Kelly, Kent, Lowndes, Pigott, Post Office, & Robson)
—— Dock Bill, Evidence . . . . . . folio 1797
—— East, Water Works Act 8vo. 1808
—— Encyclopædia . . . . . 22 vols. 8vo. 1836
—— Fishmongers' Pageant, 1616 (Lord Mayor's Day) 4to. 1844
—— Freemen of Companies 12mo. 1703
—— French Chronicle of, 1260–1343. No. 28, C. S. Pa. (G. J. Aungier) 1844
—— Gazette, 1665–1868 . . . . 290 vols. folio
—— Gentlemen of Account residing in London & the Suburbs, 1595, 28 Eliz. . . . . . . 8vo.
—— Gildhallæ Munimenta (*see* Riley)
—— Grey Friars, Chronicle of, 1189–1556. No. 53, C. S. Pa. (ed. J. G. Nichols) 1851
—— Guide, 1760, 1770, 1783 . . . 3 vols. 8vo.
—— History of (*see* Brydall, Chamberlain, Hatton, Herbert, Howell, Hughson, Lambert, Maitland, Malcolm, Pennant, & Stowe)
—— Institution, Catalogue of Library . . . .
—— Institution, Charter, 47 Geo. III., Act of Parliament, Bye-laws, &c. 8vo. 1832
—— Map of, as it appeared in 1578, published by Antiquarian Society 1738

LIST OF THE BOOKS IN THE

London, Map of, in Case (Cassell & Co.) . . . 1867
—— Quo Warranto, Rex v. Mayor of, Proceedings
folio 1696
—— Scriveners (Free) Case 4to. 1749
—— Tracts, containing :—
1. Rules for Governing Fishermen of Thames & Medway 1785
2. Orders of Commissioners of Sewers 1806
3. Reply to Statement of Fellowship Porters, contained in Report of Committee of Courts over Coal and Corn Meters 1818
4. Dowling's Report of Riots in London, of the Case of Beckwith v. Wood 1818
5. Address of the Commissioners of the Court of Requests for Southwark 1819
6. Norton's Exposition of Privileges of the City as to Claims of Non-Freemen to Deal by Wholesale within its Jurisdiction 1831
7. Tithes, Argument before the Lord Mayor, upon Dr. Owen's application under Stat. 37 Hen. VIII. for Tithes at 2s. 9d. in the Pound 1823
8. Yantlett Creek, Gurney's Report of Trial, Rex v. Montagu & others 1824
9. Orders for Regulating the Standing of Carts for Hire 1825
10. Orders for Regulating the Standing of Carts in Gracechurch Street 1827
11. Accounts of Monuments & Pictures in Guildhall . 1827
12. Table of Rates of Watermen on Thames . . . 1828
13. Rules & Bye-laws for Regulation of Watermen & Lightermen on Thames 1828
14. Substance of a Memorial of the Chartered Gas Light & Coke Company to the Commissioners of Sewers . n. d.

London University Calendar, 1832–66. 18 v. 8vo.
—— Viaduct, Holborn Bridge, Plan 1833
—— Westminster, & Southwark, Parish Clerks' Survey. 8vo. 1732
—— & Middlesex, Correspondence between Mr. Alex. Venables & Mr. Coles as to Under-sheriff of. Vol. 3, L. T.
Londonderry, Five Reports of Deputations as to Estate of Grocers' Company there . . 8vo. 1817–29
Long v. The Bishop of Capetown, Case, &c., in P. C. 8vo. 1866
—— (C. E.) C. S. Pa. No. 74
—— (Edwd.) History of Jamaica . 3 vols. 4to. 1774

Longfield (R.) & Townsend (J. F.) Irish Exche-
quer Reports, 1841–42 . . . . 8vo. 1843
Longman (T.) London Guide . . 16th ed. 12mo. 1783
Longmate (B.) Peerage, 1790–1813. 7 vols. 12mo. n. d.
Lord Chancellors, Lives of . . . . . 2 vols. 8vo. 1708
———————— Livings, List of (*see* Vol. 3, H. L.
Bills, 1863)
—— (H. W.) on Highway of the Seas in time of
War 12mo. 1862
Lords, House of, Remembrances for MSS. Orders,
&c. 1660–1717 . . . . 12mo.
Lorimer (J.) on Equal Representation : a Letter
to Lord Russell. Vol. 23, Pam.
—— The Constitutionalism of the Future, or Par-
liament the Mirror of the Nation . 2nd ed. 8vo. 1867
Loring (C. G.) Letters to Mr. E. W. Field on the
Present Relations between Great Britain & the
United States, 1862. Vol. 22, Pam.
Loughborough (*Lord*), Biography of (*see* Lawyers) 1790
—— Argument in C. P. on Fines payable
on Admission to Copyhold Estates. Vol. 2,
Col. Jur.
Louis-Philippe of France, Pedigree of . . folio 1825
Louth, Notices of 8vo. 1834
Louthian (J.) Form of Process (Scotland)
2nd ed. 8vo. 1752
Lovat Peerage, 1827–35 :—
Case of Rev. A. G. Fraser. Vol. 2, 2nd ser.
—— T. A. Fraser. Vol. 2, 3rd ser.
Evidence. Vol. 9, 1827.
———————— 19.
Lovelass (P.) on Bills 8vo. 1796
———————— Wills . . . . 7th ed. 8vo. 1790
———————— . . . . 9th ed. 8vo. 1798
———————— (Gow) . . 11th ed. 8vo. 1823
Lovesy (C. W.) on Arbitration—Master & Work-
man 12mo. 1867
Low (S.) London Charities 12mo. 1862

Lowndes (J. J.), Maxwell (P. N.) & Pollock's (C. E.) Practice Reports . . . 2 vols. 8vo. 1851–52
—— & Maxwell (P. N.) Bail Court Cases. 8vo. 1852–54
—— (L. J.) Remarks on Lord Denman's Bill for Improving the Law of Evidence. Vol. 18, Pam. 1843
—— (M. D.) London Directory, 1780, 1787, & 1792 . . . . 3 vols. 8vo.
—— (R.) on Collisions at Sea 8vo. 1867
—— (W.) on Legacy Duties 8vo. 1824
—— Remarks on Life & Writings of Plato. Vol. 13, Jac. Col. 1827
—— The Delays in the Court of Chancery considered, with practical Suggestions for Prevention or Removal. Vol. 17, Pam. 1843
—— (W. T.) Bibliographer's Manual. 2 vols. 8vo. 1834
———————— & Appendix (Bohn) 6 vols. 12mo. 1865
Lowth (*Bp. of Winchester*) Biography of Wykeham . . . . 3rd ed. 8vo. 1777
Loyalists, Compounding, Catalogue of . 12mo. 1655
Luard (H. R.) (*see* Edward the Confessor, Lives of) No. 3, M. R. Pub. 1858
—— (*see* Bp. Grossetete's Letters) 25 M. R. Pub. 1861
—— B. de Cotton. Historia Anglicana. 16 M. R. Pub. 1859
Lubé (D. G.) Equity Pleading 8vo. 1823
Luby & others (Fenians) Trial at Dublin, November 1865 . . . . 8vo. 1866
Lucas (*Rev.* C.) on the Modern Clergy . . 8vo.
—— (R. N.) Trusts & Trustees, the Perils of 12mo. 1860
Lucian of Samosata, Works of (W. Tooke) 2 vols. 4to. 1829
Luder (A.) Election Reports, 1785–90. 3 vols. 8vo. 1808
Ludlow (H.) (*see* Batten)
—— (J. M.) Joint Stock Winding-up Acts. 8vo. 1850
Luffman (J.) Charters of London 8vo. 1793
Lumley (B.) Parliamentary Practice . . . 8vo. 1838
—— (W. G.) on Annuities 8vo. 1833
—— Abridgment of Poor Law. 2 vols. 8vo. 1840–43

Lumley (W. G.) Parochial Assessments
          4th ed. 12mo. 1858
———————————————— . . . . 5th ed. 1863
—— Sanitary Laws 12mo. 1859
—— on Nuisances, &c. Removal 12mo. 1860
—— The Union Assessment Act . . . 12mo. 1864
—— Poor Removal Acts . . . . 2nd ed. 12mo. 1865
Lunacy, Law of, Letter to Lord Brougham on the Amendment, by a Phrenologist. Vol. 20, Pam. 8vo. 1843
—— Laws of, & their Crimes, Extracts from Reports of Commissioners in Lunacy. Vol. 15, Pam. 1859
—— Laws & their Crimes as they affect all Classes of Society. By the Chairman of the alleged Lunatics' Friend Society, for the consideration of the Legislature. Vol. 20, Pam. 1859
—— Report of Equity Committee of Society on the Law. Vol. 15, Pam. 1848
Lush (*Sir* R.) Practice . . . . 2nd ed. 8vo. 1840
————————————— (Stephen) 2nd ed. 8vo. 1856
————————————— (Dixon) 3rd ed. 2 vols. 8vo. 1865
Lushington (G.) Manual of Naval Prize Law. 8vo. 1866
—— (H.) on the Broad & Narrow Gauge of Railways, & Remarks on the Reports of the Gauge Committees. Vol. 21, Pam. 1846
—— (V.) Admiralty Reports, & Appeals to the Privy Council, 1859–62 . . . . . . 8vo. 1864
Lutwyche (A. J. P.) on the Principles of Pleading the General Issue 8vo. 1838
—— Registration Reports, 1843–53. 2 vols. 8vo. 1847–54
—— (*Sir* Edw.) C. P. Reports, 1682–1704
          2 vols. folio 1704
Lydgate (John) Poem, The Child of Bristow. No. 73, C. M. Vol. 4 (ed. C. Hopper) 1859
Lyms (Israel) Hebrew Grammar . 2nd ed. 8vo. 1757
Lynch (A. H.) on Chancery & Appellate Jurisdiction, Letter to Lord Melbourne. Vol. 1, Chy. Pam.

Lyndwood (W.) Provinciale, seu Constitutiones
Angliæ, 1525. Accedunt Constitutiones Angliæ
Legitimæ seu Legatinæ Othonis et Othoboni. folio 1594
———————————————————— 4th ed. folio 1679
Lyon (*Rev.* W.) History of Town & Port & Castle
of Dover 8vo. 1813
Lysons (*Rev.* D.) Historical Account of the En-
virons of London within Twelve Miles thereof
4 vols. 4to. 1795–1800
    Containing :—
History of Surrey. Vol. 1 1792
——————— Middlesex. Vols. 2 & 3 1795
——————— Herts, Essex, & Kent. Vol. 4 . . 1800
————————————————— Supplement to do.
of certain parishes, &c. in Middlesex 4to. 1800
—— Magna Britannia . . 8 vols. in 6, 4to. 1808–22
Vol. 1. Bedfordshire, Berkshire, Buckingham-
shire 4to. 1813
Vol. 2. Cambridgeshire, Cheshire . . . 4to. 1813
Vol. 3. Cornwall 4to. 1814
Vol. 4. Cumberland 4to. 1816
Vol. 5. Derbyshire 4to. 1817
Vol. 6. Devonshire 4to. 1822
—— Designs for the Improvement of the Metro-
polis 8vo. 1816

M

Macallan (A.) Digest of Scotch Law. 3rd ed. 8vo. 1834
McAlpin (W. H.) Catalogue of Dr. Lee's Library
at Hartwell 8vo. 1865
McArthur (J.) Naval Court Martial . . . 8vo. 1792
Macartney (J.) (*see* Armstrong)

Macaulay (*Lord*) Essays . . 2nd ed. 3 vols. 8vo. 1842
—— History of England, 1685-1702. 5 vols. 8vo. 1860-64
Macauley (A.) History & Antiquities of Claybrook,
&c., Leicestershire 8vo. 1791
—— (J.) (*see* E. Chitty's Equity Index)
McCleland (T.) Exchequer Reports, 1823-24. 8vo. 1825
—— & Younge (F.) Exchequer Reports, 1824-26
8vo. 1827
McCord (T.) Civil Code for Lower Canada. 12mo. 1867
McCulloch (J. R.) Commercial Dictionary . 8vo. 1844
Macdonald (A.) Masters, Workmen, Servants,
Apprentices 8vo. 1868
—— (*Sir* H.) Biography of (*see* Lawyers)
Macgregor (S.) Trial of Humphreys for Forgery
as to Stirling Peerage 8vo. 1839
McHenry (J. J. A.) Spanish Grammar . 12mo. 1854
Machiavelli (J.) Opera 4to. 1550
—— Works . . . . fol. 1680
Machyn (H.) (Citizen of London) Diary. No. 42,
C. S. Pa. 1550-63 (ed. J. G. Nichols) . . . 1848
Macintosh (*Sir* James) Life of (R. J. Macintosh)
2nd ed. 2 vols. 8vo. 1836
Mackenzie, History of Galloway . 2 vols. 8vo. 1841
—— (E.) History of Newcastle, including Gateshead 4to. 1827
—— (G.) Naval & Military Kalendar . . 12mo. 1821
—— (*Sir* G.) Scotch Pleadings since 1661 . 4to. 1672
——————————— Criminal Practice . . 8vo. 1678
——————————————————— 2nd ed. folio 1799
—— Institutions of Scotch Law . . . 12mo. 1692
——————————————— . 2nd ed. 12mo. 1723
—— Works . . . . 2 vols. folio 1716-22
—— (J. T.) Suggestions for the Reconstruction
of the Indian Government. Vol. 10, Pam. . . 1857
—— Paper read before the British Association at
Aberdeen on the Trade & Commerce of India.
Vol. 14, Pam. 1859
—— (*Lord*) Studies in Roman Law. 2nd ed. 8vo. 1865

Mackenzie (W.) on Solicitors' Bookkeeping. 12mo. 1858
—— (*Rev.* W.) Index to Laws of Isle of Man,
1422–1855 . . . . 8vo. 1861
Mackinnon (D.) Philosophy of Evidence. Vol. 2.
Jac. L. T. 1812
Maclachlan (D.) (*see* Arnold)
—— on Shipping 8vo. 1860
———————— Supplement 8vo. 1862
Maclaclan (D.) (*see* Chitty on Bills)
Maclaurin Scotch Criminal Cases, 1670–1770. 4to. 1774
—— (C.) Algebra . . . . 4th ed. 8vo. 1779
McLean (C. H.) & Robinson (Geo.) H. L. Reports, 1839 . . . . 8vo. 1840
Maclean (*Col.*) Reduction of the Will of, in a
Cause in Lunacy, Reprinted from 'Mental
Science Journal.' Vol. 20, Pam. 1861
—— (J.) C. S. Pa. No. 76 1860
Macleod (H. D.) Theory & Practice of Banking
2 vols. 2nd ed. 8vo. 1866
Macnaghten (S.) (*see* Select Cases in Chancery
temp. King)
Macnaghten (S.) & Gordon (A.) Chancery Reports, 1849–51 . . . . . . 3 vols. 8vo. 1850–52
Macpherson, P. C. Practice 8vo. 1860
—— (D.) Annals of Commerce . . 4 vols. 4to. 1865
—— (J.) Original Papers concerning Secret History of Great Britain . . 2 vols. 2nd ed. 4to. 1776
—— (Wm.) on Infants 8vo. 1842
Macqueen (J. F.) H. L. & P. C. Practice. 8vo. 1842
—— Lecture on Early History & Academic Discipline of Inns of Court & Chancery, before
Lincoln's Inn Benchers. Vol. 9, Pam. . . . 1851
—— House of Lords Reports on Scotch Appeals,
1851–65. . . . . 4 vols. 8vo. 1855–65
—— on Divorce, Marriage, Legitimacy, &c.
2nd ed. 8vo. 1860
Macquer (M. P.) Roman History abridged (translation from the French, by T. Nugent). . 8vo. 1760

Macrae (D. C.) Insolvency Practice (under Protection Acts) 12mo. 1852
Macrory (A. J.) Report of the Clough Case in Irish Exchequer. Vol. 13, Jac. Col.
—— (Edw.) Report of Patent Cases 1855–57   8vo.
Mac Skinner (S.) History of Carrickfergus
　　　　　　　　　　　　　　3rd ed. 8vo. 1829
Macworth (*Sir* H.) on Free Parliament; Reprint from G. Bowyer, Pam. Par. Proc. 1840
Madden (*Sir* F.) No. 61, C. S. Pa., C. M. Vol. 3. 1855
Maddock (H.) Chancery Reports, 1815–20
　　　　　　　　　　5 vols. 8vo. 1817–1822
————————————— Practice . 2nd ed. 2 vols. 8vo. 1820
————————————— 3rd ed. 2 vols. 8vo. 1837
—— & Geldart (T. C.) Chancery Reports, 1821
　　　　　　　　　　　　　　　　8vo. 1829
Madox (F.) Formulare Anglicanum . . .   folio 1702
—— Firma Burgi, History of Cities, &c. .   folio 1726
—— Baronica Anglica . . . .   folio 1736
—— (T.) History of the Exchequer . . .   folio 1711
————————————— 2nd ed. 2 vols. 4to. 1769
Madras Presidency, Regulations & Acts of (*see* East India Company)
—— Gazette 1868
—— Laws (*see* R. Clarke)
Magens (II.) on Insurance . . . . 2 vols. 4to. 1755
Magistrates' Assistant . . . . . 3rd ed. 8vo. 1795
Mahon (*Lord*) War of Spanish Succession . 8vo. 1823
—— Life of Condé 12mo. 1845
—— History of England, 1713–83
　　　　　　　　　　4th ed. 7 vols. 8vo. 1853
Maidlow (J. M.) & others, Six Essays, written for Prizes, on Commons Preservation, for H. W. Peek, Esq. 8vo. 1866
Maidstone, Charters to, by James 4to. 1825
Maine (H. S.) Ancient Law 8vo. 1861
Maitland (Wm.) History of London, Westminster, & Southwark . . . . 2 vols. folio 1756

Major (J.) Historia Majoris Britanniæ. J. B.
Ascensius. 4to. 1740
Malcolm (J. P.) History of London, Ancient &
Modern . . . . 4 vols. 4to. 1802
—— Lives of Topographers and Antiquaries. 4to. 1815
    Containing :—

Ashmole, Elias.	Hearne, Thomas, M.A.
Atkins, Sir Robert	Jones, Inigo
Aubrey, John	Kennet, White (Bishop of
Bentham, James, M.A.	Peterborough)
Brand, Jno., M.A.	Kilburne, Richard
Brown, Sir T., M.D.	Leigh, Charles, M.D.
Channing, Sir Henry	Lumbarde, William
Dale, Samuel	Maitland, William
Dart, John	Morant, Philip, M.A.
Drake, Francis	Newcourt, Richard
Ducarel, Andrew, LL.D.	Pennant, Thomas
Dugdale, Sir W.	Stow, John
Fuller, Thomas, D.D.	Strype, John, M.A.
Gent, Thomas	Stukeley, Wm., M.D., F.R.S.
Gough, Richard	Thoresby, Ralph
Hasted, Edward	Wood, Anthony, M.A.

Male (A.) on Elections, Law & Practice . 8vo. 1818
Malebranche (N.) Search after Truth (R. Sault)
                               12mo. 1694
Mallory (J.) on Quare Impedit. . . . . folio 1737
—— Entries . . . . . 4th ed. 2 vols. 8vo. 1791
Malmesburiensis Monachus (*see* Eulogium Historiarum), No. 9, M. R. Pub. 1858–63
Malt & Beer, Enquiry as to reducing Duties on.
Vol. 5, Pam. 1830
Malta, Ordinances, 1857–67 . . . . 3 vols. folio
Malthus (T. R.) Essay on Population . . 8vo. 1817
Malvern (*see* Chambers, J.)
Malynes (G.) Lex Mercatoria . . 3rd ed. folio 1686
Man, Isle of (*see* Pigott's Directory) 1837
—— History, &c. of . . . . . 2nd ed. 12mo. 1744
—— The Statute Laws of 8vo. 1797
(*See* Collections of Isle of Man Statutes to
1861, by Mills, Geneste, Jeffcott, Gell, Burman,
Lamothe)

Man Isle of, Report of the Commissioners of Inquiry for the Isle of Man, 1792 . . folio 1805
—— Proceedings before the Privy Council respecting the Duke of Athol's Claim on the Isle, in 1765 . . . . folio 1805
Manby (R.) on Fines. 8vo. 1837
—— (T.) Collection of Statutes . . . . folio 1767
Manchester (*see* Cheetham Hospital)
—— Collegiate & Cathedral & Parish Church & the Cathedral Commission: Answer to Commissioners. Vol. 9, Pam. 1853
—— Guide, including Salford 8vo. 1804
—— Law Society, Catalogue of Library . 8vo. 1854
—— Rectory, Division Evidence 8vo. 1850
—— Vindicated: Collection of Papers published in 'Chester Courant' (*see* 'Chester Miscellany') 12mo. 1749
Mander (J.) Derbyshire Miners Glossary . 8vo. 1824
Manipulus Vocabulorum [by Peter Levins, A.D. 1570] (H. D. Wheatley) No. 95 C. S. Pa. . 1867
Manisty (H.) Letter to Sir F. Pollock on Local Courts. Vol. 3, Pam. 1843
Manning (J.) Digest of N. P. Cases. 2nd ed. 8vo. 1820
—— Exchequer Practice, Revenue Branch
2nd ed. 8vo. 1827
—— & Ryland (A.) K. B. Reports, 1827–29
5 vols. 8vo. 1827–30
—— & Granger's (T. C.) C. P. Reports, 1840–44
7 vols. 8vo. 1841–46
—— & Scott (Jno.) C.B. Reports, 1845–50
9 vols. 8vo. 1846–57
—— (*Rev.* O.) & Bray (Wm.) History of Surrey
3 vols. folio 1804
Manlove (Edwd.) Rhymed Chronicle, containing the Customs, &c. of the Wirksworth Lead Mines (T. Tapping) . . . . 2nd ed. 8vo. 1851
Mansel (G. B.) Letter to H. Brougham, Esq., on Legal Education. Vol. 3, Law Tr. 1830

P

Mansel (G. B.) Practice on Writ of Trial
                                        12mo. 1833
—— Jurisdiction Rights & Limitations . . 8vo. 1834
—— Limitation & Prescription 8vo. 1839
Mansfield (*Earl*) Biography of, 1790 (*see* Lawyers,
 & Roscoe's Lives of Eminent British Lawyers)
—— (*Lord*) Proceedings in Parliament, occasioned
 by his Directions to Juries in Libellous matters,
 & his Lordship's Judgment in Rex *v.* Woodfall,
 for Libel, in 1770. Vol. 2, Libel L. Tr.
Mant (*Dr.* R.) Common Prayer . . 3rd ed. 4to. 1825
Manwood (J.) on Forest Laws 4to. 1615
—— on Forest Laws (Nelson) . . . 4th ed. 4to. 1717
Manzoni, I Promessi Sposi 12mo. 1845
Mapes (W.) Poems. No. 16, C. S. Pa. (T.
 Wright) 1841
—— de Nugis Curialium, No. 50 do. 1160–82 . . 1850
Maps, Catalogue of, & Topographical Drawings in
 British Museum . . . . 2 vols. 8vo. 1844
—— & Drawings in Geo. III. Library & Cata-
 logue of MSS. . . . . folio 1829
March (Jno.) on Arbitration & Awards (bound up
 with March (J.) on Slander) 1674
—— on Slander 12mo. 1674
—— Commonwealth's Friend (Amicus Rei-
 publicæ) 12mo. 1651
—— K. B. Reports, 1639–42 . . 2nd ed. 4to. 1676
Marchmont Peerage, Case of F. D. Horne. Vol. 2,
 2nd series
        Evidence—Vol. 4—1822
                  ,,   19—1838
                  ,,   17—1839
                  ,,   21—1840
                  ,,   16—1842
                  ,,   19—1843 H. L. Sess. Papers.
Margaret of Anjou, Letters of, &c. C. S. Pa.
 No. 86, (ed. C. Monro). 1863
——'s Trial (Scotch) 8vo. 1793

Marina (J.) Sobre la antigua Legislacion de Leon
y Castilla 4to. 1808
—— Juicio critico de la Novísima Recopilacion. 8vo. 1820
Marine Society's Bye-Laws 12mo. 1772
————————————————— . . . 3rd ed. 12mo. 1787
————————————————— . . . 5th ed. 12mo. 1809
Maritime Officers' Compensation (*see* East India Co.)
Marius (Jno.) on Bills. . . . . . 2nd ed. 12mo. 1670
Markham (T. H.) (*see* Day, Finlason, & Stephen)
—— Common Law Procedure Acts. 3rd ed.12mo. 1864
Marmyon Peerage, Case of L. Dymoke. Vol. 2,
2nd series, 1817
—— Evidence, Vol. 4
Marriage abroad (within prohibited Degrees) Law
Tr. Vol. 7.
—— Articles & Cross Remainders, on Construction of, in Duke of Richmond's Case. Opinion,
Argument, & Decree of Lord Chancellor Apsley.
Vol. 2, Col. Jur. (May 4, 1773)
—— 1st Report of Commissioners on Law of,
Evidence & Index . . . . folio 1848
—— with a Deceased Wife's Sister, Memorandum
in Relation to, stating the Effect of a Royal
Commission & Report. Vol. 24, Pam. . . . 1851
———————————— Observations on Debate on Bill
for Legalizing, reported in 'Times.' Vol. 24, Pam. 1851
———————————— Facts & Opinions in favour of.
Vol. 24, Pam.
—— Law Dialogues, a Day too late, or a Glance
at the Working of the Act of 1835. Vol. 24,
Pam. 1852
—— & Divorce. Nuptiæ Sacræ, or Enquiry into
the Scripture Doctrine of. Vol. 2, Jac. Col.
Marriott (*Sir* James) Admiralty Reports, temp.
Sir G. Hay & Sir James Marriott, 1776–79 8vo. 1801
—— Argument on giving Judgment in Admiralty Court as to ship 'Columbus.' Vol. 1,
Col. Jur.

Marriott (*Rev.* W.) Antiquities of Lyme, Cheshire,
  & its Vicinities 4to. 1810
Marsden (J. B.) on Mosaic Code, influence on, in
  subsequent Legislation 8vo. 1862
Marshall (C.) Reports (C. P.) 1813–16
                                        2 vols. 8vo. 1815–17
—— (J.) Analysis of Titles to Land Consolidation,
  Scotland, Act, 1868 . . . . 8vo. 1869
—— (Saml.) on Insurance. 2nd ed. 2 vols. 8vo. 1808
——————————— (*Mr. Serjt.* Shee) 4th ed. 8vo. 1861
——————————— (*Sir* W. Shee) . 5th ed. 8vo. 1865
—— (W.) on the Law of Costs 12mo. 1860
———————————————— 2nd ed. 12mo. 1862
—— Law of Railway Companies as Carriers. 12mo. 1862
Marsham (J. R.) (*see* Carrington, F. A.)
Marta (P.) Digesta novissima totius Juris con-
  troversi scientiæ . . . . . 6 vols. in 2, folio 1622
—— Tractatus de Jurisdictione per et inter Judicem
  Ecclesiasticum et Secularem exercenda . folio 1609
Martiall (J.) (*see* Calfhill, Bishop)
Martin (Adam) Familiar Epistles. L. T. . 1668–69
—— Exchequer Repertories, Orders & Decrees,
  Index of 8vo. 1819
  (Another Copy, with Mr. Rich's Additions)
—— (F.) Statesman's Year Book. 3 vols. 4th,
                5th & 6th eds. 12mo. 1866–68
—— (*Rev.* J.) History, &c. of Naseby (Northton)
                                   8vo. 1792
—— (P.) Dictionnaire françois et hollandois. 4to. 1710
————————————————— 4th ed. 4to. 1762
—— (R. M.) British Colonies. 5 vols. 2nd ed. 8vo. 1835
—— (Thos.) on Priests' Marriages . . . 4to. 1554
—— Character of Bacon, his Life & Works. 8vo. 1835
—— Introduction to Conveyancing Precedents. 8vo. 1837
—— Conveyancing Precedents 8vo. 1837
Martyn (T.) History of Thetford (Gough) . 4to. 1779
—— (W.) History of the Reign of Twenty
  English Kings—William the Conqueror to Henry
  VIII. 1066–1546 . . . . folio 1615

Mary (*Queen*) Calendar of State Papers, Domestic
Series. Ed. by Robert Lemon. Vol. 1. imp. 8vo. 1856
—— Calendar of State Papers, Foreign Series,
1553-58 . . . . imp. 8vo. 1861
—— & Queen Jane, Chronicle of. No. 48, C. S.
Pa. (ed. J. G. Nichols) 1849
—— Queen of Scots (A. J. Crosby and J. Bruce)
No. 93, C. S. P. 4to. 1867
Mascall (F.) on Intestacy 8vo. 1815
Mason (F.) Vindiciæ Ecclesiæ Anglicanæ
2nd ed. folio 1625
—— (W. F.) Reports (U.S.) 1816-30
vols. 8vo. 1836-51
—— (W. M.) Cathedral of St. Patrick, Dublin
4to. 1819
—— (W. S.) Ireland (Survey) . 3 vols. 8vo. 1814
Massay (Wm.) Common Law *v*. Common Sense
8vo. 1850
Master (*Rev*. R.) History of the College of Corpus
Christi & of the Blessed Virgin Mary, Cambridge,
with additional matters by John Lamb . 4to. 1831
Mathew (J. M.) Landlord & Tenant Manual. 8vo. 1841
Matthews (R.) on Criminal Law . . . 12mo. 1833
—— Strictures on Dissenters' Chapel Bill. Vol. 18,
Pam. 1841
Maty (*Dr*. M.) Works of Lord Chesterfield
3 vols. 8vo. 1779
Maude (F. P.) & Pollock (C. E.) on Merchant
Shipping 8vo. 1853
———————————————— 2nd ed. 8vo. 1861
———————————————— 3rd ed. 8vo. 1864
Maugham (Robt.) Outlines of Character
2nd ed. 8vo. 1823
—— on Usury. Vol. 3, Jac. Col. 1824
—— Law of Attorneys, Solicitors, & Agents. 8vo. 1825
—— on Literary Property 8vo. 1828
—— Observer & Digest, 1830-56. 57 vols. 8vo.
—— Legal Almanac . . . 6 vols. 8vo. 1835-41
—— Outlines of Criminal Law 12mo. 1837

Maugham (Robt.) Outlines of Law, Private
Wrongs 12mo. 1837
——————————— Public Wrongs . 12mo. 1837
——————— Questions on the Jurisdiction of
the Courts 12mo. 1838
—— Law of Attorneys, Solicitors, & Agents, with
Statutes, Rules, & Orders. 8vo. 1839
—— Questions on the Law 12mo. 1839
—— Year Book & Diary . . . 4 vols. 8vo. 1841–51
—— Outlines of Law of Real Property . . 12mo. 1842
—— Attorneys, &c. Act. 8vo. 1843
—— Attorney's Hand Book 12mo. 1853
—— Digest of Examination Questions, 1836–55
6th ed. 12mo. 1855
——————————————————— from 1855
8th ed. 12mo. 1861
Maule (G.) & Selwyn (W.) K. B. Reports, 1813–
17 . . . . 6 vols. 8vo. 1813–17
Maunder (S.) Treasury of Knowledge (Woodward
& others) 8vo. 1853
—— Treasury of Natural History . 5th ed. 8vo. 1858
—— Treasury of History 8vo. 1858
—— Scientific & Literary Treasury . . . 8vo. 1858
—— Biographical Treasury . . 11th ed. 12mo. 1859
—— Treasury of Geography, (W. Hughes)
12mo. 1860
Mauritius Ordinances, 1857–67 . . 3 vols. folio
Mawe (Jno.) Mineralogy of Derbyshire
8vo. 1802
Maximes du Droit public français. 2 vols. 12mo. 1772
May (*Dr.* C.) History of European States, with
Biographical Sketches . . . . . . folio 1795
—— (G.) History of Evesham 8vo. 1834
—— (J. W.) (*see* Angell)
—— (*Sir* T. E) Parliamentary Practice
2nd ed. 8vo. 1854
———————————————————— 4th ed. 8vo. 1859
———————————————————— 5th ed. 8vo. 1863

May (*Sir* T. E.) Parliamentary Practice
           6th ed. 8vo. 1868
—— (*Dr.* C.) Questions on Sugden's Vendors. 8vo. 1865
—— History of English Constitution, 1760–1860
           2 vols. 8vo. 1861–63
Maydiston (R.) Alliterative Poem on Deposition of
  Ric. II. No. 3, C. S. Pa. (ed. J. Wright) . 4to. 1838
Mayhew (C. J.) on Merger 12mo. 1861
Mayne (J. D.) Equitable Defences . . 12mo. 1854
—— on Damages 8vo. 1856
Mead (*Dr.*) Letter to Wise, with some Antiquities
  of Berkshire 4to. 1738
—— Further Observations 4to. 1742
Measures, Weights, & Coins, 3rd Report of International Association as to. Vol. 12, Pam. . 1859
Medical Circular 12mo. 1852
—— Directory, London & Provincial, 1856–59
           2 vols. 12mo.
—— Reform, Statement of Society of Apothecaries, & Address to Society of Practitioners on Medical Bill. Vol. 5, Pam. 1844–5
—— Register . . . . 8 vols. 8vo. 1860–69
Medway to the Thames, Pamphlet on Proposed
  Cut from 8vo. 1827
Meeson (R.) & Welsby (W. N.) Exchequer Reports
  & Index, 1836–47 . . . . 17 vols. 8vo. 1836–49
Melbourne Directory . . . . 2 vols. 8vo. 1859–60
Mellius (P. J.) Institutiones Juris Civilis et Criminalis Lusitani (Portugal) . . 7 vols. 8vo. 1827–29
Members of Parliament, Oaths to be taken by, Arguments on. Vol. 7, Jac. Col. 1829
—— Election of, Barnardiston *v.* Soames. Atkyns'
  Law Tr. 1741
Mence (R.) on Mutual Rights of Husband & Wife.
  Vol. 6, Law Tr.
Mercantile Community, Report, &c. by Committee
  of London Merchants. Vol. 8, Pam. 1852
Merchant Laws . . . . 2 vols. 8vo. 1761

Merewether (H. A.) Report of West Looe Election
             8vo. 1823
—— Address to Kings, Lords, & Commons as to Representative Constitution of England. Pam. Vol. 4 1830
Merewether (H. A.) & Stephens (A. J.) on Corporations & History. . . . . . 3 vols. 8vo. 1835
Meriton (G.) Landlords' Law . . 3rd ed. 12mo. 1669
Merivale (C.) Roman Empire. 5th ed. 7 vols. 8vo. 1862–64
—— (J. H.) Chancery Reports (temp. Eldon) 1813–17 . . . . 3 vols. 8vo. 1817–19
—— Letters to Mr. Courtenay on the Chancery Commission. Vol. 4, Jac. Col. 1827
—— Letters on Chancery Reform. Vol. 2, Chy. Pam. 1841
Merville (P. de) De la Coutume de Normandie, reduite en Maximes 4to. 1707
Meschen (*Dr.* T. de) on Colenso's Fallacies. Vol. 18, Pam.
Metcalfe (T.) & Perkins (J. C.) Digest of Common Law & Admiralty, & Supplement, Boston, U.S. (continued by Curtis). 8vo. 1869
Metcalfe (T.) On Contracts, U. S. . . . 8vo. 1868
Metropolis Improvement, Design by an Architect
             8vo. 1816
Metropolitan & Provincial Law Association, Proceedings of Annual Meeting. Vol. 11, Pam. . . 1857
—— Reports & Circulars . . . 2 vols. 8vo. 1852–62
—— Magazine, 1833–50 . . . 48 vols. 8vo.
Meymott (F. W.) on Southwark Court of Request Act (*see* Emerson on City Courts) 1830
Meyrick (*Sir* S. R.) History of Cardiganshire
             4to. 1808
Mézeray (F. E. de) A General Chronological History of France, translated by John Bulteel. folio 1683
—— Abrégé chronologique de l'Histoire de France; nouvelle édition, augmentée . . . 4 vols. 4to. 1740
Michael (W. H.) Sanitary Acts . . . 12mo. 1867

Michie (A.) the Case of W. H. Barber. Vol. 17,
Pam. 1847
Middleham Church, Yorkshire, Antiquities of. No.
38, C. S. Pa. (Rev. W. Atthill). . . . 4to. 1847
Middlesex, Heralds' Visitations for, taken in 1663
Middleton (*Dr.* C.) Biography of Cicero. 2 vols. 4to. 1741
Miege (G.) New State of England
        3 vols. 12mo. 1669–1755
—— Present State of Britain . . 11 vols. 8vo. 1707–48
—— Colonies of Great Britain 12mo. 1742
Mildmay (W.) on Mode of Proceeding at City
Common Hall Elections 8vo. 1743
——————————————————————— 8vo. 1819
Mill (J.) History of British India. Continuation
by W. H. Wilson . . . . . 9 vols. 8vo. 1823–48
—— (Job) on Conveyancing . . . . . folio 1746
Millar (F. C. J.) & Collier (J. B.) on Bills of Sale
          12mo. 1858
——————————————————— 2nd ed. 12mo. 1860
Miller (C.) a Plea for the Revival of the Study of
the Common Law, in a Letter to the Earl of
Derby. Vol. 27, Pam. 1862
—— Plea for Moral Philosophy & Law. Letter
to the Earl of Derby. Vol. 27, Pam. . . . 1865
—— (*Rev.* C.) Letter to Mr. Gladstone on the
duty of Government towards the Church &
Clergy. Vol. 3, Pam. 1841
—— Letter to Rev. R. Jones, comparing principles
of Parochial Assessments & the Tithe Commu-
tation Act. Vol. 6, L. T.
—— (D.) on Fines & Recoveries . . . 12mo. 1822
——————————————————— . 2nd ed. 8vo. 1825
—— (Edwd.) History of Doncaster . . . 4to. 1804
—— (Jno.) on English Government . 2nd ed. 4to. 1790
—— Enquiry into State of Civil Law . . 8vo. 1825
—— on the unsettled Condition of the Law . 8vo. 1839
—— (S.) General Orders 8vo. 1841
———————————————— 1845–50 . . . 8vo. 1850

Miller (S.) on Chancery Master's Office
Vol. 6, Pam. 1848
—— (S.) Analysis of the Reform Act . 12mo. 1832
—— Mortgage (Equitable) 8vo. 1842
—— on Land Tax . . . . . 3rd ed. 12mo. 1843
——————————— 8vo. 1849
Miller (S.) Suggestions for Equalization of the Land
& Abolition of other Taxes. Vol. 19, Pam. . 1848
—— Trial before Lord Mansfield for republishing
Junius's Letter to the King. Libel L. T. Vol. 3
Milles (T.) Catalogue of Honour . . . . folio 1610
Mills (M. A.) the Ancient Ordinances & Statute
Laws of the Isle of Man, with Copious Extracts
from the several British Statutes having reference
thereto (continued by G. Geneste) . . . 8vo. 1821
Milne (*Rev.* J.) Sectionum Conicarum Elementa
8vo. 1723
—— (Joshua) on Annuities . . . 2 vols. 8vo. 1815
Milner (*Dr.* Jno.) History of Winchester Cathedral
2 vols. 4to. 1800
Milton (Jno.) Papers relating to. No. 75, C.
S. Pa. (W. D. Hamilton) 1859
—— Prose & Poetical Works, by Rev. J. Mitford
8 vols. 8vo. 1863
Milvaine (*Bp.*) & other eminent persons in America,
Letters from, on Marriage with deceased Wife's
Sister. Vol. 24, Pam. 8vo. 1851
Milward (C. R.) Irish Ecclesiastical Reports, temp.
Radcliff, 1838–42 . . . . 8vo. 1847
Minchin (J.) & Herbert (Hon. A.) Crown Cir-
cuit Companion . . . . 9th ed. 8vo. 1820
Mines & Metals, Account of 8vo. 1721
Mining Journal. Railway & Commercial Gazette
18 vols. folio 1850–67
Minot (G.) (*see* U. S. Statutes)
—— (J.) Digest of Jamaica Laws. 33 Car. II.
to 28 Vict. 8vo. 1865
Minsheu (Jno.) Dictionary (11 Languages). folio 1617

Mirehouse (J.) on Tithes . . . 2nd ed. 8vo. 1802
—— Advowsons 8vo. 1827
Mist (N.) Journal, 1718-25 . . . 3 vols. folio
Mitchell (G.) Letters to Earl Russell respecting
the late Events at Warsaw & in Poland. Vol. 21,
Pam. 1862
Mitford (J.) Equity Pleading . . . 4 vols. 8vo. 1780
————————————— . . . 3rd ed. 8vo. 1814
————————————— (Jeremy) 4th ed. 8vo. 1822
————————————— (Smith). . . 8vo. 1847
Modern Entries . . . . folio 1734
—— Reports (Equity & Com. Law) . . folio 1730
————————————— by Thos.
Leach, 1669-1700 . . . . . 12 vols. 8vo. 1796
Moffatt's Divorce Evidence, 1832 (see Vol. 10,
Peerage Evidence)
Mohedanus. Decisiones Rotæ Romanæ . . folio 1603
Moile (N.T.) Specimen of a New Edition of State
Trials 8vo. 1838
—— Drama of Cicero 4to. 1847
Molesworth Peerage, Evidence. Vol. 6
Moleyn's (T. de) Landowner's, &c. Guide (Irish) 8vo. 1866
Molière's (J. B. P.) Œuvres (M. Bret) 6 vols. 8vo. 1773
Molloy (C.) de Jure Maritimo. 7th ed. 2 vols. 8vo. 1722
————————————— 9th ed. 2 vols. 8vo. 1769
————————————— 10th ed. 2 vols. 8vo. 1778
—— (P.) Irish Chancery Reports, temp. Hart.
1827-28 . . . . 3 vols. 8vo. 1827-33
Molyneux (E.) Equity Lectures (see Lectures,
Ireland, No. 3)
—— (W.) Case of Ireland being bound by English
Acts 8vo. 1719
Monarchy, Discourse on, as to Succession of James
II. 8vo. 1684
Monasteries, Suppression of, 1528-55 . No. 26,
C. S. Pa. (T. Wright) 1843
Monastic Life, Rule of (see C. S. Pa. No. 57)
(J. Morton) 1853

Moniteur (Le) Universel, 1868 & continued
Monro (C.) (*see* C. S. Pa. No. 86)
Monstrelet's Chronicles, translated by Johnes
                                      2 vols. 8vo. 1840
Montacute Peerage, Case of W. S. Lowndes. Vol. 2, 3rd series
Montagu (B.) (*see* Lord Bacon)
—— on Set-off 8vo. 1801
Montagu (B.) on Bankruptcy . . 4 vols. 8vo. 1805-7
———————————————— 2nd ed. 2 vols. 8vo. 1819
—— Law Tracts 8vo. 1805-29
    Containing :—

    1. Thoughts on Abolition of Punishment of Death in Bankruptcy Cases 1821
    Evidence before the Committee; Report of Committee; Act 1 Geo. 4. c. 115
    2 & 3. Letters on the Bankrupt Laws to E. B. Sugden . 1829
    4. Tract No. 3 of Society for Diffusing Information on Capital Punishment & Prison Discipline. The Effects of Capital Punishment for Forgery & Theft 1818
    5. Hanging not Punishment Enough, printed in 1701 & reprinted 1812
    6. Copyright Law, Enquiries as to the proposed Alterations in, as it affected Authors & the Universities . . 1813
    7. University Library, Enquiries & Observations respecting. 1805
    8. Corruption of Blood. Debate in the House of Commons upon, 25th April 1814
    9. High Treason. Debate in House of Commons on Sir Samuel Romilly's Bill on the Punishment for . 1813
    10. Insolvent Debtors' Bill. Enquiries respecting, with Opinions of Dr. Paley, Mr. Burke, & Dr. Johnson on Imprisonment for Debt . . . . . 2nd ed. 1816
    11. Reform of the Law 1827

Montagu (B.) on Insolvent Debtors' Bill and Opinions on Imprisonment for Debt . . 8vo. 1815
—— on Partnership . . . . . . 2 vols. 8vo. 1815
—— Insolvent Debtors . . . . 2nd ed. 2 vols. 1822
—— on the Love of Excelling & of Excellence
                                                    8vo. 1820
—— on the Bill for improving the Bankruptcy Laws. Vol. 4, Jac. Col. 1822
—— on Equity Pleading 8vo. 1824

Montagu (B.) Summary of the Law of Lien. 12mo. 1824
—— Enquiries respecting Commissioners of the Court of Bankruptcy, & the Lord Chancellor's Court. Vol. 4, Jac. Col. 1825
—— Letters to Sir R. Peel on the Report of the Chancery Commissioners as to Bankruptcy. Vol. 4, Jac. Col. 1826
——————— Part 2. Vol. 8, Jac. Col. 1827
—— on Reform. Vol. 8, Jac. Col. 1827
—— on Bankruptcy Law (Letters 2 & 3). Vol. 8, Jac. Col. 1829
—— Bankruptcy Reports, 1829-32 . . . 8vo. 1832
—— Bankruptcy System. Vol. 10, Jac. Col. . . 1834
—— Letter to Lord Cottenham on Separating Chancellor's Functions. Vol. 1, Chy. Pam. . . 1836
—— Sonnets. . . . . . . 2 vols. 12mo. 1860-61
—— & Gregg (F.) Digest of Bankrupt Laws
3rd ed. 2 vols. 8vo. 1827
—— & McArthur (J.) Bankruptcy Reports, 1828-30 . . . . 8vo. 1830
—— & Ayrton (S.) on Bankruptcy . 2 vols. 12mo. 1834
—— & Bligh (R.) Bankruptcy Reports, 1831-33
8vo. 1835
—— & Ayrton (S.) Bankruptcy Reports, 1833-37 . . . . 3 vols. 8vo. 1837-39
—— & Neale (J.) Election Law 8vo. 1839
—— & Chitty (E.) Bankruptcy Reports, 1838-39
8vo. 1840
—— Deacon (E.) & De Gex (J.) Bankruptcy Reports, 1840-44 . . . . 3 vols. 8vo. 1842-45
Montefiore (J.) Commercial Law & Notarial Precedents. 4to. 1802
Montesquieu (C. de S.) De l'Esprit des Loix
7 vols. 12mo. 1769
——————————————————— 6 vols. 12mo. 1777
——————————————————— translated by
Nugent . . . . . . 2nd ed. 2 vols. 8vo. 1752
——————————————————— 5th ed. 2 vols. 8vo. 1773

Monthemer Peerage Case of W. Lowndes. Vol. 2, 3rd series

Monthly Account. The Law Tr. 1688–89

Montrose Dukedom. Case of Earl of Crawford & Balcarres. Vol. 3, 3rd series

Montserrat, Acts of Assembly, 1668–1740 . folio 1743
——————————————— 1857–63 (imperfect) folio

Moody (W.) Crown Cases, 1824–44. 2 vols. 8vo. 1837–44

—— & Malkin (B. H.) N. P. Reports, 1826–30
              8vo. 1831

—— & Robinson (F.) N. P. Reports 1830–44
           2 vols. 8vo. 1837–44

Moore (Edw.) Index to House of Commons Journals, 1714–74 . Vols. 18–34 . . folio 1805

—— (E. F.) Reports, Privy Council, 1836–61
            10 vols. 8vo.

—— Reports, ditto, N. S. 1862–67 . 4 vols. 8vo.

—— Gorham Case 8vo. 1852

—— Westerton v. Liddell, case 8vo. 1857

—— Indian Appeals, 1837–64 . 11 vols. 8vo. 1840–69

—— (Sir F.) Cases (temp. Hen. VIII., Eliz. et Jac. I.) par Sir G. Palmer (French) . . folio 1663
——————————————————— 2nd ed. folio 1675

—— (H.) Account of Growth, Christenings & Burials of London from 1601 to 1750 . . folio 1751

—— (H.) Lawyer's Companion & Diary . 8vo. 1862

—— (J. B.) A digested Index to the Term Reports, 1785–1815. . . . . . 2 vols. 8vo. 1816

—— Reports, Common Pleas & Exchequer Chamber, 1815–27 . . . . . . 12 vols. 8vo. 1818–31

—— & Payne (J.) C. P. Reports, 1827–1831
          5 vols. 8vo. 1828–32

—— & Scott (J.) 1831–34 . . . 4 vols. 8vo. 1833–34

—— (T.) on Bankruptcy. 8vo. 1788

—— on Bankruptcy Precedents . 2nd ed. 8vo. 1789

—— on Rules & Orders in Chancery, K. B. C. P. & Exchequer to M. 1794 . . . . . . 12mo. 1794

——'s Almanac, 1801–1830 . . 2 vols. 12mo.

Morality, Essays on 12mo. 1751
Morant (P.) History of Town & Borough of Colchester . . . . folio 1748
—— Essex, History & Antiquities of, including Colchester. . . . . . . 2nd ed. 2 vols. folio 1816
—— Remarks on Mr. Selden's Mare Clausum (*see* Falle, P.)
Moray, History of Province of 8vo. 1798
More (*Dr.* J. S.) Lectures on Law of Scotland, (McLaren) . . . . 2 vols. 8vo. 1864
—— (*Sir* Thos.) Lineage (*see* Foss' Grandeur of the Law) . . . . 4to. n. d.
Moreau de St.-Méry (M. L. E.) Description de St.-Domingue . . . . 2 vols. 8vo. 1777
Morell (*Dr.* T.) (*see* Ainsworth)
Morery (L.) Historical, Geographical, & Poetical Dictionary (Le Clerk) English
2 vols. in 1, 6th ed. folio 1694
Morgan (G. O.) Chancery Orders, 1852–59. 12mo. 1859
—— Chancery Orders, Consolidated. 2nd ed. 8vo. 1860
———————————— Supplement to . . 8vo. 1861
———————————— Acts, &c. . 3rd ed. 8vo. 1862
———————————— (Morgan & Chute) . 8vo. 1868
—— & Davey (H.) on Law of Chancery Costs
8vo. 1865
—— (H. D.) on Marriage, Adultery, & Divorce
2 vols. 8vo. 1827
—— (J.) Attorney's Vade Mecum. 2nd ed. 8vo. 1787
—— (Mary) Tour to Milford Haven, Pembrokeshire 8vo. 1795
Morgan (S.) Sphere of Gentry . . . . folio 1661
Morley (W. H.), Cat. of MSS. in Arabic & Persian Languages in Asiatic Library 12mo. 1854
—— Digest of India Cases . . . . 3 vols. 1850–52
Morning Advertiser, 1852–67 . . 30 vols. folio
—— Chronicle, 1823–62 . . . . . 71 vols. folio
—— Herald, 1832–67 . . . . . 71 vols. folio
—— Post, 1832–67 . . . . . . 70 vols. folio

Morning Star, 1866-67 . . . . . . 4 vols. folio
Morris (J.) Two Lectures delivered by him at the Law Institution on the Admiralty Court. Vol. 13, Pam.; Vol. 16, Pam.
—— (R.) Letter to Mr. Justice Aston on his Animadversions upon Morris' Affidavit in Almon's Case for Libel. Libel L. T. Vol. 3 . 2nd ed. 1770
—— Digest of Practice Cases 8vo. 1847
—— & Finlaison's (W. F.) Common Law Procedure Act, 1852 . . . . . . 12mo. 1852-53
—— (W.) The Proper System of Railroads for Ceylon, a Letter to Viscount Torrington. Vol. 19, Pam. 1860
Mortgage Debt, Priority of, Case of Willoughby v. Willoughby, in Chancery. Vol. 1, Col. Jur.
Mortimer (*see* Beawes)
—— Every Man his own Broker. 6th ed. 12mo. . . 1762
Morton (Edw.) on Chancery Reform; Letter to Sir James Graham. Vol. 8, Pam. . . 8vo. 1851
—— (J.) (*see* C. S. Pa. No. 57)
—— (*Rev.* J.) Natural History of Northamptonshire . . . . folio 1712
—— (T. C.) Vendor & Purchaser . . . 8vo. 1836
Moseley (J.) on New County Courts. . . 8vo. 1846
—— on Contraband of War 12mo. 1861
—— (*Sir* O.) Tutbury, History of Castle, Town, & Priory 8vo. 1832
Mosely (Wm.) Chancery Reports, temp. King, 1726-30 . . . . 8vo. 1793
Moss (E.) Remarks on Companies with Limited Liability in 18 & 19 Vict. c. 188. Vol. 10, Pam. 1856
—— (W.) Liverpool Guide 8vo. 1797
Mossop (*Rev.* F.) Elegant Orations . . . 8vo. 1788
Moule (Thos.) on British Heraldry . . . 8vo. 1822
—— on English Counties . . . . . . folio 1837
Mounteney (B.) on Detinue. Vol. 3, Pam. 8vo. 1838
Moylan (D. C.) on Right of Search as between France, America, & Great Britain. Vol. 4, Pam. 1843

LAW SOCIETY LIBRARY. 225

Muilman (P.) History & Survey of Essex
        6 vols. 8vo. 1770-72
Mulock (T.) Railway Revelations: Letters on the
Subject of the proposed Direct London & Manchester Railway. Vol. 21, Pam. 1845
Municipal Boundaries Reports on England & Wales
        4 vols. folio 1832
———————————— Small Boroughs. folio 1832
———————————— Ireland . . . folio 1832
———————————— Scotland . . folio 1832
—— Corporation Act. 8vo. 1835
Munster (S.) Cosmographie Universelle . . folio 1552
Murder by French Midwife of her Husband. L. Tr. 1687
—— will Out, Account that the Earl of Essex
did not murder himself. L. T. 1689
Murphy (A.) Gray's Inn Journal. 2 vols in 1, 12mo. 1756
—— (F. S.) & Hurlstone (E. T.) Exchequer
Reports, 1836-37 . . . . 8vo. 1838
—— (R.) Translation of Works of Tacitus
        4 vols. 4to. 1793
Murray (John) Handbook for Southern Germany
       3rd ed. 12mo. 1843
—— Handbook for Switzerland, Savoy, and Piedmont 12mo. 1845
—— (T.) The Laws and Acts of Parliament
made by Kings James I., II., III., IV., V.,
Queen Mary, Jas. VI., Chas. I. & II. . folio 1681
Musgrave (Wm.) Memoirs of Walpole . . 8vo. 1732
—— (Sir W.) Court Register, 1660-1782 . 8vo. 1782
Music MSS., Catalogue of, in British Museum
        8vo. 1842
Musnicki (L. N. H.) Roxolana the Podolian.
Vol. 23, Pam.
Mutiny Acts, 1809-35 . . . . . 28 vols. 12mo.
—————— 1854 . . . . 12mo.
Mylne (J. W.) *Chancery Reports* (see Russell, J.)
—— & Craig (R. D.) Chancery Reports, 1837-48
        5 vols. 8vo.

Q

Mylne (J. W.) & Keen (B.) Chancery Reports,
  1831–35 . . . . 3 vols. 8vo. 1834–1837
M. (C.) on Law of Sewers 8vo. 1762
M.P.'s, Oaths to be taken by. Vol. 7, Jac. Col. . 1829
M. (R.) Commentariorum de Rebellione Anglicana
  ab anno 1640 usque ad annum 1685 Libellus 8vo. 1686
MSS. temp. Jacobi, Caroli, &c. . . . . folio

N

Napier (J.) (*see* Alcock, J. C.)
—— Lecture on Common Law Study (*see* Irish
  Pamphlets) 8vo. 1839
—— (W. F. P.) Peninsular War . 6 vols. 8vo. 1832–40
Napoléon, Code, translated by a Barrister . 8vo. 1825
Narrative, Irish, 1641–90. No. 14, C. S. Pa.
  (T. C. Croker) 1841
Nash (C.) on Railway Carrying & Carriers' Law.
  Vol. 21, Pam. 1846
—— (T.) History of Worcestershire
                      2nd ed. 2 vols. folio 1799
Natal Blue Book, 1863–67 . . . . 6 vols. folio
—— Laws & Votes, 1857–67 . . . 4 vols. folio
National Manuscripts, England & Wales, 3 parts
                            3 vols. 4to. 1868
———————————— Scotland . . . . folio
Naval Biography & Chronicle . . . 5 vols. 8vo. 1800
—— & Military Calendar 12mo. 1824
Navy, Case of Assistant Surgeons in, by a Naval
  Medical Officer . . . . 2nd ed. 1850
—— List, 1826–68 . . . 55 vols. 12mo. & 8vo.

Naylor (*Sir* George) Engravings of Arms of Gloucestershire Gentry 4to. 1792
Neale (F.) on Money-lending. Vol. 3, Law Tr. 1826
Neate's (W. J.) Letter to Sir Wm. Follett, suggesting some amendments in the proposed County Court Bill. Vol. 20, Pam. 1844
Negro Slavery, Mr. Brougham's Opinion on
Neild (Jas.) Account of Society for Debtors' Relief
         2 vols. 8vo. 1802–3
Nelson (J.) History of Islington 4to. 1811
—— (W.), Rights of the Clergy 8vo. 1716
—— Reports in Chancery, 1625–92 . . . 8vo. 1717
—— Law of Manors . . . . folio 1726
—— on Game Laws . . . . . 3rd ed. 12mo. 1736
—— Justice of the Peace . . . 12th ed. 8vo. 1745
Netler on Tithes 8vo. 1625
Netter (T.) of Walden (*see* Fasciculi Zizaniorum, No. 5, M. R. Pub.) W. W. Shirley 1858
Netterville Peerage, 1830–4, Case of A. J. Netterville. Vol. 4, 3rd series. Evidence, Vol. 6, & Vol. 23, H. L. 1861
Neuman & Baretti, Pocket Dictionary of the Spanish & English Languages 4to. 1823
Nevill (de) Testa de (*see* Record Commission)
Neville (S.) & Manning (J.) K. B. Reports, 1832–36 . . . . 6 vols. 8vo. 1834–39
—— & Perry (T. E.) K. B. Reports, 1836–38
         3 vols. 8vo. 1837–38
Nevis, Acts of, 1681–1861 . . . . . . 8vo. 1862
New Brighton, Cheshire, Plan of . . . . . .
—— Brunswick Acts, 1786–1846 & 1857-8–1860
         3 vols. 4to.
Newburgh Peerage, Cases of T. Eyre, & Princess Giustiniani. Vol. 4, 3rd series
Newcastle (*Duke of*) Letter on Neutrality in Time of War. Vol. 1, Col. Jur.
Newcastle Election Poll Books, 1833 & 1837-8
         2 vols. 8vo. 1835–8

Newcome (P.) History of St. Alban's Abbey
                                2 vols. in 1, 4to. 1793–95

Newcourt (Ric.) Repertorium, an Ecclesiastical Parochial History of the Diocese of London
                                  2 vols. folio 1708–10

Newfoundland Acts, 1858–67 (incomplete)
————— 1868 . . . . . . 8vo.

Newgate Calendar (*see* Buckler, & Barnett & Buckler) . . . . 5 vols. 4to. 1807–12

Newland (Jno.) Chancery Practice . . . 8vo. 1813
————————————————— . 2nd ed. 8vo. 1819
————————————————— . 3rd ed. 8vo. 1830

Newman (F. W.) on the Constitutional & Moral Right or Wrong of our National Debt. Vol. 27, Pam. 1849

Newmarch (W.) (*see* Christie, R.)

New Monthly Magazine, 1831–66 . 103 vols. 8vo.

Newnam (Wm.) on Conveyancing. . 3 vols. folio 1781

New Peerage . . 1st to 3rd ed. 9 vols. 8vo. 1769–85

Newport, Isle of Wight, Custom at, a Punishment for Bad Lawyers. 1812

New Reports, 1862–65 . . . . .6 vols. 8vo. 1863–65

NEWSPAPERS:—
    Albion
    Atlas
    Bell's Weekly Messenger
    Britannia
    Church and School Gazette
    City Press
    Colonial Gazette
    Courier
    Daily News
    Daily Telegraph
    Ecclesiastical Gazette
    Economist and Weekly Commercial Times
    Educational Times
    Estates Gazette and Investment Record
    Evening Herald
    Examiner
    Express
    Gazette des Tribunaux

Newspapers—*continued*
Globe
Guardian
Herapath's Railway and Commercial Journal
Illustrated London News
Illustrated Times
John Bull
Mining Journal
Mist's Journal
Moniteur Universel
Morning Advertiser
Morning Chronicle
Morning Herald
Morning Post
Morning Star
North British Advertiser
Observer
. Pall Mall Gazette
Parthenon (The)
Press (The) and St. James's Chronicle
Punch
Railway Times
Saturday Review
Spectator
Standard
Sun
Times
U. K. Solicitors' Register
Volunteer Service Gazette

New South Wales Acts, 1824–52 . 3 vols. 8vo.
———————————— 1824–65 . 5 vols. folio
———————————— Private, 1832–62 . folio 1863
———————————————— 1865–67–8
2 vols. folio
———————————— Census . . . . . . fol. 1861
———————————— (Sydney) Directory . . 8vo. 1862
———————————— Statement as to Proceedings in 1824, 5, 6
New Testament (Nicolas de Lyra. Nurembergæ)
folio 1486
Newton (*Sir* I.) Tables for Renewing Leases
6th ed. 12mo. 1808
—— Philosophical Discoveries (Maclaren) . 4to. 1748

Newton (*Dr.* R.) Characters of Theophrastus 8vo. 1754
—— (Wm.) History of Maidstone . . . 8vo. 1741
—— Map of London, temp. Hen. VIII. before the
Dissolution of the Monasteries . . . . folio 1855
—— Letterpress to London in the Olden Time,
being a Topographical Memoir of London, Westminster, and Southwark . . . . . . folio 1855
—— & Son, Registration of Designs . . . 8vo. 1844
—— Copyright of Designs 8vo. 1845
—— Inventions & Specifications . . . . 8vo.
New York Reports, Court of Appeal (*see* Selden)
—— Political Code 8vo. 1860
—— Civil Code 8vo. 1865
—— Penal Code 8vo. 1865
—— Book of Forms 8vo. 1865
—— Code of Procedure 12mo. 1867
—— Revised Statutes (J. W. Edmonds)
6 vols. 8vo. 1863-66
(And *see* America)
New Zealand Acts, 1854-6-8 . . . . . folio
——————— 1860-1-8 . . . . . folio
——————— Statistics, 1853-6-7-8 . 3 vols. folio
Nicholl (H. J.) *Railway Cases* (*see* Carrow, J. M.)
Nicholl (H. J.), Hare (T.) & Carrow (J. M.) Railway Cases . . . . 2 vols. 8vo. 1835-42
Nicholls (J.) & Doyle (E.) on Insolvency & Bankruptcy . . . . 2nd ed. 8vo. 1845
Nichols (F. M) (*see* Britton)
—— on Knighthood, Feudal & Obligatory . 4to. 1863
—— (J.) Royal Wills. 4to. 1780
—— History & Antiquities of Leicestershire
8 vols. folio 1811
—— (J. B.) Account of St. Katherine's Hospital
4to. 1824
—— Catalogue of Library of Sir Henry Hoare, at Stourhead, containing a minute account of almost every Topographical Work to be found in various publications 8vo. 1840

Nichols & others. Collectanea Topographica &
  Genealogica . . . . 8 vols. 8vo. 1834–43
—— (J. G.) (*see* C. S. Pa. Nos. 35, 39, 42, 48, 53,
  60, 77, 83, 94, 97 ; C. M. Nos. 56, 61, 73)
—— Catalogue of Camden Society Papers . 4to. 1862
Nicholson (C.) Annals of Kendal 8vo. 1832
—————— (Wm.) Historical Libraries of England,
  Scotland, & Ireland . . . . . 2nd ed. folio 1714
———————————————————— 3rd ed. folio 1736
Nicol (H.) *County Court Equity Jurisdiction* (*see*
  Pollock, C. E.)
Nicolas (N. H.) Biography of Davidson . . 8vo. 1823
—— (*Sir* N. H.) Progresses of Queen Elizabeth
  2nd ed. 3 vols. 4to. 1823
—— Notitia Historica (Tables, &c.) . . . 8vo. 1824
—— Peerage . . . . 2 vols. 12mo. 1825
—— Testamenta Vetusta. Hen. II. to Queen
  Elizabeth . . . . 2 vols. 8vo. 1826
—— Progresses of King James I. . 4 vols. 4to. 1828
—— Historical Literature 8vo. 1830
—— Scrope & Grosvenor Roll, Controversy rela-
  tive to their Court Armour, temp. Ric. II.
  2 vols. folio 1832
—— Chronology of History 8vo. 1833
—— Proceedings & Ordinances of the Privy
  Council, 1386–1542 . . . . 7 vols. 8vo. 1834–37
—— on Adulterine Bastardy 8vo. 1836
—— History of Strathern & Monteith Earldom. 8vo. 1842
Nicolson (J.) & Burn (Rd.) History of Westmore-
  land & Cumberland . . . . . 2 vols. 4to. 1777
Nightingale *v.* Stockdale, Trial (*see* Carr *v.* Hood)
Nisbet (*Sir* Jno.) Doubts & Questions, & some De-
  cisions in Court of Session, Scotland . . folio 1698
Nobility, Historical Essay on the rise of the . 8vo. 1718
Noble (*Rev.* M.) History of Cromwell
  2nd ed. 2 vols. 8vo. 1784
—————————————————— College of Arms. 4to. 1805
Nolan (M.) *Reports* (*see* Strange, Sir Jno.)

Nolan (M.) Poor Laws . . . . . 2 vols. 8vo. 1805
—— Speech on Farnboro' Road Bill. Vol. 13,
 Jac. Law Tracts 1811
Nonarum Inquisitiones, temp. Edward III. (see
 Record Commission) . . . . . . folio 1807
Nonconformist Society's Report on Parliamentary
 Debate on Dissenters' Chapel Bill . . . 8vo. 1844
Nonparochial Registers, Report of Commissioners on
 Registering Births, &c. . . . . . . folio 1838
Noorthouck (Jno.) History of London, West-
 minster, & Southwark . . . . . . folio 1773
Norburie (Geo.) On Abuses in Chancery, & Re-
 medies. Vol. 1, Hargrave's Law Tr.
Norden (Jno.) Description of Essex, 1594. No. 9,
 C. S. Pa. (ed. Sir H. Ellis) 1840
—— Speculi Britanniæ pars. Historical Descrip-
 tion of Essex, 1594 (ed. by Sir H. Ellis). No. 9,
 C. S. Pa. 4to. 1840
—— Progress of Piety. Par. S. Pa. 1847
Norfolk Poll Book, 1802 & '17 . . 2 vols. 8vo.
—— MSS. in Bodleian Library, Historical Poems
 from the 16th Century. No. 61 C. M. Vol. 3
 (ed. J. P. Collier) 1854
Norman Rolls, Rotuli Normanniæ, 1205–1417 (see
 Record Commission) 8vo. 1835
——· & Saxon Charters (see Charta Antiquæ)
—— (J. P.) Exchequer Reports (see Hurlston, E. T.)
—— on Patent Law 12mo. 1853
Normandie, Coustumes du Pais de. . . . 4to. 1586
Norris (W.) Parliamentary Bills of Costs. 12mo.
North British Advertiser, unbound
—— Kent Railway Evidence in Parliament. folio 1845
—— Peerage Case, Lady S. Doyle. Vol. 2, 2nd
 series. Evidence, Vol. 6, and Vol. 16, H. L. 1837
—— (R.) on English Law 8vo. 1824
Northamptonshire (see Peck's Stanford) 1727
Northington (Lord) Reports (see Eden, R. H., &
 Henley, Lord)

Northumberland Election Poll Book, 1747–8–1774
8vo. 1826
——————————————— 1826 . 8vo. 1827
——————————————— 1832 . 8vo. 1833
——————————————— 1847 . 8vo. 1847
—————— Peerage, Claim of J. Percy. Vol. 4, 3rd series
Norton v. Reilly, Lord Northington's Decree. Remarkable Case. Vol. 1, Col. Jur.
—— (G.) Exposition of City Privileges as to Claims of non-Freemen to deal by wholesale within its jurisdiction. See London Tr. . . . 1821
—— Commentaries on City Franchises . . 8vo. 1829
—— (J. B.) On Administration of Justice in Southern India 8vo. 1853
Norvin's Histoire de Napoléon 12mo. 1842
Norwicensis Historia Anglicana B. de Cotton. (ed. H. R. Luard) No. 16, M. R. Pub. 1859
Norwich, Removal of Assizes to, from Thetford. 8vo. 1824
Notaires, La Science des . . . . 2 vols. 4to. 1771
Nott's Grounds of Law 12mo. 1657
Nova Scotia, Journal of House of Assembly
5 vols. folio 1863–67
—————————————— of Legislative Council
5 vols. folio 1863–67
—— Law Reports of Supreme Court, 1834–41. 8vo. 1853
—— Revised Statutes 8vo. 1851
————————————— 2nd series 8vo. 1859
————————————— 3rd series 8vo. 1864
—— Statutes 1857, 8, 9, 60 . , . . 8vo. 1857–60
—— Statutes 1863, 4, 5, 6, 7 . . . . 8vo. 1863–67
Novísima Recopilacion de las Leyes de España
6 vols. 4to. 1805–29
Nowell (A.) Catechisms. Par. S. Pub. 1853
Noy (W.) Maxims. Law Tr. & A. 1641
—————————————— (Barton). 12mo. 1794
—————————————— (Bythewood) . 6th edit. 12mo. 1821
—————————————————————— . 9th edit. 8vo. 1824

Noy (W.) K. B. Reports, 1595. . . . . folio 1656
Nucius (N.) Travels. No. 17, C. S. Pa. (J. A. Cramer) 1841
Nugent Peerage. Evidence, Vol. 20, & Vol. 20, H. L. 1839
Nuptiæ Sacræ, or an Inquiry into the Scripture Doctrine of Marriage & Divorce. Vol. 2, Jac. Col.. 1821
N. (J.) Alien Priories, & of such lands as they are known to have possessed in England & Wales
2 vols. in 1, 12mo. 1779
N. (N.) on Estates Tail & Descents. Law Tr., 1641
N. (P.) An Abridgment of 49 Popish Trials, 1678–87, mostly reported in Howell's State Trials, Jardine's Edition, 1828 . . . . . 8vo. 1690

O

Oath of Adjuration, Thoughts on (*see* Adjuration)
Oaths, Forms of . . . . . 2 vols. 12mo. 1649–89
—— to be taken by M.P.'s. Jac. L. T. Vol. 7,
    collected by Mr. Sugden 1829
Oats (H. C.) Factory Acts 12mo. 1862
Obituary & Biography (Annual), 1818–26. (Vols.
    3, 6, 8 wanting) . . . . . . 6 vols. 8vo.
Observer, The, Newspaper, 1844–67. 18 vols. folio
O'Connell's (Danl.) Intercepted Letter, Treason in
    the Church. Vol. 5, Pam. 1839
—— The Queen, Lord Denman's Judgment . 8vo. 1844
Ogborne (Elizth.) History of Essex . . . 4to. 1814
Ogilby (Jno.) Itinerarium Angliæ (Road Book) folio 1675
—— & Morgan (Wm.) Traveller's Pocket Book
                                21st ed. 12mo. 1782
Ogle (J. C.) (*see* Armstrong, Rd.)
Oke (G. C.) on Solicitors' Bookkeeping . . 8vo. 1849
—— Magisterial Formulist . . . 2nd ed. 8vo. 1856
——————————————— & Addenda to
                                3rd ed. 8vo. 1862
——————————————————— 4th ed. 8vo. 1868
——· Magisterial Synopsis . . . . . 6th ed. 8vo. 1858
——————————————— Supplement to
                                7th ed. 8vo. 1861
——————————————————— 9th ed. 8vo. 1866
——————————————————— 10th ed. 8vo. 1868
—— Turnpike Laws . . . . . 2nd ed. 12mo. 1860
—— Game and Fishery Laws 12mo. 1861
Okey (C.) Analyse de l'Acte de Réforme du Parle-
    ment (Angleterre) 8vo. 1832
—— Letter to Lord Chancellor, with Forms of
    Deeds & Documents compared & exemplified.
    Vol. 1, Pam. 1835

Okey (C. H.) Laws relating to Subjects of Great
  Britain & France . . . . 2nd ed. 8vo. 1829
—— Droits d'Aubaine de la Grande-Bretagne.12mo. 1830
—— Droits etc. des Étrangers dans la Grande-
  Bretagne 12mo. 1831
Old Entries, Intrationum Liber . . . . . folio 1546
—— Bailey Sessions Papers, 1824, 5, 6, 7, 8, 1830
    6 vols. 4to.
Oldfield (T. H. B.) History of Boroughs
    2nd ed. 3 vols. 8vo. 1794–97
Oldmixon (J.) Lives of the Lord Chancellors from
  1067 to 1708. . . . . 2 vols. 8vo. 1708
Oldys (W.) & Park (T.) Harleian Miscellany
    10 vols. 4to. 1808–13
Oliphant (G. H. H.) on Horses, Racing, Wagers &
  Gaming 12mo. 1847
———————————————————— (G. R.
  Ryder) . . . . 3rd ed. 8vo. 1865
Oliver & Boyd's Edinburgh Almanac or Direc-
  tory, 1838–67 . . . . 12mo.
Oliver (*Rev.* Geo.) History of Beverley & Col-
  legiate Church of St. John 4to. 1829
—— History of Collegiate Church at Wolver-
  hampton 8vo. 1836
—— (L.), Beavan (E.) & Lefroy (T. E. P.) Rail-
  way Cases. Vols. 5, 6, & 7 . . 3 vols. 8vo. 1847–54
—— (W. A.) Manual of Shipping Law . 12mo. 1868
Omler (Edw.) *Election Cases* (*see* Knapp, J. W.)
Onslow *v.* Horne—Trial for Libel before Mr.
  Justice Blackstone. Libel L. T. Vol. 3
Onslow *v.* Morris—Trial for Defamation before
  Lord Mansfield at Guildhall in 1770. Libel
  Law T. Vol. 3
—— (A.) (*see* Buller, Sir F.)
—— Biography of Dr. Abbott 8vo. 1777
Ooddeen *v.* Oakeley, Judgment of the Lords Jus-
  tices of Appeal . . . . Vol. 21, Pam. 1862
Opinions & Cases . . . . 2 vols. 8vo. 1791

LAW SOCIETY LIBRARY. 237

Option on the Claim of Archbishops to dispose of Preferment of Bishops pending Translation. Vol. 2, L. T.
Orange, Prince of, Representation of Danger of Protestants previously to his coming. L. T. 1688-89
—— Declarations containing his reasons why he invaded England. Law T. 1688-89
—— and Princess, Prayer for. L. T. 1688-89
Ord (J. W.) History & Antiquities of Cleveland
            4to. 1846
Orders in Council, Ecclesiastical Commissioners & Acts . . . . 20 vols. 8vo. 1845-62
Ordnance Maps . . . . 2 vols. folio 1838
Oriental MSS. Cat. in British Museum
          4 vols. folio 1838-47
Originalium Rotulorum Abbreviatio, Hen. III. & Edw. III. (Playford) (*see* Record Commission)
         2 vols. folio 1803-10
Origine (De l') des Lois, des Arts et des Sciences
          2 vols. 4to. 1758
Orléanois, Carte d' (France) 1761
Orme (R.) Digest of Election Law . . . 8vo. 1796
Ormerod (G.) History of Cheshire & City of Chester, & Survey of every Township in County
          3 vols. folio 1819
Ormonde Peerage—no case—Evidence, Vol. 20
Orphans, Case of, considered 12mo. 1725
Orrery (*Earl*) Remarks on Life, &c. of Dr. Jonathan Swift . . . . 3rd ed. 12mo. 1752
Ortolan (J. L. E.) (*see* Justinian)
O'Sullivan (J.) Letter to Professor Morse on the Sole Chance left for Reunion of America. Vol. 16, Pam. 1863
Otho & Othobon, Constitutions (*see* Lyndwood)
Otto (E.) Thesaurus Juris Romani . 5 vols. folio 1725
Oude, its Spoliation 8vo. 1857
Oughton (T.) Ordo Judiciorum . . . 2 vols. 4to. 1738

Owen (*Dr.*) Argument upon his application before Lord Mayor for Tithes at 2*s*. 9*d*. in the £ (*see* London Tracts) 1823
—— (H.) & (J. B.) Blakeway's History of Shrewsbury . . . . 2 vols. 4to. 1825
—— (T.) K. B. Reports, 1583–1615 . . folio 1656
—— (Wm.) Welch Dictionary . . 2 vols. 4to. 1803
—— Trial for Libel in 1732 before Lord C. J. Lee. Vol. 3, Libel L. T.
Oxenedes, Johannis de, Chronica (ed. Sir H. Ellis) No. 13, M. R. Pub. 8vo. 1839
Oxford Calendar, 1810–67 . . . 42 vols. 8vo.
—— Graduates, 1659–1782 . . . . . . 8vo. 1772
———————— 1650–1800 . . . . . . 8vo. 1801
———————— 1659–1850 . . . . . . 8vo. 1851
—— Poll Book 8vo. 1853
—— Press, Observations on the Press (*see* Blackstone L. T. 1771)
—— University, Commissioners' Report . . folio 1852
————————————— Statutes of the 4to. 1768

P

Paget (Jno.) on Income Tax Act (bound up with
Pratt) 12mo. 1843
Paine (Thos.) Trial . . . . . 2nd ed. 8vo. 1793
Palna (G.) Dictionnaire Legislatif et Reglementaire
des Chemins de Fer. 8vo. 1864
Palaye, Mémoires sur l'ancienne Chevalerie. Vol. 2
12mo. 1759
Paley (Wm.) Principal and Agent (Gow)
2nd ed. 8vo. 1819
——————————— (J. H. Lloyd) 3rd ed. 8vo. 1833
—— on Convictions (Macnamara) . 4th ed. 8vo. 1856
————————————— . . . 5th ed. 8vo. 1866
Palgrave's (*Sir* F.) On the Rise & Progress of the
Commonwealth . . . . . . 2 vols. 4to. 1832
—— Essay on the Original Authority of the King's
Council. 8vo. 1834
—— History of Normandy & England. 2 vols. 8vo. 1851
Pall Mall Gazette, 1867-68 . . . 8 vols. 4to.
Palliser (*Capt.*) & Nangle (*Capt.*) on the Volunteer in the Field. Vol. 15, Pam. 1861
Palmer (*Sir* Gefery) K.B. Reports, 1619-53 . folio 1678
—— (Jno.) History of Siege of Manchester, reprint, 1822 . . . . 8vo. 1642
——.(J.) on Costs . . . . . . 8th ed. 4to. 1818
——————————— . . . . . . 9th ed. 4to. 1823
—— on Costs & Supplement . 10th ed. 4to. 1829-32
—— Parliamentary Costs 4to. 1823
—— Practice, House of Lords. 8vo. 1830
——————————————————— 8vo. 1841-42
—— Practice of Appeals to the Privy Council from
the Colonies. Vol. 12, Jac. Col. 1831
—— (S.) Index to the Times, 1867-69 . 4to. 1867-69
Pamphlets, Various . . . . . 28 vols. 8vo.
Pancras, Southampton, Paving Acts . . 12mo. 1801
Pandectarum Juris Civilis Digestum Novum
5 vols. folio 1566

Panormitani Abbatis Commentaria Juridica
4 vols. folio 1517
—— on Decretals . . . . 4 vols. fol. 1524
Panton v. Williams, Sir H. Jenner's judgment, supposed Forged Will Case. Vol. 1, Pam. . . . 1840
Paolo, Discourse on Inquisitioni de Venetia . 4to. 1639
Papal Bulls (see Chartæ Antiquæ)
Papists, Letter shewing that Treaties with them cannot be relied on. L. Tr. 1688–89
Paris Directory 8vo. 1846
—— (Matthew) Historia Minor. Edited by Sir F. Madden. No. 44, M. R. Pub. 1866
Parish Clerks' Survey of the Cities of London & Westminster, Southwark, & part of Middlesex & Surrey, within the Bills of Mortality . . 8vo. 1732
Parishes (see Vol. 18, House of Commons' Sessions Paper, 1840)
Park (J. A.) Insurance, Marine & Life . . 8vo. 1787
——————————————————————4th ed. 8vo. 1800
—————————————————————— . 5th ed. 1802
———————————————— 7th ed. 2 vols. 8vo. 1817
———————————— (Hildyard) 8th ed. 2 vols. 8vo. 1842
———————— (J.J.) Letters on Law Improvement. 8vo. 1830
———————— Lecture on Systems of Registration & Conveyancing. Vol. 5, L. T. 1833
—— (J. J.) History of Hampstead . . . 8vo. 1815
—— on Dower 12mo. 1819
—— Contre-projet to Humphresian Code . 8vo. 1828
—— What are Courts of Equity? Lecture on. L. T. Vol. 5 1832
—— Dogmas of the Constitution 8vo. 1833
Parker (Thomas) Laws of Shipping & Insurance
4to. 1775
—— (W. P.) *Precedents in Conveyancing* (see Bythewood, W. M.)

Parker Society's Papers, containing :—
    Ridley (Bp.) Works 1841
    Sandys (Abp.) Sermons, &c. 1841

LAW SOCIETY LIBRARY. 241

Parker Society's Papers—*continued.*

Pilkington (Bp.) Works 1841
Hutchinson (Bp.) Works 1841
Philpot (Archdeacon) Examination, &c. . . . 1842
Christian Prayers & Meditations
Jewel (Bp.) Letters (1st series) Zurich
Grindal (Abp.) Writings
Becon (Chaplain to Abp. Cranmer) Early Writings
Fulkes (Wm.) Defence of English Translation of the Bible . 1843
Hooper (Bp.) Early Writings
Cranmer (Abp.) Writings on the Lord's Supper
Becon Catechism & other Pieces
Liturgies, Catechisms, &c. temp. Edw. VI. 1844
Coverdale (Bp.) Writings of
Latimer (Bp.) Sermons
Becon's Flower of Prayer, &c.
Jewel (Bp.) 2nd series of Letters from Zurich . . . 1845
Latimer (Bp.) Remains
Jewel (Bp.) Writings of, 1st portion
Devotional Piety, temp. Queen Eliz. . . 2 vols.
Coverdale (Bp.) remaining portion of his Writings. . 1846
Reformation, English Letters relating to. Vol. 1
Cranmer (Bp.) Remains of
Calfhill's Answer to Martell's Treatise on the Cross
Jewel (Bp.) further portions of his Works
Liturgies, &c. temp. Queen Elizabeth
Reformation, concluding portion of Letters as to
Norden's Progress of Piety 1847
Jewel (Bp.) 3rd portion of his Works 1848
Bradford's Writings, 1st portion
Tyndale's Writings, 1st portion
Fulke's Answer to Martiall & Stapleton
Whitaker's Disputations on Holy Scriptures . . . 1849
Bullinger's Sermons, Decades 1 & 2, forming 1st Vol.
Bull (Bp.) Select Writings
Tyndale's Writings, 2nd portion
——————— 3rd and last Vol. 1850
Bullinger, 3rd Decade, forming Vol. 2
Jewel, 4th and last Vol.
Cooper (Bp.) Answer to Apology of Private Mass
Bullinger, 4th Decade, forming Vol. 3 1851
Private Prayers, temp. Queen Elizabeth
Whitgift (Abp.) 1st Vol. of his Works
Woolton's Christian Manual
Hooper, 2nd Vol. 1852
Bullinger, 5th Decade, forming 4th Vol.
Whitgift, 2nd Vol.
Parker (Abp.) Correspondence

R

Parker Society's Papers—*continued*.
  Whitgift, 3rd & last Vol. 1853
  Bradford, 2nd & last portion
  Nowel's Catechisms
  Rogers on the Articles (Index to 57 vols.)
Parker (*Abp.*) De Antiquitate Britannicæ Ecclesiæ
  (Drake) . . . . folio 1720
  —— Catalogue of Manuscripts of 4to. 1777
  —— (*Rev.* R.) (*see* Cantalupe, N.)
  ——(R. A.) Observations on Remuneration to
  Attorneys & Solicitors. Vol. 16, Pam. . . . 1853
Parker (*Sir* T.) Exchequer Reports, 1743-66. folio 1776
Parkhurst (R. M.) Paper read (1866) before the
  Manchester Statistical Society, as to Local Courts
  & Tribunals of Commerce. Vol. 27, Pam. . . 1866
Parkin (*Rev.* C.) *History of Norfolk* (*see* Blomefield,
  Rev. F.)
Parkins (W. T.) (*see* Beavan, Edw.)
Parkinson (G. H.) Common Law Judges' Chamber
  Practice 12mo. 1861
Parkyn's Account of Great Yarmouth (reprint) 8vo. 1776
Parliament, Acts & Ordinances, 1642-46 . folio 1646
  ————————————————— 1640-67 . folio 1667
  —— Answer to Petyt's Book of 1680 . . 12mo. 1681
  —— Bishops' Right to Vote in . . . 12mo. 1680
  —— Cases & Records in, on privilege . . 8vo. 1764
  —— Commons' Debates, 1660-1744. 21 vols. 8vo. 1733-92
  —— Debate on 'Abdicate' 12mo. 1690
  —— Debates, 1804-13 . . . 29 vols. 8vo. 1804-13
  —— Elector Denied his Vote for M.P. Ashby *v.*
  White . . . . 2nd ed. 8vo. 1721
  —— History & Debates, 1680-85 . . . . 8vo.
  —— History, 1102-1660 . . . 21 vols. 8vo. 1781-82
  —— Lords' History, 1160-1743 . 8 vols. 8vo. 1742-43
  —— Members of, from 1660-1724 . . 12mo. 1824
  —— Pamphlets on Privilege of . . . 8vo. 1839-40
    Containing :—
    1. Mr. Blundell's Letter to G. F. Young, Esq. with Con-
       siderations on Judgment in Howard *v.* Gossett . . 1839

Parliament, Pamphlets on Privilege of—*continued.*

2. Mr. Freshfield's Speech on Printed Papers ; Breach of Privilege 1839
3. Mr. C. R. Kennedy on the Privileges of the House of Commons 1840
4. Mr. Mackworth on Free Parliaments : Vindication of Right of Commons, justifying their Proceedings in Ashby *v.* White. Printed in 1704; reprinted 1840
5. Mr. T. Pemberton's Letter to Lord Langdale, on recent Proceedings of H. C. on Subject of Privilege . . 1837
6. Ditto . . . . 3rd ed. 1840
7. Mr. Pickering's Remarks on Report of a Select Committee of late H. C. on publishing Printed Papers. 2nd ed. 1838
8. Mr. Rutherford on the Judicial Privilege of the Commons on Controverted Elections considered, and its Partial Abolition vindicated 1838

—— Tracts on Privilege of 4to. 1642
Viz. :—
Collection of Rights & Privileges of Parliament & Prerogatives of Kings 1642
A Declaration of Parliament upon 5 Hen. IV., whereby the Commission of Array is supposed to be warranted (H. Elsynge) 1642
Richard Steele's Crisis; a Discourse representing the causes of the late happy Revolution, with Remarks on the Danger of a Popish Successor 1714

—— Private Bills, Instructions for passing . 8vo. 1825
—— Privileges of (*see* Anglesey)
—— Privileges of (*see* Parliamentary Pamphlets & Tracts)
—— Protests of the House of Lords, 1641–1745
4to. 1745
—— Register, 1744–1803 . 83 vols. 8vo. 1775–1804
—— Standing Orders in L. & C. 1839–49
4 vols. 12mo.
—— White & Black Lists of Houses of, & of Ireland, from 1690 . . . . 12mo. 1752
Parliamentary Alphabetical Digest & Index . . 1834
—— Debates, 1610. No. 81, C. S. Pa. 1862
—— Papers :—
House of Commons—Votes . 2 vols. folio 1745–47

Parliamentary Papers—*continued*.
Sessions Papers, namely, Selection of H. C.:—

	Votes	Bills	Papers	Total	
Papers	56	291	347		1801–26

General Index of Do.
Selections of Sessions Papers, containing Bills, Reports, &c. of House of Commons, 2 vols.

	folio	1806–7
2 vols.		1807
4		1808
3		1809
5		1810

Selections of Sessions Papers, containing Bills, Reports, &c. of House of Lords 1804–5

2 vols.	1810
1	1811
2	1812
2	1812–13

		Votes	Bills	Papers and Reports	Total		
Part of Do.							
House of	Commons	..	..	..	11	vols.	1813
——	Lords	..	2	1	3		
——	Commons	..	..	..	19		1814–15
——	Lords	..	1	1	2		
——	Commons	..	..	..	13		1816
——	Lords	..	1	1	2		
——	Commons	..	..	..	14		1817
——	Lords	..	1	1	2		
——	Commons	..	..	..	13		1818
——	Lords	..	1	1	2		
——	Commons	..	2	18	20		1819
——	Lords	..	1	..	1		
——	Commons	..	1	3	4		1819–20
——	Lords	..	1	1	2		
——	Commons	..	1	11	12		1820
——	Lords	..	1	1	2		
——	Commons	..	3	20	23		1821

LAW SOCIETY LIBRARY. 245

Parliamentary Papers—*continued.*

	Votes	Bills	Papers and Reports	Total	
House of Lords	..	1	1	2	
———— Commons	..	..	16	16	1822
———— Lords	..	3	1	4	
———— Commons	..	..	15	15	1823
———— Lords	..	3	1	4	
———— Commons	2	3	20	25	1824
———— Lords	1	4	2	7	
———— Commons	2	3	23	28	1825
———— Lords	1	2	1	4	
———— Commons	..	2	26	28	1826
———— Lords	2	2	1	5	1826–27
———— Commons	2	2	24	28	1826–27
———— Lords	1	2	2	5 vols.	
———— Commons	2	3	24	29	1828
———— Lords	1	2	2	5	
———— Commons	2	2	22	26	1829
———— Lords	1	1	3	5	
———— Commons	1	3	28	32	1830
———— Lords	1	1	..	2	
———— Commons	2	..	14	16	1830–31
———— Lords	..	2	1	3	
———— Commons	..	4	17	21	1831
———— Lords	1	1	3	5	
———— Commons	4	4	47	55	1831–32
———— Lords	..	2	3	5	
———— Commons	3	4	37	44	1833
———— Lords	1	2	5	8	
———— Commons	6	4	46	56	1834
———— Lords	1	2	1	4	
———— Commons	5	4	49	58	1835
———— Lords	1	4	4	9	
———— Commons	5	6	46	57	1836
———— Lords	1	3	12	16	
———— Commons	5	4	54	63	1837
———— Lords	1	3	12	16	

Parliamentary Papers—*continued*.

	Votes	Bills	Papers and Reports	Total	
House of Commons	5	6	47	58	1837–38
———— Lords	1	2	10	13	
———— Commons	5	5	43	53	1839
———— Lords	1	4	11	16	
———— Commons	5	3	46	54	1840
———— Lords	1	2	9	12	1841
———— Commons	4	3	29	36	1st Session 1841
———— Commons	..	1	7	8	2nd Session
———— Lords	1	3	6	10	
———— Commons	5	4	44	53	1842
———— Lords	1	2	6	9	
———— Commons	6	4	55	65 vols.	1843
———— Lords	1	4	28	33	
———— Commons	5	4	47	56	1844
———— Lords	1	4	33	38	
———— Commons	6	6	45	57	1845
———— Lords	2	3	26	31	
———— Commons	8	4	55	67	1846
———— Lords	1	3	41	45	
———— Commons	8	4	73	85	1847
———— Lords	2	4	43	49	
———— Commons	8	6	69	83	1847–48
———— Lords	2	4	43	49	
———— Commons	8	6	54	68	1849
———— Lords	2	4	39	45	
———— Commons	8	8	49	65	1850
———— Lords	2	4	40	46	
———— Commons	8	6	66	80	1851
———— Lords	1	3	36	40	
———— Commons	6	4	62	72	1852
———— Lords	2	5	81	88	
———— Commons	9	7	104	120	1852–53
———— Lords	2	4	46	52	
———— Commons	9	6	73	88	1854

LAW SOCIETY LIBRARY. 247

Parliamentary Papers—*continued.*

	Votes	Bills	Papers and Reports	Total	
House of Lords	2	4	42	48	
——— Commons	8	6	57	71	1854–55
——— Lords	2	4	51	57	
——— Commons	8	6	84	98	1856
——— Lords	1	1	16	18	1857
——— Commons	7	1	20	28	1st Session
——— Lords	2	4	30	36	1857
——— Commons	..	4	50	54	2nd Session
——— Lords	2	3	45	50	
——— Commons	7	4	76	87	1857–58
——— Lords	1	2	24	27	1859
——— Commons	6	2	31	39	1st Session
——— Lords	1	2	28	31	vols. 1859
——— Commons	..	2	43	45	2nd Session
——— Lords	·2	6	42	50	
——— Commons	8	6	74	88	1860
——— Lords	2	4	53	59	
——— Commons	8	4	86	98	1861
——— Lords	2	5	44	51	
——— Commons	8	5	70	83	1862
——— Lords	2	4	57	63	
——— Commons	8	5	84	97	1863
——— Lords	2	4	46	52	
——— Commons	8	4	78	90	1864
——— Lords	2	3	37	42	
——— Commons	8	4	63	75	1865
——— Lords	2	4	49	55	
——— Commons	9	5	72	86	1866
——— Lords	..	..	..	..	
——— Commons	6	6	70	..	1867

General Index to Sessions Papers H.C. 1801–26 1830
——————————————————— 1801–32 . 1833
General Index to Reports only H. C. 1696–34 . 1834
——————— Bills   do. H. C. 1834–44 . 1845
———————————————— H. L. 1801–45 . 1847

Parliamentary Papers—*continued.*
 General Index to Bills only H. C. 1844-50 . . 1850
 ——————— of Reports only of Committees H. C.
  1801-52 1853
 ——————— of Bills only H. C. 1801-52 . . . 1853
 ——————— of Papers H. L. 1801-52
 ——————— Public Acts H. L. 1801-52
 ——————— Local & Personal Acts H. L. 1801-52 1854
 ——————— Papers H. C. 1832-38 1840
 ——————— Divisions H. C. 1834-52
 ——————— Public Petitions H. C. 1833-52 . 1855
 ——————— to Papers H. L. 1801-59. . . . 1860
 ——————— H. C. 1852-3-61 1862
Parliamentary Reform: Letter to R. Freedom, Esq.,
 on the Redistribution, Extension, & Purification
 of the Elective Franchise, by a Revising Barrister. Vol. 9, Part 2, Pam. . . . . 1853.
—— Review for 1826. Vol. 7, Law T.
Parliamentary Writs & Writs of Military Summons,
 Edw. I. & II. [*Sir* F. Palgrave] 2 vols. in 4
 (Vol. 2, in 3 divisions) . . . . . folio 1827-34
Parliamentorum Rotuli, 6 Edw. I. to 19 Hen. VII.
 1278-1503. . . . . 6 vols. folio 1780
 —— Indices, 1278-1503 [J. Stracey, J. Pridden,
 & E. Upham] . . . . folio 1832
Parliamentum, Modus Tenendi (T. D. Hardy). 8vo. 1846
Parochial Societies, Instructions for Establishing
 National Life Annuities
Parry (*Capt.* W. E.) Journal of Second Voyage to
 discover North-West Passage, & Appendix
         2 vols. 4to. 1824-25
Parsons (Edw.) History of Leeds . 2 vols. 8vo. 1834
—— (Philip) Monuments in East Kent . . 4to. 1794
—— (Robt.) Answer to 5th Part Lord Coke's
 Reports 4to. 1606
—— (*Dr.* T.) on Contracts, U. S.
       4th ed. 2 vols. 8vo. 1860
Parthenon, The . . . . 2 vols. 4to. 1862-63

Parton (John) History of St. Giles-in-the-Fields
             4to. 1822
Pask (J.) on Registering Judgments . . 12mo. 1859
Patent Journal, 1852–68 & continued . . . 1852–68
—— Office, Catalogue of Library . 2 vols. 4to. 1857–58
—— Rolls. Rotuli Litterarum Patentium. Vol. 1,
Part. 1, 1201–16 (T. D. Hardy) (*see* Record
Commission) . . . . folio 1835
—— Rolls, The General Introduction to (T. D.
Hardy). 8vo. 1835
Patents, Abridgment of Specifications. Vols. 1 to
37 . . . . 28 vols. 12mo. 1857–69
 1. Drain Tiles & Pipes
 2. Sewing & Embroidery
 3. Manure
 4. Preservation of Food
 5. Marine Propulsion
 6. Manufacture of Iron & Steel
 7. Aids to Locomotion
 8. Steam Culture
 9. Watches, Clocks, & other Timekeepers
10. Firearms & other Weapons: Ammunition & other Accoutrements
11. Paper. Manufactures of Paper, Pasteboard, & Papier-mâché
12. Paper Cutting, Folding, & Ornamenting, including Envelopes, Cards, Paperhangings
13. Typographic, Lithographic, & Plate Printing
14. Bleaching, Dyeing, & Printing Yarns & Fabrics
15. Electricity & Magnetism; their Generations & Applications
16. Manufacture & Application of Indiarubber, Gutta-percha, &c., including Air, Fire, & Waterproof
17. Production & Applications of Gas
18. Metals & Alloys
19. Photography
20. Weaving
21. Ship Building, Repairing, Sheathing, Panelling

Patents, Abridgment of Specifications—*continued*.
  22. Bricks & Tiles
  23. Plating or Coating Metals with Metals
  24. Pottery
  25. Medicine, Surgery, & Dentistry
  26. Music & Musical Instruments
  27. Oils—Animal, Vegetable, & Mineral
  28. Spinning, including the preparation of Foreign Materials, & the doubling of Yarns & Threads
  29. Lace & other looped & netted Fabrics
  30. Preparation & Construction of Fuel
  31. Raising, Lowering, & Weighing
  32. Hydraulics
  33. Railways, from 1770 to 1863
  34. Saddlery
  35. Roads & Ways
  36. Bridges
  37. Writing
—— Descriptive Index of, for 1867 . . . 4to. 1868
—— Correspondence as to Extension of Patent Law to Colonies, 1852–61 . . . . . . 4to.
—— for Inventions. General Index to the Repertory for 1815–45 . . . . 8vo. 1846
———————————— 1617–1867. Specifications
———————————————— Drawings
———————————— Index of Patentees, 1617–1867 (Alphabetical)
———————————— Chronological, 1617–1867
———————— Index of Subject-matter, 1617–1867
———————————— Reference . . 2 vols. 4to. 1855
—— Supplement to, 1617–1852 . . . . 4to. 1858
Paterson (J.) Road Book (E. Mogg). 18th ed. 8vo. 1829
—— Compendium of English & Scotch Law
                                                     8vo. 1860
—— Country Attorney 12mo. 1861
—— Game Laws 12mo. 1864
—— (J. W.) (*see* Archbold & Shaw)
Paton (Thos. J.) on Appeals to H. L. . . 8vo. 1858

Paul (John) Landlord & Tenant (Wilson)
          4th ed. 8vo. 1778
———————————————— 7th ed. 8vo. 1791
Pauper Children, Report on Training . . . 8vo. 1841
Pawley (R.) Catalogue of Nobility created by
 Car. II. 8vo. 1662
Pawnbrokers & Usurers . . . . 2nd ed. 12mo. 1775
Payne (J.) *N. P. Reports* (*see* Carrington, F. A.)
——— *C. P. Reports* (*see* Moore, J. B.)
——— (O.) Collection of Scarce Treatises upon Metals, &c. containing 'The Art of Metals,' written originally in Spanish by A. A. Barba, translated by Earl Sandwich in 1669; that invaluable Piece of Mr. G. Plattes on a Discovery of all sorts of Mines, from Gold to Coal; Houghton's 'Complete Miner' . . . . . . 2nd ed. 12mo. 1738
——— (T.) List of Lords & Commons . 12mo. 1724–25
Peachey (J. P.) on Marriage Settlements . 8vo. 1860
Peake (T.) on Evidence 8vo. 1801
———————————————— . . . 2nd ed. 8vo. 1804
———————————————— . . . 3rd ed. 8vo. 1808
——— N. P. Reports, 1790–1812 . 2 vols. 8vo. 1820–29
Pearce (J.) on the Abuses of the Law. Vol. 2,
 Law Tracts 1814
——— (R. P.) (*see* Denison, S. C.)
Pearson (C.) Synopsis of his intended Lecture on
 Prison Discipline. Vol. 6, Pam. 1848
——— Proceedings at Meeting at London Tavern to diminish the Overcrowding of the Streets, & provide Dwellings for the Working Classes. Vol. 27, Pam. 1859
Peck (Fras.) Antiquarian Annals of Stanford, Lincoln, Rutland, & Northamptonshires
            folio 1727
——— (Wm.) Topographical History of Bawtry & Thorne 4to. 1813
——— Topographical Account of Axholme, Scampton, & Tattershall, Lincolnshire 4to. 1815

Peckwell (R. H.) Election Cases, 1796–1806
         2 vols. 8vo. 1803–5
Pecock (R. *Bp. of Chichester*) the Repressor of
 overmuch Blaming of the Clergy. Ed. C. Ba-
 bington. No. 19, M. R. Pub. 1860
Peel (*Sir* R.) Speech on the Criminal Law. Vol. 3,
 Law T. 1826
—— Speech on Recovery of Small Debts. Vol. 12,
 Jac. Col. 1827
—— Acts, arranged by a Barrister . . . 12mo. 1827
 ———————————————— 2nd ed. 12mo. 1850
Peerage. Reports from the Lords Committees
 touching the Dignity of a Peer of the Realm, &c.,
 with Appendices. 5 vols. folio, London, reprinted 1829
>Vol. 1. First Report
>Vol. 2. Second, Third, and Fourth Report. Alphabetical Digest. Index Summonitionum. Index Nominum et Locorum
>Vol. 3. Appendix 1. Part 1 (Summonitiones temp. Johan.—Edw. II.)
>Vol. 4. Appendix 1. Part 2. (Summonitiones temp. Edw. III.—Edw. IV.) Appendices 2, 3, 4
>Vol. 5. Fifth Report. Appendix 5. (Patents of Creation, &c., temp. Stephen—Edw. IV.) Index Creationum. Index Nominum. Index Locorum

—— Bill, Pamphlets on (*see* Grimaldi's Tracts)
Peerages & Baronages (*see* Cases in House of
 Lords' Appeals, & 1st, 2nd, & 3rd series; but
 see also under each name) . . . 8 vols. folio
Pegge (Saml.) Curialia, Historical Account of Royal
 Household 4to. 1784
—— Anecdotes. 8vo. 1818
—— Anonymiana . . . . . . 2nd ed. 8vo. 1819
Pell Records; Issue Roll of Thomas de Branting-
 ham, and Issues of the Exchequer (*see* Devon F.)
Pemberton (L. L.) Equity Practice by Revivor
 & Supplement 8vo. 1867
—— (T.) Letter to Lord Langdale on Parlia-
 mentary Privilege (*see* Pam. on Parly. Priv.)
           2nd ed. 1837

Pemberton (T.) Letter to Lord Langdale on Parliamentary Privilege (*see* Pam. on Parly. Priv.)
3rd ed. 1840
—— Substance of Speech on Recommitment of Bill for facilitating Administration of Justice in Chancery. Vol. 2, Ch. Pam. 1840
Penfold (C.) on the System of Rating Railways to the Relief of the Poor. Vol. 6, Pam. 1849
Pennant (T.) Account of London . . 3rd ed. 4to. 1793
—— History of Whiteford & Holyhead . . folio 1796
—— Journey from Chester to London . . 8vo. 1811
Pennsylvania, Charters to . . . . . . folio 1742
Penny (G.) Traditions of Perth 8vo. 1836
Pensions (*see* Sinecures)
People's Rights, properly maintained in the Choice of their Representatives: Address to the Electors of Westminster, by an Elector. Vol. 27, Pam. 1818
Perkins (J. W.) on Conveyancing (bound up with Littleton's Tenures) 1642
———————————————————— 14th ed. 12mo. 1758
—— Profitable Book 12mo. 1657
Perrault (C.) Les Hommes illustres de France
2 vols. folio 1696–1700
Perrin *v.* Blake, Judgment in K.B., with Judge's Arguments thereon. Vol. 1, Col. Jur.
Perry (*Sir* E.) Oriental Cases, 1841–1852 . 8vo. 1853
—— (*Capt.* Jno.) Account of Stopping-up Dagenham Breach, Essex 8vo. 1721
—— (H. & J. W.) Knapp's Election Cases, 1833
8vo. 1833
—— (M. R.) Bankrupt Gazette, 1826–67
42 vols. 8vo.
—— (T. E.) *K. B. Reports* (*see* Nevile, S.)
—— & Davison (H.) Reports of K.B. 1838–41
4 vols. 8vo. 1839–42
Perryn (*Sir* R.) Biography of (*see* Lawyers)
Perth Peerage, Case of G. D. Duke de Melfort. Vol. 2, 2nd series

Perth Peerage, Case of G. D. Duke de Melfort &
T. Drummond. Vol. 4, 3rd series.
—— Peerage, Evidence. Vol. 21, H. L. Sess.
Pa. 1846, and Vol. 20, 1846–47
—— (*Earl of*) Correspondence, 1688–96. No. 33
C. S. Pa. (W. Jerdan) 1845
Pesnelle (M.) Coutume de Normandie. Nouv. éd. 4to. 1759
Peters (R.) (*see* U. S. Statutes)
—— Reports, U. S. (*see* Curtis)
Petersdorff (C.) Abridgment of Common Law Reports, & Supplement . . . 20 vols. 8vo. 1825–44
———————————————— N. S. 6 vols. 8vo. 1861–64
—— Lectures 8vo. 1829
—— Summary of Practice 8vo. 1832
—— on Pleading 8vo. 1835
Petersfield, History of Churcher's College at. 8vo. 1823
Paterson (T. T. A.) (*see* Chambers, T.)
Petheram (W. C.) on Interrogatories . . . 8vo. 1864
Pétrarque (F.) Mémoires pour la Vie (Amsterdam)
3 vols. 4to. 1764
Petrie (Hy.) & Sharpe (*Rev.* J.) Monumenta
Historica Britannica . . . . fol. 1848
—— (S.) Cricklade Case 8vo. 1785
—— Magni Rotuli Scaccarii Normanniæ, 1184. 4to. 1830
Petroburgense, Chronicon, 1122–1286. No. 47,
C. S. Pa. (T. Stapleton) 1849
Pettus (*Sir* Jno.) Fodinæ Regales, or Laws of
Mines . . . . fol. 1670
Petyt (Wm.) Jani Anglorum Facies Nova, or,
Monuments of Antiquity as to Great Councils
of the Kingdom. 12mo. 1680
—— Rights of the Commons of England asserted
8vo. 1680
—— Book of 1680, Answers to (as to Public
Records) 12mo. 1681
Phear (J. B.) on Rights of Water, Sea, & Seashore
8vo. 1859
Philbrick (F. A.) (*see* Hopwood, C. R.)

Philipott (Thomas) Villare Cantianum, or Kent
  Surveyed 4to. 1659
Philipps (H.) Catalogue of Families raised to Power
  & Wealth by Legal Profession . . . 12mo. 1686
—— (J.) Election Cases 8vo. 1782
—— Inland Navigation . . . . . 5th ed. 8vo. 1808
—— (W.) on the Study of the Law. 2nd ed. 12mo. 1675
Philips (Jos.) Special Pleading . 2nd ed. 12mo. 1850
—— (J.) Monthly Mercury on State of Europe,
  1688-99 . . . . 10 vols. 4to. 1692-99
—— Letters on Special Pleading. 2nd ed. 12mo. 1850
Phillimore (J. G.) Private Law among the Romans:
  from the Pandects 8vo. 1863
—— (Josh.) Ecclesiastical Reports, 1809-21
                                3 vols. 8vo. 1818-27
—— (R.) on Domicil 8vo. 1847
—— *Ecclesiastical Law* (*see* Burn, R.) 1842
—— (R. J.) International Law. 4 vols. 8vo. 1851-61
Phillipart (*Sir* Jno.) General Index to Parliamen-
  tary Debates, 1803-30 . . . 2 vols. 8vo. 1832-34
Phillipps (C. S. M.) Jurisprudence . . . 8vo. 1863
—— (S. M.) on Evidence 8vo. 1814
——————————————— . . . 2nd ed. 8vo. 1815
——————————————— . . . 3rd ed. 8vo. 1817
——————————————— . 6th ed. 2 vols. 8vo. 1824
——————————————— . 7th ed. 2 vols. 8vo. 1829
—— & Amos (A.) on Evidence. 8th ed. 2 vols. 8vo. 1837
——————————————— 9th ed. 2 vols. 8vo. 1843
—— (*Sir* T.) Catalogue of MSS. Part 2 . folio
Phillips (C.) Biography of Curran . 2nd ed. 8vo. 1822
—— (C. P.) on Copyright 8vo. 1863
—— on Lunatics 8vo. 1868
—— (E.) English Dictionary . . . 4th ed. fol. 1678
—— (G.) Du Droit ecclésiastique dans ses Sources
                                        8vo. 1852
—— Angelsächsisches Recht 8vo. 1825
—— Titles & Honours conferred by George I. &
  II. 1728 (*see* Grimaldi's T. Vol. 1)

Phillips (R. S.) Guide to Crystal Palace & Park
2nd ed. 12mo. 1854
—— (T. J.) Chancery Reports, 1840–41 (*see* Craig, R. D.)
Philonomus, the Young Lawyer's Recreations
12mo. 1694
Philpot's (J.) Works. Par. S. Pa. 1842
Physicians, College of, Catalogue of Fellows, &c. of
8vo. 1835
Pickering (P. A.) Remarks on Report of Select Committee of H. C. on publishing Printed Papers (*see* Pam. on Parly. Priv.). . . . . 2nd ed. 1838
—— Decisions of H. C. & Remarks on Treating, &c. on Election of M.P.'s 8vo. 1849
—— on Popery, the Inquisition, & the Jesuits 12mo. 1851
Picket Street Proposed Lottery Scheme. 8vo. new ed.
Pigot (*Lord*) Defence of & Inquest on (*see* East India Company)
—— & Co.'s Universal Money Table & Commercial Chart Exchange Standard. . . . .
—— & Dean's Manchester, Salford, &c. Directory 8vo. 1821–22
Pigot's Directories :—
 Bedfordshire, &c. (National Commercial) 8vo. 1830–31
 Berkshire, *see* Beds, 1830–31
 Birmingham, *see* Scotland, 1837
 Buckinghamshire, *see* Beds, 1830–31
 Cambridgeshire, *see* Beds, 1830–31
 Carlisle, *see* Scotland, 1837
 Cheshire, *see* London & Provincial, 1822–23
 —— National Commercial (Northern) . 8vo. 1834
 Cornwall, *see* Beds, 1830–31
 Cumberland, *see* Cheshire, 1834
 Derbyshire, *see* London and Provincial, 1822–23
 —— 8vo. 1835–36
 Devonshire, *see* Beds, 1830–31
 Dorsetshire, *see* Beds, 1830–31
 Durham, *see* Cheshire, 1834

Pigot's Directories—*continued.*
Essex, *see* Home Counties in London Directory, 1834
Gloucestershire,*see* London & Provincial,1822–23
—— *see* Beds, 1830–31
Hampshire, *see* Beds, 1830–31
Herefordshire,*see* London & Provincial, 1822–23
—— *see* Beds, 1830–31
—— *see* Derby, 1835–36
Hertford, *see* London, 1834
Home Counties 8vo. 1834
—— *see* London, 1834
Hull, *see* Scotland, 1837
Huntingdonshire, *see* Beds, 1830–31
Isle of Man, *see* Scotland, 1837
Kent, *see* London, 1834
Lancashire, *see* London & Provincial, 1822–23
Lancashire, *see* Cheshire, 1834
Leeds, *see* Scotland, 1837
Leicestershire, *see* London & Provincial, 1822–23
—— *see* Derby, 1835–36
Lincolnshire, *see* London & Provincial, 1822–23
—— *see* Derby, 1835–36
Liverpool, *see* Scotland, &c. 1837
London, 1834–38, 1840 . . . . . 4 vols. 8vo.
—— & Provincial 8vo. 1822–23
Manchester, *see* Scotland, &c. 1837
Middlesex, *see* London, 1834
Monmouthshire, *see* London & Provincial, 1822–23
—— *see* Beds, 1830–31
Monmouthshire, *see* Derby, 1835–36
Newcastle-upon-Tyne, *see* Scotland, 1837
Norfolk, *see* London & Provincial, 1822–23
—— *see* Beds, 1830–31
Northamptonshire, *see* Beds, 1830–31
Northumberland, *see* Cheshire, 1834
Nottinghamshire, *see* London & Provincial, 1822–23

Pigot's Directories—*continued*.
Nottinghamshire, *see* Derby, 1835-36
Oxford, *see* Beds, 1830-31
Rutland, *see* London & Provincial, 1822-23
—— *see* Derby, 1835-36
Scotland, with Maps, the Isle of Man, &c. . . . 1837
Sheffield, *see* Scotland, 1837
Shropshire, *see* London & Provincial, 1822-23
—— *see* Derby, 1835-36
Somersetshire, *see* London & Provincial, 1822-23
—— *see* Beds, 1830-31
Stafford, *see* London & Provincial, 1822-23
—— *see* Derby, 1835-36
Suffolk, *see* Beds, 1830-31
Surrey, *see* London Directory, 1834
Sussex, *see* London Directory, 1834
Wales, North & South, *see* London & Provincial, 1823.
———————————— *see* Derby, 1835-36
Warwick, *see* London & Provincial, 1822-23
—— *see* Derby, 1835-36
Westmoreland, *see* Cheshire, 1834
Wiltshire, *see* London & Provincial, 1822-3
—— *see* Beds, 1830-31
Worcestershire, *see* London & Provincial, 1822-23
———————— *see* Derby, 1835-36
Yorkshire, *see* London & Provincial, 1822-23
———— *see* Cheshire, 1834
—— English Atlas (with Map of London & 14 miles round) . . . . folio 1831
Pigott (G.) & Rodwell (H.) Election Reports, 1843-45 . . . . 8vo. 1846
—— (N.) on Recoveries (Mr. Serjeant Wilson)
2nd ed. 4to. 1770
Pike (W. P.) Practice of Dublin Court of Record
12mo. 1842
—— Practical Precedents in Civil Bill Process (Ireland) 12mo. 1843
———————————————— 2nd ed. 12mo. 1851

LAW SOCIETY LIBRARY. 259

Pilgrimage of Sir R. Guylford, 1506. No. 51,
  C. S. Pa. (Sir H. Ellis) 1850
Pilkington (Jas.) View of Present State of Derby-
  shire . . . . 2 vols. 8vo. 1803
—— (*Bp.* J.) Works. Par. S. Pa. 1841
Pindar's Odes, translated by Dr. G. West
                                  4th ed. 4to. 1749
Pinto (A. J. de G.) Tratado regular e Pratico de
  Testamentos e Successores 4to. 1820
Pipe Roll, Magnum Rotulum Pipæ, 1130 (*see*
  Record Commission) 8vo. 1833
—— Rotulus Cancellarii, vel Antigraphum Magni
  Rotuli Pipæ 1201 (J. Hunter) (*see* Record
  Commission) 8vo. 1833
—— The Great Roll of the Pipe. 2, 3, & 4
  Hen. II., 1155–58. Curâ J. Hunter (*see* Record
  Commission) 8vo. 1844
  ————————————— 1 Rich. I., 1189–90
Curâ J. Hunter (*see* Record Commission) . 8vo. 1844
Pipon (*Col.* J. K.) & Collier (J. F.) Manual of
  Military Law . . . . 3rd ed. 12mo. 1863
Pitman (E. D.) on Principal & Surety . . 8vo. 1840
Pitt (C.) Report of a Trial, Pitt *v.* Milne &
  others, on a charge of Conspiracy, July 1818.
  Jac. Col. Vol. 12 1820
Placita de Quo Warranto, temp. Ed. I., II., III. in
  Curia Receptæ Scaccarii Westm. asservata (curâ
  W. Illingworth) (*see* Record Commission) folio 1818
Placitorum Abbreviatio, Ric. I. to Ed. II. (W.
  Illingworth) (*see* Record Commission) . . folio 1811
Platt (T.) on Covenant 8vo. 1829
—— on Leases . . . . 2 vols. 8vo. 1847
Playfair (W.) Baronetage included with Peerages,
  &c. viz.: Vols. 1 & 2, English Peerages; Vol. 3,
  Scotch Peerages; Vols. 4 & 5, Irish Peerages;
  Vols. 6 & 7, English Baronets; Vol. 8, Irish
  Baronets; Vol. 9, Scotch Baronets. 9 vols. 4to. 1809–11
Pleader's Assistant 8vo. 1786

Pleading, Method of 8vo. 1697
―― Rules for . . . . 2nd ed. 8vo. 1694
―――――――― . . . . 2nd ed. 12mo. 1794
Pleess (Wm.) Account of the Island of Jersey 4to. 1817
Pline le jeune, Lettres de. 8vo. 1721
Plinii Secundi Historia Naturalis 4to. 1685
Plot (Robt.) Natural History of Oxfordshire, with
   Map. 8vo. 1677
―― History of Staffordshire . . . . . folio 1686
Plowden (Edw.) K.B. Reports, temp. Edwd. VI. to
   Eliz. . . . . 2 vols. in 1, folio 1571

                            2 vols. 8vo. 1816
―― Moot Book of Queries (H. B.) . . 12mo. 1662
―― Abridgment (Ashe's) . . . . . 12mo. n. d.
―― (F.) on Enrolling Deeds 8vo. 1789
―― on Usury 8vo. 1797
―― on Tithes 8vo. 1806
Plunket (E.) Suit in Equity, and Chart . . 8vo. 1868
Plutarch's Lives of the Poets. Wrangham
                      4th ed. 6 vols. 8vo. 1826
Pocket Companion 8vo. 1735
―― Peerage (Scotch) . . . . 2 vols. 12mo. 1826
―― Peerage. . . . . 2 vols. 12mo. 1788
Pocock (G. P.) Transportation & Convict Dis-
   cipline considered, in a Letter to Earl Grey
                          Vol. 5, Pam. 1847
―― (L.) on Rate of Mortality & List of Works on
                          2nd ed. 8vo. 1842
―― (R.) History of Gravesend 4to. 1797
―― Memorials of the Tufton Family . . 8vo. 1800
Pole (*Sir* Wm.) Collection towards a History of
   Devonshire 4to. 1791
Polewart or Polwarth Peerage, Evidence. Vols. 6,
   12, & 20
Polus (Mat.) Synopsis Criticorum Sacræ Scripturæ
   (J. Leusden) . . . . 5 vols. folio 1624
Polite Intelligencer (Directory) 12mo. 1806

LAW SOCIETY LIBRARY. 261

Political Songs of England (*see* No. 6, C. S. Pa.)
—— Tracts, as to Popish Plot . . . . . folio 1680

1. Lewis (W.) his Deposition
2. Everard (Edwd.) his Deposition
3. Reading (N. Esq.) Trial
4. White (Edwd.), Harcourt (Thos. Wm.), Fenwick (John), Gowan (John), & Turner (Anthony), tried for High Treason
5. May (Thos.) & Blane (John), Trial of, Clearing Dr. Oates's Reputation
6. Turberwill (Edwd.) Information
7. De Faria (Francisco) Information
8. De Faria (Francisco) Narrative
9. Dangerfield (Thos.) Information, October 26, 1680
10. Dugdale (Stephen) Information, October 26, 1860
11. Mansell (Col. Roderick) Narrative &c. of Plot
12. Macnamara (John), Fitzgerald (Maurice), & Nash (John), Information
13. Report of Committee of H. C. for receiving Informations on Complaint of Peter Norris
14. Jemson (Robt. Esq.) Information
15. Stafford (Wm. Lord Visct.) his Speech on the Scaffold
16. Dangerfield (Thos.) Information, October 30, 1680
17. Mowbray (Laurance) Narrative
18. Dangerfield (Thos.) 2nd Narrative
19. Danby (Earl of) Reflections upon, as to Murder of Sir Edmondbury Godfrey
20. Robson (Robt.) Narrative
21. Anderson (Lionel), Russell (Wm.), Paris (Chas.), Starkoe (Henry), Corker (James,) Marshall (Wm.), Lumsden (Alex.), & Kennish (D. J.), for High Treason
22. Bourk (Hubert) Information
23. Knox (Thos. Wm. Osborne) & Lorne (John), Narrative of their Conspiracy
24. Whitehead, Harcourt, Fenwick, Gowan, & Turner, their Speeches at their Execution

Political Tracts, &c 8vo. 1804–12
Containing :—

Accounts of the Middlesex Election in 1804
Exposition of Westminster Election 1807
Sir F. Burdett's Speech as to the Duke of York . . 1809
Controverted Election as to Do. 1809
Sir F. Burdett's Plan of Reform 1809
—— Address to the Electors of Westminster . . 1810
—— His Life to 1810
—— Speech on the Address to, in 1812

Political Tracts, &c.—*continued*.
  Sir F. Burdett's Address to the Electors of Westminster 1812
  Westminster Election 1812
  Sketch of Life of Burdett
  Westminster Election, 1808
  Cartwright's Reason for Reformation
  The Royal Mystery
  Trial of Hunt, of the 'Examiner'
  —— Clifford *v.* Brandon
  Proceedings at the Common Hall 1809
  Memoirs of C. J. Fox 1806
  —— Wellington (F. L. Clarke)
  Account of Lisbon
  Memoir of Lord Nelson

Pollard (Robt.) Peerage 4to. 1793
POLL BOOKS:
  Berks. 1818
  Cambridge County. 1754, 1780, 1826
    Cambridge University. 1822, 1827
  Dorset. 1807
  Durham. 1790
  Essex County. 1722, 1724, 1763, 1780
  Gloucester City. 1816
    Bristol. 1739
  Hants. 1779, 1790
  Hereford County. 1802
  Hertfordshire. 1784, 1802, 1805
  Kent. 1734, 1754, 1790, 1796, 1802
    Maidstone. 1806-7, 1818, 1820, 1826
    Rochester. 1802, 1806
  Leicester County. 1775
    Leicester Boro'. 1768, 1796, 1826
  Norfolk. 1802
  Northumberland. 1747-8, 1774, Feb., Mar., June, and July 1826, 1832, 1847
    Newcastle-upon-Tyne. 1835-6, 1837-8
  Oxford University. 1853
  Suffolk.
    Ipswich. 1754, 1780
  Sussex.
    Lewes. 1802, 1812, 1826
  Wilts. 1818
  York County. 1807
    York City. 1741
    Hull. 1774
  Westminster. 1774, 1816

Pollexfen (*Sir* H.) K.B. Reports, 1660–83 folio 1702

Pollock (C. E.) (*see* Maude, F. P.)
—— *Practice Reports* (*see* Lowndes, J. J.)
—— County Court Practice . . . 2nd ed. 8vo. 1853
——————————————— . . . 4th ed. 8vo. 1861
——————————————— . . . 5th ed. 8vo. 1864
——————————————— . . . 6th ed. 8vo. 1868
—— & Nicol (Henry) County Court Equity Jurisdiction 8vo. 1865
Polwhele (R.) History of Devonshire . folio 1797–1806
—— History of Cornwall, with map . 2 vols. 4to. 1816
Polydore Vergil (*see* C. S. Pa. No. 29) (Sir H. Ellis) 1844
Polypus, all the Talents (bound up with Hogan's Appeal to the Public) . . . . 6th ed. 8vo. 1807
Pomey (F.) English & French Grammar
6th ed. 12mo. 1789
Pompeius. Law Dictionary; Vocabularius Juridicus (MS.) . . . . 4to. n. d.
Poor Law Commissioners' Report 8vo. 1834
Poor, Plea for. 1st Report of Leicester Square Soup Kitchen 8vo. 1850
Pope (A.) Works . . . . . . 7 vols. 8vo. 1770
—— Elegy on Man . . . . folio 1819
—— Letters to Atterbury when in the Tower of London. No. 73, C. S. P., C. M. Vol. 4 (J. G. Nichols) 1859
—— (Chas.) Laws of Customs & Excise
5th ed. 8vo. 1820
Popham (*Sir* Jno.) K.B. Reports . . . . folio 1656
———————————————— 1591–1651. folio 1682
Popish Treaties: Letter from a Gentleman at York to his Friend in the Prince of Orange's Camp, showing that they are not to be relied on. Tracts 1688–89
Population of Great Britain. Abstract Returns
6 vols. folio 1811–34
———————————— Comparative Returns, 1801–31. fo. 1831
Porter (J. S.) Lecture on the Metrical Systems as to Weights & Measures. Vol. 12, Pam. . . 1859

Portland (*Duke of*) Case as to Lease of Inglewood Forest, Cumberland, granted to him by the Lords of the Treasury 8vo. 1768
Portugal, Ordenançãoes e Leis. 9th ed. 3 vols. 4to. 1824
Possession of Ancestor continued by Heir-Apparent. His. L. T. 1761
Postlethwayte (M.) on Public Debts, Taxes, Supplies, &c. ; 8vo. 1757
Post Obit Annuity, Opinions on the Grant of a Perpetual. Vol. 2, Col. Jur.
—— Office, Acts relating to 12mo. 1793
———————— Directory, London, 1801–68. 60 vols.
———————————— Maps, 1845–67
———————————————— Suburban, 1860, 1863, & 1865 . . . . 3 vols. 8vo.
———————————————— Home Counties, 1845, 1855, 1859, 1862, & 1866 . . . . . . 5 vols. 8vo.
Pote (Josh.) Registrum Regale Sociorum et Alumnorum in Coll. Etonensi 4to. 1774
Pote (J.) History & Antiquities of Windsor Castle & the Royal College & Chapel of St. George, with the Institution, Laws, & Ceremonies of the most noble Order of the Garter 4to. 1749
Pothier (R. J.) Œuvres posthumes. . 2 vols. 4to. 1777
—— Œuvres posthumes (par Bugnet, et Table par Sirey) . . . . . 2nd ed. 11 vols. 8vo. 1861–62
Vol. 1 contains:—

1. Coutume d'Orléans
2. Des Obligations
3 & 4. Du Contrat
5. Du Contrat de Prêt
6. Du Contrat de Mariage
7. Du Mari
8. Des Successions
9. Des Personnes et des Choses
10. De la Procédure
11. Table par Sirey

—— on Partnership, Translation by O. D. Tudor, & Index 8vo. 1862
Pott (Thos.) Law Dictionary 8vo. 1803
Potter (T. R.) History & Antiquities of Charnwood Forest (Leicester) 4to. 1842

Potts (T.) Discovery & Trial of Lancashire Witches
of 1613 (Reprint) with Introduction, &c. by
James Crossley 4to. 1845
Poulson (G.) History & Antiquities of Holderness
          2 vols. 4to. 1840–41
—— History of Beverley & of the Provostry
& Collegiate Church of St. John . . . 8vo. 1829
Powell (Edmd.) The Law of the Practice of Evi-
dence . . . . 2nd ed. 12mo. 1859
——————————————— . . . 3rd ed. 8vo. 1868
—— Inland Carriers . . . . . 2nd ed. 8vo. 1861
—— (J. J.) on Powers 8vo. 1787
—— on Devises 8vo. 1788
——————— (T. Jarman) . . . 2 vols. 8vo. 1827
—— on Contracts . . . . 2 vols. 8vo. 1790
—— on Mortgage . . . . 3rd ed. 2 vols. 8vo. 1791
——————————— . . . . 4th ed. 2 vols. 8vo. 1799
—— Mortgages & Precedents (T. Coventry).
        6th ed. 3 vols. 8vo. 1826
—— (Tho.) Attorney's Academy 4to. 1623
——————————————— . . 3rd ed. 4to. 1630
—— Index to Records 4to. 1627
Power (D.) *Nisi Prius* (*see* Selwyn, W. J.)
—— Rodwell (H.) & Dew (E. L.) Election Cases,
1847–56 . . . . 2 vols. 12mo. 1853–7
Powis Barony, Case of Sir Nathl. Curson, 1st series
—— (*Earl*) Catalogue of his Hendon Estate. 8vo. 1756
Pownall (T.) Map of America 1776
Poynter (T.) on Marriage & Divorce
        2nd ed. 8vo. 1824
Practical Law Science 8vo. 1835
—— Register in Chancery . . . . . . 8vo. n. d.
—— C. P. 8vo. 1743
Practice, Chancery, Epitomised . 4th ed. 8vo. 1771
—— Complete Clerk in Court, or Practising So-
licitor 8vo. 1726
—— K. B. 8vo. 1739
——————— . . . . . . 3rd ed. 2 vols. 8vo. 1750

Practice, K. B. 8vo. 1814
——————— & C. P. 12mo. 1674
————————————— Epitomised . . . 8vo. 1757
—————————————————— 8vo. 1763
—————————————————— 8vo. 1778
—————————————————— 8vo. 1779
—— Manual of Parliamentary 12mo. 1827
Practising Attorney, or New K. B. Guide . 8vo. 1779
Prater (H.) on Law of Husband & Wife. Vol. 12,
    Jac. Col. 1834
—— on the Conflict of English & Scottish Law of
    Marriage Vol. 12, Jac. Col. 1835
—— Marriage 8vo. 1835–6
Pratt (J. T.) (*see* Bott)
—— Abstract of Courts of Requests Acts, England
    & Wales 8vo. 1824
—— Landlord & Tenant 8vo. 1826
—— Criminal Statutes . 2nd ed. 2 vols. 12mo. 1827
—— Friendly Societies 8vo. 1829
—— Income & Property Tax (bound up with Paget) 1843
————————————————————— 2nd ed. 12mo. 1843
—— Savings Bank Act 12mo. 1844
—— Savings Bank, Instructions for Establishing,
    1837 (*see* Stocks)
—— Savings Bank Law . . . 6th ed. 12mo. 1844
—— Savings Bank, Progress 12mo. 1845
—— Savings Bank, Summary of 8vo. 1846
—— Digest of Reports of Cases in continuation of
                          2 vols. 8vo. 1850–5
—— (W. T.) on Building Societies
                          2nd ed. 12mo. 1865
——————————————————— 5th ed. 12mo. 1859
—— on Highways (Kinnersley) 10th ed. 12mo. 1865
—— Law of Friendly Societies. . 7th ed. 12mo. 1867
Precedents in Chancery, 1689–1722 . . . folio 1733
Prentice (S.) (*see* Archbold's Practice by Chitty)
—— (*see* Roscoe on Evidence)
—— *Action at Law* (*see* Smith, Jno. W.)

Presbyterian Endowments, Report of Attorney-
General v. Pearson, before Lord Cottenham.
Vol. 2, L. T.
Prescott (W. H.) History of the Conquest of
Mexico . . . . 6th ed. 2 vols. 8vo. 1850
—— History of the Conquest of Peru
6th ed. 2 vols. 8vo. 1850
—— History of the Reign of Ferdinand & Isabella
the Catholic, of Spain . . 7th ed. 2 vols. 8vo. 1851
Present State of Court of Great Britain . 12mo. 1742
Press, The, Sketch of the Political History of last
Three Years. Vol. 11, Pam. 1856
———————————————— 1853–67. 14 vols. folio
—— and St. James's Chronicle, Aug. to Dec. 1868
& continued
Preston, History of, with Guild Merchant, & some
Account of Duchy & County Palatine of Lancaster
4to. 1822
—— Town of, Encomium, Happiness of Retire-
ment. Lanc. Co. T. 1733
—— (R.) on Conveyancing 8vo. 1806
———————————————— 2nd ed. 3 vols. 8vo. 1813–16
———————————————— 3rd ed. 3 vols. 8vo. 1819–29
—— Estate & Tenures . . . 2 vols. 8vo. 1820–27
—— on Abstracts of Title. 2nd ed. 3 vols. 8vo. 1823–4
Prestwich (*Sir* J.) Respublica 4to. 1787
Price (Geo.) Exchequer Reports, 1813–25
13 vols. 8vo. 1816–28
—— Exchequer Practice, Jurisdiction, &c. . 8vo. 1827
———————————————— . 8vo. 1831
—— (Rd.) on Life Annuities . . 2nd ed. 18mo. 1772
—— Life Annuities (W. Morgan) 5th ed. 2 vols.
8vo. 1792
—— (Wm.) on Minerals. . . . . . . folio 1778
Prichard (J. C.) on Insanity 8vo. 1835
Prideaux (C. G.) on Churchwardens. 6th ed. 12mo. 1857
———————————————— 7th ed. 18mo. 1863
———————————————— 10th ed. 18mo. 1865

Prideaux (C.G.) on Churchwardens. 11th ed. 18mo. 1868
—— (F.) on Conveyancing . . . 3rd ed. 8vo. 1859
—— & Whitcombe (J.) on Conveyancing
4th ed. 2 vols. 8vo. 1864

5th ed. 2 vols. 8vo. 1866
—— on Judgments & Crown Debts. 3rd ed. 12mo. 1845

4th ed. 12mo. 1865
—— (*Dr.* H.) Ecclesiastical Tracts. 2nd ed. 8vo. 1716

1. Validity of Orders of Church of England
2. The Justice of Present Established Law, giving Successor to Ecclesiastical Benefices all Profits from Day of Avoidance
3. Award of King Charles I. as to Personal Tithes, a Vindication thereof, & a Thanksgiving Sermon

—— On Tithes . . . . 2nd ed. 8vo. 1736
—— Life of 8vo. 1748
Priestley, Appeal on the Birmingham Riots . 8vo. 1791
Prince Edward's Island, Laws, 1773–1865. 5 vols.
8vo.
Prince (Alex.) Record of Patent Inventions. 8vo. 1843
—— (Jno.) Worthies of Devon . . . . . folio 1701
———————————————————— 4to. 1810
—— (J. H.) Remarks on Barring Dower. Vol. 27,
Pam. 1805
—— on Conveyancing 8vo. 1812
Princes of Wales, Chronicle of (Rev. J. Williams) 1860
(*see* Brut y Tywysogion, No. 17, M. R. Pub.)
Principal & Factor, Statement of the Laws of,
Defects, & a Remedy 1842
Prior (H. L.) on Conveyancing 8vo. 1857
Pritchard (R. A. & W. T.) Digest of Law &
Practice of the Court for Divorce & Matrimonial Causes 8vo. 1859
—— (T. S.) Handy-Book for Executors & Administrators 12mo. 1861
—— (W. T.) Admiralty Digest 8vo. 1847

Pritchard (*Dr.* R. A. Pritchard, W. T. Pritchard,
& A. Jones) . . . . 2 vols. 8vo. 1865
Private Acts from   to 1867 (incomplete) in
progress
—— Index, 1483–1831 * . . . . . . folio
—— Acts, Index to, 1801–59 . . . . . folio 1860
—— Bills, Instructions for Passing . . . 8vo. 1825
Private Bills, Report on, of House of Commons. fo. 1846
—— Prayers, temp. Queen Eliz. Par. S. Pa. . . 1851
Privileges & Regalities of Repledging. His. L.
T. 1761
Privy Council Appeal Cases, 1833–67. 71 vols. folio
—— Case of Commendams before the. Vol. 1,
Col. Jur. 1791
—— Proceedings of, & Ordinances, 1386–1542,
10 Ric. II. to 33 Hen. VIII. (Sir H. Nicolas)
(*see* Record Commission). . . 7 vols. 8vo. 1834–37
Process in Absence. His. L. T. 1761
Proclamations, 1–7 James I., 1602–9 . . folio
Proclus, Commentaries on First Book of Euclid's
Elements . . . . 2 vols. 4to. 1792
Promises & Covenants. His. L. T. 1761
Promptorium Parvulorum, sive Clericorum Lexicon
Anglo-Latinum Princeps, A.D. 1440. No. 25,
C. S. Pa. (A. Way) Vol. 1, A—L 1843
—— No. 54, C. S. Pa., Vol. 2, M—R 1853
—— No. 89, C. S. Pa., Vol. 3, R—Z 1865
Property, of (*see* His. L. T. 1761)
——————— Tax Act, 38 Geo. III. cap. 16 . folio 1798
Prophecy of Bishop Usher. T. 1688
Proposals from Abp. of Canterbury & other
Bishops to H. M., Account of. T. 1688
Proposition for compiling & amending Laws
Protestant Liturgy, a New. T. 1688
Protestants, Representations of the Dangers of, be-
fore Prince of Orange came. T. 1688–89

* This Index includes some Public, Local, & Road Acts.

Protests of Lords in 1722-23 (*see* Impeachment of Lords)
Prussian Laws, Frederician Code, translated from the French . . . . 2 vols. 8vo. 1761
Pryce (W.) Mineralogia Columbiensis . . . fol. 1778
Prynne (William) the Soveraigne Power of Parliaments and Kingdomes 4to. 1643
    And bound therewith:—
—— An Humble Remonstrance against the Tax of Ship-money, written An. 1636; printed without his privity, An. 1641, but now set out by a true copy agreeing with the originall; to right the Author 4to. 1643
—— The Opening of the Great Seale of England, &c. 1643
—— - Rome's Masterpiece, or the Grand Conspiracy of the Pope, &c. . . . . 2nd ed. 1644
—— The Popish Royall Favourite 1643
—— The Doome of Cowardisze & Treachery . . 1643
—— A Vindication of Psalme 105-15 1644
—— A Moderate Apology against a pretended Calumny, in answer to some passages in the Preheminence of Parlement 1644
—— The Falsities and Forgeries of the Anonymous Author of a late Pamphlet 1644
—— Catalogue of Printed Books written by William Prynne 1643
—— A True and full Relation of the Prosecution, Arraignment, Tryall, and Condemnation of Nathaniel Fiennes 1644
—— Twelve Considerable Serious Questions touching Church Government 1644
—— Independency Examined, Unmasked, Refuted, &c. 1644
—— A Sovereaign Antidote to prevent, appease, and determine our unnaturall and destructive Civill Warres and Dissentions 1642
—— Brevia Parliamentaria Rediviva . . . 8vo. 1662

Prynne (William) the History of King John, King
Henry III. & King Edward I. &c. . . . folio 1670
—— (*see* Cotton, *Sir* R.)
Public Acts, Abstract of, 1770–75. 3 vols. folio 1776–7
—— Index to, 1801–59 . . . . folio 1860
—— Characters, 1798–1809 . . . 10 vols. 8vo.
—— Councils of the Kingdom, & of Affairs of War
& Peace therein debated. Col. Jur. Vol. 2
—— Departments, Notes of Materials for the
History of (F. S. Thomas) . . . . . folio 1846
—— Expenditure, Increase of, How to Check It.
The Piccadilly Papers, No. 1, Vol. 15, Pam. . 1860
—— General Acts, 1224–1848 . 197 vols. folio
(Annual wanting, 18, 19, 20, 22, Car. 2)
—— General Acts, 1708–1749. . 21 vols. 12mo.
—— General Acts, 1832–1867 . . 35 vols. 8vo.
—— General Acts, Abridged, 9 Hen. III. to
9 Geo. II. . . . . 9 vols. 8vo. 1730
—— General Acts, Abridged, to 11 Geo. II.
2 vols. folio 1739
—— Institutions: Report of Proceedings at Meet-
ing, Freemasons' Tavern, to promote the Admis-
sion to, without Charge—Jos. Hume, Chairman.
Vol. 27, Pam. 1837
—— Records, Reports of Committees of House of
Commons . . . . folio 1732
——————————————————— folio 1801
—— Records, Reports from Commissioners, 1800–
1819 . . . . 2 vols. folio 1812–19
—— Records, Reports from Commissioners & Ap-
pendix of Engravings 1819
—— Records, Evidence from the Committee of
the House of Commons on the Commission . 8vo. 1836
—— Records, Report of Commissioners, 1837, folio
—— Records, Report of the Committee of the
House of Commons on the Commission . 8vo. 1837
—— of Deputy Keeper . . . . 6 vols. folio 1840–49
(And *see* Record Commission.)

Public Sale Rooms, Prospectus for establishing, in
  London. Vol. 4. Pam. 1835
Publishers, Appeal against Monopoly of. Vol. 4,
  Pam. 1835
Puffendorff's (*Baron*) Law of Nature & Nations
  (Dr. B. Kennett) . . . . . . 3rd ed. folio 1717
—— Law of Nature & Nations (Johnson) . 8vo. 1758
—— Les Devoirs de l'Homme et du Citoyen,
  traduit par Barbeyrac . . 5th ed. 2 vols. 8vo. 1735
Pugh (W. O.) Welch Dictionary 8vo. 1832
—— Welsh Grammar 8vo. 1832
Puller (C.) (*see* Bosanquet, *Sir* J. B.)
Pulling (A.) Laws of London 8vo. 1842
—— Is the Gaol the only Preventive of Crime &
  Criminals? Vol. 18, Pam. 1843
—— Observations on City Corporations Disputes . 1847
—— on Attorneys 8vo. 1849
——————————————— . . . . . 3rd ed. 8vo. 1862
—— Mercantile Joint Stock Companies' Accounts
  12mo. 1850
—— On Private Bill Litigation: Can Nothing be
  Done to Improve it? Vol. 11, Pam. 1859
—— On our Law Reporting System: Cannot its
  Evils be Prevented? Vol. 20, Pam. 1863
Pulton (F.) De Pace Regis et Regni. . . folio 1610
——————————————————— . . . folio 1615
—— Collection of the Statutes, Magna Charta to
  7 James, 1225–1610, with Notes . . . folio 1617
Punch. Vols. 47 to 53, 1864–69 & continued . 4to.
Purkis (H. W.) Telegram, Examination Questions
  & Answers, 1859–1864 . . . . 8vo. 1865
Putnam (J. P.) (*see* U. S. Digest)
—— Hale (G. S.), Smith (H. F.) & Frost (H. W.)
  United States Digest of Decisions in Common
  Law, Equity, & Admiralty Courts of U. S. &
  England, 1847–65 . . . . . 19 vols. 8vo.
—— Supplement to, of Courts of Common Law &
  Admiralty, U. S. (Boston) . . 2 vols. 8vo. 1860–61

Putnam (J.P.) Equity, U. S. (Boston). 2 vols. 8vo. 1864
    (And *see* United States Digest)
Pycroft (J. W.) Letter to Sir R. H. Inglis on Oxford University Commission. Vol. 9, Pam. Part 2
                                                            2nd ed. 1851
—— on Oxford University Commission, & Nature of Protection afforded by Legislative Incorporation. Vol. 8, Pam. 1852
—— Examination of Claim of H.M. to Seashore in Cornwall & Devon 4to. 1854
Pye (*Dr.* J.) Moral System of Moses . . 4to. 1770
Pyper (W.) Gradus ad Parnassum . . . 8vo. 1831
P. (G.) Law of Parliament 8vo. 1690

Q

Quarterly Review, 1809–1868 . . 128 vols. 8vo.
Quayle (T.) General View of the Agriculture of
 the Isle of Man 8vo. 1812
Quebec, Code of Laws for 8vo. 1774
Queen Caroline's Trial (*see* Evidence, Vol. 3; Hansard's Parliamentary Debates, 1820; & Vol. 53, House of Lords Journal for 1820)
Queenborough, Charter to . . . . . 12mo. n. d.
Queen's Bench Reports (*see* Adolphus & Ellis)
Queensbury Peerage, Case of C. Marquis & Earl of. 3rd series, Vol. 4; Evidence, Vol. 21
Queensland (Australia) Acts, 1865–67. 2 vols. folio
Quibbles of the Law . . . . . 2nd ed. 8vo. 1726
———————————— . . . . . 4th ed. 8vo. 1736
Quin (John) on Local Courts 8vo. 1831
Quintilianus (M. F.) de Institutione Oratoria Libri XII. cum notis et animadversionibus (P. Burmanni) . . . . 2 vols. 4to. 1720
Quo Warranto Proceedings in the Court of King's Bench touching the Charter of the City of London . . . . folio 1626

R

Racine (J.) Œuvres 8vo. 1829
Radcliffe (J.) Bibliotheca Chethamensis, 2 vols. 8vo. 1791
Ragged Schools relative to the Government Grants for Education: Report of Conference at Birmingham. Vol. 15, Pam. 1861

Railway Cases, Law & Equity, 1835–54 (see Nicholl, Carrow, & Oliver) . . . 7 vols. 8vo. 1840–55
—— Map of England & Wales, in case 1852
—— North Kent, Evidence in Parliament. folio 1845
—— Times, 1838–68 (in progress) . 62 vols. 4to.
—— & Land Taxation, Poor & other Rates, their Injustice & Impolicy. Vol. 21, Pam. 1844
Railways, Acts for Regulating, 1838–49 . 12mo.
Raithby (J.) Index to Statutes from Magna Charta to 49 Geo. III. . . . . 3 vols. 8vo. 1814
—— Index to Statutes from Magna Charta to 49 Geo. III. (1809) 4to. 1814
—— on the Study & Practice of the Law
2nd ed. 8vo. 1816
Raleigh (Sir W.) Biography of 12mo. 1677
—— History of the World . . . . . . folio 1687
Ram (J.) on Father's Right to Custody of his Children. Vol. 11, Jac. Col. 1828
—— on Assets, Debts, & Incumbrances . 12mo. 1832
—— on Legal Judgment 8vo. 1834
—— on Facts 8vo. 1861
Ramsay (C.) on Government 12mo. 1732
Ramshay (W.) Decisions on New Pleading Rules
8vo. 1838
Randall (C.) History of Stirling (Scotland)
12mo. 1812
Rapin (T.) History of England, Acta Regia, containing Crown Grants, &c. (S. Whatley) . folio 1732
———————————————————— (Rev.
N. Tindal) . . . . . 2nd ed. 2 vols. folio 1732
Rastell (W.) Entries 4to. 1670
—— Collection of Statutes, 9 Hen. III. to 23 Eliz. 4to. 1681
Rauthmell (Rev. Ric.) Roman Antiquities of Overborough, Lancashire. Reprint 8vo. 1824
Ravennas (P.) Juris Civilis Compendium . 4to. 1521
Rawdon (Marmaduke) of York, Life of. No. 85, C. S. Pa. [Ed. R. Davies] 1863

Rawlins (A. H.) on Chancery Orders & Improvement of Courts. Vol. 11, Jac. Col. 1831
Rawlinson (Christ.) on Corporations (W. N. Welsby)
         4th ed. 12mo. 1863
———————————————— (T. Geary) 5th ed. 12mo. 1868
—— (*Dr.* R.) Specimen of Mistakes in Dugdale's Baronage (*see* Grimaldi's Tracts, Vol. 3)
Ray (*Dr.* J.) Medical Jurisprudence
      4th ed. enlarged, 8vo. 1860
Raymond (*Lord*) K. B. Reports . . 2 vols. folio 1743
———————————————— 3rd ed. 2 vols. folio 1775
——————1694–1730 (Bayley) 4th ed. 3 vols. 8vo. 1792
———————————————— (Gale) 5th ed. 8vo. 1832
—— (*Sir* T.) K. B. Reports, 1660–1684 . folio 1696
———————————————————2nd ed. folio 1743
Rayner (J.) Tithe Cases (Exchequer) 1575–1782
        3 vols. 8vo. 1783
—— on Bankrupt Law Reform. Vol. 13, Pam.
—— (Wm.) Trial for Libel before Lord Raymond in 1732. Libel L. T. Vol. 3
Read Baronetage, Pedigree, & Proceedings. 3rd series; Evidence, Vol. 10
Reader (W.) Domesday Book of Warwickshire
           4to. 1835
Real Property, Commissioners' Report, 1829–32.
         2 vols. folio
———————— Law Questions, by a Barrister. 8vo. 1839
———————— Remarks on Framing a Code of Laws for. Vol. 5, Jac. Col. 1827
Record Commission, Return to, from Lincoln's Inn
         8vo. 1801
—— Office, Proposal for Erecting General . 8vo. 1832
———————— General Papers relating to . . 8vo. 1835
—— of Caernarvon (*see* Record Commission).
—— Commission. Publications of the Commissioners of Public Records.
Record Commission.—Publications.
 Acts of the Lords Auditors of Causes & Complaints, A.D. 1466–94. [Ed. T. Thomson] folio 1839

Record Commission—*continued.*
Acts of the Lords of Council in Civil Causes,
A.D. 1478-1495. [Ed. T. Thomson] . folio 1839
—— of the Parliament of Scotland, from 1124 to
1707. [Ed. T. Thomson & C. Innes]
11 vols. folio 1814-44
Ancient Laws & Institutes of England, comprising Laws enacted under the Anglo-Saxon kings, from Æthelbirht to Cnut, with an English translation of the Saxon; the laws called Edward the Confessor's, the laws of William the Conqueror, and those ascribed to Henry I.; also Monumenta Ecclesiastica Anglicana from the seventh to the tenth century, and the ancient Latin version of the Anglo-Saxon laws. With a Glossary, &c. [Ed. B. Thorpe] . . . . folio 1840
—— Laws & Institutes of Wales, comprising laws supposed to be enacted by Howel the Good, modified by subsequent regulations under the Native Princes, prior to the conquest by Edward I.; and analogous Laws, consisting principally of institutions which by the Statute of Ruddlan were permitted to continue in force: with an English translation of the Welsh text. To which are added a few Latin Transcripts, containing Digests of the Welsh Laws, principally of the Dimetian Code. With Indexes & Glossary. [Ed. A. Owen] . folio 1841
Calendarium Inquisitionum post mortem sive Escætarum, temp. Reg. Hen. III. ad Ric. III.; cum Appendice de quamplurimis aliis Inquisitionibus a regno Hen. III. usque Jac. I. nuper repertis. [Ed. J. Caley] . 4 vols. folio 1806-28
—— Rotulorum, Chartarum, et Inquisitionum ad quod Damnum, temp. Reg. Johan. ad Hen. VI. [Ed. J. Caley] . . . . folio 1803
—— Rotulorum Patentium in Turri Londinensi; with Indexes by S. Ayscough . . . folio 1802

278   LIST OF THE BOOKS IN THE

Record Commission—*continued.*
Calendars of the Proceedings in Chancery in the Reign of Queen Elizabeth; to which are prefixed Examples of earlier proceedings in that Court, from Ric. II. to Queen Elizabeth. [Ed. J. Bayley] . . . . 3 vols. folio 1827–32
Catalogue of the Manuscripts in the Cottonian Library in British Museum. By J. Planta
folio 1802
—— of the Harleian Manuscripts in the British Museum. [Ed. by H. Wanley, D. Casley, Rev. R. Nares & others. Index by Rev. T. H. Horne] . . . . . 4 vols. folio 1801–12
—— of the Lansdowne Manuscripts in the British Museum, with Indexes & Preface. [Ed. Sir H. Ellis] . . . . folio 1812–19
Documents illustrative of English History in the 13th & 14th centuries, &c. [Ed. H. Cole]
folio 1844
—— & Records illustrating the History of Scotland, & the transactions between the Crowns of Scotland & England, preserved in the Treasury of Her Majesty's Exchequer. Vol. 1. [Ed. Sir F. Palgrave] 8vo. 1837
Domesday Book: seu, Liber Censualis Wilhelmi primi regis Angliæ inter archivos regni in dom. Cap. West. asservatus. [Ed. A. Farley.]
2 vols. folio 1783
—— Libri Censualis vocati Domesday Book Indices. Accessit Dissertatio Generalis de ratione hujusce Libri. [Ed. Sir H. Ellis]
folio 1816
—— Libri Censualis vocati Domesday Book Additamenta ex codi. antiquiss. Exon' Domesday. Inquisitio Eliensis. Liber Winton. Boldon Book. [Ed. Sir H. Ellis] . . . . folio 1816
—— A General Introduction to Domesday Book, accompanied by Indexes of the Tenants in Chief, & Under Tenants, at the time of the

Record Commission—*continued.*
Survey, as well as of the Holders of Lands
mentioned in Domesday anterior to the for-
mation of that Record; with an Abstract of
the Population of England at the close of the
Reign of William the Conqueror, so far as the
same is actually entered; illustrated by nume-
rous notes and comments. [Ed. Sir H. Ellis]
2 vols. 8vo. 1833
Ducatus Lancastriæ Pars I. Calendarium Inquisitionum post mortem, &c. temp. Regum
Edw. I. ad Car. I. (Partes II., III., IV.) A
Calendar to the Pleadings, &c. from Hen. VII.
to end of reign of Queen Elizabeth. [Ed. R. J.
Harper, J. Caley, & W. Minchin.]
4 parts in 3 vols. folio 1823–34
Exchequer (History of), &c. (*see* Kalendars)
Fines, sive Pedes Finium; sive Finales Concordiæ
in Curia Domini Regis, 7 Ric. I.–16 John,
1195–1214. [Ed. J. Hunter] 2 vols. 8vo. 1835–44
(And *see* Rotuli.)
Inquisitionum ad Capellam Domini Regis retornatarum, quæ in publicis Archivis Scotiæ adhuc
servantur, Abbreviatio. [From about 1546
to the end of the 17th century. Ed. T. H.
Thomson] . . . . . . 3 vols. folio 1811–16
—— in Officio Rotulorum Cancellariæ Hiberniæ
asservatarum Repertorium. [Ed. J. Hardiman]
2 vols. folio 1826–29
Kalendars (The Antient) and Inventories of the
Treasury of his Majesty's Exchequer, together
with other Documents illustrating the history
of that Repository. [Ed. Sir F. Palgrave.]
3 vols. 8vo. 1836
King's Council, authority of (*see* Palgrave,
Sir F.)
Modus tenendi Parliamentum; an ancient Treatise
on the mode of holding the Parliament in England. [Ed. T. D. Hardy] 8vo. 1846

Record Commission—*continued.*

Monumenta Historica Britannica, or Materials for the History of Britain from the earliest period. Prepared and illustrated with Notes by the late H. Petrie, assisted by the Rev. J. Sharpe. [Completed & the Prefatory Matter added by T. D. Hardy.] Vol. 1 (extending to the Norman Conquest) . . . . . . folio 1848

<small>*Contents:*—Gildas, or *Gildus*; Nennius, Beda, Anglo-Saxon Chronicle, Asserius de rebus gestis Ælfredi, Chronicon Æthelwærdi, Florentiæ Wigornensis Chronicon, Simeonis Dunelmensis Historia, Henrici Huntendunensis Historia, " L'Estoire des Engles solum la translation Maistre Geffrei Gaimar," Annales Cambriæ, Brut y Tywysogion, De Bello Hastingensio Carmen.</small>

Nonarum Inquisitiones in Curia Scaccarii, temp. Reg. Edw. III. [Ed. G. Vanderzee] . folio 1807

Palgrave (*Sir* F.) upon the Original Authority of the King's Council 8vo. 1834

—— Parliamentary Writs & Writs of Military Summons, together with the Records and Muniments relating to the suit & service due & performed to the King's High Court of Parliament and the Councils of the Realm, or affording evidence of attendance given at Parliaments & Councils; with Alphabetical Digest & Index. 2 vols. in 4 (Vol. 2 in 3 divisions)
folio 1827–34

Pipe Rolls, The Great Rolls of the Pipe for the 2nd, 3rd, & 4th years of King Henry II., A.D. 1155–58, & 1st year of King Ric. I. A.D. 1189–90. Reprinted. [J. Hunter]
2 vols. 8vo. 1844

Placita de Quo Warranto, temp. Edw. I., II., III., in Curia Receptæ Scaccarii. Westm. asservata. [Ed. W. Illingworth] . . . folio 1818

Placitorum in Domo Cap. Westm. asservatorum Abbreviatio, temp. Ric. I.–Edw. II. [Ed. W. Illingworth] . . . . folio 1811

LAW SOCIETY LIBRARY. 281

Record Commission—*continued.*
Privy Council of England, Proceedings & Ordinances of, from 10 Ric. II. to 33 Hen. VIII.
1386-1542. [Ed. Sir H. Nicolas]
7 vols. 8vo. 1834-37
Registrum vulgariter nuncupatum, " The Record of Caernarvon," e Codice MS. Harleiano 696 descriptum. [Ed. Sir H. Ellis] . . . folio 1838
—— Magni Sigilli Regum Scotorum in Archivis publicis asservatum A.D. 1306-1424. [Ed. T. Thomson] . . . . folio 1814
Rotuli Chartarum in Turri Londinensi asservati; accurante T. D. Hardy. Vol. 1, pars 1, ab anno 1199 ad annum 1216. . . . . . . folio 1837
—— Curiæ Regis. Rolls & Records of the Court held before the King's Justiciars or Justices, from 6 Ric. I. to 1 John. [Ed. Sir F. Palgrave.]
2 vols. 8vo. 1835
—— Finium. Excerpta e Rotulis Finium in Turr. Lond. asservatis, Hen. III. Rege, A.D. 1216-72, curâ C. Roberts . 2 vols. 8vo. 1835-36
—— Hundredorum temp. Hen. III. et Edwd. I. in Turr. Lond. et in Curia Receptæ Scaccarii Westm. asservati. [Ed. W. Illingworth.]
2 vols. folio 1812-18
—— de Libertate ac de Misis et Præstitis regnante Joh. [cura T. D. Hardy] . . . 8vo. 1844
—— Literarum Clausarum in Turr. Lond. asservati, ab anno 1204 ad annum 1227; accurante T. D. Hardy . . . . . 2 vols. folio 1833-44
—— Rotuli Litterarum Patentium in Turri Londinensi asservati: ab anno 1201 ad annum 1216; accurante T. D. Hardy. Vol. I. Pars I. . . . . folio 1835
—— Normanniæ in Turr. Lond. asservati Joh. et Hen. quinto Angliæ Reg.; accurante T. D. Hardy. Vol. 1 de annis 1200-1205 necnon de anno 1417 . . . . 8vo. 1835

Record Commission—*continued.*
Rotuli de Oblatis et Finibus in Turr. Lond.
asservati temp. Reg. Joh.; accurante T. D.
Hardy 8vo. 1835
—— Scotiæ in Turr. Lond. et in Dom. Cap.
Westm. asservati temp. Reg. Angliæ Edw. I.-
Hen. VIII. [Ed. D. Macpherson, J. Caley,
W. Illingworth. Indexes by T. H. Horne]
       2 vols. folio 1814-19
—— Selecti ad Res Anglicas et Hibernicas spectantes, ex Archivis in Dom. Cap. Westm.
deprompti. Cura J. Hunter 8vo. 1834
Rotulorum Originalium in Curia Scaccarii Abbreviatio, temp. Reg. Hen. III. Edw. III.
[Ed. H. Playford]
       2 vols. folio 1805-10
—— Patentium et Clausorum Cancellariæ Hiberniæ Calendarium. Vol. 1, pars 1, Hen. II.-
Hen. VII. . . . . folio 1828
Rotulum (Magnum) Scaccarii, vel Rotulum Pipæ
de anno tricesimo primo Reg. Hen. I. (ut
videtur); quem plurimi hactenus laudarunt
pro Rotulo quinti anni Stephani Regis. [Ed.
J. Hunter] 8vo. 1833
Rotulus Cancellarii vel Antigraphum Magni
Rotuli Pipæ de tertio an. Reg. Joh. [Ed.
J. Hunter] 8vo. 1833
Rymer (Thomas). Fœdera, Conventiones, Litteræ
et cujuscunque generis Acta publica inter
Reges Angliæ et alios quosvis Imperatores,
Reges, Pontifices, Principes, vel Communitates,
ab ingressu Gulielmi I. in Angliam (A.D.
1066) ad nostra usque tempora habita aut
tractata; primum in lucem missa studio T.
Rymer Historiographi, et R. Sanderson;
denuo aucta, et multis locis emendata, accurantibus A. Clarke, F. Holbrooke, et J. Caley
           folio

Record Commission—*continued.*
Statutes of the Realm (from Magna Charta to end of reign Q. Anne), printed from original Records & authentic Manuscripts. [Ed. A. Luders, Sir T. E. Tomlins, J. France, W. B. Taunton, J. Raithby] . 9 vols. folio 1810-28
—— Index, Alphabetical and Chronological
folio 1824-28
Taxatio Ecclesiastica Angliæ et Walliæ, auct. P. Nich. IV. circa A.D. 1291. [Ed. T. Astle, Rev. S. Ayscough, & J. Caley]
folio 1802
Testa de Nevill, sive Liber Feodorum in Curia Scaccarii temp. Hen. III. et Edw. I. [Ed. J. Caley & W. Illingworth] . . . . folio 1807
Valor Ecclesiasticus Hen. VIII., auctoritate regia institutus cum Appendice et Indicibus (A.D. 1535). [Ed. J. Hunter]
6 vols. folio 1810-34
Records, Répertoire of (bound up with Powell's Attorneys' Academy) 1631
Recoveries, Equitable Case on Validity of, Opinions of Eminent Counsel. Vol. 1, Col. Jur.
Reddie (J.) Historical Notices of Roman Law, & its Study in Germany 8vo. 1826
—— Letter to Lord Chancellor on Expediency of giving a new Civil Code for England. Vol. 9, Jac. Col. 1828
Redesdale (*Lord*) on Chancery Commissioners' Report. Vol. 3, Jac. Col. 1826
Redfield (J. F.) on Railways (American Law)
3rd ed. 2 vols. 8vo. 1867
—— on Wills (American Law). 2nd ed. 2 vols. 8vo. 1867
Redford (G.) & Riches (T. H.) History of Uxbridge
8vo. 1818
Redington (James) Calendar of Treasury Papers preserved in H.M. Public Record Office, 1557-1696 . . . . 2 vols. imp. 8vo. 1868

Red Horse in Warwickshire (*see* Wise's Letter to
Dr. Mead) 4to. 1738-42
Rees (Abm.) Encyclopædia (by Chambers) 5 vols.
folio 1791

———————————————————————
45 vols. 4to. 1819-20
—— (*Dr.* T.) on the Regium Donum: Sketch of,
History of, & Parliamentary Grants to Poor
Dissenting Ministers 1834
Reeves (*Lord* C. J.) Instructions to his Nephew on
the Study of the Law. Vol. 1, Col. Jur. . .
—— (J.) History of English Law. 2nd ed. 5 vols.
8vo. 1787
——————————————— 3rd ed. 5 vols.
8vo. 1813-29
——————————————(W. Finlaison). Vols. 1 & 2 1869
Reform Act, Letter to Lord John Russell, with Suggestions for Amending it, by a Revising Barrister.
Vol. 4, Pam.
—— Handbook, Reforms Needed. Vol. 12, Pam. 1859
Reformation, English, Letters as to. Par. S. Pa.
—— Narratives of the. No. 77, C. S. Pa. (Fox;
& ed. J. G. Nichols) 1859
—— The New, Society and its Principles. Vol. 15,
Pam. 1861
Regalities & Privileges of Repledging. His. L. T.
Regicides' Trial 8vo. 1724
Register, Annual, or Royal Calendar, 1748-1866.
12mo.
—— East India Company (*see* East India Company)
Registration & Conveyancing Report . . folio 1850
Registrum Prioratus Wigorniensis (W. H. Hale)
C. S. Pa. No. 91 . . . . 4to. 1865
—— vulgariter nuncupatum " The Record of
Caernarvon;" e codice MS. Harleiano 696 descriptum. (Sir H. Ellis) (*see* Record Commission)
folio 1811
Registry, Reasons for a 4to. 1674

Registry Bill, Letter to an M.P. on proposed.
Vol. 5, L. T. 1831
Reguera Valdelomar. Guia para el Estudio del
Derecho patrio 4to. 1803
Reid (*Dr.* T.) Essay on Man . . . . . folio 1788
Reimes (P. de) Blonde of Oxford & Jehan of Dummartin, a Romance (ed. M. Le Roux de Lincy)
(*see* p. 49) C. S. P. No. 72 1858
Repertorium Juridicum, Notes of Cases from Edw. I.
folio 1742
Replevin . . . . 2nd ed. 8vo. 1736
Report of the Deputy Keeper of the Public Records
& the Rev. J. S. Brewer to the Master of the
Rolls, upon the Carte & Carew Papers in the
Bodleian & Lambeth Libraries 1864
—— of the Deputy Keeper of the Public Records
to the Master of the Rolls upon the Documents in
the Archives & Public Libraries of Venice. 8vo. 1866
Requests, Courts of, Return to Parliament for London, Westminster, Southwark, Palace Court, &
Tower Hamlets . . . . folio 1833
Revocation of a Will, Opinions on. Vol. 2, Col.
Jur. . . . .
Rex *v.* Montagu & others. Reprint of Trial (bound
up with Yantlett Creek) City T. 1824
—— *v.* Woodfall, Account of his Trial for Libel in
1770. Vol. 2, Libel L. T.
—— *v.* Woollycombe, Retrospect of Proceedings.
Vol. 5, L. T. 1833
Richard II., Hen. IV., V. & VI., English Chronicles
of Reigns of, 1377-1461. C. S. Pa. 64 (ed. Rev.
J. S. Davies) 1856
Richards's (Jno.) Letter to Lord Brougham in reply
to Tomkins & Jenkins. 12 Jac. Col. 1835
Richards (R. S.) Code Napoléon . . . . 8vo. n. d.
—— (Wm.) History of Lynn, Norfolk. 2 vols. 8vo. 1812
Richardson (*Dr.* Chas.) Chronological Dictionary
2 vols. 4to. 1858

Richardson (D. H.) Bankruptcy & Insolvency Costs
12mo. 1843
—— (Robt.) King's Bench Practice. 4th ed. 2 vols.
folio 1759
———————————————————— 5th ed.
2 vols. 8vo. 1769
———————————————— 6th ed. 2 vols. 8vo. 1776
—— on Wills . . . . 2nd ed. 8vo. 1769
—— Common Pleas' Practice. . . 2 vols. 8vo. 1778
—— (Wm.) Epitome of Chancery Practice. 8vo. 1838
Richelieu in Love, or Youth of Charles I., the prohibited Comedy. Vol. 23, Pam. 1852
Richmond (*Duke of*) on Construction of Marriage Articles & Cross Remainders in Duke's Case, with Mr. Booth's Opinion, Mr. Wedderburn's Argument, & Decree of Lord Chancellor Apsley. Vol. 2, Col. Jur.
—— Inventory of Wardrobe, Plate, &c., & of the Wardrobe, &c. of Catherine of Arragon at Baynard Castle. C. S. P., No. 61, C. M. Vol. 3 (ed. J. G. Nichols) 1854
Riddell (H.) on Railway Parliamentary Practice
12mo. 1846
Rider's List of Peers, &c. 12mo. 1781
Ridgway (A.) on Notarial Evidence, including the Case of Achilli *v.* Newman. Pam. Vol. 8, and Vol. 11
—— (Jas.) Baronages & Peerages . . . 8vo. 1838
—— (Wm.) Cases temp. Hardwicke, K.B. and Chancery, 1733–1736 . . . . 8vo. 1794
—— Reports, Irish House of Lords, 1784–1796
3 vols. 8vo. 1795-8
Ridley (*Bp.*) Works. Par. S. Pa. 1841
Rigge (Wm.) on Registration of Deeds . . 8vo. 1778
Riley (H. T.) Munimenta Gildhallæ Londonensis.
12 M. R. Pub. . . . . 4 vols. 8vo. 1859-62
Riots, Summary of Law of, by a Member of the Incorporated Law Society. Vol. 1, Pam. . . 1842

LAW SOCIETY LIBRARY. 287

Ripley (G.) & Dana (C. A.) New American Cyclopædia & Popular Dictionary of General Knowledge . . . . 16 vols. 8vo. 1863
—— (W. R.) on Tithes 8vo. 1846
Risdon (T.) Survey of Devon, Review of Part of, by W. Chapple 4to. 1785
—— Chorographical Survey of Devonshire. 8vo. 1811
Rishanger (Wm. de) Chronicle (J. O. Halliwell) C. S. Pa. No. 15. 1840
Ritson (J.) Maxims in Conveyancing. . . 8vo. 1804
Riverston Peerage Case of W. T. Nugent. Vol. 2, 2nd series
Road Acts, 1752-3-1797. . . . . 43 vols. folio
Roberts (C.) Calendarium Genealogicum, Henry III. & Edward I. 2 vols. 8vo. (*see* Calendar of State Papers) 1865
—— (G.) (*see* C. S. Pa. No. 41)
—— (Wm.) on Fraudulent Conveyances . . 8vo. 1800
—— on Wills. 8vo. 1809
———————. . . . . 2nd ed. 8vo. 1815
———————. . . . . 3rd ed. 8vo. 1826
—— History of Lyme Regis 8vo. 1823
—— Leeming, & Wallis's County Court Cases
                                                            8vo. 1849-51
Robertson (David) A Tour through the Isle of Man, to which is subjoined a review of the Manx History 8vo. 1794
—— House of Lords' Reports, 1707-27 . 8vo. 1807
—— (*Dr.* J. E. P.) Ecclesiastical Reports, 1844-53
                                                  2 vols. 8vo. 1852-3
—— (*Dr.* Wm.) Works, containing History of Scotland; History of the Emperor Charles V.; History of America; & History of India. 9 v. 8vo. 1824
Robinson (B. C.) on Warrants of Attorney & Cognovits. 12mo. 1844
—— (C.) Practice in Courts of Justice in England & United States, as to the grounds & form of defence in personal actions. Vol. 5 . . 8vo. 1868

Robinson (*Dr.* C.) Admiralty Reports
        3 vols. 8vo. 1799–1802
—————— 1798–1808. 4th ed. 6 vols. 8vo. 1812
—— (F.) *N. P. Reports* (*see* Moody, W.)
—— (G.) *House of Lords Cases* (*see* Maclean, C. H.)
—— Report of Earl Dalhousie *v.* McDowell Case
in House of Lords 8vo. 1840
—— Reports on Scotch Appeals to H. L.
        2 vols. 8vo. 1840–41
—— (J. C.) Alexander VII. and his Cardinals [by
John Bargrave, 1662–80] No. 92, C. S. P. . . 1867
—— (J. L.) & (C.) Canada Reports (*see* Cameron)
—— (T.) on Gavelkind 8vo. 1741
—————— . . . . 2nd ed. 8vo. 1788
—————— (Wilson) 8vo. 1822
—————— (Norwood) . . . 8vo. 1855
—— (*Rev.* T.) History of Westmoreland & Cumberland 12mo. 1709
—— The Mosaic System of Moses (bound with
Rev. T. Robinson's Westmoreland History)
—— (*Sir* Thos.) Entries of Declarations, Pleadings, &c. . . . . folio 1634
—— (Wm., *LL.D.*) History of Tottenham . 8vo. 1818
—————————————— 2nd ed. 8vo. 1840
—— History of Edmonton 8vo. 1819
—— History of Stoke Newington 8vo. 1820
—— History of Enfield . . . 2 vols. in 1, 8vo. 1823
—— Compendium of the Poor Laws, &c. . 8vo. 1827
—— Magistrates' Pocket Book (Archbold)
        2nd ed. 8vo. 1827
—— History of Hackney . . 2 vols. in 1, 8vo. 1842
—— (Wm., D.C.L.) Admiralty Reports, 1833–50
        3 vols. 8vo. 1844–50
——(W.H.) Handbook to The Peak & Buxton. 12mo. 1854
Robson (J.) (*see* C. S. Pa. No. 18)
—— (T.) British Heraldry . . . 3 vols. 4to. 1830
—— (Wm.) London Directory, 1824–42. 6th to
      23rd ed. 11 vols. 8vo.

Robson (Wm.) Court Guide 12mo. 1839
Roccus (F.) De Assecurationibus Notabilia 12mo. 1708
—— de Navibus et Naulo 12mo. 1708
Roche (C. M.) Letter to Sir R. Bethell on Defects of Present System of Land & Judicial Registration. Vol. 19, Pam. 1855
Rochefoucauld (F. duc de la) Maxims & Reflections
           12mo. 1694
Rochester, History of, & its Environs . . 8vo. 1772
——————————————————— 2nd ed. 8vo. 1817
—— Poll Book 8vo. 1807
   (And *see* Kent, 1803)
Rocque (J.) a New and Accurate Survey of London, Westminster, the Borough of Southwark, with the country about it for 19 miles in length and 13 in depth 1751
Rodd, Catalogue of Books as to Ireland . . 8vo. 1849
Rodwell (H.) (*see* Pigot, G.)
—— *Election Cases* (*see* Power, D.)
Roe (F. T.) on Election Law. 2nd ed.
         2 vols. 8vo. 1818
Rogers (A.) Mines, Minerals, & Quarries. 8vo. 1864
—— (F. N.) Elections . . . . . 2nd ed. 8vo. 1830
———————————— . . . . 6th ed. 8vo. 1841
———————————— . . . . 8th ed. 8vo. 1857
———————————— . . . . 9th ed. 8vo. 1859
———————————— (F. S. P. Wolferstan)
        10th ed. 8vo. 1868
——————————————————— 11th ed. 8vo. 1865
—— Ecclesiastical Law 8vo. 1840
—— Registration of Voters Act, with Analysis
          12mo. 1843
—— (Thos.) on Thirty-nine Articles. Par. S. Pa. 1853
Rogron (J. A.) les Codes français, Droit civil et criminel . . . . 5th ed. 2 vols. 4to. 1863
Rokeby Peerage, Evidence, Vol. 6
Roll of Bishop Swinfield, Vol. 1, 1289-90. No. 59, C. S. Pa. (Rev. J. Webb) 1853

Roll of Bishop Swinfield, Vol. 2, No. 62, C. S. Pa. 1864
Rolle (*Sir* H.) K. B. Reports, 1614–1625. 2 v. folio 1675
—— (*Mr. Serjt.*) Abridgment . . 2 vols. folio 1668
—— *Lord* Hale's Preface to. Vol. 1, Col. Jur.
Rollin's (M.) Ancient History. 18th ed. 6 vols. 8vo. 1851
Rolls, Master of the, Authority in Chancery. 8vo. 1827
Rolt (R.) History of the Isle of Man, from the
   Earliest Account to the Present Time . . 8vo. 1773
Romances (3 Metrical) No. 18, C. S. Pa. (J.
   Robson) 4to. 1841
Romanist Psalms & Hymn Book . . . 12mo. 1449
Rome, Correspondence of Foreign Governments
   with . . . . folio 1851
Romilly (*Sir* Saml.) Biography of (*see* Roscoe's
   Biography of Eminent English Lawyers)
—— (J.) (*see* Cambridge Graduati)
Roos, Peerage Cases of Lady Fitzgerald & Duke of
   Rutland. List of Proofs on Duke of Rutland's
   Claim. 1st & 3rd series, Vol. 4 ; Evidence, Vol. 6.
Roots (G.) Charters to Kingston 8vo. 1797
Roper (R. S. D.) on Legacies 8vo. 1804
—— on Legacies (White) . 3rd ed. 2 vols. 8vo. 1828
——————————————— . 4th ed. 2 vols. 8vo. 1847
—— on Husband & Wife (Jacob)
                              2nd ed. 2 vols. 8vo. 1836
Roscoe (H.) Lives of Eminent British Lawyers
                                           12mo. 1830

      Sir E. Coke   Sir J. E. Wilmot
      John Selden   Sir Wm. Blackstone
      Sir Matthew Hale   Lord Ashburton
      Lord Guilford   Lord Thurlow
      Lord Jefferies   Sir Wm. Jones
      Lord Somers   Lord Erskine
      Lord Mansfield   Sir Saml. Romilly

—— (H.) *Exch. Reports* (*see* Crompton, *Sir* C.)
—— on Real Actions . . . . 2 vols. 8vo. 1825
—— on Evidence . . . . 4th ed. 12mo. 1836
——————————————— . . . . . . 5th ed. 12mo. 1839
—— on Evidence (Smirke) . . . . 6th ed. 8vo. 1844

Roscoe (H.) on Evidence (Smirke) . 9th ed. 8vo. 1858
———————————————— . . . . 10th ed. 8vo. 1861
——————————(Mills & Markby) 11th ed. 8vo. 1866
—— on Criminal Evidence (Power) . 6th ed. 8vo. 1862
———————————————— (J . F. Stephen)
7th ed. 8vo. 1868
Roscommon, Dillon's Case, Claim to Right to Vote.
Vol. 4, 3rd series; Evidence, Vol. 2. . . . 1824–8
Rose (G.) Bankruptcy Reports temp. Eldon, 1810–
1814 . . . . 2nd ed. 2 vols. 8vo. 1821
Ross (*Sir* Jno.) Narrative of Second Voyage to Discover North-West Passage 4to. 1825
—— (T.) Guide to Hastings & St. Leonards. 12mo.
Rosse (J. W.) (*see* Blair)
Rosser (A.) Credit Pernicious. Vol. 3, Pam.
2nd ed. 1834
Rouen, Journal of the Siege of, in 1591. No. 39,
C. M. Vol. 1 [Sir T. Coningsby] (ed. J. G.
Nichols) 1846
Rough *v.* Murray, Case in P. C. 8vo. 1825
Rous (Geo.) Letter to Jurors on Lord Mansfield's
Judgment in Rex *v.* Woodfall. Libel L. T. Vol. 3.
———'s (J.) Diary, 1625–1642. No. 66, C. S. Pa.
(ed. M. A. E. Green) 1856
Rouse (R.) (*see* Bateman)
—— on Mortgage 8vo. 1844
—— Practical Conveyancer . 2nd ed. 2 vols. 8vo. 1858
——————————————— . 3rd ed. 2 vols. 8vo. 1867
—— Practical Man . . . . . 8th ed. 12mo. 1858
——————————— . . . . . 11th ed. 12mo. 1865
——————————— . . . . . 12th ed. 12mo. 1868
—— Copyhold Enfranchisement Manual
2nd ed. 8vo. 1858
———————————————————— 3rd ed. 8vo. 1866
Rousseau (J.-J. de) Œuvres. 2nd vol. only, 12mo. 1783
Routier (C.) Principes généraux du Droit civil et
coutumier de la province de Normandie . 4to. 1742
————————————————————— 2nd ed. 4to. 1748

Routier (C.) Pratiques bénéficiales : l'Usage de la
province de Normandie . . . . 2nd ed. 4to. 1757
Routledge (Geo.) Men of the Time . . . 8vo. 1865
——————————————————— 7th ed. 1868
Rowe (*Sir* W. C.) *Election Cases* (*see* Cockburn,
Sir H. E. J.)
Rowell (Robt.) Analysis of County Court Act. folio 1856
Rowland (C.) on the Laws & Customs of the Port
of London 8vo. 1842
——————————————————— 2nd ed. 8vo. 1843
—— (D.) Remarks on Case & Judgment in T.
1842, Crane *v.* Price. Vol. 18, Pam. 1842
—— Manual of the English Constitution . . 8vo. 1859
—— (*Rev.* H.) Antiquities of Anglesey. 2nd ed. 4to. 1766
Rowzee (*Dr.* L.) History of Tunbridge Wells. 12mo. 1671
Roxburgh, Dukedom : Cases of Lady Essex Kerr
& Sir J. J. Kerr. 1st series, P. C.; 3rd series,
Vol. 4; Evidence, 1st series, Vols. 10 & 12
Royal Blue Book or Directory, 1823–69 . 12mo.
—— Families of Europe (from ' Spectator ') 1863
—— Kalendar, or Court & City Register, 1744–
1869 (in progress) . . . . . 12 vols. 8vo.
Rudder (Saml.) History of Gloucestershire . folio 1779
——————————————— Gloucester . . 8vo. 1781
Rudge (R. J.) History of Evesham . . . 8vo. 1820
Ruffhead (Owen) Index to Statutes, Magna Charta
to 1770 . . . . 8vo. 1772
Rugby School, Report of Proceedings before Lord
Langdale 8vo. 1839
Rules & Orders, 1457–1743 (*see* K. B.) 2nd ed. 8vo. 1747
——————————— Chancery, 1625–1722 . . 8vo. 1729
——————————— Common Pleas 4to. 1654
——————————— C. P. 1654–1722 . . . 8vo. 1729
——————————— at Lancaster . . . 12mo. 1831
——————————————————— . . . 12mo. 1832
——————————— Equity Exchequer . . . 8vo. 1729
——————————— General, from 1828 to 1863,
printed for Members of the Society. 5 vols. 12mo.

Rules and Orders, K. B. 1604–1729 . . . 8vo. 1729
———————— 1604–1747 . . . folio 1747
———————— 1604–1794 . . . 8vo. 1795
———————— & C. P. 8vo. 1732
———————————————— 8vo. 1733
———————————————— . . 2nd ed. 8vo. 1747
———————————————— & Exchequer. 8vo. 1778
Rumsey (A.) Chart of Family Inheritance according
  to Moohummudan Law 8vo. 1867
—— Chart of Hindoo Family Inheritance, with
  explanatory Treatise 8vo. 1868
—— on County Court Jurisdiction before & after
  January 1868 . . . . 8vo. 1867
Runnington (C.) on Ejectment 8vo. 1781
Rushworth (J.) Collection of English History,
  1618–40. . . . . 2 vols. folio 1682
Russell (F.) on Arbitration . . . 2nd ed. 8vo. 1855
—————————————————— . . . 3rd ed. 8vo. 1864
—— (Jno.) Form of Process (Scotch) . . 8vo. 1768
—— (J.) *Chancery Reports* (*see* Turner, G.)
—— Reports in Chancery, 1826–28. 5 vols. 8vo. 1827–31
—— & Mylne (J. W.) Chancery Reports, 1829–31
  2 vols. 8vo. 1832–37
—— (J. A.) (*see* Chitty, E., on Contracts)
———————————————— Jos., on Bills)
—— Law of Factors & Brokers 8vo. 1844
—— & Maclachlan (D.) (*see* Chitty on Bills)
—— (late *Lord*) Defences of his Innocence. At-
  kins's L. T.
—— (R. W.) Remarks on English Enlistment
  Question 8vo. 1852
—— (*Sir* W. O.) on Crimes. 2nd ed. 2 vols. 8vo. 1826–8
———————————————— (Greaves) 3rd ed. 2 vols. 8vo. 1843
———————————————— 4th ed. 3 vols. 8vo. 1865
—— (W. O.) & Ryan (F.) Crown Cases, 1799–1824
  8vo. 1825
——'s Modern History of Europe (continued by
  Dr. Coote). . . . . 6 vols. 8vo. 1827

Russian Code, Instructions to Commissioners to
frame new (translated by M. Tatischeff) . 4to. 1768
Rutherforth (Dr. T.) Institutes of Natural Law
                                                    2 vols. 8vo. 1765
―――――――――――――― 2nd ed. 2 vols. 8vo. 1779
―― (T. B.) on Judicial Privilege of the Court on
Controverted Elections. Pam. Par. Priv. . . 1838
Rutland Papers, No. 21, C. S. Pa. 1485–1533
(W. Jerdan) 1842
Rutlandshire (*see* Peck's Stanford, Lincoln) . . . 1727
Rutter (J.) History of North-West Division of
Somersetshire 8vo. 1829
―― History of Fonthill Abbey 4to. 1832
Ryan (E.) *Crown Cases* (*see* Russell, *Sir* W. O.)
―― & Moody (W.) Nisi Prius Reports, 1823–26
                                                                                     8vo. 1827
Ryland (A.) *K. B. Reports* (*see* Dowling, Jas., &
Manning, J.)
―― Paper read at the Social Science Meeting
at Bradford, on Trade Marks fraudulently Imitated. Vol. 23, Pam. 1859
Ryley (Wm.) Placita Parliamentaria . . . folio 1661
Rymer (Thos.) & Sanderson (R.) Fœdera, Conventiones, Literæ, et Acta Publica, 1101–1654
(Ed. G. Holmes) . 3rd ed. 20 vols. in 10, folio 1745
―――――――――――――――― Fœdera, Conventiones, Literæ, et Acta Publica. 1066–1377
(Ed. J. Caley, Dr. A. Clarke & F. Holbrooke).
Vols. 1–3 in 6 parts . . . . . . folio 1816–30
(*See* Record Commission)

S

Sabbath Breaking, On (*see* Legal Recreations). . n. d.
Sabio (Don Alphonso) Las siete Partidas del Rey
       3 vols. 4to. Madrid 1807
Sacheverell (*Dr.* H.) Trial . . . . . . folio 1710
——————————————. 8vo. 1710
—————— (Wm.) An Account of the Isle of Man, to which is added a Dissertation about the Mona of Tacitus and Cæsar, and an account of the Ancient Druids, by T. Brown 12mo. 1702
Sainsbury (W. N.) Calendar of State Papers, Colonial Series, preserved in Her Majesty's Public Record Office, and elsewhere

 Vol. I.: America and the West Indies, 1574–1660.
 Vol. II.: East Indies, China, and Japan, 1513–1616.

        Imp. 8vo. 1860–62
S. Albani Monasterii Chronica et Annales temp. Hen. III. & Edwd. I., W. Rishanger, 1259–1307 (ed. H. T. Riley). 28 M. R. Pub. . . 1863–67
—— Historia Anglicana Th. Walsingham (ed. H. T. Riley) 1863
St. Christopher Acts, 1711–1857 . . . . 8vo.
———————————— 1857–1864 . . . folio 1857–64
St. Clement Dane's Paving Act, 23 Geo. III. 12mo. 1813
———————— Watching Act, 1764 . 12mo. 1778
St. David's (*Bp.*) Introduction to Arabic Alphabet
         12mo. 1809
—— Motives to Study of Hebrew. 2nd ed. 12mo. 1814
St. Germains (*Earl, & Viscount* Gage) Speeches in the House of Lords on a Marriage with a Deceased Wife's Sister. Vol. 24, Pam. . . 1851
St. George's Heraldic Visitation of Westmoreland in 1615 . . . . 12mo. 1823

St. Giles' Pound to Kilburn Turnpike Act, 23 Geo. III. . . . . 12mo.
St. Helena Ordinances, 1857–1866. Imperfect. 2 vols. folio
St. Leonard's (*Lord*) Handy Book of Property Law 12th ed. 12mo. 1858
—— Misrepresentations in Lord Campbell's Lives of Lords Lyndhurst & Brougham . . . 8vo. 1869
St. Loy, Legend of 8vo. 1820
St. Lucia Laws, 1681–1852 . . . . . 8vo. 1865
————————— 1853–1865 . . 2 vols. folio 1853–65
St. Mary, Islington, Poor Relief Act . . . 8vo. 1825
———— Lambeth, Act for Watching . 12mo. 1820
St. Pancras, Southampton, Paving Acts, 41, 55 George III. . . . . 12mo.
St. Paul's, London, the Domesday of, MCCXXII. (Archdeacon Hale). No. 69, C. S. Pa. . . . 1858
St. Palaye. Memoires of Ancient Chivalry. 12mo. 1759
St. Thomas, the Incredulity of (the Scriveners' Play at York) C. M. Vol. 4, No. 73, C. S. Pa. (ed. J. P. Collier). 1859
St. Vincent Acts, 1857–1867. . . . . 2 vols. folio
Sale (Geo.) Koran . . . . 2 vols. 8vo. 1825
Sale Rooms, Public, Prospectus for Establishing, in London. Vol. 4, Pam. 1835
Salaries, Official, H. C. Report on . . . . . folio 1850
Salford Guide (*see* Manchester) 1804
Salisbury (*Lord*) Treasurer. Speech on King James's Intention to Create his Son Prince of Wales. MS. temp. Jas. &c.
Salkeld (Wm.) K. B. Reports, 1695–1704. 2nd ed. 2 vols. in 1, folio 1721
————————————————— 3 vols. folio 1724
———————————— (Wilson) 5th ed. 3 vols. folio 1773
———————————— (W. D. Evans) 6th ed. 3 vols. 8vo. 1795
Salmasius (Cl.) De Re Militari Romanorum 4to. 1657
Salmon (N.) History of Essex . . . . . folio 1740
—— History of Hertfordshire . . . . . folio 1728

Salmon (T.) & Guthrie, Geographical Grammar. 8vo. 1777
—— (T.) Chronological Historian . 2nd ed. 8vo. 1733
—— Peerage, 1st to 3rd ed. . 3 vols. 12mo. 1751-61
—— Peerage, Irish 8vo. 1759
—— Peerage, Scotch 8vo. 1759
—— a new Abridgment, &c. of State Trials from
Rich. II. to 11 Geo. II. . . . . . . folio 1738
Salomon (D.) his Address to Court of Aldermen as
to his Admission as Alderman of Portsoken Ward.
Vol. 23, Pam.
Sampson (M. B.) Letter to J. Forbes on the Phrenological Theory of the Treatment of Criminals
Defended. . Vol. 18, Pam. 1843
Sams (Wm.) Peerage . . . . 2 vols. 12mo. 1827
Samuel (E.) Military Law 8vo. 1820
Sanchez (R. P. T.) de Matrimonio 3 vols. in 1 folio 1739
Sanders (F. W.) (*see* Atkyns)
—— on Copyhold Surrenders 8vo. 1819
—— on Uses and Trusts . . . 2nd ed. 8vo. 1799
———————————— . 4th ed. 2 vols. 8vo. 1824
———————————— (G. W. Sanders & Jno.
Warner) . . . . 5th ed. 2 vols. 8vo. 1844
—— (G. W.) Orders in Chancery and Statutes.
12 Rich. II. to 8 Vict. . . . . . 2 vols. 8vo. 1845
Sanderson (Robt.) Lectures on Oaths . . 12mo. 1655
—— (Wm.) History of Queen Mary of Scotland &
James VI. . . . . folio 1656
Sandford (F.) Abridgment of the Genealogy of the
Kings, particularly of the Royal Family, of
England 8vo. 1741
Sands, Sydney Directory 8vo. 1864
Sandys (*Abp.*) Sermons, &c. Par. Soc. Pub. . . 1841
—— (C.) on Gavelkind 8vo. 1851
Sanger (G. P.) (*see* U. S. Statutes)
Sangster (J.) on Rights & Duties of Property. 12mo. 1851
Sanitary Enquiry Report . . . . . . folio 1843
Sankey (W. G. V.) The Rights of Operatives Asserted. Vol. 27, Pam. 1838

Sapphus Poetriæ Lesbiæ Fragmenta (J. C. Wolfius) 4to. 1733
Sargant (W. L.) Letter to John Bright. Vol. 13, Pam. No. 8 1861
Sargent (R.) on the Law . . . . 2nd ed. 8vo. 1842
—— Burghersh, Sussex, or the Pleasures of a Country Life 12mo. 1855
Sarpi (Fra Paoli) Histoire du Concile de Trente (par P.-F. de Courayer) . . . 3 vols. 4to. 1751
Sarum, History & Antiquities of Old & New. 8vo. 1777
Saturday Review, 1859–1868 . . 15 vols. folio
Saul, a Dramatic Sketch 8vo. 1844
Saunders (C. T.) Address to the Law Students' Society at Birmingham. Vol. 27, Pam. . . . 1866
—— (*Sir* Edmd.) K. B. Reports, 18–24 C. II. 1667–1673 . . . . folio 1686
———————————————— (J. Williams) 3rd ed. 6 vols. 8vo. 1799–1802
———————————————— (J. Patterson & E. V. Williams) . . . 5th ed. 3 vols. 8vo. 1824
———————————————— (E. V. Williams) 6th ed. 3 vols. 8vo. 1845
—— (T. W.) The Law & Practice of Orders of Affiliation and Proceedings in Bastardy . 12mo. 1854
———————————————— 4th ed. 12mo. 1862
———————————————— 5th ed. 12mo. 1867
—— Prison Acts 12mo. 1865
—— Magistrates' Practice . . . 3rd ed. 12mo. 1867
—— & Cole's (H. T.) Bail Court Cases, 1846–1848 2 vols. 8vo. 1847–9
—— & Cox (E. W.) Consolidated Criminal Law 2nd ed. 8vo. 1862
—— (Geo.) Report of Middlesex Bridges . 4to. 1826
Sausse (M. A.) & Scully (N.) Irish Rolls Reports, temp. O'Loughlen, 1837–40 . . . . . 8vo. 1841
Savage (James) History of the Hundred of Carhampton, Somerset 8vo. 1830
———————————— Taunton . . . 8vo. 1822

Savary (M. P. L.) Dictionnaire universel de
Commerce, & Supplement . . 4 vols. folio 1730–42
Savigny (F. C. von) Private International Law.
A Treatise on the Conflict of Laws, and Limit
of their Operation in respect of Place and Time.
Translated by W. Guthrie 8vo. 1869
Savile (*Sir* Jno.) C. B. & Ex. Reports, temp.
Eliz. 1579–1594 . . . . folio 1688
Savile (H.) Correspondence. No. 71 C. S. Pa.
(ed. W. D. Cooper). 4to. 1858
Saxon & Norman Charters (*see* Chartæ Antiquæ)
Saye & Sele Peerage Cases of John Twistleton,
1st series
——————— of F. B. Twistleton, 2nd series
——————— of Col. T. Twistleton, 3rd series
Sayer (*Mr. Serjt.*) on Costs 8vo. 1768
——————————— . . . 2nd ed. 8vo. 1777
——————— Damages. . . . 12mo. 1770
Sayres, Synopsis of Blackstone. . . . . folio 1846
Scapula (J.) Greek & Latin Lexicon . . . folio 1653
Scarlett (Jno.) on Bills of Exchange. 2nd ed. 12mo. 1584
Schiller (F.) Marie Stuart 12mo. 1861
—— Wallenstein 12mo. 1852
Schoales (John) & Lefroy (S.) Irish Chancery Re-
ports, temp. Redesdale, 1802–4 . 2 vols. 8vo. 1806–21
Schomberg (J.) Naval Chronology from the time
of the Romans to 1802. . . 5 vols. in 3, 8vo. 1802
Schreiber (A.) Guide to the Rhine. 4th ed. 12mo. 1836
Schroderus (J. C.) Tragœdiæ Senecæ. . . 4to. 1728
Scobell (Hen.) Acts & Ordinances of Parliament,
1640–1657 (continuation of Pulton) . . folio 1658
—— House of Lords Remembrances and Pro-
ceedings 4to. 1689
Scotch Acts of Sederunt of Lords of Council &
Session, 1553–1790 . . . . folio 1790
—— Bankrupt Bill, Report of London Com-
mittees on 8vo. 1814
——————————— Statement of ditto . 8vo. 1814

Scotch Conveyancing System. 3rd ed. 2 vols. 8vo. 1826
———————— 3rd Report of Committee on. folio 1838
—— Decisions of Courts of Session from Institution to 1827 . . . . 4 vols. 4to. 1729
—— Decisions, Lords, 1678–1712 . 2 vols. folio 1759
——————— Dictionary of, in Court of Session, from Institution till 1764 . . . 5 vols. 12mo. 1774
—— Digest of Cases, 1815–37 . . 2 vols. 8vo. 1834–8
—— Peerages, Compendium. 1st to 7th ed.
7 vols. 12mo. 1724–64
—— Rebellion in 1745 (for account of proceedings see Chester Miscellany & Robertson's Works, Vols. 1. & 2)
Scotiæ Inquisitionum Retornatarum Abbreviatio & Indices, 1545–1699 (T. H. Thomson) (see Record Commission). . . . . . . 3 vols. folio 1811-16
—— Rotuli, in turri Lond. et in domo Capitulari Westm. asservati temp. Edw. I.–Hen. VIII. (D. Macpherson, J. Caley, & W. Illingworth) (see Record Commission). . . . 2 vols. folio 1814–19
——————— (see Chartæ Antiquæ)
Scotland. Calendar of State Papers. Ed. by M. J. Thorpe, 1509–1603 . 2 vols. imp. 8vo. 1858
—— Acts of Parliament of, 1124–1707 (T. Thompson & C. Innes) . . . 11 vols. folio 1844–24
—— Acts of Lords Auditors of Causes & Complaints, 1466–94 (Thompson) (see Record Commission) . . . . folio 1839
—— Boundaries of, House of Lords Reports on. folio 1832
—— Buik of the Croniclis of; being a Metrical version of the History of Hector Boece, by W. Stewart (W. B. Turnbull) (see No. 6 M. R. Pub.)
3 vols. 1858
—— Correspondence relating to (see State Papers)
—— Documents and Records in the Exchequer as to History of (Palgrave) (see Record Commission)
8vo. 1837
—— Index to Statutes, 1424–1707 . . . 12mo. 1707
—— Interest of, considered 12mo. 1733

LAW SOCIETY LIBRARY. 301

Scotland, New Statistics of . . . 15 vols. 8vo. 1845
—— Record Commission Correspondence . 8vo. 1836
—— Report on Labouring Population of (*see* Labouring Population)
—— National MSS. . . . . folio 1860
—— Topography of (*see* Sinclair's Statistics of Scotland)
—— Dictionary of Decisions in Court of Session, from Institution till 1764 . . . 5 vols. 12mo. 1774
——————— from Institution to 1827. 4 vols. 4to. 1829
—— The Decision of the Lords of Council and of Session, 1678-1712 . . . . . 2 vols. folio 1759
(*See* also Bell, Maclaurin, & Nisbet)
—— Reports on Public Records of, 1800-8. folio 1806-9
——————— (*see* Vols. 1 & 2, Robertson's Works)
—— System of Conveyancing in. 3rd ed. 2 vols. 8vo. 1826
Scotorum Historia . . . . fol. 1521
—— Regum Registrum Magni Sigilli, 1306-1424 (T. Thompson) (*see* Record Commission) fo. 1814
Scott (B.) Statistical Vindication of the City of London; its Fallacies Explored, its Figures Explained 8vo. 1867
—— (G.) Memoirs of Sir J. Melvill . . fol. 1683
—— (Jno.) Costs, Com. Law, Probate & Divorce, & Conveyancing 8vo. 1856
——————————————— 2nd ed. 8vo. 1860
——————————————— 3rd ed. 8vo. 1868
—— Reports, C. P., 1834-40 . . 8 vols. 8vo. 1835-41
—— New ditto, 1840-45 . . . 8 vols. 8vo. 1841-45
—— Common Bench Reports, 1850-1856
9 vols. 8vo. 1852-56
————————————— Index . . . 8vo. 1858
—— N. S. ditto, with Index, 1856-65. 20 vols. 8vo.
—— *v.* Fenoulet, Arguments and Decree of Lord Chancellor Thurlow, 1779, MS. . . . folio 1779
—— *v.* Vernon, Conditional Legacy Hargrave's Jur. Arguments, Vol. 1
—— (M. L.) & Jarnagin (M. P.) on the Law of Telegraphs, U. S. 8vo. 1868

Scott (R.) Greek & English Lexicon (*see* Liddell)
—— (*Sir* Walter) Border Antiquities of England
& Scotland . . . . 2 vols. 4to. 1812–13
Scottish Law List 1848–56
—— Widows' Fund Reports, &c. . . . 8vo. 1834
Scribner (C. H.) on Dower, U.S. . 2 vols. 8vo. 1867
Scriven (Jno.) on Copyhold and Supplement
3rd ed. 3 vols. 8vo. 1833
—— (H. Stalman) . . . 4th ed. 2 vols. 8vo. 1846
———————————————— 5th ed. 8vo. 1867
Scriven's Copyhold Act (H. Stalman) . 12mo. 1841
Scriveners' Co. Case of the Free Scriveners. 4to. 1749
Scroggs (*Sir* Wm.) on Court Leet (Vorle). 12mo. 1701
———————————————— 3rd ed. 8vo. 1714
———————————————— 4th ed. 8vo. 1728
Scrope (*Sir* Richard Le) & Grosvenor (*Sir* Robert)
Roll, being the Controversy between them, temp.
Richard II. relative to their Coat Armour, History
of the Scrope Family, &c. (Sir R. H. Nicolas)
2 vols. folio 1832
Sea Laws & Maritime Affairs, translated out of the
Italian MS. from Doctors' Commons. 3rd ed. 4to.
—— MSS. from Doctors' Commons Library. folio
—— Service Regulations & Instructions. 4th ed.
folio 1772
Secret Services of Car. II. & Jas. II., 1679–88.
No. 52, C. S. Pa. (J. Y. Akerman) 1851
Seckford (Thos.) Statutes & Ordinances of Alms-
houses at Woodbridge, Suffolk 4to. 1792
—— (R. Loder) . . . . 2nd ed. 4to. 1811
Securities upon Lands to Pay Debts. His. L. T.,
1761
Sedgwick (J.) Remarks on Vol. 1, Blackstone's
Commentaries 4to. 1807
—— (T.) on the Measure of Damages, U. S.
3rd ed. 8vo. 1858
——————————— 4th ed. (H. D. Sedgwick) 8vo. 1868
—— Statutory & Constitutional Law, U. S. 8vo. 1857
Seduction (*see* Legal Recreations)·

Seeley (J.) Description of Stowe (Bucks) . 8vo. 1827
Seely (*Rev.* T.) Letter to Bishop of London on the Case of. Pam. Vol. 5
Segar (*Sir* Wm.) on Honor, Military & Civil. folio 1602
―― Honores Anglicani 8vo. 1712
Selden (John) Barons' Privileges (*see* Scobell, H. L. Remembrances, 1589)
―― Biography of (*see* Roscoe's Lives of Lawyers)
―― Judicature in Parliament . . . . 12mo.
―― (H. R.) Reports, Court of Appeal, U. S. (New York) . . . . 6 vols. 8vo. 1851–4
―― (John) Titles of Honour . . 2nd ed. folio 1631
―――――――――――――――― . . 3rd ed. folio 1672
―― Works, by David Wilkins . . 3 vols. folio 1726

Vol. I. :—
    Dedicatio, Præfatio, & Vita Seldenii
    De Anno Civili Veteris Ecclesiæ, seu Reipublicæ Judaicæ Dissertatio
    De Jure Naturali & Gentium juxta Disciplinam Ebræorum
    De Synedriis & Præfecturis Juridicis Veterum Ebræorum
    Indices

Vol. II. :—
    De Successionibus in Bona Defunctorum; & de Successionibus in Pontificatum Ebræorum
    De Diis Syris
    Eutychii Ecclesiæ suæ Origines
    Uxor Ebraica
    Analecta Anglo-Britannica
    Janus Anglorum
    Dissertatio ad Fletam
    Judicium de decem Scriptoribus Anglicanis
    Mare Clausum: *see also* Falle (P.)
    Vindiciæ de Scriptione Maris Clausi
    Marmora Arundelliana
    Notæ in Eadmerum
    Epistolæ et Poemata

Vol. III. :—
    England's Epinomis
    Original of Duels
    Titles of Honour
    History of Tithes, MSS.
    Of the Passage in the Revelations concerning the Number 666
    Of Calvin's Judgment of the Revelations, MSS.
    Birthday of Our Saviour

Selden's Works—Vol. III. *continued.*
- Purpose of writing History of Tithes
- Of Jews sometimes living in England
- On Office of Lord Chancellor
- Barons' Privileges
- Judicature in Parliament
- Ecclesiastical Jurisdiction of Testaments
- Letter to Mr. Vincent, concerning his Discovery of Errors
- Baronies of Grey & Ruthen, Arguments, MSS.
- Notes on Drayton's Polyolbion
- Notes on Sir John Fortescue de Laudibus Legum Angliæ
- Notes on Sir Ralph de Hengham's Summæ
- Speeches in House of Lords, MSS.
- Table Talk

Selden (John) Law Tracts. . . . . . . folio 1683
- Jani Anglorum Facies Altera
- England's Epinomis
- Original of Ecclesiastical Jurisdiction of Testaments
- Administration of Intestates' Goods

Selkirk (*Earl*) Observations on Scotch Highlands
             8vo. 1805
Sellon (B. J.) King's Bench Practice
          2 vols. 8vo. 1792-6
——————— (Crompton) 2nd ed. 2 vols. 8vo. 1798
Selwyn (W.) Nisi Prius . . . . . 2 vols. 8vo. 1806
————————————— . . 2nd ed. 2 vols. 8vo. 1810
————————————— . . 3rd ed. 2 vols. 8vo. 1812
————————————— . . 5th ed. 2 vols. 8vo. 1820
————————————— . . 8th ed. 2 vols. 8vo. 1831
————————————— . . 9th ed. 2 vols. 8vo. 1838
————————————— . . 11th ed. 2 vols. 8vo. 1845
————————— (D. Power) 12th ed. 2 vols. 8vo. 1859
—— Supplement (*see* Power & Wolferstan) 8vo. 1861
Senior (N. W.) Outline of the Science of Political
 Economy 4to. 1836
—— Pamphlets . . . . . . 3rd ed. 8vo. 1831
 Containing :—
  1. Lecture on Political Economy
  2. Three Lectures on Transmission of Precious Metals
  3. Two Lectures on Population
  4. Three Lectures on the Cost of Obtaining Money
  5. Three Lectures on Rate of Wages

Senior's Pamphlets—*continued*.
6. Remarks on Emigration, with Draft of a Bill
7. Letter to Lord Howick on Legal Procedure for Irish Poor
8. Instructions for Central Board of Poor-Law Commissioners

Serjeant-at-Law, on Degree of (*see* E. W.)
—— Enquiry into the Justice of Abolishing the Rank of, dedicated to the Lord Chancellor Chelmsford, by a Barrister of the Temple. Vol. 12, Pam. 1850
Serious Questions touching Church Government (*see* Prynne, W.)
Seton (*Sir* H.) on Decrees in Equity . . . 8vo. 1830
———————————————— (W. H. Harrison & R. H. Leach) . . . . . . 2nd ed. 8vo. 1854
———————————————— 3rd ed. 2 vols. in 3, 8vo. 1862
Settlement Cases, temp. Parker, 1710–27
          2nd ed. 8vo. 1729
Sévigné (Made.) Letters . . . . 9 vols. 12mo. 1811
Sewell (R. C.) on Chancellor's Court at Oxford. 8vo. 1839
—— Sheriff Law 8vo. 1842
Sewers, Commissioners of, Memorial of Chartered Gas Light & Coke Co., London Tracts
—— City Commissioners' Order, London Tracts
—— Law of . . . . 2nd ed. 8vo. 1722
—— London Act 12mo. 1772
Seyer (*Rev.* Saml.) Memoirs of Bristol & its Neighbourhood . . . . 2 vols. 4to. 1821
Seymour (H.) Speech on Irish Church & Letter of Archdeacon Stopford to James Whiteside. Vol. 19, Pam. 1863
Shaen (Wm.) & Greville (E. K.) Bills of Chancery Costs 12mo. 1857
Shakespeare's Plays, by Samuel Johnson
          8 vols. 8vo. 1768
—— Works, by Clarke & Glover
      Cam. ed. 9 vols. 8vo. 1865–66
Shannon River, 1st, 2nd, & 4th Reports. H. L. Sess. Pa. . . . . 3 vols. folio 1837 39

x

Sharkey (P. B.) on Parliamentary Election Committees' Practice 12mo. 1866
Sharp (G.) Congregational Courts . . . 8vo. 1784
—— on Crown Law. 8vo. 1773
—— Rights of People . . . . . 2nd ed. 8vo. 1775
Sharpe (*Rev.* J.) Monumenta (*see* Petrie & Sharpe)
Shaw (Geo.) on Election Law 12mo. 1857
—— (James) Domestic Lawyer 8vo. 1831
—— (J.) Parish Law (*see* Archbold)
—— (P.) Scotch Appeal Reports, 1821–24
    2 vols. 8vo. 1826–28
—— Digest of Scotch Courts of Session & H. L. Cases, 1815–1837 . . . . . 2 vols. 8vo. 1834–38
—— & McClean (C. H.) Scotch Appeals Reports, 1835 to 1838 . . . . 3 vols. 8vo. 1836–39
—— (*Rev.* S.) History of Staffordshire & Plan
    2 vols. folio 1798
Shee (Wm., afterwards *Sir* W.) on Shipping (*see* Abbott)
Sheen (West) Rules of Customs pertaining to. Col. Jur. Vol. 2, Pam.
Shelford (L.) on Real Property Statutes
    7th ed. 8vo. 1863
—— on Lunacy 8vo. 1833
——————. . . . . . . 2nd ed. 8vo. 1847
(*See* Brydall, Collinson, Elmer, Phillips, Archbold)
—— on Highways 12mo. 1836
——————— . . . . . . 3rd ed. 12mo. 1862
—— on Husband & Wife 8vo. 1841
—— on Law of Mortmain 8vo. 1845
—— on Railways . . . . . . 2nd ed. 8vo. 1846
—— on Tithes, & Supplement . . 3rd ed. 12mo. 1848
—— on Insolvency 8vo. 1850
—— Copyhold Enfranchisement Manual . 8vo. 1853
—— on Bankruptcy . . . . . 2nd ed. 12mo. 1854
———————————. . . . 3rd ed. 8vo. 1861–63
—— Succession . . . . . . 2nd ed. 12mo. 186'
—— on Joint Stock Companies 8vo. 1863

Shelley's Case, Hargrave's Observations on. Hargrave's Law Tr. Vol. 1
Shephard (C.) Colonial Practice of St. Vincent. 8vo. 1822
Shepherd (H. L.) on Election Law . . . 8vo. 1825
Sheppard (Wm.) Court Judicature . . 12mo. 1656
—— Epitome of Statute Law . . . . . folio 1656
—— Common Assurance 4to. 1669
—— Court Keeper's Guide 12mo. 1649
——————————————— . . . 7th ed. 12mo. 1689
—— Justice of the Peace 12mo. 1654
—— Actions on the Case . . . . 2nd ed. 8vo. 1675
—— Touchstone of Precedents (R. Preston)
7th ed. 2 vols. 1820
——————————— (G. E. Atherley) 8th ed. 8vo. 1826
Sherborn Hospital, Collections relating to . 4to. 1771
Sheridan (T.) Discourse on the Use and Power of Parliament 12mo. 1685
Sheriff, The Compleat 8vo. 1696
Sheriff's Court Practice 12mo. 1657
Sheriff's Accounts (*see* Hale's Tracts)
Sheriffs, &c. Office (bound up with Grounds of the Law) 12mo. 1552
Shipley (*Rev.* O.) on Purgatory of Prisoners. 8vo. 1857
Shipping (*see* Abbott, Greenhow, James, Lees, Shee, Maude, & P. Oliver Sutherland)
Shirley (*Rev.* W. W.) Fasciculi Zizaniorum (*see* No. 5, M. R. Pub.) 1858
—— Royal, &c. Letters illustrative of Reign of Hen. III. 27 M. R. Pub. 1862-66
Shower (*Sir* B.) K. B. Reports . 2 vols. folio 1708-20
———————————————— 1708 . . . ⎫
———————————————— & Cases in ⎬ folio 1698
Parliament bound with it, 1698 . ⎭
———————————————— 1679-94 (T. Leach)
2nd ed. 2 vols. 8vo. 1794
Shropshire, Selection of Antiquities of . folio 1824
Shute (Wm.) History of Venice, collected by Thomas de Fougasses . . . . folio 1612

Sicilia, Atti del Governo, L. Generale, 1860-62. 8vo. 1862
—— Atti del Governo Dittatoriale . . . 8vo. 1864
Sickelmore (R.) History of Brighton . 12mo. n. d.
Siderfin (*Sir* T.) Q. B. Reports. 2 vols. in 1, folio 1683
                              1659-71, folio 1714
Sierre Leone Acts, 1857 & continued . . . .
Significavit, on Quashing a (*see* Attwood *v.* Eyre)
Sills (Geo.) on Composition with Creditors. 12mo. 1865
Simcox (Jno.) Election Law 8vo. 1789
Simons (H. A.) on Interpleader (bound up with Lawes on Bills of Exchange)
—— (N.) & Stuart (J.) Chancery Reports, 1822 to 1826, temp. Leach . . . 2 vols. 8vo. 1824-27
—— Chancery Reports, 1826-1852, temp. V.-CC. Leach, Hart, & Shadwell . . 17 vols. 8vo. 1829-54
———————————— new series, 1850-1852, temp. Cranworth & Kindersley . . . 2 vols. 8vo. 1851-2
Simpson (Jos.) Reflections on the Requisite for the Study of the Law . . . . 3rd ed.
    (*See* Law, Reflection on)
———————————————————— by M. Dawes
                                   5th ed. 8vo. n. d.
—— (Robt.) Collection of Fragments for a History of Derbyshire . . . . . 2 vols. 8vo. 1826
—— History & Antiquities of Lancaster . 8vo. 1852
Sinclair (*Sir* Jno.) on the Bullion Report. Jac. Col. Vol. 13
—— Statistical Account of Scotland (Edinburgh)
                             21 vols. 8vo. 1791-99
Sims (R.) Index to Pedigrees & Arms contained in the Heralds' Visitations & other Manuscripts in the British Museum (Sims) 8vo. 1849
—— Hand-Book to the Library of the British Museum 8vo. 1853
—— Manual of Public Records . 2nd ed. 8vo. 1861
Simson (Robt.) Sectionum Conicarum Libri V. 4to. 1735
Sinecures & Pensions, Report of Select Committee
                                       folio 1834

Six Codes, les (France) 8vo. 1828
Skene (*Sir* Jno.) Regiam Majestatem (Old Laws
 of Scotland) . . . . folio 1609
—— Exposition of Termes & Words in Regiam
 Majestatem 4to. 1641
Skinner (R.) King's Bench Reports, 1671–1697
 folio 1728
Skirrow (Wm.) on the Exclusion of the Queen from
 the Liturgy. Jac. Col. Vol. 1
Sladden (W.) Registry Laws of Canada . 8vo. 1857
Slander, Liberty of the Press on. Libel Law Tracts,
 Vol. 1
Slane Peerage Evidence. Vol. 3, 2nd series, 1827
Slater (Isaac) Directory for Manchester . 8vo. 1858
———————————————— Scotland . . 8vo. 1867
Slaughter (M.) Railway Intelligence, No. 11. 8vo. 1861
Slave Trade Abolition, Briefs, Evidence, &c. 1788–
 1807 . . . . 18 vols. folio
Slave Laws of Jamaica 8vo. 1828
Sleigh (W. C.) Personal Wrongs & Legal Remedies
 12mo. 1860
—— Handy Book of Criminal Law, applicable
 chiefly to Commercial Transactions . . 12mo. 1860
Sliford (Wm.) Court Register 8vo. 1741
Smale (J.) & Giffard (J. W. De L.) Chancery
 Reports, temp. V.-C. Stuart, 1852–57. 8vo. 1855–58
Small Boroughs, Boundary Commissioners' Parlia-
 mentary Reports on . . . . folio 1832
Smee (Jno.) Tax Acts . . . . . 2 vols. 8vo. 1723–97
Smethurst (J. M.) on Locus Standi . . 12mo. 1866
———————————————————— . . . 12mo. 1866
Smirke (E.) (*see* Roscoe on Evidence)
Smith (Adam) Wealth of Nations. Vol. 2 only
 8vo. 1791
—— (*Dr.* A.) Life & Essays (*see* D. Stewart) 4to. 1795
—— (C.) English Atlas . . . . folio 1835
—— (*Dr.* Chas.) History of Cork (Dublin)
 2nd ed. 8vo. 1774

Smith (*Dr.* Chas.) History of Kerry (Dublin) 8vo. 1774
———————————————— Waterford (Dublin)
8vo. 1774
—— (C. M.) on Master & Servant . . . 8vo. 1852
———————————————— 2nd ed. 8vo. 1860
—— (Edmd.) Elementary Views of Conveyancing
12mo. 1863
—— (H. F.) Digest, U. S. (*see* United States Digest)
—— (H. S.) Register of Contested Elections. 12mo. 1841
—— (J. G.) Hints for the Examination of Medical Witnesses 12mo. 1829
—— (*see* Erskine)
—— (*Rev.* J. J.) Catalogue of MSS. of Gonville & Caius College Library, Cambridge. 8vo. 1849
—— (J. O.) The Lawyer & his Profession. 12mo. 1860
—— (J. P.) K. B. Reports, 1803–1806. 3 vols.
8vo. 1803–6
—— (J. T.) Letter to Metropolitan Sanitary Commissioners. Pam. Vol. 17
—— (James W.) on Public Meetings
—— (Jno. Thos.) Antiquities of Westminster & St. Stephen's Chapel 4to. 1807
—— (Jno. Wm.) on Mercantile Law . . 8vo. 1834
———————————————— 2nd ed. 8vo. 1838
———————————————— 3rd ed. 8vo. 1843
———————————————— (J. M. Dowdeswell) . . . . 4th ed. 8vo. 1848
———————————————— 5th ed. 8vo. 1853
———————————————— 6th ed. 8vo. 1859
———————————————— 7th ed. 8vo. 1865
—— Leading Cases on Various Branches of the Law
2 vols. 8vo. 1837
———————————————— 2nd ed. 2 vols. 8vo. 1841
———————————————— (J. S. Willes & H. S. Keating) . . . . . 3rd ed. 2 vols. 8vo. 1849
———————————————— 4th ed. 2 vols. 8vo. 1856
———————————————— (F. R. Maude & T. E. Chitty) . . . . . 5th ed. 2 vols. 8vo. 1862

LAW SOCIETY LIBRARY. 311

Smith (Jno. W.) Leading Cases in Various Branches
  of the Law) . . . . . 6th ed. 2 vols. 8vo. 1867
—— Action at Law (D. B. Ring) . 3rd ed. 12mo. 1848
———————————— (E. Wise) . . 5th ed. 12mo. 1854
———————— (S. Prentice) . 6th ed. 12mo. 1857
———————————————— 7th ed. 12mo. 1860
———————————————— 8th ed. 12mo. 1863
———————————————— 9th ed. 12mo. 1866
———————————————— 10th ed. 12mo. 1868
—— on Contracts (J. G. Malcolm) . 2nd ed. 8vo. 1855
——————————————— . 3rd ed. 8vo. 1860
——————————————— . 4th ed. 8vo. 1865
——————————————— . 5th ed. 8vo. 1868
—— Landlord & Tenant 8vo. 1855
————————————— (F. P. Maude) 2nd ed. 8vo. 1866
—— (John Sidney) Chancery Practice. 2 vols. 8vo. 1834
————————————————— Vol. 2 only 1835
————————————————— 2 vols. 8vo. 1837
—————————————————3rd ed. 2 vols. 8vo. 1844
—— Chancery Practice, Handbook of . . 8vo. 1848
————————————————— 5th ed. &
intended as 2nd ed. of the Handbook . . 8vo. 1855
————————————————— 6th ed. 8vo. 1857
—— & Smith (Alfred) Chancery Practice, Handbook of . . . . 7th ed. 2 vols. 8vo. 1862
—— Equity Principles 8vo. 1856
—— (Josiah) Evidence in Divorce Case. Vol. 10,
Peerage Cases
—— (Josiah W.) on Fines 12mo. 1846
—— Manual of Equity Jurisprudence. 2nd ed. 12mo. 1849
————————————————— 3rd ed. 12mo. 1854
————————————————— 5th ed. 12mo. 1856
————————————————— 6th ed. 12mo. 1861
————————————————— 7th ed. 12mo. 1864
————————————————— 8th ed. 12mo. 1866
————————————————— 9th ed. 12mo. 1868
—— on Real & Personal Property . . . 8vo. 1855
————————————————— 2nd ed. 8vo. 1859
————————————————— . 3rd ed. 8vo. 1865

Smith (Josiah W.) Manual of Common Law &
Bankruptcy 12mo. 1862
────── Manual of Bankruptcy . . . 12mo. 1864
────── Manual of Common Law 2nd ed. 12mo. 1864
──── (P.) (*see* Best)
──── (Thos.) History of St. Marylebone. . 8vo. 1833
──── (Toulmin) Parliamentary Remembrancer
2nd ed. folio 1860–65
──── Nuisances Removal . . . . 3rd ed. 12mo. 1861
──── (Wm.) List of Bankrupts, 1786–1806. 8vo. 1806
──── (*Dr.* Wm.) Dictionary of Antiquities
2nd ed. 8vo. 1851
──────────── the Bible . . . 3rd ed. 4to. 1863
──────────── Biography & Mythology
3rd ed. 8vo. 1864
──── Dictionary of Greek & Roman Geography
2nd ed. 8vo. 1854
──── Latin & English Dictionary 8vo. 1863
──── (Wm.) Irish Chancery Receiver's Duties &
Office 8vo. 1828
──────────────── Rules & Orders, 1639
to 1839 . . . . 12mo. 1839
──────────────────── &c. . 12mo. 1843
──────────────── Regulation Act, 1850,
12mo. 1850
──── Irish Equity Orders 8vo. 1845
──── Remarks on Law Reform. Law Tr. Vol. 6
──── History of Warwickshire 4to. 1829
Smithers (H.) Liverpool, its Commerce, &c. 4to. 1825
Smithfield Market Question fully considered. Pam.
by Clericus, 1837
──── Plan of Market Improvements 1851
Smollett (*Dr.* T.) History of England from Revo-
lution to death of George II., in continuation
of Mr. Hume's History . . . . 4 vols. 8vo. 1830
Smyth (Rd.) Obituary of such persons as he knew,
1627–74 (ed. Sir H. Ellis)(*see* C. S. Pa. No. 44) 1849
──── (*Sir* T.) De Republica Anglorum, the Maner
of Governments 4to. 1584

Smyth (*Capt.* W. H., afterwards Admiral) Notices of the Manor and Mansion of Hartwell . 4to. 1851
——————————————————— Cycle of Celestial Objects contained at Hartwell Observatory 4to. 1860
——————————————— Sidereal Chromatics from Bedford Cycle 8vo. 1864
—— (*see* McAlpin for Law Catalogue of Hartwell House)
—— (*Lieut.* W.) & Lowe (F.) Journey from Lima to Para 8vo. 1835
Sneyd (C. A.) (*see* C. S. Pa. No. 37)
Social Science, Transactions of Society (*see* Hastings) . . . . 6 vols. 8vo. 1862-68
—— Journal (*Dr.* E. Lankester) 1865-6 . 8vo. 1866
——————————— Sessional Papers for promoting
8vo. 1866
Solicitor, A, on Descent & Distribution . . 8vo. 1834
—— Compleat 12mo. 1668
——————————— (*See* also Practick) . 4th ed. 8vo. 1672
Solicitor's Compleat Entering Clerk . . . 8vo. 1683
—— Guide . . . . 2 vols. 12mo. 1776
—— Duty to teach Client to manage his own Business 12mo. 1668
Solicitors, Essay in Vindication of. Jac. L. T. Vol. 5 1826
—— Journal, 1857-68 . . . . . 12 vols. 4to.
—— & Attorneys, List of ; Tables of Fees, &c. presented to H. C. . . . . 2 vols. folio 1729-32
—— Additional Lists, ditto . . . . . folio 1830
(*See* Attorneys, & also Law Lists)
—— Practice in Chancery Epitomised
4th ed. 8vo. 1775
—— Register (*see* Window) . . . 2 vols. 4to.
—— Country, Suggestions to 8vo. 1837
Somers (*Lord*) Collection of scarce and valuable Tracts relating to the History and Constitution of these Kingdoms (Walter Scott).
2nd ed. 13 vols. 4to. 1809-15

Somers (*Lord*) on Duty of Grand Juries. Libel
L. T. Vol. 1
—— Life of (*see* Roscoe's Lives of Lawyers)
Somner (Henry) Reflections on the Decline of Eloquence in England. Pam. Vol. 5
—— (Wm.) Antiquities of, or Survey of the ancient City of Canterbury 4to. 1640
—— on Gavelkind . . . . . . 2nd ed. 4to. 1726
—— Life of, by W. Kennett (bound up with Somner, H. on Gavelkind)
Sortain (*Rev.* J.) Life of Lord Bacon . . 12mo. n. d.
Southwark, Parish Clerks' Survey of London, Westminster, & 8vo. 1732
Southampton, Charter to, 1641 . . . . 12mo. 1810
South Australia, Acts & Ordinances of Government & Legislative Council of, 1837–56. 3 v. fo.
—— Acts of the Parliament of, 1857–1867
12 vols. 4to.
South Sea Bubbles . . . . 3 vols. 8vo. 1711
—— Company, Abstract of Acts . . . 12mo. 1718
—— Scheme, History of the Company, &c. (D. Templeman) 8vo. 1735
—— Stock, 1822 (*see* Unclaimed Dividends)
Spackman (W. F.) Railway Interest . . . 8vo. 1845
Spain. Calendars of Letters, Despatches, & State Papers, 1485–1525 (edited by G. A. Bergenroth)
3 vols. imp. 8vo. 1862–68
Spanish Laws, Catalogue of, in Lincoln's Inn Library 8vo. 1847
Spark (T.) Lactantii Lucii Cœlii Opera . . 8vo. 1684
Special Cases in Chancery, 1625–1714
3 vols. in 1, folio
—— 69–1693 . . . . 8vo. 1694
Spectator, The, commencing Vol. 14 & continued
Speed (John) The Theatre of the Empire of Great Britain . . . . folio 1696
Spelman (*Sir* Henry) Views of English Towns
(2 copies) 4to. 1656
—— Glossarium Archæologicum . 3rd ed. folio 1687

Spelman (*Sir* Henry) Life & Posthumous Works
(E. Gibson) . . . . folio 1698
CONTAINING :—
Feuds & Tenures
Ancient Government of England
Parliaments
Origin of the Four Terms of the Year
Answer to Archbishop Abbot's Apologie as to Death of
Peter Hawkins
On Origin of Testaments and Wills and Probates
Icenia: sive Norfolciæ Descriptio Topographica
Comitum Marescallorum Angliæ Catalogus
De Milite Dissertatio
Historia Familiæ de Sharnburn
Dialogue concerning the Corn of the Kingdom
A Catalogue of the Dwellings of the Archbishops & Bishops

Spence (Geo.) Enquiry into the Origin of the Laws
of Modern Europe & Political Institutions.   8vo. 1826
—— An Essay on the Origin of English Laws. 8vo. 1812
—— Equitable Jurisdiction of the Court of
Chancery . . . . 2 vols. 8vo. 1846-9
—— on Evils & Abuses in Chancery. Chancery
Pam. Vol. 1 1831
—— 1st Address on State of Courts, & Suggestions
for Remedy. Chancery Pam. Vol. 2 1839
—— 2nd ditto
—— 3rd ditto, & Observations on Proposition of
' Quarterly Review ' 1840
—— Speech on Chancery Reform. L. T. Vol. 4 &
Pam. Vol. 3
—— (*Rev.* Mr.) Polymetis ; or an Enquiry on the
Works of the Roman Poets . . . . . folio 1747
Spencer, Bagshaw *v.*, Case of, in Chancery. Col.
Jur. Vol. 1
Spiers (*Dr.* A.) French & English Dictionary
2 vols. 8vo. n. d.
Spike (E.) on Master & Servant (C.B.Clayden) 12mo.
Spiller (B.) Index to Statutes, 1801-28 . . 4to. 1829
Spilsbury (W. H.) Lincoln's Inn & its Library
12mo. 1850
Spinks (*Dr.*) Ecclesiastical & Admiralty Reports,
1853-5 . . . . 2 vols. 8vo. 1855

Spotswood (John) *or* (Spotiswoode) History of
  Church of Scotland . . . . . . 3rd ed. folio 1668
Spottiswood (John) Form of Scotch Process . 12mo. 1711
—— Introduction to the Knowledge of the Stile of
  Writs in use in Scotland . . . . 5th ed. 8vo. 1765
Sprange (John) Tunbridge Wells Guide . 12mo. 1797
—————————————————————————— . 12mo. 1801
Sprat (*Dr.* Thos.) Voyage to England, from the
  French of J. Sorbiere 12mo. 1665
—— History of Royal Society of London
   3rd ed. 4to. 1722
Spurzheim (G.) Philosophical Principles of Phrenology . . . . 3rd ed. 8vo.
—— Phrenology, or Doctrine of the Mind
   3rd ed. 8vo. 1825
—— Sketch of the Natural Laws of Man . 12mo. 1825
Stair (*Visct.*) Institutions of the Law of Scotland
   4th ed. 2 vols. folio 1826–31
Stafford Peerage Case. Vol. 2, 2nd series. Evidence.
  Vols. 3, 10, 12, 1808–25
—————————————— Genealogical Table . . . 8vo. 1818
—— (*Visct.* Wm.) his Speech on the Scaffold.
  Political Tr. 1688
Staffordshire, The Widow of the Wood . 12mo. 1755
Stammers (J.) The Bar Practice vindicated in the
  case of Reg. *v.* Disraeli. Vol. 27 Pamp. . . . 1838
Stamp (G.) Index to Statutes . 2nd ed. 12mo. 1853
- —————————————————————— . . 3rd ed. 8vo. 1862
  (*See* Ruffhend, Ruithby, Vardon, Spiller)
Stamp Office Law List (*see* Law List)
Standard, The, Newspaper 1832
Standing Orders in Parliament, Lords & Commons
  (*see* Bigg & also Vacher)
Stanhope (*Earl*) Life of Wm. Pitt. 4 vols. 12mo. 1862
Stanley, House of, History of, Isle of Man, & Travels of Sir W. Stanley 8vo. 1793
—— (*Sir* Wm.) Travels (bound up with History
  of House of Stanley)
Stannaries of Cornwall, Laws of the . . 12mo. 1752

Stannaries of Cornwall, Laws of the . 2nd ed. 8vo. 1824
—————————————————— further ed. 8vo. 1836
Stapleton (A. G.) Biography of George Canning
         2nd ed. 3 vols. 8vo. 1831
—— (Thos.) Plumpton Correspondence, temp.
Edwd. IV., Rich. III., Hen. VII. & VIII.,
1461–1551-2 (*see* C. S. Pa. Nos. 4, 34, 47)
Stapylton (M. B.) Conveyancing Precedents (*see*
Davidson, E.)
Stark (A.) History of Gainsborough & Stow. 8vo. 1817
Starkey (Hy.) Trial for High Treason. Political Tr. 1688
Starkie (Thos.) on Criminal Pleading. 2 vols. 8vo. 1814

         2nd ed. 2 vols. 8vo. 1822
—— Nisi Prius Reports, 1814–1823 . 3 vols. 8vo. 1823
—— Law of Evidence in Civil & Criminal Pro-
ceedings . . . . 2nd ed. 8vo. 1833
———————————————————— 3rd ed. 8vo. 1842
—— on Slander & Libel . . 2nd ed. 2 vols. 8vo. 1830
————————————— 3rd ed. (H. C. Folkard). 8vo. 1869
State Law, or Doctrine of Libels. Libel Tracts,
Vol. 1
—— Papers, temp. Hen. VIII. 11 vols. 4to. 1830–52

  Vol. 1 contains Domestic Correspondence
  „ 2 & 3 „ Correspondence relating to Ireland
  „ 4 & 5 „ Correspondence relating to Scotland
  „ 6–11 „ Foreign Correspondence

*———————— British & Foreign, from 1812 to
1857 (& to be continued) . . . 46 vols. 8vo.
——— General List of, from Vol. 1 to Vol. 21,
1820 . . . . 8vo. 1842
——————————— Index, Vol. 1 to Vol. 42, 1373–
1853 . . . . 8vo. 1865

 * This publication is intended to comprise the principal documents which have been made public relating to the political and commercial affairs of nations and to their relations with each other, from the termination of the war in 1814 to the latest period. The above collection was presented by Lord Stanley.

State Treaties, 1688-1771 . . . . . 2 vols. 8vo. 1772
  (And *see* Brown & Hertslet, & Vol. 146, House of
  Common Papers, up to 1826)
—— Trials, Specimen of (new ed. by Moile) 8vo. 1838
  ——————— Rich. II. to Geo. II. 6 vols. folio 1719-30
  ————————————————————— 3rd ed. 8vo. 1735-42
  ——————— 1163-1820, by Howell & Howell (Jun.)
                              34 vols. 8vo. 1816-28
  ——————— A New Abridgment & Critical Review
  of, from Rich. II. to 11 Geo. II., with Index, &c.
  by Mr. Salmon . . . . folio 1738
  ——————— Index, by Jardine
Statham (Nicholas) Abridgment of the Law (per
  me R. Pynson) . . . . n. d.
Stationers' Company Almanac. 68 vols. 12mo. 1792-1860
                              & continued
Statutes at Large, 1224-1868 . . 46 vols. 4to.
———————Index to, from 1225-1809 (Raithby).4to.
—— of the Realm . . . . . 10 vols. folio 1810-22
—— 2 & 3 Wm. IV. to 1868 . . 37 vols. 8vo.
—— of Hen. VIII., 1509-46 . . . . . folio 1595
  (*See* also Rastell, Keble, Pulton, Scobell, Tothill,
  Cromwell, Acts of; & *see* Acts & Ordinances
  & Public General Acts)
  ——————— Indexes to (*see* Ruffhead, Raithby, Vardon,
  Spiller, Stamp)
Statute of Uses, Case on Operation of. Har. L. Tr.
  Vol. 1
Staunforde, or Stanford, (W.) Exposition of the
  King's Prerogative 8vo. 1627
—— Les Plees del Coron 4to. 1607
Staunton (*Sir* Geo.) Embassy to China. 2 vols. 4to. 1797
—— The Fundamental Laws of the Penal Code of
  China 4to. 1810
Steers (Jno.) on Parish Law 8vo. 1830
————————————————————(H. J. Hodgson) 8vo. 1857
Steele (R.) The Crisis, a Discourse representing the
  Just Causes of the late Happy Revolution, 1711
  (*see* Parl. Tr.)

Stemmata Chicheliana, Genealogical Account of some Families so named, with Supplement (*see* Buckler) . . . . folio 1765
Stephen (*Sir* G.) on Bankruptcy & Credit Trade. Pam. Vol. 8
—— Jurymen's Guide 12mo. 1845
—— (H. J.) Commentaries on Laws of England, partly founded on Blackstone . 4 vols. 8vo. 1841 45
———————————————————2nd ed. 4 vols. 8vo. 1848
———————————————————— (Jas. Stephen) 3rd ed. 4 vols. 8vo. 1853
———————————————————— 4th ed. 4 vols. 8vo. 1858
———————————————————— 5th ed. 4 vols. 8vo. 1863
———————————————————— 6th ed. 4 vols. 8vo. 1868
—— Principles of Pleading in Civil Action
5th ed. 8vo. 1843
———————————————————— (J. Stephen & F. F. Pinder) . . . . . . 6th ed. 8vo. 1860
———————————————————— (F. F. Pinder) 7th ed. 8vo. 1866
—— (James) Common Law Procedure Act, 1860 (bound up with Finlason) (*see* Day, Markham)
—— Questions for Law Students on 6th ed. Stephen's Commentaries 8vo. 1869
—— (J. F.) a General View of the Criminal Law of England 8vo. 1863
Stephanus (Hen.) Thesaurus Linguæ Latinæ
2 vols. folio 1573
———————————————————— Græcæ
5 vols. folio 1573
Stephens (A. J.) The Law of Nisi Prius, Evidence in Civil Actions, & Arbitrations & Award
3 vols. 8vo. 1842
—— Ecclesiastical & Eleemosynary Statutes, Hen. III. to 1844 . . . . 2 vols. 8vo. 1845
—— Ecclesiastical Courts 12mo. 1853
—— on Laws relating to the Clergy. 2 vols. 8vo. 1848
—— (*see* Merewether, H. A.)
Sterne (Laurence) Works . . . . 8 vols. 12mo. 1795

Stevens (John) History of Ancient Abbeys, &c.
2 vols. folio 1722
—— (Addenda to Sir Wm. Dugdale's Monasticon Anglicanum) . . . . 3 vols. folio 1718-23
Stevens (*Capt.* John) Spanish & Eng. Dictionary. 4to. 1726
—— (   ) on Devises & Revocations . . 8vo. 1829
Stevenson (*Rev.* Jos.) Calendar of State Papers, Foreign Series, of the Reign of Elizabeth, preserved in Her Majesty's Public Record Office, &c.
Vol. I.—1558-1559.   Vol. IV.—1561-1562.
Vol. II.—1559-1560. Vol. V.—1562.
Vol. III.—1560-1561.
Imp. 8vo. 1863-67
—— (*see* Abingdon Monastery, No. 2, M. R. Pub.)
Vols. I. & II. 1858
—— Letters, &c. illustrative of English Wars in France during Reign of Henry VI. No. 22, M. R. Pub. . . . . 2 vols. 1861-64
—— (Pearce) on Infant Custody Bill. L. T. Vol. 6
—— (Wm.) View of the Agriculture of Surrey 8vo. 1809
—— History & Antiquities of Ely Cathedral (*see* Bentham, J.)
Stewart (Duncan) on the Law & Practice of Bankruptcy 12mo. 1832
—— (Dugald) Essays on Philosophical Subjects, by Dr. Adam Smith, & Account of his Life. 4to. 1795
—— (*Sir* James) Abridgment of the Acts of Parliament & Convention, from 1424 to 1707 12mo. 1707
———————————————————— continued
by A. Bruce, from 1707 to 1726 . . . 12mo. 1726
—— (James) on Conveyancing. 3 vols. 8vo. 1827-31
—————————————— 2nd ed. 3 vols. 8vo. 1829-32
—— Precedents in Conveyancing (*see* Bythewood, W. M.)
—— Principles of the Law of Real Property, according to Blackstone's Text. 8vo. 1837
—— The Principles of the Law of Real & Personal Property upon Blackstone's Text . 2nd ed. 8vo. 1840
—— on Rights of Persons, according to the Text of Blackstone 8vo. 1839

LAW SOCIETY LIBRARY. 321

Stewart (James) on Law of England Reform. 8vo. 1842
—— (J. S.) *Scotch Appeal Cases* (*see* Craigie, J.)
—— (W.) History of H. Boece (*see* Turnbull)
Stillingfleet (Edw. *Bp.* of Worcester) Ecclesiastical Cases . . . . 2 vols. 8vo. 1698–1704
——————————————— 2nd ed. 2 vols. 8vo. 1702–4
—— (*Bp.*) Works & Life . . . . 6 vols. folio 1710
Stirling, History of 12mo. 1812
Stockdale (Jno.) Parliamentary Guide . . 8vo. 1784
—— Trial for Libel on H. C. 8vo. 1790
Stock (J. S.) Observations on the Case of Lady Hewley's Charity. L. T. Vol. 3 1836
Stockdale *v.* Hansard, Consideration on Judgment (*see* Blundell)
Stoddart (*Sir* Jno.) Letter to Lord Brougham on the Opinion of the Judges in the Irish Marriages. Reg. *v.* Willis 8vo. 1844
Stokes (Anthony) View of Constitution of British Colonies in America 8vo. 1783
—— (Whitley) on Lien of Attorneys & Solicitors, &c. 12mo. 1860
—— Power of Attorneys (*see* Bythewood, W. M.)
Stone (J.) Petty Sessions Practice . . . 12mo. 1836
—— Metropolitan Police Manual . . . 12mo. 1841
—— (Samuel) Justice's Manual . . 9th ed. 8vo. 1862
————————————————— . 11th ed. 8vo. 1865
————————————————— . 12th ed. 8vo. 1867
————————————————— . 13th ed. 8vo. 1868
Story (Josh.) Commentaries on American Law (Boston) 3 vols. 8vo. 1833
————————————————— Abridged. 8vo. 1833
—— on Equity Jurisprudence. 3rd ed. 2 vols. 8vo. 1833
————————————————— 7th ed. 2 vols. 8vo. 1857
————————— (J. F. Redfield) 9th ed. 2 vols. 8vo. 1866
—— on Bailments . . . . . (Boston) 8vo. 1839
————————— (E. H. Bennett) . 7th ed. 8vo. 1863
—— on Conflict of the Laws 8vo. 1835
————————————————— . . . 5th ed. 8vo. 1857

Y

Story (Josh.) on Conflict of the Laws (J. F.
  Redfield) . . . . 6th ed. 8vo. 1865
—— on Agency . . . . 5th ed. 8vo. 1857
—— on Bills of Exchange . . . . 4th ed. 8vo. 1860
—— on Equity Pleading 8vo. 1838
———————————————(E. B. Bennett) 6th ed. 8vo. 1857
—— on Partnership, U. S. . . . 5th ed. 8vo. 1859
———————————————(J. C. Gray) 6th ed. 8vo. 1868
—— on Promissory Notes . . . . 5th ed. 8vo. 1859
———————————————. . . . 6th ed. 8vo. 1868
—— (W. W.) Life & Letters of Joseph Story
  2 vols. 8vo. 1815
—— Circuit Court Reports, 1839–45, U. S. (see
  Curtis) . . . . 3 vols. 8vo. 1851–55
—— on Sales of Personal Property . 2nd ed. 8vo. 1853
—— on Contracts . . . . . . 4th ed. 2 vols. 8vo. 1856
Stow (John) Survey of London . . 2nd ed. 4to. 1603
———————————————(by Anthony Munday)
  3rd ed. 4to. 1618
———————————————(by Anthony Munday
  & Henry Dyson) . . . . . . 4th ed. folio 1633
———————————————(J. Strype) 6th ed. 2 vols. folio 1754
—— Life of (see Malcolm's Lives)
—— Family, &c. Prayers 8vo. 1840
—— Biblical Catechism . . . . 2nd ed. 12mo. 1841
—— a Version of the Psalms . . 3rd ed. 8vo. 1842
—— Thoughts on the Gospel 8vo. 1846
—— Reflections on the Epistles of St. Paul. 8vo. 1847
—— Thoughts on the Liturgy . 2 vols. 12mo. 1850–56
—— A Hermit's Narrative of Opinions on Divine
  Revelation & Christianity 8vo. 1861
Stowe, Bucks, Description of (see Seeley) . 8vo. 1827
Strange (*Sir* John) Queen's Bench Reports
  2 vols. folio 1754
———————————————(J. Strange) 2nd ed. 2 vols. 8vo. 1782
———————————————1716–49 (Nolan) 3rd ed. 2 vols. 8vo. 1795
Strange (*Sir* Thos.) on Hindu Law; with an Intro-
  duction by J. D. Mayne (Madras) . . 8vo. 1859

Strangford (*Viscount*) No. 55 C. S. P., C. M. Vol. 2
Strathmore Peerage. Case, Vol. 3, 2nd series.
 Evidence, Vol. 7. 1821
Strawberry Hill, Catalogue of the Contents of
 (Earl Waldegrave's) 4to. 1842
Street (G.) Indian & Colonial Mercantile Directory
 8vo. 1867-68
Strickland (Geo., M.P.) An Alarm on the Rights
 of the Poor in Danger from the Supposed Law
 Reform. Vol. 5, L. T. 1833
Striking in the King's Palace(*see* Legal Recreations)
Stroud (F.) County Court Practice in Bankruptcy
 12mo. 1862
Strype (John, M.A.) Stow's Survey of London
 6th ed. 2 vols. folio 1754
—— Life of (*see* Malcolm's Lives)
Stuart (James) Historical Memoirs of the City of
 Armagh 8vo. 1819
—— Letter to Directors of East India Company
 (*see* East India Company) 4to. 1778
—— (J.) *Chancery Reports* (*see* Simons, N.)
—— (*Dr.* G.) View of Society in Europe . 4to. 1778
—— History of Scotland from the Establishment
 of the Reformation till Queen Mary's Death
 2 vols. 4to. 1782
—— Observations concerning the Public Law &
 Constitutional History of Scotland . . . 8vo. 1799
Stubbs (W.) & Talmash (G.) Crown Circuit Com-
 panion 8vo. 1738
———————————————————— 3rd ed. 8vo. 1762
—— (W., M.A.) Gesta Regis Henrici Benedicti
 Abbatis. Vols. I., II. (*see* M. R. Pub. No. 49) 1867
—— Chronica Magistri Rogeri de Houedene.
 Vol. I. (*see* M. R. Pub. No. 51). 1868
Stukeley (*Dr.* Wm.) History of Stonehenge. folio 1740
—— Itinerarium Curiosum; or an Account of the
 Antiquities, &c. observed in Great Britain. folio 1776
—— Life of (*see* Malcolm's Lives)

Style (Wm.) Modern Reports (1645–1655) in the
Upper Bench Courts . . . . folio 1658
——— Practical Register of the Common Law
4th ed. 8vo. 1707
Suetonius (C. Tranquillus) Opera 4to. 1684
Sudlow (J. J. J.) Inaugural Address at Islington
Institution, 1837. Pam. Vol. 5
Suffolk, Agriculture of 8vo. 1804
Sugden (E. B., afterwards *Sir* E. B. Sugden, now
Lord St. Leonards) on Vendors & Purchasers of
Estates 8vo. 1805
————————————————————— 4th ed. 8vo. 1813
————————————————————— 7th ed. 8vo. 1826
————————————————————— 8th ed. 8vo. 1830
————————————————————— 9th ed. 2 vols. 8vo. 1834
————————————————————— 10th ed. 3 vols. 8vo. 1839
————————————————————— 11th ed. 2 vols. 8vo. 1846
————————————— (a Concise & Practical View)
8vo. 1851
————————————————————— 13th ed. 8vo. 1857
————————————————————— 14th ed. 8vo. 1862
(For Questions on, *see* May)
——— Letters on Sale & Purchase of Estates
2nd ed. 8vo. 1812
————————————————————— 5th ed. 8vo. 1829
——— On Powers . . . . 4th ed. 8vo. 1826
————————————————————— 5th ed. 8vo. 1831
————————————————————— 6th ed. 2 vols. 8vo. 1836
————————————————————— 7th ed. 2 vols. 8vo. 1845
————————————————————— 8th ed. 8vo. 1861
——— a Letter to C. Butler, on Presuming a Surrender of Terms. Jac. Col. Vol. 1, 4th ed. . . 1820
——— Reply to J. Williams upon the 'Abuses of
Chancery.' Jac. Col. Vol. 1 1825
——— Letter to J. Humphreys on the Law of Real
Property. Jac. Col. Vol. 4 1826
——— Speech in the House of Commons on the
Court of Chancery. Jac. Col. Vol. 8 . . . 1831

Sugden (E. B.) Letter to Lord Melbourne on Appellate Jurisdiction of Court of Chancery & House of Lords. Chan. Pam. Vol. 1 1835
—— on Property Law, as Administered by the House of Lords 8vo. 1849
—— Answer to the Question, 'Shall We Register Our Deeds?' Pam. Vol. 8 1852
—— on Real Property Statutes 8vo. 1852
—— Handy Book of Property Law. 6th ed. 12mo. 1858
——————————————————— 7th ed. 12mo. 1863
—— (Henry) on Law of Wills, as altered by 7 Wm. 8vo. 1837
—— Collection of Oaths to be taken by M.P.s Vol. 7, Jac. L. Tr.
Suits in Chancery by Subpœna. Har. L. T. Vol. 1 (And see Chancery)
—— at Law, Observations on Expense, with Plan for a Remedy. Col. Jur. Vol. 1
Sullivan (F. S.) Lectures on Feudal & English Law 4to. 1772
——————————————————— (G. Stuart) 2nd ed. 4to. 1776
—— & Pigott, Trial of (see Trials of Fenians)
Sully (*Duke* of) Memoirs . . . . 5 vols. 8vo. 1819
Summonitiones ad Parliamentum . . 5 vols. folio 1829
(*See* Peerage Report on Dignity of Peer of the Realm.)
Sumner (Charles) Reports, U. S. (*see* Curtis)
Sun Newspaper . . . . 1842 & continued
Supersedeas, Grant of the Office of. Lord Bacon's Argument on the Writ de Rege Inconsulto. Col. Jur. Vol. 1
Supreme Authority, Submission to. L. T. 1688
Surgeons, Assistant, in Navy, Case of. Pam. Vol. 1. 2nd ed. 1850
Surtees (Robt.) History of Durham. 4 vols. folio 1816–40
Surveyor's Dialogues . . . . . 4th ed. 8vo. 1738
Sussex Election Poll Books 8vo. 1784–1826

Sussex Election Poll Books 1802
—————————————————————— 8vo. 1805-16
Sussex, East. 8vo. 1837
Sutherland (W.) Britain's Glory, or, Shipbuilding
   Unvailed . . . . 2nd ed. folio 1729
Swabey (*Dr.* M. C. M.) Reports, Admiralty, 1855-
   1859 . . . . 8vo. 1860
       (Continued by Lushington)
—— & Tristram (*Dr.* T. H.) Reports, Probate &
   Divorce Court, 1858-1866. . . 4 vols. 8vo. 1860-66
Swan (Robt.) on Jurisdiction of the Ecclesiastical
   Courts relating to Probates & Administrations . 1830
Swanston (C. T.) Chancery Reports, temp.
   Eldon, 1818-19 . . . . . . 3 vols. 8vo. 1820-27
Sweet (Geo.) Index, Precedents in Conveyancing
—— (*see* Bythewood, W. M.)
—— Concise Precedents in Conveyancing
                          2nd ed. 8vo. 1845
—— Supplement to Title 'Purchase Deeds' in
   Jarman & Bythewood on Conveyancing . 8vo. 1850
—— (Joseph) on County Courts 8vo. 1835
—— (S. W.) Memoir of, 1841. Vol. 7, L. T.
Swinburne (Henry) on Testaments & Wills
                            4th ed. 4to. 1677
————————————————————— 5th ed. folio 1728
————————————————————— 6th ed. folio 1743
—— on Spousals or Matrimonial Contracts . 4to. 1686
—— (Thomas) Critical Examination of Mr. Cantrell's Remarks on Separate Use Clause.
L. T. Vol. 6
Swinden (Henry) History of Great Yarmouth. 4to. 1772
Swinfield (Rd. De, *Bishop* of Hereford) Roll of
   Houschold Expenses of. Vol. 1, No. 59 C. S.
   Pa. (ed. Rev. J. Webb) 1853
——————————————————————— Vol. 2, No. 62
   C. S. Pa. (ed. Rev. J. Webb) 1854
Swift (*Dr.* Jonathan) Works, with Notes & Life
   (Sir W. Scott) . . . . 2nd ed. 19 vols. 8vo. 1824

Sydenham (Jno.) History of Poole & a Description
of Corfe Castle, by a near Resident . . 8vo. 1829
Sykes (John) Local Records or Historical Registry
of Durham & Northumberland, Newcastle-upon-
Tyne & Berwick-upon-Tweed 8vo. 1824
——————————————————— 2 vols. 8vo. 1833
Symonds (Rd.) Diary of the Marches of the Royal
Army during the Civil War. C. S. Pa. No. 74
(C. E. Long). 1859
Symons (E. W.) on the Law relating to Merchant
Shipping 12mo. 1839

T

Taaffe Peerage Case 4to. 1856-57
Tacitus (C. C.) Works, translated by A. Murphy
4 vols. 4to. 1793
—— Opera et Notæ (J. Pichon; Paris) 4 vols. 4to. 1682
Tacking, Opinion on the Doctrine of, Col. Jur. Vol. 2
Tagore (P. C.) Vivada Chintamani, Commentary
on the Hindoo Law prevalent in Mithila . 8vo. 1863
Tait's (Wm.) Magazine, 1832-4 . . 4 vols. 8vo.
——————————— 1834-60, N. S. 27 vols. 8vo.
Talbot (*Ld.* C.) Cases temp. (J. G. Williams)
2nd ed. folio 1753
———————————————————— 3rd ed. 8vo. 1792
Talfourd (T. N.) (*see* Dickinson, W.)
Tamlyn (Jno.) Reports (Rolls) 1820-30 . . 8vo. 1831
—— Observations on the Law of Inheritance.
Vol. 5, L. T. 1834
—— On Entails 8vo. 1825
Tanner (*Dr.* Thos.) Notitia Monastica, or an Ac-
count of all the Abbeys, Priories, &c. in England
& Wales, & Colleges & Hospitals founded before
1540 (J. Nasmith) . . . . folio 1787
Tanjore, King of, Papers as to Restoration (*see* East
India Company)

Tapia (Eugenio de) Febrero novísimo, ó Librería
de Jueces, Abogados, y Escribanos. 9 vols. 4to. 1828–30

Tapp (W. J.) on Maintenance & Champerty,
principally as affecting Contracts . . 12mo. 1861

Tapping (Thos.) The Cost Book, its Principles &
Practice 12mo. 1853

—————————————————— 2nd ed. 12mo. 1854

——— on the High Peak Mineral Customs and
Mineral Courts Act, 1851 . . . . 12mo. 1851

——— on the Derbyshire Mining Customs and Mineral Courts Act 12mo. 1854

——— Colliery & Ore Mine Inspection & Truck Acts
12mo. 1861

(And *see* Manlove)

Tasmania, Acts of Legislature of, 1857–1866-7
4 vols. folio

Tate (W.) The Calculations of Life Annuities &
the Public Funds simplified & explained. Tract
1819 (bound up with Stocks & Annuities)

Taswell (Wm.) Autobiography of, 1651–82. C. M.
Vol. 2, No. 55, C. S. P. (P. Elliott) 1852

Tatischeff (M.) (*see* Russian Code)

Tatham *v.* Wright, Trial before Mr. B. Gurney
(*see* Barwick)

Tattershall (G.) & Chambers (T.) Metropolitan
Buildings Act 12mo. 1844

Taunton (W. P.) Reports, 1807–19. 8 vols. 8vo. 1814–23

Taxatio Ecclesiastica Angliæ et Walliæ, auctoritate
P. Nicholai IV. A.D. 1291 (T. Astle, S. Ayscough, & J. Caley). See Record Commission
folio 1802

Taxation, History of, 1688–1770

Taxes, Consolidating Duties of Commissioners of.
. 8vo. 1803–17

——— History of, &c. . . . . 8vo. n. d.

——— (*see* Cunningham, Davenant, Postlethwayte)

Tayler (Geo.) Appeals to Superior Courts by Case
12mo. 1865

Taylor (Arthur) The Glory of Regality, Treatise on the Anointing & Crowning Kings & Queens of England 8vo. 1820
—— (A. G.) Medical Jurisprudence. 6th ed. 12mo. 1858
—————————————————— Enlarged ed. 8vo. 1865
—— (Edgar) The Book of Rights, or Constitutional Acts & Parliamentary Proceedings affecting Civil & Religious Liberty. 8vo. 1833
—— Memoir, 1839. Vol. 7, L. T.
—— (J.) Elements of Civil Law. . 2nd ed. 4to. 1755
—— (J. S.) Manual on Winding up Companies. 8vo. 1865
—— (Jno. Pitt) Law of Evidence as administered in England & Ireland, with Illustrations from American & other Foreign Laws . 2 vols. 8vo. 1848
————————————————— 3rd ed. 2 vols. 8vo. 1858
————————————————— 4th ed. 2 vols. 8vo. 1864
————————————————— 5th ed. 2 vols. 8vo. 1868
—— (J. R.) Correspondence as to Widening Chancery Lane. Pam. Vol. 7
—— (R.) Index Monasticus; or the Abbeys & other Monasteries, Alien Priories, &c. in Diocese of Norwich & Kingdom of East Anglia . folio 1821
—— (Silas) on Gavelkind, with History of Wm. the Conqueror, written temp. Hen. I. . 4to. 1663
—— (Tom) Local Government & Public Health Acts, 1858 . . . . 8vo. 1858
Teesdale (H.) Map (in case) of Lancashire, divided into Hundreds & Parishes . . . . . folio 1830
Teignmouth (*Lord*) Sketches of the Coasts & Islands of Scotland and of Isle of Man. 2 vols. 8vo. 1836
Temple (C.) Suggestions for Reform of Court of Chancery & Appellate Jurisdiction of House of Lords. Pam. Vol. 7.
—— (L.) on Carriers (*see* Chitty, T.)
—— on Pleading (*see* Chitty, T.)
—— (*Sir* W.) Works & Life . . . 2 vols. folio 1750
—— Inner, Library Catalogue 8vo. 1833
—— Middle, Library Catalogue 8vo. 1863

Tenant Law . . . . 7th ed. 8vo. 1718
—— 8vo. 1733
—— . . . . 14th ed. 8vo. 1753
—— . . . . 15th ed. 8vo. 1760
—— . . . . 17th ed. 8vo. 1777
Tenures (*see* Legal Recreations)
Terentius (P.) Afer Comœdiæ (Birmingham) 4to. 1772
Tertullianus (S. F.) Opera Omnia cum J. Parnellii
 Notis (Colon.) . . . . folio 1617
Term Reports (*see* Durnford & East)
Terms in Gross, Opinions on. Col. Jur. Vol. 2
Terrien (Guillaume) Commentaires du Droict civil
 de Normandie (Rouen). . . . . . folio 1654
Testa de Nevill, sive Liber Feodorum in Curia Scac-
 carii, temp. Hen. III. & Edw. I. (J. Caley & W.
 Illingworth) (*see* Record Commission) . . folio 1807
Testamentos & Successores (*see* Pinto)
Thames, Remarks on, Encroachments in, near Dur-
 ham Yard 8vo. 1771
—— Water Company, Report of Commissioners
 (*see* List of Attorneys) 1783
—— Watermen & Lightermen, Rules for Regu-
 lating (*see* London Tracts) 1828
Thanet, Tour through Isle of, and Description of
 Churches and Monuments 4to. 1793
Thellusson's Will, Arguments in (*see* Hargrave's
 Jur. Arguments & Appendix)
Theloall (S.) Registrum Brevium (no name on title
 page) . . . . 4th ed. folio 1687
Theobald (Wm.) Interpleader 12mo. 1833
—— Poor Law Amendment Act . . . 12mo. 1834
—— Law of Principal and Surety. . . . 8vo. 1832
—— What is Special Pleading? Letter to Lord
 Denman. Law Tracts, Vol. 5.
Theophrastus, Characters of (*see* Newton)
Thesaurus Juris Romani (Otto) . . 5 vols. folio 1725
Thom (Alex.) Irish Almanac & Official Directory
 of Great Britain & Ireland . 20 vols. 8vo. 1850–69

Thom (A.) British Directory & Official Handbook
of U. K. With County & Borough Register for
England & Wales 8vo. 1862
Thomas (F. S.) Hand Book to Public Records
8vo. 1853
Thomas (F. S.) Historical Notes, Henry VIII. to
Anne, 1509–1714 . . . . 3 vols. 8vo. 1856
—— Notes & Materials for the History of Public
Departments . . . . folio 1846
—— (J. P.) Universal Jurisprudence . . 8vo. 1828
——————————————————— 2nd ed. 8vo. 1829
—— of Elmham, Historia Monasterii S. Augustini
Cantuariensis (C. Hardwick) 8 M. R. Pub. . . 1858
Thoms (W. J.) Anecdotes & Traditions of Early
English History. C. S. Pa. No. 5. . . 4to. 1838
—— (see C. M. Vol. 2, No. 55, C. S. P.)
Thompson (*Sir* A.) Biography of (*see* Eminent
Lawyers)
—— Liber Placitandi, or Entries . . . . folio 1674
—— (A.) (*see* Geoffrey of Monmouth)
—— (R.) Court Guide 12mo. 1844
—— (G. A.) Geographical & Historical Dictionary
of America & West Indies, containing Trans-
lation of the Work of Don Antonio de Alcedon
5 vols. 4to. 1815
—— Maps of America & West Indies . . folio 1815
—— (J.) Historical Sketches of Bridlington
12mo. 1821
—— (P.) Collections for Topographical & His-
torical Account of Boston, Lincoln . . . 8vo. 1820
——————————————————————— 4to. 1820
Thomson (James) Law Reports of Decisions of the
Supreme Court in Nova Scotia, 1833–41 . 8vo. 1853
—— (H. B.) Institutes of the Law of Ceylon
2 vols. 8vo. 1866
—— Laws of War 12mo. 1854
—— (R.) Essay on Magna Charta . . . 8vo. 1829
Thoresby (R.) Life of (*see* Malcolm's Lives)

Thoresby (R.) Ducatus Leodiensis, or the Topography of Leeds & Parts Adjacent (T. D. Whitaker; York) . . . . . . 2nd ed. folio 1816
(*See* Whitaker for continuation)
Thornber (Wm.) Historical & Descriptive Account of Blackpool, Lan. 12mo. 1837
—— Account of Blackpool, Lan. (bound up with Lanc. Co. T.) . . . . 3rd ed.
Thornton Romances. C. S. Pa. No. 30 (ed. J. O. Halliwell) 1844
—— (Edwd.) Gazetteer of Territories under the Government of the East India Company, & the Native States on the Continent of India. 4 v. 8vo. 1854
—— Trial of (*see* J. Cooper)
—— (J. B.) Digest of Conveyancing, Testamentary, & Registry Laws of all the States of the Union, U. S. 8vo. 1847
—— (Thos.) Notes of Cases, Ecclesiastical & Maritime Courts, 1841–50 . . . 7 vols. 8vo. 1843–50
Thoroton (R.) The Antiquities of Nottinghamshire folio 1677
—— History of Nottinghamshire, with large additions (J. Throsby) . . . . 3 vols. 4to. 1797
Thorpe (B.) (*see* Anglo-Saxon Chronicle)
—— (M. J.) Calendar of State Papers relating to Scotland, preserved in Her Majesty's Public Record Office . . . . Imp. 8vo. 1858

> Vol. 1. The Scottish Series, of the Reigns of Henry VIII., Edward VI., Mary, and Elizabeth, 1509–1589
> Vol. 2. The Scottish Series, of the Reign of Elizabeth, 1589–1603; an Appendix to the Scottish Series, 1543–1592; and the State Papers relating to Mary, Queen of Scots, during her Detention in England, 1568–1587

Threatening Letters (*see* Legal Recreations)
Thring (Henry) Succession Duty Act . . 12mo. 1853
—— Land Drainage Act, 1861 . . . 12mo. 1862
—— Law & Practice of Joint Stock Companies
  2 vols. 12mo. 1861–63
  ——————————————— 2nd ed. 12mo. 1867

Thring (Henry) Law & Practice of Joint Stock
   Companies. Supplement to 12mo. 1867
Throsby (J.) Select Views in Leicestershire. 2 v. 4to. 1789
Thrupp (John) Anglo-Saxon Home from 5th to 11th
   Century 8vo. 1862
Thurlow (*Lord*) Biography of (*see* Lawyers &
   Roscoe's Lives)
Tickell (*Rev.* John) History of the Town & County
   of Kingston-upon-Hull from its Foundation,
   Edward I. 4to. 1798
Tidd (Wm.) Practical Forms, K. B. . . . 8vo. 1799
—————————————————————— . . . 8vo. 1809
—— Practice of the Courts of C. P. & Ex.
                            4th ed. 8vo. 1814
—————————————————————— 5th ed. 8vo. 1819
—————————————————————— 6th ed. 8vo. 1824
—— Practice of Court of K. B. in Personal
   Actions. 2nd part only 8vo. 1794
—————————————————— with Reference to Cases in C. P. . . 3rd ed. 2 vols. 8vo. 1803
—————————————————— with Forms
   on Replevin & Ejectment . . . 2nd ed. 8vo. 1804
—————————————————— with Reference to Case in C. P. . . 4th ed. 2 vols. 8vo. 1808
—————————————————— & C. P. on
   Personal Actions . . . 5th ed. 2 vols. 8vo. 1812
—————————————————— 6th ed. 1 vol. only, 8vo. 1817
—————————————————————— & Law &
   Practice of Extent & Rules of Court & Modern
   Decisions in Exchequer . 7th ed. 2 vols. 8vo. 1821
—————————————————— 8th ed. 2 vols. 8vo. 1824
—————————————————— & Ejectment
                            9th ed. 2 vols. 8vo. 1828
—————————————————— Appendix. 8vo. 1828
—————————————————— Supplement. 8vo. 1830
—————————————————— 2nd Supplement
   & General Rules of the Courts 8vo. 1832
—— Practice of Superior Courts on Personal
   Actions & Ejectments 8vo. 1833

Tidd (Wm.) New Practice of K. B., C. P. & Ex. in
  Personal Actions & Ejectments 8vo. 1837
—— Practical Forms & Entries of Proceedings,
  Q. B., C. P., Ex. . . . . 8th ed. 8vo. 1840
—— Observations on Uniformity of Process Act
                                              12mo. 1832
Tidswell (R. T.) & Littler (R. B. M.) Practice &
  Evidence in Divorce & Matrimonial Causes 12mo. 1860
Tierney (*Rev.* M. A.) History & Antiquities of
  Castle & Town of Arundel, including the Bio-
  graphy of its Earls. 2 vols. in 1. . . . 8vo. 1834
Tilsley (Hugh) Stamp Laws 8vo. 1847
—————————————— with Supplement. 2nd ed. 8vo. 1850
—— New Stamp Act, Supplement to. 6th ed. 8vo. 1854
—— Digest of the Stamp Acts. 7th ed. . 8vo. 1859
———————————————————————— 8th ed. 8vo. 1860
———————————————— (E. H. Tilsley). 9th ed. 8vo. 1865
Tim Bobbin's Works. (*see* Corry)
Timber for Navy, Quota to be provided by County
  of Dorset (*see* MS. temp. James)
Timbs (J.) Year Book of Facts on Science & Art
                                              12mo. 1868-9
Times Newspaper (1805 wanting) . . . 1795-1868
—— Index to (*see* Palmer)
Tindal (Wm.) History & Antiquities of the Abbey
  & Boro' of Evesham 4to. 1794
Tite (Wm.) Letters collected from the Autography
  in his Possession. Vol. 5, C. M. No. 87, C. S. P. 1854
Tobago, Acts of Legislature of, 1857-65 . folio
Todd (J. & G.) Description of York, particularly
  the Cathedral (imperfect). . . 9th ed. 12mo. 1823
—— (J. H.) (*see* C. S. Pa. No. 20)
Tolcher (R. H.) Report, Henry *v.* Great Northern
  Railway, 1857 . . . . 8vo. 1858
Toller (Saml., afterwards *Sir* Saml.) on Executors
                                    2nd ed. 8vo. 1806
——————————————— (by Whitmarsh) 4th ed. 8vo. 1818
——————————————————————— 5th ed. 8vo. 1822
——————————————————————— 7th ed. 8vo. 1838

Toller (Saml., aft. *Sir* Saml.) on Tithes . . 8vo. 1808
——————————————(by Wooddeson) 8vo. 1816
Tomkins (F.) Institutes of Roman Law. Part 1
              8vo. 1867
—— (Isaac) & Jenkins (Peter) Letter on Primogeniture. Law Tracts, Vol. 5
Tomlins (T. E.) Repertorium Juridicum, being a General Index to all the Cases & Pleadings contained in all the Reports, Year Books, &c.
           2 vols. 8vo. 1788
—— Digested Index of Term Reports, K. B. 1785–98 . . . . 8vo. 1799
———————————————— K. B. & C. P.
           2nd ed. 8vo. 1800
—— Digest, K. B. & C. P. 1783–1811. 4th ed. 8vo. 1812
—— Law Dictionary. 4th ed. 2 vols. . . 4to. 1835
Tontine of 1789, List of Nominees of 1809–18. 4to.
Tooke (Jno. Horne) Trial 8vo. 1795
—— (Thos.) on High & Low Prices of the last Thirty Years . . . . 2 vols. 8vo. 1823
—— (Wm.) Monarchy in France, its Rise, Progress, & Fall. 8vo. 1855
—— Tookiana, Militia Mea Multiplex. . . 12mo. 1860
Topographica & Genealogica Collectanea (*see* Nichols) . . . . 8 vols. 1834–43
Toone (Wm.) Magistrate's Manual, Summary of the Duties, &c. of a Justice of the Peace
           4th ed. 8vo. 1828
Torrens (R. R.) on Registration of Title to South Australia Real Property 12mo. 1859
Tothill (W.) The Transactions of the High Court of Chancery (Sir R. O. Holborne) temp. Hen. VIII. 12mo. 1820
—— Transactions or Reports in Chancery. 12mo. 1830
Tottill (R.) Magna Charta, 1224–1303 . . 12mo. 1556
———————————— 1225–1585 . 12mo. 1587
Tottie (T. W.) Statements, the Trusts & Administration of Lady Hewley's Charities. L. T. Vol. 3.
Touchstone Precedents (*see* Sheppard)

Toulmin (G. G.) Statutes & Orders relating to
Practice & Pleading in Chancery . . . 8vo. 1847
Tower (*Dr.*) Observations on Juries & Law of
Libel (Libel L. T.)
Townesend (Geo.) Tables to most Precedents of
Pleadings, Writs, & Return of Writs . . folio 1667
—— A Preparation to Pleading . . 3rd ed. 8vo. 1713
————————————————— . . 3rd ed. 8vo. 1721
Townsend (A.) (*see* Bradford)
—— (Fras.) Calendar of Knights from 1760
8vo. 1828
—— (G. H.) Manual of Dates 8vo. 1862
—— (Jos.) Journey through Spain in 1786–7
Vol. 3 only, 8vo. 1792
—— (J. F.) *Reports* (*see* Longfield, Robt.)
Townshend (H.) Historical Collections, an exact
account of the Proceedings of the four last Parliaments of Queen Elizabeth, comprehending the
Speeches of Mr. Secretary Cecill, Sir Francis
Bacon, Sir Walter Raleigh, Sir Edward Hobby,
& divers others . . . . folio 1680
Tractatus ex Variis Juris Interpretibus Collecti
cum Indicibus . . . . 17 vols. in 13, folio 1549
Tractatus Varii utriusque Juris 4to. 1512
Tracts. Law Tracts & Arguments . . . 4to. 1641
Containing:—
1. Fuller's Argument against Ecclesiastical Commission
2. Sir F. Bacon's Cases of Treason
3. Sir H. Yelverton's Argument touching Propriety of Good
& Loyal Impositions
4. Doderidge's Complete Parson
5. Crompton's Star Chamber Cases
6. Noy's Maxims
7. N. N. on Estates Tail & Descents
8. Queen Elizabeth's Injunctions to Clergy & Laity, 1599
9. Brooke, R., Reading on Statute of Treason, Magna Carta,
C. 16
10. Life of Henry III.

Tracts (Law) 4to. 1688–9
1. Proceedings against the Bishop of London before the Ecclesiastical Commissioners in 1686

Tracts (Law)—*continued.*
2. Letter from a Gentleman at York to his Friend in the Prince of Orange's Camp, showing that Popish Treaties are not to be relied on
3. Representations of the Dangers to the Protestants before the coming of the Prince of Orange
4. Apology for the Church of England as to the spirit of persecution of which she is accused
5. The Prince of Orange's Declaration, containing his reasons for invading England
6. Animadversions upon the Prince of Orange's Declaration containing his reasons for invading England
7. Another Declaration
8. Letter from French Ministers who had fled into Germany on account of late Persecution
9. Account of Proposals from the Archbishop of Canterbury and other Bishops to his Majesty
10. Prince of Orange's Third Declaration, dated at Sherburn Castle, November 28, 1688
11. Prayers for the Prince & Princess of Orange
12. Enquiry as to Submission to Supreme Authority
13. Enquiry whether we owe Allegiance to the King, and are bound to treat with him and call him back
14. Letter to a Member of the Convention
15. Answer to it
16. Vindication of the Church of England & the Penal Laws; Reflections upon the New Test Act, & the Reply thereto
17. Three Letters from Jesuits
18. Account of the Death of the Earl of Essex
19. Murder will out; or an Account that the Earl of Essex did not murder himself, but was murdered by others
20. A Hellish Murder committed by a French Midwife on the body of her Husband in January 1687
21. The Character of a Trimmer
22. Colonel Henry Martin's Familiar Epistles
23. The Monthly Account
24. The Dream
25. A New Protestant Liturgy
26. Prophecy of Bishop Usher
27. The Laws in Sir Edward Hale's Case
28. Lord C. J. Herbert's Law on Sir Edward Hale's Case examined

Tracts, (Law) . . . . 8 vols. 8vo.
Vol. 1.   CONTENTS.
No. 1. Law of Descent in Fee Simple (Wm. Blackstone, Esq.) . 1759
2. On Forfeiture and High Treason . . . 3rd ed. 1748
3. Are Tenants by Copyhold Freeholders, and entitled to Vote for Knights of the Shire? 1758

Tracts (Law)—*continued.*
4. Proposals to Parliament for remedying the Charge &c. of Suits at Law and in Equity, 7th ed., by an Attorney . n.d.
5. A Discourse concerning Treasons and Bills of Attainder, 2nd ed. 1717

Vol. 2.
No. 1. Mr. Concanen's Observations on the Use and Abuse of the Practice of the Law, 3rd ed. . . . . . n.d.
2. Mr. James Pearce on the Abuses of the Law, particularly by Actions of Arrest 1814
3. Mr. D. W. Harvey's Letter to the Burgesses of Colchester 1822
4. Mr. Robt. Maugham on the Principles of the Usury Laws and of the Authorities in their favour 1824

Vol. 3.
No. 1. Mr. J. S. Stock's Observations on the Case of Lady Hewley's Charity in the Atty.-Gen. v. Shore . . . 1836
2. Atty.-Gen. v. Shore, Rev. Josh. Hunter's Defence of the Trustees of Lady Hewley's Foundations . . . 1834
3. Substance of Speech of C. P. Cooper, Esq. as Counsel for the Rev. Charles Welbeloved in Atty.-Gen. v. Shore . 1834
4. Mr. T. W. Tottie's plain Statement of the Trusts and recent Administrations of Lady Hewley's Charity . . 1834
5. Correspondence between Mr. Alderman Venables & Mr. Coles respecting the office of Under-Sheriff of London & Middlesex 1821
6. Mr. Jas. Yates's Letter to the Vice-Chr. of England in reply to His Honor's remarks relative to the British and Foreign Unitarian Association in his Judgment in Atty.-Gen. v. Shore 1834
7. Forms of Schedule & Award on the Enfranchisement of Copyhold Lands and the discharge of Heriots by Local Commissioners on requisition of the parties interested . 1835
8. Mr. G. B. Mansell's Letter to Henry Brougham, Esq. on the present state of Legal Education 1830

Vol. 4.
No. 1. The History &c. & present Legal Position of the English Presbyterians; published by the English Presbyterian Association 1834
2. Presbyterian Endowments: Report of the hearing of the case of the Wolverhampton Meeting-House, Atty.-Gen. & Mander v. Pearson, before Lord Cottenham . . 1836
3. Dr. T. Rees' History of the Regium Donum & Parliamentary Grant to poor Dissenting Ministers in England & Wales; with a Vindication of the Distributor & Recipients from the charge of Political Subserviency . . 1834
4. Copy Mr. Yates's Letter, same as in Vol. 3.
5. Letter to Benjn. Hawes, Esq., being Strictures on the Minutes of Evidence taken before the Select Committee on the British Museum, by Edwd. Edwards . . . 1836

Tracts (Law)—continued.

6. Substance of the Speech of George Spence, Esq. on Chancery Reform, on Sir Chas. Wetherell's Motion in the H. C. 17 June 1830
7. Mr. Spence's Speech in H. C., 30 Nov., on Sir Edwd. Sugden's Motion for Returns as to the Court of Chancery 1830

Vol. 5.

No. 1. Arrest for Debt, Law of, by an Attorney
2. Arrest, Law of, Remarks on, Abolition of, & Imprisonment for Debt, by a Barrister 1830
3. Register Bill, Letter to an M.P. on the proposed; being a reply to a Circular Letter printed at Northallerton . 1831
4. Registering Births, &c. Observations on Lord John Russell's Bill, by Mr. Jas. Yates 1836
5. Equity—What are Courts of Equity? a Lecture delivered at King's College, London, by J. J. Park, Esq. . . 1832
6. Primogeniture: a Letter to Isaac Tomkins & Peter Jenkins by Timy. Winterbottom, 2nd ed. 1835
7. Registration and Conveyancing System: Lecture delivered at King's College, London, by J. J. Park, Esq. . . 1833
8. Arrest & Imprisonment for Debt—Thoughts on the Present State of the Law 1828
9. Deeds of Composition by Insolvent Traders, Proposal for an Act, &c., by S. Ayrton, Esq. 1833
10. Rex v. Woollcombe—Retrospect of the Proceedings in this Prosecution ats. V. A. Sir Edmund Coddrington at Devonport . . . . n.d.
11. Local Courts Bill of Lord Brougham, examined by H. B. Denton, Esq. 1833
12. Legal Practitioners, Thoughts on the Present Condition of, by one of the Prescribed 1834
13. Inheritancy, Observations on the Law of, by J. Tamlyn, Esq. 1834
14. Real Property, Observations on the proposed new Code relating to, by R. Dixon, Esq. 1837
15. Public Bills, a Letter to Lord Melbourne on the present mode of Legislation as to, by M. J. West, Esq. . . 1836
16. What is Special Pleading? Letter to Sir T. Denman, (L.C.J.) in Answer to this Question, with a Proposal for Emendations in the Forms of Actions by W. Theobald, Esq. . 1832
17. Law Reform—An Alarm on the Rights of the Poor, & the Property of the Rich in Danger, from a supposed, by G. Strickland, Esq. 1833

Vol. 6.

No. 1. Quintillian's Institutes of Oratory, Book 5, c. 7, concerning Witnesses, their examination, & cross-examination, by W. M. Best, Esq. 1836

Tracts (Law)—*continued.*

2. Cases illustrating the Conflict between the Laws of England & Scotland, with regard to Marriage, Divorce, & Legitimacy, by H. Prater, Esq. 1835
3. Bankruptcy Reform, in a series of Letters addressed to Sir R. Peel, by C. Fane, Esq. 1838
4. The Mutual Rights of Husband & Wife, with the Draft of a Bill to replace that of Mr. Serjt. Talfourd for the Custody of Infants, by R. Mence, Esq. . . . 1838
5. Observations on the doctrine applicable to the Separate Use & Non-anticipation Clauses as carried out in Tullett *v.* Armstrong, by Benson Blundell . . . 1839
6. Remarks on the Separate Use Clause, addressed in a Letter to the Lord Chancellor, with a view to the Cases of Tallet *v.* Armstrong & Scarborough *v.* Bowman, by J. T. Cantrell, Esq. 1839
7. Examination of Mr. Cantrell's remarks on the Separate Use Clause, in a Letter addressed to the Law Students of England, by Thos. Swinburne, Esq. 1839
8. Observations on points relating to the Amendment of the Law of Patents, by C. S. Drewry, Esq. . . . 1839
9. The principles of Mr. Shaw Lefevre's Parochial Assessment Bill & the Tithe Commutation Act compared in a Letter to the Rev. R. Jones, one of the Commissioners, to the Rev. C. Miller 1839
10. Remarks on Law Reform, addressed more particularly to the General Reader, by W. Smith, Esq. . . . 1840
11. A Plain Letter to the Lord Chancellor on the Infant Custody Bill, by P. Stevenson, Esq. . . . 1839

Vol. 7.

No. 1. Remarks on the Law of Bailment, by J. B. Wallace . 1840
2. Lectures on the Sources from which Pedigrees may be traced from the Norman Conquest, by S. Grimaldi, Esq.; delivered at the Incorporated Law Society, Dec. . . 1835
3. Memoir of Edgar Taylor, Esq., reprinted from Legal Observer of 29th Sept. 1839
4. Memoir of Samuel White Sweet, Esq. 1841
5. Proposed Alterations in the Law of Copyright
6. Judges' Circuit Expenses in 1707
7. Legal Antiquities—Writ of Protection to an Attorney of K. B., 1 Ric.—Bill of Costs of, 1608 1839
8. On the Law as to Marriages abroad between English Subjects within the prohibited degrees, from Legal Observer for Jan. 1840
9. The Court of Bequests, by Wm. Hutton, author of the 'History of Birmingham'; with a Memoir . . . 1840
10. Parliamentary Review for 1826

LAW SOCIETY LIBRARY. 341

Tracts (Law)—*continued.*

Vol. 8.
No. 1. Substitute for Sir J. Campbell's Summary Law for obtaining Judgment on Bonds, Bills, & Notes, by an Attorney 1835
2. Westminster Hall Courts, Facts for the consideration of Parliament before final adoption of a Plan perpetuating the Courts of Law on a site injurious & costly to the suitor 1840
3. The Law Courts & New Houses of Parliament, Extracts from the Evidence taken before the Select Committee of the House of Commons in 1841 & 1842, proving the necessity of removing the Courts to the neighbourhood of the Inns of Court 1843
4. Review of the Evidence taken before the Select Committee of the House of Commons on the proposal to remove the Courts of Law to the Inns of Court . . . 1842
5. Consideration on Ecclesiastical Courts Reform, in reference to the Government Bill before the House of Commons, by Harvey Gun 1844

Tracts (Law), A Collection of, by E. Jacob, Esq.
13 vols. 8vo.
Vol. 1. CONTENTS.
No. 1. Historical Questions exhibited in the Morning Chronicle, Jan. 1818
2. T. Canning on Assignments of Interests of Husband & Wife 1826
3. Mr. Sugden on presuming a Surrender of Terms . 4th ed. 1820
4. Mr. Amos on the Case of King *v.* Geddington . . . 1823
5. Mr. W. Skirrow on the exclusion of the Queen from the Liturgy 1821
6. Hon. Mr. Eden's Analysis of Bankrupt Law Consolidation Bill 1823
7. Mr. Eden's Observations on the Bankrupt Laws . . 1824
8. Mr. Wright's Letter on Bill for recovering Small Debts . 1821
9. Examination of Article in Edinburgh Review respecting Lord Eldon, by a Barrister 1823
10. On the Practice of Chancery in Cases of Libellous, &c., Publications, from Edinburgh Review . . . 1823
11. Mr. Wright's Observations on Judges of the Court of Chancery, &c. 1823
12. Enquiry as to Delays of Chancery 1824
13. Mr. Sugden's Reply to Mr. Williams upon the Abuses of Chancery 1825
14. Mr. Bentham's indications respecting Lord Eldon . . 1825
15. Mr. Hayes on the Law of Real Property 1825

Tracts (Law)—*continued.*
Vol. 2.
No. 1. Case of the President of Queen's College, Cambridge—
(Mr. C. Bowdler) 1821
2. Mr. Gurney's Report of Sir J. Nicholl's Judgment in
Kemp *v.* Wickes. 1810
3. Nuptiæ Sacræ, or an Enquiry into the Scripture Doctrine of
Marriage & Divorce, addressed to Parliament . . 1821
4. The Philosophy of Evidence, by Mr. D. McKinnon . . 1812
5. An Enquiry into the Plans; &c.; of American Mining
Companies 1825
6. Grammar Schools considered with reference to a Case
lately decided by the Lord Chancellor (Mr. S. Bannister) 1820
7. Remarks on the Indians of North America in a Letter
to an Edinburgh Reviewer (Mr. S. Bannister) . . 1822

Vol. 3.
No. 1. Reasons against the Repeal of the Usury Laws . . 1825
2. Mr. Maugham on the Usury Laws 1824
3. Mr. F. Neale on Money-lending 1826
4. Mr. Peel's Speech on the Criminal Law 1826
5. The Case between Lincoln's Inn, the Court of King's
Bench, & Mr. T. J. Wooler, by Mr. W. . . . 1826
6. Eldoniana, by Dr. Fea 1826
7. Considerations on the Report of the Chancery Commissioners, by Lord Redesdale 1826

Vol. 4.
No. 1. Mr. Montagu's Observations on the Bill for improving the
Bankrupt Law 1822
2. Mr. Fonblanque on Bill for consolidating the Bankrupt
Law 1824
3. Mr. Montagu's Enquiries respecting the Courts of Commissioners of Bankrupt & the Lord Chancellor's Court . 1825
4. Mr. Montagu's Letters on Report of the Chancery Commissioners 1826
5. Mr. Walters on Delays in Chancery 1826
6. Mr. Merivale's Letter on the Chancery Commission . 1827
7. Mr. J. Wilks's Letters on the Chancery Question & the
New Bill 1827
8. Mr. Sugden's Letter to Mr. Humphreys on the Real
Property Laws 1826

Vol. 5.
No. 1. Observations on the Chancery Bar 1816
2. Essay in vindication of the Solicitors 1826
3. Mr. Carrighan on the doctrines and practice of the Court
of Chancery 1826
4. Remarks on framing a Code of Laws for Real Property,
by a Barrister 1827
5. Mr. Dixon on proposed New Code for Real Property . 1827

Tracts (Law)—*continued.*
6. Mr. Beaumont on the Code for Real Property . . . 1827
7. Mr. Espinasse on Defects of the Law 1827
8. Mr. Jones (the Marshal) on the Insolvent Debtors Act . 1827
9. Mr. H. Dance's Letter to Mr. Jones . , . . 1827
10. Account of Tunbridge School, Kent 1827
Vol. 6.
No. 1. Mr. C. E. Dodd's Questions on the Law of Elections . 1826
2. Mr. Ralph Barnes's Enquiry as to Equity Practice & the Law of Real Property 1827
3. Mr. G. Long's Reflections on the Law of England . . 1827
4. Lord Eldon's Judgment in Wellesley v. the Duke of Beaufort 1827
Vol. 7.
No. 1. Mr. J. E. Blunt's History of the Jews in England . . 1830
2. Mr. J. George's View of the Law affecting unincorporated Joint Stock Companies 1825
3. Mr. A. Amos's Introductory Lecture on the study of English Law 1829
4. Mr. W. Hayes' Letter to Mr. Amos on the above . . 1830
5. Sir A. Halliday's Letter on the number of Lunatics & Idiots in England & Wales 1829
6. Mr. G. M. Burrows' Letter on Evidence, &c., on Lunacy of Mr. E. Davies 1830
7. Mr. W. W. Whitmore's Letter to the Electors of Bridgenorth on the Corn Laws 1826
8. The Grand Vizier unmasked—Remarks on Mr. Canning's claim to public confidence 1827
9. The Poll at Cambridge Election, May 1827, by Mr. H. Gunning 1827
10. Mr. E. B. Sugden's Extracts from Acts of Parliament relating to Oaths to be taken by M.P.'s . . . 1829
11. An Observer's Estimate of Mr. Brougham's Local Court Bill 1830
Vol. 8.
No. 1. Mr. B. Montagu's Letters on the Report of the Chancery Commission 1827
2 & 3. Mr. B. Montagu's Letters on the Bankrupt Law . . 1829
4. Mr. F. Griggs's Costs in Bankruptcy 1826
5. Mr. F. Griggs's Suggestions for Alterations in the Bankrupt Law 1831
6. Mr. C. S. Cullen on Reform of the Bankrupt Court, 2nd ed. 1830
7. Mr. B. Montagu on Reform of the Law 1827
8. Mr. H. Dance on Law Expenses 1830
9. Strictures on the Orders of the Court of Chancery . . 1829
10. Mr. R. M. Hume on Chancery Delays & their Remedy . 1830
11. Sir E. B. Sugden's Speech in House of Commons, 16th Dec. 1830, on the Court of Chancery 1831

Tracts (Law)—*continued.*
  12. Mr. G. Spence on the Evils & Abuses of the Court of
       Chancery, & proposed Amendments 1831
  13. Abstract of a Bill for the Reformation of the Court of
       Chancery 1831
       Vol. 9.
No. 1. Common Law Commission, proposed Regulations, &c., as
       to Process, &c. 1829
   2. Mr. Serjt. E. Lawe's suggestions for Alterations of the
       Law on Practice, Pleading, &c. 1827
   3. The Hon. W. Long Wellesley's View of the Court of
       Chancery 1830
   4. A Barrister's Letter on the Judges of the Court of Chan-
       cery 1829
   5. Mr. John Reddie's Letter to the Lord Chancellor on the
       expediency of the proposal to form a New Civil Code
       for England 1828
       Vol. 10.
No. 1. Mr. J. Halcombe's Report of the Trial Rowe *v.* Grenfell . 1826
   2. Mr. R. H. Coote's Letter to the Real Property Commis-
       sioners on the proposed General Registry . . . 1829
   3. Mr. W. P. Wood's Letter to the Real Property Commis-
       sioners in answer to some objections advanced against a
       General Register 1829
   4. Mr. J. Hodgkin's Observations on the proposed Establish-
       ment of a General Register 1829
   5. Mr. G. Bentham's Observations on the Registration Bill
       addressed to the Real Property Commissioners . . 1831
   6. Contributory Remarks on a General Registry, by Mr. W.
       W. Humphry 1830
       Vol. 11.
No. 1. Mr. W. Hayes on the Doctrine of Equity as to Separate
       Estate, &c. 1836
   2. Mr. J. D. Chambers on the Errors in the Reform Act . 1832
   3. Mr. R. G. Hall's Observations on the Inexpediency of a
       General Metropolitan Registry 1834
   4. Mr. J. Ram's Observations on a Father's Right to the
       Custody of his Children 1828
   5. Mr. W. Eagle on 2nd & 3rd Wm. 4 relating to Moduses
       & Exemptions from Tithes 1834
   6. Mr. R. M. Hume on Chancery Delays and their Remedy . 1826
   7. Substance of Lord Langdale's Speech in House of Lords,
       18th June, 1836, on 2nd reading of Bill for Better Ad-
       ministration of Justice in Chancery . . . 1836
   8. Mr. Brougham's Speech in House of Commons, 7th Feb.
       1828, on the present State of the Law . . . 1828
   9. A few Hints on the consideration of the system of Bank-
       ruptcy as administered by the Commissioners . . n.d.

LAW SOCIETY LIBRARY. 345

Tracts (Law)—*continued.*
10. Mr. B. Montagu's Letters to Sir Edward Sugden on the
    Court of Commissioners & Court of Review . . 1834
11. Mr. W. Courtenay's Observations on the projected Improvements in the Court of Chancery 1828
12. General Orders, Rules, &c., for Remedy of Abuses in the
    Court of Chancery, by A. H. Rawlins, Esq. . . . 1831
13. Mr. W. Glover on Lord Brougham's Law Reforms & Courts
    of Social Jurisdiction . . . . . 2nd ed. 1834
14. Observations regarding the office of Master of the Court
    of Chancery 1831

Vol. 12.
No. 1. Substance of Sir R. Peel's Speech in House of Commons,
    20th June, 1827, on Small Debts Bill 1827
2. Mr. F. Hill's Letter on the Stannary Courts of Cornwall . 1835
3. Mr. H. Prater on the Conflict of Laws of England &
    Scotland as to Marriage, &c., & Law of Husband &
    Wife 1835
4. Mr. H. Prater's Essay on the Law of Husband & Wife . 1834
5. Mr. E. Burke's Letter on Attacks made upon him & his
    Pension 1831
6. Mr. E. Burke's Opinions on Reform 1831
7. Mr. John Palmer on the Practice on Appeals from the
    Colonies to the Privy Council 1831
8. Mr. W. H. Bosanquet's Letter on the Production of Documents on Motion before Hearing 1836
9. Mr. P. W. Crowther's History of the Law of Arrest & Bail 1828
10. Orders to regulate Practice, &c., in Chancery . . . 1828
11. Mr. Chas. Pitt's Report of Trial for a Conspiracy in 1818 1820
12. Mr. J. Richard's Letter in reply to Tomkins & Jenkins . 1835
13. Lord Henley's Plan of Church Reform 1832

Vol. 13.
No. 1. Opinions of H. Brougham, Esq., on Negro Slavery . . 1830
2. Mr. A. J. Macrory's Report of the Clough Case in the
    Irish Exchequer in April, 1836 1836
3. Du Calcul des Probabilités, par C. F. de Bioquilley . . 1805
4. Die Creignisse Warschau, August 1831 (Johann Czyniski) 1832
5. Sir John Sinclair's Observations on the Report of the
    Bullion Committee . . . . . 2nd ed. 1810
6. Evidence, &c., on the Petition of the Proprietors of Collieries in South Wales taken before a Committee of the
    House of Commons, May 1810 1810
7. Substance of Mr. Nolan's Speech before a Committee of
    the House of Commons on the Farnborough Road Bill . 1811
8. Mr. T. L. Follett's Elements to the Science of Good
    Government 1833
9. Mr. W. Lowndes' Remarks on the Life & Writings of
    Plato 1827

Tracts (Law) on Libel . . . 4 vols. 8vo. 1680–1771
Containing—
Vol. 1.   CONTENTS.
No. 1. Lord John Somers on the Trust, Power, and Duty of
Grand Juries. First printed 1681; reprint 1771
2. Grand Juryman's Oath and Office explained . . . 1680
3. Sir John Hawles on the Duty of Petty Juries; or, the
Englishman's Rights 1764
4. State Law on the Doctrine of Libels . . . . n. d.
5. The Liberty of the Press as it respects Personal Slander
2nd ed. n. d.
6. The Doctrine of Libels and the Duty of Juries . . 1752
7. A Letter to Mr. Almon concerning Libels, General Warrants, the Seizure of Papers and Sureties for the Good
Behaviour . . . . 7th ed. 1771
8. A Summary of the Law of Libel 1771
9. The Lords' Protest in the case of Wilkes, touching Privilege of Parliament in Matters of Libel . . . 1765
Vol. 2.
No. 1. Enquiry into Power of Juries on Trials for Libel by
Indictment or Information 1792
2. Considerations on matter of Libel, suggested by Mr. Fox's
notice to Parliament, by Jno. Leach, Esq. . 2nd ed. n. d.
3. Observations on Rights and Duties of Juries, and Remarks
on the Law; by Dr. Towers 1784
4. Discussion on the Law of Libels 1785
Vol. 3.
No. 1. Rayner's Trial before Lord Raymond, for a Libel, in . 1732
2. Zenyer's Trial at New York, for a Libel upon the Chief
Justice of the Province, in 1735
3. Owen's Trial for a Libel, in 1765, before Lord Chief
Justice Lee
4. Almon's Trial, in 1770, before Lord Mansfield, for selling
Junius's Letters
5. Morris's Letter to Mr. Justice Aston on account of his
Animadversions upon Morris's Affidavit in Almon's Case 1770
6. The Proceedings in the Action of Onslow v. Horne, for a
Defamatory Libel, tried before Mr. Justice Blackstone . 1770
7. Proceedings in Parliament occasioned by Lord Mansfield's
Directions to Juries in Libellous Matters; with copy of
his Lordship's Judgment in the K. v. Woodfall, on an
information for Printing a Libel, in 1770; with an
account of Two Motions in K. B. in consequence of the
Verdict given on his Trial; with Adversion to cases of
Owen and Almon, and what passed on Baldwin's Trial
8. Account of Trial Onslow v. Horne, for Defamation, before
Lord Mansfield at Guildford, in 1770
9. Miller's Trial before Lord Mansfield, for publishing
Junius's Letters to the King

Tracts (Law) on Libel—*continued.*
10. Rous's Letter to Jurors upon Lord Mansfield's Judgment
 in Rex v. Woodfall, with a Copy of it . . 2nd ed. 1785
11. Mr. Erskine's Speech for a New Trial in case of Dean of
 St. Asaph, for a Libel, before Mr. Justice Buller . . 1784
12, 13. Mr. Dawes' Two Letters on the Dean's case and on Libel;
 with Sir Wm. Jones's Dialogue on the Principles of
 Government 1785
 Vol. 4.
No. 1. Mr. Bowles' Considerations on the Rights of Judge and
 Jury in Trials for Libel 1791
 2. Mr. Bowles's Letter to Mr. Fox on his motion in the House
 of Commons for a Bill respecting Libel . 2nd ed. 1792
 3. Mr. Bowles's 2nd Letter to Mr. Fox on the matter of Libel,
 and Dangerous Tendency of his Bill 1792
 4. Mr. Bowles' Appendix to his 2nd Letter, being Brief
 Deductions from First Principles applicable to matter
 of Libel 1792
 5. Enquiry into Extent of Power of Juries on Trials of In-
 dictments or Information for Seditious or Criminal
 Writings or Libels; extracted from Papers published in
 1776, concerning the Province of Quebec
 6. Debates in both Houses of Parliament upon Mr. Fox's
 Bill for Removing Doubts respecting the Functions of
 Juries in cases of Libel; with the Protest against the
 Bill, and a copy of it

Trade & Credit, Remarks on Present State of.
 Pam. Vol. 3 1840
Tradesmen's Lawyer . . . . . 2nd ed. 12mo. 1709
Transtagano (A. V.) Dictionary, Portuguese &
 English . . . . 2 vols. 4to. 1773
Travelling Laws 12mo. 1718
Treason, Cases of, Bacon L. T.
—— Discourse on, L. T. Vol. 1 . . . 2nd ed. 1717
Treasury Papers, Calendar of, 1557–1696 (edited '
 by Joseph Redington) . . 2 vols. imp. 8vo. 1868
Treaties & Grants, Collection of (*see* East India
 Company)
—— of Peace, Alliance, & Commerce between
 Great Britain & other Powers from 1688 to Pre-
 sent Time . . . . 2 vols. 8vo. 1772
—— State, Extract from such as relate to the
 Duty & Conduct of Commanders of Ships of
 War 4to. 1741

Tredinnick (Rd.) Review of Cornish Copper Mining
 Enterprise . . . . 2nd ed. 8vo. 1858
Tredgold (T.) Elementary Principles of Carpentry
 2nd ed. 4to. 1828
Trelawny Papers, temp. Car. I. C. M. Vol. 2,
 No. 55 (ed. W. D. Cooper) 1853
Tremaine (*Sir* John) Pleas of the Crown . folio 1723
Trevan (J.) System of Swindling, 1847. Pam.
 Vol. 5
Trevelyan Papers, 1442–1643 (*see* C. S. Pa. Nos.
 67 & 84; ed. J. P. Collier) . 2 vols. 4to. 1857–63
Trevisa, Chronicles of England (*see* Higden) folio 1577
Trevor (C. C.) Taxes on Succession & Digest of
 Statutes & Cases 8vo. 1856
 ——————————————————— 2nd ed. 8vo. 1860
Trevoux de (*see* De Trevoux)
Trials, Central Criminal Court (*see* Barnett &
 Buckler)
—— Remarkable . . . . folio 1584–1685
 Containing Trials of—
  FitzHarris (Edwd.) *for Treason*
  Plunket (*Dr.* Oliver) *for Treason*
  Shaftsbury, *Earl of* (Anthony) *for Treason*
  Colledge (Stephen) *for High Treason*
  Stayley (William) *for Treason*
  Russell (*Lord* William) *for Treason*
  Walcot (Thos.) *for Treason*
  Hone (Wm.) *for Treason*
  Rous (Jno.) *for Treason*
  Blague (*Capt.*) *for Treason*
  Delamere (*Baron*) *for Treason*
  Armstrong (*Sir* T.)
  Gascoyne (*Sir* T.) *for Treason*
  Hambden, (John) *for Misdemeanor*
  London (*Bishop of*) *v.* Hickeringill, *for Barratry*
  Braddon (Laurance) *for Misdemeanor, &c.*
  Speke (Hugh) *for Misdemeanor, &c.*
  Parry (*Dr.* William) *for Treason*
  Danby (*Earl*) *Answer of and Arguments for Ball, Impeachment
   for High Treason*
  L'Estrange (Roger) *a Papist, Depositions proving him*
  Stapleton (*Sir* M.) *for Treason*
  Thwing (Thos.) *for Treason*

Trials, Remarkable—*continued.*
Pressicks (Mary) *for Treason*
Castlemaine (*Earl*) *for Treason*
Stafford (*Viscount* Wm.) *for Treason*
Wakeman (*Sir* G.) ⎫
Corker   ⎬ Observations on their *Tryall, by T.*
Marshall   ⎭   *Ticklefoot*

Tryals, History of most remarkable Tryals in Great Britain and Ireland in Capital Cases, both by the unusual methods of Ordeal, Combat, and Attainder, and by Ecclesiastical, Civil, and Common Law 8vo. 1715
    Trials of—
Queen Emma *by Ordeal*
Lancaster (Thomas, *Earl of*) *for Treason*
Rygeway (Cecely de) *for Murder*
Annesly (*Sir* M.) & Thos. Catrington *by Combat*
Hereford (*Duke of,* afterwards Henry IV.) *by Combat*
FitzAlan (*Earl of* Arundel) *for Treason*
Cambridge (Richard, *Earl of*) *for Treason*
Oldcastle (*Sir* John) *for Heresy*
Hunne (Richard) *for Heresy* after his death
Horsey (*Dr.*) *for Murder*
Stafford (*Duke of* Buckingham) *for Treason*
Queen Anne Boleyn *for Adultery*
Nicholson (John) *for Heresy*
Cromwell (T., *Earl of* Essex). History *of Attainder*
Howard (*Duke of* Norfolk). History *of Attainder*
Newton, Mr., & Mr. Hamilton *by Combat*
Mrs. Arden *for Murder*
Seymour (Thomas, *Lord*) *for Treason*
Somerset (Edward, *Duke of*) *for Felony*
Throgmorton (*Sir* N.) *for Treason*
Parry (*Dr.*) *for Treason*
Plaintiff & Defendant, *Combat,* between Champions of
Queen of Scots (Mary) *for Conspiring*

Trials by Combat and Forms to be observed
—— Collection of, for High Treason, Murder, Rapes, &c. . . . . . temp. 1603–1721, folio
    Containing Trials of—
Atkins (S.) *for Murder*
Audley (*Lord*) *for Rape*
Baynton (Sarah) *for Forcible Marriage*
Berry (Henry) *for Murder*
Borosky (Geo.) *for Murder*

Trials, Collection of—*continued.*
Broding (Giles) *for Rape*
Carnwath (*Earl*) *for Treason*
Charles (*King*) *for Treason*
Cowper (Spencer) *for Murder*
Conningsmark (*Count*) *for Murder*
Coke (Arundel) *for slitting Mr. Crispe's Nose*
Derwentwater (*Earl*) *for Treason*
Fitzpatrick *for Rape*
Green (Robert) *for Murder*
Hartwell (Jno.) *for Forcible Marriage*
Hill (Lawrence) *for Murder*
Kenmure (*Viscount*) *for Treason*
Marson (John) *for Murder*
Mead (Wm.) *for a Tumult*
Nairn (*Lord*) *for Treason*
Nithisdale (*Earl*) *for Treason*
Penn (Wm.) *for a Tumult*
Raleigh (*Sir* W.) *for Treason*
Reason (Hugh) *for Murder*
Rogers (Wm.) *for Murder*
Russel (*Lord*) *for Treason*
Sidney (Algernon) *for Treason*
Spurr (Jno.) *for Forcible Marriage*
Stern (Jno.) *for Murder*
Stevens (Ellis) *for Murder*
Swendsen (H.) *for Forcible Marriage*
Teanter (Robt.) *for Murder*
Vratz (Christn.) *for Murder*
Widdington (*Lord*) *for Treason*
Wintoun (*Earl*) *for Treason*
Woodbourne (Jno.) *for slitting Mr. Crispe's Nose*

—— Select Collection of . . . . 2 vols. 8vo. 1744
  The contents of these Volumes are selections from Howell's State Trials
  See also State Trials
—— of Irish Fenians—
  Reg. *v.* Sullivan & Pigott
  —— Halpin
  —— Warren
  Luby & others

The following Trials will be found either under their respective Titles or the name of Reporter:—
Adams *v.* Malkins. *Is a Scrivener liable to the Bankrupt Laws?* [HURD.]

Trials—*continued.*
Annesley (Craigdenn) *v.* Anglesey Civil Ejectment.
Brodie & Smith. *Robbery.* [CREECK.]
Beaurain *v. Sir* Wm. Scott. *Excommunication.*
Bather Doed *v.* Rrayne. *Ejectment.* [WALSH.]
Bishops, The Seven. *Libel.*
Burrell, *Bart., v.* Nicholson. *Is Richmond Terrace Extra-parochial?*
Cardigan, *Earl of. Felony.*
Carr *v.* Hood. *Libel.*
Clarendon, *Earl of. Treason.*
Clayton & Duchy of Cornwall. *Case as to a Lease.*
Cochrane, *Lord. Conspiracy.*
Criminal Trials, 1831.
Gibson (Doed) *v.* Hargrave. *Ejectment.*
Grindall (Doed) *v.* Grindall. *Ejectment.*
Gunpowder Plot. [JARDINE.]
Hanson. *Conspiracy.* [JONES.]
Hewley (*Lady*). *Charity Proceedings in H. L.*
Howe, Wm. *Libel.*
Johnston, *Lieutenant-Colonel. Mutiny.*
Margarot. *Sedition.*
Morgan *v.* London Dock Company. *Tort.*
Nightingale *v.* Stockdale. *Libel.* (*See* Carr *v.* Hood.)
Paine. *Libel.* [GURNEY.]
Papists. P. N., 1690.
Regicides.
Rex *v.* Bebb. *Extent.* [HUGHES.]
Rex *v.* Kinsman & others. *Conspiracy.* [FRASER.]
Rex *v.* City. *Proceedings on Quo Warranto.*
Rex *v.* Montague. *As to Yantlett Creek.* [GURNEY.]
Rex *v.* Woodfall. Parliamentary Proceedings, vol. 2, Lib. L. Tr.
Rex *v.* Woollcombe. Retrospect of Proceedings, vol. 5, L. Tr.
Stirling Peerage—Humphrys. *Forgery.*
Sacheverell (*Dr.*)
Stockdale. [GURNEY.]
Witches, at Bury St. Edmunds.
Tatham *v.* Wright. *Will.*
Thornton. *Murder.*
Tooke (Horne). [GURNEY.]
Watson & others. *Treason.*
Winter & others. 1606.
Zulueta. *Slave Trading.*

—— State . . . . new ed. by Moile, 12mo. 1836
—— (celebrated) Scotch. Arnot (Hugo) 1336 to 1784 . . . . 4to. 1785
Aikenhead (Thomas). *Blasphemy.*
Armstrong (John). *Murder.*

Trials (celebrated) Scotch—*continued.*

Auchmonty (Charles). *Treason.*
Blair (Alexander). *Incest.*
Borthwick (Francis). *Blasphemy.*
Carmichael (Robert). *Murder.*
Carnegie (James). *Murder.*
Chistler (John). *Murder.*
Clark (George) & John Ramsay. *Murder.*
Connocher (John). *Clandestine Marriage.*
Cornwall (Archibald). *Attempting to hang up the King's Picture on the Gallows.*
Crichton (Andrew). *For disputing the King's authority.*
Cumming (George). *Murder.*
Dickson (John). *Parricide.*
Douglas (Archibald). *Murder.*
Dow. *Stealing Wine.*
Drummond (Robert). *Libel.*
Drysdale (William). *Incest.*
Falconer (John). *Using false keys.*
Fleming (John). *Slander of the King.*
Flight (Alexander). *Insult.*
Forbes (*The Master of*). *Treason.*
Fraser (*Capt.* Simon). *Treason.*
Fraser (*Lord* Charles). *Treason.*
Fraser (John). *Adultery.*
Gillespie (John & others). *Murder.*
Gowry (John, *Earl of*). *Conspiring to murder the King.*
Gray (James). *Murder.*
Green (*Capt.* Thomas & his Crew). *Piracy.*
Guthrie (John). *Adultery.*
Huitley (Margaret). *Adultery.*
Henderson (George). *Forgery.*
Horne of Spott. *Murder.*
Johnston (Agnes). *Murder.*
Ker (*Sir* James). *Clandestine Marriage.*
Macdonald (Archibald). *Treason.*
Macgregor (*Laird of*). *Slaughtering Laird of Luss's friends.*
Macgregor (Malcolm). *Murder.*
Macgregor (Patrick Roy). *Number of crimes.*
McIver & McAllum. *Destroying ships.*
McLeod (Mrs.). *Forgery.*
Morton (*Earl of*). *Murder.*
Mowbray (David). *Tumult within burgh.*
Mowbray (Francis). *Doom for Treason.*
Murdock (John). *Adultery.*
Niven (John). *Leasing making.*
Ogilvie the Jesuit. *Saying Mass.*
Ormistone (*Laird of*). *Murder.*

Trials (celebrated) Scotch—*continued.*
Piscatorii (Leonardo). *Shooting.*
Ramsay (John) & George Clark. *Murder.*
Robertson (Patrick). *Adultery.*
Rois (Thomas). *Publishing a pasquinade.*
Rutherfoord (Andrew). *Murder.*
Ruthven (Alexander). *Conspiring to Murder.*
Scott (Thomas) & Henry Yuir. *Keeping Q. Mary a prisoner.*
Skeene (James). *Treason.*
Stewart (James). *Murder.*
Stewart (John). *Leasing making.*
Storey (James). *Murder.*
Tarbet (John). *Murder.*
Taylor (Daniel) & others. *For not praying for King George.*
Tennant (Francis). *Seditious pasquinade.*
Thomson (John). *Treason.*
Wallace (John). *Saying Mass.*
Wilson (James). *Incest.*

Trimmer, Character of a. Law Tracts 1688
Triennial Act, Speeches against (*see* Impeachment of Lords)
Trinidad, Laws of, 1831-48 . . . . . 8vo. 1852
—— Ordinances of Council Government, compiled by Commissioners, 1857-1865 . . 2 vols. folio
——————————————— 1866-7 (unbound)
Trinity House, Charters to 8vo. 1730
——————————————— 8vo. 1825
Tripier (L.) Les Codes français . . 5th ed. 8vo. 1864
Tristram (*Dr.* T. H.) Reports (*see* Swabey)
Trollope (*Rev.* W.) History of Christ's Hospital. 4to. 1834
Troplong (M.) Droit civil expliqué. Des Donations entre Vifs et des Testaments. 2nd ed. 4 vols. 8vo. 1862
—— Droit civil expliqué. Du Cautionnement et des Transactions 8vo. 1846
—— Droit civil de la Contrainte par corps en matière civile et de commerce 8vo. 1847
—— Droit civil du Dépôt et du Séquestre et des Contrats aléatoires . . . . 8vo. . 1845
—— de l'Échange et du Louage
3rd ed. 2 vols. 8vo. 1859
—— du Mandat 8vo. 1846

Troplong (M.) Droit civil du Contrat de Mariage
et des Droits respectifs des Époux

3rd ed. 3 vols. 8vo. 1857
—— Droit civil expliqué. Du Nantissement, du
Gage et de l'Antichrèse 8vo. 1847
—— de la Prescription . . 4th ed. 2 vols. 8vo. 1857
—— du Prêt 8vo. 1845
—— des Priviléges et Hypothèques, & Supplément

5th ed. 5 vols. 8vo. 1854-6
—— du Contrat de Société civile et commerciale

2 vols. 8vo. 1843
—— de la Vente . . . . 5th ed. 2 vols. 8vo. 1856
Troutbeck (*Rev.* John) A Survey of the Antient
& Present State of the Scilly Islands, Cornwall

12mo. 1793
Trover & Conversion 12mo. 1696
Troward (Nich.) Election Statutes . . . 8vo. 1790
Trower (C. F.) Debtor & Creditor, with Table of
Courts in England & Wales for the Recovery of
Debts 8vo. 1860
—— Law as to Building Churches, Parsonages, &
Schools 8vo. 1867
Truro Election Proceedings, collected from the
'West Briton' 8vo. 1830-33
Trye (John) Filacer's Office of K. B., Jus Filizarii

12mo. 1684
Tucker (Josiah) A Treatise on Civil Government. 8vo. 1781
Tudor (O. D.) Leading Cases on Real Property,
Conveyancing, & Construction of Wills & Deeds

8vo. 1856
—————————————————— 2nd ed. 8vo. 1863
—— The Charitable Trusts Act, 1853, with a
Summary of the Law of Charities . . 12mo. 1854
—————————————————— 2nd ed. 12mo. 1862
—— - Leading Cases on Mercantile & Maritime Law

8vo. 1860
—————————————————— 2nd ed. 8vo. 1868
—————————————————— *see* White
—————————————————— in Equity. 3rd ed. 2 vols. 8vo. 1866

Tuke (*Dr.* T. H.) on Insanity 12mo. 1854
—— (John) Map of Yorkshire (in case) . . . 1782
—— General View of the Agriculture of the North
Riding of Yorkshire 8vo. 1800
Tunbridge School, Account of, 1827. Jac. Col.
Vol. 5 . . . . 2nd ed.
Tunnicliff (Wm.) Topographical Survey of Counties of Somerset, Gloucester, Worcester, Stafford,
Chester, & Lancaster. 8vo. 1789
Turks & Caicos Islands, Ordinances 1861-66
Turmines (H.T.A) Rambles on the Isle of Sheppey
12mo. 1843
Turnbull (W. B.) Calendar of State Papers,
Foreign Series, of the Reign of Edward VI. preserved in Her Majesty's Public Record Office.
1547-53 . . . . imp. 8vo. 1861
—— Calendar of State Papers, Foreign Series, of
the Reign of Mary, preserved in her Majesty's
Public Record Office, 1553-58 . . imp. 8vo. 1861
—— (*see* Buik of Chroniclis, with History of H.
Bocce) No. 6, M. R. Pub. 1858
Turner (F.) The Contract of Pawn . . . 8vo. 1866
—— (Geo.) & Russell (J.) Chancery Reports,
temp. Eldon, 1822-4 . . . . 8vo. 1832
—— (Samuel) Present Practice & Costs of the
Court of Chancery (R. H. Venables)
3rd ed. 8vo. 1804
—— Epitomes of the Practice of Courts of Chancery, K. B., C. P., Equity, Ex.; & the Solicitor's
Guide concerning Bankrupts, 1806-9 . 8vo.
——————————————————— 1806-12. 8vo.
—— Practice & Costs in Court of Chancery (R.
Venables) . . . . . . 4th ed. 2 vols. 8vo. 1810
——————————————— 5th ed. 2 vols. 8vo. 1817
——————————————— 6th ed. 2 vols. 8vo. 1825
—— (Sharon) History of England during Middle
Ages . . . . 5 vols. 8vo. 1825
—— History of the Anglo-Saxons. 5th ed. 3 vols.
8vo. 1828

Turner (Sharon) History of England from Henry
    VIII. to Elizabeth . . . . . 4 vols. 8vo. 1827-9
—— (Thos.) Counsel to Inventors of Improvements
                                                12mo. 1850
—— Patents & Registration 8vo. 1851
—— on Amendment of the Patent Laws. Pam.
    Vol. 8
Turnley (J.) The Spirit of the Vatican illustrated
    by Historical & Dramatic Sketches . . 8vo. 1845
Turnor (E.) Collections for the History of the Town
    & Soke of Grantham, containing Authentic
    Memoirs of Sir Isaac Newton 4to. 1806
—— (L.) History of Town & Boro' of Hertford
                                                 8vo. 1830
Turnpike Act, St. Giles Pound to Kilburn. 23
    Geo. III. . . . . 12mo.
—— Statutes 8vo. 1828
Twells (P.) Chancery Reports (see Hall, F. J.)
Twiss (Horace) The Public & Private Life of Lord
    Chancellor Eldon. . . . . . 3 vols. 8vo. 1844
—— (Dr. Travers) Laws of Nations . . . 8vo. 1861
Twysden (Sir R.) on Government of England. C.
    S. Pa. No. 45 (ed. J. M. Kemble) 1849
Tyler (R. H.) Commentaries on the Law of Infancy
    & the Law of Coverture (Albany, U. S.). 8vo. 1868
—— Ecclesiastical Law, U. S. 8vo. 1866
Tymms (S.) (see C. S. Pa. No. 49).
Tyndale (Wm.) Writings. Par. S. Pa.
                                  3 vols. 8vo. 1848-50
Tyrwhitt (R. P.) & Tyndale (T. W.) Digest of
    Statutes & Supplement, Magna Charta
                                  3 vols. 4to. 1822-6
—— Index to Sir E. Coke's Reports, 1225-1821,
    by Thomas & Fraser. Vol. 7. Coke's Reports . 1827
—— Exchequer & Exchequer Chamber Reports,
    1830-35 . . . . 5 vols. 8vo. 1832-7
—— & Granger (T. C.) Exchequer & Exchequer
    Chambers Reports, 1835-6 . . . . . 8vo. 1837

Tyrrell (E.) Chronicles of London from 1089 to
- 1483, written in 15th Century, from MSS. in
British Museum 4to. 1827
Tytler (*Hon.* A. F.) Essay on Military Law &
Courts Martial . . . . . . 2nd ed. 8vo. 1806

U

Uckfield Union, Poor Law Auditors' Report. 8vo. 1836
Udall (Henry) County Court Acts (9 & 10 Vict.
c. 95) . . . . 2nd ed. 12mo. 1847
Ulster, Irish Society in (*see* Irish Society)
Umfreville, Pedigree of 4to. 1859
Unclaimed Dividends of Bank Stock . . 8vo. 1805-22
———————————— & Names of Proprietors of
South Sea Stock 8vo. 1823
———————————— on Bank Stock, &c. . 8vo. 1808
———————————————————— (Walsh) 12mo.
Underdown (E. M.) The Law of Art Copyright
12mo. 1863
Unions (*see* Parishes)
Uniformity, Act of (*see* Common Prayer)
United States (*see* America)
Universal Pocket Companion . . 3rd ed. 12mo. 1760
Upcott (Wm.) A Bibliographical Account of the
Principal Works relating to English Topography
4 vols. 4to. 1818
Urlin (R. D.) Manual of the Law relating to Office
of Trustee . . . . 3rd ed. 12mo. 1868
Urquhart (Geo.) Experienced Solicitor in the House
of Lords . . . . folio 1773
—— (D.) Reflections on Thoughts & Things. 8vo. 1844
Uses & Trusts, Law of 1734
Usher (*Bp.*) Prophecy of 1688. L. T.
Usury Laws, Reasons against the Repeal of. Jac.
Col. Vol. 3

V

Vacarius (M.) Descriptio Juris Romani . . 8vo. 1820
Vacher (T. B.) & Sons, on Controverted Elections
            12mo. 1847
——————————— List of Private Bills in
 Parliament, 1853-68
—— Digest of Stamp Duties & Summary of Decisions thereon . . . . . . 5th ed. 12mo. 1862
————————————————— 6th ed. 12mo. 1865
—— Standing Orders, Lords & Commons, 1848-69
           12mo. 1848–69
Vaizey (J. S.) Lord St. Leonards Act to Amend the
 Law of Property & to Relieve Trustees. 12mo. 1860
Valin (M. R. J.) Nouveau Commentaire sur l'Ordonnance de la Marine . . . . . 2 vols. 4to. 1760
Vallière (*Duc de*) Catalogue des Livres de la Bibliothèque (par De Bure) . . . . . 3 vols. 8vo. 1783
Valor Ecclesiasticus, temp. Henry VIII. :—
 Vol. I. Canterbury, Rochester, Bath & Wells, Bristol, Chichester, London . . . . folio 1810
 „ II. Winchester, Salisbury, Oxford, Exeter, Gloucester
            folio 1814
 „ III. Hereford, Coventry, Lichfield, Worcester, Norwich, Ely . . . . folio 1817
 „ IV. Lincoln, Peterborough, Llandaff, St. David's, Bangor, & St. Asaph . . . . folio 1821
 „ V. York, Chester, Carlisle, Durham . . . folio 1825
 „ VI. Appendix (divers Dioceses) and Indexes, with the Introduction* by Mr. Hunter . . . folio 1834
   (*See* Record Commission)

Van der Linden (J.) Guide to Demerara Law,
 translated from the Dutch 8vo. 1814
—— Institutes of the Laws of Holland, translated
 by J. Henry 8vo. 1828
Van Dieman's Land Company, 3rd Report. 8vo. 1828
Van Espen (Z. B.) Jus Ecclesiasticum Universum
 (J. P. Gibert) . . . . . 10 vols. in 5, folio 1769

* The Introduction is placed at commencement of Vol. 1.

Van Heythuysen (F. M.) Chancery Pleadings. 8vo. 1816
——————————————————(E. Hughes)
2nd ed. 2 vols. 8vo. 1828
—— Epitome of Law Library . . 2nd ed. 12mo. 1826
Vapereau (G.) Dictionnaire des Contemporains
3rd ed. 8vo. 1865
Varenius (B.) Géographie générale (4th vol. only)
12mo. 1755
Vardon (Thos.) Index to House of Commons Journal, 1820-37 . . . . folio 1839
—————————————— Local & Personal & Private Acts, 1798-1839 . . . . 8vo. 1840
Vattel (Emer de) Law of Nations (Latin)
2 vols. in 1, 4to. 1759
———————————————————— (English) 8vo. 1797
Vaughan (R.) British Antiquities Revived: a Friendly Contest touching the Sovereignty of the Three Princes of Wales in Ancient Times. 4to. 1834
——(*Sir* Jno.) C. P. Reports, 1666-73 . . folio 1677
Vaux Peerage Evidence, 1836
Veal (Jno.) Record & Writ Practice. 2nd ed. 12mo. 1845
Venables (*Alderman*) Correspondence as to Office of Undersheriff. L. T. Vol. 3
Venice. Report of the Deputy Keeper of the Public Records to the Master of the Rolls, upon the Documents in the Archives & Public Libraries of Venice 8vo. 1866
Ventris (*Sir* P.) C. P. Reports. 2nd ed. 2 vols.
folio 1701
———————————————— 3rd ed. 2 vols. folio 1701
———————————————— . . . . 4th ed. 1726
Verney (*Sir* Ralph) Verney Papers, Notes of Long Parliament, temp. Car. C. S. Pa. No. 31 . . . 1845
———————————————— 1639. C. S.
Pa. No. 56 (J. Bruce) 1853
Vernon (C.) Considerations for Regulating the Exchequer 12mo. 1642
—— (G. W.) and Scriven (J. B.) Irish Common Law Reports, 1786-8 . . . . 8vo. 1790

Vernon (Thos.) Chancery Reports . . 2 vols. folio 1726
———————————————— 1680–1790 (Jno.
Raithby) . . . . 3rd ed. 2 vols. 8vo. 1828
Vesey, or Vezey (Fras., Sen.) Chancery Reports
            2 vols. folio 1771
————————————————— 1746–55. 2nd ed. 2 vols. 1773
————————————— (R. Belt) 4th ed. 2 vols. 8vo. 1818
——————— —————— Supplement to (R. Belt) 8vo. 1825
Vesey (Fras., Jun.) Chancery Reports, 1789–1817
        2nd ed. 19 vols. 8vo. 1812–27
—— Chancery Reports, Index to (by a Barrister). 8vo. 1822
————————————— Supplement to (J. E.
Hovendon) . . . . 2 vols. 8vo. 1827
—— & Beames (J.) Chancery Reports, temp.
Eldon, 1812–14 . . . . 2nd ed. 3 vols. 8vo.
Vickers (J. W.) Municipal Corporations Directory
              8vo. 1866
Victor (B.) The Widow of the Wood . . 12mo. 1765
Victorian Acts (*see* Adamson)
—— Statutes, Public, 1829–66 . . 3 vols. 4to. 1866
———————— Private 4to. 1866
Vidian (A.) Entries . . . . folio 1684
Vieyra (A.) Portuguese & English Dictionary
           2 vols. 4to. 1773
Villargues (Rolland de) Les Codes criminels
interprétés . . . . 2nd ed. 8vo. 1864
Viner (Chas.) Abridgment of Law and Equity
          23 vols. folio
——————————————————— Supplement to
        6 vols. 8vo. 1789–1806
Vinnius (A.) Institutionum Imperalium Commentarius 4to. 1709
Virgilii Georgica Hexaglotta . . . . . folio 1827
Virgin Islands, Ordinances, 1856–66 . . folio
Virginia, Acts of Assembly . . . . . folio 1727
—— Laws of . . . . folio 1732
—— Code of Laws, U. S. 8vo. 1849
Vitrian (J.) Las Memorias de Felipe de Comines
         2 vols. in 1, folio 1643

Vizard (John) Compendium of Principles in Philosophy and Divinity 8vo. 1836
—— (Wm.) Letter to Mr. Courtenay on Practice in Chancery. Chy. Pam. Vol. 1
—— Remarks in a Letter to the Speaker on the Inconveniences of the Present Mode of Proceeding on Private Bills in Parliament, with Suggestions for a Remedy (*see* West) . . 8vo. 1825
Voet (J.) ad Pandectas Commentarius
      6th ed. 2 vols. folio 1734
Voltaire (F. M. A. de) Œuvres. 70 vols. 8vo. 1784–9
Volunteer Service Gazette, 1861-7, 6 vols. folio
Vowell (J.) alias Hoker, Antique Description and Account of City of Exeter 4to. 1765
Vulliamy (L.) Sculpture in Architecture . folio 1818
—— Bridge of the Trinità at Florence (bound with the above) 1822

W

Waddilove (A.) on Probate Act 8vo. 1857
—— Digest of Ecclesiastical Law 8vo. 1849
Wainwright (J.) History of Strafford & Tickhill, Doncaster & Conisbrough, Yorkshire . . 4to. 1829
Wake (*Dr.* W.) Epistles of the Fathers . . 8vo. 1693
—— (Robt.) History of Southwold, Suffolk
      2 vols. 8vo. 1839
Wakefield (E. G.) on Punishment of Death. 8vo. 1831
—— (Edw.) Account of Ireland, Statistical & Political . . . . 2 vols. 4to. 1812
Waldegrave (*Earl*) Catalogue of Contents of Strawberry Hill 4to. 1842
Wales, Cambrian Directory 8vo. 1800
—— South, Evidence on Petition of Proprietors of Collieries in. Vol. 13, Jac. Col. 1810
—— Great Session, Jurisdiction & Practice. 8vo. 1795

Wales, Jurisdiction of K.B. over Latitat (Discourse against) Hargrave's L. T. Vol. 1
—— Princes of (*see* 'Spectator,' March 7, 1863)
—————— Friendly Contests as to (*see* Penglenn's British Antiquities)
—— Ancient Laws & Statutes of . . . folio 1841
Walesby (F. P.) on Instruments of War. Vol. 5, Pam. . . . . 3rd ed. 1841
Walker (G. A.) Burial Ground Incendiarism, the last Fire at the Bone House, in the Spa Fields Golgotha. Vol. 17, Pam. 1856
—— (John) English Dictionary . . 5th ed. 4to. 1810
Walford (J. G.) on Customs 8vo. 1846
Walkley (Thos.) Catalogue of Dukes, &c. 12mo. 1658
—— Order of the Lords 4to. 1628
Wallace (Geo.) on Scotch Peerages . . . 8vo. 1785
—— (J. B.) Remarks on the Law of Bailments. L. T. Vol. 7 1840
Wallia. Extentæ ad Walliam Spectantes (the Record of Caernarvon) 26 Edward III. (Sir H. Ellis) . . . . folio 1838
(This volume contains Leges & Consuetudines Walliæ & Extentæ Com. Meryoneth)
(*See* Record Commission.)
—————— Rotuli (*see* Chartæ-Antiquæ)
Walliæ & Angliæ Taxatio Ecclesiastica (*see* Chartæ Antiquæ)
Waller (Wm.) on Mines of Sir Casbery Price in Cardiganshire 8vo. 1688
—— (Dr. J. F.) Report of Proceedings at a Visitation held in Trinity College, Dublin, to hear Appeals of Dr. Shaw & another . . 8vo. 1858
Wallis (Jno.) Account of Northumberland
2 vols. 4to. 1769
Walsh (F.) List of Unclaimed Dividends in Bank Stock, &c. 8vo. 1808
—— (F. N.) Report of Trial of Burrell *v.* Nicholson, the Non-parochiability of Richmond Terrace, Westminster 8vo. 1834

Walsh & Son, Report of Trial Morgan *v.* London
Dock Company 8vo. 1860
Walsingham (T.) Historia Anglicana, Chronica
Monasterii S. Albani, 1272-1422. 28 M. R. Pub.
2 vols. 8vo. 1863
Walters (J. B.) on Chancery Delays & Conduct of
Solicitors. Vol. 4, Jac. Col. 1826
Walthoe (J.) Law Catalogue . 3 vols. 12mo. 1716-26
War & Peace Debates in the Public Councils of
the Kingdom. Vol. 2, Col. Jur.
Warburton (J.) & others, History of Dublin
2 vols. 4to. 1818
————'s Tracts 8vo. 1789
Ward (R.) on Investments 8vo. 1852
—— (*Lord*) Justice of the Peace. . 3 vols. 4to. 1709
—— (*Rev.* W. P.) Isle of Man & Diocese of
Sodor & Man, antient & authentic Records &
Documents relating to the Civil & Ecclesiastical
History of that Island 12mo. 1837
Warkworth, Chronicles of Edward IV. 1461-74.
C. S. P. No. 10 (J. O. Halliwell) . . . 4to. 1839
Warlter (J.) Table on Statute of Limitations
8vo. 1862
Warner (*Rev.* R.) Translation of Domesday for
Hants 4to. 1789
—— History of Hampshire . . . . 2 vols. 4to. 1793
—— Topography of S. W. parts of Hants . 8vo. 1798
—— History of the Isle of Wight 8vo. 1795
—— Walk through Wales 8vo. 1798
Warren (Saml.) on Attorney's Duties . . 8vo. 1848
—— Election Law & Practice . 2 vols. 8vo. 1852-3
—— Law Studies 8vo. 1833
———————————— 8vo. 1835
———————————— . . . . . 3rd ed. 2 vols. 8vo. 1863
—— Select Extracts from Blackstone's Com-
mentaries 8vo. 1837
—— Charge to Grand Jury at Hull, Epiphany
Sessions. Vol. 9, Pam. 1854
—— (John) Trial of (*see* Trials of Fenians). 8vo. 1867

Warry (G. D.) on Railway Ratings . . . 8vo. 1866
Warton (*Rev.* T.) Specimen of a History of Oxfordshire. . . . . 2nd ed. 4to. 1783
—— History of Kiddington, Oxford. 3rd ed. 4to. 1815
—— Biography of Sir Thos. Pope . . . 8vo. 1772
Water Report of Directors of London Watford Spring Water Company. Vol. 9, Pam. Part 2, 1852
—————— Microscopical Examination, &c. of the Thames & other Waters. Vol. 9, Pam. Part 2 1852
—— Company (*see* Thames)
Waterlow & Sons' Standing Orders of H. L. & C. on Private Bills 12mo. 1856
Watkins (John) History of Bideford, Devon. 8vo. 1792
—— (C.) on Conveyancing . . . . 2nd ed. 4to. 1804
———————————— (Morley & Coote). 3rd ed. 8vo. 1819
———————————— (Preston). 3rd ed. 8vo. 1819
———————— MSS. Notes (Preston).4th ed. 8vo. 1823
———————————— (Merefield). 8th ed. 8vo. 1833
———————————— (White). 8th ed. 8vo. 1838
—— on Copyhold (R. G. Vidal). 3rd ed. 2 vols. 8vo. 1826
—— Descent (J. Williams) . . 4th ed. 8vo. 1837
Watson (G.) (*see* Bacon, Francis, Viscount St. Albans)
—— (James) & others, Trial for High Treason (*see* Fairburn) 8vo. 1817
—— Paramythia, or mental Pastimes collected in Russia 12mo. 1821
—— (*Rev.* John) History of Halifax, Yorkshire. 4to. 1775
—— (*Dr.* Wm.) Clergyman's Law . 3rd ed. folio 1725
————————————————— . . 4th ed. folio 1747
—— (Wm.) Common Pleas Rules, 1654–1736. 8vo. 1736
—— (White) Delineation of the Strata of Derbyshire, bound up with (Mawe, J.) . . . 4to. 1811
—— Partnership 8vo. 1794
——————— . . . . 2nd ed. 8vo. 1807
—— Historical Account of Wisbech & the circumjacent Towns and Villages in Isle of Ely . 8vo. 1827

Watson (W. H.) on Sheriff 8vo. 1827
—— on Arbitration 8vo. 1825
———————————————— . . . . . . .2nd ed. 8vo. 1836
———————————————— . . . . 3rd ed. 8vo. 1846
Watts (*Dr.* Robert) Bibliotheca Britannica. 4 vols.
4to. 1821
Waylen (James) Chronicles of Devizes, Wilts. 8vo. 1839
Weatherfield (G. M.) County Court Law   12mo. 1867
Weatherley, Guide to Probate Court. 2nd ed. 8vo. 1858
Weever (John) Ancient Funeral Monuments. 4to. 1767
Webster (*Dr.* N.) English Dictionary. 2 vols. 4to. 1832
—— History of Metals 8vo. 1671
—— (Edwd.) Parliamentary Costs . . 12mo. 1859
————————————————————— 2nd ed. 8vo. 1864
————————————————————— 3rd ed. 12mo. 1867
—— (Thos.) on Patents 8vo. 1841
—— Patent Cases. . . . . . . 2 vols. 8vo. 1844–5
Wedderburn (Alex.) Statistics of New Brunswick
4to. 1835
Wedgwood (*Dr.* W. R.) and Homan (J. S.) Law
Manual for Notaries and Bankers (New York)
8vo. 1867
Weekly Reporter, 1852–69 . . 17 vols. 4to. 1853–69
—— (Digest) 1852–9 . . . . . 2 vols. 4to.
Weekly Bankrupt List, 1811–12
Wegener's Defence of Hereditary Right according
to the Lex Regis of Prince Christian of Denmark.
Vol. 9, Pam. 1853
Weights (Decimal) Memorial on, to Mr. Disraeli,
March 12. Vol. 12, Pam. 1859
Weir ( ) Greenock (*see* Denholme, J.) . . 8vo. 1829
Wellbeloved (C.) Eboracum, or York under the
Romans 8vo. 1842
Welch (J.) List of Westminster Scholars, 1561–
1788, & MSS. to 1824 . . . . . . 4to. 1788
Welford (R. G.) on Chancery Practice . . 8vo. 1842
Wellesley (*Hon.* W. L.) View of Chancery. Vol.
9, Jac. Col. 1830

Wellesley v. Duke of Beaufort, Lord Eldon's Judgment. Vol. 6, Jac. Law Tr.
Wells (G.) Law & History of Drainage of Bedford Level Fens . . . . 2 vols. 8vo. 1830
Wellington Despatches (ed. by his Son, Duke of Wellington) . . . . 10 vols. 8vo. 1858
Welsby (W. N.) (*see* Archbold)
—— (*see* Bateman on Highways)
—— Hurlstone (E. T.) & Gordon (J.) Exchequer Reports, 1847–54. . . . . 9 vols. 8vo. 1849–54
—— & Beavan (E.) (*see* Chitty's Statutes)
Wendell (J. L.) Blackstone's Commentaries, adapted to the American Student. 4 vols. 8vo. 1852
Wendt (E. E.) Papers on Maritime Legislation
8vo. 1868
Wentworth (T.) on Executors . . 4th ed. 12mo. 1656
———————————————— (J. M. Manley)
12mo. 1676
———————————————— 8vo. 1763
———————————————— (Jeremy) 14th ed. 8vo. 1829
——(John) Pleading . . . . 10 vols. 8vo. 1799
Wesket (John) on Marine Insurance . . 4to. 1781
West (afterwards *Lord Chancellor*) Enquiry as to manner of creating Peers 8vo. 1719
—— (M. J.) on Public Bills, Letter to Lord Melbourne. Law Tr. Vol. 5 1836
—— (Edwd.) on Extents 8vo. 1817
—— v. Erissey, Case of, in Exchequer T. 1726, on Marriage Articles. Vol. 1, Col. Jur.
—— India Company Charter 12mo. 1826
—— Dock & London Dock Bills. Evidence. folio 1797–99
—— Indies, History (*see* Martin's British Colonies)
—— Administration of Justice in. Report . folio 1826
—— & Spanish Provinces of North America. Map
—— (M. J.) Letter to Viscount Melbourne on Legislation as to Public Bills (*see* Vizard on Private Bills) 8vo. 1836
—— (R.) & Buhler (J. G.) Digest of Hindu Law
8vo. 1867

West (Thos.) Antiquities of Furness Abbey, Lancashire 4to. 1744
——————————————— (W. Close) 8vo. 1818
—— (James) Guide to the Lakes of Cumberland & Westmoreland (Pennington) . 7th ed. 8vo. 1799
—— (M. J.) H. L. Reports, 1839–41 . . 8vo. 1842
—— Chancery Reports (temp. Hardwick) 1786–89 8vo. 1817
—— (Wm.) Symbolæographia 8vo. 1590
Westbrook (R. A.) Volunteer, the Question considered, its Importance, & Consequence of Neglect. Vol. 15, Pam. 1861
Westhead (J. P. B.) on 18th Chapter of Leviticus; Marriage with Deceased Wife's Sister. Vol. 24, Pam. 1850
Western Australia, Ordinances, 1858–66. 2 v. 4to.
——————————————— Index to, 1832–62. 4to. 1862
Western (T. G.) London Tithe Cases . . 8vo. 1823
—— (*Lord*) Facts & Arguments in Favour of a more Frequent Delivery of the Gaols. Vol. 18, Pam. 1842
Westlake (Jno.) Private International Law. 8vo. 1858
Westminster, Instructions to Jury, for Execution of their Office, 1800 . . . . 8vo. 1801
—— Courts at, Removal of, Facts as to. Vol. 4, Pam.
—— Hall Courts, Facts for the Consideration of Parliament before the Final Adoption of a Plan perpetuating the Courts of Law on a Site injurious & costly to the Suitors. L. Tr. Vol. 8 . . 1840
—— Hall & New Houses of Parliament, Extracts from Evidence taken before Committee of House of Commons in 1841–42, proving the Necessity of Removing the Courts to the Neighbourhood of the Inns of Court, 1843. L. T. Vol. 8
—— Review of the Evidence, & Extracts therefrom, reprinted from 'Legal Observer.' L. T. Vol. 8 1842

Westminster Election Poll Books (*see* Suffolk)
            8vo. 1754
————————————————— 8vo. 1780
————————————— (*see* Hertford)
—— & Foreign Quarterly Review, 1835–51
            39 vols. 8vo.
————————————————— N. S. 1852–67,
            32 vols. 8vo.
—— Sewers, Statute, &c. of 8vo. 1826
————— & Laws of 8vo. 1839
—— Power of Court to demand Fees, Mullin's Letter on 8vo. 1836
—— Plan 1840
—— Survey of Parish Clerks of London, Westminster, & Southwark 8vo. 1732
West Sheen, Petersham, & Ham, the Rules of Customs prevailing at. Vol. 2, Col. Jur.
Westmoreland (*see* Whitaker's History of Richmond)
Wetenhall (J. B.) Price of Stocks, &c. 1832–67
            17 vols. folio
Wharton (F.) on Homicide, U. S. 8vo. 1855
—— (C. F.) Legal Maxims 8vo. 1866
—— Peerage Case. Claim of Mr. Baillie. 1st series, p. 416. Evidence, p. 425
————————————— Evidence, Vols. 13 & 17 House of Lords Sessions Papers
————————————— of C. K. Vol. 3, 3rd series, p. 570
—— (T. J.) Digest of Cases, & Rules of Practice of 3rd Circuit Court, U. S. 8vo. 1822
—— (*Sir* G.) Britain, Chronology, 1600–61
            12mo. 1661
—— (J. J. S.) Articled Clerk's Manual
         8th ed. 12mo. 1858
—— Law Dictionary . . . . . 2nd ed. 8vo. 1859
————————————— . . . . . 3rd ed. 8vo. 1864
————————————— . . . . . 4th ed. 8vo. 1867

Wharton (*Dr.* Richard) on Political Economy
          2nd ed. 8vo. 1852
Wheatley (*Rev.* Chas.) Illustration of the Book of
 Common Prayer 8vo. 1810
—— (H. D.) *see* C. S. Pa. No. 95 1867
Wheaton (*Dr.* H.) International Law in Europe
 & America, U. S. (W. R. Lawrence) . . 8vo. 1863
—————————————— (Dana) 8th ed. 8vo. 1866
—— Reports, U. S. (*see* Curtis)
Wheeler (J.) History of Manchester, Lanc. 8vo. 1836
Whishaw (J.) Dictionary 8vo. 1829
—— (Fras.) Map of Hendon, & Book of References
            4to. 1828
—— Plan for Viaduct for Holborn Bridge . . . 1833
—— Map of London, showing as at Fire in 1661,
 & Present State . . . . since 1831
—— (F.) Railway Analysis 8vo. 1837
—— (J.) Reform Act(bound up with Waller).12mo. 1832
Whiston (Wm.) Theory of the Earth. 4th ed. 8vo. 1725
—— Sacred History of the Old & New Testament
         6 vols. 8vo. 1745–46
Whitaker (Jno.) History of Manchester
         2 vols. 4to. 1771–73
—— (*Dr.* T. D.) History of Craven Deanery folio 1812
—— History of Leeds (R. Thoresby)
        2nd ed. 2 vols. folio 1816
—— Lien 8vo. 1812
—— History of Richmondshire & parts of York-
 shire, Lancashire, & Westmoreland
         2 vols. folio 1823
—— Loidis & Elmete; continuation of Thoresby's
 History of Leeds, embracing Aredale and Wharf-
 dale, and the Vale of Calder, Yorkshire
         Vol. 2, folio 1816
—— History of Whalley, Clitheroe, & Cartmell
         3rd ed. 4to. 1818
—— (*Dr.* Wm.) Disputations on Holy Scripture.
 Par. S. Pa. 8vo. 1849

White (Chas.) Peerage 8vo. 1825
—— (F. M.) Report on Regina v. Goodchild on Rating Tithe Commutation Rent Charge . 8vo. 1838
—— (F. T.) and Tudor (O. D.) Leading Cases in Chancery 8vo. 1849
———————————— 2nd ed. 2 vols. 8vo. 1858
———————————— 3rd ed. 2 vols. 8vo. 1866
—— (Rev. G.) History of Selbourne, Hants
4to. 1813
—— (G. T.) on Revivor 8vo. 1843
—— (J. B.) on Anti-Religious Libel Law . 8vo. 1834
—— Civil Service Guide . . . 5th ed. 12mo. 1862
—— (J. M.) as to Select Vestries, &c. Pam. Vol. 4 1834
—— Letter to Mr. Stewart on Enfranchisement of Copyholders 8vo. 1839
—— Parochial Settlements . . . Vol. 4, Pam. 1835
—— (Jno.) Address to the People and Church of Scotland in reply to Sir James Graham and the Government on the Law of Patronage. Vol. 23, Pam. No. 5 1843
—— (Wm.) History, Gazetteer, and Directory of Hampshire and the Isle of Wight . . 8vo. 1859
———————————————————— of W. R. of Yorkshire, with York City and Port of Hull . . . . 2 vols. 12mo. 1837-38
———————————— of East and North Ridings & See of Ripon, &c. 8vo. 1840
Whitelock (Sir B.) on Government . 2 vols. 4to. 1766
—— Memorials of English Affairs, temp. Car. I. to Restoration of Car. II. . . . 4 vols. 8vo. 1853
—— (Sir Jas.) Liber Famelicus of. C. S. Pa. No. 70 (J. Bruce) 1858
Whitgift's (Abp.) Works. Par. S. Pa.
3 vols. 4to. 1851-2-3
Whitmarsh (F.) on Bankruptcy . 2nd ed. 8vo. 1817
Whittle (F. A.) History of Bolton, Lanc. . 8vo. 1865
Whitton (Wm.) Chancery Fee Guide (Irish) 8vo. 1843

Whitmore (W. W.) Letter on the Corn Laws.
Vol. 7, Jac. Col. 1826
Whitworth (Chas.) List of Lords & Officers of
State 8vo. 1765
—— Nobility 12mo. 1763
Whyte (Fras.) for the Sacred Law of England
12mo. 1652
Wickstead (J.) Table of Costs 8vo. 1829
Wicliffe's Apology for the Lollards. No. 20, C.
S. Pa. (J. H. Todd) 1842
Wigan, Charters relating to 4to. 1808
Wightwick (Jno.) Exchequer Reports, 1810-11
8vo. 1819
Wigram (Jas.) on Discovery 8vo. 1836
—— Wills 8vo. 1831
———— (H. Wigram). 8vo. 1837
———— (W. K. Wigram) . . 4th ed. 8vo. 1858
Wigtoun Peerage Cases of H. Flemyng, Esq., &
State of the Evidence. 1st series, p. 543-63.
Vol. 4, p. 505 1780
Wilcock (J. W.) on Municipal Corporations. 8vo. 1827
Wilkinson (R.) on the Reform Act, 1867 . 8vo. 1868
Willcock (J. W.) Laws of Inns, &c. . . . 12mo. 1829
—— Medical Law 8vo. 1830
—— Poor Laws 8vo. 1829
—— on the Office of Constable 8vo. 1827
Wight (Alex.) Inquiry into Rise, &c. of Parlia-
ment, chiefly in Scotland 4to. 1784
Wigorniensis Registrum Prioratus (W. H. Hale)
No. 91, C. S. Pa. 1865
Wilberforce (R. J.) on Church Courts and Church
Discipline 8vo. 1845
Wilden Ferry to the Mersey—Opposition to in-
tended Canal 4to. 1766
Wilde (*Sir* F. T.) Lecture in Hall of Incorporated
Law Society, 1833. Pam. Vol. 3
—— Supplement to Barton's Conveyancing(C.Bar-
ton, jun.) . . . . . . 3rd ed. 3 vols. 8vo. 1826

Wilkins (David) Leges Anglo-Saxonicæ . folio 1731
—— Works of Selden . . . . . 3 vols. folio 1726
—— (M. J.) & others. Revised Statutes of Nova
  Scotia. 2nd series 8vo. 1859
Wilks (J., Jun.) Four Letters to Lord Lyndhurst
  on the Chancery Questions. Jac. Col.
  Vol. 4, 1827
Wilkinson (Jas. Jno.) on the Funds . . . 8vo. 1839
—— Limitation of Actions 8vo. 1829
—— on Replevin 8vo. 1825
—— on Shipping, Building, &c. 8vo. 1842
—— (*Rev.* J.) Views in Cumberland, Westmore-
  land, & Lancaster . . . . folio 1821
—— (M.) Chancery Practice of Durham . . 8vo. 1807
—— (R.) London, Illustrated 4to. 1819
—— (Robt.) Representation of the People Act. 8vo. 1868
Will (J. S.) Practice of the Referees' Courts in
  Parliament 8vo. 1866
—— on County Courts 8vo. 1868
Willes (*Sir* John) C. P. Reports (C. Durnford)
  1734–58 . . . . folio 1799
Williams (David) History of Monmouthshire, illustrated by John Gardnor 4to. 1796
—— (E. V.) on Executors . . . . 2 vols. 8vo. 1832
———————————— . 2nd ed. 2 vols. 8vo. 1838
———————————— . 3rd ed. 2 vols. 8vo. 1841
———————————— . 4th ed. 2 vols. 8vo. 1849
———————————— . 5th ed. 2 vols. 8vo. 1856
———————————— . 6th ed. 2 vols. 8vo. 1866
—— (F. S.) Improvements of Equity Jurisdiction
  8vo. 1852
—— (John) on Rise, &c. of Northern Governments
  2 vols. 4to. 1777
—— Opinion on Devise of Real & Personal Estate,
  1791. Vol. 1, Col. Jur.
—— (J. G.) (*see* Cases, temp. Talbot, Lord C.)
—— (Joshua) on Personal Property . . . 8vo. 1848
———————————— 2nd ed. 8vo. 1855

Williams (Joshua) on Personal Property
                                                     3rd ed. 8vo. 1856
—————————————————— 4th ed. 8vo. 1860
—————————————————— 5th ed. 8vo. 1864
—————————————————— 6th ed. 8vo. 1866
—— on Real Property 8vo. 1845
—————————————— . . . . 3rd ed. 8vo. 1852
—————————————— . . . . 5th ed. 8vo. 1859
—————————————— . . . . 6th ed. 8vo. 1862
—————————————— . . . . 7th ed. 8vo. 1865
—————————————— . . . . 8th ed. 8vo. 1868
—— Law Questions . . . . . 7th ed. 8vo. 1866
—— on Real Assets 8vo. 1861
—— Paper on the True Remedy for the Evils affecting the Transfer of Land, read before the Juridical Society, 1862. Vol. 19, Pam.
—— (P.) Reports in Chancery, 1695–1734
                                4th ed. 3 vols. 8vo. 1787
————————————————— (Cox)
                                5th ed. 3 vols. 8vo. 1793
————————————————— (J. B. Monro, W. L. Lowndes, & Jas. Randall). 6th ed. 3 vols. 8vo. 1826
—— (R. G.) (see Chitty, T., on Pleading)
—— & Bruce (G.) Jurisdiction & Practice of the High Court of Admiralty 8vo. 1868
—— (Dr. S. W.) Chinese Commercial Guide
                                         5th ed. 8vo. 1863
—— (T.) Every Man his own Lawyer. 2nd ed. 8vo. 1818
—— (T. W.) Conveyances' Precedents . . 8vo. 1788
————————————————————— . . 8vo. 1792
—— Justice of the Peace . 2nd ed. 4 vols. 8vo. 1808
—— Digest of Statutes, 9 Hen. III. to 30 Geo. III.
                                            2 vols. 4to. 1791
———————————————— 42 Geo. III.
                                            3 vols. 4to. 1791–93
Willich (C. H.) Tithe Commutation Tables. 8vo. 1837–66
—— Table for realising Property . 3rd ed. 8vo. 1853
—————————————— Annuities & Successions. 12mo. 1856

Willis (Browne, *LL.D.*) History of Buckingham
4to. 1755
—— (B.) Survey of Cathedrals. 3 vols. in 2, 4to. 1742
—— Survey of St. Asaph (by E. Edwards)
2 vols. 8vo. 1801
—— (C.) Notitia Parliamentaria . . . 12mo. 1715
—— (J. W.) on Interrogatories 8vo. 1816
—— on Duties and Responsibilities of Trustees
8vo. 1827
Wilmore (G.) on the Statutes at Large—Confusion worse Confounded. Vol. 9, Pam. 1852
Willmore (G.) & Bedell (E.) Mercantile & Maritime Guide 8vo. 1856
—— Wollaston (F. L.) & Davison (H.) K. B. Reports, 1837 1839
————————————— & Hodges (W.) 8vo. 1840
—— Is Trial by Jury worth keeping? Vol. 7, Pam. 1850
Willoughby of Parham, Peerage Case of H. Willoughby. 3rd series, Vol. 4, p. 519
—— *v*. Willoughby, Case on Prior Mortgage, Debts. Vol. 1, Col. Jur.
Wilmot (F. E.) on Preliminary Education for Profession of Arms. Vol. 10, Pam. 1856
—— (*Sir* J. E.) Biography of (*see* Roscoe's Lives of Lawyers)
—— Memoir, Notes, Opinions, &c. Judgments, 1757–70 . . . . 4to. 1802
Wilson (Geo.) on Fines & Recoveries. 2nd ed. 8vo. 1773
———————————— 3rd ed. 8vo. 1780
—— (*Serjt.* G.) King's Bench & other Reports, 1742–74 . . . 2nd ed. 3 vols. in 2, folio 1779–84
———————————— 3rd ed. 3 vols. 8vo. 1799
———————————— 1746–69
4th ed. 3 vols. 8vo. 1792
—— (*Dr.* H. B.) History of Merchant Taylors' School 4to. 1814
—— Parish of St. Lawrence Pountney . . 4to. 1831
—— on Sequestration. Vol. 1, Pam. 1836

Wilson (*Dr.* H. B.) on Fabric, &c. of St. Mary's,
Aldermanbury. Vol. 1, Pam. 1840
—— Letter to the Parishioners of St. Thomas the
Apostle. Vol. 7, Pam.
—— (J.) & Shaw (P.) House of Lords Reports,
Scotch Appeals, 1825–34. . . 7 vols. 8vo. 1829–39
—— (John) on the Monarchy 12mo. 1684
—— Chancery Reports, 1818-19. 2 vols. in 1, 8vo. 1820
—— Equity Exchequer Reports, 1807–17 . 8vo. 1818
—— (Joseph) Memorabilia Cantabrigiæ, or an
Account of the different Colleges in Cambridge,
&c. 8vo. 1803
—— (Joshua) Biographical Index to House of
Commons 8vo. 1806
—— (Robt.) Outlines of a Plan for the Transfer
of Real Property. Vol. 4, Pam. 1844
—— on Registration of Title to Land . . 8vo. 1860
—— Proposal to the Land Transfer Commissioners
8vo. 1868
—— (T.) & Spence (R.) Eboracum, or History of
York, and Description of Cathedral. 2 vols. 8vo. 1788
—— (*Rev.* T.) Archæological Dictionary
2nd ed. 8vo. 1793
—— (W.) Paper on Prisons, read at the National
Association at Birmingham
Wiltshire, View of, during Election, 1818 . 8vo. 1818
—— Election Poll Book 8vo. 1818
Wimbledon Manor, Extracts from the Court Rolls
of, extending from 1 Edw. IV. to 1666; selected
for use of the Wimbledon Common Committee
8vo. 1866
Winch (*Sir* H.) Entries . . . . folio 1650
—— C. P. Reports, 1622–25 . . . . . folio 1657
Windham (Wm.) Extract of Speech on Mr. Cur-
wen's Reform Bill in 1809. Vol. 12, J. L. T. 1831
Window (   ) Solicitors' Register of the United
Kingdom, 1840-45 . . . . . . 2 vols. 4to.
Wing (V.) Sheet Almanac, 1744-1820 . . folio

Wingate (Edmond) Maximes of Common Law. folio 1658
Winiwarter (J. M. C. de) General Civil Code of
  Austria 8vo. 1866
Winslow (F.) on Lunatics 12mo. 1845
Winstanley (J. W.) Practice of the Chancery of
  Lancashire. 8vo. 1855
Winterbotham (T.) (*see* Tomkins & Jenkins)
Winter & others, Trial, Popish Plot . . . 8vo. 1606
Winterton (Rad.) Poetæ Minores Græci . 12mo. 1684
Wise (E.) Supplement to Burn's Justice . 8vo. 1852
—— (F.) Letter to Dr. Mead as to Antiquities in
  Berks, Bucks, Warwickshire, & Oxon . 4to. 1738
—— Further Observations 1742
Witches, Trial of 8vo. 1682
Witham Institution, Lecture at, on Education.
  Vol. 5, Pam. 1845
Withy (Robt.) on Annuities 8vo. 1800
Witt (F. de) General Atlas . . . . . . folio
Wolferstan (F. S. P.) & Dew (E. L.) Election
  Cases, 1857–58 . . . . 12mo. 1859
—— & Bristow (S. B.) do. 1856–64 . . 12mo. 1865
Wolverhampton, Plan of (*see* Vol. 2, Shaw's Staffordshire)
Women, the Laws of, Resolutions of Women's
  Rights 8vo. 1632
—— & Children employed in Agriculture. Report
                                                      8vo. 1843
Wood (Ant. à) Athenæ Oxonienses, 1500–1690
                       2 vols. in 1, folio 1691–92
———————————— new ed. [the third] by
  P. Bliss . . . . 4 vols. 4to. 1813–20
—— (*Dr*. Wm.) Remarks on Insanity, Plea of &
  Management of. Vol. 9, Pam.
—— (E.) on Conveyancing. 4th ed. 3 vols. folio 1779
———————————— 5th ed. 3 vols. folio 1790
—–— (H.) Decrees on Tithes, 1650–1797. 4 vols.
                                                      8vo. 1798
—— (Jas.) Will Appeal Case, P. C. 6. 2 vols. folio 1840

LAW SOCIETY LIBRARY. 377

Wood (Jno.) History of Bath. 2nd ed. 2 vols. 8vo. 1749
—— (Thos.) Institutes of the Laws of England
           2nd ed. folio 1722
           6th ed. folio 1738
           7th ed. folio 1745
           10th ed. folio 1772
—— (T. L.) Letter to W. L. Lindsay, Esq., on London Health & London Traffic. Vol. 11, Pam.
—— (W. P.) on General Registry, Answers to Objections against. Vol. 10, Jac. Col. . . . 1829
—— (Sir W. P.) Lecture at Exeter Hall to Young Men's Christian Association on Truth and its Counterfeits. Vol. 23, Pam. 1856
Woodburn (S.) Environs of London, Ecclesiastical Topography of the. . . . . 2 vols. in 1, 4to. 1807
Woodcroft (B.) Appendix to English Reaping Patents 4to. 1855
Wooddesson (R.) Vinerian Lectures on the Laws of England . . . . 3 vols. 8vo. 1792
———————————————— (Dr. W. R. Williams) . . . . . 2nd ed. 2 vols. 12mo.
—— (see Toller)
Woodfall (Wm.) Landlord & Tenant. 2nd ed. 8vo. 1804
———————————————— 3rd ed. 8vo. 1811
———————— (S. B. Harrison) . new ed. 8vo. 1831
———————— (S. B. Harrison & F. L. Wollaston)
          4th ed. 2 vols. 8vo. 1840
———————— (F. L. Wollaston) 5th ed. 2 vols. 8vo. 1843
———————— (F. L. Wollaston) . 6th ed. 8vo. 1849
———————— (Hy. Horn) . . . 7th ed. 8vo. 1856
———————— (W. R. Cole) . . 8th ed. 8vo. 1863
———————————————— 9th ed. 8vo. 1867
Woodlock (Wm.) Irish Jurist, 1862–66. 5 vols. 4to.
Woods & Forests, Observations on Land Revenue
               4to. 1707
—— Account of all Manors, &c. . . . . folio 1787
—— 17 Reports of Commissioners, & Index
            2 vols. folio 1787

Woods & Forests, 4 Reports of Surveyor-General
of H. M. Land Revenue, 1797–1809 . . folio 1812
—— 12 Reports of Commissioners, 1812–35
　　　　　　　　　　　　　2 vols. folio
—— Report of Select Committee . . . . folio 1834
—— 4 Reports of Commissioners, 12–15. folio 1835–38
—— 8 Reports of Commissioners, 16–23
　　　　　　　　　　　2 vols. folio 1839–46
—— 3 Reports of Commissioners, 24–26. folio 1847–49
—— (G.) An Account of the Past and the Present State of the Isle of Man, including a topographical descriptive outline of its Laws and a History of the Island 8vo. 1811
Wooller (T. J.) Report as to his Admission to Lincoln's Inn. Vol. 3, Jac. Col. 1826
Woolley (Wm.) Collection of Statutes as to Hull & Sealcoates, Yorkshire 8vo. 1836
Woolrych (H. W.) on Common Rights . . 8vo. 1824
———————————————— 2nd ed. 8vo. 1850
—— Law Officers, series from 1558–1824 . 12mo. 1826
—— on Sewers & Waters 8vo. 1830
———————————— & Drainage. 3rd ed. 8vo. 1864
—— on Window Lights 12mo. 1833
—— on Enclosure Act 12mo. 1837
—— on Criminal Law 12mo. 1837
———————————— as amended by the Statutes of 1861 . . . . 8vo. 1863
—— on Party Walls 8vo. 1845
—— Metropolitan Building Act 12mo. 1856
—— Local Management Act 12mo. 1863
Woolsey (R.) on Mayor's Court Attachment. 8vo. 1816
Woolton (D. John) Christian Manual. Par. S. Pa.
　　　　　　　　　　　　　12mo. 1851
Wordsworth (C.) on Elections 8vo. 1832
————————————————— . . 2nd ed. 8vo. 1835
—— Election Practice 8vo. 1832
————————————————— . . . 12mo. 1865
—— Digest of Election Cases 8vo. 1834

Wordsworth (C.) General Rules and Orders of the
Courts 8vo. 1834
———————————————————— 2nd ed. 8vo. 1835
—— on Joint Stock Companies. . 2nd ed. 12mo. 1837
———————————————— . 4th ed. 8vo. 1845
———————————————— . 5th ed. 8vo. 1854
———————————————— . 6th ed. 8vo. 1856
———————————————— . 7th ed. 12mo. 1857
———————————————— . 8th ed. 8vo. 1860
———————————————— . 10th ed. 8vo. 1865
—— Registration of . . . . . 2nd ed. 8vo. 1843
—— Railways, &c. Companies requiring Sanction
of Parliament . . . . 6th ed. 8vo. 1851
—— on Compensation 8vo. 1863
————————————— . . . . 2nd ed. 12mo. 1866
Worrall (Jno.) Law Catalogue 12mo. 1732
———————————————— 12mo. 1736
—— & Brooke (E.) . . . . . . 2 vols. 12mo. 1788
Worsley (F.) Examination of P. Taylor's Thesis
on Expediency of Passing an Act to Permit
Defendants, their Wives, &c. to Testify on Oath
in Criminal Courts. Vol. 13, Pam.
—— (*Sir* Richd.) History of the Isle of Wight. 4to. 1781
Wotton (Thomas) English Baronetage
1st ed. 3 vols. 12mo. 1721
. ————————————— 2nd ed. 4 vols. in 5 8vo. 1741
Wratislaw (A. H.) on Middle-Class & Non-Gremial
Examinations. Vol. 13, Pam. 1860
—— (W. F.) Biography of the Family . . 4to. 1845
Wright (A.) Court Hand Restored. 3rd ed. 4to. 1786
———————————————————— 4th ed. 4to. 1845
—— (*Rev.* G. S.) Guide to Giant's Causeway,
Antrim 12mo. 1823
—— (Jas.) History of Rutlandshire . . . folio. 1684
—— (*Sir* M.) on Tenures . . . 3rd ed. 8vo. 1768
—— (Thos.) on Anglo-Saxon Literature . 8vo. 1839
—— (T.) (*see* C. S. Pa. Nos. 3, 6, 16, 24, 26, 50)
8vo. 1839

Wright (Thos.) History of Essex . . 2 vols. 4to. 1836
—— Political Songs of England. John to Edw.
II. 1199–1307. C. S. Pa. No. 6 1839
—— Political Poems & Songs relating to English
History, Edw. III. to Ric. III. No. 14 M. R.
Pub. . . . . 2 vols. 8vo. 1859–61
—— (W.) Observations to Mr. Preston on
Chancery Delays & Judges. Vol. 1, Jac. Col. . 1823
—— on Small Debts Bill. Vol. 1, Jac. Col. . . 1821
—— (W.) on Study and Practice of the Law
          3rd ed. 12mo. 1824
Writs, MSS. Register of . . . . 4to.
Wyatt (Jno.) Practical Register in Chancery. 8vo. 1800
Wycliffe (Jno.) (*see* C. S. Pa. No. 20. ed. J. H.
Todd) 1842
Wyld (Jas.) Map of the World . . . . folio 1843
—— Atlas of the World . . . . folio 1853
Wyndham (H. P.) Domesday Book of Wilts. 8vo. 1788
—— Tour through Wales (Sir R. C. Hoare). 4to. 1781
Wynne (E.) Eunomus, or Dialogues on the Law
& Constitution of England. 2nd ed. 4 vols. 8vo. 1785
—— (*Sir* Jno.) Family History of Gwedir. 12mo. 1770
—— (W.) Life of Sir L. Jenkins. . 2 vols. folio 1724
W. (E.) The Body of the Common Law of England 12mo. 1655
—— Observations touching the Antiquity & Dignity
of the Degree of Serjeant-at-Law . . . 8vo. 1765
—— on Justice 12mo. 1661

X

Xenophon. Opera—Anabasis. Vol. 3 only. 12mo. 1839

Y

Yale (G.) on Mining Claims and Water Rights in
California, U. S. 8vo. 1867
Yantlett Creek Trial, Rex v. Montagu (bound up
with London Tracts) 1824
Yates (James) Letter to Vice-Chancellor of England on Lady Hewley's Charity. Vol. 1, L. T.
—— Observations on Lord Russell's Bill for Registering Births. Vol. 3, L. T. 1836
—— (*Rev.* Rd.) Bury St. Edmund's, Monastic
History, &c. of Cathedral 4to. 1805
—— (Wm.) Plan of Lancashire 4to. 1786
Year Books. [Reports of Law Cases from the
Reign of Edward II. to 27 Henry VIII., with
references to the Abridgments of Brooke, Fitzherbert, and Statham, with Indices
11 Parts, in 9 vols. folio 1678–80

> Part I. [Edw. II. Mem. in Scacc. 1–19 Edward I.] Les Reports des Cases argue et adjudge in le temps del Roy Edward le Second, et auxi Memoranda del' Exchequer en temps le Roy Edward le Primer. Sylong les ancients Manuscripts ore remanant en les maines de Sir Jehan Maynard, Chevaler, Serjeant de la Ley, al sa Tres Excellent Majesty Le Roy Charles le Second.
> Part II. [1–10 Edw. III.] Le premier Part de les Reports des Cases en Ley, que furent argues en le temps de le tres Haut et Puissant Prince Roy Edward le Tierce. Ore nouvelment imprimes, corriges & amendes, avec les notations & references a l'abregement de l' tres Reverend & tres Sages Juges de cest Royaulme Brook & Fitzherbert.
> Part III. [17–39 Edw. III.] Le second Part de les Reports.
> Part IV. [40–50 Edw. III.] Les Reports des Cases en Ley que furent argue à quadragesimo ad quinquagesimum annum de tres Haut & Puissant Prince Roy Edward le Tierce. Ore novelment imprimes, corriges & amendes, avec les notations et references al Brook, Fitzherbert, et Statham.

Year Books—*continued*.

Part V. [1-51 Edw. III.] Le Livre des Assises et Pleas del Corone, moves & dependants devant les Justices sibien en lour Circuits come aylours, en temps du Roy Edward le Tiers, avec une Table des principals matters des Pleas del' Corone. Or nouvelment imprime et corrigé; avec une nouvelle Table de touts les principals Cases contenus in cest Livre, & les Titles sous queux Sir Robert Brook les Pleas de ceo ad abbregé: colges, & proprement escrits en le margin de chacun Plea.

Part VI. [Henry le IV. & Henry le V.] Les Reports des Cases en Ley que furent argues en le temps de Tres Haut & Puissant Princes les Roys Henry le IV & Henry le V. Ore novelment imprimes, corriges & amendes, avec les notations & references al Brook, Fitzherbert, & Statham.

Part VII. [1-20 Henry VI.] La premiere part des Ans du Roy Henry le VI. Or nouvellement perusee & corrigee avec les notes marginales. Et une profitable Table annexee a ceo.

Part VIII. [21-39 Henry VI.] Les Reports des Cases contenus in les Ans vingt premier & apres en temps du Roy Henry le VI. Communement appelles, The Second Part of Henry the Sixth, novelment revus et corriges in divers lieux. Avec une table perfecte des choses notables contenus en ycel'. Auxi vous aves in cest impression les Cases icy referres aux abridgments de Brook & Fitzherbert.

Part IX. [1-22 Edw. IV.] Les Reports des Cases en Ley que furent argues en temps du Roy Edward le Quart. Avec les notations de Tres Reverend Judges Brook & Fitzherbert. Et autre references n'unques devant imprimee. Ovesque un Table perfect des choses notables contenus en ycel.

Part X. [5 Edw. IV.] Les Reports des Cases en Ley en le cinque An du Roy Edward le Quart. Communement appelle Long Quinto. Novelment imprimee et corrigee, ovesque references al Brook et un Table perfect.

Part XI. [Edw. V.-Henry VIII.] Les Reports des Cases en les ans des Roys Edward V, Richard III, Henrie VII & Henry VIII. Touts qui par cy devant ont este publies. Or nouvellement imprime, corrige, et revieue: ovesque plusieurs bonnes Notes en la marge par tout le Livre; qui referrent les Cases al Abbregement de Brook, & autres livres des Ans. Aussi avec plusieurs notes fort profitables or nouvellement addez en l'autre marge, referrantes aux autres Reports, et livres del Ley, & aussi aux mesmes livres des Ans.

Year Books. 20 & 21, 1292-3, & 30 & 31, & 32 & 33
of Edw. I. 1302-5 (edited & translated by Alfred
J. Horwood;) 31 M. R. Pub. . 3 vols. 8vo. 1863-66
Yelverton (Sir H.) Argument respecting Impositions, Law. T. 1641
Yelverton (Sir H.) K. B. Reports . . . folio 1661
——————————————————. 2nd ed. folio 1674
——————————————————. 3rd ed. folio 1734
Yonge (W.) Diary of No. 41, C. S. Pa. 1604-28
(G. Roberts) 4to. 1848
Yool (G. V.) on Waste, Nuisance, and Trespass
8vo. 1863
York, Election Poll Book 8vo. 1727
——————————————— 8vo. 1754-80
——————————————— 8vo. 1807
Yorke (C.) on Forfeiture. . . . 2nd ed. 8vo. 1746
———————————— with an Appendix con-
cerning Estates tail in Scotland . 3rd ed. 8vo. 1748
———————————— . . . . . 4th ed. 12mo. 1788
—— on the Law of the Nobility of the Realm. 12mo. 1642
Yorkshire, from Camden Magna Brit. . . 4to. n. d.
Young (C.) Table of Precedency 8vo. 1841
—— (Rev. G.) History of Whitby & Streones-
halh Abbey, &c. . . . . 2 vols. 8vo. 1817
—— (Jno.) Catalogue of Autograph Letters 4to. 1863
—— (Wm.) Statutes as to Justices of the Peace
12mo. 1660
—— Clerk's Manual 12mo. 1672
—— (see Nova Scotia Statutes)
Younge (Edw.) Equity Exchequer Reports, 1830-
32 . . . . 8vo. 1833
—— Report Small v. Attwood 8vo. 1833
—— (E.) & Collyer (Jno.) Equity Exchequer
Reports, 1834-40 . . . . 4 vols. 8vo. 1836-40
———————————————— Chancery Reports,
V.-C. Bruce, 1841-44 . . . 2 vols. 8vo. 1843-44
—— & Jervis (J.) Exchequer Reports, 1826-30
3 vols. 8vo. 1828-30

Z

Zabrocki (*Lieut.* C. D. B.) Account of General Georgey's Surrender to the Russians. Vol. 9, Pam.

Zenger, Trial at New York for Libel before C. J. of the Province, in 1735. Vol. 2, Tracts on Libel 1738

Zizaniorum Fasciculi Magistri Johannis Wyclif cum Tritico, ascribed to Thos. Netter. (Ed. by W. W. Shirley.) 3 M. R. Pub. . . . 8vo. 1858

Zouch (R.) Civil Law 12mo. 1652

—— Peerage Case and Pedigree of Sir C. Bisshopp, & Appendix. Vol. 4, 3rd series, p. 520, &c. Evidence, Vol. 13

Zulueta (P. de) Trial for Slave Trading. . 8vo. 1844

REPORTS,

IN ALL THE COURTS IN CHRONOLOGICAL ORDER.

REPORTER	Period	Vols.	Size	Date
HOUSE OF LORDS.				
Colles	1697 to 1713	1	8vo	1789
Brown	1701 to 1779	7	folio	1779 to 1783
——	1701 to 1779	7	8vo	1784
—— (Tomlin's) . 2nd edit.	1702 to 1800	8	8vo	1803
Shower	. .	1	folio	1698 to 1708
—— . . . 3rd edit.	1694 to 1699	1	folio	1740
Dow	1812 to 1818	6	8vo	1814 to 1819
Bligh	1819 to 1821	4	8vo	1823 to 1827
—— New Series	1827 to 1837	11	8vo	1829 to 1837
Dow & Clark	1827 to 1832	2	8vo	1830 to 1832
Clark & Finnelly	1831 to 1846	12	8vo	1835 to 1846
—————— N. S.	1847 to 1850	2	8vo	1849 to 1851
.	1850 to 1866	9	8vo	1853 to 1866
Index of Cases, 1814 to 1865	. .	1	8vo	1868
West	1839 to 1841	1	8vo	1842
Law Reports	1866 to 1868	3	8vo	1866 to 1868
Leahy's Report of Lord Denman's Judgment in O'Connell v. Regina	1844	1	8vo	1844
SCOTCH APPEAL CASES.				
Robertson	1707 to 1727	1	8vo	1807
Craigie, Stewart, & Paton	1726 to 1821	6	8vo	1849 to 1856
Shaw's	1821 to 1824	2	8vo	1826 to 1828
Robinson's	1840 to 1841	2	8vo	1840 to 1842
Bell's	1842 to 1852	6	8vo	1849 to 1856
Wilson & Shaw	1832 to 1834	2	8vo	1838 to 1839
Shaw & M'Clean	1835 to 1838	3	8vo	1836 to 1839
M'Clean & Robinson	1839	1	8vo	1840

REPORTER	Period	Vols.	Size	Date
SCOTCH APPEAL CASES *—continued.*				
Robinson's Report of Dalhousie *v.* M'Douall . . .	1840	1	8vo	1840
Macqueen	1851 to 1865	4	8vo	1855 to 1866
Law Reports	1866 to 1868	3	8vo	1866 to 1868
PRIVY COUNCIL APPEALS.				
Acton	1809 to 1811	2 in 1	8vo	1811
Serjeant Rough's Case *v.* Murray .	. .	1	8vo	1825
Knapp	1829 to 1836	3	8vo	1831 to 1836
Moore, E. F.	1836 to 1846	15	8vo	1837 to 1866
—————— N. S. . . .	1862 to 1866	4	8vo	1864 to 1866
—————— Indian Appeals .	1837 to 1866	11	8vo	1867
—————— The Gorham Case .	1852	1	8vo	1852
—————— Westerton *v.* Liddell	. .	1	8vo	1857
Hodge's Report of Long *v.* Bishop of Cape Town . . .	. .	1	8vo	1866
Law Reports	1865 to 1868	2	8vo	1866 to 1868
IRISH HOUSE OF LORDS.				
Ridgway	1784 to 1796	3	8vo	1795 to 1798
CHANCERY.				
Brookes' New Cases (March) .	Temp. Hen. 8, &c.	1	12mo	1651
Tothill (Holborne's) . . .	Temp. Hen. 8, &c.	1	12mo	1820
Dickens	1559 to 1792	2	8vo	1803
———	. .	1	12mo	1650
Cary	Temp. Eliz.	1	12mo	1820
Rayner's Tithe Cases . . .	1575 to 1782	3	8vo	1783
Nelson	1625 to 1692	1	8vo	1717
Special Cases	1625 to 1714	3 in 1	folio	1736
———	1670 to 1706	1	folio	1742
Freeman, (Hovenden) . 2nd edit.	1660 to 1706	1	8vo	1823
Cases in . . . 3rd edit.	1660 to 1678	3 in 1	folio	1735
———, Special	1669 to 1693	1	8vo	1694
——— . 3rd edit.	. .	3 in 1	folio	1736
Choice Cases	1672	1	12mo	1672
Finch, Sir H. (his own time) .	1673 to 1680	1	folio	1725
Vernon, ed. W. P. Williams and W. Melmoth . .	1681 to 1719	2	folio	1726 to 1728
Vernon, (Raithby) . 3rd edit.	1680 to 1719	2	8vo	1828
Precedents in Chancery . .	1669 to 1722	1	folio	1733
—————— Finch, 2nd ed. .	. .	1	8vo	1786

REPORTER	Period	Vols.	Size	Date
CHANCERY—*continued.*				
Williams (P.) (Cox) 4th edit.	1695 to 1734	3	8vo	1787
—— (Cox) . . 5th edit.	. .	3	8vo	1793
. .	. .	1	folio	1734
—— 6th ed. Munro, Lowndes, & Randall	. .	3	8vo	1826
Gilbert, Lord C. B. . 2nd edit.	1706 to 1725	1	8vo	1742
———————— (K. B. & Chy)	1713 to 1714	1	8vo	1760
Select Cases, Temp. King . .	1724 to 1733	1	folio	1740
———————— (Macnaghten) 2nd edit.	. .	1	folio	1850
Mosley, Temp. King . . .	1726 to 1730	1	8vo	1793
Equity Cases abridged . .	1732	1	folio	1732
Cases, Temp. Talbot (Williams) 2nd edit.	. .	1	8vo	1753
———————————— 3rd edit.	1733 to 1737	1	8vo	1792
Atkyns, Temp. Hardwicke . .	1736 to 1754	3	folio	1765
———————— . .	. .	3	8vo	1781
———————— (Sanders) 3rd edit.	. .	3	8vo	1794
West, Temp. Hardwicke . .	1736 to 1739	1	8vo	1817
Kelynge, Lord W. . . .	1730 to 1735	1	folio	1764
Barnardiston, T.	1740 to 1741	1	folio	1742
Vesey, senior, Temp. Hardwicke	. .	2	folio	1771
———————— 2nd edit.	1746 to 1755	2	folio	1773
——, Belt's, and Supplement. 4th edit.	. .	3	8vo	1818 to 1825
Eden (Lord Henley) . . .	1757 to 1766	2	8vo	1827
Wilmot, Sir E., Notes & Judgments	1757 to 1770	1	4to	1802
Ambler	1760 to 1756	1	folio	1790
—— (Blunt) 2nd edit. . .	1737 to 1783	2	8vo	1828
Equity Cases abridged. 4th edit. . .	. .	2	folio	1756
(Vol. I. 5th edit.; Vol. II. 2nd edit. . . .	1769 to 1793	2	folio	1769 to 1793
Brown	1778 to 1785	4	folio	1785
—— . . . 2nd edit.	1778 to 1794	4	folio	1794
—— (Belt's) . . 5th edit.	1778 to 1794	4	8vo	1820
Cox . . . . 5th edit.	1783 to 1796	2	8vo	1816
Vesey, junior, with Index & Hovenden's Supplement, 2nd edit.	1789 to 1817	22	8vo	1827
Vesey & Beames, Temp. Eldon, 2nd edit.	1812 to 1814	3	8vo	1818
Cooper, G.	1815	1	8vo	1815
Merivale, Temp. Eldon . .	1815 to 1817	3	8vo	1817 to 1819
Daniel (Equity Exchequer) . .	1817 to 1820	1	8vo	1824
Swanston	1818 to 1819	3		1821 to 1827

c c 2

REPORTER	Period	Vols.	Size	Date
CHANCERY—*continued.*				
Wilson (Vol. I. pts. 1, 2, 3; Vol. II. pt. 1.)	1818 to 1819	- -	8vo	1820
Jacob & Walker	1819 to 1821	2	8vo	1821 to 1823
Jacob	1821 to 1822	1	8vo	1828
Turner & Russell . . .	1822 to 1824	1	8vo	1832
Russell	1826 to 1828	5	8vo	1827 to 1831
Russell & Mylne	1829 to 1831	2	8vo	1832 to 1837
Younge (Equity Exchequer) .	1830 to 1832	1	8vo	1833
Mylne & Keen	1831 to 1835	3	8vo	1834 to 1837
Cooper, C. P., Select Cases, Temp. Brougham . .	1832 to 1834	1	8vo	1835
Younge's Report, Small *v.* Atwood	.1833	1	8vo	1833
Railway Cases, Law & Equity .	1835 to 1847	4	8vo	1835 to 1848
Cooper, C. P., Points of Practice .	1837 to 1838	1	8vo	1841
Mylne & Craig	1837 to 1848	5	8vo	1837 to 1848
Rugby School, Report of Proceedings before Lord Langdale	1839	1	8vo	1839
Craig & Phillips	1840 to 1841	1	8vo	1842
Phillips	1841 to 1849	2	8vo	1847 to 1849
Cooper, C. P., Temp. Cottenham .	1846 to 1847	1	8vo	1847
Cripps' Clergy Law Cases . .	1846 to 1850	1	8vo	
Hall & Twells, Temp. Cottenham .	1848 to 1850	2	8vo	1850 to 1851
Macnaghten & Gordon ditto .	1849 to 1851	3	8vo	1850 to 1852
Equity Reports	1853 to 1855	3 in 4	8vo	1854 to 1855
De Gex, Macnaghten, & Gordon .	1851 to 1857	8	8vo	1853 to 1864
De Gex & Jones	1857 to 1859	4	8vo	1858 to 1861
De Gex, Fisher, & Jones . .	1859 to 1861	3	8vo	1861 to 1867
De Gex, Jones, & Smith (Vol. III. pt. 1, 1865.)	1862 to 1865	2	8vo	1865 to 1866
Law Reports, Chancery Appeals .	1865 to 1868	3	8vo	1866 to 1868
———————— Equity .	1865 to 1868	6	8vo	1866 to 1868
Henry *v.* Gt. Western Railway Company (Tolcher's Report) .	1857	1	8vo	1858
New Reports, Equity & Com. Law	1862 to 1865	6	4to	1865
Weekly Reporter, Law & Equity .	1852 to 1868	16	4to	1853 to 1858
——————— Digest . .	1852 to 1859	2	4to	
ROLLS COURT.				
Tumlyn, Temp. Leach . .	1829 to 1830	1	8vo	1831
Keen, Temp. Langdale . .	1836 to 1839	2	8vo	1837 to 1839
Beavan, Temp. Langdale & Romilly (*Subsequent Reports are included in* CHANCERY.)	1838 to 1866	35	8vo	1840 to 1867

REPORTER	Period	Vols.	Size	Date
CHANCERY—*continued.* **VICE-CHANCELLORS' COURTS.**				
Maddock, Temp. V. CC. Plumer & Leach	1815 to 1822	6	8vo	1817 to 1829
Simons & Stuart, Temp. V. C. Leach	1822 to 1826	2	8vo	1825 to 1827
Simons, Temp. V. C. Leach . .	1826 to 1852	17	8vo	1829 to 1854
Simons (N.S.), Temp.V.CC. Shadwell, Cranworth & Kindersley .	1850 to 1852	2	8vo	1851 to 1852
Drewry, Temp. V. C. Kindersley.	1852 to 1859	4	8vo	1852 to 1860
Drewry & Smale, Temp. V. C. Kindersley	1859 to 1865	2	8vo	1862 to 1867
Younge & Collyer, Temp. V. C. K. Bruce	1841 to 1844	2	8vo	1843 to 1845
Collyer, Temp. V. C. K. Bruce .	1844 to 1846	2	8vo	1845 to 1847
De Gex & Smale, Temp. V. CC. Bruce & Parker . . .	1846 to 1852	5	8vo	1846 to 1852
Smale & Giffard, Temp. V. C. Stuart	1852 to 1857	3	8vo	1855 to 1858
Giffard, Temp. V. C. Stuart. .	1858 to 1864	4	8vo	1860 to 1867
Hare, Temp. V. CC. Bruce, Wigram, Turner & Wood . .	1841 to 1853	11	8vo	1847 to 1853
Kay, Temp. V. C. Wood . .	1853 to 1854	1	8vo	1854
Kay & J., V. C. Wood . .	1854 to 1858	4	8vo	1857 to 1859
Johnson, V. C. Wood . . .	1858 to 1860	1	8vo	1860
Johnson & Heming, V. C. Wood .	1859 to 1863	2	8vo	1861 to 1863
Heming & Miller, V. C. Wood .	1862 to 1865	2	8vo	1864 to 1866
IRISH CHANCERY.				
Scholes & Lefroy, Temp. Redesdale	1802 to 1804	2	8vo	1806 to 1821
Ball & Beatty	1807 to 1814	2	8vo	1824
Hogan (Rolls)	1816 to 1833	2	8vo	1828 to 1838
Beatty, Temp. Hart . . .	1827 to 1829	1	8vo	1829
Molloy, Temp. Hart . . .	1827 to 1828	3	8vo	1827 to 1833
Lloyd & Goold, Temp. Plunkett .	1834 to 1836	1	8vo	1839
Drury and Walsh . . .	1837 to 1840	2	8vo	1839 to 1842
Sausse & Scully, Temp. O'Loughlen (Rolls) .	1837 to 1840	1	8vo	1841
Irish Equity	1838 to 1850	13	8vo	1839 to 1848
Flannagan & Kelly (Rolls) . .	1840 to 1842	1	8vo	1843
Connor & Lawson . . .	1841 to 1843	2	8vo	1842 to 1844
Drury & Warren . . .	1841 to 1843	4	8vo	1843 to 1846
Drury, Temp. Sugden . . .	1843	pt. 1	8vo	1843
Jones & Latouche, Temp. Sugden .	1844 to 1846	3	8vo	1846 to 1849
Lloyd & Goold, Temp. Sugden .	1845	1	8vo	1846
Irish Chancery, N. S. . . .	1850 to 1866	17	8vo	1852 to 1867

REPORTER	Period	Vols.	Size	Date
IRISH CHANCERY—*continued.*				
Irish Chancery (Select Cases), Drury	Temp. Napier	1	8vo	1860
——— Law Reports	1867 to 1868	2	8vo	1867 to 1868
QUEEN'S BENCH.				
Year Books in Eleven Parts, forming 9 vols., viz.				
Part 1. 1 to 19 Edw. 2	1307 to 1325	1	folio	1678
2. First 10 years of Edw. 3.	1327 to 1336	1	folio	1679
3 & 4. 17th to 50th Edw. 3.	1343 to 1376	1	folio	1679
5. Liber Assisarium, or Pleas of the Crown	Temp. Ed. 3.	1	folio	1679
6. ———	Temp. H. 4. and 5.	1	folio	1679
7 & 8. ———	Temp H. 6.	1	folio	1679
9. ———	Annals Ed. 4.	1	folio	1680
10. ———	Long Ed. 4. Quinto.	1	folio	1680
11. ———	Temp. Ed. 5, to R. 3. H. 7. and 8.	1	folio	1679
Ashe's Index	. .	2	folio	1614
Moore, Sir F.	1485 to 1617	1	folio	1662
——— Palmer. 2nd edit.	1615	1	folio	1675
Edward 4, Temp. 5 Anno	1465	1	folio	1638
Keilway (Croke) Temp. Hen. 7 & 8 3rd edit.	1496 to 1574	1	folio	1688
Dyer, translated by Vaillant	1513 to 1593	3	8vo	1794
——— . . . 2nd edit.	1527 to 1581	1	folio	1672
Plowden	1548 to 1571	1	folio	1571
———	1548 to 1578	2	8vo	1816
Coke (in French)	1568 to 1611	4	4to	1601 to 1672
———	. .	4	folio	1697
——— (Wilson)	1572 to 1615	7	8vo	1793
——— Ashe's Table of	. .	1	12mo	1696
——— New Ed. with Notes by Thomas and Frazer, Index by Tyrwhitt	. .	6	8vo	1826
Godbolt	1574 to 1638	1	4to	1653
Croke	1581 to 1641	3	4to	1661
——— (Grimstone) 2nd edit.	. .	3	folio	1669
Leonard	1582 to 1615	1	folio	1658
——— (Hughes) 2nd edit.	. .	4 in 2	folio	1687
Owen	1583 to 1615	1	folio	1656
Gouldsborough	1585 to 1603	1	4to	1653
Popham	1591 to 1651	1	folio	1682
Noys	1595	1	folio	1656

REPORTS. 391

REPORTER	Period	Vols.	Size	Date
QUEEN'S BENCH—*continued.*				
Yelverton	1602 to 1613	1	folio	1661
——— . . . 2nd edit.	. .	1	folio	1674
——— . . . 3rd edit.	. .	1	folio	1735
Bulstrode . . . 2nd edit.	1603 to 1649	1	folio	1688
Coke's 5th Report, Answer to (Parsons) . . . }	1606	1	folio	1606
Rolle, Sir H.	1614 to 1625	2	folio	1675
Bridgman, Sir Jno. . . .	1615 to 1620	1	folio	1659
Palmer, Sir G.	1619 to 1653	1	folio	1678
Ley	1619 to 1629	1	folio	1659
Jones, Sir W.	1620 to 1641	1	folio	1675
Latch	1625 to 1628	1	folio	1661
March . . . 2nd edit.	1639 to 1643	1	4to	1675
Saunders	1642 to 1673	1	4to	1686
———	. .	6	8vo	1799
——— (Patteson & Williams) 5th edit. }	. .	3	8vo	1824
Styles	1645 to 1655	1	8vo	1658
Alleyn	1646 to 1649	1	folio	1681
Kelyng, Sir John, Temp. Car. II..	. .	1	folio	1708
Siderfin, Sir T.	. .	2 in 1	folio	1683
———	1659 to 1671	1	folio	1714
Raymond, Sir T. . . .	1660 to 1684	1	folio	1696
——— . . . 3rd edit.	. .	1	folio	1743
Pollexfen	1660 to 1683	1	folio	1702
Levinz's	. .	2	folio	1702
——— . (Sulkold) 2nd edit.	1660 to 1696	3 in 2	folio	1722
Keble	1661 to 1671	3	folio	1685
Ventris . . . 2nd edit.	. .	2	folio	1701
——— . . . 4th edit.	1668 to 1692	2 in 1	folio	1726
Parker (Temp. Geo. I.). 2nd edit.	. .	1	folio	1729
Modern (Leach's) . 5th edit.	1669 to 1700	12	8vo	1796
Jones, Sir T. . . 2nd edit.	1670 to 1685	1	folio	1729
Freeman. Law & Equity by Dixon	1670 to 1706	2 in 1	folio	1742
Skinner	1671 to 1697	1	folio	1728
Shower	. .	2	folio	1708 to 1720
——— . . . 2nd edit.	1679 to 1694	2	folio	1792
Comberbach	1685 to 1695	1	folio	1724
Carthew	. .	1	folio	1728
——— . . . 2nd edit.	1688 to 1639	1	folio	1741
Holt, Sir Jno.	1688 to 1710	1	folio	1738
Raymond, Lord . . .	. .	2	folio	1743
——— . . . 3rd edit.	1694 to 1730	2	folio	1775
——— (Bayley) 4th edit.	. .	3	8vo	1792
——— (Gale) 5th edit.	. .	1	8vo	1832
Salkeld	1695 to 1704	2 in 1	folio	1721

REPORTER	Period	Vols.	Size	Date
QUEEN'S BENCH—*continued.*				
Salkeld . . . 2nd edit.	. .	3 in 1	folio	1724
——— (Wilson) . 5th edit.	. .	3 in 1	folio	1773
——— (Evans) . 5th edit.	. .	3	8vo	1795
Comyn (Rose's) . . 2nd. edit.	1695 to 1739	2	8vo	1792
Cases, Temp. Holt (W. B.'s) 3rd edit.	1703 to 1705	1	folio	1733
Settlement Cases, Temp. Parker. 2nd edit.	1710 to 1727	1	8vo	1729
Fortescue	1711 to 1731	1	folio	1748
Strange	. .	2	folio	1754
——— . . . 2nd edit.	. .	2	8vo	1782
——— (Nolan) . . 3rd edit.	1716 to 1747	2	8vo	1795
Barnardiston, R. . . .	1724 to 1734	2	folio	1744
Fitzgibbon	1728 to 1732	1	folio	1732
Burrow's Settlement Cases, 2nd edit.	1732 to 1776	1	4to	1786
Cunningham . . 2nd edit.	1733 to 1736	1	folio	1770
Lee's Cases, Temp. Hardwicke .	1733 to 1736	1	8vo	1815
Ridgway's Cases, Temp. Hardwicke	1733 to 1745	1	8vo	1794
Andrews (Vernon) . . .	1738 to 1790	1	8vo	1791
——————— . . . 2nd edit.	. .	3 in 2	folio	1779 to 1784
Wilson . . 3rd edit. (Vol. I. K. B., II. and III. C. P.)	1743 to 1773	3	8vo.	1799
——————— 4th edit.	. .	3	8vo.	1792
Blackstone, Wm. . . .	1746 to 1779	2	folio	1781
——————— (Elsley's) 2nd ed.	. .	2	8vo	1828
Sayer	1751 to 1757	1	folio	1775
Kenyon's Notes (Hanmer) . .	1753 to 1759	2	8vo.	1819 to 1825
Burrow	1756 to 1770	4	folio	1766
——— . . . 3rd edit.	1756 to 1772	5	folio	1777 to 1780
——— . . . 4th edit.	. .	5	8vo	1790
——— . . . 5th edit.	. .	5	8vo	1812
Loft's	1771 to 1774	1	folio	1776
Cowper . . . 2nd edit.	1774 to 1778	2	8vo	1800
Caldecott's Settlement Cases .	1776 to 1785	1	4to	1786
Douglas	1779 to 1781	1	folio	1733
———	. .	1	folio	1786
——— . . . 3rd edit.	1778 to 1781	2	8vo	1790
——— . (Frere) 4th edit.	1778 to 1785	4	8vo	1813 to 1831
Davies' Patent Cases . . .	1785	1	8vo	1816
Durnford & East, or Term Reports	1785 to 1800	8	folio	1800
——————— 4th edit.	. .	8	8vo	1794 to 1802
Cases & Opinions . . .	. .	2	8vo	1791
Hunt's Annuity Cases . . .	1794	1	8vo	1794
East	1801 to 1814	16	8vo	1801 to 1814
Smith	1803 to 1806	3	8vo	1803 to 1806
Maule & Selwyn	1813 to 1817	6	8vo	1813 to 1817

REPORTER	Period	Vols.	Size	Date
QUEEN'S BENCH—*continued.*				
Barnewall & Alderson	1818 to 1822	5	8vo	1818 to 1822
Chitty	1819 to 1820	2	8vo	1820 to 1823
Dowling & Ryland	1822 to 1828	9	8vo	1822 to 1831
Barnewall & Cresswell	1823 to 1830	10	8vo	1823 to 1832
Manning & Ryland	1827 to 1829	5	8vo	1827 to 1830
Danson & Lloyd's Commercial Cases	1828 to 1829	1	8vo	1830
Lloyd & Welsby's Commercial Cases	1829 to 1830	1	8vo	1830
Barnewall & Adolphus.	1830 to 1834	5	8vo	1831 to 1835
Dowling's Practice Reports	1830 to 1841	9	8vo	1833 to 1842
Neville & Manning	1832 to 1836	6	8vo	1834 to 1839
Adolphus & Ellis	1834 to 1841	12	8vo	1835 to 1842
Harrison & Wollaston	1835 to 1837	2	8vo	1836 to 1837
Neville & Perry	1836 to 1838	3	8vo	1837 to 1838
Smith's Leading Cases		2	8vo	1837
——— 2nd edit.		2	8vo	1841
——— (Keating & Willis) 3rd edit.		2	8vo	1849
——— (Willis & Keating) 4th edit.		2	8vo	1856
——— (Maude & Chitty) 5th edit.		2	8vo	1862
——— 6th edit.		2	8vo	1867
Perry & Davison	1838 to 1841	4	8vo	1839 to 1842
Willmore, Wollaston, & Davison	1839	1	8vo	1839
Willmore, Wollaston, & Hodges	1840	1	8vo	1840
Adolphus & Ellis (Queen's Bench Reports)	1841 to 1852	18	8vo	1842 to 1856
Dowling's Practice, New Reports	1841 to 1843	2	8vo	1843 to 1844
Gale & Davison	1841 to 1843	3	8vo	1841 to 1843
Davison & Merivale	1843 to 1844	1	8vo	1844
Dowling & Lowndes	1843 to 1849	7	8vo	1845 to 1856
Sanders & Cole (Bail Court Reports)	1846 to 1848	2	8vo	1847 to 1849
Jebb's Report of Dr. Hampden's Case	1848	1	8vo	1848
Bittleston & Wise, New Practice Cases	1844 to 1848	3	8vo	1844 to 1848
Lowndes, Maxwell, & Pollock	1850 to 1851	2	8vo	1851 to 1852
——— & Maxwell	1852 to 1854	1	8vo	1852 to 1854
Roberts, Leeming, & Wallis, County Court Cases		1	8vo	1849 to 1851
Ellis & Blackburn, Q. B. Reports	1852 to 1858	8	8vo	1853 to 1859
———, Blackburn, & Ellis, Q. B. Reports	1858 to 1859	1	8vo	1860
——— & Ellis, Q. B. Reports	1858 to 1861	3	8vo	1865 to 1867
Common Law Reports	1853 to 1855	5	8vo	1854 to 1855
Webster's Patent Cases, Temp. Elizabeth to 1854		2	8vo	1844 to 1855
Macrory's Patent Reports		1	8vo	1852 to 1855

REPORTER	Period	Vols.	Size	Date
QUEEN'S BENCH—*continued.*				
Best & Smith, Q. B. Reports	1861 to 1865	5	8vo	1862 to 1866
Law Reports	1865 to 1868	3	8vo	1866 to 1868
COMMON PLEAS.				
Benloe & Dalison	1440 to 1574	1	folio	1689
Saville, Sir J.	1579 to 1594	1	folio	1687
Anderson, Sir E. 2 Parts.	Temp. Eliz.	1	folio	1664 to 1665
Brownlow & Goldesborough Part I.	Temp. Eliz. and James I.	1	4to	1651
——————— 3rd edit. Parts I. and II.	Temp. Eliz. and James I.	1	4to	1675
Hobart, Sir H.		1	folio	1641
——————— 4th edit.	1613 to 1644	1	folio	1678
Hutton . . . 2nd edit.	1616 to 1628	1	folio	1682
Winch, Sir H.	1622 to 1625	1	folio	1657
Littleton	1626 to 1632	1	folio	1683
Hetley, Sir T.	1628 to 1631	1	folio	1657
Bridgman, Sir O.	1660 to 1667	1	8vo	1823
Carter	1664 to 1688	1	folio	1688
Vaughan	1666 to 1673	1	folio	1677
Lutwyche, Sir E.	1682 to 1704	1	folio	1704
Cook, Cases & Rules	1706 to 1740	1	folio	1742
Barnes, Notes of Cases		2	8vo	1754
——————— 2nd edit.		1	4to	1772
——————— 3rd edit.	1753 to 1756	1	8vo	1790
Willes	1734 to 1758	1	folio	1799
Blackstone, H. . . 3rd edit.	1788 to 1796	2	8vo	1801
Bosanquet & Puller . 3rd edit.	1796 to 1804	3	8vo	1826
———————, New Reports 2nd edit.	1804 to 1807	2	8vo	1827
Taunton	1807 to 1819	8	8vo	1814 to 1823
Marshall	1813 to 1816	2	8vo	1815 to 1817
Moore, J. B.	1815 to 1827	12	8vo	1818 to 1831
Broderip & Bingham	1818 to 1822	3	8vo	1821 to 1823
Bingham	1822 to 1834	10	8vo	1824 to 1834
Moore & Payne	1827 to 1831	5	8vo	1828 to 1832
Moore & Scott	1831 to 1834	4	8vo	1833 to 1834
Bingham, New Cases	1834 to 1840	6	8vo	1835 to 1841
Scott	1834 to 1840	8	8vo	1835 to 1841
Hodges	1835 to 1837	3	8vo	1836 to 1839
Arnold	1838 to 1839	1	8vo	1840
Manning & Granger	1840 to 1844	7	8vo	1841 to 1846
Scott's New Reports	1840 to 1845	8	8vo	1841 to 1845

REPORTER	Period	Vols.	Size	Date
COMMON PLEAS—*continued.*				
Manning, Granger, & Scott, Common Bench Reports	1845 to 1850	9	8vo	1847 to 1856
Scott's, C. B.	1850 to 1856	9	. .	1852 to 1856
———— Index to the 18 vols.		1	8vo	1858
———— C. B., New Series	1856 to 1865	20	8vo	1857 to 1866
Lutwyche's Registration Cases	1843 to 1853	2	8vo	1847 to 1854
Keane & Grant Do.	1854 to 1862	1	8vo	1863
Hopwood & Philbrick Do.	1863 to 1867	1	8vo	1867
Law Reports	1865 to 1868	3	8vo	1866
EXCHEQUER.				
Eagle & Younge	1204 to 1820	4	8vo	1826
Jenkyns 2nd edit.	1220 to 1623	1	folio	1734
Gwillim 2nd edit.	1285 to 1824	4	8vo	1825
Rayner's Tithe Cases	1575 to 1782	3	8vo	1783
Lane	1605 to 1612	1	folio	1657
Wood's Decrees on Tithes	1650 to 1797	4	8vo	1798
Hardres	1655 to 1660	1	folio	1693
Bunbury	. . .	1	folio	1755
————	1714 to 1760	1	8vo	1791
Parker	1743 to 1766	1	folio	1776
Anstruther	1791 to 1796	3	8vo	1797
Forrest	1800 to 1801	1	8vo	1802
Wightwick	1810 to 1811	1	8vo	1819
Price	1813 to 1825	13	8vo	1816 to 1828
Wilson (Equity Exchequer)	1817	1	8vo	1818
Assessed Taxes, Decisions of the Judges	1823 to 1865	7	folio	1823 to 1865
M'Cleland	1823 to 1824	1	8vo	1825
M'Cleland & Younge	1824 to 1826	1	8vo	1827
Younge & Jervis	1827 to 1830	3	8vo	1828 to 1830
Crompton & Jervis	1830 to 1832	2	8vo	1832 to 1833
Tyrwhitt	1830 to 1835	5	8vo	1832 to 1837
Crompton & Meeson	1832 to 1834	2	8vo	1834 to 1835
Crompton, Meeson, & Roscoe	1834 to 1836	2	8vo	1835 to 1836
Tyrwhitt & Granger	1835 to 1836	1	8vo	1837
Gale	1835 to 1836	2	8vo	1836 to 1838
Meeson & Welsby, & Index	1836 to 1847	17	8vo	1836 to 1849
Murphy & Hurlstone	1836 to 1837	1	8vo	1838
Horn & Hurlstone	1838 to 1839	1	8vo	1840
Welsby, Hurlstone, & Gordon	1847 to 1856	9	8vo	1848 to 1854
Hurlstone & Gordon	1854 to 1856	2	8vo	1855 to 1856
———— & Norman	1856 to 1862	7	8vo	1857 to 1862

REPORTER	Period	Vols.	S'ze	Date
EXCHEQUER—*continued.*				
Hurlstone & Coltman . . .	1862 to 1865	3	8vo	1863 to 1866
Law Reports	1865 to 1868	3	8vo	1866 to 1868
NISI PRIUS.				
Clayton	1651	1	12mo	1651
Peake	1790 to 1812	2	8vo	1820 to 1829
Espinasse	1793 to 1807	6	8vo	1796 to 1811
Campbell	1807 to 1816	4	8vo	1809 to 1816
Starkie	1815 to 1823	3	8vo	1816 to 1823
Holt	1815 to 1817	1	8vo	1818
Gow . . . 2nd edit.	1818 to 1820	1	8vo	1828
Manning's Digest of N. P. Cases 2nd edit.	1820	1	8vo	1820
Ryan & Moody	1823 to 1826	1	8vo	1827
Carrington & Payne . . .	1823 to 1839	9	8vo	1825 to 1847
Moody & Malkin . . .	1826 to 1830	1	8vo	1831
Moody & Robinson . . .	1830 to 1844	2	8vo	1837 to 1844
Carrington & Marshman . .	1842	1	8vo	1843
Carrington & Kirwan . . .	1843 to 1852	3	8vo	1845 to 1852
Foster & Finlason . . .	1856 to 1867	4	8vo	1860 to 1867
See also BULLER, SELWYN, & A. J. STEPHENS' " NISI PRIUS."				
IRISH COMMON LAW, &c.				
Davies, Sir John . . .	1603 to 1610	1	8vo	1762
Vernon & Scriven . . .	1786 to 1788	1	8vo	1790
Jebb, Crown Cases Reserved .	1822 to 1840	1	8vo	1841
Hayes (Exchequer) . . .	1830 to 1832	1	8vo	1837
Alcock & Napier . . .	1831 to 1833	1	8vo	1834
Heyes & Jones (Exchequer) .	1832 to 1834	1	8vo	1843
Cooke & Alcock	1833 to 1834	1	8vo	1834
Jones (Exchequer) . . .	1834 to 1838	2	8vo	1838 to 1847
Hudson & Brooke . . .	1837 to 1838	1	8vo	1839
Jones & Carey (Exchequer) .	1838 to 1839	1	8vo	1840
Irish Law	1838 to 1850	13	8vo	1839 to 1852
Jebb & Symes . . .	1838 to 1841	2	8vo	1840 to 1842
Millward, Ecclesiastical, Temp. Radcliff	1838 to 1842	1	8vo	1847
Armstrong, M'Arthur, & Ogle (N.P.	1840 to 1842	1	8vo	1843
Jebb & Rourke	1841 to 1842	1	8vo	1843
Longfield & Townsend (Exchequer)	1841 to 1842	1	8vo	1843
Irish Circuit Cases . . .	1841 to 1843	1	8vo	1843

REPORTER	Period	Vols.	Size	Date
IRISH COMMON LAW—*contd.*				
Shee's Reports	1841 to 1843	1	8vo	1843
Irish Common Law Reports (N.S.)	1850 to 1867	17	8vo	1852 to 1867
—— Law Reports . . .	1867 to 1868	2	8vo	1867 to 1868
BANKRUPTCY.				
Rose, Temp. Eldon . 2nd edit.	1810 to 1814	2	8vo	1821
Buck, do. . . .	1816 to 1820	1	8vo	1820
Glyn & Jameson . . .	1821 to 1823	2	8vo	1824 to 1828
Montagu & M'Arthur . . .	1828 to 1830	1	8vo	1830
Montagu	1829 to 1832	1	8vo	1832
Deacon & Chitty . . .	1832 to 1835	4	8vo	1834 to 1837
Montagu & Bligh . . .	1832 to 1833	1	8vo	1835
Montagu & Ayrton . . .	1833 to 1838	3	8vo	1835 to 1839
Deacon	1835 to 1840	4	8vo	1837 to 1840
Montagu & Chitty . . .	1838 to 1839	1	8vo	1840
Montagu, Deacon, & De Gex .	1840 to 1844	3	8vo	1842 to 1845
De Gex, Temp. V. C. Bruce .	1844 to 1848	1	8vo	1850
Fonblanque (of Commissioners) .	1840 to 1850	1	8vo	1852
Bankruptcy & Insolvency . .	1853 to 1854	1	8vo	1855
ECCLESIASTICAL.				
Lee	1752 to 1758	2	8vo	1833
Haggard (Consistorial) . .	1789 to 1802	2	8vo	1822
Phillimore	1809 to 1821	3	8vo	1818 to 1827
Addams	1822 to 1826	3	8vo	1823 to 1826
Haggard (Ecclesiastical) . .	1827 to 1832	3	8vo	1829 to 1832
Curties	1834 to 1844	3	8vo	1834 to 1844
Panton *v.* Williams, Sir H. Jenner's Judgment. *See* Pamphlets	.	.	.	1840
Thornton, Notes of Cases . .	1841 to 1850	7	8vo	1843 to 1850
Croke's Report of Horner & Liddiard	.	1	8vo	1800
Robertson	1844 to 1853	2	8vo	1852 to 1853
Spinks, (Ecclesiastical & Admiralty)	1853 to 1855	2	8vo	1855
Deane	1855 to 1857	1	8vo	1858
PROBATE & DIVORCE COURTS.				
Swabey & Tristram . . .	1858 to 1866	4	8vo	1860 to 1867
Tristram & Searle Law Rep. .	1865 to 1868	1	8vo	1868

REPORTER	Period	Vols.	Size	Date
ADMIRALTY.				
Marriott	1776 to 1779	1	8vo	1801
Robinson, C.	. .	3	8vo	1799 to 1802
——— . . . 4th edit.	1798 to 1808	6	8vo	1812
Edwards	1808 to 1810	1	8vo	1812
Greene	. .	1	8vo	1818
Dodson . . . 4th edit.	1811 to 1822	2	8vo	1815 to 1828
Haggard	1822 to 1832	3	8vo	1825 to 1840
Robinson, W.	1838 to 1850	2	8vo	1844 to 1852
Swabey	1855 to 1859	1	8vo	1860
Lushington	1859 to 1862	1	8vo	1864
Browning & Lushington . .	1863 to 1865	1	8vo	1868
Browning, L. R. . . .	1865 to 1866	1	8vo	1866
Admiralty & Ecclesiastical . .	1865 to 1868	2	8vo	1867 to 1868
ELECTION CASES.				
Anonymous	1741	1	8vo	1741
———	1774	1	8vo	1744
Glanville, 21 & 22 James I. .	. .	1	8vo	1775
Petrie's Cricklade Case . .	. .	1	8vo	1735
Douglas, Ld. Glenbervie 2nd edit	1775 to 1776	4	8vo	1802
Luders	1785 to 1790	3	8vo	1808
Fraser	1790 to 1791	1	8vo	1791
Peckwell	1796 to 1806	2	8vo	1805
Disney's Cases and Acts . .	. .	2	8vo	1833 to 1812
Corbett & Daniell . . .	1819	1	8vo	1821
Cockburn & Rowe . .	1833	1	8vo	1833
Perry & Knapp . . .	1833	1	8vo	1833
Knapp & Omler . . .	1834 to 1835	1	8vo	1837
Wordsworth's Digest . . .	1834	1	8vo	1834
Delane's Decisions of Revising Courts }	1836	1	8vo	1836
Falconer & Fitzherbert . .	1837 to 1838	1	8vo	1839
Barrow & Austen . . .	1842	1	8vo	1844
Barrow & Arnold . . .	1843 to 1846	1	8vo	1846
Pigott & Rodwell . . .	1843 to 1845	1	8vo	1846
Power, Rothwell & Dew . .	1847 to 1856	2	12mo	1852 to 1856
Wolverston & Dew . . .	1857 to 1858	1	12mo	1859
CROWN CASES.				
Kelyng, Sir J., Temp. Car. II. .	. .	1	folio	1708
Leach	1730 to 1788	1	8vo	1789

REPORTER	Period	Vols.	Size	Date
CROWN CASES—*continued.*				
Leach . . . 3rd edit	1730 to 1800	2	8vo	1800
Forster . . . (*Dublin*)	1767	1	8vo	1767
Forster (Dalison) . 2nd edit	. .	1	8vo	1776
Russell & Ryan	1799 to 1824	1	8vo	1825
Lewen	1822 to 1838	2	8vo	1834 to 1839
Moody	1824 to 1824	2	8vo	1837 to 1844
Denison . *continued* by Pearce	1844 to 1852	2	8vo	1850 to 1852
Temple & Mew (Crm & Appl Cses)	1848 to 1851	1	8vo	1853
Dearsley	1850 to 1856	1	8vo	1856
Dearsley & Bell	1856 to 1858	1	8vo	1858
Bell	1858 to 1860	1	8vo	1863
Cox, E. W.	1843 to 1868	1	8vo	1846 to 1868
Leigh & Cave	1861 to 1865	1	8vo	1866
Law Reports	1866 to 1868	1	8vo	1866 to

INDEX TO SUBJECTS.

ABBEYS :—
  Aberconway—C. M. No. 39.
  Bec—Bourget.
  Bury St. Edmunds—Gillingwater.
  Easby (Y.)—Bowman.
  Evesham—Tindall.
  ——— Macray, No. 29, M. R. Pub.
  Faversham—Lewis.
  Fonthill—Rutter.
  Furness—West.
  Hyde, Winchester—Edwards, No. 45, M. R. Pub.
  Peterborough—C. S. P. No. 47.
  Westminster—Dart.
  Whitby—Charlton.
ABBOT (ABP.), LIFE OF—Onslow.
ABBREVIATIO PLACITORUM—Rec. Com.
"ABDICATED," DEBATE ON IN PARLIAMENT, 1695.
ABERDEEN, ANNALS OF—Kennedy.
ABINGDON FREE GRAMMAR SCHOOL, MEMORIAL OF—Blundell.
ABINGDON MONASTERII CHRONICON—Stevenson, No. 2, M. R. Pub.
ABRIDGMENTS — Doctor & Student, Bacon, Brooke, Cay, Comyns, Davenport (of Coke), Fitzherbert, Godolphin, Ireland (of Coke), Petersdorff, Plowden, Rolle, Statham, & Viner.
ABRIDGMENTS, PUBLIC ACTS.
ABSENCE, PROCESS IN—Vol. 2, His. L. Tr.
ABSTRACTS OF TITLE. *See* Preston.
ACCIDENTS & NEGLIGENCE—Hay.
ACCOUNTS—Cory.
ACTIONS ON THE CASE—Sheppard.
ACTIONS AT LAW—Boote, Chitty, Kerr, Smith.
ACTIONS AT LAW, LIMITATION OF (IRISH) BILL—Ferguson.
ACTIONS AT LAW (U.S.)—Angell.
ACTS, PUBLIC GENERAL, 1224—1867.
ACTS, PUBLIC & PRIVATE, INDEX, 1224—1867.
ACTS, PUBLIC & PRIVATE, INDEX, 1483—1831.
ACTS (SIR R. PEEL), ARRANGED BY A BARRISTER.
ACTS & ORDINANCES, COLLECTION OF, IN CONTINUATION OF PULTON—Scobell.
ADMINISTRATION OF JUSTICE IN WEST INDIES, REPORT—H. C.

ADMIRALTY :—
  Compendium—Horne.
  Court, Lectures on—J. Morris.
  Digest—Greene.
  Jurisdiction—Edwards.
  Law & Practice (in U. S.)—Conkling.
  Practice—F. Clerke, Coote, Williams & Bruce.
  Statute Laws—Horne.
ADMIRALTY REPORTS—Dodson, Edwards, Haggard, Lushington, Marriott, Robinson (C.), Robinson (W.), Spinks, Swabey.
ADULTERINE BASTARDY—Nicolas.
ADULTERY—Morgan.
ADVOCATE, THE—Cox.
ADVOWSONS—Mirehouse.
AFFILIATION—Saunders.
AFRICA, MAP OF—Arrowsmith.
AGENCY—Paley, Story, Theobald.
AGENCY & TRUSTS—Brown (W.)
AGHABOE, ACCOUNT OF—Ledwich.
AGRICULTURAL CUSTOMS OF COUNTIES—Kennedy & Granger.
AGRICULTURE, INCLOSURES A CAUSE OF IMPROVEMENT—Howlett's Tr.
AGRICULTURE, WOMEN & CHILDREN EMPLOYED IN, REPORT, 1845.
AGRICULTURAL CLASSES, ON IMPROVEMENT OF—Dean.
AGRICULTURAL, &c. LIBRARY—Baxter.
AGRICULTURE OF THE ISLE OF MAN, VIEW OF—Quayle.
ALBERT, PRINCE, v. STRANGE, JUDGMENT (PROPERTY IN WORKS OF ART)—Cooke.
ALCEDON, ANT. DE—Thompson.
ALCHESTER, HISTORY OF—Dunkin.
ALGEBRA—Hammond, Maclaurin.
ALMANACK, BRITISH, & COMPANION.
  Collections.
  Dublin.
  Dublin—Thom.
  Edinburgh (New).
  London.
  Moore's.
  Stationers' Company, 1792-1867.
ALUMNI ETONENSES—Harwood.
AMBASSADORS, PROCEEDINGS AGAINST—Howell

INDEX TO SUBJECTS.

AMBROSDEN, ANTIQUITIES OF—Kennett.
AMÉRICA, HISTORY OF (Greek).
AMERICA, U. S. & GREAT BRITAIN—*Correspondence.*
AMERICA (NORTH), HISTORY OF—Hinton.
AMERICA (NORTH). *See* Robertson's Works.
AMERICA, NORTH & SOUTH, MAP—Arrowsmith.
AMERICA, MAP OF—Pownall.
AMERICA, TOUR IN—Faux.
AMERICAN (NEW) CYCLOPÆDIA OF GENERAL KNOWLEDGE—Ripley & Dana.
AMERICAN LAW.
  Admiralty, &c.—Conkling, Sprague.
  Bailments—Story.
  Banking Laws of New York—Cleaveland.
  Bills of Exchange—Story.
  Commentaries—Story.
  Consular Regulations, U.S.
  Contracts—Story, Parsons, Metcalfe.
  Conflict of Laws—Story.
  Conveyancing—Thornton.
  Copyright—Curtis, Law.
  Corporations—Angell & Ames.
  Criminal Law—Bishop.
  Damages—Sedgwick.
  Dictionary—Bouvier.'
  Digests—Abbott, Putnam.
  Easements—Washburn.
  Equity Jurisprudence—Story.
  ———— *Pleading*—Story.
  Evidence—Greenleaf.
  Fire Decisions—Littleton & Blatchley.
  Highways—Angell & Durfee.
  Homicide—Wharton.
  Institutes—Bouvier.
  Insurance, Fire & Life—Angell.
  ———————— *Marine*—Duer.
  International Law—Wheaton.
  Law, First Book of, U.S.—Bishop.
  Limitation of Actions, Law & Equity—Angell.
  Marriage & Divorce—Bishop.
  Medical Jurisprudence—Ray.
  Mortgage, Real and Personalty—Hilliard.
  Mining Claims & Water Rights—Yale.
  Naval Courts Martial—Harwood.
  Nations—Wheaton.
  Notarial Manual—Wedgwood & H.
  Partnership—Story.
  Patents—Curtis, Law.
  Practice—Robinson.
  Prize Cases—Blatchford.
  Promissory Notes—Curtis, Story.
  Railways—Redfield.
  Real Property—Hilliard.
  Sales of Personalty—Story, Hilliard.
  Telegraphs—Scott & Jarnagin.
  Tidal Waters—Angell.
  Torts—Hilliard.
  Virginia Code.
  New York ditto.
  Wills—Redfield.
  Statutory & Constitutional Law—Sedgwick.
  Statutes, U.S.—Peters, Minot, Sanger.
  ———— *New York*—Edmonds.

AMERICAN LAW:—
  U.S. Leading Cases—Hare & Wallace.
  U. S. Law Dictionary—Bouvier.
  ———— *Register*—Livingston.
  ———— *Digests*— Abbott, Putnam & Smith, Metcalfe & Perkins.
AMERICAN REPORTS:—
  Circuit Courts—Gallison, Mason, Story Sumner.
  Reports—Curtis, Dallas, Cranch, Wheaton Peters, Howard.
  New York Court of Appeal—Selden, Johnson (Chy.)
AMERICAN REVIEW.
AMERICAN REUNION, LETTER TO PROFESSOR MORSE ON—O'Sullivan.
ANALECTA ANGLO-BRITANNICA—Selden, vol. 2.
ANCESTORS' POSSESSION, HEIR'S PRIVILEGE—Vol. 1, His. L. Tr.
ANCIENT CALENDARS & INVENTORIES OF EXCHEQUER—Rec. Com.
ANCIENT CHARTERS, CALENDAR—Ayloffe.
ANCIENT FUNERAL MONUMENTS—Weever.
ANCIENT HISTORY—Rollin.
ANCIENT LAWS OF ENGLAND, 1840—Rec. Com
ANCIENT LAW—Maine.
ANCREN RIWLE (OF MONASTIC LIFE)—Morton No. 57, C. S. Pa.
ANDERSON TRIAL (TREASON)—Pol. Tr.
ANECDOTES OF DUKE OF BEDFORD, 1796.
ANECDOTES & TRADITIONS OF EARLY ENGLISH HISTORY—Thom, C. S. Pa. No. 9.
ANGELSÄCHSISCHES RECHT—Phillips.
ANGLESEA, ANTIQUITIES OF—Rowland.
ANGLIÆ ET WALLIÆ TAXATIO ECCLESIASTICA—Rec. Com.
ANGLICANA DE REBELLIONE COMMENTARII—R. M.
ANGLICANI, HONORES—Dugdale.
ANGLICANUM MONASTICON—Dodsworth & Dugdale, Dugdale by Caley, Ellis & Bandinel.
ANGLICANUM MONASTICON, ADDENDA TO DUGDALE—Stevens.
ANGLORUM JANI FACIES NOVA.
ANGLO-SAXON CHRONICLE—Thorpe, No. 23, M. R. Pub.
ANGLO-SAXON HOME—Thrupp.
ANGLO-SAXON LAWS—Wilkins.
ANGLO-SAXON LITERATURE—Wright.
ANJOU, MARGARET OF, LETTERS, &c.—Monro, C. S. Pa. No. 86.
ANNALS OF ABERDEEN—Kennedy.
ANNALS OF COMMERCE—Macpherson.
ANNALS OF FIRST FOUR YEARS OF QUEEN ELIZABETH—Hayward, C. S. Pa. No. 7.
ANNALS OF ENGLAND, 1508-1558—Godwin.

ANNALS OF EUROPE, 1739-1743.
ANNALS OF KENDAL—Nicholson.
ANNALS OF STAMFORD—Peck.
ANNALES CAMBRIÆ—Williams, No. 20, M. R. Pub.
ANNUAIRE ALMANACH DU COMMERCE, PARIS—Bottin.
ANNUAL REGISTER—Dodsley.
ANNUAL REGISTER, OR ROYAL KALENDAR.
ANNUITIES — Baily, Benwell, Hunt, Kelly, Lumley, Milne, Price, Tate, Withy.
ANNUITIES & SUCCESSIONS, TABLES FOR—Willich.
ANNUITY ACT—Hunt.
ANNUITY PERPETUAL POST OBIT, ON GRANT OF —Vol. 2, Col. Jur.
ANTIGUA, ACTS OF.
ANTIQUARIAN REPERTORY—Astle & others.
ANTIQUARIAN REPERTORY—Grose & others.
ANTIQUIS DE LEGIBUS LIBER—Stapleton, No. 34, C. S. Pa.
ANTIQUITATE DE BRITANNICÆ ECCLESIÆ — Parker.
ANTI-RELIGIOUS LIBEL LAW—White.
ANTRIM COUNTY STATISTICAL SURVEY — Dubourdieu.
ANTRIM COUNTY, HISTORY OF NORTHERN COAST OF—Hamilton.
APPEAL CASES TO H. L.
APPEALS TO H. L.—Paton.
APPEAL CASE (WOOD'S WILL)—P. C.
APPEAL CASES—P. C.
APPEAL TO THE PUBLIC—Hogan.
APPEAL AGAINST THE MONOPOLY OF PUBLISHERS.
APPEAL TO SUPERIOR COURTS—Taylor.
APPELLATE JURISDICTION—Burge, Cooper, Dax.
APOLOGY FOR ABP. ABBOT, &c.—Spelman.
APOLOGY, A MODERATE—Prynne.
APOPHTHEGMS—Bacon.
APOTHECARIES SOCIETY ON MEDICAL REFORM BILL.
APPORTIONMENT—Lewin.
ARABIC ALPHABET, INTRODUCTION TO—Bishop St. David's.
ARATUS, TRANSLATION OF—Lamb.
ARBITRATION & AWARDS—Archbold, Caldwell, Kyd, March, Russell, Watson.
ARCHBISHOP, ON OPTION PENDING BISHOP'S TRANSLATION.
ARCHBISHOPS & BISHOPS, DWELLINGS OF—Spelman.
ARCHÆOLOGICAL DICTIONARY—Wilson.
ARCTIC REGIONS, EXPEDITION TO—Buck.
ARITHMETIC—Bonnycastle.

ARMAGH, HISTORY OF—Stuart.
ARRAGON, CATHERINE OF, INVENTORY OF WARDROBE—Nichols, C. M., Vol. 3, No. 61.
ARREST, HISTORY OF LAW OF—Crowther.
ARREST, ABOLITION OF—Ings.
ARMS, ANCIENT USAGE OF—Dugdale.
ARMS, ON EDUCATION FOR PROFESSION OF—Wilmot.
ARMY LIST, ANNUAL—Hart.
ARMY LIST, MONTHLY—Hart.
ARMY LIST, QUARTERLY—Hart.
ARMY & CIVIL SERVICE LIST, INDIA.
ARTICLED CLERKS' MANUAL—Wharton.
ARTICLES, THIRTY-NINE—Rogers.
ARTIFICIAL ELECTRICITY—Boccaria.
ARUNDELLIANA MARMORA—Selden, 2nd vol.
ARUNDEL, SUSSEX, HISTORY OF—Tierney.
ASHBURTON, LORD, BIOGRAPHY OF—Roscoe.
ASHMOLE, ELIAS, LIFE OF—Malcolm.
ASHURST, SIR WILLIAM, SPEECH TO—Atkyns, L. Jr.
ASIA, MAP OF—Arrowsmith.
ASSESSMENTS, PAROCHIAL—Lumley.
ASSETS, &c.—Ram, Williams.
ASSIZES, AS TO ADJOURNING THERE FROM LANCASTER—Vol. 20, Pam.
ASSOCIATE IN ARTS, NEW OXFORD EXAMINATION—Acland.
ASSURANCE, COMMON—Sheppard.
ASTON (MR. JUSTICE), LETTER TO HIM—Morris. Vol. 2, Libel L. Tr.
ATTACHMENT, FOREIGN—Locke, Brandon.
ATHOLL (DUKE OF), CASE AS TO ISLE OF MAN —Hargraves, J. A.
ATHOLL (DUKE OF), CLAIM ON ISLE OF MAN, 1765.
ATKINS (SIR R.), LIFE OF—Malcolm.
ATLAS & MAPS—Arrowsmith.
ATLAS, ENGLISH—Bowen, Pigot.
ATLAS, GENERAL—Jansson, Lavoisne.
ATTERBURY, LETTERS TO HIM WHEN IN THE TOWER—C. M. Vol. 4.
ATTORNEY & ARTICLED CLERKS, EXERCISES BETWEEN—Hobler.
ATTORNEY, WRIT OF PROTECTION TO, IN K.B. 1 RIC.—Law Tr. vol. 7.
ATTORNEY, BILL OF COSTS (OF 1608)—Law. Tr. vol. 7.
ATTORNEY & SOLICITOR, COMPLETE, ENTERING CLERK.
ATTORNEYS, SOLICITORS, & AGENTS, LAW OF —Beasley, Jones, Maugham, Morgan, Powell, Pulling, Stokes, Warren.
ATTORNEYS, LIST OF FEES OF OFFICERS, 1730

INDEX TO SUBJECTS.

ATTORNEYS, REMUNERATION TO—Parker.
ATTORNEY GENERAL v. PEARSON ON ENGLISH ENDOWMENTS, REPORT—Vol. 2, L. Tr.
ATTWOOD v. EYRE (CHANCERY), SIGNIFICAVIT —Col. Jur.
AUBREY, BIOGRAPHY OF—Britton.
AUBREY, LIFE OF—Malcolm.
AUCTION LAWS—Excise Ed.
AUCTIONS—Babington, Bateman.
AUCTIONEERS' &c. DIRECTORY—Allnutt.
AVEBURY (WILTS), DRUIDS' TEMPLE AT.
AUSTRIA & ENGLAND, ALLIANCE—Howell, C.P.
AUSTRIA, CIVIL CODE—Winiwater.
AUSTRALIA, AGRICULTURAL CO. ACT & CHARTER.
AUSTRALIA, SOUTH, ON REGISTRATION OF TITLE IN—Torrens.
AUTHORS, ON PLAN FOR ENCOURAGING—Jordan.
AUTHOR (ANONYMOUS), FALSITIES &C. OF— Prynne.
AWARD (FORM OF), COPYHOLD ENFRANCHISEMENT.
AWARDS. See Arbitration.
AXHOLME, &C. (LINCOLN), ACCOUNT OF—Peck, Vol. 1, L. Tr.
AYRTON, BOND PRACTICE IN BANKRUPTCY.

BACON, CHARACTER OF, HIS LIFE & WORKS— Martin.
BACON, LIFE OF—Sortain.
BACON (F. R.) THE "OPUS TERTIUM, &C."— Brewer, No. 4, M. R. Pub.
BAGSHAW v. SPENCER, CHANCERY, 22 G. 2ND. —Col. Jur.
BAHAMAS, LAWS OF—Anderson.
BAIL—Coke, Highmore.
BAIL COURT, REPORTS OF CASES—Chitty, Dowling, Dowling, N.S., Dowling & Lowndes, Lowndes, Maxwell & Pollock, Lowndes & Maxwell.
BAILMENTS—Nicholls, Jones, Story, Wallace.
BALE'S KING JOHN, A PLAY—Collier, C. S. P. No. 2
BANBURY, HISTORY OF—Beesley.
BANBURY PEERAGE, CASE, EVIDENCE, &C.
B——KS, SIR J., LETTER TO W. B., 1719— Gosling.
BANKERS & BANKING—Grant, Macleod.
BANKERS & NOTARIES, LAW MANUAL (NEW YORK)—Wedgwood & Homan.
BANKING SYSTEM OF NEW YORK—Cleaveland.
BANKRUPTCY, ON ABOLITION OF PUNISHMENT OF DEATH—Montagu.
BANKRUPTCY, ENQUIRIES RESPECTING—Montagu.

BANKRUPTCY, BILL Montagu.
BANKRUPTCY, LETTE Montagu.
BANKRUPTCY, LETTER Montagu.
BANKRUPTCY & INSOL Eden, Vol. 1,
BANKRUPTCY & INSO 13, Pam.
BANKRUPTCY & INSO A. Edgar & M
BANKRUPTCY & INSOL SECT.—Ford,
BANKRUPTCY & CREDI
BANKRUPTCY Act, A DITORS UNDER-
BANKRUPTCY BOND P
BANKRUPTCY COURT, MIT—Fane, Vc
BANKRUPTCY, SUGGES —Gregg, Vol.
BANKRUPTCY, LETTER Laidman, Vol.
BANKRUPTCY PRECEDI
BANKRUPTCY COURT Jac. L. Tr.
BANKRUPTCY COURT R. PEEL, &C.-
BANKRUPTCY COURT R CHANCELLOR— 8, Jac. L. Tr.
BANKRUPTCY LAW R Pam.
BANKRUPTCY DIRECTO
BANKRUPTCY LIST—B
BANKRUPTCY REGISTE
BANKRUPTCY SYSTEM-
BANKRUPTCY TREATIS Cooke, Davis, Eden, Evans, Goodinge, Gree & Roche, K Montagu, Mon & Gregg, M Stewart, Strou
BANKRUPTCY:—
Reports of Cases- & Chitty; De De Gex, Macn Gex, Fisher, & Montagu & Bligh; Monta & Chitty; Mon Rose.
Digest of Cases—
BANKRUPTCY LAW (Sc
BANKRUPTCY LAW, D

BAR (THE) SKETCHES OF JUDGES—A POEM.

BAR (THE) THE ATTORNEY & THE CLIENT—2nd Report Law Amt. Society, 20 V. Pam.

BAR (THE) PRACTICE, VINDICATION OF, IN THE CASE OF REG. *v.* D'ISADI—Stammers.

BARBADOES, CHANCERY ORDERS, LAW OF, & ACTS.

BARBER, W. H. CASE OF, IN 1847—Michie.

BARFOOT & BURGESS, REVIEW OF FACTS IN LITIGATION AS TO FARNHAM QUAY.

BARON DE BODE'S ADDRESS TO H. C. AS TO FRENCH CLAIMS.

BARONAGE (*See* Peerage)——Dugdale.

BARONS' PRIVILEGES—Selden, vol. 3.

BARONETAGES—Almon, Betham, Burke, Debrett, Kimber, Playfair.

BARONETAGES, ENGLISH—Playfair.

BARONETAGES, IRISH – Playfair.

BARONETAGE, SCOTCH.—Playfair.

BARONETAGE, READE, Evidence.

BARONIA ANGLICA—Madox.

BARRISTER & ATTORNEY, DISTINCTION—Harle.

BASINGSTOKE, HANTS, HISTORY OF THE HOLY GHOST CHAPEL AT.—Tr.

BASTARDY—Saunders.

BATH, ANTIQUITIES OF—Guidot.

BATH P. O. DIRECTORY. *See* Gloucestershire—Kelly.

BATH, HISTORY OF—Wood.

BAWTRY, HISTORY &c. OF YORK—Hunter, Peck.

BEAMES' TRANSLATION OF GLANVILLE.

BECKWITH *v.* WOOD, LONDON RIOTS REPORT.—Dowling.

BEDFORD CYCLE, SIDEREAL, CHROMATICS FROM.—Smyth.

BEDFORD DOMESDAY BOOK.—Rec. Com. Vol. 1.

BEDFORD LEVEL DRAINAGE, LAW, HISTORY, &c., OF—Cole.

BEDFORDSHIRE P. O. DIRECTORY—Kelly.

BEDFORDSHIRE DIRECTORY—Pigot.

BEDFORDSHIRE, HISTORY OF—Lysons.

BENEDICT OF PETERBOROUGH—Stubbs, No. 49, M.R. Pub.

BENEFICES. SALE OF: PAPER OF MR. A. WADDILOVE IN CONNECTION WITH AUGMENTATION OF BENEFICES BILL—Law Amendment Society.

BENEFICES (ECCLESIASTICAL), VALUATION OF—Bacon, Ecton.

BENEFICES, JUSTICE OF PRESENT ESTABLISHED LAW, GIVING SUCCESSOR TO, THE PROFITS FROM DAY OF AVOIDANCE- Prideaux, Tr.

BENEFIT BUILDING & FREEHOLD LAND SOCIETIES, LAW, &c.—Barry.

BENEFIT BUILDING SOCIETIES—Stone.

BENGAL GAZETTE.

BENGAL PRESIDENCY, REGULATIONS & ACTS.

BENTHAM (J.) LIFE OF—Malcolm.

BENTHAM, HISTORY OF ELY CATHEDRAL, SUPPLEMENT TO—Stevenson.

BENTINCK, LORD G., EXAMINATION OF CERTAIN FALLACIES IN MR. D'ISRAELI'S LIFE OF.

BERKELEY MSS., HISTORY OF CASTLE &c.—Fosbrooke.

BERKELEYS, LIVES OF THE—Smyth.

BERKSHIRE DIRECTORY (P. O.)—Kelly.

BERKSHIRE DIRECTORY—Pigot.

BERKSHIRE DOMESDAY BOOK.

BERKSHIRE GENEALOGIES—Berry.

BERKSHIRE, HISTORY OF—Lysons.

BERKSHIRE, LETTER TO WISE, WITH SOME ANTIQUITIES OF—Dr. Mend.

BERMUDA ACTS.

BERMUDA, LAWS OF—Darrell.

BERWICK-UPON-TWEED, HISTORY—Fuller.

BESSEY (LADY), SONG OF LANCASHIRE—Tr.

BEVERLEY, HISTORY OF COLLEGIATE CHURCH—Oliver.

BEVERLEY, HISTORY OF—Poulson.

BIBLE—D'Oyley & Mant.

BIBLE, DEFENCE OF ENGLISH TRANSLATION—Fuller.

BIBLICAL CATECHISM—Stow.

BIBLIOGRAPHER'S MANUAL—Lowndes.

BIBLIOTHECA BRITANNICA—Watts.

BIBLIOTHECA CHETHAMENSIS—Radcliffe.

BICESTER, HISTORY OF—Dunkin.

BIDEFORD (DEVON), HISTORY OF—Watkins.

BIDDINGS, OPINIONS AS TO ABOLISHING PRACTICE OF, PAPER OF MR. SERJT. WOOLRYCH—Law Amt. Society.

BIOGRAPHY:—
  Ashburton, Lord.
  Bacon, Lord.
  Berkeleys, The
  Blackstone, Sir W.
  Canning, George
  Chatham, Earl.
  Cicero—Sir R. Cotton.
  Curran.
  Davidson—Dolland.
  Dugdale, Sir Wm.
  Eldon, Lord Chancellor.
  Gaspar Collinius.
  Gilbert, Lord C. B.
  Jenkins, Sir L.
  King, Sir John.
  Mackintosh, Sir James.
  Mansfield, Earl.
  More, Sir Thomas.
  Pitt.
  Pope, Sir T.
  Raleigh, Sir W.

BIOGRAPHY:—
  Smith, Dr. A.
  Story, Joseph.
  Stillingfleet, Bp.
  Sir J. Brompton.
  Sutton, T. Esq.
  Taswell, Dr. W.
  Waynflete, Bp.
  Wratislaw Family.
  Wykeham, Bp.
AUTOBIOGRAPHY—20 vols. 12mo., N.D.
  Mrs. Mary Robinson & Mrs. Charlotte Clarke, vol. 1.
  Robert Drury, vol. 2.
  George Bury Doddington, vol. 3.
  David Hume, Wm. Lilly, & François Marie Arouet Voltaire, vol. 4.
  Madame du Barris, vols. 5, 6, 7, & 8.
  Goldini, vols. 9 & 10.
  Augustus Von Kotzebue, 11 & 12.
  James Lackington, vol. 13.
  Benvenuto Cellini, vols. 14 & 15.
  Theobald Wolfe Tone, vol. 16.
  James Hardy Vaux, vol. 17.
  Edward, Lord Herbert (of Cherbury), Prince Eugene (of Savoy), vol. 18.
  George Whitefield, vol. 19.
  Captain John Creighton & Thomas Ellwood, vol. 20.
See also ANNUAL BIOGRAPHY & OBITUARY.
  Campbell, Lord; Lord Chancellor.
  Campbell, Lord Chief Justice.
  Chalmers.
  Davenport.
  Eminent Lawyers.
  Foss's Judges.
  Illustrious Dead.
  Kippis's Biographical Dictionary.
  Malcolm's Lives.
  Maunder's Dictionary.
  Roscoe's Eminent Lawyers.
BIOGRAPHIA BRITANNICA—Dr. Kippis.
BIOGRAPHICAL NOTICES OF AUTHORS — See Opinions of Eminent Lawyers.
BIOGRAPHY OF DR. ABBOTT—Chalmers.
BIOGRAPHY OF AUBREY.
BIOGRAPHY OF DOLLAND.
BILLS OF EXCHANGE—Bayley, Byles, Chitty, Cunningham, Lawes, Lovelace, Mazins, Scarlett, Story.
BILLS OF SALE—Beaumont, Miller & Collier
BILLS (PRIVATE) INSTRUCTIONS FOR PASSING.
BIRMINGHAM (P O.) DIRECTORY—Kelly.
BIRMINGHAM, HISTORY OF—Hutton.
BIRMINGHAM LAW STUDENTS, ADDRESS TO, AT—Saunders.
BIRMINGHAM MANUFACTURES: COMMENTS IN CONNECTION WITH, AND THE WRITER—Gill.
BIRMINGHAM, RECORDER OF, HIS CHARGE TO THE JURY—M. D. Hill.
BIRMINGHAM RIOTS, APPEAL—Priestley.

BIRTHS, &c., REPORTS OF COMMISSIONERS ON REGISTERING.
BIRTHS, REGISTRATION OF—Glen.
BLACKPOOL, HISTORY OF—Hutton, Thornber.
BLACKSTONE'S COMMENTARIES FOR AMERICAN STUDENTS—Wendell.
BLACKSTONE'S ANALYSIS—Field.
BLACKSTONE, REMARKS ON—Sedgwick.
BLACKSTONE, SELECT EXTRACTS FROM—Warren.
BLACKSTONE, SYNOPSIS OF—Sayer.
BLANDFORD, FIRE—Blake.
BLOCKADE—Deane.
BLONDEL (R.) NARRATIVE OF EXPULSION OF ENGLISH FROM NORMANDY. No. 32, M. R. Pub.—Stevenson.
BODLEIAN LIBRARY, MSS. IN—Dodsworth.
BOECE (H.), METRICAL VERSION OF THE HISTORY OF—Stevenson. No. 6, M. R. Pub.
BOHN, A PRIVATE LETTER OF—Prynne.
BOLTON, LANCASHIRE, HISTORY OF—Whittle.
BOMBAY GAZETTE.
BOMBAY PRESIDENCY, REGULATIONS & ACTS—See pp. 31 & 112.
BOOKKEEPING, SOLICITORS'—Kain, Mackenzie, Oke.
BOOTH, MR. & COUNSEL'S OPINION ON CASE ON STATUTE OF USES—V. 1, Col. Jur.
BORDER LAWS—Bp. of Carlisle.
BOROUGHS, &c., HISTORY OF—Brady, Oldfield.
BOROUGH COURT RULES—Carey.
BOSTON (LINCOLN), HISTORY OF—Thompson.
BOUNDARIES & FENCES—Hunt.
BOWELL'S INFORMATION. Pol. Tr.
BRADFIELD, HISTORY &c. OF CHAPELRY OF—Hunter.
BRAKELONDA CHRONICLE OF JOC. DE, 1173–1202. No. 13, C. S. Pu.—Rokewode.
BRAMBER, HISTORY OF—Cartwright.
BRAND (JOHN) LIFE OF—Malcolm.
BREAD, WHAT SHOULD BE ITS PRICE?—James.
BRECKNOCKSHIRE, HISTORY OF—Jones.
BREWER'S "OPUS TERTIUM" & "OPUS MINUS." See No. 15, Rolls.
BRICKS & TILES, p. 249. Abridgment Patents.
BRIDLINGTON (YORK), HISTORICAL SKETCHES OF—Thompson.
BRIEVES. L. Tr.
BRIGHT (J.) LETTER TO HIM FROM A CONSTITUENT—Sargent.
BRIGHTON, HISTORY OF—Sickelmore.
BRISTOL P.O. DIRECTORY—Kelly.
BRISTOL, HISTORY OF—Corry, Evans.
BRISTOL, MEMORIALIST—Tyson.

BRISTOL & ITS NEIGHBOURHOOD, MEMOIRS OF—Sayer.
BRISTOW, THE CHILD OF, A POEM—Lydgate.
BRITAIN, PRESENT STATE OF, 1707-1748—Miege.
BRITAIN, DO. OF COURT OF—Chamberlain.
BRITAIN, (GREAT) & AMERICA (U.S)—Correspondence.
BRITANNIA—Blome, Camden.
BRITANNICIS DE REBUS COLLECTANEA, & APPENDIX—Leland.
BRITISH NORTH AMERICA ALMANAC.
BRITISH ARMY, ON DISPLACEMENT OF, ADDRESS TO—Lieut.-Col. Dickson.
BRITISH ANTIQUITIES REVIVED—Vaughan.
BRITISH ARTISTS, ROYAL INSTITUTE OF, ON DILAPIDATIONS.
BRITISH COLONIES—Martin.
BRITISH COLONIES, VIEW OF—Stokes.
BRITISH COLONIES, LAW OF—Clarke, Howard.
BRITISH & FOREIGN STATE PAPERS & INDEX, 1812-1857.
BRITISH COMPENDIUM: BARONAGES & PEERAGES.
BRITISH CONSULS ABROAD—Tyson.
BRITISH DOMINIONS IN NORTH AMERICA OR CANADA—Bourchette.
BRITISH GUIANA ORDINANCES.
BRITISH IMPERIAL KALENDAR.
BRITISH INTERESTS IN SPAIN, BY A BONDHOLDER.
BRITISH ISLES, *Map of*—Knipe.
BRITISH LIBERTIES—Care.
BRITISH MUSEUM, HANDY BOOK TO LIBRARY OF—Sims.
BRITISH MUSEUM, LETTER TO MR. HAWES AS TO—Edwards.
BRITISH MUSEUM READING ROOM, OBSERVATIONS—Hoskin.
BRITISH TOPOGRAPHY—Gough.
BRITON'S RIGHTS—Barrow.
BRITTANIE LE LIVRE DE REIS DE—Glover, No. 42, M.R. Pub.
BRITTON (JOHN), ACCOUNT OF TESTIMONIAL DINNER TO—Jones.
BROKER, EVERY MAN HIS OWN—Mortimer.
BROKERS, &c.—Keyzer, Russell.
BROMLEY & HOLWOOD HILL, KENT, HISTORY OF—Dunkin & Kempe.
BROUGHAM (LORD) LETTER TO, IN REPLY TO TOMKINS & JENKINS—Richards.
BROUGHAM (LORD) LAW REFORM—Glover, v. 11, Jac. Law Tr.

BROWN (J. T.) LIFE OF—Malcolm.
BRUCE'S HISTORY OF ARRIVAL IN ENGLAND OF EDW. IV., 1471. No. 1, C.S.P.
BUBBLES, SOUTH SEA.
BUCKINGHAM, DOOMSDAY BOOK, &c.—Bawden.
BUCKINGHAM, DEANERY OF WYCOMBE—Langley.
BUCKINGHAM, VILLIERS, DUKE OF, HIS FALL, &c.—Grim Tr. Vol. 1.
BUCKINGHAM, HISTORY OF—Willis.
BUCKINGHAMSHIRE, SHEFFIELD, DUKE OF, FAMILY HISTORY—Grim Tr. Vol. 3.
BUCKINGHAMSHIRE, HISTORY OF LIPSCOMBE.—Lysons.
BUCKINGHAMSHIRE POST OFFICE DIRECTORY—Kelly.
BUCKINGHAMSHIRE DIRECTORY—Pigot.
BUCKWORTH v. THIRKELL, IN R.B. IN REPLEVIN RESERVED AT CAMBRIDGE ASSIZES, 1783. Col. Jur.
BUILDERS' PRICE BOOK—Laxton.
BUILDING CHURCHES, PARSONAGES, & SCHOOLS—Trower.
BUILDING SOCIETIES—Barry, Innes, Pratt, Stone.
BULL (MR. JOHN) FAMILIAR EPISTLES TO.
BULLION REPORT—Sir John Sinclair.
BULLS, PAPAL, &c. *See* Chartæ Antiquæ.
BURCESTER, ANTIQUITIES OF—Kennett.
BURGHERSH, SUSSEX; OR, THE PLEASURES OF A COUNTRY LIFE—Sargent.
BURIAL BOARDS, LAWS OF—Glen.
BURIALS, LAWS OF—Baker.
BURKE'S ANSWER TO ATTACKS ON HIM AS TO HIS PENSION.
BURRELL v. NICHOLSON, TRIAL AS TO NONPAROCHIALIBILITY OF RICHMOND TERRACE, WESTMINSTER—Walsh.
BURTON DE ANNALES, 1001-1263—Luard. No. 36, M.R. Pub.
BURY ST. EDMUNDS, HISTORY OF—Battely.
BURY ST. EDMUNDS & ABBEY—Gillingwater.
BURY ST. EDMUNDS CATHEDRAL, MONASTIC HISTORY &c. OF—Rev. R. Yates.
BURY, WILLS & INVENTORIES—Timms. No. 49, C.S.P.
BUTLER & BOND, CASE AS TO COMMITMENT OF HEIR, & ARGUMENT—Hare, J. A.
BUXTON, HISTORY OF, AND GUIDE TO THE PEAK—Jewett.
BUXTON, HANDBOOK OF, AND THE PEAK—Robertson.
BYE-LAWS OF MARINE SOCIETY.

CAITHNESS, EARLDOM—Hargrave, Jur. Arg. Vol 1
CALAIS, CHRONICLE OF—Nichols, No. 35, C.S.P.

CALENDARS, UNIVERSITIES OF—
  Cambridge.
  Durham.
  London U. College.
  Oxford.
CALENDARS (ANCIENT) AND INVENTORIES OF THE EXCHEQUER.—Rec. Com.
CALENDARS OF PROCEEDINGS IN CHANCERY, TEMP. ELIZABETH.—Rec. Com.
CALENDARS OF ANCIENT CHARTERS—Ayloffe.
CALENDARS OF CHARTER ROLLS.—Rec. Com.
CALENDARIUM INQUISITIONUM POST MORTEM—Rec. Com.
CALENDARIUM INQUISITIONUM AD QUOD DAMNUM—Rec. Com.
CALENDARIUM CATHOLICUM—1662.
CALIFORNIA, LAWS OF—Garfield & Snyder.
CALIFORNIA, PRACTICE ACT—Labatt.
CAMBRENSIS, WORKS OF—Brewer, No. 21 M.R. Pub.
CAMBRIA TRIUMPHANS—Enderbie.
CAMBRIÆ ANNALES—Williams, No. 20 M.R. Pub.
CAMBRIAN DIRECTORY.
CAMDEN'S ERRORS AND CAMDEN'S ANSWERS—Brooke
CANADA Co. ACT.
  Charter, &c.
  Statutes & Index.
CAMPBELL'S (LORD) MISREPRESENTATIONS—Lord St. Leonards.
CANADA (L.), STATUTES.
  Index—Wickstead.
  Ac's.
  Table to Acts—Wickstead.
  Directory.
CANADA (U.), CIVIL CODE FOR.
CANADA, REGISTRY LAWS—Staddon.
CANADA, STATUTES.
CANADA, ACCOUNT OF, AND STATISTICAL DITTO—Gourlay
CANADA, REPORTS (CH. 7)—Grant.
CANADA, REPORTS, K. B.—Harrison & Robinson.
CANADA, REPORTS, C. P.—Jones.
CANALS, PLANS IN GRT. B.—Carey.
CANON LAW—Ayliffe, Durand, Gregory XIII. Lancelott, Oughton.
CANON LAW OF ENGLISH CHURCH—Johnson.
CANON AND CIVIL LAW. Latin Tr. on.
CANON AND COMMON LAW PARALLEL.—Fulbecke.
CANTERBURY (Abp.) PROPOSAL OF, TO H. M. ACCOUNT OF—Tr. 1688-9.
CANTERBURY, ANTIQUITIES OR SURVEY—Somner.
CANTERBURY, HISTORY OF—Dart.
CANTERBURY AND ROCHESTER, REPERTOIRE OF ENDOWMENTS IN DIOCESES OF—Ducarel.

CANTUARIENSIS, MONASTERII ST. AUGUSTINI, HISTORIA, BY THOMAS OF ELMHAM. Hardwick. No. 8, M.R. Pub.
CAPGRAVE (J.), LIBER DE ILLUSTRIBUS HENRICIS—Hingeston. No. 7, M.R. Pub.
CAPETOWN (BP. OF), LONG v., CASE—Hodges.
CAPITAL PUNISHMENT AND PRISON DISCIPLINE—Tract.
CAPTURES—Lee.
CARDIGANSHIRE, HISTORY OF—Meyrick.
CAREW (SIR GEO.), LETTERS TO—Maclean, No. 88, C. S. P.
CAREW v. BURRELL, SUSSEX ASSIZES REPORT—Cooke.
CAREW PAPERS, CALENDAR OF—Brewer & Bullen. Cal. St. Pa.
CARHAMPTON, SOMERSET, HISTORY OF—Savage.
CARLISLE DIRECTORY—Pigot.
CARLISLE, HISTORY OF—Jefferson.
CARLISLE (EARL), LETTERS TO—Eden.
CARNARVON, RECORD OF—Rec. Com.
CAROLINE (QUEEN), EVIDENCE ON TRIAL—See Vol. 3 Hans. Deb. & H. L. Journal, 1820.
CARPENTER (JNO.), LIFE OF—Brewer..
CARPENTRY, PRINCIPLES OF—Tredgold.
CARRIBBY ISLANDS, HISTORY OF—Davies.
CARRICKFERGUS, HISTORY OF—MacSkinner.
CARRIERS, LAW OF (GENERAL)—Chitty & Temple.
CARRIERS, LAW OF (INLAND)—Powell.
CARRIERS, LAW OF (RAILWAY COS. AS)—Marshall.
CARTE & CAREW PAPERS—Hardy & Brewer. Cal. St. Pa.
CARTMELL, HISTORY OF—Whitaker.
CARTE D'ORLEANOIS—France.
CARTS, ORDERS TO REGULATE STANDING—City Tracts.
CARTWRIGHT'S DIARY—Hunter, No. 22, C. S. P.
CASTLES, HISTORY &C. OF—
  Arundel—Tierney.
  Berkeley—Fosbrooke.
  Corfe Castle—Sydenham.
  Dover—Darell.
  Easby—Bowman.
  Richmond (York). *See* Easby.
  Tutbury—Moseley.
  Warwick—Field.
  Windsor—Pote.
See TITLE CATALOGUES.

CATECHISM—Nowell, P. S. P.
CATECHISMS, &C., TEMP. EDWARD VI.
CATECHISMS, &C., TEMP. ELIZABETH.
CATHEDRALS, SURVEY OF—B. Willis.
  Ely—Bentham.
  Gloucester, 4to.
  Rochester—Thorpe.
  St. Patrick (Dublin)—Mason.
  St. Paul's (London)—Dugdale.

CATHEDRALS:—
  Salisbury—(Dodsworth).
  Winchester—Milner.
  York—Judd, Ribton.
CATTLE MARKET, PROPOSED, AT ISLINGTON.
CATTLE PLAGUE LAW—Cox.
CATTLE PLAGUE & DRAINAGE—Constable.
CAVENDISH, FAMILY HISTORY OF—Kennett.
CECIL (SIR R), HIS CORRESPONDENCE WITH JAMES VI.—Bruce 78, C. S. P.
CECIL (SIR R.) LETTERS TO SIR G. CAREW—No. 88, C. S. P.
CELTIC RECORDS OF IRELAND, ANALYSIS OF— Donovan's Annals.
CENTRAL CRIMINAL COURT TRIALS—Buckler, Buckler & Barnett.
CEYLON RAILROADS— Morris.
CEYLON, INSTITUTE OF LAWS OF—Thomson.
CHANCELLERIE D'ANGLETERRE, COMMENTAIRES DE LA—Cooper.
CHANCELLORS' FUNCTIONS, ON SEPARATING— Montague.
CHANCELLORS (LORD), LIVES of 1067-1708— Oldmixon.
CHANCELLORS (LORD), LIVES OF—Lord Campbell, Foss. CATALOGUE OF—Dugdale, Hardy.
CHANCELLOR, ON OFFICE OF—Selden, 3rd vol.
CHANCERY, ON ABUSES.
CHANCERY, ON ABUSES AND REMEDIES IN—Norbury, Hur. L. T.
CHANCERY, ON ABUSES IN COURT OF—Sir E. B. Sugden.
CHANCERY, ACTS—Headlam.
CHANCERY, CASE OF BAGSHAW AND SPENCER IN —No 15. Vol. 1 Col. Jur.
CHANCERY, LORD LANGDALE'S SPEECH ON 2ND REPORT OF ADMINISTRATION OF JUSTICE BILL IN—Vol. 1, Chy. Pam.
CHANCERY, MR. PEMBERTON'S DO. ON RECOMMITMENT OF BILL—Vol. 2, Chy. Pam.
CHANCERY ADMINISTRATIVE JURISDICTION— Haddan.
CHANCERY, APPELLATE JURISDICTION—Lynch, Dax, Burge.
CHANCERY, APPELLATE JURISDICTION, REPLY TO WILLIAMS—Sir E. B. Sugden.
CHANCERY CHAMBERS REGULATIONS—Bloxam.
CHANCERY, COURT OF, 3 ADDRESSES—Spence.
CHANCERY, COURT OF, SUPPLEMENT TO—Spence.
CHANCERY, CALENDARS OF PROCEEDINGS IN, TEMP. ELIZABETH—Rec. Com.
CHANCERY CHAMBER PRACTICE—Bloxam, Cox.
CHANCERY COMMISSION, LETTERS ON—Morevale.

CHANCERY COMMISSION, LETTERS ON REPORT OF —Montague.
CHANCERY COMMISSIONERS' REPORT—Lord Redesdale.
CHANCERY, CLERK'S TUTOR IN—Browne.
CHANCERY, BILLS OF COSTS IN—Coleman, Morgan & Davey, Shaen & Greville.
CHANCERY, ON DOCTRINE OF COSTS—Beames.
CHANCERY, DEFECTS IN—by a Solicitor, &. Cooper.
CHANCERY, DELAYS—Beckwith.
CHANCERY, DELAYS IN MASTER'S OFFICES— Cooper.
CHANCERY, DELAYS—Hume.
CHANCERY, DELAYS IN REGISTRARS' OFFICE— Lewis.
CHANCERY, DELAYS, SUGGESTIONS FOR PREVENTION—Lowndes.
CHANCERY, DELAYS, & CONDUCT OF SOLICITORS —Walters.
CHANCERY, DELAYS, & JUDGES' OBSERVATIONS ON—W. Wright.
CHANCERY, DOCTRINE & PRACTICE—Carrighan.
CHANCERY, EVILS & ABUSES IN—Spence.
CHANCERY, FEE GUIDE (IRISH)—Whitton.
CHANCERY (CHAMBER) FORMS—Cox.
CHANCERY, FORMS & PRECEDENTS — Ayckbourne, Tripp.
CHANCERY, PROJECTED IMPROVEMENTS IN— Courtenay.
CHANCERY LANE, ON WIDENING—Taylor.
CHANCERY, LEGAL JUDICATURE IN, STATED— Burrough.
CHANCERY, ON MASTERS IN—Har. L. T.
CHANCERY, ON MASTERS' OFFICE—Master.
CHANCERY ORDERS—Beames, Beavan, Carew, Cooke, Miller, Morgan & Chute, Orders, Sanders.
CHANCERY, ORDERS & RULES TO M. 1794— Moore.
CHANCERY, ORDERS & STATUTES—Kennedy.
CHANCERY, ORDERS & IMPROVEMENTS OF COURTS—Rawlins.
CHANCERY, ORDINANCES IN—Bacon.
CHANCERY, PLEADING—Drewry, Lewis, Lube, Mitford, Story, Van Heythuysen, Welford.
CHANCERY, PRACTICAL REGISTER—Wyatt.
CHANCERY PRACTICE, LETTER—W. Vizard.
CHANCERY PRACTICE—Ayckbourn, Bohun, Braithwaite, Brown, Daniell, Drewry, Gilbert, Goldsmith, Grant, Hands, Harrison, Headlam, Hinde, Jarman, Johnes, Maddock, Newland, Smith, Tothill, Tripp, Williams, Wyatt.

CHANCERY, PRIVILEGES, IN MSS.—Lord Ellesmere & others.
CHANCERY QUESTION, LETTERS—John Wilkes.
CHANCERY, QUESTIONS & ANSWERS—Grant.
CHANCERY REFORM—Garrett, Johnes, Merevale, Morton.
CHANCERY REFORM, & ITS OFFICERS—Spence.
CHANCERY REFORM, SPEECH—Spence.
CHANCERY REFORM, & APPELLATE JURISDICTION, SUGGESTIONS—Temple.
CHANCERY, COURT OF. *Reports of Cases*—Ambler, Atkyns, Barnardiston, Brown (W.), Carey, Cases in Chancery, Cases temp Talbot, Cooper (G.), Cooper (C. P.), Coke, Cox, Craig & Phillips, Comyns, De Gex, Macnaghten & Gordon, De Gex & Jones, De Gex, Fisher, & Jones, De Gex, Jones, & Smith, Dickins, Dyer, Eden, Finch, Fitzgibbons, Freeman, Gilbert, Hall & Twells, Jacob, Jacob & Walker, Kelynge (W.), Lofft, Macnaghten & Gordon, Milne & Craig, Modern Reports, Merivale, Mosely, Moore (Sir F.), Mylne & Keen, Nelson, Peere Williams, Phillips, Pollexfen, Popham, Precedents in Chancery, Reports in Chancery, Ridgeway, Russell, Russell & Mylne, Salkeld, Select Cases, Smith (J. P.), Strange, Swanston, Tothill, Turner & Russell, Ventris, Vernon, Vesey & Beames, Vesey jun., Vesey sen., West, Willes, Wilson.

Court of Appeal—De Gex & Jones; De Gex, Jones, & Smith; De Gex, Macnaghten & Gordon.

Rolls Court—Beavan, Keen, Tamlyn.

Vice-Chancellor Lord Cranworth—Simons.

Vice-Chancellor of England—Drewry, Maddock, Simons & Stuart, Simons.

Vice-Chancellor Sir G. J. Turner—Hare.

Vice-Chancellor Sir J. L. Knight-Bruce—Collyer, De Gex & Smale, Holt (W.), Younge & Collyer.

Vice-Chancellor Sir J. Parker—De Gex & Smale.

Vice-Chancellor Sir J. Stuart—Giffard, Smale & Giffard.

Vice-Chancellor Sir J. Wigram—Hare, Holt (W.).

Vice-Chancellor Sir R. T. Kindersley—Drewry, Drewry & Smale, Simons.

Vice-Chancellor Sir W. P. Wood—Hare, Hemming & Miller. Johnson & Hemming, Kay, Kay & Johnson.

CHANCERY, SPEECH ON COURT OF—Sir E. B. Sugden.
CHANCERY, REGULATION ACT (IRISH)—Smith.
CHANCERY, AS TO RELIEF IN, AGAINST JUDGMENTS, OPINIONS—MSS. temp. Jas.
CHANCERY COURT, SATIRICAL POEM—Blewitt.

CHANCERY COURT, S1 OF—Barry.
CHANCERY COURTS, SUING—Edwards.
CHANCERY COURTS, ON Har. L. T.
CHANCERY COURT, TIM Braithwaite.
CHANCERY COURT, VIE'
CHANDOS (DUKE OF), C
CHANDOS PEERAGE—B
CHANNEL ISLANDS DIR1
CHARACTER, OUTLINES
CHARACTERS (PUBLIC),
CHARACTERISTICS OF V1
CHARITABLE TRUSTS A Finlason, Tudo1
CHARITIES, LAW OF—I
CHARITIES OF BRISTOL,
CHARITIES, ENDOWED,
CHARITIES OF LONDON,
CHARITIES, ENDOWED (
CHARITIES, REPORTS O Pu. II. C.
CHARITABLE TRUSTS, CHAPEL BILL—
CHARITABLE USES—H1
CHARLES I. COLLECTI &c. 1643.
CHARLES I., SIR E. L Langmead, N Vol. 4.
CHARLES I. & REBELL1
CHARLES I. & REVOLU
CHARLES I. LETTERS MARIA—Bruce,
CHARLES I.—Bruce, C
CHARLES II. FIVE LE1 No. 87, C. S. F
CHARLES II. & JAME Ackerman. N
CHARLES II.—Greene,
CHARLES V., HISTORY
CHARNWOOD FOREST,
CHARTÆ ANTIQUÆ—I
CHARTERS, ANCIENT Madox.
CHARTERS, GREAT, I stone.
CHARTERS OF BRITISH
CHARTERS TO CAMBR1
CHARTERS TO CHIPP1
CHARTERS TO CINQUE

INDEX TO SUBJECTS. 411

CHARTERS TO CINQUE PORTS—Jeaks.
CHARTERS TO CIVIL ENGINEERS.
CHARTERS TO EAST INDIA CO.
CHARTERS, ESTABLISHING COURTS IN INDIA.
CHARTER TO THE BANK OF ENGLAND.
CHARTER TO THE BANK, REPORT OF, 1832.
CHARTER TO GLASTONBURY.
CHARTER TO KINGSTON, SURREY—Roots.
CHARTER TO THE DUCHY OF LANCASTER—Hardy.
CHARTER TO LEICESTER CORPORATION.
CHARTER TO LONDON CORPORATION—Suffman.
CHARTER TO LONDON INSTITUTION.
CHARTER TO MAIDSTONE (by James).
CHARTER TO PENNSYLVANIA, N. A.
CHARTER TO QUEENBOROUGH.
CHARTER TO ROCHESTER—Thorpe.
CHARTER TO ST. ALBANS—Farrington.
CHARTER TO SOUTHAMPTON.
CHARTER TO TRINITY HOUSE, DEPTFORD.
CHARTER TO WEST INDIA Co.
CHARTER TO WIGAN, 1808.
CHARTER PARTIES—Lawes.
CHARTER ROLLS, CALENDARS—Rec. Com.
CHAUNCEY (SIR H.), LIFE OF—Malcolm.
CHELSEA, HISTORY OF—Faulkner.
CHESHIRE, HISTORY OF—Sir J. Dodridge, Hanshall, Holt, Sir P. Leycester, Lysons, Ormerod.
CHESHIRE DIRECTORY—Pigot.
CHESHIRE P. O. DIRECTORY—Kelly.
CHESTER COURANT, IN VINDICATION OF MANCHESTER.
CHESTER, DOMESDAY BOOK—Vol. 1, Rec. Com.
CHESTER, CITY OF, HISTORY OF—Hemingway.
CHESTER, JOURNEY FROM TO LONDON—Pennant.
CHFSTER, SURVEY OF—Tunnicliffe.
CHESTERFIELD (LORD), WORKS OF—Maty.
CHICHESTER, HISTORY OF—Hay.
CHICHESTER (PECOCK, BP. OF), REPRESSOR—Babington, No. 19, M. R. Pub.
CHICHELE (ABP.), LIFE OF—Buckley.
CHIEF JUSTICES, &c., LIST OF—Dugdale.
CHIEF JUSTICES, LIVES OF—Lord Campbell.
CHINA, EMBASSY TO—Sir G. Staunton.
CHINA, PENAL LAWS OF—Sir G. Staunton.
CHIVALRY (ANCIENT), MEMOIRES—St. Palaye.
CHILDREN, FATHERS' RIGHT TO CUSTODY OF—Bain.

CHILDREN, REPORT ON TRAINING PAUPER—II. C. Sess. Pa.
CHITTY'S STATUTES, ADDENDA TO—Beavan & P.
CHOLMELEY, WILLIAM, REQUEST OF AN ENGLISH-MAN, 1553—No. 55, C. S. P., C. M. Vol. 2.
CHRIST'S HOSPITAL, HISTORY OF—Trollope.
CHRISTIAN MANUAL—Dr. J. Woolton, P. S. P.
CHRISTIAN PRAYERS & MEDITATIONS—P. S. P.
CHRONICON PETROBURGENSE—Stapleton, No. 47, C. S. P.
CHRONICLES OF EDWARD IV.—Warkworth, No. 10, C. S. P.
CHRONICLES OF ENGLAND—Capgrave, No. 1, M. R. Pub.
CHRONICLES OF ENGLISH KINGS—Sir R. Baker.
CHRONICLES OF ENGLAND, 1189-1558—Grafton.
CHRONICLES—Holingshed.
CHRONICLES (JOHNES' TRANSLATION)—Monstrelet.
CHRONICLE (FRENCH) OF LONDON—Aungier, No. 28, C. S. P.
CHRONICLE OF GREY FRIARS OF LONDON—Nichols, No. 53, C. S. P.
CHRONICLE OF LONDON BRIDGE.
CHRONICLE OF LONDON—Tyrrell.
CHRONICLE OF REIGNS OF RICHARD II., HENRY IV., V., VI.,—Davies, No. 64, C. S. P.
CHRONICLE OF REIGNS OF HENRY VII. & VIII. —Hopper, No, 73, C. S. P.
CHRONICLE OF QUEEN JANE & QUEEN MARY—Nichols, No. 47, C. S. P.
CHRONICLES OF REBELLION IN LINCOLNSHIRE—Nichols, No. 39, C. S. P., C. M. Vol. 1.
CHRONICLES & ANNALS OF W. RISHANGER—Riley, No. 28, M. R. Pub.
CHRONOLOGICAL HISTORIAN—Salmon.
CHRONOLOGY, OR UNIVERSAL HISTORY—Aspin, Blair.
CHRONOLOGY OF HISTORY—Nicolas.
CHURCH OF ENGLAND, APOLOGY FOR.
CHURCH OF ENGLAND, BUILDING, LAW AS TO &c.—Trower.
CHURCH OF ENGLAND, VINDICATION & LAWS OF.
CHURCH OF ENGLAND, VALIDITY OF ITS ORDERS —Prideaux.
CHURCH OF ENGLAND, LETTER TO MR. GLADSTONE ON THE DUTY OF THE GOVERNMENT TOWARDS THE—Miller.
CHURCH & CLERGY LAW—Cripps.
CHURCH COURTS & CHURCH DISCIPLINE—R. J. Wilberforce.
CHURCH DICTIONARY—Dr. W. F. Hook.
CHURCH GOVERNMENT, QUESTIONS TOUCHING—Prynne.

CHURCH REFORM—Lord Henley.
CHURCH & STATE—Grim, Tr.
CHURCH, TREASON IN THE, LETTER—O'Connell.
CHURCHWARDENS, LAW OF—Prideaux.
CHURCH LANGTON, HISTORY OF—Hanbury.
CID (LE)—Corneille.
CICERO, DRAMA OF—Moile.
CICERO, BIOGRAPHY OF—Middleton.
CINQUE PORTS—Brayley.
CIRCUIT COMPANION—Dogherty.
CIRCUIT COURT REPORTS (U.S.)—Gallison.
CIRCUMSTANTIAL EVIDENCE—Willis.
CITIES, &c., HISTORY OF—Brady.
CITIZEN'S POCKET CHRONICLE—J. S. E.
CITY CHARITIES (PUBLIC)—Highmore.
CITY, COMMON HALL ELECTIONS—Mildmay.
CITY FRANCHISES, COMMENTARIES ON—Norton.
CITY ORDERS AS TO COURTS—City Tracts.
CITY PRIVILEGES—Green.
CITY PRIVILEGES, EPITOME—Hughson.
CITY PRIVILEGES, EXPOSITION OF—Norton.
CITY REMEMBRANCER.
CITY SEWER COMMISSIONERS, MEMORIAL TO—City Tracts.
CIVIL BILL PROCESS, IRISH PRECEDENTS—Pyke.
CIVIL LAW—Ayloffe, Bowyer, Brown, Domat, Fulbecke, Irving, Mackenzie, Miller, Phillimore, Taylor, Wood, Zouch.
CIVIL POLICY, NATURE OF.
CIVIL SERVICE GUIDE—White.
CIVIL WAR, A, TO PREVENT—Prynne.
CLAYBROOK, &c., HISTORY OF, &c.—Macauley.
CLAVIS CALENDARIA—Brady.
CLERGY, INSTRUCTIONS TO THE—Hodgson.
CLERGY LIST—Cox.
CLERGY LAW—Cripps, Stephens, A. S.
CLERGY & LAITY, INJUNCTIONS TO—Queen Elizabeth.
CLERGYMAN'S HANDBOOK—Dale.
CLERGYMAN'S LAW—Watson.
CLERGYMAN (MODERN)—Lucas.
CLERGYMEN, THE RIGHTS OF—Nelson.
CLERKENWELL, DISCOVERY OF JESUITS AT—Nichols, Nos. 55 & 73, C. S. P., C. M. Vols. 2 & 4.
CLERKENWELL, HISTORY OF—Cromwell.
CLERK'S MANUAL (THE YOUNG).
CLEVELAND, HISTORY OF—Grave, Ord.
CLINTON PEERAGE CASE.
CLITHEROE, HISTORY OF—Dr. T. D. Whittaker.

CLOUGH, CASE IN IRISH EXCHEQUER REPORT—Macrory.
CLOSE ROLLS, ROTULI LITTERARUM CLAUSARUM, Rec. Com.—T. D. Hardy.
CODE OF PROCEDURE OF NEW YORK, 1867.
CODEX DIPLOMATICUS (HISTORICAL SOCIETY)—Kemble.
CODEX LEGUM—Lindenbrogius.
CODEX JURIS ECCLESIASTICI ANGLICANI—Gibson.
COIN, SIR R. COTTON'S SPEECH ON—Howell, C. P.
COIN OF THE KINGDOM, DIALOGUE—Sir H. Spelman.
COKE (SIR E.), BIOGRAPHY OF—Roscoe.
COKE (LORD), REPORTS.
COKE (LORD), ANSWER TO 5TH PART—Parsons.
COKE (SIR E.) PROCEEDINGS AT OATLANDS—Gardiner, No. 87 C. S. P., C. M. Vol. 5.
COKE'S COMMENTARIES UPON LITTLETON—Hargrave & Butler.
COKE'S COMMENTARIES, ANALYSIS—Fisk.
COLCHESTER, HISTORY OF—Carter.
COLCHESTER, HISTORY OF—Cromwell.
COLCHESTER, HISTORY OF TOWN & BOROUGH—Morant.
COLCHESTER, BURGESSES, LETTER TO—D. W. Harvey.
COLENSO'S FALLACIES—De Meschen.
COLLATERAL CONSANGUINITY, ESSAY ON—Blackstone.
COLLECTANEA CANTABRIGIENSIA—Bloomfield.
COLLECTANEA TOPOGRAPHICA & GENEALOGICA—Nicholls & others.
COLLEGE OF ARMS, HISTORY OF—Noble.
COLLEGIATE &c. CHURCH OF MANCHESTER, ANSWERS—Vol. 9, Pam.
COLLIERS & COLLIERIES—Fowler.
COLLIERIES OF SOUTH WALES, EVIDENCE OF—H. C.
COLLISIONS AT SEA—Lowndes.
COLONIAL LAW—Burge, Earnshaw, Clarke, Howard.
COLONIAL OFFICE LIST (1868).
COLONIAL STATUTES—Dowling; and see each Colony.
COLONIAL SERIES, CALENDAR STATE PAPERS, AMERICAN, EAST INDIES &c.—Sainsbury.
COLONIAL POLICY—Mr. H. Brougham.
COLONIES OF ENGLAND, Mr. ADDERLEY—Vol. 18, Pam.
COLONIES, STEAM TO—Jerningham.
COLLOQUIA FAMILIARIA—Erasmus.
COLUMBUS (SHIP), SIR JAS. MARRIOTT'S JUDGMENT—Vol. 1, Col. Jur.
COMBATS, &c., LEGALITY OF—Howell, C. P.

COMMENDAMS, CASE OF. *See* Vol 2, Stillingfleet.
COMMENDAMS, CASE OF, BEFORE P. C.—Vol. 1, Col. Jur.
COMMERCE—Anderson, Macpherson.
COMMERCIAL DICTIONARY—McCulloch, Savary.
COMMERCIAL FORMS—Crabbe, Montefiore.
COMMERCIAL LAW—Beawes, Chitty, Levi, Malynes, Montefiore, Smith.
COMMERCIAL TREATISES—Hertslet.
COMMENTARIA JURIDICA—Panormitanus.
COMMENTARIES UPON LITTLETON—Lord Coke, Hargreave, Hargrave & Butler, Thomas
COMMENTARIES OF LORD COKE, SYNOPSIS—Sir H. Davenport.
COMMENTARIES ON THE COMMON LAW—Broome.
COMMENTARIES, AMERICAN—Kent.
COMMENTARIES, ENGLISH LAW—Sir W. Blackstone.
COMMENTARII IN CORPUS JURIS CIVILIS—Albericus de Rosato.
COMMENTARII IN INSTITUTIONES—Vinnius.
COMMENTARII AD PANDECTAS—J. Voet.
COMMENTARIUS JURIS ANGLICANI—Clarke, C.
COMITES MARESCALLI ANGLIÆ—Sir H. Spelman.
COMŒDIÆ—Terentius.
COMINES (DE) FILIPE.
COMMON ASSURANCE LAW—Sheppard.
COMMON LAW.—Bacon, Broom, Glisson & Gulston, Gregory, Hale, Jacob, Miller, Napier, Smith, J. W.
   Practice—Archbold. Bagley, Broom, Chitty, Crompton, Day, Finlason, Gray, Harrison, Holland & Chandless, Kerr, Kime, Lawrence, Lush, Markham, Morris & Finlason, Stephen, Tidd.
   Digests of Cases—Coventry & Hughes, Evans, Fisher, Hammond, Harrison, Jeremy, Moore, Repertorium Juridicum.
COMMON LAW v. COMMON SENSE—Massey.
COMMON LAW, IRELAND—Napier.
COMMON LAW &c. COURTS—Boothby.
COMMON PLEAS.
   Reports of Cases—Anderson, Arnold, Barnes, Bentoe, Bingham, Blackstone (Sir W.), Bosanquet & Puller, Bridgman (Sir J.), Bridgman (Sir O.), Broderip & Bingham, Brooke (Sir R.), Brownlow & Gouldsborough, Campbell, Carter, Comyns, Cooke, Cooke (Sir G.), Coke, Dalison, Dyer, Espinasse, Fitzgibbons, Fortescue, Freeman, Granger & Scott, Harrison & Rutherford, Hetley, Hodges, Hutton, Jones (Sir W), Keilway, Kelynge (W.), Leonard, Ley, Littleton, Lutwyche, Manning, Manning & Granger, March, Marshall, Modern Reports, Moore (J. B.), Moore (Sir F.), Moore & Payne, Moore & Scott, Noy, Owen, Palmer, Plowden, Pollexfen, Popham, Practical Register, Raymond (Lord), Raymond (Sir T.) Salkeld, Savile, Scott, Siderfin, Starkie, Strange, Taunton, Vaughan, Ventris, Willes, Wilson, Winch, Year Books.

COMMON PLEAS, HISTORY OF—Gilbert.
COMMON PRAYER & UNIFORMITY ACT (1724)
COMMON PRAYER—Bayley, Mant.
COMMON PRAYER, ILLUSTRATION OF BOOK OF—Wheatly.
COMMON RIGHTS—Woolrych.
COMMONERS, HISTORY OF THE—Burke.
COMMONERS & COMMONS, LAW OF, 1780.
COMMONS OF ENGLAND, RIGHTS OF, ASSERTED—Petyt.
COMMONS PRESERVATION, SIX ESSAYS—Maidlow and others.
COMMONS & WASTE LANDS—Elton.
COMMONWEALTH, ABUSES AGAINST, 1629.
COMMONWEALTH, ON USE, &c.—Palgrave.
COMMONWEALTH'S FRIEND—March.
COMPANION, UNIVERSAL POCKET (1760).
COMPANIES ACT, 1862—G. L. Browne.
COMPANIES ACT, 1867—G. L. Browne.
COMPANIES—Browne, Digby, Taylor, Shelford, Thring, Wordsworth.
COMPENDIOUS MEASURER—Hutchinson.
COMPENSATION—Ingram, Lloyd, Wordsworth.
COMPOSITION DEEDS, ACT FOR—Ayrton.
COMPOSITION DEEDS—De Gex & Smith, Forsyth, Griffith, Holland, Sills.
CONCILE DE TRENT—Sarpi.
CONCILIA MAG. BRIT. ET HIBERNIÆ—D. Wilkins.
CONCILIUM BASILIENSE—Brant.
CONDE, LIFE OF—Mahon.
CONFLICT OF LAWS—Burge, Story.
CONGREGATIONAL COURTS—Sharp.
CONICARUM SECTIONUM ELEMENTA—Milnes.
CONISBROUGH (York) HISTORY OF Wainwright
CONSOLATO DEL MARE—Battiste.
CONSTABLE, ON THE OFFICE OF—Willcock.
CONSTANTINOPLE & DELHI, MAP OF DISTRICT BETWEEN—Arrowsmith.
CONSTITUTION—Amos, De Lolme, Rowland.
CONSTITUTION, BRITISH—Lord Brougham.
CONSTITUTION, TEXT BOOK OF—Creasy.
CONSTITUTION, DOGMAS OF—Park.
CONSTITUTION, HISTORY OF, 1760-1860—May.
CONSTITUTIONAL LAW—Broom.
CONSTITUTIONALISM OF THE FUTURE—Lorimer.

CONTINENTAL GUIDE—Bradshaw.
CONTRABAND OF WAR—Deane, Moseley.
CONTRACTS—Addison, Chitty, Dixon, Leake, Metcalfe (U.S.) Powell, Smith, Parsons (U.S.), Story (U.S.).
CONTRACTS, SPECIFIC PERFORMANCE OF—Fry.
CONTRACT OF SALE—Blackburn.
CONTRE PROJET TO HUMPHRYSIAN CODE—Park.
CONTRIBUTORIES—Farrar.
CONVEYANCING, THEORY, &c., OF—Vol. 2, Col. Jur.:—Barry, Barton, Bridgman, Butler, Bythewood & Jarman, Clayton, Coventry, Covert, Crabb, Crisp, Davidson & others, Davidson & Stapylton, R. G., Greenwood, Hayes, Herne, Horseman, Housman, Hughes, Jarman (*see* Bythewood), Lilly, Martin, Mill, Newnam, Perkins, Preston, Prideaux, Prince, Prior, Ritson, Roberts, Rouse, B. Smith, Stewart, Sweet (*see* Bythewood & J.), Watkins, Wood, Wilde's Supp. to Barton, Williams.
CONVEYANCING (AMERICAN)—Thornton.
CONVICT DISCIPLINE, COMS. REPORT, 1863—Law Amt. Soc.
CONVICTIONS—Hulton, Oke, Paley.
COOPER (C. P.)—Speech.
COUNCILS (PUBLIC) OF THE KINGDOM—L. T. No. 2, No. 16.
COPYHOLD—Bray, Carter, Fisher, Rouse, Scriven, Shelford, Watkins.
COPYHOLD ENFRANCHISEMENT ACT—Cudden.
COPYHOLD SURRENDERS—Saunders.
COPYHOLD ESTATES, FINES ON ADMISSION—Vol. 2, Col Jur.
COPYHOLDER (THE COMPLETE)—Coke.
COPYHOLDERS, CONSIDERATIONS ON—Blackstone.
COPYHOLDERS, ARE THEY FREEHOLDERS?—Blackstone.
COPYHOLDS, ENFRANCHISEMENT—J. M. White.
COPYHOLDS, ON SURRENDER OF—Vol. 2, Col. Jur.
COPYRIGHT OF DESIGNS—Newton.
COPYRIGHT (IN ENGLAND & AMERICA)—Curtis.
COPYRIGHT BILL, SUGGESTIONS ON.
COPYRIGHT LAW, AS TO AUTHORS—Montague's Tr.
COPYRIGHT LAW, PROPOSED ALTERATION IN.
COPYRIGHT LAW—Crawford, Phillips, Underdown.
COPYRIGHT AND PATENT LAW—Fraser.
CORNWALL:—
P. O. Directory—Kelly, Pigot.
Domesday Book—Vol. 1, Rec. Com.
Facsimile of Ditto—Sir H. James.
History of—Borlase, Carew, Sir J. Dodrige, Gilbert, Lysons, Polwhele.
Natural History, &c.—Borlase.
Stannary Courts of—F. Hill.
Stannary Courts, Laws, &c.

CORNWALL & SCILLY, HISTORY OF—Heath.
CORK, HISTORY OF—Smith.
CORN LAWS, LETTER—Whitmore.
CORN TRADE, ON THE DECLINE OF—Howlett's Tr.
CORONER—Baker, Greenwood, Ormerod, Impey, Jervis.
CORONER'S COURT, ITS USES, &c.—Dempsey.
CORONERS, OFFICE OF, & SHERIFF—*See* Grounds of the Law.
CORONER, AS TO ELECTION OF, 1831.
CORPORATION BOUNDARIES—England & Wales.
CORPORATION BOUNDARIES—Ireland.
CORPORATION ACT (Municipal).
CORPORATION, CONDUCT OF LONDON, AS TO ITS BRIDGE—1823.
CORPORATIONS—Angell & Ames (U.S.), Grant, Kyd, Rawlinson, Willcock.
CORPORATIONS MUNICIPAL—Merewether & Stephens.
CORPUS JURIS CANONICI—Gregorie, Lancellott.
CORPUS JURIS CIVILIS—Hermannus.
CORPUS JURIS CIVILIS—1681 & 1700.
CONISBROUGH (YORK), HISTORY OF—Wainwright.
CORRESPONDENCE:—
Parker (Bp.)—P. S. P.
Plympton—Stapleton, No. 4, C. S. P.
Leycester—Bruce, No. 27, C. S. P.
Perth—Jerdan, No. 33, C. S. P.
COSMOGRAPHIE UNIVERSELLE—Munster.
COST BOOK—Tapping.
COSTS, BANKRUPTCY—Gregg, Richardson.
COSTS, CHANCERY—Coleman, Shaen & Greville, Morgan & Davey.
COSTS, COMMON LAW—Day, Evans, Gray, Hullock, Jennings & Heckforde, Le Riche, Lloyd, Marshall, Palmer, Sayer, Scott, Wickstead.
COSTS, PARLIAMENTARY—Norris, Palmer, Webster.
COTTONI POSTHUMA—Howell.
COTTON FROM INDIA, SUPPLY—Browne.
COTTON, CULTIVATION OF—Devencenze.
COTTON, CULTIVATION OF—Cordovas.
COUNTRY ATTORNEY—Gray, Paterson.
COUNTRY SOLICITOR—Gray.

COUNTY COURTS:—Columbine, Cox & Lloyd, Davis, Greenwood, Mosely, Pollock, Sweet, Udall, Will.
County Court Bill—Neate.
County Court Act, Remarks on—Joyce.
County Court Extension Bill, Substitute—Beake.
County Court Act, Analysis, 1856—Nowell.
County Court, On Working of—Vigil.
Equity Jurisdiction—Batten & Ludlow, Gibbons & Harvey, Pollock & Nicol.
Jurisdiction, before & after January 1, 1868—Rumsey.
Rules—Rumsey.
Reports of Cases—Roberts, Leeming & Wallis.
COUNTY KALENDAR—Churton.
COUNTY VOTER'S MANUAL—James.
COURSE OF PROCEEDING—Bohun.
COURT OF GREAT BRITAIN, PRESENT STATE OF.
COURT GUIDE—Boyle, Robson, Thompson.
COURT HAND RESTORED—Wright.
COURT KEEPER—Greenwood, Jacob.
COURTS LEET & BARON—Kitchen, Scriven, Scroggs, Sheppard.
COURTS MARTIAL—MacArthur, Tytler.
COURT MARTIAL ON DOUGLAS.
COURT REGISTER—Musgrave, Sliford.
COURTS—L. Tr.
COURTS OF K. B. & C. P. PROCESS THEREFROM—Sir M. Hale.
COURTS, EVIDENCE ON REMOVAL OF, EXTRACTS FROM.
COURTS, LETTER WHERE TO SIT—Smith & Trail.
COURTS, ON JURISDICTION OF—Maugham.
COURTS, QUESTIONS ON JURISDICTION OF—Maugham.
COURTS, FEES OF OFFICERS OF—List.
COURTS OF LAW & EQUITY, ON ASSIMILATION OF—Aston.
COVENANTS—Platt.
COWARDICE & TREACHERY, DOOM OF—Prynne.
CRANCH'S REPORTS (U.S.). *See* Curtis.
CRANE *v*. PRICE, REMARKS—Rowland.
CRAVEN—Whitaker.
CREDIT, PERNICIOUS—Rosser.
CREDIT & TRADE, REMARKS ON.
CREDITOR & DEBTOR: SUGGESTIONS.
CREDITOR & DEBTOR, ON LAW OF—Henley.
CREDITOR & DEBTOR, ARRANGEMENTS—Trower, De Gex & Smith, Forsyth.
CREDITORS, ON COMPOSITION WITH—Griffiths, Holland, Sills.
CRICKLADE CASE—Petrie.

CRIME & CRIMINALS, IS GAOL THE PREVENTION?—Pulling.
CRIME & INSANITY—Burn.
CRIMES—Russell.
CRIMINAL CASES, AS TO PERMITTING DEFENDANTS &C. TO TESTIFY—Law Amt. Society.
CRIMINAL CASES, ON AMTS., AS TO PROCEDURE IN—Law Amt. Society.
CRIMINAL ACTS—Jervis.
CRIMINAL INFORMATION—Cole.
CRIMINAL JURISPRUDENCE—Beccaria, Roscoe.
CRIMINAL JUSTICE—Cotter.
CRIMINAL JUSTICE, COURTS OF, IN JAMAICA—Davis.
CRIMINAL LAW Archbold, Bishop (U.S.), Carrington, Chitty, Cole, East, Greaves, Hawkins, Matthews, Pulton, Roscoe, Russell, Sleigh, Saunders & Cox, Starkie, Stephen, Woolrych.
On Improvement of—Foote.
Outlines of—Maugham.
Speech on—Sir R. Peel.
CRIMINAL LAW REPORTS OF CASES—Cox, Lewin.
CRIMINAL PLEADING & EVIDENCE—Archbold.
CRIMINAL STATUTES—Pratt, Archbold.
CRIMINALS, THEORY OF TREATMENT OF—Sampson.
CRISIS—S'r Richd. Steele. *See* Tr. on Parliamentary Privileges.
CRITIC (BRITISH).
CROMWELL(O.)& THE ENGLISH COMMONWEALTH, HISTORY OF—Guizot.
CROMWELL, HISTORY OF—Noble.
CROMWELL (R.) & THE HISTORY OF THE RESTORATION OF CAR. II.—Guizot.
CROWN ASSISTANT—Dogherty.
CROWN CASES—Bell. Denison, Dearsly, Dearsly & Bell, Foster, Leach, Leigh & Cave, Moody, Russell & Ryan.
CROWN CIRCUIT COMPANION—Minchin & Herbert, Stubbs & Talmash.
CROWN, GRANTS &C. FROM THE, DURING REIGN OF EDW. V.—Nichols, No. 60, C. S. P.
CROWN LAW—Sharp.
CROWN, PLEAS OF THE—East, Hale, Hawkins, Tremaine.
CROWN, SUCCESSION TO—Doleman.
CROYDON—Ducarel, Garrow.
CUMBERLAND:—
D rectory—Pigot.
P. O. Dire tory—Kelly.
Estates of Greenwich Hospital in. See Greenwich.
Guide & D.rectory—Jollie.

History of—Hutchinson, Lysons, Robinson.
Survey of Lakes of—Clarke.
Views in—Rev. J. Wilkinson.
CUMBERLAND & WESTMORLAND :—
Domesday Book, *for Parts of*—Bawdwen.
History of—Nicholson & Burn.
Guide to Lakes of—West.
CUBIALIA, ACCOUNT OF ROYAL HOUSEHOLD—Pegge.
CURSITOR BARON—Foss.
CURRAN, BIOGRAPHY OF—Phillips.
CUSTOMS OF GOODS IMPORTED, &C., LD. C. J. HALE - Har. L. T.
CUSTOMS, STATUTES, AND RATES—Carkess.
CUSTOMS, LAWS, &C., OF LONDON.
CUSTOMS—Baldwin, Walford.
CUSTOMS AND EXCISE LAWS—Pope.
CUT FROM THE MEDWAY TO THE THAMES—Pamphlet V.
CYCLOPÆDIA, NEW AMERICAN—Ripley & Dana.

DACRE *v.* DACRE, CASE—Hargr. J. A.
DALE (SAMUEL), LIFE OF—Malcolm.
DALLAS, REPORTS (U.S.). *See* Curtis.
DAMAGES—Mayne, Sayer, Sedgwick, U.S.
DAGENHAM REACH (ESSEX), STOPPING UP—Parry.
DANBY (EARL OF), AS TO MURDER OF SIR E. GODFREY—Pol. Tr.
DANGERFIELD, INFORMATION OCT. 1680, AND 2ND NARRATIVE—Pol. Tr.
DANUBIAN PRINCIPALITIES, CORRESPONDENCE—Bratiano.
DATES, MANUAL OF—Townsend, Haydn.
DAVERS (M. M.), ENQUIRY AS TO LETTER SO SIGNED OF 3/2/1613—(J.B.) C. M. Vol. 5, No. 87, C.S.P.
DAVEY'S CASE, LETTER ON—Barrow, Dr.
DAVEYS (SIR JOHN), ARGUMENT—MSS. temp. Jas.
DAVIDSON, BIOGRAPHY—Nicolas.
DAVIS (DR. JOHN) ARGUMENT—No. 68, C. S. P., Caulfield.
DEATH, PUNISHMENT OF—Wakefield.
DEBATES IN PARLIAMENT, HISTORY—1102-1660.
DEBATES IN LORDS—1160-1743.
DEBATES IN COMMONS—1660-1744.
DEBATES IN COMMONS ON BILL FOR PUNISHMENT OF HIGH TREASON, 5/4/1813—Mont. Tr.

DEBATES IN COMMONS O 25/4/1814—Mo
DEBT, EXECUTION FOI His. L. Tr.
DEBT, PERSONAL, EXE L. Tr.
DEBT, SECURITIES TO F
DEBTOR, EXECUTION DEATH OF—L.
DEBTORS' RELIEF SOCIE
DEBTOR & CREDITOR, —De Gex & S Sills, Trower.
DEBTOR & CREDITOR,
DECEASED WIFE'S SIST
DECISIONS—Linglois.
DECIMAL WEIGHTS—M
DECREES IN EQUITY—
DECRETALS—Panormit
DEEDS & DOCUMENTS,
DEEDS & ENROLLING—
DEE's (DR.), DIARY—]
DEFAMATION—Cooke.
DE FARIA, INFORMAT Pol. T.
DE LEGIBUS—Bracton.
DELITTE (DEI) E DELLA
DENT (JOHN), LIFE OF
DENMARK & GERMANY
DEPTFORD, TRINITY H
DERBY :—
  Collection for His.
  Derby, &c., *Tour*—
  Domesday Book—
  P. O. Directory—
  History &c. of—
  Lysons.
  Miners' Glossary—
  Mining Customs—
  Mineralogy of—N
  Strata, De'ineatio
  Survey—Holt.
  View of—Pilking
DERBYSHIRE, DOMESDA
DERBYSHIRE—Davies,
DERWENTWATER (EAR MENT AGAINST—Lords.
DESBOROUGH, HUNDRE
DESCENT—Blackstone,
DESCENT & DISTRIBUT
DESIGN FOR METROPO Architect.
DETINUE - Mounteney.
DEVISES—Gilbert, Pov

INDEX TO SUBJECTS. 417

DEVISE OF REAL & PERSONALTY, OPINION—
  Col. Jur.
DEVIZES (WILTS), ANTIQUITIES OF—Davis.
DEVIZES, CHRONICLES OF—Waylan.
DEVON, DOMESDAY BOOK—Vol. 1, Rec. Com.
DEVON, WORTHIES OF—Prince.
DEVONSHIRE :—
  Directory—Kelly.
  Collection towards a History of—Sir Wm. Pole.
  History of—Polwhele, Lysons.
  Survey of—Risdon, by Chapple.
  Chorographical Survey of—Risdon.
DEVOTIONAL PIETY, TEMP. Q. ELIZ.—Par. S. Pa.
DIALOGUES, SURVEYORS'.
DIALOGUES BETWEEN WHIG AND TORY 1718. *See* Gosling.
DIALOGUES ON MARRIAGE LAW OF 1835—Vol. 24, Pam.
DIARIES :—
  Dee (Dr.)—No. 19, C. S. Pa.
  Cartwright (Bp.)—No. 22, C. S. Pa.
  Yonge (W.)—No. 41, C. S. Pa.
  Machyn (H.)—No. 42, C. S. Pa.
  Rous (J.)—No. 66, C. S. Pa.
  Symonds (R.)—No. 74, C. S. P.
  Lake (Dr. Edwd.)—No. 39, C. M.
DICTIONARIES :—
  America & West Indies—Thompson.
  Antiquities, Gr. & Rom.—W. Smith.
  Archæological—Britton, Hickes.
  Bible—W. Smith.
  Bibliographical—Hazlitt, Lowndes, Moule, Watts.
  Biographical—Allibone, Bayle, Chalmers, Davenport, Hole, Kippis, Maunder, Routledge, W. Smith, Wilson.
  Chronological—Richardson.
  Church—Hook.
  Classical—Lemprière.
  Commercial—McCulloch, Savary (Fr.).
  Critical—Bayle, Hickes.
  Dates—Haydn.
  Dutch—Halma.
  Encyclopædias—Britannica, London, Rees, (Chambers).
  English—Halliwell, Johnson, (Todd), Junius, Phillips, Walker, Webster.
  Extinct Peerage—Burke.
  Faillettes des—(French) Bedaredde.
  Flemish—Halma.
  French—Boyer, De Trevoux, Furetiere, Spiers.
  General—Bayle.
  Geographical—Bouillet (Fr.), Edinburgh Gazetteer, Morery, W. Smith (Gr. & Rom.), Varenius.
  German—Flugel.
  Glossarial—Boucher, Du Cange, Mander (Derbyshire), Spelman.
  Greek—Dehèque, Hedericus, Liddell & Scott, Scapula.
  Historical—Bouillet, Morery.

DICTIONARIES—*continued.*
  Italian—Baretti, Graglia.
  Landed Gentry—Burke.
  Languages eleven—Minsheu.
  Latin—Ainsworth, Facciolatus, W. Smith.
  Law, English—Blount, Cunningham, Holthouse, Jacob, Pompeius, Pott, Tomlins, Whishaw.
  Law, Scotch—Bell, Skene.
  Law, American—Bouvier.
  Lexicons — Calvinus (Jur.), Facciolatus (Lat.), Hedericus (Gk.), Hoffmannus (J.), Liddell & Scott (Gk.)
  Marine—Falconer.
  Norman French—Kelham.
  Portuguese—Vieyra.
  Scotch—Jamieson.
  Spanish—Castellane, Neuman & Baretti, Stevens.
  Thesaurus—Bridgman, Ecton (Eccl.) Stephanus (Lat. & Gk.)
  Welsh—Owen, Pugh.
MAUNDER'S TREASURIES :
  Knowledge.
  Natural History.
  History.
  Scientific & Literary.
  Biography.
  Geography.
DIGESTA NOVISSIMA TOTIUS JURIS—Marta.
DIGESTS :—
  Admiralty—Green, Notanda (Edwards), Pritchard.
  Common Law—Burchell, Chitty & Forster, Comyns, Coventry, Evans, Fisher, Guise, Hammond, Harrison, Jeremy, Jurist, Manning, Moore, Notanda (Edwards).
  Ecclesiastical—Waddilove.
  Equity—Bridgman, Chitty, Evans, Fisher, Jagge, Jurist, Notanda (Edwards).
  House of Lords—Clark, Kinnear (Scotch).
  Real Property—Cruise.
  Poor Law—Const.
  Records—Jones, Martin.
  Scotch Law—Alexander, Bell, Kinnear, Shaw.
  Statutes—Gabbett, Chitty by Welsby & Bearan, Crabb, Raithby, Ruffhead, Stamp, Vardon, Williams.
DIGNITIES—Beatson, Betham, Cruise, Haydn.
DILAPIDATIONS—Royal Institute of British Artists.
DILAPIDATIONS & NUISANCES—Elmes, Gibbon, Grady.
DIRECTORIES :—
  Annuaire Almanach de Commerce—Bottin.
  Auctioneers', &c.—Allnutt.
  Bombay.
  Boston (U.S.)
  Cambrian.
  Canada.
  Derbyshire—Pigot.
  Devonshire—Pigot.
  Devonshire, P. O.—Kelly.
  Dorsetshire—Pigot.

DIRECTORIES (*continued*):—
 Dorsetshire, P. O.—Kelly.
 Durham—Kelly.
 Durham, P. O. See Westmoreland—Kelly.
 Westmoreland—Pigot.
 Fashionable, or Royal Blue-Book.
 Joint Stock Companies'—Barker.
 Madras—Gratz.
 Medical London and Provincial.
 Municipal Corporations'—Vickers.
 Paris. See Bottin's Annuaire.
 Polite Intelligence.
 P. O.—Kelly.
 P. O. Suburban—Kelly.
 British—Thom.
 London — Johnstone, Kelly, H. Kent, Pigot, Robson.
 London & Provincial — Holden, Pigot, Robson.
DISCOURSES ON ENGLISH LAW—Sir H. Finch.
DISCOVERY—Hare, Wigram.
DISPATCHES OF DUKE OF WELLINGTON—Col. Greenwood & Duke of Wellington.
DISPUTATIONS—Bellarmine.
DISSENTERS' CHAPELS BILL:—
 Proceedings.
 Report on, Parliamentary Debate on.
 Strictures on—Matthews.
DISSERTATIO AD FLETAM—Selden, 2nd vol.
DISTRESS—Bradby, Bullen, Gilbert.
DISTRIBUTION & DISSENT—By a Solicitor.
DISEASE & CRIME, CONNECTION BETWEEN—M. D. Hill.
DIVIDENDS, UNCLAIMED.
DIVISION OF COUNTIES, PROPOSED REPORT—England, Ireland, 1832.
DIVORCE EVIDENCE—Smith's Divorce.
DIVORCE, LAW OF — Bilton, Bishop (U.S.), Browne, Browning, Inderwick, McQueen, Morgan, Paynter, Pritchard, T. Tidswell & Littler.
DOCTORS' COMMONS SOCIETY, ACCOUNT OF—MSS., Ducarel.
DOCTOR & STUDENT, ABRIDGMENT.
DOCUMENTS ILLUSTRATING ENGLISH HISTORY IN 13TH & 14TH CENTURIES—H. Cole. Rec. Com.
DOCUMENTS (ECCLESIASTICAL)—No. 8, C. S. Pa.
DOCUMENTS, PRODUCTION OF—Bosanquet.
DOMESDAY—Bawdwen, Ellis, Henshall, Kelham Rec. Com. Wyndham.
DOMICILE—Cole, Phillimore.
DONCASTER (YORK), HISTORY OF—Hunter, Miller, Wainwright.
DON QUIXOTE—Cervantes.
DORMANT PEERAGES—Banks.
DORSET:—
 Domesday Book for—Vol. 1, Rec. Com.
 Domesday Book for, &c.—Bawdwen & Hutchins, Vol. 2, Rec. Com.

DORSETSHIRE:—
 History of—Boswell.
 Antiquities of—Coker.
 Antiquities of — Hutchins.
 Directory—Kelly, Pigot.
DOUGLAS' CASE, H. L. 1769, ARGUMENT—Co Jur.
DOVER, TOWN—Lyon.
DOVER CASTLE—Darell.
DOVERCOURT—Dale.
DOWER—Park.
DOWER, REMARKS ON BARRING—Prince.
DOOM OF COWARDICE AND TREACHERY—Prynn
D'OYLEY FAMILY, HISTORY OF—Bayley.
DRAIN TILES & PIPES—Vol. 1, Abr. Pat.
DRAINAGE, LAND—Thring, Woolrych.
DRAINING & EMBANKING—Dugdale.
DRAKE (FRANCIS), LIFE OF—Malcolm.
DRAKE (SIR F.), SERVICES AGAINST SPAIN I 1567 [R. LENG]—Hopper, 87, C. S. P C. M. Vol. 5.
DRAYTON'S POLYOLBION, NOTES ON—Selden 3rd vol.
DRUIDS' TEMPLE AT AVEBURY, WILTS, A POEM O:
DRUNKEN BURNABEE'S JOURNAL—Brathwaite.
DUBLIN:—
 Archbishops, Memoirs of—D'Alton.
 History of—Warburton & others, Harris
 County, History of—D'Alton.
 History of Cathedral of St. Patrick—Mason.
 Court of Record, Precedents in—Pyke.
 Visitation at, on Dr. Shaw's Appeal, Proceedings.
DUCAREL (ANDREW), LIFE OF—Malcolm.
DUCATUS LANCASTRIÆ CALENDARIUM, INQUISITIONUM POST MORTEM, &C.—Rec. Com.
DUELS, ORIGIN OF—Selden, 3rd vol.
DUGDALE'S INFORMATION—Pol. T.
DUGDALE'S (SIR WILLIAM) LIFE, &C.—Hamper, Malcolm.
DUGDALE'S PEERAGE, SPECIMENS OF MISTAKE IN—Rawlinson.
DUKEDOM OF ROXBURGH, CASES & EVIDENCE.
DUKEDOM OF SUSSEX, CASE OF SIR A. F. D'ESTE
DUNWICH, &C., HISTORY OF—Gardiner.
DURHAM YARD, REMARKS ON ENCROACHMENTS ON THAMES, NEAR.
DURHAM COAL MINES—Holmes.
DURHAM ESTATES, GREENWICH HOSPITAL.
DURHAM, HISTORY OF—Hutchinson, Surtees.
DURHAM & NORTHUMBERLAND, LOCAL RECORD OF—Sykes.
DURHAM DIRECTORY—Kelly, Pigot.
DUTCH TRADE—Huet.
DUTIES ON MALT & BEER, ENQUIRY AS TO—Vol. 5, Parl.

EARTH, THEORY OF THE—Whiston.
EARTH, THE, & MANKIND—Howard.
EASEMENTS—Gale, Gale & Whatley.
EASEMENTS & SERVITUDES (U.S.)—Washbourne.
EAST INDIA COMPANY:—
  Acts of Governor, &c.
  Acts of, Bombay.
  Acts of, Calcutta.
  Acts of, Madras.
EAST INDIA ARMY LIST.
EAST INDIA REGISTER.
EAST LONDON WATER WORKS ACT.
EAST & WEST LOOE, HISTORY OF—Bond.
EBORACUM, OR, YORK UNDER THE ROMANS—Wellbeloved.
ECCLESFIELD (YORKSHIRE), HISTORY OF—Hunter.
ECCLESIASTICAL COMMISSION, ARGUMENT AGAINST—Fuller.
ECCLESIASTICAL COMMISSIONERS, PROCEEDINGS AGAINST BISHOP OF LONDON.
ECCLESIASTICAL COMMISSIONERS, ON A SCHEME OF THE DEAN & CHAPTER OF CARLISLE.
ECCLESIASTICAL COMMISSIONERS, ACTS & ORDERS IN COUNCIL. See p. 113.
ECCLESIASTICAL COURTS IN CASES OF MARRIAGE, EFFECT OF SENTENCES—Har. L. T.
ECCLESIASTICAL COURTS, ON THE CONSTITUTION, &c. OF—A. J. Stephens.
ECCLESIASTICAL COURTS—Swan.
ECCLESIASTICAL DOCUMENTS—Hunter.
ECCLESIASTICAL DIRECTORY & CLERICAL GUIDE.
ECCLESIASTICAL FORMS—Law.
ECCLESIASTICAL JURISDICTION, DISCOURSE ON—Atkyns T.
ECCLESIASTICAL JURISDICTION — Clarke, Edwards.
ECCLESIASTICAL JURISDICTION OF TESTAMENT.—Selden, 3rd vol.
ECCLESIASTICAL LAWS, ANSWER TO ARGUMENT OF H. C. MEMBERS—Howell, C. P.
ECCLESIASTICAL LAWS, ABRIDGMENT—Godolphin.
ECCLESIASTICAL LAWS—Burn, Cripps, Dale, Degge, Doddridge, Gibson, Grey, Harding, Hodgson, Oughton, Rogers, Stephens, Stillingfleet, Tyler (U.S.), Van Espen.
ECCLESIASTICAL PRACTICE—Clark, Cockburn, Consett, Coote.
ECCLESIASTICAL REFORM—Gem.
ECCLESIASTICAL LAW:—
  Reports of Cases, &c.—Addams, Curteis, Deane, Haggard, Phillimore, Robertson, Spinks.
  Digest of Cases—Waddilove.
ECCLESIASTICAL LAW, IRELAND—Bullingbroke.
  Reports of Cases—Milward.

ECCLESIASTICAL & ELEEMOSYNARY STATUTES, HENRY V., 1844—A. J. Stephens.
ECCLESIASTICAL STATUTES AT LARGE—Law.
ECCLESIASTICAL TRACTS—H. Prideaux.
ECCLESIASTICUS VALOR—Rec. Com.
EDINBURGH REVIEW, ARTICLE ON LORD ELDON IN.
EDINBURGH ALMANAC & DIRECTORY—Oliver & Boyd.
EDUCATION, LECTURE ON, AT WITHAM—Vol. 5, Pam.
EDUCATION, REPORT AS TO GRANTS FOR RAGGED SCHOOLS.
EDUCATION, STRICTURES ON—Baines.
EDUCATIONAL TIMES.
EDMONTON, HISTORY OF—Robinson.
EDWARD THE CONFESSOR, LIVES OF—No. 3, M. R. Pub., Luard.
EDWARD I., YEAR BOOKS—No. 31, M. R. Pub., Horwood.
EDWARD III., HISTORY OF—Barnes.
EDWARD III. TO RICHARD III., POEMS, &c.—Wright, 14 M. R. Pub.
EDWARD IV., CHRONICLE OF—Warkworth. No. 10, C. S. P.
EDWARD IV., HISTORY OF ARRIVAL OF—Bruce, No. 1, C. S. P.
EDWARD V., GRANTS TEMP.—Nichols, No. 60. C. S. P.
EDWARD VI., MARY, ELIZABETH, CAL. ST. PA. DOM. SER.—R. Lemon.
EDWARD VI., CAL. ST. TH. FOR. SER.—Turnbull.
EGERTON PAPERS—Collier. No. 12, C. S. Pa.
EJECTMENT—Adams, Cole, Runnington.
ELECTOR DENIED HIS VOTE, DEBATE ON. See p. 115.
ELECTION OF MEMBERS OF PARLIAMENT—Barnardiston & Soames.
ELECTION, CONTESTED REGISTER—Smith, H. S.
ELECTION, CONTROVERTED—Parker.
ELECTION DICTIONARY—Chambers.
ELECTION CASES DIGEST—Wordsworth.
ELECTION LAW—Chambers, Clerk, Cunningham, Disney, Dodd, Heywood, Lewis, Montagu & Neale, Orme, Roe, Rogers, Sharkey, Shaw, Sheppard, Simeon, Warren, Wordsworth.
EECTION LAW, SCOTLAND—Bell.
ELECTION LAW, REPORTS OF CASES—Barron & Austin, Barron & Arnold, Corbett & Daniell, Cockburn & Rowe, Douglas, Falconer & Fitzherbert, Fraser, Glanville, Knapp & Ombler, Luder, Puckwell, Perry & Knapp, Philipps, Power, Pedwell & Dew, Wolferstan & Lew, Wolferstan & Bristow. See Register, App. Ca.
City of London—Mildmay.

ELECTION & REGISTRATION OF VOTERS—Bretherton, Shaw.

ELECTION, CONTROVERTED, PRIVILEGE OF, H. C. IN—Rutherford.

ELECTION COMMITTEES—Pickering.

ELECTION REGISTRATION.

ELECTION PETITIONS—Hands.

ELECTION POLL BOOKS.

ELECTION REGISTRATION CASES—Pigott & Rodwell, Lutwyche, Keane & Grant, Hopwood & Philbrick.

ELECTION STATUTES—Tooward.

ELDON (LORD), LIFE OF—Twiss.

ELDON (LORD), ARTICLE ON—Edinburgh Review.

ELDONIANA, DIALOGUE—Dr. Fox.

ELECTRICITY (ARTIFICIAL)—Beccaria.

ELECTRICITY & MAGNETISM, THEIR GENERATIONS, &c.—Vol. 15, Abr. Pat.

ELIZABETH (PRINCESS), ACCOUNT OF—No. 55, C. M. Vol. 2, Strangford.

ELIZABETH (QUEEN), ANNALS OF FIRST FOUR YEARS OF [Sir F. Hayward]—Bruce, No. 7, C. S. P.

ELIZABETH, CAL. ST. PA. DOM. SER.—Green and Lemon.

ELIZABETH, CAL. ST. PA. FOR. SER —Stevenson.

ELIZABETH & JAMES VI., LETTERS OF—Bruce. No. 46, C. S. Pa.

ELIZABETH, LETTERS TEMP.—Bruce. No. 78, C. S. Pa., Chamberlain.

ELIZABETH, PROGRESSES OF—Nicolas.

ELIZABETH, TEMP., CAL. OF PROCEEDINGS IN CHANCERY—Rec. Com.

ELY CATHEDRAL, HISTORY, &c. OF—Bentham.

ELY, ISLE OF, TOWNS, &c. OF, HISTORY OF—Watson.

ELOQUENCE, ON DECLINE OF—Somner.

EMIGRATION, REMARKS ON—Senior, Pam.

EMIGRATION, EXTENT OF—Bate.

EMIGRATION, ON IMPORTANCE OF—Bate.

ENCHIRIDIUM, SEU INSTITUTIONES—Corvinus.

ENCYCLOPÆDIA BRITANNICA, 8TH EDITION, 1860.

ENCYCLOPÆDIA, LONDON.

ENFIELD, HISTORY OF—Robinson.

ENGLAND :—
Ancient Government of—Sir H. Spelman, Dillon.
Lord Great Chamberlain, Memoir.
Lord Great Chamberlain, Percy, Claim to.
Validity of Orders of Church of—Prideaux T.
Church of, & Penal Laws, 1633.
Expediency as to giving New Civil Code—Reddie.

ENGLAND :—
Representative Constitution of, Address—Merewether.
Dictionary of, Carlisle.
Enlistment Question, Remarks on.
Epinomus—Selden, 3rd vol.
Foreigners resident in, 1618-88.—Cooper. No. 82, C. S. P.
Genealogy of the Royal Family—Sandford.
Great Seal of, Opening of—Prynne.
Glory—Brooke.
Government of—Twysden, C S. Pa.
General History of—Baker, Boyer, Brady, Camden, Campbell, Capgrave, Chronicles of Great Britain and Ireland. M. R. Ed. Cole, Dalrymple, Froude, Fuller, Gale, Godwin. Grafton, Hallam, Hardy, Hearne, Heylyn, Higden, Holinshed, Hume, Kemble, Kennett. Leland, Lingard, Macaulay, Macpherson, Mahon, Major, Martin, May, Palgrave, Rapin, Rowland, Rushworth, Smollett, Speed, Stow, Stukeley, Turner, Tyrrell, Whitelock, Wright.
Historical Library—Nicholson.
Italian Account of, 1550—Sneyd, No. 37, C. S. P.
Italian Relation of—Sneyd, No. 37, C.S. Pa.
Knights Hospitallers in, 1338—Larking, No. 65, C. S. P.
Laws of Amos, Bacon, Bayly, Blackstone, Bracton, Britton, Brydall, Coke, Collectanea Juridica, Cowell, Cox, Crabb, Doctor & Student, Doddridge, Finch, Fleta, Fortescue, Francillon, Glanville, Gregory, Grounds & Rudiments, Haleg, Hargrave, Hawke, Holt, Horseman, Jacob, Kerr, Lambard, Law Amendment Society, Law Tracts. Miller, Montague, Noy, Perkins, Reeves, Selden, Sheppard, Smith, Spelman, Spence, Stephen, Sullivan, Van Heythuysen, Wingate, Wood, Woodeson, Wynne.
Law Dictionaries—Blount, Bouvier (U.S.), Cowell, Cunningham. Holthouse, Jacob, Tomlins, Wharton, Whishaw.
New State of, 1691-1712—Miege.
Notes on History of, 1509-1714—Thomas.
Political Songs of—T. Wright.
Polychronicon of—Higden.
Worthies of—Fuller.

ENGLAND & GERMANY, RELATIONS BETWEEN.

ENGLAND, IRELAND, & SCOTLAND, HISTORICAL LIBRARIES—Nicholson.

ENGLAND & IRELAND, COLLECTANEA CURIOSA—Gutch.

ENGLAND & IRELAND, DIGEST OF STATUTE LAW OF—Gabbett.

ENGLAND & SCOTLAND, BORDER ANTIQUITIES—Sir W. Scott.

ENGLAND & SPAIN, STATE PAPERS RELATING TO, 1485-1509. Bergenroth, Cal. St. Pa.

ENGLAND & SPAIN, QUESTION OF PROCEEDINGS BETWEEN—Howell C. P.

ENGLAND & WALES, ATLAS—Smith.

ENGLAND & WALES, BOUNDARY, PARLIAMENTARY REPORTS.
ENGLAND & WALES, ECCLESIASTICAL REVENUES REPORTS.
ENGLAND & WALES, RAILWAY MAP OF.
ENGLISH LAW, LETTER AS TO STUDY OF—Hayes.
ENGLISH & IRISH LAW, COMPARATIVE VIEW—Ayres.
ENGLISH & SCOTCH LAW, COMPENDIUM—Paterson.
ENGLISH LAWYER—Giffard.
ENGLISH AFFAIRS, CAL. OF STATE PAPERS RELATING TO, 1202-1509—M.R. Pub.
ENGLISH & FOREIGN FUNDS, &c., CORRESPONDENCE—Fenn.
ENGLISH & FRENCH EXERCISES—Pomey.
ENGLISH INHABITANTS IN AMERICA, LAWS USED BY.
ENGLISH JUDGES, BIOGRAPHY OF—Foss.
ENGLISH LIBERTIES—Care.
ENGLISH REAPING PATENTS, APPEAL—Woodcroft.
ENGLISH REFORMATION, LETTERS.
ENGLISH-SAXON GRAMMAR—Elstob.
ENGLISH SYNONYMS—Carlisle, Crabb.
ENGLISH TOPOGRAPHY — Britton, Carlisle, Gough, Lewis, Moule, Nicholls.
ENGLISH TOWNS, VIEW OF—Spelman.
ENTAILS—Tamlyn.
ENTRIES—Aston, Brown, Brownlow, Clift, Coke, Hansard, Levinz, Lilly, Mallory, Modern, Old, Rastell, Robinson, Thompson, Vidian, Winch.
EPISTLES OF THE FATHERS—Wake.
EPISTLES, REFLECTIONS ON THE—Stow.
EPISTOLÆ ET POEMATA—Selden, 2nd vol.
EQUAL REPRESENTATION, LETTER ON—Lorimer.
EQUITY—Adams, Ayckbourn, Barton, Beames, Daniel, Drewry, Fonblanque, Ford, Francis, Goldsmith, Gresley, Griffith, Haddon, Haynes, Home, Hunter, Jarman, Lewis, Lubé, Pemberton, Plunket, Seton, Smith, Snell, Spence, Story.
EQUITY ACTS—Jemmett.
EQUITY COSTS—Beames, Coleman.
EQUITY COSTS, BILLS OF—Shaen & Greville, Morgan & Davey.
EQUITY COURTS, SPEECH ON—Freshfield.
EQUITY DIGEST — Bridgman, Chitty, Evans, Jeremy, Repertorium Juridicum, Evans.
EQUITY JURISDICTION, IMPROVEMENT OF—F. S. Williams.

EQUITY JURISDICTION IN COUNTY COURTS—Batten & Ludlow, Davis, Gibbon & Harvey, Gilmour, Pollock & Nicol, Rumsey, Will.
EQUITY JURISPRUDENCE—Jeremy, Smith, Story, Spence.
EQUITY, LEADING CASES IN—Tudor, White & Tudor.
EQUITY LECTURES, IRELAND—Molyneux.
EQUITY, WHAT ARE COURTS OF—Park.
EQUITY MASTERS' OFFICES—Report of Law Amendment Society.
EQUITY ORDERS, IRELAND—Smith.
EQUITABLE DEFENCES—Gilmour, Mayne.
EQUITABLE RECOVERIES, OPINIONS ON.
ERROR, WRITS OF, IN CRIMINAL CASES—Har. J. A.
ERSKINE (LORD), BIOGRAPHY OF—Roscoe.
ESSAYS — Bacon, Hume, Lord Macaulay, Morality, Abp. King on Evil.
ESSEX :—
  Directory—Kelly.
  Directory, Home Counties—Pigot.
  Domesday Book—Vol. 2, Rec. Com.
  Genealogies—Berry.
  History of—Lysons, Morant, Muilman, Norden, Ogborn, Salmon, Wright.
ESSEX (EARL), DID NOT MURDER HIMSELF—L. T.
ESTATE IN FEE SIMPLE DEFEASIBLE, OPINION—C. J.
ESTATE TABLES — Inwood, Sir I. Newton, Willich.
ESTATES—Sir H. C. Chambers, Sugden.
ESTATES TAIL & DESCENTS—Law Tract, N.
ESTATES & TENURES—Preston.
ETONENSES ALUMNI—Harwood.
ETCHINGHAM FAMILY, History of—Hall.
ETYMOLOGIUM ANGLICANUM—Junius.
EUCLID'S ELEMENTS, Commentaries on, 1st Book—Proclus.
EUCLID'S ELEMENTS—Simson.
EUNOMUS—E. Wynne.
EUROPE, ANNALS, 1739-1743 :—
  History—Alison, Russell.
  Introduction to Literature of—Hallam.
  Map of—Arrowsmith.
  Modern, Laws of—Spence.
  View of Society in—Gr. G. Stewart.
EUROPEAN CONSTITUTIONS—La Croix.
EUROPEAN CONVENTION AS TO DOMICILE—Woolrych.
EUROPEAN DIRECTORY—Kelly.
EUROPEAN STATES, HISTORY OF—May.
EUTYCHII ECCLESIÆ SUÆ ORIGINES—Selden, Vol. 2.

EVERARD'S DEPOSITION—Pol. T.
EVERYTHING, ENQUIRE WITHIN FOR.
EVESHAM (WORCESTERSHIRE), HISTORY OF—May, Rudge.
EVESHAM ABBEY (WORCESTERSHIRE), HISTORY OF—Tindal.
EVESHAMENSIS CHRONICON ABBATIÆ—Thomas de Marlberge. No. 29, M. R. Pub.
EVIDENCE—Best, Davis (County Courts), Gilbert, Greenleaf, Gresley, Hare, Moffat, Peake, Phillips, Phillips & Amos, Powell, Roscoe (Civil & Criminal), Starkie, Taylor, Wigram, Will.
EVIDENCE ON LONDON DOCK BILL.
EVIDENCE ON MANCHESTER RECTORY DIVISION.
EVIDENCE, PHILOSOPHY OF—Mackinnon.
EVIDENCE, REMARKS ON BILL—Lowndes.
EVIDENCE OF DEFENDANTS, &c.—F. Worsley.
EXAMINATION QUESTIONS, DIGEST—Maugham.
EXCELLING, &c., LOVE OF—Montagu.
EXCHEQUER CALENDARS (ANCIENT) & INVENTORIES OF THE PUBLIC RECORDS—Sir F. Palgrave.
EXCHEQUER, CONSIDERATIONS FOR REGULATING—C. Vernon.
EXCHEQUER HISTORY & PRACTICE—Burton, Dax, Fowler, Gilbert, Madox, Manning, Price, Vernon.
EXCHEQUER, ORIGINALIA AND MEMORANDA ROLLS—Jones.
EXCHEQUER REPERTORIES, ORDERS AND DECREES, INDEX OF—Martin.
EXCHEQUER:—
Reports of Cases—Ambler, Anstruther, Benloe, Blackstone (H.), Bosanquet & Puller, Brooke, Bunbury, Comyns, Coke, Crompton, Crompton & Jervis, Crompton & Meeson, Davies, Dyer, Fitzgibbon, Forrest, Fortescue, Freeman, Gilbert, Godbolt, Hardres, Holt (Sir J.), Hurlstone & Coltman, Hurlstone & Gordon, Hurlstone & Norman, Jenkins, Kelwey, Lane, Leonard, Ley, Littleton, McCleland, McCleland & Younge, Meeson & Roscoe, Meeson & Welsby, Modern Reports, Moore (Sir F.), Parker, Plowden, Price, Raymond (Sir T.), Salkeld, Savile, Siderfin, Strange, Tyrrwhitt, Tyrrwhitt & Granger, Ventris, Welsby, Willes, Year Books, Younge & Jervis.
Equity—Daniell, Wilson, Younge, Younge & Collyer.
EXCHEQUER EQUITY (IRELAND) ORDERS.
EXCISE EDITION OF AUCTION LAWS.
EXCISE BOARD, ORDERS—Hersee.
EXCISE LAWS—Bateman.
EXAMINATION QUESTIONS, DIGEST OF—Maugham.

EXECUTIONS—Gilbert.
EXECUTORS, CAN THEY MAKE CONVEYANCE WITHOUT HEIR?—L. Jour. T.
EXECUTORS, ON CLAIM TO RESIDUE—L. Jour. T.
EXECUTORS, REMEDIES FOR RECOVERING RENT—L. Jour. T.
EXECUTORS & ADMINISTRATORS—Pritchard, Toller, Wentworth, Sir E. V. Williams.
EXECUTORY LIMITATIONS, SOUNDNESS OF—L. Jour. T.
EXETER, ANTIQUITIES OF—Powell.
EXETER CROWN COURTS, AS TO MALPRACTICES IN—Bird.
EXETER DEANERY CASE, REPORT—R. Barnes.
EXETER, HISTORY OF—Jenkins, Izaacke.
EXETER & DEVON CHARITIES, HISTORY OF—Izaacke.
EXETER ELECTION, MOBIAD—Brice.
EXETER (BISHOP OF), ON CHURCH DISCIPLINE BILL—A. J. Stephens.
EXETER (BISHOP OF), SPEECH ON BILL FOR MARRIAGE WITH DECEASED WIFE'S SISTER—Sleigh.
EXON DOMESDAY BOOK—Vol. 4, Rec. Com.
EXPENSES OF JOHN OF BRABANT & H. & T. OF LANCASTER—No. 55, C. M. Vol. 2.
EXTENT, OLD & NEW—L. T.
EXTENTS—Tidd, West.
EXTINCT BARONETAGES—Burke.
EXTINCT PEERAGE—Almon, Bankes, Bolton, Burke.
EXTRADITION—Clarke, Egan.

FABER v. STORNEY, ON JUDGMENT—Serjt. Jones.
FABLES—Æsop.
FACTS FOR PARLIAMENT, AS TO WESTMINSTER COURTS—Vol. 8, L. T.
FACTS—Ram.
FACTOR & PRINCIPAL, STATEMENT.
FACTORS & BROKERS, PAPERS ON—Freshfield.
FACTORS & BROKERS, LAW OF—Russell.
FACTORY ACTS—Oats.
FAMILIAR EPISTLES—Martin.
FAMILIES (ROYAL) OF EUROPE—Spectator.
FAMILY HISTORY GWEDIR—Sir John Wynne.
FARES, HACKNEY CARRIAGE, 1867.
FARM, LAW OF THE—Dixon.
FARNBOROUGH ROAD BILL, SPEECH ON—Nolan
FAVERSHAM, HISTORY OF—Jacob.
FAVERSHAM ABBEY, &c., HISTORY OF—Lewis.

FEES OF HOUSE OF COMMONS—Reports.
FELLOWSHIP PORTERS, REPLY—City T.
FELTON'S EXECUTION—Grimaldi T.
FENCES—Hunt.
FERDINAND & ISABELLA, REIGN OF—Prescott.
FEUDAL DIGNITIES—Betham, Borthwick.
FEUDAL LAW—Craig. Sullivan.
FEUDAL PROPERTY—Sir J. Dalrymple.
FEUDS & TENURES—Sir H. Spelman.
FILACER'S OFFICE—Frye.
FINANCE—Cohen.
FINES ON ADMISSION TO COPYHOLDS, ARGUMENT—Col. Jur.
FINES, LAW OF—Browne, Cruise, Hands, Manby, Miller, Pigott, Smith.
FINE ROLLS:—
 Concordiæ Finales, Vol. 1—Rec. Com.
 Excerpta—Rec. Com.
 Rotuli de Oblatis—Rec. Com.
FINES LEVATI, READING ON—Coke.
FIRE ASSURANCE—Bunyon.
FIRE DECISIONS, U.S.—Littleton & Blatchley.
FIREARMS, &c.—Vol. 10, Abr. Pat.
FIRMA BURGI—Madox.
FISHMONGERS' PAGEANT (London).
FISHERMEN OF THAMES, RULES—City T.
FISHERY & GAME LAWS—Oke, Paterson.
FISHERIES—Oke.
FISK'S COKE UPON LITTLETON.
FIXTURES—Amos & F., Jerard, Grady.
FLEET REGISTERS—Burn.
FODINÆ REGALES, LAWS OF MINE—Pettus.
FŒDERA CONVENTIONES LITERÆ, &c.—Rymer. Rec. Com.
FOOD, PRESERVATION OF—Vol. 4, Abr. Pat.
FONTHILL ABBEY, HISTORY OF—Rutter.
FOREST LAWS—Manwood.
FORFEITURE—Blackstone, York.
FOREIGN ATTACHMENT—Brandon.
FOREIGN COPYRIGHT—Bohn.
FOREIGN & DOMESTIC SERIES, COLLECTION OF LETTERS, &c.—Brewer, Cal. St. Pa.
FOREIGN SERIES, COLLECTION OF LETTERS, &c.—Turnbull, Cal. St. Pa.
FOREIGN ENLISTMENT ACT—Gibbs.
FOREIGN GOVERNMENTS, CORRESPONDENCE OF, WITH ROME—Sess. Pa.
FOREIGN QUARTERLY & WESTMINSTER REVIEW, N. S.
FOREIGNERS, RESIDENT IN ENGLAND, 1618–88—Cooper, No. 82, C.S.P.
FOREIGNERS, FRENCH LAWS AS TO—Henry.
FORESTALLING - Illingworth.

FORGERY, TRIAL OF DUNN FOR—Vol. 1, Col. Jur.
FORMULARE ANGLICANUM—Madox.
FORMS—Archbold.
 Common—Hall.
 Magisterial—Oke.
 Pleading—Bullen & Leake, Chitty.
FORMS, ORDERS & PRECEDENTS, CHANCERY—Ayckbourn, Daniel, Greening.
FOTHERINGHAY, HISTORY OF—Bunney.
FOX v. MACKRETH, APPEAL TO H. L.—Har. Jur. Ar.
FRAMLINGHAM, HISTORY OF—Loder & Hawes.
FRANCHISES, COUNTY, &c.—Dennes.
FRANCE:—
 Almanach Annuaire du Commerce—Bottin.
 Bibliographie—De Bure.
 Brevets d' Invention, Repertoire—Houard.
 Cadière & Girardin, Procez—Le Hugo.
 Catalogue de la Bibliothèque de France—M. le Duc Palliers, De Bure.
 Catalogue of Books on Law of France in Lincoln's Inn Library.
 Classiques français—G. Cordoue.
 De l'Homme et du Citoyen les Devoirs—Puffendorff.
 Dictionary, Old French Law—Kelham.
 Dictionnaire de Droit normand - Houard.
 Dictionnaire des Chemins de Fer - Palaa.
 Dictionnaire des Faillites—Bedarride.
 Droits, &c. des Etrangers dans le Grand Brétagne—Okey.
 France, America, & Great Britain; Right of Search—Morglan.
 France & England, Conference between Ambassadors of.
 France, History of—Mezeray.
 France & Great Britain, Digest of Law between Subjects of—Okey.
 France, Belgium, & part of Switzerland, Map—Arrowsmith.
 France, The Monarchy of—Tooke.
 French Exercises—Formy.
 French Grammar—Brasseur, Pomey.
 Œuvres posthumes—Pothier.
FRANCE, LAW OF:—
 Absence, de l'—Demolombe.
 Adoption, de l'—Demolombe.
 Assurances—Emerignon.
 Chancellerie d'Angleterre, Cour de la Lettres—Cooper, Boyer, Collard.
 Causes célèbres—Richer.
 Codes, les, français—Tripiers.
 Codes, Six, in French.
 Code de Commerce—Alauzet.
 Code Napoléon, translated—Barrett, Barrister, Gilbert, Richards.
 Codes, les, criminels—Villargues.
 Code pénal—Adolphe & Helie.
 Code du Droit civil et criminel—Rogrons.
 Code de la Procédure civile et criminelle—Gilbert.
 Code d' Instruction criminelle, &c.—Gilbert.
 Code maritime des Prises—Le Beau.

France, Law of (*continued*)
  Collection des Loix, A.D. 420-1789—Isambert.
  Commentaire de la Marine—Vulin.
  Commentaires du Droit civil de Normandie—Terrien.
  Commerce, Bourses de—Bedarride.
  Commerce, des Faillites et Banqueroutes—Bedarride.
  Commerce maritime—Bedarride.
  Commerçants—Bedarride.
  Commissionnaires—Bedarride.
  Contrat—Pothier.
  Coutumes anglo-normandes—Houard.
  Décisions nouvelles—Denizart.
  D'stinction des Biens—Demolombe.
  Droit administratif—Dufour. [Okey.
  Droit d'Aubaine de la Grande-Bretagne—
  Droit canon—Durand.
  Droit civil français—Duvergier, Toulliers.
  Droit civil, Cautionnement—Troplong.
  Droit civil, Contrainte—Troplong.
  Droit civil, l'Échange—Troplong.
  Droit civil, Mandat—Troplong.
  Droit civil, Prêt—Troplong.
  Droit civil, Contrat de Mariage—Troplong.
  Droit civil, Nantissement—Troplong.
  Droit civil, Prescription—Troplong.
  Droit civil du Dépôt et du Séquestre—Troplong.
  Droit civil des Donations et des Testaments—Demolombe, Troplong.
  Droit civil des Priviléges et Hypothèques—Troplong.
  Droit (Du) ecclésiastique—Phillips.
  Droit international—Fœlix.
  Achats et Ventes—Bedarride.
  Institutions de Droit—Argot.
  L'Instruction criminelle—Hélie.
  Juridiction commerciale—Bedarride.
  Jurisprudence commerciale—Girod et Clariond.
  Lettre de Change—Bedarride.
  Lois de la Procédure—Carré.
  Loix de l'Esprit—Montesquieu.
  Loix de l'Esprit, translated—Nugent.
  Mari—Pothier.
  Mariage, du Contrat—Pothier, Demolombe.
  Maximes, Droit public français.
  Minorité—Demolombe.
  Notaires, la Science des—Ferrière.
  Obligations, Des—Pothier.
  Origine (De l') des Lois etc.
  Orléanois, Carte d'.
  Orléans, Coutumes d'—Pothier.
  Paternité et Filiation—Demolombe.
  Personnes et Choses—Pothier.
  Prêt du Contrat—Pothier.
  Procédure—Pothier.
  Publication—Demolombe.
  Servitude—Demolombe.
  Société du Contrat—Troplong.
  Sociétés—Bedarride.
  Successions—Pothier.
  Successions—Demolombe.
  Vente—Troplong.

Fraud—Hovenden, Roberts.
Frederician Code of Prussia.
Freemen of Companies of London.
Free Parliaments—Sir H. Mackworth.
Free Scriveners, Company's Case.
Freeton (Yorkshire), History of—Hunter.
French Dictionary—Boyer, Furetière.
Friend (Sir John), Trial.
Friendly Societies—James, Pratt, Stone.
Fuel, Preparation, &c.—Vol 20, Abr. Pat.
Fulham, History of—Faulkner.
Fulke's Answer to Martiall & Stapleton—Par. S. Pa.
Fuller, Life of—Malcolm.
Funds—J. J. Wilkinson, Fairman, Keyser.
Funeral Monuments—Weever.
Furness Abbey, Antiquities of—West.

Gainsborough, History of—Stark.
Gaius—Tomkins and Lemon.
Galloway, History of—Mackenzie.
Galway, History of—Hardiman.
Game Laws—Chitty, Deacon, Leigh, Locke, Nelson, Oke, Paterson.
Game & Fishery Laws—Oke.
Gaming—Oliphant.
Gaol Delivery, Facts for more frequent—Lord Western.
Garter, Knights of, History of—Buswell.
Gas Light & Coke Co., Memorial to Sewers Commissioners.
Gas, Production &c. of—Vol. 17, Abr. Pat.
Gateshead, History of—Mackenzie.
Gavelkind—Robinson, Sandys, Somner, Taylor. *See* Elton's Tenures.
Gazettes:—
  Dublin.
  Edinburgh.
  London.
  Ecclesiastical Estates.
  Pall Mall.
  Perry (Bankruptcy).
Gazette, Mining Journal. Railway and Commercial.
Gazetteers:—
  Edinburgh Imperial—Blackie.
  Johnston (General).
  Indian—Thornton.
  Longsdale Hundred &c.—C'arke.
  Yorkshire—Clarke, White.

GENEALOGIES:—
  Berks—Berry.
  Essex—Berry.
  Hampshire—Berry.
  Hertfordshire—Berry.
  Kent—Berry.
  Sussex—Berry.
GENEALOGICUM CALENDARIUM TEMP. HEN. III. & ED. I.—Roberts.
GENEALOGICAL, HISTORICAL, &c. DICTIONARY.
GENEALOGICA & TOPOGRAPHICA COLLECTANEA— Nichols & others.
GENEALOGICAL TABLES—Betham.
GENERAL ATLAS—Arrowsmith, De Witt.
GENERAL DICTIONARY—Bayle.
GENERAL GAZETTEER—Johnston.
GENERAL ISSUE—Charnock, Lutwyche.
GENERAL RECORD OFFICE, PROPOSAL FOR— Cooper.
GENERAL REGISTRY—Bentham, Coote & Harrington, Hodgkin, Humphry, W. P. Wood.
GENERAL REGISTRY, TRACTS ON & REASONS FOR.
GENT, LIFE OF—Malcolm.
GENTLEMEN OF ACCOUNT RESIDING IN LONDON, &c., 1595.
GENTLEMAN'S MAGAZINE.
GENTOO CODE OF LAWS IN INDIA, 1776-81.
GENTRY, SPHERE OF—Morgan.
GENTRY—Burke.
GEOFFREY OF MONMOUTH, HISTORY OF— Thompson.
GEOGRAPHY—Bouillet, Fenning & Collyer, Gregory, Salmon & Guthrie, Varenius.
GEOMETRY—Gregory.
GEOMETRY: ELEMENTS OF EUCLID.
GEORGE III. LIBRARY, MAPS, &c. IN, & CAT. OF MSS.
GEORGEY (GEN.), ACCOUNT OF SURRENDER— Vol. 8, Pam., Lieut. C. D. B. Zabrocki.
GEORGICA HEXAGLOTTA—Virgil.
GERMAN DICTIONARY—Flügel.
GERMANY, MAP OF—Arrowsmith.
GERMANY & ENGLAND, RELATIONS BETWEEN— Gardiner, No. 90, C. S. Pa.
GESTA BRITANNORUM, CHRONOLOGY, 1600-1661 —Wharton.
GIBSON, DOE D., v. HARGREAVES, REPORT OF TRIAL—Fraser.
GILDHALLÆ MUNIMENTA—Riley, No. 12, M. R. Pub.
GLASGOW, HISTORY OF—Gibson.
GLASGOW & GREENOCK, HISTORY OF — Denholme.
GLASTONBURY, CHARTER TO.

GLOBES, EXERCISES ON THE—Butter.
GLOBES, USE OF THE—Dilworth.
GLOBES, PAIR OF THE.
GLOSSARIUM ARCHÆOLOGICUM—Spelman.
GLOSSARIUM AD SCRIPTORES INFIMÆ LATINITATIS—Du Cange.
GLOSSARY—Boucher.
GLOSSARY OF WORDS IN RECORDS—Brady.
GLOUCESTERSHIRE, DOMESDAY BOOK FOR— Bawdwen.
GLOUCESTERSHIRE, HISTORY OF — Atkins, Fosbrooke, Rudder.
GLOUCESTERSHIRE, SURVEY OF—Tunnicliffe.
GLOUCESTERSHIRE DIRECTORY—Pigot, Kelly.
GLOUCESTERSHIRE GENTRY, ENGRAVINGS OF ARMS OF—Sir G. Naylor.
GLOUCESTER, History of—Rudder.
GLOUCESTRIÆ MONASTERII S. PETRI HISTORIA & CARTULARIUM—Hart, No. 33, M. R. Pub.
GODALMING RABBIT WOMAN, HISTORY—André.
GODMANCHESTER, HISTORY OF—Fox.
GOLD COMPANIES & THE COST BOOK—Higgins.
GOLD, DISCOVERIES, &c., LETTERS—Smee.
GORHAM CASE—Moore.
GORHAM CASE, REVIEW OF—Chambers.
GOSLING'S LISTS OF LORDS, KNIGHTS, &c.— Grim. T.
GOSPELS, THOUGHTS ON THE—Stow.
GOUGH, LIFE OF—Malcolm.
GOVERNMENT—Sir R. Filmer, Follett, Jones, Ramsay, Tucker, Whitelock.
GOVERNMENT OF INDIA, A PRESIDENT THE BEST.
GRÆCUM LEXICON—Hedericus.
GRACECHURCH STREET, ORDER AS TO CARTS IN —City T.
GRADUS AD PARNASSUM—Pyper.
GRAMMAR SCHOOLS—Bannister, Carlisle.
GRANDE BRETAGNE, DROITS, &c. DES ÉTRANGERS —Okey.
GRANDE BRETAGNE, DROITS D'AUBAINE—Okey.
GRAND JURIES, CHARGE TO— Sir J. Astry.
GRAND JURIES, TRUST POWER, &c. OF—Lord Somers.
GRANDEUR OF THE LAW—Foss.
GRANT FAMILY, HISTORY OF.
GRANTHAM, HISTORY OF—Turner.
GRAVESEND, HISTORY OF—Pocock.
GRAY'S INN JOURNAL—Murphy.
GREAT BRITAIN. See England.
GREAT SESSION OF WALES, JURISDICTION, &c. OF—C. Abbott.

GREAT BRITAIN, LAWS RELATING TO SUBJECTS OF—Okey.
GREAT BRITAIN & U. S., LETTERS ON RELATIONS BETWEEN—Loring.
GREECE, HISTORY OF—Grote.
GREEK & ENGLISH LEXICON—Liddell & Scott.
GREEK & LATIN LEXICON—Scapula.
GREENOCK, HISTORY OF—Weirs.
GREENOCK & GLASGOW, HISTORY OF—Denholme.
GREENWICH HOSPITAL, ESTATES OF, IN DURHAM.
GREENWICH PARISH, GIFTS TO—Kimbell.
GRESHAM'S (SIR T.) WILL.
GREVILLE FAMILY, HISTORY OF—Edmonson.
GREY & RUTHEN BARONIES, ARGUMENTS—Selden, 3rd vol.
GRINDALL (ABP.), REMAINS—Par. S. Pa.
GROCERS' Co.'s ESTATES, REPORTS.
GROCERS' Co.'s ESTATES, ACCOUNT OF—Heath.
GROSSETESTE (BP.)—Luard. No. 25, M. R. Pub.
GROTIUS ON DUTCH JURISPRUDENCE—Herbert.
GROUNDS OF LAW—Hawke, Nott.
GUELPH, HISTORY OF HOUSE—Halliday.
GUERNSEY, HISTORY OF — Berry, Dicey, Le Marchant.
GUIA PARA EL ESTUDIO DEL DIRECHO PATRIO— Reguera Valdelomar.
GUIDES :—
    Civil Service—White.
    Demerara Law—Lindon.
    Hastings & St. Leonard's.
    Lakes of Cumberland & Westmoreland— Jollie.
    Liverpool—Moss.
    London—Baldwin, Hitch, Kelly, Kent, Longman, Lowndes, Pigot, Robson.
    Manchester & Salford.
    Mercantile & Maritime.
    Parliamentary—Stockdale.
    Peak—Jowitt.
    Probate Court—Weatherley.
    P.O.
    To Juries & Jurymen—Sir G. Stephen.
    Tunbridge Wells—J. Strange.
GUILDHALL, ACCOUNT OF LIBRARY, WORKS OF ART, IN.
GUILDFORD HOSPITAL, ACCOUNT OF—Abbott.
GUILFORD (LORD), BIOGRAPHY OF—Roscoe.
GUNPOWDER TREASON, DISCOVERY—Bp. Lincoln.
GUYLFORDE (SIR R.) PILGRIMAGE—Ellis. No. 51, C. S. P.
GWEDIR FAMILY, HISTORY OF—Sir John Wynne.

HACKNEY, HISTORY—Robinson.
HACKNEY CARRIAGE FARES.
HALE (SIR M.), BIOGRAPHY—Roscoe.
HALE'S (SIR EDWARD) CASE—28, L. T.
HALE (LORD), PREFACE TO ROLLE'S ABRIDGMENT.
HALIFAX (YORK), HISTORY OF—Watson.
HALLAMSHIRE, HISTORY—Hunter.
HAM, CUSTOMS—Col. Jur.
HAMILTON'S FAMILY—Aiton.
HAMMERSMITH, HISTORY—Faulkner.
HAMPSHIRE :—
    Directory—Kelly, Pigot.
    Domesday—Rec. Com.
    Genealogies—Berry.
    History—Warner.
    Topography—Warner, White.
HAMPSTEAD, HISTORY—Park.
HAMPSTEAD & HIGHGATE ROAD ACT.
HAND (THE)—Bell, Bridgwater Treatises.
HANDBOOKS—Lord St. Leonard's, Pritchard, Thomas.
HANGING NOT PUNISHMENT ENOUGH—Montague, Law T.
HANSWORTH, HISTORY—Hunter.
HARDWARE DISTRICT DIRECTORY—Kelly.
HARDWICK (LORD)—Campbell, Foss.
HARLEIAN MISCELLANY—Oldys & Park.
HARLEY (LADY B.), LETTERS—Lewis. No. 58, C. S. P.
HARTLEPOOL, HISTORY—Sharp.
HARTWELL NOTICES—V.-Admiral Smyth.
HARTWELL OBSERVATORY—V.-Admiral Smyth.
HARWICH, HISTORY—Dale.
HASTED, LIFE OF—Malcolm.
HASTINGS & ST. LEONARD'S, GUIDE—Ross.
HAWKSTEAD, HISTORY—Sir J. Cullum.
HAYWARD, ANNALS OF QUEEN ELIZABETH. No. 7, C. S. P.
HEARNE, LIFE OF—Malcolm.
HEBREW CRITICISM—Clarke.
HEBREW GRAMMAR—Lyons.
HEBREW, ON STUDY OF—Bishop of St. David's
HEIR-APPARENT, POSSESSION—His. L. T.
HEIRS, REPRESENTATIVE OF—His. L. T.
HENDON ESTATE, CAT.—Earl Powis.
HENDON, MAP—Cooke, Whishaw.
HENGRAVE (SUFFOLK)—Gage.
HENRY II., LIFE OF — [Benedict of Peterborough] Stubbs. No. 29, M. R. Pub.

HENRY III., ROYAL, &c. LETTERS OF HIS REIGN
—Shirley. No. 27, M. R. Pub.
HENRY IV. & EDW. I., CALENDARIUM GENEA-
LOGICUM—Roberts.
HENRY IV.—[Capgrave] Hingeston. Nos. 7, 18,
M. R. Pub.
HENRY V.—Cole, Hingeston. Nos. 11, 7,
M. R. Pub.
HENRY VI.—Stevenson. No. 22, M. R. Pub.
HENRY VII.—Bacon, Hingeston. No. 7, M. R.
Pub.
HENRY VII., BULL OF INNOCENT VIII.—Col-
lier. No. 39, C. S. P.
HENRY VII. & VIII.—No. 73, C. M. Vol. 4,
Godwin.
HENRY VIII., STATE PAPERS TEMP.—Cal. St.
Pa. Brewer.
HENRY v. GT. W. RAILWAY, REPORT—Tolsher.
HERALDIC ARCHITECTURE—Donaldson.
HERALDRY—Bolton, Boutell, Brooke, Dugdale,
Edmondson, Gwillim, Milles, Moule,
Robson, Segar, Selden, Yorke.
HERBERT (LORD C. J.), LAW EXAMINED IN SIR
E. HALE'S CASE.
HEREFORDSHIRE:—
Domesday—Com. Rec.
Directory—Kelly, Pigot.
History of Duncumb—Lodge.
HERMIT'S OPINIONS—Stow.
HERTFORDSHIRE:—
Domesday—Bawdwen, Com. Rec.
Directory—Kelly, Pigot.
Genealogies—Berry.
History of—Chauncy, Clutterbuck, Lysons,
Salmon, Turner.
HEWLEY CHARITY, SPEECH—C. P. Cooper.
HEWLEY CHARITY, HISTORY—Tottie, Hunter
& Gurneys, Stock.
HEXAMETER (ENGLISH), TRANSLATIONS.
HIGH COMMISSION, COURT OF—Burn.
HIGDEN (H.), POLYCHRONICON.
HIGHGATE GRAMMAR SCHOOL—J. G.
HIGH PEAK, CUSTOMS—Tapping.
HIGHWAYS—Angell & Durfee (U.S.), Bate-
man, Glen, Oke, Pratt, Shelford.
HINDU LAW—S. G. Grady, Sir Wm. Jones,
Sir T. Strange, T. L. Strange, Tajore.
Digest—J. G. Buhler & West.
Inheritance, Treatise—Rumsey.
HISTORICAL, &c. DICTIONARY.
HISTORICAL LAW TRACTS.
HISTORICAL LITERATURE—Nicolas.
HISTORICAL COLLECTION—Townshend.
HISTORY, ANCIENT—Rollin.
HISTORY, CHRONOLOGY OF—Nicolas.
HISTORY PRIOR TO CONQUEST—Vergil.

HOGLANDIA, DESCRIPTION—Holdsworth.
HOLBORN BRIDGE VIADUCT, PLAN—Whishaw.
HOLDERNESS, HISTORY—Poulson.
HOLLAND, INSTITUTES—Dr. J. Van der Linden.
HOLWOOD HILL, HISTORY—Dunkin & Kempe.
HOLYHEAD, HISTORY—Pennant.
HOLY SCRIPTURES, DISPUTATIONS—Dr. Wm.
Whitaker.
HOME COUNTIES DIRECTORY—Kelly, Pigot.
HOMICIDE (U.S.)—Wharton.
HOMER & ENGLISH METRE, ESSAY—Barter.
HOMMES ILLUSTRES, FRANCE—Perrault.
HOMME, LES DEVOIRS DE L'—Puffendorff.
HONESTY, &c., ANATOMISED—Howell, C. P.
HONOR, CATALOGUE OF—Milles, Segar.
HONORES ANGLICANI—Segur.
HONOUR, LAWS OF—Gosling.
HOOK (DR.), SERMON PREACHED BEFORE THE
QUEEN.
HORÆ JURIDICÆ SUBSECIVÆ—Butler.
HORTICULTURE—Baxter.
HORSES, LAW OF—Oliphant.
HOSPITALS:—
Cheetham, Manchester.
Greenwich.
Guildford—Abbot.
HOUSE OF COMMONS:—
Biographical Index to—Beatson, Joshua
Wilson.
Career in—Harle.
Committees—Frere.
Declaration of Sympathy for Subjects
abroad—MS. temp. James.
Determination on Election Cases.
General Index of Bills, 1801-44.
Divisions, 1834-52.
Journals, 1547-1837, viz.—
Cunningham . . Vols. 1 to 7
Flaxman . . . „ 8—11
Forster . . . . „ 12—17
Moore . . . . „ 18—34
Dunn . . . . „ 35—55
Bromey . . . „ 56—75
Vardon . . . . „ 76—92
Papers, 1801-62.
Petitions, 1833-52.
Reports, 1696-1834.
Reports only of Committees, 1801-52.
Divisions—Pickering.
Journals & Indexes.
Precedents—Hatsell.
Printed Papers, Howard v. Gossett.
On the Privileges of Subjects—Howell C. P.
Reports on Established Church.
Report on Fees of.
Report on Private Bills.
Report on Finance.
Report on Sanitary Inquiry.
Report on Sinecures, &c.
Report on Small Boroughs.

HOUSE OF LORDS:—
　Biographical Index of—Beatson.
　Jurisdiction of the—Sir M. Hale.
　Remembrances, &c.—Scobell.
　General Index of Public Acts.
　　Local & Personal.
　　Of Bills, &c.
　　Of Papers, 1801-60.
　General Index of Journals, viz.—
　　Vols. 1 to 10
　　,, 11 — 19
　　,, 20 — 35—Brodie.
　　,, 36 — 52
　　,, 53 — 64
　　Of Public Bills, 1833-63.
　　Miscellaneous, 1833-63.
　Law of—M'Queen, May.
　Digest of Cases—Clark.
　Appeals from Scotland—Bell, Craigie, Macqueen, Maclean & Robertson, Paton, Robertson, Shaw & Maclean, Stewart & Paton, Shaw, Wilson & Shaw.
　Reports of Cases on Appeal—Bligh, Brown, Colles, Clark & Finelly, Clark, Dow, Dow & Clark, Shower, Willes.
HOUSE PROPERTY, HINTS—Cross.
HOVEDEN, ROGER DE — Stubbs. No. 51, M. Pub.
HOWARD FAMILY, ANECDOTES—C. Howard.
HOWARD *v.* GOSSETT, BLUNDELL—Vol. 1, Pam. on Par. Priv.
HOWARD, REPORT ON PRINTED PAPERS.
HOWARD'S REPORTS (U.S.). *See* Curtis.
HULL:—
　Charge to Grand Jury—Warren.
　Directory—Kelly, Pigot.
　History—Frost, Tickell, White.
HULL & SEALCOATES STATUTES—Woolley.
HUNTINGDON PEERAGE—Bell.
HUNTINGDONSHIRE DIRECTORY—Kelly, Pigot.
HUNTINGDONSHIRE, VISITATION OF—Ellis. No. 43, C. S. Pa.
HUNTINGDON, DOMESDAY.
HUSBAND & WIFE, LAW OF—Bright, Mence, Prater, Roper, Shelford.
HYDRAULICS—Vol. 32, Abr. Pat.
HYDRAULIC EXPERIMENTS—Beaufoy.
HYDE ABBEY (WINCHESTER), HISTORY—Edwards, No. 45, M. R. Pub.

ICENIA—Spelman.
IDIOTS—Collinson, Phillips, Shelford.
ILIAD—Homer.
IMBANKING—Dugdale.
IMPEACHMENT OF LORDS.
IMPEACHMENT OF WARREN HASTINGS — The Oracle.

IMPERIAL GAZETTEER—Blackie.
IMPERIAL KALENDAR, BRITISH.
IMPOSITIONS, ARGUMENT AS TO—Sir W. Yelverton.
IMPRISONMENT FOR DEBT—Farley.
INCHIQUIN (EARL), APPEAL—Har. Jur. Arg.
INCLOSURES—Cooke, Howlett's T., Woolrych.
INCOME AND PROPERTY TAX LAW—Davies, Paget, Pratt.
INDEPENDENCIES EXAMINED—Prynne.
INDEXES :—
　Abbeys—Taylor.
　Chancery, Modern.
　Com. Law, &c.—Chitty & Forster.
　Com. Law Reports, 1726.
　Com. Law T. Rep.—Moore, Tomlin.
　Equity—Chitty, Jagoe.
　Law Reports. See Admiralty, Chancery, &c.
　Pedigrees—Sims.
　Records—Hawkins.
　Statutes—Raithby, Stamp.
　The Times.
　Unrepealed Statutes—Archer.
INDEX VILLARIS—Adams.
INDIA :—
　Acts of Company, Governor-General, &c.
　Administration of Justice—Norton, Pam. Vol. 10.
　Appeals to P. C.—Moore.
　Gazetteer—Thornton.
　Gentoo Code of Laws in 1776 & 1781.
　Government—Mackenzie.
　History of—Mill, Dr. W. Robertson, Wilson.
　Law of—Alcock, Field.
　Law of, Digest—Morley, Perry.
　Map of—Arrowsmith.
　Oriental Cases—Perry.
　Succession Act—Hyde.
　Summary—Theobald.
　Trade & Commerce—Mackenzie.
　Wealth—Hare.
INDIA REGISTER.
INDIA RUBBER, &c., MANUFACTURE, &c. OF—Vol. 16, Abr. Pat.
INDICTABLE OFFENCES—Boothby.
INDUSTRIOUS CLASSES DWELLINGS—C. Pearson.
INFANTS—Chambers, Ebsworth, Macpherson.
INFANT CUSTODY BILL, LETTER—Stevenson.
INGLEWOOD FOREST, LEASE TO DUKE OF PORTLAND.
INHERITANCE, LAW OF—Tamlyn.
INJUNCTIONS—Drewry, Eden, Kerr.
INLAND NAVIGATION, HISTORY OF.
INNER TEMPLE, APPEAL TO—Harvey, Hayward.
INNS OF COURT & CHANCERY, LECTURE—Macqueen.

INNS OF COURT—Addison, Herbert, Ireland.
INNS OF COURT, HISTORICAL MEMORANDA.
INNS, &C., LAWS OF—Willcock.
INQUISITIONUM AD QUOD DAMNUM CALENDARIUM
 —Rec. Com.
INQUISITIONUM POST MORTEM CALENDARIUM—
 Rec. Com.
INQUISITIONUM IN CANCELLARIA HIBERNICA
 REPERTORIUM—Rec. Com.
INQUISITIONES NONARUM TEMP. EDW. III.—
 Rec. Com.
INQUISITIONUM RETORNATARUM ABBREVIATIO
 SCOTIÆ - Rec. Com.
INSANITY — Connelly, Prichard, Tuke, Ray
 (Medical Jurisprudence).
INSANITY & CRIMINAL LUNATICS—Dr. Wood.
INSOLVENCY—Burges, Cooke, Kendall, Macrae,
 Nicholls, Shelford.
INSOLVENT DEBTORS BILL, &c.—Montagu.
INSOLVENT DEBTORS ACT—Jones.
INSOLVENT DEBTORS ACT, LETTER TO MR.
 JONES—H. Dance.
INSOLVENT DEBTORS, LAW & PRACTICE—
 Burges, Cooke, Gill, Kendall, Macrae,
 Shelford.
INSTITUTES—Justinian, Ortolan.
 American Law—Bouvier.
 English Law—Coke.
 English Law, Commentaries on — Har-
 greave & Butler.
INSTITUTIONES JURIS CANONICI—Lancellott.
INSTITUTIONES JURIS CIVILIS LUSITANI —
 Mellius.
INSTITUTIONES—Vinnius.
INSTITUTION DE DROIT FRANÇAIS—Argou.
INSURANCE, FIRE—Angell, Beaumont, Bunyon,
 Ellis.
INSURANCE, GENERAL — Emerigon, Magens,
 Park.
INSURANCE, LIFE—Angell, Beaumont (U.S.),
 Bunyon, Ellis, Farren.
INSURANCE, Marine—Arnould, Burn, Duer,
 Lees, Magens, Marshall, Park, Parker,
 Wesket.
INTERNATIONAL COMMERCIAL LAW—L. Levi.
INTERNATIONAL LAW—Austen, Burlamaqui,
 Bynkershoek, Chitty, Cutler, Felix,
 Hamel, Kent, Levi, Phillimore, Puffen-
 dorf, Rutherforth, Selden, Twiss, Vattel,
 Westlake, Wheaton.
INTERNATIONAL LAW, PRIVATE — Savigny by
 Guthrie.
INTERPLEADER—Simons, Theobald.
INTERROGATORIES—Petheram, Willis.
INTEREST OF HUSBAND IN ESTATE OF WIFE—
 Col. Jur.

INTEREST TABLES—Lawson.
INTESTACY—Mascall.
INTESTATES' GOODS, ADMINISTRATION—Selden's
 T.
INVENTIONS & SPECIFICATIONS—Newton.
INVENTORS, COUNSEL TO—Turner.
IRELAND :—
 Antiquities of—Ledwich.
 Boundaries—Parliamentary Reports.
 Calendar of State Papers, 1509-85 —
 Hamilton.
 Case of—Molyneux.
 Dictionary of—Carlisle.
 Dublin Directory—Thom.
 Ecclesiastical Revenues — Parliamentary
 Reports.
 Invasion of—Todd, No. 48, M. R. Pub.
 Lectures, &c.—Lascelles.
 Memoirs (Sir J. Barrington).
 Population of—Howlett's T.
 Records, Celtic—Donovan.
 Statistical Surveys of—Mason, Wakefield.
 Topography of—Beaufort.
 Ultimate Remedy for—Lascelles.
 Reports of Cases:—
 High Court of Parliament—Ridgeway,
 Vernon & Scriven.
 Court of Chancery—Ball & Beatty, Beatty,
 Connor & Lawson, Drury, Drury &
 Warren, Drury & Walsh, Jones &
 Latouche, Lloyd & Gould [temp.
 Plunkett], Lloyd & Gould [temp. Sug-
 den], Molloy, Schoales & Lefroy.
 Rolls Court—Flanagan & Kelly, Hogan,
 Sausse & Scully.
 King's or Queen's Bench—Alcock & Napier,
 Cooke & Alcock, Davies, Hudson &
 Brooke, Jebb & Bourke, Jebb & Symes,
 Vernon & Scriven.
 Nisi Prius—Armstrong, Macartney &
 Ogle.
 Exchequer--Hayes, Hayes & Jones, Jones,
 Jones & Carey, Longfield & Townsend.
 Crown Cases Reserved—Jebb.
 Ecclesiastical—Milward.
 Digest of Cases—Archer.
 Law Treatises—Beasley, Bullingbroke,
 De Moleyns, Ferguson, Molyneux,
 Napier.
 History—Dalrymple, Donovan, Hamilton,
 Cal. St. Pa., Hennessy, 46 M. R. Pub.,
 Todd, 48 M. R. Pub., Wakefield.
IRISH AFFAIRS, CHRONICLE OF.
IRISH ANTIQUARIAN RESEARCHES — Sir W.
 Betham.
IRISH CHANCERY, FEES IN, SCHEDULE.
IRISH CHANCERY, ORDERS IN.
IRISH COMMON LAW DIGEST—Archer.
IRISH CHURCH—Vol. 19, Pam.
IRISH ECCLESIASTICAL LAW—Bullingbroke.
IRISH ESTATES OF DRAPERS' COMPANY—Re-
 ports.
IRISH JURIST—Woodlock.

430   INDEX TO SUBJECTS.

IRISH NARRATIVE—Croker, No. 14, C. S. Pa.
IRISH POOR—Senior.
IRISH RECORDS—Beasley.
IRISH RECORDS, INDEX TO—King.
IRISH SOCIETY, ULSTER.
IRISH SOCIETY, ORIGIN, &c.
IRISH STATUTES.
IRISH STATUTES, APPENDIX TO—Ball.
INVESTMENTS—Ward.
IPSWICH & VILLAGES NEAR, HISTORY—Clarke.
IRON, REAL VALUE OF—Cort.
IRON & STEEL, MANUFACTURE OF—Abr. Put. Vol. 6.
ISÆUS, SPEECHES OF—Jones.
ISLE OF WIGHT DIRECTORY. *See* DORSET—Kelly
ISLINGTON, HISTORY OF—Nelson.
ISLINGTON INSTITUTE, INAUGURAL ADDRESS OF J. J. J. SUDLOW.
ISSUE ROLLS OF THE EXCHEQUER—Devon.
ITALIAN ACCOUNT OF ENGLAND—Sneyd, No. 37, C. S. Pa.
ITALIAN & ENGLISH DICTIONARY—Graglia.
ITALIAN TRANSLATION OUT OF, AS TO MARITIME AFFAIRS—Barretti.
ITINERA ANGLIÆ—Ogilby, Leland.
ITALY & GERMANY—Vol. 10, Pam.
ITALY, SOUTH, & MAP—Arrowsmith.
ITALY, THE CASE OF THE WAR IN, STATED, 1718.
ITALY:—
   History, Venice—Shute.
   History, Romans—Merivale.
   History, Rome—Gibbons.
   Law of—Bowyer.
   Law, Codice Civile—Borsari.
   Law, Codice Civile, Procedure—Borsari.
   Law, Atti, Manifesti.
   Law, Leggi e Decreti.
   Law, L·ggi e Trattati—Zappala.
   Law, Sentenze, Corte di Cassazione.
   Law, Sicilia, Atti Gov. Generale.
   Law, Toscane e Lucca, Decisioni, Giurisprudenza.
   Tuscany, Edict of Grand Duke.

JAGHIRE (LORD CLIVE'S), OPINIONS ON—Vol. 1, Col. Jur.
JAMAICA:—
   Acts of Assembly.
   Courts of Criminal Justice—A Solicitor.
   History of—Long.
   Laws—H. F.
   Laws, Digest of—Minott.
   Laws, 1857-67.
   Reports of Cases.
   Slave Laws.

JAMES I., PROCLAMATIONS.
JAMES I., PROGRESSES OF—Nicolas.
JAMES II., AS TO HIS SUCCESSION.
JAMES II. & CHAS. II., SECRET SERVICES OF—Akerman, No. 52, C. S. Pa.
JAMES VI. & ELIZABETH, LETTERS—Bruce, No. 46, C. S. Pa.
JAMES VI., CORRESPONDENCE WITH SIR R. CECIL—Bruce, No. 78, C. S. Pa.
JANE (QUEEN) & QUEEN MARY, CHRONICLES—Nichols, No. 48, C. S. Pa.
JANI ANGLORUM FACIES NOVA—Petyt, Selden.
JEFFERIES (LORD), BIOGRAPHY OF—Roscoe.
JEFFERIES, SPEECH OF—Vol. 2, Col. Jur.
JENKINS (SIR L.), LIFE OF—Wm. Wynne.
JERSEY:—
   History of—Falle, Plcoss.
   Laws, &c.—Le Cras.
JESUITS.
JESUITS' COLLEGE AT CLERKENWELL, DISCOVERY—No. 55, C. M. Vol. 2, & No. 73, C. M.
JESUITS, LETTERS FROM, 1688-9.
JEWELL (BP.), LETTERS, &c.—Par. S. Pa.
JEWS, SOMETIME LIVING IN ENGLAND—Selden, Vol. 3.
JEWS, EMANCIPATION OF—Vol. 6, Pam.
JEWS, HISTORY—Blunt.
JODDRELL'S TITHE CASE, ABBOTT ON—Vol. 1, Pam.
JOHNSON'S COBBLER OF PRESTON—Lanc. Co. T.
JOHNSON'S WORKS, OXFORD EDITION.
JOINT STOCK BANKS—Grant, Macleod.
JOINT STOCK COMPANIES—Cox, Pulling, Shelford, Thring, Wordsworth.
JOINT STOCK COMPANIES, WINDING UP—Ludlow, Taylor.
JOINT STOCK COMPANIES' DIRECTORY—Barker.
JONES (INIGO), LIFE OF—Malcolm.
JONES (SIR WM.), BIOGRAPHY—Roscoe.
JOURNALS:—
   Dr. Davies—Caulfield, No. 68, C. S. P.
   Education.
   Gray's Inn.
   House of Commons.
   House of Lords.
   Indexes to. See Letter I.
   Law.
   Mining.
   Mist's.
   Parry's Arctic.
   Patent.
   Rouen, of Siege of, 1591—[Sir T. Coningsby] Nichols. No. 39, C. S. P.
   Solicitors'.
JOURNEY FROM CHESTER TO LONDON—Pennant.

JUDGMENTS, 2ND BOOK OF—Huxley, Townsend.
JUDGMENTS & CROWN DEBTS—Prideaux.
JUDGMENTS, ON REGISTERING—Pask.
JUDGES' CHAMBERS, DEBATE ON—Vol. 3, Pam.
JUDGES' CIRCUIT, EXPENSES OF—Cooper, No. 73, C. S. P.
JUDGES' CHAMBERS, PRACTICE AT—Bagley, Cox.
JUDGES, CIRCUITS OF THE.
JUDGES, LIVES OF THE—Lord Campbell, Foss, Phillips, Townsend.
JUDGMENTS—Pask, Prideaux, Townsend.
JUDICATURE IN PARLIAMENT—Selden, 3rd vol.
JUDICIAL EVIDENCE—Bentham.
JUDICIUM DE DECEM SCRIPTORIBUS ANGLICANIS—Selden, Vol. 2.
JUICIO CRÍTICO DE LA NOVÍSIMA RECOPILACIÓN—Marina.
JUNIUS' LETTERS, ALMON'S TRIAL FOR SELLING—Libel L. T. Vol. 3.
JURIES:—
   Debate on Bill—Vol. 3, Libel L. T.
   Duty of—Vol. 1, Libel L. T.
   Duty of, or Englishman's Right—Sir John Hawles.
   Grand—Sir G. Stephen, Vol. 2, Libel L. T.
   Grand, Power of—Libel L. T.
   Proceedings in Parliament—Vol. 2, Libel L. T.
JURIES—Cary.
JURE, DE, MARIS—Ld. C. J. Hale, Har. L. T.
JURE, DE, NATURALI & GENTIUM, JUXTA DISCIPLINAM EBRÆORUM—Selden, Vol. 1.
JURE, DE, BELLI AC PACIS—Grotius.
JURIS CIVILIS, COMPENDIUM—Ravennas, P.
JURIS CIVILIS, DIGESTUM NOVUM, PANDECTA.
JURIS ROMANI DESCRIPTIS—Vacarius.
JURISDICTION COMMERCIALE—Bedarride.
JURISDICTION OF COURTS—Crompton, Maugham.
JURISDICTION OF COURTS, QUESTIONS ON—Crompton, Maugham.
JURISDICTION OF K. B. IN WALES—Author unknown.
JURISDICTION, RIGHTS AND LIMITATIONS—Mansel.
JURISPRUDENCE—Austin, Phillips, Thomas, Wheaton.
JURY, TRIAL BY—Bentham, Cary, Dufour, Hawles, Somers, Stephen, G. Willmore.
JURYMEN'S (GRAND) OATH EXPLAINED.
JUS FEUDALE—Craig.
JUS GRÆCO-ROMANUM TAM CANONICUM QUAM CIVILE—Leunclavius.
JUS ROMANUM—Bynkershoek.
JUSTICE, THE COMPLETE.
JUSTICE, EXECUTIVE, THOUGHTS ON.

JUSTICE. MIRROR OF, AND TRANSLATION—Horne, W. H.
JUSTICE OF THE PEACE, CASE, LAW—Archbold, Arnold, Boyd, Burn, Dalton, Higges, Horne, Lambard, Nelson, Oke, Robinson, Saunders, Sheppard, Snowden, Stone, Lord Ward, T. W. Williams, Wise.
JUSTICE OF THE PEACE, STATUTES AS TO—W. Younge.
JUSTICE & ITS MISCARRIAGES—J. Turner.
JUSTICE, EN, L'ART DE PROCEDER, CIVILE QUM CRIMINELLE—L. Lassere.

KEMP v. WICKS, SIR J. NICHOLLS' JUDGMENT, REFUSAL TO BURY CHILD.
KENDAL, ANNALS OF—Nicholson.
KENNETT, LIFE OF—Malcolm.
KENNINGTON MANOR, PETITION TO, DUCHY OF CORNWALL.
KENSINGTON, HISTORY OF—Faulkner.
KENT:—
   Description of—Brayley.
   Directory—Kelly. *See* HOME COUNTIES, Pigot.
   Domesday Book.
   Gaol Delivery in 1788—MSS.
   Gazetteer—Bagshaw.
   Genealogies—Berry.
   History of—Harris, Hasted, Ireland, Lambard, Lysons, Parsons, Philipot.
   North, Railway Evidence.
   Proceedings in 1640.
   Papers relating to Proceedings in, in 1642-6.
   Surrey & Sussex Domesday Book—Hanshall & Wilkinson.
   Tenures of—Elton.
KERRY, HISTORY OF—Smith.
KEW GARDENS, DESCRIPTION OF—Sir W. Hooker.
KIDDINGTON, HISTORY—Warton.
KILBURN TO ST. GILES'S POUND, ROAD ACT.
KING JAMES' INTENTION TO CREATE HIS SON PRINCE OF WALES, LORD TREASURER SALISBURY'S SPEECH—MSS. King James.
KING JAMES, JUDGMENT BETWEEN LD. CHANC. ELLESMERE & LD. COKE—Col. Jur.
KING, ENQUIRY AS TO ALLEGIANCE TO.
KING JOHN, A PLAY [Bale], Collier, No. 2, C. S. P.
KINGDOM, THE DANGER WHEREIN IT STOOD, AND THE REMEDY—Howell's C. P.
KING'S (OR QUEEN'S) BENCH, JURISDICTION OF, OVER WALES.

432 INDEX TO SUBJECTS.

KING'S (OR QUEEN'S) BENCH & C. P., DISCOURSES
—Ld. C. J. Hale, Har. L. T.

KING'S (OR QUEEN'S) BENCH PRACTICE. *See*
COMMON LAW.

KING'S (OR QUEEN'S) BENCH PRACTICE OF THE
CROWN SIDE—Gude, Corner, Grady &
Scotland, Hands.

KING'S (OR QUEEN'S) BENCH :—
Reports of Cases—Adolphus & Ellis, Aleyn,
Andrews, Barnardiston, Barnewall &
Alderson, Barnewall & Adolphus, Barnewall & Creswell, Benloe, Best & Smith,
Blackstone (Sir W.), Brooke, Bulstrode,
Caldecott, Carthew, Coke, Comberbach,
Comyns, Cowper, Croke, Cunningham,
Davison & Merivale, Douglass, Dowling
& Ryland, Durnford & East (Term
Reports), Dyer, East, Ellis & Blackburn; Ellis, Blackburn, & Ellis; Ellis
& Ellis, Fitzgibbons, Freeman, Fortescue, Gale & Davison, Godbolt, Gouldsborough, Hobart, Holt (Sir J.), Jones
(Sir T.), Jones (Sir W.), Keble, Keilway,
Kelyng (Sir J.), Kelynge (W.). Kenyon,
Latch, Leonard, Levintz, Ley, Lofft,
Manning & Ryland, March, Maule &
Selwyn, Modern Reports, Moore (Sir F.),
Neville & Manning, Neville & Perry,
Noy, Owen, Palmer, Peere-Williams,
Perry & Davison, Plowden, Pollexfen,
Popham, Raymond (Lord), Raymond
(Sir T.), Ridgeway (temp. Hardwicke),
Rolle, Salkeld, Saunders, Shower, Siderfin, Skinner, Smith (J. P.), Strange,
Style, Ventris, Wilson (G.), Year Books,
Yelverton.

KING'S COLLEGE HOSPITAL REPORT.

KING'S COUNCIL—Palgrave.

KINGS OF ENGLAND, HOW THEY HAVE SUPPORTED THEIR ESTATE—Howell's C. P.

KING'S INN, DUBLIN—Duhigg, Littledale.

KINGS (ENGLISH) HAVE CONSULTED PARLIAMENT
AS TO THEIR CHILDREN'S MARRIAGE—
Howell's C. P.

KINGS, POWER OF—Sir R. Filmer.

KING'S PREROGATIVE—Sir W. Staunforde.

KINGSTON-ON-HULL—Tickell.

KINGSTON, DUCHESS OF, WILL, OPINION ON CASE
—Col. Jur.

KINGSTON, SURREY, CHARTER TO—Roots.

KIRBY MOOR SIDE, HISTORY—Eastmead.

KNARESBOROUGH, HISTORY—Calvert.

KNIGHTHOOD, BRITISH ORDERS — Ashmole,
Burke, Clarke, Nichols.

KNIGHTS OF THE BATH—Anstis.

KNIGHTS HOSPITALLERS IN ENGLAND—Larking
& Kemble- No. 65, C. S. Pa.

KNIGHTS, KALENDAR OF—Townsend.

KNOX & OTHERS, NARRATIVE OF THEIR CONSPIRACY—Pol. T.

KORAN, THE—Sale.

KYTELER (A.), PROCEEDINGS AGAINST—Wright.
No. 24, C. S. P.

LABOURING CLASSES, EMPLOYMENT—Dean.

LACE, &c., FABRICS–No. 29, Abr. Pat.

LACOCK ABBEY, HISTORY—Bowles.

LACTANTIUS—Spark.

LADY HEWLEY'S CHARITY, LETTER—Yates.

LAKE (DR. EDWARD), DIARY—No. 39, C. M.

LAKE (SIR EDWARD), INTERVIEW WITH CAR. I.
—No. 73, C. M. Vol. 4.

LAKE (SIR THOMAS), LETTER—No. 87, C. M.
Vol. 5.

LAMBARD, LIFE—Malcolm.

LAMBETH (ST. MARY), ACT.

LAMBETH, HISTORY—Allen.

LAMBETH PALACE, HISTORY—Herbert & Brayley.

LANCASHIRE :—
Account of Inland Navigation.
Agriculture of—Dickson.
Chancery Practice—Winstanley.
Charters of its Duchy—Hardy.
Description of—Cooke.
Domesday Book for Amounderness, &c., in
—Bawdwen.
Dialect—Corry.
Directories—Baines, Kelly, Pigot.
Gazetteer—Clarke.
History—Britton, Corry, Gregson, Whitaker, Wilkinson.
Natural History—Leigh.
Plan of—Yates.
Plot.
Survey—Holt.
Witches, Trial—Potts (reprint), Crossley.

LANCASTER, HENRY & THOMAS OF, & JOHN OF
BRABANT, EXPENSES — Burtt. No. 55,
C. S. P., C. M. Vol. 2.

LANCASTER, HISTORY OF—Simpson.

LANCASTER, MAP OF—Binns.

LANCASTER, SURVEY OF—Tunnicliffe.

LANCASTER, RULES OF C. P. AT.

LANCASTRIÆ DUCATUS, CALENDARIUM INQUISITIONUM—Rec. Com.

LAND DRAINAGE ACT—Thring.

LAND, REGISTRATION OF TITLE TO—Wilson.

LAND REGISTRY, WORDS TO OWNERS—Vol. 11,
Pam.

LAND REVENUES, OBSERVATIONS—Woods & F.

LAND, SECURITIES ON DEBT—His. L. T.

LAND, SUGGESTIONS TO GIVE TITLE TO.

LAND TAX—Miller.

LAND TENANCY— Kennedy & Granger.

LAND, TITLE TO—Law Jour. T.
LAND, TITLE AND TRANSFER OF—Atkinson, Ayrton, Bruce, Fitch, Goodeve.
LANDED GENTRY OF ENGLAND, ADDRESS—Vol. 11, Pam.
LANDED GENTRY, DICTIONARY OF THE—Burke.
LANDLORD'S LAW—Mereton.
LANDLORD & TENANT—Archbold, Mathew, Paul, Pratt, Smith, Woodfall.
LAND, IRELAND—De Moleyns.
LANDOWNER'S, &c. (IRISH) GUIDE—De Moleyns.
LAND TAXATION & RAILWAYS, INJUSTICE—Vol. 8, Pam.
LANGTOFT (P.) CHRONICLE, TO DEATH OF EDWD. I.—T. Wright, No. 47, M. R. Pub.
LANKESTER (DR.), JOURNAL OF SOCIAL SCIENCE. *See* Hastings.
LATHAM HOUSE, SIEGE OF.
LATHAM SPA, ACCOUNT OF—Borlase.
LATIMER, SERMONS & REMAINS—Par. S. Pa.
LATIN DICTIONARIES—Ainsworth, Bridgeman, Ducange, Eaton, Otto, Facciolati, Stephanus.
LAUDIBUS, DE, LEGUM ANGLIÆ—Fortescue.
LAW AMENDMENT SOCIETY:—
 Address—Vol. 20, Pam.
 5th Report—Vol. 20, Pam.
 18th Report, 1860–1—Vol. 23, Pam.
 Mr. Serjt. Burke on Literature, &c.—Vol. 20, Pam.
LAW ASSOCIATION, METROPOLITAN & PROVINCIAL, REPORTS, 1852–62.
LAW:—
 (*Britton*) *the French Text*—F. M. Nichols.
 Law, its Abuses—Pearce.
 Lord Brougham's Letter on the Making the Law—Vol. 6, Pam.
 Mr. Brougham on State of the Law.
LAWS OF ENGLAND. *See* England, Laws of:—
 Considerations as to Amendment of Law—Har. L. T.
 Discourse on Enchiridion Legum.
 Economy of the Law—Cochrane.
 Elementary Principles of—Harris.
 Grandeur of the Law—Foss.
 Introduction to English Law.
 Language of the Written Code.
 Law & Equity, Grounds & Rudiments of, digested.
 Law & County Courts—Finlaison.
 Law Courts, &c., Evidence taken before H. C.—Vol. 9, Pam.
 Law Dictionary, or Termes de la Ley—T. B.
 Law Errors.
 Law Expenses, Remarks—H. Dance.
 Law, Imprisonment, Letters on—Park.
 Law Institute, Dublin, Papers—Vol. 16, Pam.

LAWS OF ENGLAND—*continued*
 Law Library, Epitome of—Van Heythuysen.
 Law Life and Literature—Barter.
 Law List—Brown, Stamp Office.
 Law of East India Company.
 Law Officers, Series 1558–1824—Woolrych.
 Law as to Gamesters.
 Law Code for Quebec.
 Law of Great Britain—Curson.
 Law of Women.
 Law of Nature & Nations—Burlemaqui, Chitty, Grotius, Phillimore, Puffendorf, Rutherforth, Vattel, Wheaton.
 Law Quibbles.
 Law Reform—Field, Montague, L. T., Strickland, Smith.
 Law Reporting—Daniel, Pulling.
 Law Science, Practical.
 Law, Speech on the, 1828—Ld. Brougham.
 Law Study—Bridgman, Napier, Phillips, Simpson, Stuart, Wright.
 Law Study & Practice—Raithby.
 Law Times, & Index to.
 Law Tracts—Bacon, Blackstone, Coke, Collectanea Jur., Hargrave, Jacob, Col., Law Journal, Montagu.
 Law Writers' Report—Vol. 20, Pam.
 On Defects of the Law—Espinasse.
 On the Profession of Law—Lewis.
 Outlines of Character—Maugham.
 Principles of the English Law—Sergeant.
 Public Wrongs, &c.—Maugham.
 Questions on the Law—Maugham.
 Quotations from Blacksto e—Jones.
 Scotch Law Decisions—Bell.
 Study of Law, Instructions on—Ld. C. J. Reeves, Col. Jur., Warren.
 Tenant Law.
 Unsettled Condition of Law—Miller.
LAWYERS, BAD, PUNISHMENT FOR—Hants Co. T.
LAWYERS' COMPANION & DIARY—Finlason.
LAWYERS' COMPANION—Moore.
LAWYERS, EMINENT, OPINIONS OF—Chalmers.
LAWYERS, PSEUDO, LETTER ON—Lewis.
LAWYER'S, YOUNG, RECREATIONS—Philonomus.
LAWYER, DOMESTIC—Shaw.
LAWYER, HONEST. *See* Eminent Lawyers.
LAWYER, EVERY MAN HIS OWN—Jacob, T. Williams.
LAWYER, THE, & HIS PROFESSION—Smith.
LAWYER, THE TRADESMAN'S.
LEAMINGTON & WARWICK, HISTORY OF—Field.
LEASES, &c. ACT—Brickdale.
LEASES—Chambers, Davison, Platt.
LEASES, TABLES FOR RENEWING—Newton.
LEADING CASES:
 Common Law—Smith.
 Equity—Tudor, White & Tudor.

LEADING CASES—*continued*.
  Conveyancing—Tudor.
  Mercantile—Tudor.
  U. S.—Hare & Wallace.
LEARNING, ADVANCEMENT OF—Lord Bacon.
LEARNING, FAME, &c. TRIBUTE TO—Cort.
LECTURA, BARTOLUS DE SAXO-FERRATO.
LECTURES ON JURISPRUDENCE—Petersdorff, F. S. Sullivan.
LECTURES DELIVERED IN HALL OF I. L. S.—S. F. T. Wilde.
LEECHDOMS, &c.—Cockayne, No. 35, M. R. Pub.
LEEDS DIRECTORY—Pigot.
LEEDS, HISTORY OF — Parsons, Thoresby, Dr. T. D. Whitaker.
LEGACIES—Gwynne, Hanson, Lowndes, Roper, Shelford, Trevor.
LEES, REPORT ON INQUEST—Dowling.
LEGAL ALMANAC—Maugham.
LEGAL DISCONTENT—Vol. 15, Pam. No. 6.
LEGAL DISCONTENT, THOUGHTS ON - Vol. 3, L. T.
LEGAL EDUCATION, LETTER—Haddon.
LEGAL EDUCATION, LETTER—Mansel.
LEGAL REPORT OF PARLIAMENTARY COMMITTEES.
LEGAL REPORT, ESTATE CASES COLLECTED—Law Jour. T.
LEGAL FORMS—Hall.
LEGAL GUIDE, ECCLESIASTICAL.
LEGAL JUDGMENT—Ram.
LEGAL MAXIMS—Bacon, Broom, Francis, Noy, Wharton, Wingate.
LEGAL OBSERVER & DIGESTS—Maugham.
LEGAL PRACTITIONERS, CONDITION—Vol. 3, L. T. No. 12.
LEGAL PROMPTER—Ibbotson.
LEGAL PERIODICALS :—
  Irish Jurist.
  Justice of the Peace.
  Law Advertiser.
  Law Chronicle.
  Law Journal, O. & N. Series.
  Law Jurist & Weekly Notes of Cases & Legal News, O. & N. Series.
  Law Magazine & Review.
  Law Times, O. & N. Series.
  Law Times, Digest, N. S.
  Lawyer & Magistrate's Magazine.
  Legal Observer.
  Legation Magazine.
  Monthly Law Magazine.
  Notanda.
  Solicitor's Journal.
  Weekly Reporter & Digest.
  Weekly Notes of Cases, Law Report.
LEGES ANGLO-SAXONICÆ—D. Wilkins.
LEGAL STUDIES—Hoffman.

LEGISLACION DE LEO
LÉGISLATION, TRAITÉ
LEGIBUS, DE ANTIQUIS Pa.
LEGIBUS, DE—MSS., (
LEGITIMACY—Macque
LEIGH, Life—Malcoln
LEICESTER SQUARE So
LEICESTER :—
  Corporation Char
  Domesday Book.
  Memoirs & Antiq
LEICESTERSHIRE :—
  History—Curtis,
  Leicestershire, &c
  Directories—Kell
LENG, ROBERT — Ho C. M. Vol. 5.
LETTRE DE CHANGE—
LEWES, &c., HISTORY
LEVIATHAN—Hobbes.
LEWIS'S DEPOSITION A T. 1680.
LEX MERCATORIA—Be
LEXICONS :—
  Greek & Englis Scott.
  Greek & Latin L
  Lexicon Græcum
  Lexicon Juridicu
  Law Lexicon—W
  Lexicon Universa
  Universal Latin Forcellini.
LEYCESTER CORRESPO C. S. Pa.
LIBEL CASES, LETTER L. T.
LIBEL CASES, PROCE ON LORD MANS 3, Libel L. T.
LIBEL CASES, DUTY OF T. No. 4.
LIBEL, DOCTRINE OF.
LIBEL, POWER OF JUR
LIBEL LAW—Jones.
  Discussion on—V
  Liberty of the P 1, Libel L. T.
  Summary of—Vo
  Summary of, on 1 Libel L. T., D
LIBEL, CONSIDERATIO L. T., Leach.
LIBEL BILL, LETTER: Bowles.

LIBEL BILL, DEBATE ON FUNCTIONS OF JURIES
—Vol. 4, Libel L. T.
LIBEL, SPEECH IN DEAN OF ST. ASAPH'S CASE,
MR. ERSKINE—Vol. 3, Libel L. T.
LIBEL, TRIAL OF ZENGER AT NEW YORK FOR—
Vol. 3, Libel L. T.
LIBEL & SLANDER—Cooke, Starkie.
LIBER FAMELICUS, SIR JAS. WHITELOCK—Bruce, No. 70, C. S. P.
LIBER REGIS—Bacon.
LIBER VALORUM—Ecton.
LIBERTY, CIVIL & RELIGIOUS—Hakewell, Jenkins, G. Sharp.
LIBRARY COMPANION—Dibden.
LIBRARY, EPITOME OF LAW—Van Heythuysen.
LIEN, LAW OF—Cross, Montagu, Whitaker.
LIEN, ATTORNEYS—Stokes.
LIFE ANNUITIES—Fortune, Milne, Price. *See* ANNUITIES.
LIFE ASSURANCE—Bunyon, Beaumont, Ellis, Farren.
LIFE ASSURANCE, REMARKS ON ACTS—Chaplain.
LIFE ASSURANCE SOCIETY, ECONOMIC, REPORT.
LIFE ASSURANCE SOCIETY, EQUITABLE, DEED OF SETTLEMENT.
LIFE CONTINGENCIES—Farren.
LIFE & FIRE INSURANCE, & ANNUITIES— Ellis.
LIFE & ESSAYS OF DR. A. SMITH.
LIFE OF A LAWYER, WRITTEN BY HIMSELF.
LIFE OF SIR JAS. MACKINTOSH—R.J. Mackintosh.
LIGHTS, WINDOW—Latham.
LIMA TO PARA, JOURNEY—Smyth.
LIMERICK, HISTORY OF—Ferrar.
LIMITATION OF ACTIONS—Angell (U.S.), Ferguson (Irish), Mansel, J. Wilkinson.
LIMITATIONS & PRESCRIPTIONS—Gibbons.
LIMITED LIABILITY COMPANIES, REMARKS ON— Moss.
LINCOLN'S INN & ITS LIBRARY—Spilbury.
LINCOLN'S INN LIBRARY:—
Catalogue of Books in.
Catalogue of French Law Books in—

LINCOLNSHIRE:—
Chronicles of Rebellion in 1470—Vol. 1, No. 39, C. M.
Directory—Kelly, Pigot.
Domesday Book for—Bawdwen.
LINCOLN, DOMESDAY BOOK—Vol. 1, Rec. Com.
LINDSEY, DOMESDAY BOOK—Vol. 1, Rec. Com.
L'ISTHME DE SUEZ, SON PERCEMENT—De Semencourt.
LISTS:—
Army—Hart.
Bankrupt—Smith.
Clergy—Cox.
Colonial Office.
Foreign Office—Hertslet.
Indian Army.
Law List.
Law List, Australia.
Law List, Scotch.
Lords & Commons—Cave, Payne.
Lords & Officers of State—Whitworth.
Navy.
Nobility—Whitworth.
Nominees of Tontine.
Unclaimed Dividends.
LITERARY FUND, SUMMARY OF FACTS—Vol. 11, Pam.
LITERARY LIFE, REMINISCENCES OF—Dibden.
LITERARY MEN, LETTERS OF EMINENT—Ellis, No. 23, C. S. Pa.
LITERARY PROPERTY, DONALDSON *v.* BECKETT, CASE IN H. L.—Maugham.
LITERATURE—Hallam.
LITURGIES, CATECHISMS, &C. TEMP. EDWD. VI. & ELIZABETH—Par. S. Pa.
LITURGY, THOUGHTS ON THE—Stow.
LIVERPOOL:—
Athenæum Library Catalogue.
Corporation v. Corporation of London, Arguments—Har. Jur. Arg.
Directory—Kelly.
Guide—Moss.
History—Enfield.
Its Commerce &c.—Smithers.
LIVERPOOL TO LEEDS, PLAN OF PROPOSED CANAL.
LIVES, &c. OF ILLUSTRIOUS DEAD IN 1711-12.
LIVES OF LORD ELDON, BACON, THE BERKELEYS, PITT (EARL STANHOPE), SIR J. MACKINTOSH, SPELMAN, STORY. *See* also Lives of Eminent Lawyers, & Roscoe's Biography.

LOCAL GOVERNMENT ACT—Taylor.
LOCAL MANAGEMENT ACT—Cooke, Woolrych.
LOCAL, PERSONAL, & PRIVATE ACTS, INDEX— Vardon.
LOCOMOTION, AIDS TO—Vol. 7, Abr. Pat.
LOGIC, PURE—Jevons.
LOLLARDS, APOLOGY FOR THE WICLIFFE—Todd, No. 20, C. S. Pa.
LONG PARLIAMENT, NOTES OF—No. 31, C. S. Pa., Sir R. Verney.

LONDON:—

Antiquities of. See Stillingfleet's Eccl. Law.
Bridge, Chronicles of.
Bridge, Proceedings as to.
Charities—Highmore, Low.
Charities, Endowed.
Charter to Bank.
Charters—Luffman.
Christenings & Burials—Morris.
Chronicles, Grey Friars, 1189-1556—Nichols, No. 53, C. S. Pa.
Chronicle temp. Hen. VII. & VIII.—No. 39, C. S. Pa., C. M. Vol. 4.
Chronicles of London—Tyrrell.
Citizen's Pocket Chronicle—J. F. S.
City of London Courts—Emerson.
City of London Remembrancer—Nichols.
College of Arms, History—Noble.
Collier Dock Act.
Companies—Maitland.
Corporation Disputes—Pulling.
City Privileges—Norton, Hughson.
Dictionary of London—Elmes.
Directories—Hitch, Johnson, Kelly, Kent, Lowndes, Pigot, Robson, Suburban, P.O.
Domesday of St. Paul's—Archdeacon Hale, No. 69, C. S. Pa.
Encyclopædia.
Environs—Lysons, Woodburn.
East London Water Works Acts.
Fishmongers' Pageant.
Franchises—Norton.
Freemen of Companies.
French Chronicle, 1260-1343—No. 28, C. S. Pa.
Gentlemen of Account resident, 1595.
Gildhallæ Munimenta—Riley, No. 12, M. R. Pub.
Gresham's, Sir T., Will.
Grocers' Company—Heath.
Grey Friars of London—No. 53, C. S. Pa.
Guide—Longman.
Health & Traffic, Letter—T. L. Wood.
History—Brydall, Brayley, Chamberlain, Gwynn, Hatton, Hughson, Maitland, Malcolm, Newton, Noorthouck, Pennant, Stow, Strype.
Hospitals:—
St. Katharine—Nichols.
Royal—Firth.
Christ's—Trollope.

LONDON—continued.
Inns of Court, Antiquities of—Herbert, Ireland.
Laws & Customs—Bohun, Brandon, Greene, Harrison, Locke, Norton, Pulling, Rowland.
Liberties of City—Jacob.
London Illustrated—Wilkinson.
London Institution, Charter to.
London against the King, Quo Warranto (City lost its Charter).
London v. King's Lynn, Case of the latter —Har. Jur. Arg.
London University Calendar.
Merchants, Report.
Merchant Taylors' School—Hessey, Wilson.
Map in 1578—Soc. of Antiq.
Map—Duncker, Greenwood, Hatton, Horwood, Newton, Rocque, Whishaw.
Map of London, in Case—Cassell, P. O. Directory.
Proceedings against Bishop of London before Ecclesiastical Commissioners — No. 1, T. 1688-9.
Parochial History—Newcourt.
Pamphlets.
Plan of London—Wyld.
Plan for Holborn Viaduct.
Physicians, Catalogue of College of— Goodall.
Present State of London—Delaune.
Public Sale Rooms, Prospectus for.
Reports of City Special Cases—Calthrop.
Royal Society of London, History of—Dr. T. Sprat.
St. Laurence Pountney, History—Wilson.
St. Paul's, History—Dugdale.
Scriveners' Company, Case.
Sewers Act.
Sewers (City), Commissioners' Order as to.
Sewerage Question—Booth.
Survey, Parish Clerks—Rocque.
Temple—Addison.
Tithe Cases—Weston.
Tracts relating to City.
Trade Tokens, Catalogue—Beaufoy.
Vindication of—Scott.

LONDON & MIDDLESEX:—
Correspondence as to Sheriff of.
Description—Brayley.

LONDON & WESTMINSTER:—
Improved—Gwynne.
Inns of Court—Ireland.
Parish Clerks' Survey.
Survey of Cities of—Rocque.

LONDON & SOUTHWARK, HISTORY OF—Noorthouck.

LONDON DOCK & WEST INDIA DOCK BILLS, EVIDENCE.

LONDON & WATFORD SPRING WATER COMPANY, REPORT OF DIRECTORS OF.

LONDON TO NORWICH & YARMOUTH, SECTIONS OF EASTERN COUNTIES INTENDED RAILWAY.

LONDONDERRY, REPORTS, GROCERS' COMPANY.

LORD CHANCELLORS, CATALOGUE OF—Hardy.
LORD KEEPERS OF THE SEAL & CHANCELLORS.
LORDS WHO COMPOUNDED FOR ESTATES, LIST OF—Dring.
LORDS, HOUSE OF:—*See also* House of Lords.
  Appellate Jurisdiction—Cooper, Hall, Macqueen, Palmer, Urquhart.
  Order of the—Walkley.
  Protests, 1722-3.
  Reports.
  Report on Marriages, Townshend's Case.
  Spiritual, &c. List—Gosling.
LOUTH, NOTICES OF.
LOWESTOFT, HISTORY OF—Gillingwater.
LOYALTY, ON REWARD OF—Sir J. D. Hay.
LUBY & OTHERS, TRIAL (FENIAN).
LUNACY—Archbold, Brydall, Collinson, Cooper, Elmer, Highmore, Phillips, Shelford, Winslow.
  As Affecting all Classes.
  Extracts of Report.
  Law Amendment Society, Report.
  Letter by a Phrenologist.
  Suggestions on Asylums—Dr. Leech.
LUNATICS, &C., LETTER ON NUMBER OF, IN E. & W.—Halliday.
LUSHINGTON' (DR.), JUDGMENT IN BANDA & KIRWEE BOOTY.
LÜTZEN, BATTLE OF, LETTER DESCRIBING—Fleetwood.
LYME, ANTIQUITIES OF—Marriott.
LYME REGIS, HISTORY OF—Roberts.
LYNDHURST (LORD), MEMOIR—Gibson.
LYNN, HISTORY OF—Richards.
LYTTELTON (LORD), WORKS OF—Ayscough.

MACHYN'S DIARY—Nichols, No. 42, C. S. Pa.
MACNAMARA & OTHERS, INFORMATION—Pol. T.
MADRAS GAZETTE:—
  Laws—Clarke.
  Regulations & Acts.
  Trevelyan's, Sir C., recall.
MAGAZINES :—
  Blackwood's.
  British Critic.
  Colburn's New Monthly.
  Colburn's United Service.
  European.
  Fraser's.
  Gentleman's.
  Law Magazine, Monthly.
  Law Magazine & Review.
  Legulean.
  Magistrate & Lawyer's.
  Metropolitan.
  Tait's.
  U. S. Journal.

MAGISTRATES :—*See* Justice of the Peace.
  Reports of Cases—Bittleston & Wise; Carrow, Hamerton, & Allen; Dowling & Ryan; Manning & Ryland; Nolan; Neville & Manning; Neville & Perry.
MAGISTRATES' AID. *See* Justice.
MAGNA CARTA & CARTA DE FORESTA—Blackstone.
MAGNA CHARTA & STATUTA ANTIQUA.
MAGNA CHARTA, ESSAY ON—Thompson.
MAGNA CHARTA, STATUTES—Tothill.
MAHOMET, ALCORAN—Sale.
MOOHUMMUDAN LAWS, CHART OF—Rumsey.
MAIDSTONE, HISTORY OF—Newton.
MAIDSTONE, CHARTER TO, BY JAMES.
MAINTENANCE & CHAMPERTY—Tapp.
MAITLAND, LIFE—Malcolm.
MALVERN, HISTORY OF—Chambers.
MAN, ESSAY ON—Pope, Reid.
MAN, NATURAL LAWS OF—Dr. G. Spurzheim.
MARY ST., LAMBETH, ACT.
MAN, GLIMPSES AT ORIGIN, &C. OF—Heyworth.
MAN, ISLE OF :—
  Description of—King.
  Antiquities—Johnstone.
  Directory—Pigot.
  History — Bullock, Feltham, Hargrave, Quayle, Robertson, Rolt, Sacheverell & Brown, Stanley, Woods.
  Laws—Burman, Geneste, Gill, Jeffcott, Johnson, Lamothe, Mackenzie, Mill, Ward.
MANCHESTER :—
  Cathedral & Church, &c., Answer to Commissioners—Vol. 9, Pam.
  Cheetham Hospital, Founder's Will.
  Directories—Kelly, Slater.
  History—Aikin, Wheeler, Whitaker.
  History of Siege—Palmer.
  Salford, &c. Directory—Pigot & Deans.
MANDAMUS—Impey.
MANDAT, EXPLIQUÉ DU—Troplong.
MANKIND—Sir M. Hale.
MANSFIELD (LORD), JUDGMENT IN REX *v.* WOODFALL, LETTER—Rous.
MANSFIELD (LORD), BIOGRAPHY OF—Roscoe.
MANORS, LAWS OF—Nelson.
MANORS, RIGHTS OF LORDS OF. *See* Gurdon on Parliament.
MSS., HISTORY OF THE COURT OF EXCHEQUER.
MSS., DESCRIPTION OF ANCIENT TALLIES.
MARCHES, JURISDICTION OF THE—Bacon.
MANURE—Vol. 3, Abr. Pat.
MAPES, DE NUGIS CURIALIUM—Wright, No. 50 C. S. Pa.

MAPES, POEMS—Wright. No. 16, C. S. Pa.
MAPS:—
Delhi & Constantinople, District between—Arrowsmith.
Maps, &c. in Geo. III. Library.
Maps & Drawings, Cat. of, in Brit. Mus.
Ordnance.
P. O.—Kelly (London).
MARI, DU—Pothier.
MARE CLAUSUM—Selden, Vol. 2.
MARGAN, DE, ANNALES—Luard. No. 36, M. R. Pub.
MARIAGES, TRAITÉ DES—Demolombe.
MARIAGE, DU CONTRAT DE—Pothier.
MARIAGE, DU CONTRAT DE, EXPLIQUÉ—Troplong.
MARINE, COMMENTAIRE SUR L'ORDONNANCE DE 1A—Valin.
MARINE INSURANCE — Arnold, Burn, Duer (U.S.), Wesket.
MARINE LAW—Burn, Molloy.
MARINE PROPULSION—No. 5, Abr. Pat.
MARITIME AFFAIRS & SEA LAWS, TRANSLATED OUT OF THE ITALIAN.
MARITIME AFFAIRS, MS. FROM DES. COMS. LIBRARY.
MARITIME LEGISLATIVE PAPERS—Wendt.
MARITIME OFFICERS OF E. I. Co., COMPENSATION TO—Debate.
MARITIME WARFARE—Thompson.
MARITIMO, DE JURE—Molloy.
MARLBERGE (T. DE) CHRONICON ABBATIÆ EVESHAMENSIS—No. 29, M. R. Pub. Macray.
MARLBOROUGH (DUKE OF), HISTORY—Alison.
MARMYON FAMILY, HISTORY—Bankes.
MARRIAGE ARTICLES, CONSTRUCTION OF, IN DUKE OF RICHMOND'S CASE, & OPINION—Vol. 2, L. T.
MARRIAGE SETTLEMENTS—Atherley, Peachy.
MARRIAGE, Law OF—Atherley, Bishop (U.S.), Macqueen, Morgan, Poynter, Shelford, Swinburne.
Commissioners' Report.
Conflict, English & Scotch—Prater.
Ireland—Stoddart.
MARRIAGE WITH DECEASED WIFE'S SISTER—Several Pam. comprising Vol. 24.
MARRIAGE & DIVORCE, ENQUIRY INTO, SCRIPTURE DOCTRINE OF—Vol. 2, Jur. L. T.
MARSHALLING ASSETS—Cook, Jarman, Ram, Roper, Spence, Story, Williams.
MARTIAL LAW—Finlason, Samuel, Tytler.
MARTIALL & STAPLETON, ANSWER TO—Fulkes, Par. S. Pa.
MARTIALL'S TREATISE OF THE CROSS, ANSWER TO—Calfhill, Par. S. Pa.

MARY (QUEEN) CAL. ST. PA. DOM. SER.—Lemon.
MARY (QUEEN) COL. ST. PA. FOR. SER.—Turnbull.
MARY (QUEEN) & JANE (QUEEN), CHRONICLE—Nichols, No. 48, C. S. Pa.
MARYLEBONE, SURVEY OF—Britton.
MASTER OF THE ROLLS, AUTHORITY IN CHANCERY.
MASTER & SERVANT—Smith, Spike, by Claydon.
MASTER'S OFFICE, CHANCERY—Bennett, Hargrave.
Common Law—Dax.
Ireland—Beasley.
MATRIMONIO, DE—Sanchez.
MATRIMONY, BANNS OF—Greaves.
MAUNDER'S WORKS. See TREASURIES.
MAXIMS—Bacon, Broom, Francis, Noy, Wharton, Wingate.
MAXIMES DU DROIT PUBLIC FRANÇAIS.
MAXIMS & REFLECTIONS—La Rochefoucauld.
MAXWELL (COL. R.), INFORMATION—Pol. T. 1680.
MAY & ANOTHER, TRIAL.
MAYOR'S (LORD) COURT PRACTICE—Brandon, Daly.
MSS. CATALOGUE—Hardy.
MSS. HARLEIAN—Catalogue.
MEASURES, WEIGHTS, & COINS, PLAN OF INTERNATIONAL ASSOCIATION—Browne.
MEASURING MADE EASY—Goode.
MECHANICS' INSTITUTE, ADDRESS TO ST. PIERRE SOCIETY, CALAIS—Taylor.
MEDICAL EVIDENCE ANALYSED—Smith.
MEDICAL INQUIRER, AMERICAN—Chitty.
MEDICAL JURISPRUDENCE—Brady, Chitty, Guy, Ray, Taylor, Willcock.
MEDICAL PROFESSION, EXAMINATION OF BILL—Dr. Forbes.
MEDICAL REGISTER.
MEDICAL WITNESSES, HINTS FOR EXAMINATION OF—Smith.
MEDICINE, SURGERY, & DENTISTRY—No. 25, Abr. Pat.
MELSA, CHRONICON MONASTERII DE—Bond, No. 43, M. R. Pub.
MEMOIRS:—
H. Butterworth.
Lord Lyndhurst—Gibbs.
Sir J. Melville.
Duke of Sully.
Mr. Sweet.
Sir J. E. Wilmot.
MÉMOIRES—Brantome.

MÉMOIRES POUR LA VIE—Pétrarque.
MEMORIALS OF ENGLISH AFFAIRS—Whitelock.
M.P.'s, OATHS TO BE TAKEN BY—Vol. 7, Jac. L. T.
MEN'S LIVES, SECURITY FOR—Vol. 1, Libel L. T., Lord Somers.
MEN OF THE TIME—Routledge.
MERCANTILE, &C. ACCOUNTS—Pulling.
MERCANTILE GUARANTEES—Fell.
MERCANTILE & MARITIME GUIDE—Willmore & Bedell.
MERCANTILE LAW. See COMMERCIAL LAW, Reports of Cases, Danson & Lloyd, Lloyd & Welsby, Ross.
MERCANTILE & MARINE LAW, LEADING CASES IN—Tudor.
MERCHANT'S MANUAL—Hobler.
MERCHANT SEAMEN—Symons.
MERCHANT SHIPPING — Abbott, Greenhow, Holt, James, Lees, Maclachlan, Maude & Pollock, Oliver, Shee, Symons.
MERCHANT TAYLORS' SCHOOL:—
Account—Hessey.
History—Dr. H. B. Wilson.
MERGER—Mayhew.
MERSEY, INTENDED CANAL TO, FROM WILDEN FERRY.
MERYONETH COMITATUS EXTENTÆ. See RECORD OF CAERNARVON.
METALS, HISTORY—Webster.
METALS & ALLOYS—Vol. 18, Abr. Pat.
METALS, PLATING OR COATING WITH—No. 23, Abr. Pat.
METALS & MINES, ACCOUNT OF.
METALS, MINES, &C., COLLECTION OF TREATISES UPON—Barba, Payne.
METRICAL ROMANCES, THREE—Robson, No. 18, C. S. Pa.
METROPOLIS, DESIGN FOR IMPROVEMENT of—By an Architect.
METROPOLIS, MAP OF COUNTY COURTS—Davis.
METROPOLITAN BUILDING ACT—Cooke, Tattershall & Chambers, Woolrych.
METROPOLITAN LOCAL MANAGEMENT ACT—Woolrych.
METROPOLITAN MAGAZINE.
METROPOLITAN POLICE MANUAL—Stone.
METROPOLITAN FARES FOR HACKNEY CARRIAGES.
METROPOLITAN POOR LAW—Glen.
METROPOLITAN, GENERAL, REGISTRY—Hall.
METROPOLITAN SANITARY COMMISSIONERS — Smithson.
MEXICO, MAP OF—Arrowsmith.
MEXICO, CONQUEST OF—Prescott.
MIDDLE AGES—Hallam.

MIDDLE CLASS & NON-GREMIAL EXAMINATIONS —A. H. Wratislaw.
MIDDLEHAM CHURCH ANTIQUITIES — Atthill, No. 38, C. S. Pa.
MIDDLESEX, DOMESDAY BOOK FOR—Bawdwen.
MIDDLESEX:—
Bridges, Report of—Saunders.
Directories. See *Home Counties*—Kelly, Pigot.
Herald, Visitation for, 1660.
History—Lysons.
MIDDLESEX & LONDON, DESCRIPTION OF— Brayley.
MIDDLE TEMPLE LIBRARY, CATALOGUE.
MILFORD HAVEN, TOUR TO—Morgan.
MILITARI, DE RE ROMANORUM—Salmasius.
MILITARY LAW—Griffith, Piper & Collier, Samuel, Tytler.
MILITIA MEA MULTIPLEX—Tookians.
MILITIA LAWS—Prendergast.
MILITARY ENGINEER.
MILITARY & NAVAL CALENDAR.
MILLAR v. TAYLOR, REPORT ON LITERARY PROPERTY—Burrow.
MILTON, PAPERS RELATING TO.
MILTON, PROSE & POETICAL WORKS.
MINER, COMPLETE—Houghton.
MINERAL LAWS—Houghton.
MINERALS, &C.—Price.
MINERALOGIA COLUMBIENSIS—Pryce.
MINES—Arundell, Bainbridge, Collier, Pettus, Rogers, Tapping.
MINES, MINERALS, & QUARRIES.
MINES OF SIR C. PRICE IN CARDIGANSHIRE— Waller.
MINING ENTERPRISE—Tredennick.
MINING JOURNAL.
MINISTERS, FRENCH, WHO FLED ON PERSECUTION.
MINORITÉ, DE LA—Demolombe.
MISCELLANY—Bentley, Camden, Harleian.
MIST'S JOURNAL.
MODERN PLEADER—Impey.
MODUS TENENDI PARLIAMENTUM—Hardy.
MONARCHY, LETTER TO THE QUEEN—Brougham
MONARCHY, ON THE—John Wilson.
MONASTERIES:—
Abingdon—Stevenson, No. 2, M. R. Pub.
De Melsa—Bond, No. 43, M. R. Pub.
De Waverleia—Luard, No. 36, M. R. Pub.
De Wintonia—Luard, No 36, M. R. Pub.
[*Rishanger*] *St. Alban's*, Riley—No. 28, M. R. Pub.

MONASTERIES—*continued.*
  St. Alban's, [*Walsingham*] Riley, No. 28, M. R. Pub.
  St. Peter, Gloucester—Hart, No. 33, M. R. Pub.
  St. Augustine, Canterbury — Hardwick, No. 8, M. R. Pub.
MONASTERIES, SUPPRESSION OF, 1528-55—Wright, No. 26, C. S. P.
MONASTIC INSTITUTIONS — Dugdale, Stevens, Tanner, Willis.
MONASTICI ANNALES—Luard, No. 36, M. R. Pub.
MONEY, PROVINCE OF, HISTORY.
MONMOUTH, HISTORY OF—Heath.
MONMOUTHSHIRE :—
  Directories—Kelly, Pigot.
  History—Coxe, Williams & Gardner.
MONEY, COST OF OBTAINING—Senior, Pam.
MONEY LENDING—Male.
MONITEUR, LE, UNIVERSEL.
MONTHLY, THE, ACCOUNT.
MONTHLY, NEW, MAGAZINE.
MONTHLY MERCURY—Phillips.
MONTHLY RECORD, BIRTHS, &c.
MONTREAL ALMANACK.
MONTROSE DUKEDOM—Lord Lindsay.
MONUMENTA HISTORICA BRITANNICA—Petrie & Sharp.
MONUMENTA FRANCISCANA — Brewer, No 4, Rolls.
MONUMENTS, ANCIENT FUNERAL—Weever.
MOOHUMMUDAN LAW, CHART OF FAMILY INHERITANCE—Rumsey.
MOOT BOOK—Plowden, Gregory.
MORAL PHILOSOPHY & LAW, PLEA FOR, LETTER—Miller.
MORANT, LIFE—Malcolm.
MORE (SIR THOS.), LINEAGE—Foss.
MORGAN'S CALCULATIONS OF ACCUMULATIONS—Har. Jur. Arg.
MORGAN *v.* LONDON DOCK COMPANY, TRIAL—Walsh & Son.
MORNING ADVERTISER.
MORNING CHRONICLE.
MORNING HERALD.
MORNING POST.
MORNING STAR.
MORTALITY, LAW OF—Farren.
MORTALITY, RATE OF—Powell.
MORTGAGE, CASE ON PRIOR WILLOUGHBY *v.* WILLOUGHBY.
MORTGAGES—Coote, Davison, Fisher, Hillier (U.S.), Powell, Rouse.

MORTGAGES, EQUITABLE—Miller.
MORTMAIN, STATUTES, CASES—Col. Jur.
MORTMAIN—Highmore, Shelford.
MOSAIC CODE, INFLUENCE IN LEGISLATION—Marsden.
MOSES, SYSTEM OF—Robinson.
MOSES, MORAL SYSTEM OF—Pye.
MOWBRAY'S NARRATIVE—Pol. T.
MUNICIPAL CORPORATION & PUBLIC HEALTH ACTS—Bullock, Rawlinson, Welsby.
MUNICIPAL CORPORATIONS — Merewether & Stephens, Willcock.
MUNICIPAL LAW—Arnold.
MURDER BY A FRENCH MIDWIFE, 1687.
MUSIC & MUSICAL INSTRUMENTS—Vol. 26, Abr. Pat.
MUTINY—Report for Relief of Sufferers in India.
MUTUAL LAW ASSOCIATION, ADDRESS TO—Kennedy.
MYDDELTON *v.* LORD KENYON, ARGUMENT—Har. Jur. Arg.
MYSORE REVERSION—Major Bell.
MYTHOLOGY—Lemprière, Smith.

NABOB OF THE CARNATIC, PETITION — Har. Jur. Arg.
NAMES, FICTITIOUS—Hamst.
NANTISSEMENT, DU—Troplong.
NAPOLÉON, HISTOIRE—Norsius.
NARRATIVES :—
  Expulsion of English from Normandy—Stevenson, No. 32, M. R. Pub.
  Irish—Croker, No. 14, C. S. Pa.
  Oppression of Islanders of Jersey.
  Reformation -- [Foxe] Nichols, No. 77, C. S. Pa.
  Second Arctic Voyage—Sir J. Ross.
NASEBY—Martin.
NATAL—Laws.
NATIONS, LAWS OF—*See* International Law.
NATIONAL COLONIAL SOCIETY ON EMIGRATION REPORT—Vol. 18, Pam.
NATIONAL DEBT, ON THE—Vol. 27, Pam., Newman.
NATIONAL LIFE ANNUITIES, CALCULATIONS—Bennett, Tate.
NATIONAL MSS., ENGLAND AND WALES.
NATIONAL MSS., SCOTLAND.
NATURA BREVIUM—Fitzherbert.
NATURAL LAW—*See* INTERNATIONAL LAW.
NATURALISATION—Hansard.
NATURALIS HISTORIA PLINII SECUNDI.

NAVAL BIOGRAPHY & CHRONICLE.
NAVAL CHRONOLOGY—Schombergh.
NAVAL COURT-MARTIAL—McArthur.
NAVAL EXPOSITION—Blankley.
NAVAL & MILITARY KALENDAR—Mackenzie.
NAVAL PRIZE LAW MANUAL—Lushington.
NAVAL PRIZE LAW—Katchenovsky.
NAVIBUS, DE, ET NAULO—Roccus.
NAVIGATION, INLAND—Phillips.
NAVY, CASE OF ASSISTANT SURGEONS IN.
NAVY, CRIMINAL LAW OF—Thring.
NAVY TIMBER, DORSETSHIRE, LETTER AS TO QUOTA—MS. temp. James.
NATURIS, RERUM DE, A. NECKHAM—Wright, No. 34, Rolls.
NE EXEAT REGNO, WRIT OF—Beames.
NEGLIGENCE & ACCIDENTS—Hay.
NEGRO SLAVERY, MR. BROUGHAM ON.
NETTER (T.), FASCICULI ZIZANIORUM—Shirley, No. 5, M. R. Pub.
NEWBURY, HISTORY—Bunny.
NEW BRIGHTON, PLAN OF.
NEW BRUNSWICK ACTS.
NEWCASTLE COAL TRADE—Gardiner.
NEWCASTLE-UPON-TYNE, HISTORY—Brand, Mackenzie.
NEW COLONIES—Bannister.
NEWCOURT, LIFE OF—Malcolm.
NEW FOREST—Lewis.
NEWFOUNDLAND ACTS.
NEWGATE KALENDAR.
NEW MONTHLY MAGAZINE—Colburn.
NEWSPAPERS. *See* List in Catalogue.
NEWPORT (I. OF WIGHT), CUSTOM AT—Hants Co. Tr.
NEW PROTESTANT LITURGY — No. 25, T. 1688-9.
NEW SOUTH WALES :—
  Crown Lands, 2nd Letter on License Fees—Vol. 18, Pam., Hamilton.
  Proceedings in 1824-6.
  Census, 1861.
  Sydney Directory.
NEW STAR CHAMBER CASES—Crompton, Law T. Vol. 1.
NEW TESTAMENT, 1486.
NEW YORK :—
  Codes & Forms.
  Reports, Court of Appeal—Selden.
  Chancery Reports—Johnson.
  Revised Statutes—Edmonds.
NEW ZEALAND, ACTS & STATISTICS.
NICHOLAI (P.), IV. TAXATIO ECCLESIASTICA ANGLIÆ ET WALLIÆ—Rec. Com.

NINE DAYS' WONDER—Kemp, No. 11, C. S. Pa.
NISI PRIUS—Buller, Duncombe, Espinasse, Manning, Onslow, Selwyn, Stephens.
NISI PRIUS REPORTS—Campbell, Carrington & Payne, Carrington & Kirwan, Carrington & Marshman, Dowling & Ryland, Espinasse, Foster & Finlason, Gow, Moody & Matkin, Moody & Robinson, Holt, Ryan & Moody, Peake, Starkie.
NOBILITY — Brooke, Dale, Dugdale, Milles, Pawley, Whitworth.
  Law of the York.
  Historical Essay on the Rise of. See PEERAGES.
NOBILITY & GENTRY, LAW—Brydall.
NOLAN'S SPEECH ON FARNHAM ROAD BILL— Vol. 13, L. T.
NON COMPOTES MENTIS—*See* LUNACY.
NONARUM INQUISITIONES, EDW. III.—Vanderzee, Rec. Com.
NORFOLCIÆ, DESCRIPTIO TOPOGRAPHICA — Sir H. Spelman.
NORFOLK :—
  MSS. of an Historical Poem—Vol. 3, No. 61, C. M.
  Directory. See CAMBRIDGESHIRE—Kelly, Pigot.
  Domesday Book—Vol. 2, Rec. Com.
  History—Blomefield & Parkins.
NORMAN & SAXON CHARTERS. *See* CARTÆ ANTIQUÆ.
NORMAN DICTIONARY—Kelham.
NORMAND DROIT, DICTIONNAIRE DE—Houard.
NORMAN ROLLS—Carte, Rec. Com., Petrie.
NORMANDIE :—
  Coutumes du Pais de.
  Commentaires du Droict civil de—Terrien.
  Coutume—Pesnelle.
  La Coutume reduite en Maximes—P. de Merville.
  Principes généraux du Droit civil et coutumier—Routier.
  Pratiques—C. Routier.
NORMANDY & ENGLAND, HISTORY—Palgrave.
NORMANDY, EXPULSION OF ENGLISH FROM — Blondel, Stevenson, No. 32, Rolls.
NORTHAMPTON DOMESDAY BOOK.
NORTHAMPTONSHIRE :—
  Directory—Kelly, Pigot.
  History—Baker, Bridges.
NORTHAMPTONSHIRE, &c. TOUR—Bray.
NORTH AMERICAN INDIANS—Bannister.
NORTH BRITISH ADVERTISER.
NORTH & SOUTH AMERICAN STATES, A CHAPTER FROM THE HISTORY OF—Gibbs, Vol. 16, Pam.

NORTH & SOUTH AMERICA, MAP OF—Arrowsmith.
NORTHERN GOVERNMENTS—J. Williams.
NORTHINGTON (LD.), DECREE IN NORTON v. REILLY—No. 18, Vol. 1, Col. Jur.
NORTH KENT RAILWAY, EVIDENCE.
NORTHUMBERLAND:—
Directories—Kelly, Pigot.
History—Hodgson, Hutchinson, Wallis.
NORTHUMBERLAND & DURHAM, LOCAL RECORDS—Sykes.
NORTON v. REILLY—Decree of Ld. Chancellor Northington—Vol. 1, No. 18, Col. Jur.
NORWICH, HISTORY OF—Blomefield.
NORWICENSIS MONACHI B. DE COTTON, HISTORIA ANGLICANA—Luard, No. 16 M. R. Pub.
NOTABILIA DE ASSECURATIONIBUS—Roccus.
NOTÆ IN EADMERUM—Selden, Vol. 2.
NOTANDA—Edwards.
NOTAIRES, LE SCIENCE DES.
NOTARIAL & COMMERCIAL LAW PRECEDENTS—Montefiore.
NOTARIAL EVIDENCE—Ridgway, Pam. Vol. 8.
NOTARY—Brooke.
NOTARIES & BANKERS' LAW MANUAL, NEW YORK—Wedgwood & Homan.
NOTES OF CASES:—
Ecclesiastical &c. Law—Thornton.
From Edward I.
For History of Public Departments—Thomas.
History of E., 1509-1714.
Law Journal.
Law Reporting.
Long Parliament—No. 31, C. S. Pa., Verney.
NOTITIA HISTORICA—Nicolas.
NOTITIA MONASTICA—Tanner.
NOTITIA PARLIAMENTARIA—B. Willis.
NOTTINGHAM:—
Domesday Book—Vol. 2, Rec. Com.
History—Deering.
NOTTINGHAMSHIRE:—
Directory—Kelly, Pigot.
Domesday Book—Bawdwen.
History—Thorston.
Tour—Bray.
NOVA SCOTIA:—
History—Haliburton.
Journal of House of Assembly.
Journal of Legislative Council.
Reports of Supreme Court—Thompson.
Revised Statutes—Campbell & others.
Revised Statutes, 2nd Series—Wilkins & others, Young & Others.
NUCIUS' TRAVELS—Cramer, No. 17, C. S. Pa.

NUGIS, DE, CURIALIUM—Mapes, Wright. No. 50, C. S. Pa.
NUPTIÆ SACRÆ, OR DOCTRINE OF MARRIAGE—Vol. 2, L. T.
NUISANCES—Gibbons, Glen, Keane, Lumley, Smith, Yool.

OATHS, FORM OF.
OATHS TO BE TAKEN BY M.P.'s—Jac. L. T. Vol. 2.
OATHS IN CHANCERY—Braithwaite.
OATHS OF JURYMEN—Vol. 1, Libel L. T.
OATHS, LECTURES ON—Sanderson.
OBITUARY, 1627-74—Smith.
OBITUARY, ANNUAL, 1761-2.
OBLIGATIONS, DES—Pothier.
OBSERVER, LEGAL—Maugham.
OBSERVER NEWSPAPER.
O'CONNELL v. REGINA, JUDGMENT—Leahy.
OCCUPATION, OR GLANCE AT PROPERTY TAX, &c.—Arrowsmith.
ODES—Pindar.
ODYSSEY—Homer.
OFFICERS IN THE ARMY—Prendergast.
OFFICIAL SALARIES, H. C. REPORT.
OILS, ANIMAL, &c.—No. 27, Abr. Pat.
OLD & NEW TESTAMENT, SACRED HISTORY—Whiston.
OLDYS & PARK, HARLEIAN MISCELLANY.
OLD WHIG—Vol. 2, Grim. T.
OODDEEN v. OAKELEY, JUDGMENT—Vol. 21, Pam.
OPERATIVES, RIGHTS—Sankey.
OPINIONS ON ESTATE IN FEE—Vol. 2, Col. Jur.
OPINION ON REVOKING WILL—Vol. 2, Col. Jur.
OPTION (THE), CLAIM OF ABP. TO DISPOSE OF SEES—Vol. 2, Col. Jur.
OPUSCULA JURIDICA—Bynkershoek.
OPUS MINUS & OPUS TERTIUM—Brewer, No. 15, Rolls.
ORANGE (PRINCE OF), PAPAL TREATIES CANNOT BE RELIED ON—T. 1688-9.
ORANGE (PRINCE OF), DANGERS OF PROTESTANTS BEFORE HE CAME—T. 1688-9.
ORANGE (PRINCE OF), REASONS WHY HE INVADED ENGLAND—T. 1688-9.
ORANGE (PRINCE & PRINCESS OF), PRAYER FOR—T. 1688-9.
ORATIONS, ELEGANT—Mossop.
ORATORY LECTURES—Lawson.

ORDINANCES:—
   British Guiana.
   Ceylon.
   Falkland Islands.
   Gibraltar.
   Malta.
   Mauritius.
   St. Helena.
   Victoria.
   Western Australia.
ORDINANCES, &c. OF P. C.
ORDINANCES OF H. C. AS TO SEQUESTRATED ESTATES, &c.—MS. temp. Jas.
ORDO JUDICIORUM—Oughton.
ORDERS IN BANKRUPTCY, 1842-68.
ORDERS IN CHANCERY—Cox.
ORDERS IN CHANCERY, IRISH—Smith.
ORDERS IN CHANCERY & STATUTES—Morgan, Morgan & Chute, Sanders.
ORDERS IN COUNCIL, ECCLESIASTICAL COMMISSIONERS ACTS.
ORDERS IN COUNCIL AS TO ELECTION OF CORONERS.
ORDER OF THE GARTER, HISTORY—Ashmole.
ORIGIN, &c. OF U.S. COURTS—Conkling.
ORIGINALIA RECORDS, INDEX TO—Jones.
ORIGINES JUDICIALES—Dugdale.
ORLÉANS, COUTUME D'—Pothier.
ORPHANS, CASE OF, CONSIDERED.
ORPHANS' LEGACY—Godolphin.
OTHO, CONSTITUTIONS OF—Lyndewood.
OUDE, SPOLIATION OF.
OUTLINES OF LAW, PRIVATE WRONGS—Maugham.
OUTLINES OF LAW, PUBLIC WRONGS—Maugham.
OUTLINES OF CRIMINAL LAW—Maugham.
OVERBOROUGH, ROMAN ANTIQUITIES—Rauthmell.
OWN TIME, HISTORY—Burnett.
OXEN BRIDGE, THE, OF BREDE PLACE—Cooper, W. D.
OXENEDES, J., DE CHRONICA—Sir H. Ellis, No. 13, M. R. Pub.
OXONIENSES ATHENÆ—Wood.
OXFORD:—
   Blonde of—De Lincy, No. 72, C. S. Pa.
   Calendar.
   Chancellor's Court of Oxford—Sewell.
   Domesday Book for Oxford—Bawdwen.
   Edward, Earl of Oxford. See IMPEACHMENT OF LORDS.
   Election Poll Book.
   Exeter College Case—Vol. 2, Stillingfleet.
   Munimenta Academica—Anstey, No. 50, M. R. Pub.
   New Oxford Examination—Acland.
   Oxford Press, Observations on—Blackstone.

OXFORD—*continued.*
   Speech in H. C. at Oxford in 1st Charles I.—Howell's C. P.
   Statutes of the University.
   University Commission—Pycroft.
   University Commission, Letter—Pycroft.
   University Commissioners' Reports.
OXFORDSHIRE:—
   Directory—Kelly, Pigot.
   History—Brewer, Kennett, Plot, Warton, Wood.

PAUL'S, ST., CATHEDRAL, HISTORY—Dugdale, Ellis, Hale, No. 69, C. S. P.
PACE DE REGIA, ON THE LAW—Pulton.
PACKING SPECIAL JURIES—Bentham.
PALACES:—
   Croydon—Ducarel.
   Crystal Palace.
   Hampton Court.
   Lambeth.
   Westminster.
   Windsor.
PALL MALL GAZETTE.
PANDECTÆ RERUM JUDICATARUM—Ærodius.
PANTON v. WILLIAMS, JUDGMENT—Vol. 1, Pam.
PAPAL ROYAL FAVORITE—Prynne.
PAPER-CUTTING, &c.—Vol. 12, Abr. Pat.
PAPER, MANUFACTURES OF, &c.—Vol. 11, Abr. Pat.
PAPERS, C. S.—Egerton, Howard, Kent (Proceedings), Milton, Rutland, Trelawney, Trevelyan, Verney.
PAPISTS, TREACHERY OF. *See* PRYNNE.
PARAMYTIA—Watson.
PARIS, MAP OF, & ENVIRONS. *See* S. De Fers Deson.
PARIS (M.) HISTORIA MINOR—Madden, No. 44, M. R. Pub.
PARISH CLERKS' SURVEY of LONDON, WESTMINSTER, & SOUTHWARK.
PARISH LAW—Archbold, Cripps, Prideaux, Shaw, Steer, Duncan.
PARISH OFFICER—Jacob.
PARISHES, LIST OF—Vol. 18, 1840, H. C. Pa.
PARKER (BP.), CORRESPONDENCE—Par. S. Pa.
PARLIAMENT:—
   Acts of Parliament, Abridged—Scobell, Williams.
   Acts & Ordinances.
   Address to Parliament against Charitable Trusts Bill.
   Aids—Har. Jur. Arg.
   Answer as to Bishops Voting in Parliament.
   Bankruptcy, Commissioners' Reports.
   Bills—Bramwell.
   Bills, H. L. & H. C.

PARLIAMENT—*continued.*
Bills of Costs—Norris, Palmer.
Cases & Records—Hatsell.
Committee's Report on Fees in Law & Equity.
Committee's Report on Legal Education.
Debate on 'Abdicate.'
Debates—Barrow, Townshend.
Debates in Parliament, 1610—C. S. Pa.
Debat s in Parliament, 1804-13—Hansard.
Declaration of Parliament on Commission of Array, 1641—Elsynge.
Elector denied his Vote.
Free Parliament—Macworth.
General Index to Debates in Parliament—Phillipart.
Guide—Stockdale.
History—Gurdon, Hakewil, Hale, Howell, May, Oldfield, Pettus, Petyt, Prynne, Smith, Spelman, Wight, Willis.
History & Debates, L. & C.—1680-85.
Journals of H. C. & H. L. & Indexes.
Judicature in Parliament, Treatise, MSS.
Locus Standi—Smethurst.
Manual of Parliament.
Members of Parliament—Beatson, Dodd, White.
Mirror of Parliament—Burrow.
Parliamentary Records—Cotton.
Parliamentary Reform—Bagehot, Stapleton.
Parliamentary Register.
Parliamentary Register—Beatson.
Parliamentary Register, Irish.
Parliamentary Review, 1826—L. T. Vol. 7.
Parliamentary Sessions Paper, H. C. H. L., & Indexes.
Parliamentary Votes, H. C. & H. L.
Parliamentary Writs & Writs of Military Summons.
Practice—Bramwell, Bristowe, Elsynge, Fawcett & Littler, Halcomb, Lumley, Macqueen, May, Palmer, Will.
Precedents—Bourke, Ellis, Hatsell, Petyt.
Privilege—Ld. Anglesey, Atkyns, Blundell, Cotton, Ferrall, Freshfield, Hakewell, Hardy, Hatsell, Howell's C. P., Kennedy, MSS., Pemberton, G. P. Prynne, Ryley, Rymer, Selden, Smith.
Proceedings in Parliament—Crew.
Protests of H. L.
Remonstrance to Parliament—J. Jenkins.
Its Rise and Power—Sheridan.
Reports of H. C., 1715-1800, *& Index.*
Site for Houses of Parliament—Fowler.
Standing Orders in Parliament—Biggs, Vacher.
Writs—Palgrave, Rec. Com.
Verney's Notes on Long Parliament—Bruce, No. 31, C. S. P.

PAROCHIAL ASSESSMENTS—Carwardine, Lumley.

PAROCHIAL ASSESSMENTS BILL & TITHE COMMUTATION ACT, LETTER—Miller.

PAROCHIAL REGISTERS—Bigland.

PAROCHIAL SETTLEMENTS—Sir E. J. Gambier, J. M. White.

PAROCHIAL SETTLEMENTS, LAWS OF, BY EQUITABLE ESTATE—Rous.

PAROCHIAL SOCIETIES, INSTRUCTIONS FOR ESTABLISHING NATIONAL LIFE ANNUITIES.

PARSON, THE COMPLETE—Doddridge.

PARSON ABERONI, APOLOGY FOR, 1719—Gosling.

PARSON'S COUNSELLER—Degge.

PARTIES TO SUITS IN EQUITY—Calvert.

PARTHENON, THE.

PARTNERSHIP—Collyer, Dixon, Gow, Lindley, Montagu, Pothier, Story (U.S), Watson.

PARTNERSHIP, LIMITED LIABILITY—Field, Pam. Vol. 9.

PASTORALS, HEXAMETRICAL EXPERIMENTS—Virgil.

PARTY WALLS—Woolrych.

PARVULORUM PROMPTORIUM—Way, C. S. Pa. Nos. 35, 47, 54.

PATENTS:—
Alphabetical Index of Patents.
Alphabetical Index of Patentees.
Chronological Index of Patents.
Subject Matter, Index of.
Reference to Patents.
Specifications & Drawings, 1617-1867.
Abridgment of Specifications.
Supplement to Abridgment of Specifications.
General Index to Repertory of Patents, 1815-45.
Journal of Patents, 1852-68.
Law of Patents—Browne, Byrne, Campin, Carpmael, Curtis (U.S.), Davis, Drewry, Godson, Hindmarch, Holroyd, Norman, Prince, Turner, Webster.
Law of Patents & Copyright—Fraser.
Privileges, Laws of, in Europe, &c.—Loosey.
Reports of Cases—Davies, Carpmael, Webster, Macrory.

PATENTIUM ROTULORUM CALENDARIUM—Ayscough, Rec. Com.

PATENT LAWS, CORRESPONDENCE, PATENT COMMISSIONERS.

PATENT ROLLS, INTRODUCTION TO—T. D. Hardy.

PATENT ROLLS—1201-1216, Vol. 1, Pt. 1, T. D. Hardy.

PATENT ROLLS, REPERTORY OF, IN IRISH CHANCERY—Erck.

PATERNITÉ, ET DE LA FILIATION—Demolombe.

PAWN, ON CONTRACT OF—Turner.

PEACE & WAR—Grotius.

PEDIGREES:—
See *Berry's Genealogies.*
Pedigrees from the Norman Conquest, Lectures—Grimaldi.
Pedigree of Louis-Philippe of France.
Pedigree of Umfreville.

PEER, REPORT ON THE DIGNITY OF.

!AGES & BARONAGES, 1ST, 2ND, & 3RD
SERIES :—
Airlie, Case & Evidence.
Airth, Case & Evidence.
Anglesey, Case & Evidence.
Annandale, Case & Evidence.
Athenry, Case & Evidence.
Aylmer, Case and Evidence.
Balfour of Burleigh, Case.
Balrath, De, Case.
Banbury, Case & Evidence.
Barnewall, Case & Evidence.
Beaumont, Case & Evidence.
Belhaven, Case.
Berkeley, Case & Evidence.
Berners, Case & Evidence.
Borthwick, Case & Evidence.
Botetourt, Case.
Bowes, Case.
Brandon, Case.
Bray, Cases & Evidence.
Buttevant, Evidence only.
Camoys, Case & Evidence.
Cassillis, Cases.
Chandos, Case & Evidence.
Clifford, Case.
Clinton, Case.
Crawford & Lindsay, Cases & Evidence.
Devon, Case & Evidence.
De Lisle, Case & Evidence.
Dunboyne, Case.
Dundonald, Case.
Ely, Evidence on Claim to Vote.
Fairfax of Cameron, Case.
Fitzwalter, Case & Evidence.
Gardner, Evidence only.
Glencairne, Case.
Grandison, Cases & Evidence.
Great Chamberlain, Lord, of England, Cases.
Hamilton, Duke of, Case.
Hastings, Cases & Evidence.
Herries, Case & Evidence.
Howard de Walden, Cases and Evidence.
Huntly, Case & Evidence.
Inchiquin, Case.
Ireland, Lord Stewardship of, Case—
Lord Shrewsbury.
Killie, Evidence.
Killeen, Act 27 Henry VI.
Kilmorey, Claim to Vote, Evidence.
Lauderdale, Case.
Leicester, Case.
Leigh, Case & Evidence.
Lennox, Dukedom, Case.
Lovat, Case & Evidence.
Marchmont, Case & Evidence.
Marmyon, Case & Evidence.
Molesworth, Evidence.
Montacute, Case.
Monthermer, Case.
Montrose, Dukedom, Case.
Netterville, Case & Evidence.
Newburgh, Cases.
Norbury, Claim to Vote.
North, Case & Evidence.
Northumberland, Percy's Case.
Nugent, Evidence.
Ormond, Evidence.

PEERAGES & BARONAGES—continued.
Perth, Case & Evidence.
Polwarth, Evidence.
Powis, Case.
Queensbury, Case & Evidence.
Riverston, Case.
Rokeby, Evidence.
Roos, Cases & Evidence.
Roscommon, Cases and Evidence.
Roxburgh, Cases & Evidence.
St. Clair, Case.
Say & Sele, Case.
Shrewsbury & Waterford, Case & Evidence.
Sinclair, Case & Evidence.
Southesk, Cases.
Slane, Cases & Evidence.
Spinie, Case.
Stafford, Cases, Evidence, & Genealogical Table.
Stirling, Case.
Strange, Case.
Strathallan, Case.
Strathmore & Kinghorn, Case & Evidence.
Sussex, Dukedom, Case.
Sydney of Penshurst, Perry's Case.
Taaffe, Case.
Tracey, Case & Evidence.
Vaux of Harrowden, Case & Evidence.
Wharton, Cases & Evidence.
Wigtown, Cases & State of Evidence.
Willoughby of Perham, Case.
Zouch, Case & Evidence.

PEERAGE, THE OLD WHIG ON STATE OF—Gosling.
PEERAGE BILL, CONSIDERATIONS ON IT—Gosling.
PEERAGE BILL, PAMPHLETS ON—Gosling.
PEERAGE, LIMITATION OF, SECURITY OF LIBERTIES, 1720.
PEERAGE, BUCHAN, PETITION OF SIR C. MACKENZIE.
PEERAGES & BARONIES, WORKS ON THE—Almon (Extinct), Almon, Banks, Barlow, Bolton, Brown, Burke (British), Collins, Debrett, Dugdale, English Compendium, Edmondson, Fielding, Guthrie, Jacob, Kearsley, Kimber, Longmate, New, Sir H. Nicolas, Playfair, Pocket, Pollard, Ridgway, Salmon, Sams, West, C. White.
PEERAGES & BARONETAGES, WORKS ON THE—Burke, Debrett, Lodge, Playfair.
PEERAGE, IRISH—Compendium, Kimber, Lodge, Longmate, Playfair, Salmon.
PEERAGE, SCOTCH — Compendium, Kimber, Pocket Companion, Playfair, Salmon.
PEERS, CREATING, MANNER OF—West.
PEERS, LIST OF—Rider.
PELL RECORDS—Devon.
PEMBROKESHIRE, HISTORY—Fenton.
PENAL CODE, PREPARED BY INDIAN LAW COMMISSIONERS.
PENAL CODE, FRENCH.
PENAL LAW—Lord Auckland

PENAL STATUTES—Addington.
PENAL STATUTES, ABRIDGED—Clarke.
PENAL STATUTES, ENQUIRY AS TO DISPENSING WITH—Atkyns' T.
PENNANT, Life—Malcolm.
PEOPLE'S RIGHTS—Sharp.
PENINSULAR WAR—Napier, Wellington.
PENNSYLVANIA, CHARTERS TO.
PERIODICALS NOT LEGAL:—
Annals of Europe.
Annual Register.
Historical Register.
Present State of Britain—Chamberlain.
New State of England—Meige.
Present State of Britain—Meige.
Present State of Court of Great Britain.
PERJURY, PARDON FOR—Har. Jur. Arg.
PERPETUAL POST OBIT ANNUITY, OPINIONS—Col. Jur. V. 2.
PERPETUITIES—Lewis, Shelford.
PERRIN v. BLAKE—JUDGMENT—Mr. Justice Blackstone, Col. Jur. V. 1.
PERRY'S CASE OF PRIVILEGE ON H. L. COMMITTAL—Har. Jur. Arg.
PERSONAL ESTATE, TRANSMISSION OF, LECTURE—Senior, Pam.
PERSONAL PROPERTY, ON SALES OF—Benjamin, Story (U.S.), Jos. Williams.
PERSONS, RIGHTS OF—Stewart.
PERSONNES, DES, ET DES CHOSES—Pothier.
PERTH, TRADITIONS OF—Penny.
PERTH (EARL OF), CORRESPONDENCE—Jerdan, No. 33, C. S. Pa.
PERTH (EARL OF), CORRESPONDENCE—No. 33, C. S. Pa.
PERU, CONQUEST OF—Prescott.
PETERHAM, CUSTOMS—Vol. 2, Col. Jur.
PETER'S REPORTS U.S. See CURTIS.
PETERSFIELD, HISTORY OF CHURCHER'S COLLEGE AT.
PETROBURGENSE, CHRONICON—Stapleton, No. 47, C. S. Pa.
PETTY BAG OFFICE, FORMS OF WRITS—Abbott.
PETTY JURIES—Sir J. Hawles.
PETYT, ANSWER TO HIS BOOK OF 1680.
PEWS, ENGLISH.
PHILADELPHIA, CHARTERS TO.
PHILOSOPHY—Bacon, Boyle, Newton, Vizard.
PHILPOTS (ARCHDEACON), EXAMINATION, &c. OF.
PHOTOGRAPHY—Vol. 19, Abr. Pat.
PHRENOLOGY, PRINCIPLES OF—G. Spurzheim.
PHRENOLOGY, DOCTRINE OF THE MIND—G. Spurzheim.
PHRENOLOGY, MANUAL OF—Bust, J. Deville.

PICCADILLY PAPERS, THE CHURCH QUESTION.
PICCADILLY PAPERS, ON CHECKING PUBLIC EXPENDITURE.
PICKET STREET PROPOSED LOTTERY, SCHEME.
PIETY, DEVOTIONAL, TEMP. ELIZABETH—Par. S. Pa.
PIETY, ITS PROGRESS—Norden, Par. S. Pa.
PIGOTT (LORD), DEFENCE OF.
PIGOTT (LORD), CORONER'S INQUEST ON. See E. I. Co.
PIGOTT'S DIRECTORY. See Johnston, Hitch, Kelly, Kent, Lowndes, Robson, Suburban, Thompson.
PILGRIMAGE—Sir R. Guylford.
PIPE, GREAT ROLL OF THE—Pub. Rec.
PITT, LIFE OF—Earl Stanhope.
PLACITA PARLIAMENTARIA—Ryley.
PLACITANDI DOCTRINA, S. E.[UER].
PLANS, WESTMINSTER SEWERS, HOLBORN VIADUCT.
PLATO, REMARKS ON LIFE—Lowndes.
PLEADER, ENGLISH—Bowman.
PLEADER—Herne.
PLEADER, ASSISTANT TO.
PLEADER'S GUIDE (ANSTEY).
PLEADING:—
Method of Pleading—Browne (W.), Bullen & Lawes, Leake, Chitty, Clift, Euer, Finlason, Greening, Lutwyche, Mallory, Petersdorff, Philips, Ramshay, Robinson, Stephen, Theobald, Townesend, Wentworth, Williams, Winch.
Rules for Pleading, 1694.
Criminal Pleading—Archbold, Roscoe, Starkie.
Equity Pleading—Drewry, Mitford, Montague, Story (U.S.).
PLEAS OF THE CROWN—F. East, Hale, Hawkins, Sir W. Staunforde, Tremaine.
PLEBEIANS—Grimaldi T. Vol. 2.
PLESHY, HISTORY OF—Gough.
PLINE LE JEUNE, LETTRES DE.
PLUMPTON CORRESPONDENCE—Stapleton, No. 4, C. S. Pa.
POCKET COMPANION.
POCKET CONVEYANCER—Bird.
POEMS & TRANSLATIONS—Sir J. Denham.
POEMS—Mapes, No. 16, C. S. Pa.
POETRY, ART OF—Barter.
POETS, LIVES OF THE—Plutarch.
POISONS, PAPER READ AT BRITISH ASSOCIATION, BIRMINGHAM—W. Wilson.
POLICE, ORIGIN OF—Fielding.
POLICE OF THE METROPOLIS—Colquhoun.
POLICE & CRIMINALS—Mr. Serjeant Adams.

INDEX TO SUBJECTS. 447

POLITICAL ECONOMY — Senior, A. Smith, Whately.
POLITICAL HISTORY, SKETCH OF—The Press.
POLITICAL INDEX, OR REGISTER—Beatson.
POLITICAL SONGS, EDW. III.—RIC. III. — Wright, No. 14, M. R. Pub.
POLL BOOK, Berkshire, Cambridge, Bristol, Chelmsford, Dorsetshire, Durham, Essex, Gloucester, Hampshire, Herefordshire, Hertfordshire, Hull, Ipswich, Kent, Leicester, Norfolk, Northumberland, Newcastle, Oxford, Rochester, Suffolk, Sussex, Westminster, Wiltshire, York, Yorkshire.
POLYCHRONICON—Higden, with Trevisa, Babington, No. 41, Rolls.
POLYDORE VERGIL—Ellis, No. 29, C. S. Pa.
POLYMATIS ON ROMAN POETS—Spence.
POMPEII—Donaldson.
PONTEFRACT, HISTORY—Boothroyd.
POOLE CASTLE, HISTORY—Sydenham.
POOR, LABOURING :—
   Local Reports, E. & W.
   Local Reports, Scotland.
   Report on, of Great Britain.
POOR, DISCOURSES ON THE—Sir M. Hale.
POOR, EXAMINATION OF MR. PITT'S SPEECH ON CONDITION OF—Howlett's Tr.
POOR, HISTORY OF THE—Eden.
POOR LAW—Archbold, Bott, Burn, Foley, Glen, Leigh, Lumley, Nolan, Robinson, Theobald.
POOR LAW COMMISSIONERS, REPORT ON LOCAL TAXATION.
POOR LAW COMMISSIONERS, INSTRUCTIONS FOR CENTRAL BOARD OF—Senior.
POOR, PLEA FOR THE.
POOR & POOR RATES—Howlett's Tr.
POOR RATES, CASES OF EXEMPTION — E. Griffiths, Lumley.
POOR RATE, DIMINUTION—Greedy.
POOR REMOVAL ACTS—Lumley.
POPULATION, LECTURE—Senior.
POPULATION, ESSAY ON—Malthus.
POPULATION OF GREAT BRITAIN, RETURN.
POPULATION OF GREAT BRITAIN, COMPARATIVE RETURN.
POPISH RECUSANTS, &c. AS TO—Howell's C. P.
POPE INNOCENT VIII., BULL—Collier, No. 39, C. S. P. C. M., Vol. 1.
POPE NICOLAS IV. TAXATION—Rec. Com.
POPE'S BRIEF, CONCLUSIONS—Cooper.
POPE'S (ALEX.) LETTERS TO ATTERBURY — Nichols, No. 73, C. S. P. Vol. 4, C. M.
POPERY, INQUISITION & JESUITS—Pickering.

POPERY, CATHOLIC BALLAD—MSS. temp. James.
PORTIBUS (DE) MARIS—Har. L. Tr.
PORTLAND (EARL OF) & OTHERS—Impeachment of Lords.
PORTLAND (DUKE OF), AS TO LEASE TO.
PORTSOKEN WARD, ADDRESS OF ALDERMAN SALOMON—Vol. 23, Pam.
PORTUGAL :—
   Institutiones Juris Civilis Lusitani—Mello.
   Law of Portugal, Direito Civil—Carneiro.
   Ordenações e Leis.
   Tratado regular e practico de Testamentos e Successões.
POST OFFICE, ACTS RELATING TO.
POST OFFICE, DIRECTORIES—Kelly.
POTTERY—Vol. 24, Abr. Pat.
POWERS—Chance, Powell, Sugden.
PRACTICAL LAW, OUTLINES OF—Fleming.
PRACTICAL MAN—Rouse.
PRACTICAL REGISTER IN CHANCERY—Wyatt.
PRACTICAL REGISTER, CHANCERY & COMMON LAW—Lilly.
PRACTICARUM OBSERVATIONUM LIBRI II. — Gaill.
PRACTICE :—
   Parliamentary, H. L. — May, McQueen, Palmer.
   H. L. & P. C.—May, McQueen, Macpherson, Palmer.
   Parliamentary, H. C.—Bramwell, Bristow, Halcomb, Lumley, Manual, Palmer, Vincent & West.
   Parliamentary Practice, H. C., Referees' Court—Fawcett, Sharkey, Will.
   Chancery — Ayckbourn, Barnes, Barry, Batten & Ludlow, Bohun, Browne, Daniel, Field, Ford, Gilbert, Goldsmith, Grant, Hadden, Harrison, Hinde, Jarman, Kennedy, Maddock, Newland, Pemberton, Prideaux, Richardson, Smith, Turner, Wyatt, Welford.
   Clerk in Court of Chancery.
   Chancery Practice in Libellous Publications—Vol. 1, Libel L. Tr.
   Chancery Practice in Masters' Office—Bennett.
   Practising Solicitor in Chancery.
   Receiver, Duties & Office of, Irish—Smith.
   Chancery Record & Writ—Veal.
   Chancery Practice of Durham—Wilkinson.
   Chancery, of Lancashire.
   Attorneys—Bohun.
   Practice of the Courts, K. B.—Archbold, Bayley, Chitty, Chapman, Crompton, Harrison, Impey, Lee, Lush, Prentice, Richardson, Sellon, Tidd, (New) Tidd, (Supplement) Tidd, (Supplement & Rules) Tidd.
   Practical Forms, K. B.—Archbold, Chitty, Tidd.

PRACTICE—continued.
  Practical Forms, K. B., 8th edit.
  K. B., Filacer's New Guide, or Practising Attorney.
  K. B. Office—Fry.
  K. B. & C. P., or Institutio Legales—Bohun, Dowling.
  K. B. & C. P. Practice Epitomised.
  K. B. & C. P., Writ of Trial—Mansell.
  K. B. & C. P., Questions—Impey, Turner.
  K. B., Criminal—Archbold, Bolton, Corner, Grady & S., Gude, Hands.
  C. P.—Archbold, Harrison, Impey, Richardson.
  C. P., Practical Register.
  Exchequer—Burton, Day, Edmunds, Fowler, Manning, Turner.
  Exchequer, Jurisdiction, &c.—Price.
  Exchequer, Equity Side—Turner.
  Divorce & Matrimonial Causes—Bilton, Browne, Browning, Inderwick, Macqueen, Pritchard, Shelford, Swabey, Tidswell & Littler.
  Common Law Judges Chambers—Bagalley, Parkinson.
  Equity Judges Chambers—Bloxam.
  Summary of Practice—Petersdorff.
  Admiralty—Clarke, Coote, Macpherson, Williams & Bruce.
  Bankruptcy—Archbold, Christian, Cooke, Davis, Deacon, Doria & McCrae, Eden, Evans, Flather, Fonblanque, Gooding, Griffith, Green, Gregg, Hazlitt, Kendall, Koe & M., Montagu, Montagu & Ayrton, Roche, Shelford, Smith, Stewart, Turner, Whitmarsh.
  Conveyancing—Barry, Clayton, Cornish, Coventry, Greenwood, Housman, Hughes, Lucas, Prideaux, Prior, Rous, Smith.
  Conveyancing Practice, Observations in MSS.—Butler.
  Country Attorney's Practice—Archibald, Gray.
  County Courts—Batten & Ludlow, Davis, Gilmour, Rumsey, Pollock & Nicol, Stroud, Will.
  Cases, Digest of—Morris.
  Ecclesiastical—Burn, Clarke, Cockburn, Const, Rogers, Shelford.
  Election—Cox, Rogers, Wordsworth.
  Insolvency & Bankruptcy Practice—Cooke, Cox & Lloyd, Nicholls & Doyle.
  Insolvency Practice under Protection Acts—Macrae.
  Practice in Lord Mayor's Court—Brandon, Daly.
  Practice in Sheriff's Court—Harrison, Lewis.
  Practice of Lord Mayor & Sheriff's Courts.
  Practice of the Palace Court—Abrahams.
  Probate Court—Chadwick, Coote, Coote & Tristram, Cox, Dodd & Brooks, Falconer, Forster, Gwynne, Hill, Hudson, Jebb, Shelford, Tilsley, Trevor, Waddilove, Weatherley.
  Proctor's Practice—Floyer.
  Practice, Pleading, &c. Suggestions for Altering Law of.

PRACTICE—continued.
  Scotch Law Practice—Hope.
  Sessions (Petty) Practice—Stone.
  Sessions (Quarter) Practice—Archbold, Leeming & Cross.
PRATIQUES BÉNÉFICIALES, L'USAGE DE NORMANDIE—Routier.
PRATIQUE DE PROCÉDURE CIVILE ET CODE DE COMMERCE—Gilbert.
PRACTICE, &c. OF CALIFORNIA—Garfield & Snyder.
PRAYER, COMMON, WITH ACT OF UNIFORMITY.
PRAYER-BOOK—Mant, Bayley, Wheatly.
PRAYERS (PRIVATE), TEMP. QUEEN ELIZABETH—Par. S. Pa.
PRAYERS, &c. (FAMILY)—Stow.
PSALMS, VERSION OF THE—Stow.
PRECEDENCY, TABLE OF—Younge.
PRECEDENTS IN CONVEYANCING—Barry, Bridgman, Bythewood & Jarman, Bythewood (Stewart's), Coventry, Crabb, Davidson, Hayes, Horsman, Hughes, Jarman (Sweet's), Martin, Preston, Prideaux, Roberts, Sheppard, Stewart, Sweet, Watkins, Williams, Woods.
PRECEDENT BOOK—Atkinson.
PRECEDENTS IN IRISH CHANCERY, MASTERS' OFFICE—Beasley.
PREROGATIVE (ROYAL)—Allen, Fortescue, James I., Staunforde.
PRESBYTERIANS (ENGLISH), HISTORY—Vol. 2, L. Tr.
PRESS (THE) NEWSPAPER.
PRESS & ST. JAMES'S CHRONICLE.
PRESS, LIBERTY OF THE, IN SLANDER—Vol. 1, Libel L. Tr.
PRÉSCRIPTION, DE LA—Troplong.
PRESCRIPTIONS & LIMITATIONS—Gibbons.
PRESENT STATE OF BRITAIN—Chamberlain, Miege.
PRESENT STATE OF COURT OF GREAT BRITAIN—Miege.
PRESENT STATE OF ENGLAND—Miege.
PRESUMPTION—Best.
PRESTON, HISTORY OF.
PRESTON, COBBLER OF—Johnson.
PRESTON, ENCOMIUM OF, &c.—Lan. Co. Tr.
PRESTON'S ESSAY ON ESTATES, ANALYSIS—L. J. P.
PRÊT, DU CONTRAT DE—Pothier.
PRÊT, DU—Troplong.
PRICES OF STOCKS—Wetenhall.
PRICES, HIGH & LOW—Tooke.
PRIDEAUX (DR.), LIFE OF—Souverton.
PRIDEAUX (DR.), SERMON, THANKSGIVING.
PRIESTS' MARRIAGES—Marten.

PRIMOGENITURE, LETTER ON—Tomkins & Jenkins.
PRINCE CHRISTIAN OF DENMARK, DEFENCE.
PRINCESS ELIZABETH, HOUSEHOLD ACCOUNT.
PRINCES OF WALES. See Spectator, 1863.
PRINCIPAL & AGENT—Paley, Story.
PRINCIPAL & SURETY—Fell, Pitman, Theobald.
PRINTED REPORTS, REMARKS ON—Freshfield, Pickering.
PRINTS of John Bell, Esq.; W. Bray, Esq.; Eldon, Earl of; Sir Thomas More; The Hon. Spencer Perceval; Godfrey Sykes, Esq.
PRISONS—Glen, Saunders.
PRISON DISCIPLINE—C. Pearson.
PRISONERS, ON PURGATORY OF—Shipley.
PRIVATE ACTS, TABLE—Bramwell.
PRIVATE BILLS:—
 Sessions List of, 1853-68—Vacher.
 Instructions for passing.
 Legislation—Pulling.
 Report of House of Commons on.
PRIVATE MASS, ANSWER TO APOLOGY FOR—Cooper, Par. S. Pa.
PRIVATE WRONGS, LAW—Addison, Maugham, Sleigh.
PRIVILEGE OF HEIR-APPARENT—His. L. Tr.
PRIVILÉGES (DES) ET HYPOTHÈQUE—Troplong
PRIVILEGES, H. C., CASES AND RECORDS ON—Kennedy, Pemberton.
PRIVILEGES, JUDICIAL, OF COMMONS—Rutherforth (T. B.), 1838.
PRIVY COUNCIL, PROCEEDINGS, &C. OF—Nicolas.
PRIVY COUNCIL, PRACTICE OF—Coote, Macpherson. McQueen, Williams & Bruce.
 Reports of Cases—Knapp, Moore.
PRIZE COURTS & LAW, NAVAL—Acton, Katchenovsky, Lushington.
PROBABILITÉS (DES) DU CALCUL.
PROBATE COURT PRACTICE—Chadwick, Coote, Coote & Tristram, Cox, Dodd & Brooks, Falconer, Foster, Gwynne, Hill.
PROBATE COURTS COSTS—Carew, Hudson, Jebb, Shelford, Waddilove.
PROBATE COURT DUTIES—Trevor.
PROBATE COURT, REPORTS OF CASES—Swabey & Tristram.
PROCÉDURE (DE LA)—Pothier.
PROCESS (SCOTCH) FORM OF—Louthian.
PROFITABLE BOOK—Perkins.
PROGRESS OF PIETY—Norden.
PROGRESS OF COMEDY, RICHELIEU IN LOVE—Vol. 23, Pam.

PROHIBITED DEGREES, MARRIAGES—Vol. 7, L.T.
 See also Marriage with Deceased Wife's Sister—Vol. 24, Pam.
PROMESSI SPOSI—Manzoni.
PROMISES & COVENANTS—His. L. Tr.
PROMISSORY NOTES—Byles, Chitty, Story (U.S.)
PROMPTORIUM PARVULORUM SIVE CLERICORUM—Way, Nos. 25, 54, 89, C. S. Pa.
PROMISSORY NOTES (U.S.)—Story.
PROPERTY, HISTORY OF—His. L. Tr. No. 3.
PROPERTY, PERSONAL—Morton, Smith, Williams.
PROPERTY, TABLE FOR VALUING—Sir I. Newton, Willich.
PROPERTY, REAL—Burton, Cruise, Hayes, Humphrey, Shelford, Smith, Sugden, Tudor, Williams.
PROPERTY, RIGHTS & DUTIES OF—Sangster.
PROPERTY, LAW OF—Butler, Hunter, Sugden, Lord St. Leonards, Vaisey.
PROPERTY AS ADMINISTERED IN THE LORDS—Sir E. B. Sugden.
PROPHECY OF BISHOP USHER—Tr. 1688-9.
PROTECTOR CROMWELL, ACTS OF.
PROTESTANT (NEW) LITURGY—Tr. 1688-9.
PROTESTANTS, DANGER PRIOR TO PRINCE OF ORANGE COMING—Tr. 1688-9.
PROTESTS OF THE H. L., 1641-1745.
PROVINCIAL DICTIONARY—Halliwell.
PROVINCIAL DICTIONARY, SCOTLAND—Jamieson.
PROVINCIALE—Lyndwood.
PRUSSIAN CODE, FREDERICIAN.
PUBLICATION, &C. (DE LA)—Demolombe.
PUBLIC ACTS, TABLE OF—Biddle, Jacob, Stamp.
PUBLIC BILLS, LETTER—West.
PUBLIC COUNCILS OF THE KINGDOM—Vol. 2, Col. Jur.
PUBLIC CONFIDENCE, CLAIM TO—G. Canning.
PUBLIC DEBTS, TAXES, SUPPLIES, &C.—Postlethwayte.
PUBLIC DEPARTMENTS, NOTES FOR HISTORY OF—Thomas.
PUBLIC FUNDS, EPITOME OF THE—Fenn, Fortune, Wilkinson.
PUBLIC HEALTH—Baker, Glen.
PUBLIC INSTITUTIONS, ADMISSION TO, WITHOUT CHARGE—Vol. 27, Pam.
PUBLIC MEETINGS—Smith.
PUBLIC RECORDS:—
 Account of Public Records—Cooper.
 Answer to Petyt's Book as to Public Records.
 Public Records as Sources of Genealogies—Grimaldi.
 Public Records of the Four Courts at Westminster—Illingworth.

PUBLIC RECORDS—*continued.*
  Handbook of Public Records—Thomas.
  Hibernia Reports.
  Manual of Public Records—Sims.
  Report of Commissioners on Public Records.
  Report of H. C. Committee on Public Records, 1832 & 1837.
  Report of Evidence of H. C. Committee on Commission.
  Report of Deputy Keeper, Appendix of Engravings.
  And *See* Records Com. Pub.

PUBLIC WRONGS, OUTLINES OF LAW OF—Addison, Maugham, Sleigh.

PUNCH.

PUNISHMENT—Beccaria.

PURE LOGIC—Jevons.

PUPILLA OCULI—De Burgo.

PUTNEY COLLEGE, LETTER ON EDUCATION AT—Cowie.

QUARE IMPEDIT—Mallory.

QUARTER SESSIONS AMENDMENT, LETTER—Greaves.

QUARTER SESSIONS PRACTICE—Archbold, Dickinson, Leuming & Cross.

QUARTER SESSIONS, TABLE OF PUNISHMENTS AT—Dugdale.

QUEBEC, CANADA, CODE OF LAWS FOR.

QUEENBOROUGH, CHARTER TO.

QUEEN ANNE'S BOUNTY, ACCOUNT OF—Hodgson.

QUEEN ELIZABETH—Nicolas.

QUEEN ELIZABETH, PRIVATE PRAYERS—Par. S. Pa.

QUEEN HENRIETTA MARIA, LETTER OF CAR. I. TO—Bruce, No. 63, C. S. P.

QUEEN MARY II. & JAMES I., HISTORY OF—Sanderson.

QUEEN (THE), ON EXCLUDING H.M. FROM THE LITANY—Skirrow.

QUEEN (THE) ATS. O'CONNELL, JUDGMENT.

QUEEN CAROLINE, TRIAL OF. *See* Evidence H. L. Journal 1820, and Hans. Par. Debates for 1820.

QUEEN'S BENCH PRACTICE—Archbold, Chitty, Crompton, Harrison, Lush, Prentice.

QUEEN'S BENCH REPORTS—Best & Smith, Ellis & Ellis.

QUEENSLAND (AUSTRALIA), ACTS.

QUERIES—Plowden.

QUESTIONS, HISTORICAL—Morning Chronicle.

QUESTIONS FOR LAW STUDENTS—Barnham, Halliday, Maugham.

QUESTIONS ON REAL PROPERTY—By a Barrister.

QUESTIONS ON SUGDEN'S VENDORS—May.

QUESTIONS & ANSWERS—Leguliau, Maugham, Purkis.

QUESTIONS & ANSWERS ON CHANCERY PRACTICE.

QUOTATIONS OCCURRING IN BLACKSTONE, TRANSLATED—Jones.

QUO WARRANTO, PROCEEDINGS IN THE CITY.

QUO WARRANTO—Cole, Grady & Scotland.

QUO WARRANTO, PLACITA DE—Pub. Rec.

RACING & GAMING—Oliphant.

RAILWAYS:—
  American Law of Railways—Redfield.
  Analysis—Whishaw.
  Atlas, Plans & Sections—Irish.
  Broad, &c. Gauge, Remarks—Lushington.
  Railways, Canals, &c. in E. & W., Maps.
  Carrying & Carriers, Laws—Nash.
  Railway Consolidation Acts—Briggs, Cox, Tayler.
  Railway Guide & Maps—Bradshaw.
  Railway Intelligence—Slaughter.
  Railway Interest—Spackman.
  Railway Journal—Herapath.
  Law of Railways—Chambers & Paterson, Collier, Frend & Ware, Hodges, Hodgson, Penfold, Riddell, Shelford, Wurry, Wordsworth.
  Railway Litigation—A'Beckett.
  Railways, 1770–1863, Vol. 33—Abr. Pat.
  Railway Times.
  Railway Regulation Acts (Biggs).
  Railway Shareholder's Manual—Tucks.
  Railway Revelations—Mulock.

RAISING, LOWERING, & WEIGHING—Vol. 31, Abr. Pat.

RALEIGH (SIR WALTER), BIOGRAPHY.

RATING SMALL TENEMENTS—Glen.

RAWDON (W.), OF YORK, LIFE—Davies, No. 85.

RAWLINSON'S TRANSLATION OF HERODOTUS.

READING, ESSAY ON—Cocking.

READING, (N.) TRIAL—Political Tracts.

READING, BERKS, HISTORY OF—Coates.

READING ON THE STATUTE, 1723.

REAL ACTIONS—Roscoe.

REAL ASSETS—Joshua Williams.

REBELLION (THE GREAT), HISTORY—Earl Clarendon, Green.

REAL & PERSONAL ESTATE, DEVISE OF, OPINIONS—Williams.

REAL & PERSONAL PROPERTY—Beaumont, Burton, Cruise, Dixon, Fearne, Humphrey, Hunter, Lewis, Shelford, Smith, Tyrrell, Williams.

INDEX TO SUBJECTS. 451

REAL PROPERTY LAW—Hayes, Hilliard (U.S.),
Stewart, Joshua Williams.
Outlines of—Maugham.
Leading Cases in—Tudor.
Letter—Sir E. B. Sugden.
Questions—Joshua Williams.
Commissioners' Report on.
Statutes — Browell, Shelford, Sir E. B. Sugden.
Suggestions on, to Commissioners—Tyrrell.
Transfer, Plan for—R. Wilson.

REALM, STATUTES OF THE, MAGNA CHARTA TO 13TH ANNE, ALPHABETICAL & CHRONOLOGICAL INDEX.

RECEIVER IN CHANCERY—Bennett.

RECORD COMMISSION, LETTERS ON—Cole.

RECORD COMMISSION, RETURN FROM LINCOLN'S INN TO.

RECORD OFFICE (GENERAL), PROPOSAL FOR.

RECORD OFFICE (GENERAL), PAPERS RELATING TO.

RECORD & WRIT PRACTICE—Braithwaite.

RECORDS, PUBLIC—Ayloffe, Cooper, Cotton, Hawkins, Jones, Martin, Powell, Prynne, Thomas.

RECORDS IN EQUITY—Seton.

RECOVERIES—Brown, Col. Jur., Cruise, Pigott, Wilson.

RECREATIONS, LEGAL, BY A BARRISTER—Philonomus.

REDEEMING PROPERTY MORTGAGED—James.

REDESDALE (LORD), CONSIDERATIONS ON CHANCERY.

REES, SEALEY & HARVEY, LETTER TO BISHOP OF LONDON.

REEVES (L. C. J.), INSTRUCTIONS TO HIS NEPHEW ON LEGAL STUDY.

REEVES, HISTORY OF THE LAW.

REFORM :—
Reform Acts — Chambers, Miller, Okey, Whishaw, Wilkinson.
Reform Bills of 1866-7, History of—H. Cox.
Extract of Speech, Bill of 1809—William Windham.
Handbook of Reform needed—Vol. 12, Pam.
Letter to Lord J. Russell, by a Revising Barrister.
Manhood Suffrage, &c.—Stodart.
Parliamentary Reform, Letter on the Redistribution &c., of the Franchise, by a Revising Barrister.
Reform of Native States of India—Vol. 9, Pam.

REFORMATION, HISTORY—Burnet.

REFORMATION, NARRATIVES OF THE—[Foxe] Nichols, No. 77, C. S. P.

REFORMATION, NEW; SOCIETY—Vol. 15, Pa.

REGALITY, GLORY OF—Taylor.

REGISTER—Styles.

REGISTER OF WRITS, MSS.

REGISTERING ANNUITY MEMORIALS, CASES AND PRACTICE—Hunt.

REGISTERING BIRTHS—Glen, Yates.

REGIUM DONUM, HISTORY, &c.—Dr. Rees.

REGISTRATION OF ASSURANCES—Humphrey.

REGISTRATION & CONVEYANCING, LECTURES — Park.

REGISTRATION & CONVEYANCING, REPORT OF H. C. ON.

REGISTRATION OF DEEDS AND TITLES—Cooper, Jenkins, Plowden, Rigge, Roche, Sugden, Turner, Wilson.

REGISTRATION OF DESIGNS—Newton.

REGISTRATION OF JUDGMENTS—Pask, Prideaux.

REGISTRATION OF TITLES TO LAND—Bruce, Jackson.

REGISTRATION OF VOTERS ACT — Bretherton, James, Rogers, Wordsworth.

REGISTRUM BREVIUM—Theloall.

REGISTRUM MAGISTRUM MAGNA SIGILLIS.

REGISTRUM PRIORATUS WIGORNIENSIS—W. H. Hale, No. 91, C. S. P.

REGISTRUM REGALE—Pote.

REGISTRY, REASONS FOR A—L'Estrange.

REGISTRY BILL, LETTER ON.

REGULA GENERALIS—Bosanquet, Jervis.

REI VENATICÆ SCRIPTORES—Kempher.

RELIGION, PETITION OF HOUSE OF COMMONS 1625 TO THE KING—MSS. temp. James.

REMAINS :—
Cranmer, P. S. Pa.
De Dominabus, &c.—Grindall.
Latimer, P. S. Pa.

REMAINDERS—Fearne, Lewis.

REMONSTRANCE TO PARLIAMENT—Jenkins.

REMOVAL OF COURTS AT WESTMINSTER, FACTS AS TO—Vol 4, Pam.

REMOVAL OF COURTS, REVIEW OF EVIDENCE.

REPLEDGING—His. L. Tr.

REPLEVIN—Vol. 1, Col. Jur., Gilbert, Wilkinson.

REPLEVIN AND DISTRESS—Bradby.

REPORTERS—Wallace.

REPORTS, Proposal to Analyse—C. P. Cooper.

REPORTS OF CASES IN ALL THE COURTS—Law Reports.

REPORTS, ANALYSING, LETTERS RELATIVE TO—C. P. Cooper.

REPORTS ON JOINT STOCK CASES—Cox.

REPOSITORY—Hampshire.

REPERTORIUM OF RECORDS. *See* Powell's Attorney's Academy.

REPRESENTATION OF HEIRS, LIMITED & UNIVERSAL—His. L. Tr.

G G 2

REPRESENTATION OF THE PEOPLE—Wilkinson.
REPUBLICA, DE, ANGLORUM—Sir T. Smythe.
REPUBLICA, DE, ROMANO-GERMANICA—Lampadius.
REQUESTS, COURT OF:—
   Act—Hutton, Pratt.
   Returns to Parliament.
REPUBLICA—Prestwich.
RETORNA BREVIUM—R. G.
REVELATIONS—Calvin's Judgment of the, MSS. 3rd Vol.—Selden.
REVIEWS:—
   Edinburgh.
   Law Magazine & Review.
   Quarterly.
   Saturday.
   Westminster.
REVISING BARRISTERS, LETTER—Kennedy.
REVISING COURTS, DECISIONS—Delane.
REVIVOR—White.
REVIVOR & SUPPLEMENT—L. L. Pemberton.
RIC. I. (CŒUR DE LION) CHRONICLES, &C. OF HIS REIGN—Stubbs, No. 38, M. R. Pub.
RIC. II. POEM ON DEPOSITION OF—[Maydiston] (Wright) No. 3, C. S. Pa.
RIC. II. HEN. IV. V. & VI. ENGLISH CHRONICLES OF REIGNS OF—Davies, No. 64, C. S. Pa.
RIC. III. HEN. IV.-VII. LETTERS TEMP.—Robson, No. 18, M. R. Pub.
RICARDI DE CIRENCESTRIA, SPECULUM DE GESTIS REGUM ANGLIÆ—Mayor, No. 30, M. R. Pub.
RICHBOROUGH, ANTIQUITIES OF—Batteley.
RICHER, CAUSES CÉLÈBRES.
RICHMOND & SOMERSET (DUKE OF), NARRATIVE OF WARDROBE — Nichols, C. M. Vol. 3, No. 61, C. S. P.
RICHMOND (YORK), HISTORY OF—Bowman.
RICHMOND, REGISTRUM HONORIS DE—Gale.
RICHMONDSHIRE, &c HISTORY OF—Dr. T. D. Whitaker.
RIGHTS, &C. OF PARLIAMENT, &c. *See* Tr. on.
RIGHT OF BISHOPS TO VOTE IN PARLIAMENT.
RIGHTS, BOOK OF—Taylor.
RIGHT TO BEGIN & RIGHT TO REPLY—Best.
RIOTS, SUMMARY OF LAW OF—By a Member of J. L. S.
RIPON (SEE OF), HISTORY OF. *See* White.
RIVERS:—*See* Waters, Law of.
ROAD BOOK — Ogilby, Ogilby & Morgan, Paterson.
ROAD, RULE OF THE—Holt.
ROBERTS, ON INCREASE OF—Fielding.
ROBSON'S NARRATIVE—Pul. Tr.

ROCHESTER, CHARTERS, &C., OF—Thorpe.
   Cathedral, Antiquities of, Custumale Roffinse—Thorpe.
   History of.
ROCHESTER & CANTERBURY, REPERTOIRE OF ENDOWMENTS—Ducarel.
ROLL—[Bishop Swinfield,] Webb, No. 59 & 62, C. S. Pa.
ROLLE'S ABRIDGMENT, PREFACE TO—Lord Hale, Col. Jur.
ROLLS (ROTULI CHARTARUM, &c.) : — *See* Record Commission.
ROLLS OF PARLIAMENT:—*See* Parliament.
ROLLS LIBERTY COMMITTEE, ON LAND TAX.
ROLLS, MASTER OF THE, AUTHORITY IN CHANCERY.
ROMANÆ DECISIONES—Mohedanus.
ROMAN CATHOLICS, LAWS—Anstey.
ROMAN CIVIL LAW—Ayloffe.
ROMAN EMPIRE, RISE & FALL OF—Gibbon, Merivale.
ROMAN & GREEK ANTIQUITIES—Dr. Smith.
ROMAN & GREEK BIOGRAPHY & MYTHOLOGY—Dr. Smith.
ROMAN & GREEK GEOGRAPHY—Dr. Smith.
ROMAN HISTORY—Gibbon, Macquier.
ROMAN LAW—Bevor, Lord Mackenzie, Phillimore, Reddie.
ROMAN LAW, INSTITUTES OF—Tomkins.
ROMANCES—Thornton, No. 30, C. S. P.
ROMANS, PRIVATE LAW—Phillimore.
ROME, ANTIQUITIES OF—Basil.
ROME'S MASTERPIECE—Prynne.
ROMILLY (SIR J.), BIOGRAPHY—Roscoe.
ROTULORUM CALENDARIUM PATENTIUM—Rec. Com.
ROTULI CURIÆ REGIS—Rec. Com.
ROTULI DOMINABUS ET PUERIS, IN 12 Cos. 1185—Grimaldi.
ROTULI HUNDREDORUM, TEMP. HEN. III. & EDW. I.—Rec. Com.
ROTULI DE LIBERATE AC DE MISIS ET PRŒSTITIS REGNANTE JOH.—T. D. Hardy.
ROTULI LITTERARUM PATENTIUM—Rec. Com.
ROTULI NORMANNIÆ—Rec. Com.
ROTULI PARL. 6 EDW. I. TO 19 HEN. VII. & INDEX—Rec. Com.
ROTULI WALLIÆ. *See* Chartæ Antiquæ, Pub. Rec.
ROTULORUM ORIGINALIUM ABBREVIATIO. *See* Chartæ Antiquæ, Rec. Com.
ROTULUS CANCELLARII—Pipe Roll, Rec. Com.
ROUEN, JOURNAL OF SIEGE OF — [Sir T. Coningsby] Nichols, No. 39 C. S. P., C. M., Vol. 1.

Rous, Diary—Green, No. 66, C. S. P.
Rowe v. Grenfell, Trial—Halcomb.
Roxalana, the Podolian—Musarck.
Royal Family of England, History, Abridged.
Royal Families of Europe, History—Spectator.
Royal Kalendar.
Royal Prerogative—Allen.
Royal Wills—Nichols.
Rugby School, Proceedings before Lord Langdale.
Rules & Orders :—
   K. B. & C. P.
   K. B. & C. P., & Exchequer.
   C. P., 1453–1743.
   C. P., 1654–1756—Watson.
   General from 1728 — Printed by this Society.
   Of C. P. at Lancaster.
Rural Deans, Origin, &c.—Dansey.
Russell (Lord), Defence of—Atkyn's Tracts.
Russian New Code, Instructions to Commissioners to frame.
Russia, Pamphlet on, by Duke of Coburg
Rustica, de re—Cato.
Rutlandshire :—
   Directory. See Cambridgeshire — Kelly, Pigot.
   Domesday Book—Bawdwen, Rec. Com.
   History—Laird, T. Wright.
Rutland Papers—Jerdan, No. 21, C. S. Pa.

St. Alban's Abbey, History—Newcomb, Newcourt.
St. Alban's, Charter—Farrington.
St. Alban's, Chronicles of—Riley, No. 28, M. R. Pub.
St. Asaph :—
   Dean of, Case—M. Dawes.
   Survey of—Willis.
St. Domingo—Moreau.
St. Giles-in-the-Fields, History of—Parton.
St. Katherine's Hospital, Account of—Nichols.
St. Lawrence Pountney, History of Parish—Wilson.
St. Loy, Legend of—Heraud.
St. Mary's, Aldermanbury, on Fabric, &c., of—Wilson.
St. Mary's, Islington, Arranging Ecclesiastical Burdens Act.
St. Marylebone Borough, History of—Smith.

St. Mary Redcliffe Church, on Rebuilding—Britton & Hoskin.
St. Paul's Cathedral :—
   Domesday—Archdeacon Hale.
   History—Sir Wm. Dugdale.
St. Peter's Harbour & Port, Guernsey, History of.
St. Saviour, Southwark, History—Concanen and Morgan.
St. Thomas the Apostle, City, Letter—Dr. Wilson.
St. Thomas, the Incredulity of—The Scriveners' Play at York—Collier, No. 73, C. S. P., C. M., Vol. 4.
St. Vincent Colonial Practice—Shephard.
St. Winifred, Life of—Fleetwood.
Sale, Contract of—Blackburn, Hilliard (U.S.) Hughes, Sugden.
Sale of Personal Property — Benjamin, Story, U.S.
Sale Rooms, Proposed Public.
Salford Hundred, P. O. Directory. See Lancashire—Kelly.
Salmon Fisheries—Baker.
Salisbury Cathedral, Guide—Dodsworth.
Salvage—James.
Sanitary Laws—Lumley, W. H. Michael.
Santillane (de)—Le Sage.
Sarum, Old & New, History, &c., of.
Saturday Early Closing, Correspondence—Taylor.
Saturday Review.
Savings' Banks :—
   Law of—Pratt.
   Progress—Pratt.
   Summary of Law—Pratt.
Saville Correspondence—Cooper, No. 71, C. S. Pa.
Saviour, Our, On the Birthday of—Vol. 3, Selden.
Savoy—Murray.
Saxon & Norman Charters. See Chartæ Antiquæ.
Scampton, Lincoln :—
   Account of—Peck.
   History—Illingworth.
Scarborough :—
   Directory—Kelly.
   History of—Hinderwell.
Scheme, South Sea.
Schools—Abingdon, Tunbridge Wells.
Schools :—
   Abingdon.
   Arundel.
   Endowed Grammar School.
   Highgate.

SCHOOLS—*continued.*
   Merchant Taylors'.
   Tunbridge Wells.
SCIENCES, DES, DES LOIX, ET DES ARTS, DE L'ORIGINE.
SCILLY ISLANDS & CORNWALL—Heath, Troutbeck.
SCINDE RAILWAY CO., REPORT.
SCIRE FACIAS—Foster.
SCOTCH ACTS, OF, LORDS AUDITORS SEDERUNT.
SCOTCH ACTS OF PARLIAMENT, ABRIDGMENT—Alexander.
SCOTCH APPEALS TO H. L.—Bell, Kinnear.
SCOTCH BANKRUPT BILL, REPORT.
SCOTCH BARONAGE—Sir R. Douglas.
SCOTCH CHRONICLES, BUIK OF—[Stewart] Turnbull, No. 6, M. R. Pub.
SCOTCH CHURCH—Buchanan, Spotswood, White.
SCOTCH CRIMINAL CASES—Maclaurin.
SCOTCH TRIALS—Arnot.
SCOTCH LAW :— System of Conveyancing and 3rd Report.
SCOTLAND :—
   Accidents, Law of—Hay.
   Acts of Parliament—Murray, Alexander, Stewart and Bruce.
   Alphabet of Sequestrations—Gilmour.
   Appeals to H. L.—Paton.
   Bankruptcy, Law of—Kinnear.
   Boundaries, Reports on, H. L.
   Calendar of State Papers relating to—Thorpe.
   Criminal Law, Practice of—Alison, Mackenzie.
   Dictionary of Law—Bell.
   Digest of Bankruptcy Law—Alexander.
   Digest of H. L. Cases—Kinnear, Shaw.
   Digests of Law—Bell, Macallan.
   Directories—Slater, Pigot.
   Election Law—Bell.
   Evidence—Dickson.
   Feudal Property, Law of—Dalrymple.
   Forfeiture, Law of.
   Form of Process—Louthian, Russell, Spottiswood.
   History [Bocce] — by Turnbull, Bruce, Buchanan, Fordun, Forsyth, Robertson, Stuart, Selkirk, Teignmouth.
   Interest of, considered.
   Language—Jamieson.
   Law—Bell, Burton, Erskine, Mackenzie, More, Murray, Paterson, Stair, Stuart.
   Law Lists—1844, &c. continued.
   Maps.
   Ministers of—Sir W. Scott, Sir J Sinclair, Spottiswood.
   Parochial Ecclesiastical Law—Duncum.
   Pleadings—Mackenzie.
   Peerage of—Sir R. Douglas, Wallace.
   Proposal for Council of Trade—Law.
   Rebellion in 1745—See Chester Miscellany.
   Record Commissions Correspondence.
   Records, Public.

SCOTLAND—*continued.*
   Reports of Cases, H. L. — Robertson, Craigie, Stewart and Paton, Shaw and Wilson, Shaw and Maclean, Maclean and Robinson, Robinson, Bell, Macqueen, Law Reports.
   Sequestrations, Record of—Gilmour.
   Sovereignty asserted—Craig.
SCOTIÆ ROTULI—Ed. I. to Hen. VIII., Pub. Rec.
SCOTT v. VERNON, ARGUMENTS—Har. Jur. Ar.
SCOTTISH SURNAMES, HISTORY OF EXTINCT—Buchanan.
SCOTTISH WIDOWS' FUND, REPORTS, &c.
SCRIPTURES, HOLY, DISPUTATIONS—P. S. Pa. Whitaker.
SCRIVENERS (FREE) OF LONDON.
SCRIVENERS' GUIDE—Covert.
SCROPE & GROSVENOR ROLL—Nicolas.
SCULPTURE IN ARCHITECTURE—Vulliamy.
SEA LAWS—Battista, Grotius, Hule, Holt, Lowndes, Molloy, Roccus, Selden.
SEA LAWS & MSS., FROM DOCTORS' COMMONS LIBRARY.
SEA SERVICE, REGULATIONS, &c.
SEA SHORE—Phear, Pycroft.
SEALS OF ENGLAND—Brydall.
SEARCH AFTER TRUTH—Malebranche.
SECTIONES CONICÆ—Simson.
SECULAR DIARY—Barstow.
SECURITIES, TACKING—C. Jur.
SELBORNE, HISTORY OF—Rev. G. White.
SELDEN (JNO.), BIOGRAPHY OF—Roscoe.
   Of passage in No. 666 MS., 3rd Vol.—Selden.
   On Mr. Vincent's Discoveries of Errors, 3rd Vol.
   Works—David Wilkie.
SELECT VESTRIES—J. M. White.
SELF MURTHER—Adams.
SENECÆ TRAGŒDIÆ—Schroderus.
SEPARATE ESTATE, DOCTRINE OF EQUITY AS TO —Hayes.
   Use Clause, Tullett v. Armstrong—B. Blundell.
   Use Clause, Letter to Lord Chancellor—Cantrel.
SEQUESTRATION—Rev. H. B. Wilson.
SERJEANT-AT-LAW, ON DEGREE OF, E. W.—By a Member of the Temple.
SERMON, PREACHED BEFORE THE QUEEN—Dr. Hook.
SERMONS—Bullinger, Keble, Latimer, Sandys.
SERVITUDE (DE)—Demolombe.

INDEX TO SUBJECTS. 455

SESSIONAL PAPERS, OF SOCIAL SCIENCE ASSO-
CIATION.
SESSIONS PAPERS:—
 Houses of Parliament.
 Old Bailey. See Burnett & Buckler II.
SESSIONS OF THE PEACE—Dickenson, Leeming
 & Cross.
SET-OFF—Montagu.
SETTLED ESTATES, &c., ACT—Brickdale.
SETTLEMENTS—Atherley, Blythewood.
SETTLEMENTS, MARRIAGE & OTHER FAMILY—
 Peachy.
SETTLEMENTS, PARISH — Reports of Cases,
 Burrow, Caldecott, Settlement Cases,
 temp. Parker.
SEWERS:—
 Law of Sewers—C. M., Callis, Woolrych.
 Orders of Commissioners of Sewers.
 Statute, &c. of Westminster.
SEWING & EMBROIDERY—Vol. 2, Abr. Pat.
SHADWELL (V. C.), CEASING TO ADJOURN FOR
 COUNSEL—Cooper.
SHAFTESBURY, HISTORY—Adams.
SHARES IN COS., SALE & TRANSFER OF—K. E.
 Digby.
SHAREHOLDERS' MANUAL—Bradshaw.
SHARNBURN, DE, HISTORIA FAMILIÆ—Sir H.
 Spelman.
SHEET ALMANAC—Wing.
SHEFFIELD, *Directory. See* Birmingham —
 Kelly.
SHEFFIELD:—
 Directory—Pigot.
 History, &c. of—Hunter.
SHELLEY'S CASE, OBSERVATIONS ON RULE IN—
 Har. L. Tr.
SHEPHEARD, THE ASSASSIN, ANSWER TO HIS
 SPEECH, 1718. *See* Gosling.
SHEPPY, ISLE OF, RAMBLES IN—Turmine.
SHERBORNE HOSPITAL, DURHAM, COLLECTIONS
 RELATING TO.
SHERIFFS' ACCOUNTS—Sir M. Hale.
SHERIFFS, LAW OF—Atkinson, Dalton, Impey,
 Sewell, Watson. *See* Institutions 1556.
SHERIFF & CORONER, LAW OF—Impey.
SHERIFF & CORONER, OFFICE OF. *See* Grounds
 of the Law.
SHIP-BUILDING, &c.—Vol. 21, Abr. Pat.
SHIP-BUILDING, SUTHERLAND.
SHIP MONEY, REMONSTRANCE AGAINST TAX—
 Prynne.
SHIPPING (MERCHANT), LAW MANUAL—Green-
 how.

SHIPPING—Abbott, Holt, James, Lees, Mac-
 lachlan, Maude & Pollock, Oliver, Par-
 ker, Roccus, Shee, Symons, Wilkinson.
SHREWSBURY, CASE OF EARL OF, & WATERFORD
 CLAIMING OFFICE OF LORD STEWARDSHIP
 OF IRELAND.
SHREWSBURY, HISTORY OF—Phillips, Owen &
 Blakeway.
SHROPSHIRE:—
 Antiquities.
 Directory—Kelly, Pigot.
 Domesday—Rec. Com., Vol. 2.
 Map—Baugh.
SICILY, LAWS OF. 1862.
SIERRA LEONE, ACTS, 1857 & continued.
SIMONY—Cunningham.
SKETCH, DRAMATIC—Saul.
SKETCHES OF EMINENT JUDGES, &c. — Foss,
 Roscoe.
SLANDER & LIBEL—Marsh, Starkie.
SLAVERY & SLAVE TRADE, ABOLITION OF,
 BRIEFS, &c., ON COMPENSATION.
SLAVE TRADING, TRIAL OF ZULUETA FOR.
SLEAFORD, HISTORY OF—Creasy.
SLESWIG & HOLSTEIN QUESTION, RASLOFF'S
 REPLY—Vol. 14, Pam.
SMALL DEBTS BILL—W. Wright.
 Speech of Sir R. Peel on—Vol. 12, Jac. L. Tr.
SMITHFIELD MARKET QUESTION—Pamphlet by
 Clericus.
SMITHFIELD MARKET, PLAN OF CORPORATION
 IMPROVEMENTS FOR.
SMYTHE'S LIVES OF THE BERKELEYS.
SMYTH (R.), OBITUARY—Ellis, No. 44, C. S. P.
SOCIAL SCIENCE TRANSACTIONS—Hastings.
SOCIÉTÉ, DU CONTRAT DE—Troplong.
SOCIÉTÉS, DES—Bedarride.
SOLICITORS (*See* Attorneys):—
 Assistant in Chancery—Hands.
 Book-keeping—Kum, Mackenzie, Managing
  Clk., Oke.
 Complete Solicitor.
 Country Solicitors, Suggestions to.
 Duty to teach Client to manage his Business.
 Essay in vindication of Solicitors.
 Experienced Solicitor in H. L.—Urquhart.
 Guide to Solicitors in Chancery.
 Practice—Gray.
 Register of U. K.—Winslow.
SOMERS (LORD), BIOGRAPHY OF—Roscoe.
SOMERS (JNO. LORD), IMPEACHMENT OF.
SOMERSETSHIRE:—
 Directory—Kelly, Pigot.
 Domesday Book.
 History—Collinson, Rutter.
 Survey of—Tunnicliffe.
SONNETS—Montagu.
SOPHISMS OF FREE TRADE—By a Barrister.

SORTIER'S VOYAGE, COMMENTS ON—Spratt.
SOUTHAMPTON, CHARTER TO.
SOUTHAMPTON ESTATE, PAVING ACT, ST. PANCRAS.
SOUTH AUSTRALIA, ON REGISTRATION IN—Torrens.
SOUTH GERMANY—Murray.
SOUTH OF EUROPE, &c., MAP—Arrowsmith.
SOUTH SEA COMPANY:—
  Abstracts of Acts of.
  Dividends Unclaimed.
  Stock.
SOUTHERN SECESSION, LETTER TO MAURY—Cowell.
SOUTH WALES, COLLIERIES OF, EVIDENCE.
SOUTHWARK:—
  Court of Requests Act—Meymott.
  Court of Requests, Address to Commissioners. See City Tr.
  Election—Clifford.
  Etymology of Southwark—Lindsay.
  History of Southwark—Maitland.
  Southwark, London, & Westminster—Noorthouck.
  Southwark, London, & Westminster, Survey of, Parish Clerks.
SOUTH WINFIELD, HISTORY—Blore.
SOUTHWOLD, &c. HISTORY—Wake.
SOVEREIGN'S PERSON, REQUIRED IN STATE COUNCILS—Howell, C. P.
SPA FIELDS BURIAL GROUND—Walker.
SPAIN:—
  Calendar State Papers as to Affairs of Spain—Bergenroth.
  Codigo del Comercio.
  Codigo de las Costumbres maritimas de Barcelona.
  Ensayo historico-critico sobre la antigua Legislacion y principales Cuerpos legales de los Reynos de Leon y Castilla—Marina.
  Febrero novisimo, ó Libreria de Jueces, Abogados y Escribanos—Tapia.
  Guia para el Estudio del Derecho Patria—Reguera Valdelomar.
  Institutes of Civil Law of Spain, translated by Johnson—Asso & Manuel.
  Journey through Spain—Townsend.
  Juicio critico de la novisima Recopilacion—Marina.
  Las Memorias de Felipe de Comines, traducidas del Frances por Vitrian.
  Las Siete Partidas del Rey—Don Alphonso el Sabio.
  Ley de Enjuiciamiento sobre los Negocios y Causas de Comercio.
  Ley hipotecaria of Spain—Greene.
  Leyes del fuero juzgo, ó Re apilacion de las Leyes de las Wisi-Godos Españoles—Llorenté.
  Modelos de la Literatura española—Del Nine.

SPAIN—continued.
  Novisima Recipolacion de las Leyes de Españo.
SPANISH & ENGLISH DICTIONARY—Barrette, Castelluma.
SPANISH GRAMMAR—McHenry.
SPANISH LAWS. See Mr. Woodhouse's Observations on, at end of large Library Catalogue.
SPANISH PROVINCES & WEST INDIES, MAP OF.
SPECIAL PLEADING, LETTER—Corrie.
SPECIFIC PERFORMANCE—Fry.
SPEECHES:—
  Lord Brougham.
  E. Burke.
  Speeches in H. L.—MS., Selden, 3rd vol.
  On Reform, in 1792—E. Burke.
  On Reform, in 1809—Windham, Vol. 12, Jac. L. T.
  G. Canning (to his Liverpool Constituents).
  Lord Erskine.
SPECTATOR, THE.
SPINNING—Vol. 28, Abr. Pat.
STRAFFORD (VISCOUNT), SPEECH OF—Pol. Tr.
STAFFORD:—
  Domesday Book—Rec. Com.
  Survey of—Erdeswick, Tunnicliffe.
STAFFORDSHIRE:—
  Directory—Kelly, Pigot.
  History—Holt, Plot, Shaw.
STAMFORD, HISTORY OF—Howgrave.
STANFORD, ANTIQUARIAN ANNALS OF—Peck.
STAMP ACT—Hughes.
STAMP DUTIES—Heraud.
  Digest—Vacher.
STAMP LAWS—Chamberlain, Chitty, Coventry, Impey, Tilsley.
STAMP LAWS, REPLY TO CHARGE ON STATE OF LAW & COMMERCIAL REMEMBRANCER.
STANDARD (THE) NEWSPAPER.
STANDING ORDERS IN PARLIAMENT, 1848—Biggs, Vacher.
STANLEY (SIR WM.), TRAVELS OF & HISTORY OF ISLE OF MAN, &c.
STANNARIES OF CORNWALL, LAWS OF, RULES, &c.
STAPLETON (T.), PLUMPTON CORRESPONDENCE—No. 4, 34, 47, C. S. Pa.
STAR CHAMBER—Hudson, Vol. 2, Col. Jur.
STAR CHAMBER (NEW) CASES—Crompton.
STATE PAPERS:—
  British & Foreign State Papers—Presented by Lord Stanley.
  Calendars—(Editors) Bergenroth, Brewer, Bruun, Brown, Bruce, Green, Hamilton, Lemon, Roberts, Sainsbury, Stevenson, Thorpe, Turnbull.
  Collection by Lord Clarendon.

INDEX TO SUBJECTS. 457

STATE TREATIES—Brown.
   Extracts from. See Hertslett.
STATE TRIALS—Howell, Salmon.
   Specimen of a New Edition of—Moiles.
STATE TRIALS — (U. S.) temp. Washington & Adams.
STATE WORTHIES—Fuller, Lloyd.
STATUTES :—*Abridgments*—Cay, Pulton.
   Collections—Henry VIII, Rastill, Keble, Fulton, Scobell, Tothill, Cromwell, Acts and Ordinances.
   Pub. Gen. at Large, 4to.
      Black Letter, Fo.
      of the Realm, large Fo., Rec. Com.
      Do.   8vo.
      Road Acts, Fo.
      Loc. & Per., Fo.
   Abridgment (Penal)—Clarke.
   Digests. Pub. Genl.—Archer, Chitty, Crabb, Ibbotson. Raithy, Ruffhead, Williams.
   Indexes, Pub. Genl.—Raithby, Ruffhead, Spiller, Stamp.
   Key to Pub. Gen.—Farton.
   Index, Pub. & Priv. MSS.
      Do.   *do.*   H. L.
      Do.   *do.*   H. C.
      Do. Priv.—Bramwell, Vardon.
   Treatises on — Addington, Atkyns, Barrington, Dwarris.
   Irish—Fo. & Index. Ball.
      8vo.   *do.*
   Scotland, Acts of Parliament of, Abridgment—Alexander, Stewart & Bruce.
      Do. Recd. Commiss.—Fo.
      Do. Lords Auditors - Fo.
      Do. Lords of Sessions—Fo.
STATUTE BOOK :—
   Memorandum respecting our—Cooper.
   Relating to the Admiralty.
   Bankruptcy.
   Election Cases.
      Do. Irish.
   Confusion worse confounded—G. Wilmore.
   Law Epitome—Sheppard.
   Letter on Scheme to Consolidate—Sir F. Dwarris.
   Statutes of New York Revised.
      Do. and Index—(U. S.) Peters & others.
STATUTORY & CONSTITUTIONAL LAW (*See* U. S.)—Sedgwick.
STEAM CULTURE—Vol. 6, Abr. Pat.
STEELE (SIR RICHARD)—Crisis.
STERNE, WORKS OF.
STEWART'S LETTERS TO DIRECTORS—E. I. Co.
STEWARTS, GENEALOGY OF—Crawford, A. Stewart.
   Refutation of do., in a Letter to do.
STILLINGFLEET (BISHOP OF WORCESTER) DISCOURSES. FATHER OF ED. — Dr. Jas. Stillingfleet.
   Ecclesiastical Cases.
   Works & Life of.

STIRLING PEERAGE CASE—Bankes.
STIRLING, SCOTLAND, HISTORY OF—Randall.
STOCKDALE *v.* HANSARD, PAMPHLET ON PARLIAMENTARY PRIVILEGE—Ferrall.
STOCK EXCHANGE, LAW, &C., OF—Keyzer.
STOCK TABLES—Blewert.
STOCKS & ANNUITIES—Fairman.
STOCKS, &C., PRICE OF—Wetenhall.
STOCKTON-ON-TEES, ANTIQUITIES OF—Brewster.
STOKE NEWINGTON, HISTORY—Robinson.
STONEHENGE, HISTORY—Jones, D. W. Stukeley.
STOPPAGE IN TRANSITU—Houston.
STORY (JOSH.), LETTERS & LIFE OF—W. H. Story.
STOW, HISTORY OF—Stark.
STOWE (JOHN), LIFE OF—Malcolm.
STOWE, DESCRIPTION OF—Seeley.
STRAFFORD, HISTORY OF—Wainwright.
STRATFORD, HISTORY OF SHAKESPEARE'S RESIDENCE—Halliwell.
STRATHERN & MONTEITH PEERAGE—Nicolas.
STRYPE (JOHN), LIFE—Malcolm.
STUART, MARIA—Schiller.
STUDENT'S GUIDE TO PRELIMINARY EXAMINATION—Benham.
STUDY & PRACTICE OF THE LAW—W. Wright.
STUKELEY (WM.) LIFE—Malcolm.
SUBURBAN DIRECTORY—Kelly.
SUCCESSION DUTIES—Hanson, Hudson, Shelford, Tilsley, Thring, Trevor.
SUCCESSION, EVIDENCE—Hubback.
SUCCESSION TABLES—Finlaison.
SUCCESSIONS, DES—Demolombe, Pothier.
SUDLOW (MR.) HIS INAUGURAL ADDRESS AT ISLINGTON INSTITUTION.
SUEZ CANAL, AS TO OPENING ROUTE TO THE EAST: LETTER TO LORD PALMERSTON.
SUFFOLK :—
   Agriculture of
   Directory—Kelly, Pigot.
   Domesday Book, Vol. 2—Rec. Com.
SUFFOLK TRAVELLER—Kirby.
SUIT IN EQUITY—Burton, Hunter, Plunkett.
SUIT AT LAW—Boote, Kerr, Smith.
SUITS, EXPENSE OF, & PLAN FOR A REMEDY—Col. Jur.
SULLY (DUKE OF) MEMOIRS.
SUMMARY CONVICTIONS—Arnold, Oke, Paley.
SUMNER'S REPORTS, U.S.
SUN (THE) NEWSPAPER.
SUPERIOR COURTS, LETTER SUGGESTING SITE FOR, IN TEMPLE—Greene.

SUPPLEMENT & REVIVOR—Pemberton, White.
SUPREME AUTHORITY, INQUIRY AS TO SUBMISSION TO.
SURETYSHIP—Fell, Lawrence, Pitman.
SURGEONS, ASSISTANT, IN THE NAVY—by a Naval Medical Officer.
SURRENDERS OF TERMS—Sanders, Sugden, Jac. L. T., Vol. 1.
SURREY:—
  View of Agriculture.
  Directory. See *Home Counties*—Kelly, Pigot.
  Domesday Book—Henshall.
  History of—Allen, Brayley, Garrow, Lysons, Manning & Bray.
SURVEYORS, DIALOGUES.
SURVEYS:—
  Antrim—Dubourdieu.
  St. Asaph's Cathedral—Willis.
  Canterbury Sumner.
  Cornwall—Gilbert.
  Cumberland Lakes—Clarke.
  Derbyshire, Survey of Agriculture—Holt.
  Devon—Risden.
  Devon, Chorographical Survey—Risden.
  Essex—Muilman.
  Ireland—Mason.
  Kent—Tunnicliffe.
  Lancashire—Holt.
  London—Lamburd, Parish Clerks, Stowe, Strype.
  Scilly Islands—Troutbeck.
  Somerset, Worcester, Gloucester, Chester, Stafford, Lancaster—Tunnicliffe.
  Stafford—Erdeswick.
  Suffolk—Kirby.
  Whitby—Young.
  Worcester City—Green.
SUSSEX:—
  Directory. See *Home Counties*—Kelly, Pigot.
  Domesday Book—Henshall.
  Families, Age of Ed. II. IV.—Cooper.
  Genealogies—Berry.
  History of—Dallaway, Hay, Horsfield.
SUTTON, BIOGRAPHY OF Bearcroft.
SWEET (S. W.) MEMOIR OF, FROM LEGAL OBSERVER.
SWIFT (DR.) REMARKS ON LIFE, &C. OF—Earl Orrery.
SWINDLING, ON SYSTEM OF—Teevan.
SWINFIELD (BP.), ROLL—C. S. P., No. 62, Rev. J. Webb.
SWITZERLAND—Murray.
SYDNEY DIRECTORY—Sands.
SYMBOLOGÆ GEOGRAPHIA—West.
SYMONDS (RICHARDS), DIARY OF—C. S. P., No. 64, Ed. C. E. Long.

SYNEDRIIS, DE, ET PRÆFECTURIS JURIDICIS VETERUM EBRÆORUM—Selden, Vol. 1.
SYNONYMS, ENGLISH—Crabb.
SYNOPSIS CRITICORUM SACRÆ SCRIPTURÆ.—Polo.
SYON & ISLEWORTH, HISTORY—Aungier.
SYRIS, DE DIIS—Selden, Vol. 2.
SYSTEM OF EDUCATION, OBSERVATIONS ON—Vol. 5, Pam.

TABLE ON STATUTE OF LIMITATIONS Warlter.
TABLE TALK—Selden, Vol. 3.
TABLE, UNIVERSAL MONEY—Pigott.
TABLES FOR PURCHASING ESTATES, &c.—Inwood, Sir I. Newton, Stock, Willich.
TABLES, GENEALOGICAL—Betham.
TABLES, INTEREST—Laurie.
TABLES FOR TITHE COMMUTATION—Willich.
TABULÆ CURIALES—Foss.
TACITUS, TRANSLATION OF—Murphy.
TACKING, OPINIONS ON DOCTRINE OF—Col. Jur. Vol. 2.
TALENTS, ALL THE—Polypus.
TANJORE, KING OF, AS TO RESTORATION OF. See E. I. Co.
TASMANIA ACTS.
TASWELL (DR. W.), AUTOBIOGRAPHY OF—Vol. 2, C. M. No. 55.
TATTERSHALL, ACCOUNT OF—Peck.
TAUNTON, HISTORY OF—Savage.
TAUNTON DEANE, CUSTOM OF MANOR OF—Locke.
TAX ACTS, COLLECTION OF—Snee.
TAX TABLES—Kearsley.
TAXES, HISTORY OF—Cunningham, Davenant.
TAXES, CONSOLIDATING DUTIES OF COMMISSIONERS OF.
TAYLOR (M. A.), LETTER TO HIM AS TO CHANCERY JUDGES.
TAYLOR (EDGAR), MEMOIR OF.
TELEGRAM—Purkis.
TEMPLE (THE), HISTORY—Addison, Burge.
TENANT—See Landlord & Tenant.
TENANT RIGHT HOLDERS QUESTION, PROPOSAL, 2 LETTERS—Vol. 25. Pam. F. P. Jones.
TENANTS' PRIVILEGES. See Gurdon on Parliament, Vol. 2.
TENURES—Bacon, Blunt, Coke, Gilbert, Littleton, Wright.
TENURES, IRELAND—Moleyns.
TERMS, ORIGIN OF THE—Sir H. Spelman.
TERMS IN GROSS, &c. OPINION ON—Col. Jur.

TERMS, ON PRESUMING SURRENDER OF—Sir E. B. Sugden.
TERMES DE LA LEY—T. B.
TESTA SIVE LIBER FEODORUM, TEMP. HEN. III. ET ED. I.—Pub. Rec., De. Nevill.
TESTAMENT, NEW—Nicolas de Lyra, D'Oyley & Mant.
TESTAMENT, NEW & OLD, SACRED HISTORY OF THE—Whiston.
TESTAMENTA VETUSTA, HEN. II. TO Q. ELIZ.—Nicolas.
TESTAMENTARY JURISDICTION BILL—Vol. 12, Pam., Falconer.
TESTAMENTS, ORIGINAL ECCLESIASTICAL JURISDICTION OF—Selden Tr.
TESTAMENTS & WILLS, ORIGIN OF—Sir H. Spelman.
TESTAMENTS (DES), ET DES DONATIONS ENTRE VIFS—De Demolombe.
TESTAMENTS (DES)—Troplong.
TESTAMENTOS & SUCCESSORES—Pinto.
TEWKESBURY, HISTORY OF—Bennett.
THAMES WATER COMPANY, REPORT OF COMMISSIONERS.
THAMES & OTHER WATER, REPORT ON MICROSCOPICAL EXAMINATION—Vol. 9, Pam.
THAMES CONSERVANCY, HISTORY—Binnell.
THAMES, REMARKS ON ENCROACHMENTS NEAR DURHAM YARD.
THAMES FISHERMEN, RULES.
THAMES WATERMEN, TABLE OF RULES.
THANKSGIVING SERMON, 1702, AT NORWICH—Prideaux Tr.
THANET, ISLE OF, & CINQUE PORTS, HISTORY—Brayley.
THANET, ISLE OF, HISTORY—Lewis.
THANET, ISLE OF, TOUR THROUGH, & DESCRIPTION OF CHURCHES & MONUMENTS.
THEOKESBERIA DE ANNALES—Luard, No. 36, M. R. Pub.
THELUSSON'S WILL, EXTRACTS, CASE & ARGUMENTS—Har. J. A.
THESAURUS GRAMMATICO-CRITICUS ET ARCHÆOLOGICUS—Hickessii.
THESAURUS RERUM ECCLESIASTICUM—Ecton.
THESAURUS JURIDICUS—Bridgman.
THESAURUS JURIS ROMANI—Otto.
THESAURUS LINGUÆ GRÆCÆ—Stephanus.
THESAURUS LINGUÆ LATINÆ—Stephanus.
THÉÂTRE (LA), COMMENTAIRES SUR—Corneille.
THEOPHRASTUS, CHARACTER OF—Newton.
THETFORD, HISTORY OF—Bloomfield, Martyn.
THETFORD TO NORWICH, ON REMOVAL OF ASSIZES.

THINGOE HUNDRED—Gage.
THOMSON (SIR A.), BIOGRAPHY OF—Roscoe.
THORNE, HISTORY—Peck.
THORNTON ROMANCES—No. 30, C. S. P., Halliwell.
THORNTON, TRIAL OF, ON APPEAL OF MURDER—Cooke.
THORESBY (RALPH), LIFE OF—Malcolm.
THOUGHTS, &c., REFLECTIONS ON—Urquhart.
THURLOW (LORD), BIOGRAPHY OF—Roscoe.
TIBULLUS, CATULLUS, ET PROPERTIUS.
TICKHILL, HISTORY OF—Wainwright.
TIDAL WATERS, PROPERTY IN—Angell.
TIM BOBBIN'S WORK—Corry.
TIME, CALCULATION OF—Harry.
TIMES NEWSPAPER, INDEX—Palmer.
TITHES:—
  Agriculture, Influence of upon Tithes—Howlett's Tr.
  Argument of Dr. Owen before Lord Mayor—City Tr.
  Award of King Charles I.—Prideaux Tr.
  Bill as to Tithes, and Baron Wood's Observations—Curwen.
  Case—Hume v. Pearson.
  Commutation Act—Bosanquet.
  Rent Charge Report—F. M. White.
  Collection of—Jones.
  Decrees—Wood.
  History of MSS., and purpose of writing—Selden, 3rd Vol.
  Law of—Bateman, Bearblock, Bohun, Bosanquet, Cunningham, Degge, Eagle, Mirehouse, Prideaux, Ripley, Selden, Shelford, Toller.
  Reports of Cases—Eagle & Young, Gwillim, Rayner, Western, Wood.
  Rating, &c.—Serjt. T. D'Oyley.
  Rating to the Poor, Observations on Jones's Pamphlet—Blake.
  Tables—Willich.
TITE (WM.), LETTERS FROM HIS COLLECTION OF AUTOGRAPHS—5 C. M. No. 87.
TITLE, ABSTRACTS OF—Lee, Preston.
TITLE DEEDS—Dixon.
TITLES OF HONOUR—Selden, & Vol. 3 of his Works.
TITLES & HONOURS CONFERRED BY GEO. I. & II., &c.—Phillips, Grimaldi's Tr.,Vol. 1.
TITLES OF LANDED ESTATES, REMARKS OF LIVERPOOL LAW SOCIETY, VOL. 11.—Pam.
TIVERTON, HISTORY—Dunsford.
TIXALL, HISTORY OF—Sir T. Clifford.
TOBAGO, LAWS OF.
TODMORDEN—Law, Lanc. Coy. Tr.
TOLERATION ACT—Furneaux.
TOLLS, ON MORTGAGE OF—Law Journal Tr. See Gunning.

INDEX TO SUBJECTS.

TONTINE—List of Nominees of.
TYPOGRAPHICA ET GENEALOGICA COLLECTANEA—Nichols.
TOPOGRAPHIC, LITHOGRAPHIC, & PLATE PRINTING—Vol. 13, Abr. Pat.
TYPOGRAPHERS & ANTIQUARIES, LIVES OF—Malcolm.
TOPOGRAPHY—Britton, Gough, Upcott.
TORTS—Addison, Hilliard, Sleigh.
TORTURE, READING ON USE OF—Jardine.
TOTTENHAM, HISTORY OF—Robinson.
TOUCHSTONE—Sheppard.
TOWER OF LONDON, HISTORY OF—Bayley.
TRACTS:—
  Sir R. Atkyns.
  Blackstone.
  Col. Jur.
  Derbyshire (County)—Grimaldi.
  Hale (Lord).
  Hargraves.
  Hampshire (County)
  Historical.
  Howlett.
  Jacob's Collection.
  Lancashire (County).
  Law Journal.
  Law, Parliamentary & Political.
  Libel Law.
  London (City).
  Political.
  Selden.
  Somers (Lord).
  Warburton.
  Wilts (County).
TRACTATUS EX VARIIS JURIS INTERPRETIBUS COLLECTIO.
TRACTATUS VARII UTRIUSQUE JURIS.
TRACTATUS DE JURISDICTIONE—Marta.
TRADE—Child, Davenant, Postlethwayt.
TRADITIONS & ANECDOTES OF EARLY ENGLISH HISTORY—C. S. Pa. No. 5, Thoms.
TRADE MARKS—Lloyd.
TRADE MARKS FRAUDULENTLY IMITATED—Ryland.
TRAGŒDIÆ SENECÆ—Schroderus.
TRANSACTIONS & CHANCERY PRACTICE—Tothill.
TRANSACTIONS OF ASSOCIATION FOR PROMOTING SOCIAL SCIENCE—Hastings.
TRANSPORTATION & CONVICT DISCIPLINE—Pocock.
TRANSPORTATION ACT—Ayrton, Bruce.
TRANSFER OF LAND:—
  Observations on Act for Simplifying—Towgood.
  Paper read before Juridical Society, on Remedies for the Evils affecting the Transfer of Land—Joshua Williams.
TRATADO REGULARÉ PRATICO DE TESTAMENTOS É SUCCESSORES—Pinto.
TRAVELLER'S POCKET BOOK—Ogilby & Morgan.
TRAVELLING, LAWS OF.
TRAVELS OF NUCIUS—Cramer, C. S. Pa., No. 17.
TREASON—Brooke, Holbourne, Yorke.
TREASON, CASES OF—Bacon.

TREASON IN THE CHURCH, O'CONNELL'S LETTER, Vol. 5, Pam.
TREASON, DISCOURSE ON—Blackstone.
TREASURY PAPERS, CALENDAR OF—Redington. Cal. St. Pa.
TREASURIES:—
  Biography—Maunder.
  Geography — Maunder, continued by Hughes.
  History—Maunder.
  Natural History—Maunder.
  Scientific & Literary Treasury—Maunder.
  Treasury of Knowledge, & Library of Reference—Maunder; new Edition—Woodward & others.
TREATIES, COLLECTION & HISTORIES—Hertslett, Rymer. Treaties, 1688-1772.
TREATIES & GRANTS, EAST INDIA COMPANY.
TREATIES WITH PAPISTS, NOT TO BE RELIED ON—Tr. Law, 1688.
TREATIES, STATE COLLECTION. See Brown, State Papers.
TREATISES—Bridgwater.
TREES & WOODS—Craig.
TRELAWNEY PAPERS—Cooper, C. M., Vol. 2, No. 55.
TRENT, COUNCIL OF—Sarpi.
TRESPASS—Yool.
TREVELYAN PAPERS—Collier, C. S. Pa., Nos. 67 & 84.
TRIAL BY JURY, THE DARK SIDE OF, Vol. 12, Pam.—Brown.
TRIALS. See Trials in Catalogue.
TRIMMER, CHARACTER OF A, 1688.
TRIENNIAL ACT, SPEECHES AGAINST REPEALING. See Impeachment of Lords.
TRINIDAD, LAWS OF.
TRINITY HOUSE, DEPTFORD, COMPENSATION FOR SKERRIES LIGHTHOUSE.
TRINITY HOUSE, CHARTER TO.
TRIPOS, 3 DISCOURSES—Hobbs.
TROKELOWE, DE JOHANNIS, CHRONICA—Riley, No. 28, Rolls.
TROWBRIDGE, HISTORY—Bodman.
TRURO, PROCEEDINGS AT ELECTION.
TRUSTEES — Hampson, Hill, Hunter, Ince, Langley, Lewin, Paizey, Willis.
TRUSTEES, RELIEF—Clarke.
TRUSTS—Cooke, Lewin, Sanders.
TRUSTS & TRUSTEES, PERILS OF—Lucas.
TUFTON FAMILY, MEMOIRS OF—Pocock.
TULLET v. ARMSTRONG, EXAMINATION OF SEPARATE USE CLAUSES—T. Swinburne.
TUNBRIDGE WELLS:—
  Guide—Spranger.
  History—Amsinck, Rowzee.

INDEX TO SUBJECTS. 461

TUNBRIDGE SCHOOL—Vol. 5, Tracts.
TURBERVILLE, INFORMATION—Pol. Tr.
TURNPIKE LAWS—Bateman, Oke.
TUSCANY, CRIMINAL LAW REFORM—Beccaria.
TUTBURY, HISTORY OF—Moseley.
TWYSDEN, ON GOVERNMENT OF ENGLAND — Kemble, No. 45, C. S. Pa.

USURY—Bentham, Byles, Kelly, Maugham, Plowden.
USURY LAWS, REASON AGAINST REPEAL OF—Vol. 3, Jac. L. T.
UXBRIDGE, HISTORY OF—Redford & Riches.
UXOR EBRAICA—Selden, Vol. 2.

UCKFIELD UNION, POOR-LAW AUDITORS' REPORT AS TO.
ULTRA-ROMANISTS & EXTRACT LETTERS—C. P. Cooper.
ULSTER, REPORTS OF DEPUTATION OF IRISH SOCIETY IN.
UNCLAIMED DIVIDENDS, LISTS OF.
UNCLAIMED PROPERTY, REGISTER OF—De Bernandy.
UNDERSTANDING—Locke.
UNIFORMITY OF PROCESS ACT—Tidd.
UNION ASSESSMENT ACT—Castle, Lumley.
UNITED PROVINCES, MAP—Eadon.
UNITED SERVICE MAGAZINE—Colburn.
UNITED STATES - Law Register, Livingston. See America.
UNITED STATES, REPORTS OF SUPREME COURTS—Cranch, Curtis, Dallas, Howard, Mason, Peters, Story, Wheaton. See under each name in Cat.
UNITED STATES, DECISIONS IN ADMIRALTY & MARITIME CAUSES—Stringer.
UNIVERSITY ELECTION, CAMBRIDGE POLL BOOKS.
UNIVERSITY LIBRARY, INQUIRIES & OBSERVATIONS RESPECTING—Montagu Tracts.
UNIVERSAL CAMBIST—Kelly.
UNIVERSAL GEOGRAPHY—Arrowsmith, Edinb. Gazetteer, A. K. Johnston, Maunder, Sullivan & Guthrie, Dr. Smith, Ripley & Dance.
UNIVERSAL JURISPRUDENCE—Thomas.
UNIVERSAL MONEY TABLE—Pigott.
UNIVERSAL POCKET COMPANION.
UNIVERSAL REGISTER OFFICE, FOR SALE OF PROPERTY, PLAN FOR—Fielding.
UNREFORMED PARLIAMENT, HISTORY—Bagehot.
USES—Bacon, Carthew, Col. Jur., Cruise, Duke, Gilbert, Jones, Sanders.
USES, STATUTE OF, BOOTH & OTHERS, OPINIONS ON Col. Jur.
USHER (BISHOP), PROPHECY, 1688, L. T. No. 26.
USURERS & PAWNBROKERS.

VACCINATION ACTS—Fry.
VADE MECUM, ENTERING CLERK's—Browne.
VALLIÈRE (DUC DE LA) CATALOGUE DE LA BIBLIOTHÈQUE.
VALOR ECCLESIASTICUS—Rec. Com.
VALOUR, ANATOMISED BY SIR P. SIDNEY—Howell. C. P.
VAN DIEMEN'S LAND, 3RD REPORT AS TO.
VATICAN, SPIRIT OF THE—Turnley.
VENDOR & PURCHASER:—
 Personal Property—Benjamin, Blackburn, Morton.
 Real Property—Dart, Sugden.
VENETIA, DISCORSO ON INQUISITIONI DE—Paolo.
VENICE, DOCUMENTS IN LIBRARIES AT—Hardy. Cal. St. Pa.
VENICE, HISTORY—Fougasses.
VENTE, DE LA—Troplong.
VENTILATION, IMPORTANCE OF.
VERGIL, POLYDORE—Ellis, No. 29, C. S. Pa.
VERNEY PAPERS—Bruce, No. 31, C. S. Pa.
VERNONS, BIOGRAPHY OF—Haylyn.
VICISSITUDES OF FAMILIES—Burke.
VICTORIA, AUSTRALIA, ACTS—Adamson.
VICTORIA STATUTES.
VICTUALLERS (LICENSED)—Horry.
VILLA VOLFISCELLI, OR THE SHUT SCHOOL—Vol. 28, Pam., Hamilton.
VINDICATION OF THE RESIGNERS—Vol. 2, Grim. Tr.
VINDICIÆ ECCLESIÆ ANGLORUM—Mason.
VINDICIÆ DE SCRIPTIONE MARIS CLAUSI—Selden, Vol. 2.
VINERIAN LECTURES—Wooddesson.
VIRGINIA, ACTS AND LAWS OF ASSEMBLY, WITH CODE—U. S.
VIRTUE & MERIT, ENGRAVING CONCERNING.
VOCABULARIUM ANGLO-SAXONICUM—Benson.
VOLUNTEER SERVICE GAZETTE.
VOLUNTEER IN THE FIELD—Palliser & Pringle.
VOLUNTEER, THE QUESTION CONSIDERED—Westbrook.

INDEX TO SUBJECTS.

VOTE FOR M.P., ELECTOR DENIED HIS, DEBATE ON.
VOTE, HOW SHALL WE? INQUIRY INTO MEASURES OF LORD DERBY IN 1859.
VOTERS, REGISTRATION OF—Bretherton.

WAGES, RATE OF, LECTURE—Pam., Senior.
WAGERS & GAMING—Oliphant.
WALES:—
  Ancient Laws & Statutes of Wales—Rec. Com.
  Dictionary of Wales—Carlisle.
  Discourse against Jurisdiction over Wales, by Latitat—Har. L. Tr.
  History of Wales—Sir J. Dodridge, Evans, Jones.
  Itinerary through Wales—Baldwin.
  North & South Wales Directory—Pigot.
  Practice of Great Session, Wales—C. Abbott.
  Princes of Wales, Chronicles of (Brut y Tywysogion) No. 17, M. R. P.
  Tour through Wales—H. P. Wyndham.
  Walk through Wales—Warner.
WALKER'S CASE, LORDS, PROTEST IN, TOUCHING PARLIAMENTARY PRIVILEGE IN LIBEL MATTERS—Vol. 1, Lib. L. Tr.
WALLENSTEIN—Schiller.
WALPOLE, MEMOIRS OF—Musgrave.
WALPOLE'S CASE, MUTUAL WILLS—Har. J. A.
WALSINGHAM (T.) CHRONICA MONASTERII ST. ALBANI—Riley, No. 28, M. R. Pub.
WALTHAM ABBEY, HISTORY OF—Farmer.
WANTING HUNDRED, TOPOGRAPHY—Clarke.
WAR:—
  Laws of War—Thompson.
  Letter as to Capture of Neutrals' Vessels, &c., in time of War—Duke of Newcastle. Vol. 1. Col. Jur.
  On Contraband of War—Moseley.
  On Captures in War—Lee.
  On Instruments of War—Walesby.
  War of Spanish Succession—Lord Mahon.
WAR & PEACE—Grotius.
WARKWORTH, CHRONICLE OF FIRST 13 YEARS OF EDW. IV.—Halliwell, No. 10, C. S. Pa.
WARRANTS OF ATTORNEY, &C.—Robinson.
WARRANTS OF ATTORNEY, &C., ON PUBLICATION OF NOTICES OF—Ford.
WARSAW & POLAND, LETTERS RESPECTING LATE EVENTS AS TO—Mitchell.
WARWICK & LEAMINGTON, HISTORY OF—Field.

WARWICKSHIRE:—
  P. O. Directory—Kelly.
  P. O. Directory, Hardware District—Kelly.
  Directory—Pigot.
  Domesday Book—Vol. 1. Rec. Com. Reader.
  History—Aston, Dugdale, Smith.
  Tour—Bray.
WASTE, IMPEACHMENT OF, LAW ARGUMENT—Bacon.
WASTE, NUISANCE & TRESPASS—Yool.
WATCHES, CLOCKS & OTHER TIMEKEEPERS—Vol. 9, Abr. Pat.
WATER & WATERCOURSES—Angell, Phear, Woolrych.
WATER SUPPLY—Homersham.
WATERFORD, HISTORY OF—Smith.
WATERMEN, &C., RULES FOR REGULATIONS OF ON THAMES—City Tr.
WAURIN, CHRONICLES, &C., OF GREAT BRITAIN WITH TRANSLATION—Hardy, Nos. 39 & 40, M. R. Pub.
WAVERLEIA (DE), ANNALES MONASTERII—Hardy, No. 36, M. R. P.
WATSON (MR.), MOTION ON CHANCERY COMPENSATION, Vol. 3, Pam.
WAYNFLETE (BISHOP OF WINCHESTER), BIOGRAPHY OF—Chandler.
WAYS—See Highways.
WEALTH OF NATIONS—Smith.
WEAVING—Vol. 20, Abr. Pat.
WEED (THURLOW), REPLY TO HIM ON THE AMERICAN QUESTION—Fairplay.
WEIGHTS & MEASURES, LECTURES ON THE METRICAL SYSTEM FOR—Porter.
WELSH DICTIONARY—Pugh.
WELSH GRAMMAR—Pugh.
WELSH GREAT SESSION PRACTICE—Abbott.
WELSH (THE) MOUSE TRAP—Houldsworth.
WELLESLEY v. DUKE OF BEAUFORT, JUDGMENT OF—Lord Eldon.
WEST DERBY HUNDRED, P. O. DIRECTORY—Kelly. See Lancashire.
WEST v. ERISSEY, ON MARRIAGE ARTICLES—Vol. 1, Col. Jur.
WEST INDIA CO., CHARTER TO.
WEST INDIES, SIX MONTHS' RESIDENCE IN—Coleridge.
WEST INDIES & SPANISH PROVINCES OF NORTH AMERICA, MAP OF—Arrowsmith.
WEST LOOE, ELECTION REPORT—Merewether.
WEST SHEEN, CUSTOMS—Col. Jur.
WESTERN AUSTRALIA, ORDINANCES.
WESTMINSTER ABBEY, HISTORY—Dart.

WESTMINSTER ANNOYANCE JURIES, INSTRUC-
    TIONS.
WESTMINSTER, ANTIQUITIES OF, &C.—Smith.
WESTMINSTER ELECTORS, ADDRESS TO, ON RIGHT
    TO CHOOSE REPRESENTATIVES.
WESTMINSTER, FEES OF OFFICERS OF COURTS AT.
WESTMINSTER, HISTORY OF—Brayley & Britton,
    Maitland.
WESTMINSTER, LAWS OF COURT OF—Dugdale.
WESTMINSTER SCHOLARS—Welch.
WESTMINSTER SEWERS, POWER OF COURT OF,
    TO DEMAND FEES—Mullins.
WESTMINSTER, LONDON & SOUTHWARK, HIS-
    TORY OF—Noorthouck.
WESTMINSTER, LONDON & SOUTHWARK, SUR-
    VEY OF PARISH CLERKS OF.
WESTMORLAND :—
    P. O. Directory—Kelly.
    Directory—Pigot.
    History—Robinson.
    Survey of Lakes—Clarke.
    Views in—Wilkinson.
    Visitation of in 1615—St.George's Herald.
WESTMORLAND & CUMBERLAND :—
    Domesday Book—Bawdwen.
    Guide to Lakes of—Nicholson & Burn.
    History of—West.
WESTERTON v. LIDDELL, REPORT OF IN P. C.—
    Moore.
WHALLEY, HISTORY—Whitaker.
WHEATFIELD, HISTORY—Chubb.
WHEATON'S INTERNATIONAL LAW, U.S.—Law-
    rence, Dana.
WHEATON'S REPORTS. See Curtis.
WHITBY, HISTORY OF, & OF ITS ABBEY—
    Charlton.
WHITBY, & STREONESHALH ABBEY, HISTORY OF
    —Young.
WHITGIFT (ABP.), WORKS—Par. S. Pa.
WHITE & BLACK LISTS—Butler.
WHITE & BLACK LISTS OF HOUSES OF PARLIA-
    MENT, & OF IRELAND—Butler.
WHITEFORD, HISTORY—Pennant.
WHITEHEAD & OTHERS, SPEECHES AT EXECU-
    TION—Pol. Tr.
WHITLOCK (SIR J.), LIBER FAMELICUS.
WHISTON, &C, HISTORY, &C. See HALLAM-
    SHIRE—Hunter.
WHITWORTH v. GARGANI. JUDGMENT OF LORD
    COTTENHAM—Browell.
WIFE'S ESTATE, REAL & PERSONAL, HUSBAND'S
    INTEREST IN—Vol. 2, L. Tr.
WIFE'S INTEREST, ON ASSIGNMENT OF—Canning.
WIGAN, THE MAYOR OF, TALE BY BUTLER—
    Lanc. Coy. Tr.
WIGAN, CHARTER TO, 1808.

WIGHT, ISLE OF :—
    Historical Guide—Buller.
    History—Albion, Warner, Sir R. Worsley.
    Gazetteer & Directory—White.
WIGORNIENSIS, REGISTRUM PRIORATUS—Hale,
    C. S. Pa., No. 81.
WILL, REVOCATION OF, OPINION ON—C. J.
WILL, REDUCTION OF, OF COL. MACLEAN, IN
    CAUSE IN LUNACY—Vol. 20, PRM.
WILLS ACT—Deane, H. Sugden.
WILLS, LAW OF—Allnutt, Deane, Gilbert, Haw-
    kins, Hayes & Jarman, Inderwick, Jar-
    man, Lovelass, Richardson, Roberts,
    Redfield (U.S.), Roper, Shelford, H.
    Sugden, Swinburne, Wigram.
WILLS, AMERICAN LAW OF—Redfield.
WILLS FROM DOCTORS' COMMONS—Nichols &
    Bruce, No. 83, C. S. Pa.
WILLS & INVENTORIES FROM BURY ST. ED-
    MUND'S—Tymms, No. 49, C. S. Pa.
WILLS, ROYAL—Nichols.
WILTS :—
    Catalogue of Books as to Wilts—Britton.
    P..O. Directory—Kelly, Pigot. See Hamp-
        shire.
    Domesday Book—Rec. Com., Wyndham.
    Natural History of—Aubrey.
    Modern - Sir R. C. Hoare.
    Poems—Duck (a Wiltshire Thresh'r.)
    View of the County of, during Election of
        1818.
WILLOUGHBY v. WILLOUGHBY, PRIORITY OF
    MORTGAGE DEBT—Col. Jur.
WILMOT (SIR J. E.) BIOGRAPHY OF—Roscoe.
WILMOT, NOTES.
WILMOT, OPINIONS & JUDGMENTS.
WILSON (SIR J.), BIOGRAPHY OF—Roscoe.
WILTON (LORD GREY OF), LIFE.
WIMBLEDON COMMON COMMITTEE, EXTRACT OF
    COURT ROLLS FOR THEIR USE. See also
    Essays by Maidlow & others.
WICKER v. MITFORD, ARGUMENT ON APPLICA-
    TION FROM CHANCELLOR TO H. L.—
    Har, L. Tr.
WINCHESTER CATHEDRAL, HISTORY — Milner.
    Account of, From Milner.
WINCHESTER, HYDE ABBEY, CHRONICLE &
    CHARTULARY—Edwards, No. 45, M. R.
    Pub.
WINDING-UP JOINT STOCK COMPANIES—Browne,
    Taylor, Thring.
WINDOW LIGHTS – Latham, Woolrych.
WINDSOR CASTLE, &C., HISTORY, &C.—Pote.
WINDSOR & ITS NEIGHBOURHOOD, HISTORY—
    Hakewell.
WINTONIA, DE ANNALES MONASTERII—Luard,
    No. 36, M. R. Pub.

WIRKWORTH LEAD MINES, RHYMED CHRONICLE, CUSTOMS, &C. OF—Manlove.
WISE'S LETTER TO DR. MEAD AS TO THE RED HORSE, WARWICKSHIRE.
WISE (E.), SUPPLEMENT TO BURN'S JUSTICE.
WISBEACH & TOWNS, &C., IN ISLE OF ELY, HISTORY—Watson.
WITCHES, TRIAL OF—Sir M. Hale.
WITHAM INSTITUTION, LECTURES AT, ON EDUCATION—Vol. 5, Pam.
WITNESSES' EXAMINATION—Best, Smith.
WOBURN, HISTORY OF—Dodd.
WOLVERHAMPTON:—
   History of Collegiate Church—Oliver.
   Plan of. See Shaw's Staffordshire, Vol. 2.
WOMEN, LAW OF.
WOOD, AUTOBIOGRAPHY, LIFE OF—Malcolm.
WOOD, THE WIDOW OF THE—B. Victor.
WOODBRIDGE, STATUTES, &C. of SECKFORD'S ALMSHOUSES, AT—Loder.
WOODS & FORESTS:—
   17 Reports of Commissioners, 1787—1793.
   26 Reports Commissioners, 1812—1849.
   Report, Se'ect Committee, 1834.
   4 Reports of Surveyor-General of Land Revenue, 1797—1809.
WOOLRYCH (MR. SERJEANT), PAPER AS TO OPENING BIDDINGS—LawAmendment Society.
WORCESTERSHIRE:—
   P O. Directory—Kelly, Pigot.
   Domesday Book—Vol. 1, Rec. Com.
   History—Nash.
   Survey—Tunnicliffe.
WORCESTER:—
   History of City, &c.—Green.
WORKING CLASSES' DWELLINGS, &C., PROCEEDINGS AT MEETING AT LONDON TAVERN—Vol. 27, Pam., C. Pearson.
WORLD, ATLAS OF THE—Jas. Wyld.
WORLD, HISTORY OF THE—Sir W. Raleigh.
WORLD, MAP OF THE—Arrowsmith, Jas. Wyld.
WRIT, DE REGE INCONSULTO, ARGUMENT ON, IN CASE OF GRANT OF OFFICE OF SUPERSEDEAS IN C.P. LORD BACON—Col. Jur.
WRITING, ORIGIN OF—Astle.
WRITS:—
   Collection of Writs—Antrobus & Impey, Fitzherbert, Natura Brevium, Officina Brevium. Registrum Omnium Brevium, J. C., Thelnall.
   Forms of Writ - J. C.
   Writ of Summons to Parliament.
   Supplement to Style of Writs—Spottiswoode.

WRONGS & REMEDIES—Addison, Sleigh.
WYCOMBE DEANERY, &C. HISTORY OF—Langley.
WYE, EXCURSIONS DOWN THE—Heath.

YARMOUTH (GREAT):—
   Account—Parkyns.
   History—Swinden.
YARNS & FABRICS, BLEACHING, DYEING & PRESSING—Vol. 14, Abr. Pat.
YEAR BOOK, STATESMAN'S—Martin.
YEAR BOOK OF FACTS—Timbs.
YEAR BOOK & DIARY—Maugham.
YEAR BOOKS. See Reports, & Edw. I.—Horwood, No. 31, M. R. Pub.
YORK CATHEDRAL:—
   History—Todd.
   History & Description—Wilson & Spencer.
YORK, HISTORY OF—Drake.
YORK, THE SCRIVENERS' PLAY AT, THE INCREDULITY OF ST. THOMAS—Collier, C. M. Vol. 4, No. 73, C. S. P.
YORKSHIRE:—
   General View of the Agriculture of W.R.—Tuke.
   W. N. & D. Ridings, P. O. Directory.
   W. Riding & York City Directory—Kelly.
   Directory—Pigot.
   Dictionary of—Langdale.
   Diocese, Bona Notabilia of—Lawton.
   Domesday Book—Vol. 1, Rec. Com., Bawdwen.
   Ecclesiastical History—Burton.
   Gazetteer—Clarke.
   W.R. & York City, History, &c.—Wm. White.
   History—Allen, Bigland.
   History of Parts of—Whitaker.
   History of E. & W. Ridings—White.
   Map—Teesdale.
   W. R. Survey—Holt.
YORKSHIRE, &C., TOUR—Bray.
YORK, NEW, BANKING SYSTEM OF—Cleaveland.
YOUNGE'S DIARY—Roberts, No. 41, C. S. Pa.
YOUNG (JNO. ESQ.), CATALOGUE OF AUTOGRAPH LETTERS EXHIBITED IN THIS LIBRARY.
YOUNG CLERK'S, THE, GUIDE—Sir R. H.
YOUNG MEN'S CHRISTIAN ASSOCIATION, LECTURE TO, AT EXETER HALL—Sir W. P. Wood.

www.ingramcontent.com/pod-product-compliance
Lightning Source LLC
Chambersburg PA
CBHW022106300426
44117CB00007B/604